John Willis
Theatre World
1982–1983 SEASON

VOLUME 39

CROWN PUBLISHERS, INC.

ONE PARK AVENUE • NEW YORK, NEW YORK 10016

TO
ALBERT HIRSCHFELD

who, since 1925, has applied his genius, satirical wit and humor, and love of performers to recording theatrical history with uniquely irreverent line drawings that are deservedly known as masterpieces.

CONTENTS

EDITOR: JOHN WILLIS
Assistants: Stanley Reeves, John Sala
Staff Photographers: Joseph Abeles, Bert Andrews, J. M. Viade, Van Williams
Designer: Peggy Goddard

Page opposite: (clockwise from top left) Carol Channing in "Hello, Dolly!," James Earl Jones, Christopher Plummer in "Othello," Yul Brynner in "The King and I," Richard Kiley in "Man of La Mancha," Jane Alexander, Henry Fonda in "First Monday in October," the genius himself, Al Hirschfeld by Al Hirschfeld, Katharine Hepburn, Dorothy Loudon in "West Side Waltz," Liza Minnelli in "The Act."

Ken Page (center) and other members of the cast of "Cats"

Martha Swope Photo

1983 TONY-AWARD-WINNING MUSICAL
(see page 17)

THE SEASON IN REVIEW
June 1, 1982 through May 31, 1983

After two seasons of record-breaking boxoffice receipts, the charts showed a 10% decrease in gross. The average admission price rose $2.80, and 18% fewer tickets were sold. Broadway experienced the worst slump in ten years. Production costs continued to soar and several theatres stood empty. There was no longer the theatre shortage that existed two years ago. It was a depressing season of quick flops, including five one-night stands. There seemed to be a dearth of producers who love theatre more than boxoffice receipts. There was a scarcity also of new playwrights: only three wrote original plays for Broadway. Some did write for regional and Off-Broadway theatres, and a few plays were fortunate enough to be transplanted on "the Great White Way." Some producers tried to blame the economy and reduced tourism for the slump, but "the road" was also in the doldrums. There were high-quality actors in low-quality material. Not a single production opened to unanimous raves from the critics. Of the 51 openings, only 15 remained at the end of the season with 9 holdovers from previous years.

The Pulitzer Prize for best play went to "'night, Mother" by Marsha Norman. The New York Drama Critics Circle honored "Brighton Beach Memoirs," the English import "Plenty," and the Off-Broadway musical "Little Shop of Horrors." The American Theatre Wing's "Tony" Awards went to "Torch Song Trilogy" (Best Play) and its author-star Harvey Fierstein (Outstanding Actor in a Play), "Cats" (seven "Tonys" including Best Musical, and Outstanding Featured Actress Betty Buckley), Jessica Tandy (Outstanding Actress in a Play) in "Foxfire," "On Your Toes" for Outstanding Reproduction, and to its star Natalia Makarova for Outstanding Actress in a Musical, "My One and Only" for Outstanding Choreography, Outstanding Actor and Featured Actor in a Musical, Tommy Tune and Charles "Honi" Coles, respectively. "Tonys" for Outstanding Featured Performers in a Play went to Judith Ivey in "Steaming" and Matthew Broderick in "Brighton Beach Memoirs." The latter play was honored with a "Tony" for direction. Again, the presentation ceremonies were produced by Alexander H. Cohen, and televised around the world on Sunday, June 5, 1983 from the newly-christened Gershwin Theatre.

Other productions worthy of mention are the revivals of "You Can't Take It with You" with Jason Robards and Colleen Dewhurst, "A View from the Bridge" with Tony LoBianco, "The Caine Mutiny Court-Martial" with John Rubinstein, William Atherton, Stephen Joyce and Michael Moriarty, "Present Laughter" with George C. Scott, and "The Queen and the Rebels" with Colleen Dewhurst. Elizabeth Taylor and Richard Burton appeared together on Broadway for the first time in "Private Lives," and Liv Ullmann assayed "Ghosts," proving that film stars do not guarantee a legitimate theatre hit. Radio City Music Hall tried going "legit" with a production of "Porgy and Bess," but it was an unfortunate decision. Lanford Wilson's new play "Angels Fall" was moved with its outstanding cast from the Circle Repertory Theatre to Broadway without its anticipated success.

Among those giving outstanding performances and not already mentioned are Jane Alexander, Karen Allen, Maureen Anderman, Christine Andreas, Kathy Bates, Brian Bedford, David Birney, Karla Burns, Kate Burton, Keith Carradine, John Cullum, Jeffrey DeMunn, Denny Dillon, Elizabeth Franz, Peter Gallagher, Daniel Gerroll, Al Green, Harry Groener, Roxanne Hart, Anthony Heald, George Hearn, Edward Herrmann, Bruce Hubbard, Barnard Hughes, Zeljko Ivanek, Anne Jackson, Page Johnson, Susan Kingsley, Christine Lahti, Angela Lansbury, Joseph Maher, George N. Martin, Ben Masters, Lonette McKee, Bill Moor, Stephen Moore, Meg Mundy, Kate Nelligan, Ken Page, Anne Pitoniak, Chita Rivera, Nicolas Surovy, Brian Tarantina, Linda Thorson, Twiggy, Margaret Tyzack, Eli Wallach and Fritz Weaver.

Off Broadway and Off-Off Broadway presented material superior to most of Broadway's offerings. In addition, lower prices for tickets, and performances by prestigious actors helped make its season more rewarding than Broadway's. Notable musicals were "Charlotte Sweet," "Broadway Scandals of 1928," "Bugles at Dawn," "New Faces of 1952," "Upstairs at O'Neal's," "Snoopy," "The Gilded Cage," "It's Better with a Band" and "A Bundle of Nerves." Outstanding plays were "Edmond," "Blood Moon," "Extremities," "Fool for Love," "The Fox," "Greater Tuna," "Herringbone," "The House of Ramon Iglesia," "It's Only a Play," "Jeeves Takes Charge," "Life with Father," "Mary Barnes," "The Middle Ages," "The Music Keeper," "My Astonishing Self," "The Other Side of the Swamp," "Painting Churches," "Poppie Nongena," "Quartermaine's Terms," "Regard of Flight," "Skirmishes," "Standing on My Knees," "The Singular Life of Albert Nobbs," "Talking With," "Top Girls," "Triple Feature," "True West," "The Transfiguration of Benno Blimpie," "Vieux Carre," "Wild Life" and "The Wisteria Trees."

Praiseworthy performers Off Broadway include Terry Alexander, Kathy Baker, Suzanne Bertish, Philip Bosco, Fran Brill, Joanne Camp, Keith Charles, Glenn Close, Dana Delany, Donal Donnelly, Edward Duke, Giancarlo Esposito, Christine Estabrook, Laura Esterman, Peter Evans, Brenda Forbes, Ellen Greene, Ed Harris, Jo Henderson, Bill Irwin, Dana Ivey, Eugene Lee, John Malkovich, Lynn Milgrim, Jan Miner, Joe Morton, Carrie Nye, Jenny O'Hara, Jim Piddock, Remak Ramsay, Pamela Reed, David Rounds, James Russo, Eva Marie Saint, Susan Sarandon, Joe Sears, Marian Seldes, Gary Sinise, Marianne Tatum, Holland Taylor, Anne Twomey, Jaston Williams, Treat Williams and Walter Willison.

Because of shrinking federal funds and corporate donations, the number of dollars available brought heated competition, and eventual demise to some of the theatrical organizations. Many continued to operate on reduced budgets and presented quality productions. The Phoenix Theatre, founded by T. Edward Hambleton and Norris Houghton, was one of the casualties after thirty years. The Dramatists Guild in association with Circle Repertory Theatre presented its second annual Young (under 19) Playwrights Festival bringing hope and encouragement to potential future Broadway playwrights. As a salute to Britain, Norman Marshall at the No Smoking Playhouse sponsored a five-day marathon in which all known works of Shakespeare were read or performed non-stop. The New York Yiddish Theatre celebrated its centennial, and Equity Library Theatre its fortieth year of producing and providing showcases for members of its union, Actors Equity Association.

Among the year's events that should be noted are: the effort to preserve legitimate theatres gained momentum. Because of bitter controversy over demolition of the Helen Hayes, Morosco, and Bijou theatres, Mayor Edward Koch appointed a committee to advise the city on theatre demolition, construction, renovation and preservation. . . . The New York State and City Center auditoriums were renovated, and sight lines and acoustics were improved. . . . The Alvin became the Neil Simon Theatre, the Uris became the Gershwin, the Little Theatre became the new Helen Hayes Theatre, and Off-Broadway's Roundabout Stage 2 became the Susan Bloch Theatre in honor of the late publicist. . . . New York Consumer Affairs Department accused theatres of selling balcony seats as "rear mezzanine" and were ordered to desist. . . . The indiscriminate standing ovation at curtain call seemingly was becoming the custom. . . . The League of New York Theatres and Producers filed an anti-trust suit against the Dramatists Guild for "fixing, controlling, regulating and dictating royalties, minimum prices and terms for subsidiary rights." The Guild countersued. . . . Actors Equity presented a Declaration of Intent, and plan for a national theatre to provide professional productions at a nominal cost around the 50 states. . . . The death of Tennessee Williams, one of the world's great playwrights, brought an untimely end to his legacy of literary wealth.

BROADWAY PRODUCTIONS
(June 1, 1982 through May 31, 1983)

BLUES IN THE NIGHT

(RIALTO THEATRE) Conceived and directed by Sheldon Epps; Set, John Falabella; Costumes, David Murin; Lighting, Ken Billington; Conductor, Charles Coleman; Casting/Musical Director/Supervisor/Vocal Arrangements, Chapman Roberts; Co-Musical Director/Arranger/Orchestrator, Sy Johnson; Producers, Mitchell Maxwell, Alan J. Schuster, Fred H. Krones, M2 Entertainment; Associate Producer, Joshua Silver; Assistant to Producers, James Hannah; Sound, Bill Merrill, Tay MacLaren; Production Assistants, Rebecca Harrison, Ronnie Yeskel; Wardrobe, Mary Ellen Bosche; General Management, M2 Entertainment; Press, Judy Jacksina, Glenna Freedman, Diane Tomlinson; Company Manager, Paul Matwiow; Stage Managers, Zoya Wyeth, William D. Buston, Jr., David Brunetti. Opened Wednesday, June 2, 1982.*

CAST

Woman #1	Leslie Uggams
Woman #2	Debbie Shapiro
Woman #3	Jean DuShon†
Saloon Singer	Charles Coleman

Standbys: Ann Duquesnay, David Brunetti

A musical in two acts. The action takes place in a Chicago hotel during 1938.

*Closed July 18, 1982 after 53 performances and 13 previews.
† Ruth Brown during previews

Carol Rosegg Photos

Right: Leslie Uggams

Debbie Shapiro

Jean DuShon

TORCH SONG TRILOGY

(THE LITTLE THEATRE) By Harvey Fierstein; Director, Peter Pope; Sets, Bill Stabile; Costumes, Mardi Philips; Lighting, Scott Pinkney; Musical Direction/Arrangements, Ned Levy; Original Music, Ada Janik; Producers, Kenneth Waissman, Martin Markinson, John Glines, Lawrence Lane with BetMar and Donald Tick; Associate Producer, Howard Perloff; Assistant Director, Judy Thomas; Technical Supervisor, Jeremiah J. Harris; Sound, Richard Fitzerald, John Sullivan; Wardrobe, Kathy Powers; Hairstylist, Andre Tavernise; Production Assistant, George Phelps; General Assistant, Barbara Hodgen; Casting, Hughes/Moss; General Management, Theatre Now; General Manager, Edward H. Davis/Dorothy Finn; Press, Betty Lee Hunt/Maria Cristina Pucci, James Sapp; Stage Managers, Herb Vogler, Billie McBride. Opened Thursday, June 10, 1982.*

CAST

Lady Blues	Susan Edwards
Arnold Beckoff	Harvey Fierstein†1
Ed	Court Miller†2
Laurel	Diane Tarleton
Alan	Paul Joynt†3
David	Fisher Stevens
Mrs. Beckoff	Estelle Getty

STANDBYS and UNDERSTUDIES: Susan Edwards (Laurel), Diane Tarleton (Lady Blues), Christopher Stryker (Alan/David), Sylvia Kauders (Mrs. Beckoff), Scott Oakley (Keyboard), Richard DeFabees (Arnold), Peter Ratray (Ed)

A play in three acts. Part I: "The International Stud" takes place backstage at a night club, in a bar, Ed's apartment, Arnold's apartment, from January to November. Part 2: "Fugue in a Nursery": A year later in Arnold's apartment, and in various rooms of Ed's farmhouse. Part 3: "Widows and Children First": Five years later in Arnold's apartment, and on a bench in the park.

*Still playing May 31, 1983. Awarded 1983 "Tonys" for Best Play and Best Actor in a Play (Harvey Fierstein).

†Succeeded by: 1. Richard DeFabees, Donald Corren, Jonathan Hadary, David Garrison, 2. Robert Sevra, Peter Ratray, David Orange, Court Miller (returned), 3. Christopher Stryker.

Gerry Goodstein Photos

Top: (L) Court Miller, Harvey Fierstein
(R) Harvey Fierstein, Diane Tarleton

Harvey Fierstein, Estelle Getty

7

CLEAVAGE

(PLAYHOUSE THEATRE) Book, Buddy and David Sheffield; Music and Lyrics, Buddy Sheffield; Director, Rita Baker; Musical Numbers Staged by Alton Geno; Conductor/Musical Arrangements, Keith Thompson; Sets, Morris Taylor; Lighting, Scenery and Costume Supervision, Michael Hotopp, Paul DePass; Costumes, James M. Miller; Producer, Up Front Productions: Braxton Glasgow III, William J. O'Brien III, Morgan P. O'Brien, David E. Fite; Assistant to Producer, Catherine A. Adams; Technical Supervisor, Jeremiah Harris; Wardrobe, Bruce Catt; Sound, Theodore Jacobi; General Manager, Theatre Now, William Court Cohen, Eddie Davis, Norman E. Rothstein, Ralph Roseman, Charlotte W. Wilcox; Press, Susan L. Schulman; Assistant Company Manager, Kathryn Frawley; Stage Managers, Gary Ware, Arlene Grayson. Opened Wednesday, June 23, 1982.*

CAST

Daniel David	Marsha Trigg Miller
Tom Elias	Jay Rogers
Mark Fite	Sharon Troyer Scruggs
Terese Gargiulo	Dick Sheffield
	Pattie Tierce

MUSICAL NUMBERS: Cleavage, Puberty, Only Love, Surprise Me, Reprise Me, Boys Will Be Girls, Give Me an And, Just Another Song, Believe Me or I'll Be Leavin' You, The Thrill of the Chase, Lead 'Em Around by the Nose, Sawing a Couple in Half, Bringing Up Badger, Voices of the Children, All the Lovely Ladies, Living in Sin, Finale

A musical in two acts.

*Closed June 23, 1982 after 1 performance and 6 previews.

Martha Swope Photos

Top: (rear) Jay Rogers, Marsha Trigg Miller, Daniel David (standing C), Mark Fite, Pattie Tierce, (front) Tom Elias, Terese Gargiulo, Sharon Troyer Scruggs

PLAY ME A COUNTRY SONG

(VIRGINIA THEATRE) Book, Jay Broad; Music and Lyrics, John R. Briggs, Harry Manfredini; Director, Jerry Adler; Choreography, Margo Sappington; Sets, David Chapman; Costumes, Carol Oditz; Lighting, Marc B. Weiss; Musical Direction/Vocal Arrangements, Phil Hall; Sound, Robert Kerzman; Development Supervision, Milton Moss; Producer, Frederick R. Selch; Casting Director/Associate Producer, Cheryl Raab; Wardrobe, Josephine Zampedri; Production Assistants, Andrea Selch, Jeannie Banker; General Manager, Robert S. Fishko; Press, Michael Alpert, Marilynn LeVine, Mark Goldstaub, Alan Hale, Rebecca Robbins; Stage Managers, Alisa Adler, Jonathan Weiss. Opened Sunday, June 27, 1982.*

CAST

Norm	Reed Jones
Ellen	Mary Gordon Murray
Tony	Stephen Crain
Fred	Jay Huguely
Howard	Ronn Carroll
Lizzie	Louisa Flaningam
Frances	Karen Mason
Penny	Mary Jo Catlett
Buster	Kenneth Ames
Meg	Candace Tovar
Jerome	Rene Clemente
Hank	Rick Thomas

UNDERSTUDIES: Kevin Scannell (Fred/Howard/Tony/Hank), Susan Powers (Mary Gordon Murray/Meg), Brad Miskell (Norm/Buster/Jerome), Brooks Almy (Lizzie/Penny/Frances)

MUSICAL NUMBERS: Sail Away, Rodeo Dreams, Why Does a Woman Leave Her Man, Eighteen-Wheelin' Baby, Waitin' Tables, Playing for Position, Just Thought I'd Call, Sing-a-Long, If You Don't Mind, Play Me a Country Song, Coffee Beer and Whiskey, Only a Fool, You Can't Get Ahead, You Have to Get It Out to Get Away, Big City, My Sweet Woman, All of My Dreams, Rodeo Rider

A musical in two acts.

*Closed June 27, 1982 after 1 performance and 14 previews.

Kenneth Ames, Rene Clemente, Louisa Flaningam
Top Right: Mary Gordon Murray, Candace Tovar, Louisa Flaningam

9

THE GRAND KABUKI

(METROPOLITAN OPERA HOUSE) Artistic Directors, Nakamura Utaemon VI, Nakamura Kanzaburo XVII, Onoe Kuroemon II; General Managers, Chikashi Mogi, Hitoshi Kadoi, Nobuyuki Onuma; Technical Directors, Shunichiro Kanai, Sadahide Hosaka; Lighting, Kuyotsune Soma, Miyuki Iwabuchi; Stage Manager, Jerry Rice, Takeshiba Shoji; Company Manager, John H. Wilson; Press, Marilynn LeVine, Mark Goldstaub, Alan Hale, Rebecca Robbins; Production Supervisor, Dan Butt; Lighting Supervisor, Ronald Bates. Opened Tuesday, June 29, 1982.*

ACTORS

Nakamura Utaemon VI, Nakamura Kanzaburo XVII, Nakamura Tomijuro V, Nakamura Fukusuke VIII, Nakamura Matsue V, Ichikawa Ebizo X, Bando Tamasaburo V, Nakamura Kankuro V, Nakamura Kangoro, Nakamura Kosanza, Nakamura Komasuke, Nakamura Nakasuke, Nakamura Komaji, Nakamura Nakajiro, Gando Yakichi, Nakamura Sukegoro, Ichikawa Masuju, Ichikawa Masusuke, Nakamura Shikimatsu, Nakamura Tomishiro, Nakamura Utashi, Kagaya Utae, Arashi Kitsusaburo, Nakamura Utaju, Nakamura Utaju, Nakamura Nakaichiro, Bando Noriwaka

REPERTOIRE: Narukami, Migawari-Zazen, Sumidagawa, Kumagai Jinya, Bo-Shibari, Kumagai Jinya, Kanjincho, Masakado

*Closed July 10, 1982 after limited engagement of 12 performances.

Shochiku Photos

Banda Tamasaburo in "Narukami"
Top: "Masakado"

SEVEN BRIDES FOR SEVEN BROTHERS

(ALVIN THEATRE) Book, Lawrence Kasha, David Landay; Lyrics, Johnny Mercer; Music, Gene de Paul; New Songs, Al Kasha, Joel Hirschhorn; Based on the MGM film and "The Sobbin' Women" by Stephen Vincent Benet; Choreography and Musical Staging, Jerry Jackson; Director, Lawrence Kasha; Sets, Robert Randolph; Costumes, Robert Fletcher; Lighting, Thomas Skelton; Sound, Abe Jacob; Musical Director, Richard Parrinello; Orchestrations, Irwin Kostal; Dance Arrangements, Robert Webb; Presented by Kaslan Productions; Associate Producers, Martin Gould, Bernard Hodes; Assistant to Producers, Beth Riedmann; Wardrobe, Dolores Childers; Props, Charles Zuckerman; Assistant Conductor, Jerry Sternbach; Hairstylist, Juan Rodriguez; General Management, Marvin A. Krauss, Gary Gunas, Eric Angelson, Steven C. Callahan; Press, David Powers, Barbara Carroll; Stage Managers, Polly Wood, Jack Ritschel. Opened Thursday, July 8, 1982.*

CAST

Adam	David-James Carroll
Benjamin	D. Scot Davidge
Ephraim	Jeffrey Reynolds
Caleb	Lara Teeter
Daniel	Jeff Calhoun
Frank	Michael Ragan
Gideon	Craig Peralta
Mr. Bixby	Fred Curt
Mrs. Bixby	Jeanne Bates
Preacher	Jack Ritschel
Mr. Perkins	Gino Gaudio
Indian	Conley Schnaterbeck
Milly	Debbie Boone
Ruth	Sha Newman
Martha	Laurel van der Linde
Sarah	Linda Hoxit
Liza	Jan Mussetter
Alice	Nancy Fox
Dorcas	Manette LaChance
Jeb	Russell Gielsenschlag
Zeke	Kevin McCready
Carl	Don Steffy
Matt	Gary Moss
Luke	James Horvath
Joel	Clark Sterling
Dorcas' Sister	Marylou Hume
Mrs. Perkins	Marykatherine Somers
Townsboy	David Pavlosky

UNDERSTUDIES: Cheryl Crandall (Milly), Gino Gaudio (Adam), Russell Giesenschlag (Gideon), Gary Moss (Daniel), Don Steffy (Benjamin), Kevin McCready (Frank), Clark Sterling (Ephraim), James Horvath (Caleb), Marylou Hume (Alice/Sarah), Marykatherine Somers (Dorcas/Ruth/Mrs. Bixby), Stephanie Stromer (Liza/Martha), David Pavlosky (Luke/Zeke), Conley Schnaterbeck (Carl/Matt), Sam Singhaus (Jeb/Joel), Jack Ritschel (Bixby/Perkins), Jeanne Bates (Mrs. Perkins)
MUSICAL NUMBERS: Bless Your Beautiful Hide, Wonderful Wonderful Day, One Man, Goin' Courting, Social Dance, Love Never Goes Away, Sobbin' Women, The Townsfolk's Lament, A Woman Ought to Know Her Place, We Gotta Make It Through the Winter, Spring Dance, Glad That You Were Born, Wedding Dance

A musical in 2 acts and 18 scenes. The action takes place in the Pacific Northwest during the 1850's.

*Closed July 11, 1982 after 5 performances and 15 previews.

David Friedman Photos

Top Right: Debby Boone (center), (back row) Lara Teeter, D. Scott Davidge, Jeff Calhoun, Jeffrey Reynolds, (middle row) Sha Newman, Manette LaChance, Jan Mussetter, Laurel van der Linde, (front) Craig Peralta, Nancy Fox, Linda Hoxit, Michael Ragan

Jeff Calhoun, Debby Boone, Michael Ragan, Jeffrey Reynolds

PRESENT LAUGHTER

(CIRCLE IN THE SQUARE THEATRE) By Noel Coward; Director, George C. Scott; Set, Marjorie Bradley Kellogg; Costumes, Ann Roth; Lighting, Richard Nelson; Producers, Theodore Mann, Paul Libin; Casting, Lynn Kressel; Wardrobe, Millicent Hacker, Hiram Ortiz; Hairstylist, Lyn Quiyou; Press, Merle Debuskey, David Roggensack; Company Manager, William Conn; Stage Managers, Michael F. Ritchie, Duncan Scott. Opened Thursday, July 15, 1982.*

CAST

Daphne Stillington	Kate Burton †1
Miss Erikson	Bette Henritze†2
Fred	Jim Piddock
Monica Reed	Dana Ivey †3
Garry Essendine	George C. Scott †4
Liz Essendine	Elizabeth Hubbard
Roland Maule	Nathan Lane†5
Henry Lyppiatt	Richard Woods†6
Morris Dixon	Edward Conery
Joanna Lyppiatt	Christine Lahti†7
Lady Saltburn	Georgine Hall†8

STANDBYS AND UNDERSTUDIES: Mart Hulswit (Essendine), Linda Noble (Daphne/Miss Erikson), Jerry Mettner (Fred/Roland), Norma Taylor (Joanna/Liz/Monica/Lady Saltburn)

A comedy in three acts and four scenes. The action takes place sometime before World War II in London in Garry Essendine's studio.

*Closed Jan. 2, 1983 after 175 performances and 32 previews.
†Succeeded by: 1. Harriet Hall, 2. Myra Carter, 3. Betty Henritze, 4. Mart Hulswit during Mr. Scott's illness, 5. Ken Jennings, 6. John Newton, 7. Anne Swift, 8. Barbara Lester

Brownie Harris Photos

Left: Christine Lahti, George C. Scott

George C. Scott, Kate Burton

Dana Ivey

John Neville, Edward Binns, Liv Ullmann

GHOSTS

(BROOKS ATKINSON THEATRE) By Henrik Ibsen; Adapted by Arthur Kopit; Director, John Neville; Set, Kevin Rupnik; Costumes, Theoni V. Aldredge; Lighting, Martin Aronstein; Producers, John F. Kennedy Center, CBS Broadcast Group and James Nederlander; Casting Director, Terry Fay; Production Coordinator, Chic Silber; Sound, Kenneth Persson; Wardrobe, Gerald Scarbrough; Hairstylists, Diane Stokes, Stephen LoVullo, Roy Helland; Production Assistant, Patricia Fay; General Manager, Alan Wasser; Press, John Springer, Meg Gordean; Stage Managers, Mitchell Erickson, John Handy. Opened Monday, Aug. 30, 1982.*

CAST

Regina Engstrand, Mrs. Alving's maid	....	Jane Murray
Jacob Engstrand, a carpenter	....	Edward Binns
Pastor Manders	....	John Neville
Mrs. Helen Alving	....	Liv Ullman
Oswald Alving, her son	....	Kevin Spacey

STANDBYS AND UNDERSTUDIES: Tom Klunis (Manders/Engstrand), Madeleine Potter (Regina), John Bellucci (Oswald)

A drama presented with one intermission. The action takes place at Mrs. Alving's country house, beside one of the large fjords in Western Norway.

*Closed Oct. 2, 1982 after 40 performances and 8 previews.

Jack Buxbaum Photos

Kevin Spacey, Liv Ullmann

YOUR ARMS TOO SHORT TO BOX WITH GOD

(ALVIN THEATRE) Conceived from the "Gospel of St. Matthew" by Vinnette Carroll; Music and Lyrics, Alex Bradford, Micki Grant; Director, Vinnette Carroll; Sets and Costumes, William Schroder; Lighting, Richard Winkler; Sound, R. Shepard, Jim Esher; Musical Direction/Arrangements, Michael Powell; Orchestrations/Dance Music, H. B. Barnum; Choreography, Talley Beatty; Restaged by Ralf Paul Haze; Presented by Barry and Fran Weissler; Associate Producer, Jerry R. Moore; Co-Producers, Anita MacShane, Urban Arts Theatre; Production Coordinator, Daniel F. Kearns; Wardrobe, Dolores Gamba; General Managers, Alecia A. Parker, Patricia M. Morinelli; Press, Burnham-Callaghan, Owen Levy, Lynda Kinney, Jay Schwartz; Company Manager, Stephanie S. Hughley; Stage Managers, Robert Borod, Jonathan Weiss, Leslie Hardesty Sisson. Opened Thursday, Sept, 9, 1982.*

CAST

Patti LaBelle, Al Green, Julius Richard Brown, Nora Cole, Jamil K. Garland, Elijah Gill, L. Michael Gray, Ralf Paul Haze, Cynthia Henry, The Bobby Hill, Rufus E. Jackson, Elmore James, Linda James, Tommi Johnson, Janice Nunn Nelson, Dwayne Phelps, Quincella, Kiki Shepard, Leslie Hardesty Sisson, Marilynn Winbush

MUSICAL NUMBERS

Beatitudes, We're Gonna Have a Good Time, Me and Jesus, There's a Stranger in Town, Running for Jesus, We Are the Priests and Elders, Something Is Wrong in Jerusalem, It Was Alone, I Know I Have to Leave Here, Be Careful Whom You Kiss, Trial, It's Too Late, Judas' Dance, Your Arms Too Short to Box with God, Give Us Barrabas, See How They Done My Lord, Come on Down, Veil of the Temple, Can't No Grave Hold My Body, Didn't I Tell You, Couldn't Keep It to Myself, When the Power Comes, Everybody Has His Own Way, Down by the Riverside, I Love You So Much Jesus, As Long as I Live, On That Day, The Band

A musical in two acts.

*Closed Nov. 7, 1982 after 69 performances and 11 previews

Martha Swope Photos

Right: Patti LaBelle, Al Green

Patti LaBelle

Al Green

A DOLL'S LIFE

(MARK HELLINGER THEATRE) Book and Lyrics, Betty Comden, Adolph Green; Music, Larry Grossman; Director, Harold Prince; Musical Director, Paul Gemignani; Orchestrations, Bill Byers; Choreography, Larry Fuller; Hairstylist/Makeup, Richard Allen; Casting, Joanna Merlin; Sound, Jack Mann; Scenery, Timothy O'Brien, Tazeena Firth; Costumes, Florence Klotz; Lighting, Ken Billington; Presented by James M. Nederlander, Sidney Shlenker, Warner Theatre Productions, Joseph Harris, Mary Lea Johnson, Martin Richards, Robert Fryer in association with Harold Prince; Original cast album on RCA Records and tapes; Production Coordinator, Arthur Masella; Assistant Conductor, Tom Fay; Wardrobe, Stephanie Edwards; General Manager, Howard Haines; Press, Mary Bryant, Becky Flora, Philip Rinaldi; Stage Managers, Beverley Randolph, Richard Evans, Steven Kelley. Opened Thursday, Sept. 23, 1982.*

CAST

Nora	Betsy Joslyn
Actor/Torvald/Johan	George Hearn
Otto	Peter Gallagher
Eric	Edmund Lyndeck
Astrid	Barbara Lang
Audition Singer/Selma/Jacqueline	Penny Orloff
Conductor/Gustafson/Escamillo/Audition Singer/ Loki/Zetterling	Norman A. Large
Stage Hand/Dr. Berg/Audition Singer/Ambassador	David Vosburgh
Dowager	Diane Armistead
Musician/Mr. Kloster	Gordon Bovinet
Camilla Forrester	Willi Burke
Assistant Stage Manager/Helga	Patti Cohenour
Prison Guards	John Corsaut, David Cale Johnson
Helmer's Maid/Waitress	Carol Lurie
Musician/Waiter	Larry Small
Waiter/Audition Singer/Muller	Paul Straney
Maid/Widow	Olga Talyn
Ivar	Jim Wagg
Emmy	Kimberly Stern
Bob	David Seaman
Woman in white	Lisa Peters
Woman in red	Peri Gill
Woman in black	Patricia Parker
Man in black	David Evans

UNDERSTUDIES: Patti Cohenour (Nora), Norman A. Large (Actor/-Torvald/Johan), Larry Small (Otto), Willi Burke (Astrid), Olga Talyn (Jacqueline), Kevin Marcum, Sisu Raiken (Swings), Patricia Parker (Camilla), Lisa Peters (Woman in red), Katie Ertmann (Ivar/Emmy/Bob)
MUSICAL NUMBERS: Prologue, A Woman Alone, Letter to the Children, New Year's Eve, Stay with Me, Nora, Arrival, Loki and Baldur, You Interest Me, Departure, Letter from Klemnacht, Learn to Be Lonely, Rats and Mice and Fish, Jailer Jailer, Rare Wines, No More Mornings, There She Is, Power, At Last, The Grand Cafe, Finale.
A musical in 2 acts and 16 scenes. The action takes place at a rehearsal of Ibsen's "A Doll's House" in 1982.

*Closed Sept. 26, 1982 after 5 performances and 18 previews.

Martha Swope Photos

**Top Right: Betsy Joslyn, George Hearn
Below: (C) Peter Gallagher**

Peter Gallagher, Betsy Joslyn

THE QUEEN AND THE REBELS

(PLYMOUTH THEATRE) By Ugo Betti; Translated by Henry Reed; Director, Waris Hussein; By special arrangement with Ken Marsolais and Lita Starr; Set, David Jenkins; Costumes, Jane Greenwood; Lighting, John McLain; Presented by Circle in the Square (Theodore Mann, Artistic Director; Paul Libin, Managing Director); Casting, Lynn Kressel; Wardrobe, Dorthula McQueen; Production Assistant, John Blinstrub Fisher; Company Manager, William Conn; Press, Merle Debuskey, David Roggensack; Stage Managers, Ken Marsolais, Buzz Cohen. Opened Thursday, Sept. 30, 1982.*

CAST

The Porter	Sean Griffin
A Traveller	Peter Michael Goetz
An Engineer	Donald Gantry
Raim	Scott Hylands
Argia	Colleen Dewhurst
General Biante	Clarence Felder
Maupa	Anthony DeFonte
Elizabetta	Betty Miller
The Boy	Christopher Garvin
Soldiers	Marek Johnson, Campbell Scott, Stanley Tucci
Travellers	Jeffrey Holt Gardner, Jack R. Marks, Etain O'Malley, Fiddle Viracola

A drama in two acts. The action takes place in a large hall in the main public building of a hillside village at the present time.

*Closed Nov. 7, 1982 after 45 performances and 19 previews.

Martha Swope Photos

Top: Clarence Felder, Colleen Dewhurst, Anthony DeFonte, Campbell Scott, Marek Johnson

Peter Michael Goetz, Colleen Dewhurst

CATS

(WINTER GARDEN) Based on "Old Possum's Book of Practical Cats" by T. S. Eliot; Music, Andrew Lloyd Webber; Director, Trevor Nunn; Associate Director/Choreography, Gillian Lynne; Design, John Napier; Lighting, David Hersey; Sound, Martin Levan; Musical Director, Rene Wiegert; Production Musical Director, Stanley Lebowsky; Presented by Cameron Mackintosh, The Really Useful Company, David Geffen, The Shubert Organization; Executive Producers, R. Tyler Gatchell, Jr., Peter Neufeld; Casting, Johnson/Liff; Orchestrations, David Cullen, Andrew Lloyd Webber; Original cast album on Geffen Records; Company Manager, James G. Mennen; General Management, Gatchell & Neufeld; Assistant Musical Director, Keith Herrmann; Production Assistant, Nancy Hall Bell; Wardrobe, Adelaide Laurino; Hairstylists, Leon Gagliardi, Ann Miles, Charles McMahon, Richard Orton; Assistant Choreographer, Jo-Anne Robinson; Press, Fred Nathan, Eileen McMahon, Anne S. Abrams; Stage Managers, David Taylor, Lani Sundsten, Sally J. Greenhut. Opened Thursday, Oct. 7, 1982.*

CAST

Alonzo	Hector Jaime Mercado
Bustopher Jones/Asparagus/Growltiger	Stephen Hanan
Bombalurina	Donna King
Carbucketty	Steven Gelfer
Cassandra	Rene Ceballos
Coricopat/Mungojerrie	Rene Clemente
Demeter	Wendy Edmead
Etcetera/Rumpleteazer	Christine Langner
Grizabella	Betty Buckley
Jellylom./Griddlebone	Bonnie Simmons
Jennyanydots	Anna McNeely
Mistoffolees	Timothy Scott
Munkustrap	Harry Groener
Old Deuteronomy	Ken Page
Plato/Macavity/Rumpus Cat	Kenneth Ard
Pouncival	Herman W. Sebek
Rum Tum Tugger	Terrence V. Mann
Sillabub	Whitney Kershaw
Skimbleshanks	Reed Jones
Tantomile	Janet L. Hubert
Tumblebrutus	Robert Hoshour
Victoria	Cynthia Onrubia
Cats Chorus	Walter Charles, Susan Powers, Carol Richards, Joel Robertson

STANDBYS AND UNDERSTUDIES: Hector Jaime Mercado (Plato), Janet L. Hubert (Grizabella/Demeter), Marlene Danielle (Cassandra/-Demeter/Tantomile/Bombalurina), Diane Fratantoni (Cassandra/Sillabub/Etcetera/Griddlebone), Steven Hack (Coricopat/Carbucketty/-Pouncival), Herman W. Sebek (Coricopat/Alonzo), Bob Morrisey (Munkustrap/Skimbleshanks/Rum Tum Tugger/Alonzo), Steven Gelfer (Bustopher), Whitney Kershaw (Tantomile/Victoria), Rene Ceballos (Bombalurina), Susan Powers (Jennyanydots), Walter Charles (Old Deuteronomy), Rene Clemente (Mistoffolees)

MUSICAL NUMBERS: Jellicle Songs for Jellicle Cats, The Naming of Cats, Invitation to the Jellicle Ball, Old Gumbie Cat, Rum Tum Tugger, Grizabella the Glamour Cat, Bustopher Jones, Mungojerri and Rumpleteazer, Old Deuteronomy, The Awefull Battle of the Pekes and Pollicles, Marching Song of the Pollicle Dogs, Jellicle Ball, Memory, Moments of Happiness, Gus the Theatre Cat, Growltiger's Last Stand, Skimbleshanks, Macavity, Mr. Mistoffolees, Journey to the Heaviside Layer, The Ad-Dressing of Cats

A musical in 2 acts and 21 scenes.

*Still playing May 31, 1983. Winner of 1983 "Tonys" for Best Musical, Best Musical Book, Best Musical Score, Best Musical Director, Best Supporting Musical Actress (Betty Buckley), Best Costume Design, Best Lighting Design.

Martha Swope Photos

Top Right: Ken Page (center)

Betty Buckley

GOOD

(BOOTH THEATRE) By C. P. Taylor; Director, Howard Davies; Setting and Costumes, Ultz; Lighting, Beverly Emmons; Music arranged by George Fenton; Musical Director, Michael Dansicker; American production designed in association with John Kasarda (Set) and Linda Fisher (Costumes); Presented by David Geffen, Warner Theatre Productions, Elizabeth I. McCann & Nelle Nugent, and The Shubert Organization; By arrangement with the Royal Shakespeare Theatre of Stratford-Upon-Avon, England; Production Coordinator, Mary Nealon; Wardrobe, Betty Lee Matelli; Hairstylist, Frank Paul/Patrik D. Moreton; Casting, Johnson/Liff; General Management, McCann & Nugent; Company Manager, Carolyne A. Jones, Jane Tamlyn; Press, Joshua Ellis, David LeShay, Cindy Valk, Solters/Roskin/Friedman; Stage Managers, Janet Beroza, Stephen Brady, Jane Tamlyn, Brian Meister. Opened Wednesday, Oct. 13, 1982.*

CAST

Halder	Alan Howard
Sister/Elizabeth	Kate Spiro
Mother	Marjorie Yates
Maurice	Gary Waldhorn
Helen	Meg Wynn-Owen
Anne	Felicity Dean
Freddie	Pip Miller
Hitler/Bok	David Howey
Doctor/Despatch Rider	Timothy Walker
Bouller/Eichmann	Nicholas Woodeson

UNDERSTUDIES: Irene Hamilton (Mother/Helen), David Howey (Halder), Catherine Riding (Sister/Elizabeth), Kate Spiro (Anne), Paul Teague (Doctor/Bouller/Hitler/Bok/Despatch Rider/Eichmann), Timothy Walker (Freddie), Nicholas Woodeson (Maurice).

A drama in two acts.

*Closed Jan. 30, 1983 after 141 performances and 14 previews.

Mike Martin, Sophie Baker Photos

Left: Felicity Dean, Alan Howard

Nicholas Woodeson, Alan Howard

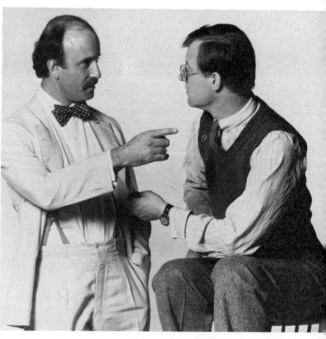

Gary Waldhorn, Alan Howard

THE WAKE OF JAMEY FOSTER

(EUGENE O'NEILL THEATRE) By Beth Henley; Director, Ulu Grosbard: Set, Santo Loquasto; Costumes, Jennifer von Mayrhauser; Lighting, Jennifer Tipton; Casting, McCorkle Sturtevant; Sound, David Rapkin; Presented by FDM Productions, Francois DeMenil/Harris Maslansky, Elliot Martin, Ulu Grosbard, Nan Pearlman, Warner Theatre Productions; Associate Producer, Arla Sorkin Manson; Assistant to the Director, John Gilliss; Wardrobe, Mary Eno; Hairstylist, Ken Davis; General Manager, James Walsh; Company Manager, Susan Bell; Press, Jeffrey Richards, C. George Willard, Robert Ganshaw, Ted Killmer, Helen Stern; Stage Managers, Franklin Keysar, Wendy Chapin. Opened Thursday, Oct. 14, 1982.*

CAST

Marshael Foster	Susan Kingsley
Leon Darnell	Stephen Tobolowsky
Katty Foster	Belita Moreno
Wayne Foster	Anthony Heald
Collard Darnell	Patricia Richardson
Pixrose Wilson	Holly Hunter
Brocker Slade	Brad Sullivan

STANDBYS AND UNDERSTUDIES: Annalee Jefferies (Marshael/-Katty/Collard), Gregory Grove (Wayne/Leon), Bing Russell (Brocker), Mary Anne Dorward (Pixrose)

A play in 2 acts and 5 scenes. The action takes place at the present time throughout the house and yard of Marshael Foster in Canton, Mississippi.

*Closed Oct. 23, 1982 after 12 performances and 12 previews.

Peter Cunningham Photos

Top: Susan Kingsley, Holly Hunter, Patricia Richardson, Belita Moreno, Stephen Tobolowsky, Anthony Heald

Anthony Heald, Brad Sullivan, Stephen Tobolowsky

ROCK 'N' ROLL!
The First 5,000 Years

(ST. JAMES THEATRE) Conceived by Bob Gill and Robert Rabinowitz; Musical Continuity and Supervision, John Simon; Special Consultant, Dick Clark; Direction and Choreography, Joe Layton; Scenery, Mark Ravitz; Costumes, Franne Lee; Lighting, Jules Fisher; Sound, Bran Ferren; Orchestrations/Dance and Vocal Arrangements, John Simon; Musical Direction, Andrew Dorfman; Media, Gill & Rabinowitz; Co-Choreographer, Jerry Grimes; Hairstylist, Lyn Quiyou; Casting, Johnson/Liff; Producers Associate, Robin Ullman; Presented by Jules Fisher and Annie Fargue in association with Dick Clark, Inc., Fred Disipio; Associate Producers, Charles Koppelman, Martin Bandier; Technical Coordinator, Arthur Siccardi; Wardrobe, Joseph Busheme, Donald L. Brassington; Props, Gregory Martin; Assistant Choreographer, Ka-Ron Brown; Production Assistant, Victor Lukas; Musical Coordinator, John Monaco; Associate Orchestrator, Steven Wexler; General Management, Marvin A. Krauss, Eric Angelson, Gary Gunas, Steven C. Callahan; Press, The Merlin Group, Cheryl Sue Dolby, Joel W. Dein, Merle Frimark, Dennis Decker; Stage Managers, Peter Lawrence, Jim Woolley, Sarah Whitham. Opened Sunday Oct. 24, 1982.*

CAST

Rob Barnes, Joyce Leigh Bowden, Ka-Ron Brown, Sandy Dillon, Andrew Dorfman, Rich Hebert, Lon Hoyt, William Gregg Hunter, Bill Jones, Jenifer Lewis, Dave Macdonald, Wenndy Leigh Mackenzie, Karen Mankes, Bob Miller, Michael Pace, Raymond Patterson, Marion Ramsey, Jim Riddle, Shaun Solomon, Tom Teeley, Russell Velazquez, Barbara Walsh, Patrick Weathers, Carl E. Weaver, Lillias White

MUSICAL NUMBERS: Love Is a Many Splendored Thing, Tutti Frutti, Rock around the Clock, Blueberry Hill, Wake Up Little Susie, Great Balls of Fire, Johnny B Goode, Heartbreak Hotel, Hound Dog, Love Me Tender, Why Do Fools Fall in Love, Sh-Boom, Will You Still Love Me Tomorrow, Da Doo Ron Ron, The Twist, Land of a Thousand Dances, I'll Be There, You Keep Me Hanging On, Proud Mary, A Hard Day's Night, I Got You Babe, Good Vibrations, Here Comes the Sun, The Sunshine of Your Love, Blowin' in the Wind, Like a Rolling Stone, Whiter Shade of Pale, Mrs. Robinson, White Rabbit, Respect, The Night They Drove Old Dixie Down, People Got to Be Free, Cry Baby, Forever Young, Everybody's Talking, Joy to the World, Both Sides Now, Higher and Higher, Tubular Bells, I Feel the Earth Move, Satisfaction, When Will I Be Loved, My Generation, You've Got a Friend, Nothing from Nothing, Say It Loud I'm Black and Proud, Summer in the City, Whole Lotta Love, Star Spangled Banner, Boogie Woogie Bugle Boy, I Feel Like I'm Gonna Die Rag, American Pie, Imagine, School's Out, Rock and Roll All Night, Benny and the Jets, Space Oddity, Take a Walk on the Wild Side, Everybody Is a Star, Stayin' Alive, Love to Love You Baby, I Will Survive, On the Run, Jocko Homo, Message in a Bottle, Our Lips Are Sealed, Concrete Shoes, Rock and Roll Music

A musical in two acts.

*Closed Oct. 31, 1982 after 9 performances and 23 previews.

Martha Swope Photos

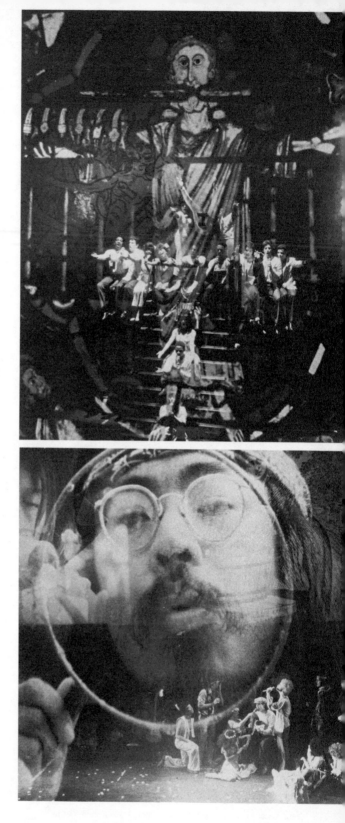

THE SHOWGIRL

(TOWN HALL) Book, Samuel Steinberg; Music and Lyrics, Nellie Casman; Additional Music, Alexander Lustig; Lyrics and New Musical Numbers, Yankele Alperin; Director, Michael Greenstein; Musical Direction, Renee Solomon; Choreography, Yankele Kaluski; Scenery, Lydia Pincus-Gani; Costumes, George Vallo; English Narration, Roz Regalson; Presented by Raymond Ariel, David Carey; Production Manager, Raymond Ariel; Press, Max Eisen, Madelon Joyce Rosen; Opened Sunday, Oct. 24, 1982.*

CAST

Mme. DuBois/Bella/Fifi/Drunkard	Mary Soreanu
Oscar Lampert	Karol Feldman
Jenny (Narrator)	Lydia Saxton
Serkeh	Shifra Lerer
Itzik	Yankele Alperin
Sol	Adrian Mandel
Frimeh	Reizel Bozyk
Nisan	Michael Michalovic
Fred	David Carey
Iser	David Ellin
Naftoli	Karol Latowicz
Jenny as a child	Hallie Lightdale, Orly Jaffe

MUSICAL NUMBERS: Overture, Excuse Me Sir, Childishness, A Jewish Song, Today Is a Holiday, Purim, I'll Always Remember You, Shteytl, I Love the Theatre, French Medley, I Will Wait for You, Just a Little Bit of Health, Five Cents, Finale.

A musical in two acts with a prologue. The action takes place in Brooklyn and Paris in 1945, 1925 and 1934.

*Closed Jan. 2, 1983 after 60 performances to tour.

Gerry Goodstein Photos

David Carey, Michael Michalovic, Mary Soreanu
Top Right: Mary Soreanu

TWICE AROUND THE PARK

(CORT THEATRE) By Murray Schisgal; Director, Arthur Storch; Sets, James Tilton; Costumes, Ruth Morley; Lighting, Judy Rasmuson; Sound, David S. Schnirman; Presented by Peter Witt, Margo Korda, Warner Theatre Productions in association with John F. Kennedy Center for the Performing Arts; General Manager, Victor Samrock; Props, Val Medina; Wardrobe, Allan Collins; Press, Joe Wolhandler, Kathryn Kempf; Stage Managers, John Vivian, Max Storch. Open Thursday, Nov. 4, 1982.*

CAST

Act I
"A Need for Brussels Sprouts"
Leon Rose .... Eli Wallach
Margaret Heinz .... Anne Jackson

The action takes place at the present time in an apartment on Manhattan's West Side

Act II
"A Need for Less Expertise"
Edie Frazier .... Anne Jackson
Gus Frazier .... Eli Wallach
Dr. Oliovsky's Voice .... Paulson Mathews

The action takes place at the present time in an apartment on Manhattan's East Side

STANDBYS: Ben Kapen, Donna Dundon

*Closed Feb. 20, 1983 after 124 performances and 4 previews.

Martha Swope Photos

**Right: Eli Wallach, Anne Jackson
in "A Need for Less Expertise"**

Eli Wallach in "A Need for Brussels Sprouts"

Eli Wallach, Anne Jackson in "A Need for Less Expertise"

FOXFIRE

(ETHEL BARRYMORE THEATRE) By Susan Cooper and Hume Cronyn; Based on materials from the Foxfire Books edited by Eliot Wigginton; Music Composed and Directed by Jonathan Holtzman; Director, David Trainer; Set, David Mitchell; Costumes, Linda Fisher; Lighting, Ken Billington; Sound, Louis Shapiro; Presented by Robert Lussier, Warner Theatre Productions/Claire Nichtern, Mary Lea Johnson, Sam Crothers; Props, Leo Herbert; Wardrobe, Benjamin Wilson; General Management, Belbrook Management; Company Manager, Thomas Shovestull; Press, David Powers, Leo Stern; Stage Managers, Martha Knight, James M. Arnemann. Opened Thursday, Nov. 11, 1982.*

CAST

Annie Nations	Jessica Tandy
Hector Nations	Hume Cronyn
Prince Carpenter	Trey Wilson
Holly Burrell	Katherine Cortez
Dillard Nations	Keith Carradine
Doctor	James Greene
Musicians	Marc Horowitz (Banjo), Ken Kosek (Fiddle), Roger Mason (Bass)

UNDERSTUDIES: Bess Gatewood (Holly), Terrance O'Quinn (Prince/Dillard), James Greene (Hector)

A play in two acts. The action takes place in Rabun County, Georgia, at the present time, and before that.

*Closed May 15, 1983 after 213 performances and 11 previews. Miss Tandy received a 1983 "Tony" Award for her performance as Best Actress in a Play.

Zoe Dominic Photos

Right: Hume Cronyn, Jessica Tandy, Keith Carradine (front)

James Greene, Jessica Tandy, Hume Cronyn

Katherine Cortez, Jessica Tandy

23

84 CHARING CROSS ROAD

(NEDERLANDER THEATRE) By Helene Hanff; Adapted and Directed by James Roose-Evans; Set, Oliver Smith; Costumes, Pearl Somner; Lighting, Marc B. Weiss; Presented by Alexander H. Cohen, Hildy Parks, Cynthia Wood; Co-Producer, Roy A. Somlyo; Presented in association with Michael Redington; Production Associate, Seymour Herscher; Casting, Meg Simon/Fran Kumin; Company Managers, Charles Willard, Jodi Moss; General Manager, Roy A. Somlyo; Press, Merle Debuskey, David Roggensack, Sid Garfield; Stage Managers, Robert L. Borod, Christopher A. Cohen. Open Tuesday, Dec. 7, 1982.*

CAST

Helene Hanff	Ellen Burstyn
Frank Doel	Joseph Maher
Cecily Farr	Ellen Newman
Megan Wells	Jo Henderson
George Martin	William Francis
William Humphries	Mark Chamberlin
Maxine Stuart	Jo Henderson
Joan Todd	Etain O'Malley
Matthew	Thomas Nahrwold

STANDBYS AND UNDERSTUDIES: Elizabeth Perry (Helene), Miller Lide (Frank), Etain O'Malley (Cecily/Megan/Maxine), Thomas Nahrwold (Humphries)

A play in two acts. The action takes place in the New York apartment of Helene Hanff and in Marks & Co., booksellers, 84 Charing Cross Road, London, England, between 1949 and 1971.

*Closed Feb. 27, 1983 after 96 performances and 15 previews.

Martha Swope Photos

Left: Ellen Burstyn, Joseph Maher

Ellen Burstyn, Jo Henderson, Ellen Newman, Mark Chamberlin, Joseph Maher (seated)

HERMAN VAN VEEN: ALL OF HIM

(AMBASSADOR THEATRE) Concept, Herman van Veen, Michel Lafaille; English Adaptation and Lyrics, Christopher Adler; Director, Michel Lafaille; Set, Gerard Jongerius, Ed DeBoer; Costumes, Ellen van der Horst; Lighting, Rob Munnik; Sound, Hans van der Linden; Musical Direction, Erik van der Wurff; English Translations, Patricia Braun; Presented by Joost Taverne, Michael Frazier, Ron van Eeden in association with Harlekyn U.S.A. Company; Associate Producer, Patricia Braun; General Manager, Frank Scardino; Technical Consultant, Jeremiah Harris; Press, Joshua Ellis, Cindy Valk, Matthew Messinger, Solters/Roskin/-Friedman; Jan Greenberg; Stage Manager, Luc Hemeleers. Opened Wednesday, Dec. 8, 1982.*

MUSICAL NUMBERS

A Girl, A Loose Woman, Cranes, Do You Remember, Hello, Heroes, Hole-in-One, I Don't Want Any Help, I Won't Let That Happen to Him, Jacob Is Dead, Kitchen Sink, Ode to Suicide, Parade of Clowns, Sarabande, Station, Tell Me Who I Was, The Back of Life, The Fence, The Interview, The Rules of the Asylum, Time Passed Her By, What a Day

A musical show in two acts performed by Herman van Veen.

*Closed Dec. 12, 1982 after 6 performances and 1 preview.

Jan Swinkels Photos

Herman van Veen (also top)

STEAMING

(BROOKS ATKINSON THEATRE) By Nell Dunn; Director, Roger Smith; Set, Marjorie Bradley Kellogg; Costumes, Jennifer von Mayrhauser; Lighting, Pat Collins; Sound, David Rapkin; Incidental Music, Richard Hartley; Dialect Coach, Elizabeth Smith; Casting, Mary Colquhoun; Production Associate, Vivian Dreifuss; Wardrobe, Mary Eno; Production Assistant, Crawford Mills; General Manager, Robert S. Fishko; Company Manager, Susan Bell; Press, Seymour Krawitz, Patricia Krawitz; Stage Managers, Steve Zweigbaum, Scott Glenn. Opened Sunday, Dec. 12, 1982.*

CAST

Violet	Pauline Flanagan
Bill	John Messenger
Nancy	Linda Thorson
Mrs. Meadow	Polly Rowles
Dawn	Lisa Jane Persky
Josie	Judith Ivey
Jane	Margaret Whitton

A play in 2 acts and 7 scenes. The action takes place in a Turkish bath in London during the late 1970's.

*Closed Feb. 5, 1983 after 65 performances and 3 previews. Miss Ivey received a 1983 "Tony" Award for Best Featured Actress in a Play.

Martha Swope Photos

Right: Judith Ivey, Linda Thorson, Pauline Flanagan

Linda Thorson, Polly Rowles, Judith Ivey, Margaret Whitton

MONDAY AFTER THE MIRACLE

(EUGENE O'NEILL THEATRE) By William Gibson; Director, Arthur Penn; Sets, John Lee Beatty; Costumes, Carol Oditz; Lighting, F. Mitchell Dana; Incidental Music, Claude Kerry-White; Presented by Raymond Katz, Sandy Gallin and the John F. Kennedy Center; Technical Supervisor, Jeremiah Harris; Props, Paul Biega; Wardrobe, William Campbell; Hairstylist, Phyllis Della, Bobby Miller, Peg Schierholz; Production Assistant, Anne Beck; Casting, Howard Feuer, Jeremy Ritzer; General Managers, Joseph Harris, Ira Bernstein, Peter T. Kulok, Steven E. Goldstein; Press, Solters/Roskin/Friedman, Joshua Ellis, David LeShay, Cindy Valk, Matthew Messinger; Assistant to the Director, Jeffrey B. Davis. Opened Tuesday, Dec. 14, 1982.*

CAST

Helen .... Karen Allen
John .... William Converse-Roberts
Annie .... Jane Alexander
Pete .... Matt McKenzie
Ed .... Joseph Warren

UNDERSTUDIES: Geraldine Baron (Annie), Denise Lute (Helen), Francoise De La Giroday (John/Pete), Paul Haggard (Ed)

A drama in three acts. The action takes place during the early part of this century, in Boston environs—first Cambridge, then Wrentham, Massachusetts.

*Closed Dec. 18, 1982 after 7 performances and 9 previews.

Martha Swope Photos

Right: Joseph Warren, Jane Alexander

Karen Allen, Jane Alexander, William Converse-Roberts

A LITTLE FAMILY BUSINESS

(MARTIN BECK THEATRE) Adapted by Jay Presson Allen from a play by Barillet and Gredy; Director, Martin Charnin; Set, David Gropman; Costumes, Theoni V. Aldredge; Lighting, Richard Nelson; Production Associate, Harvey Elliott; Presented by Harry Saltzman, Arthur Cantor, Warner Theatre Productions, in association with Center Theatre Group-/Ahmanson Theatre; Production Assistants, Virginia Mayers, Max Cantor, Tom Siracusa, David Kuhn, Nazeli Asarian, Alexander Fraser; Props, George Wagner, Jr.; Wardrobe, Frank Green; Hairstylists, Lyn Quiyou, Hiram Ortiz; Assistants to the Director, Carol Secretan, Lee Costello; General Manager, Alan Wasser; Company Manager, Harvey Elliott; Press, Arthur Cantor; Stage Managers, Frank Hartenstein, Edward R. Fitzgerald. Opened Wednesday, Dec. 15, 1982.*

CAST

Lillian	Angela Lansbury
Ben	John McMartin
Nadine	Sally Stark
Scott	Anthony Shaw
Connie	Tracy Brooks Swope
Sal	Theodore Sorel
Works Committee:	
Marco	Tony Cummings
Sophia	Hallie Foote
Vinnie	Gordon Rigsby
Joe	Donald E. Fischer

UNDERSTUDIES: Gordon Rigsby (Ben/Sal), Hallie Foote (Nadine/-Connie), Tony Cummings (Scott), Donald E. Fischer (Marco)

A comedy in 2 acts and 5 scenes. The action takes place at the present time in the morning room of the Ridley home in Cobbsville, Massachusetts.

*Closed Dec. 26, 1982 after 13 performances and 23 previews.

Martha Swope Photos

John McMartin, Angela Lansbury

Top: Anthony Shaw, Angela Lansbury,
John McMartin, Tracy Brooks Swope

ALMOST AN EAGLE

(LONGACRE THEATRE) By Michael Kimberley; Director, Jacques Levy; Set and Costumes, Karl Eigsti; Lighting, Roger Morgan; Presented by Frederick M. Zollo, Susan R. Rose, Gail Berman, William P. Suter, Nicholas Paleologos, Melvyn J. Estrin, Sidney Shlenker; Associate Producers, Paul D'Addario, Barbara Livitz; Props, Peter Gardner; Wardrobe, Mark Immens; Casting, Jane Iredale; Assistant to the Producers, Bruce Condie, Jay Schwartz; Production Associate, Georgianne Walken; Production Assistants, Monica Landry, Linda Pilz; General Manager, Theatre Now, William Court Cohen, Edward H. Davis, Norman E. Rothstein, Ralph Roseman; Company Manager, Robb Lady; Press, Judy Jacksina, Glenna Freedman, Marcy Granata, Diane Tomlinson, Susan Chicoine; Stage Managers, Steve Beckler, Deborah Clelland. Opened Thursday, Dec. 16, 1982.*

CAST

Billy Spencer .... Jeffrey Marcus
Terry Mathews .... Scott Simon
Mark Lillard .... John P. Navin, Jr.
Shawn Haley .... Neill Barry
The Colonel .... James Whitmore

STANDBYS AND UNDERSTUDIES: Ed Setrakian (Colonel), Mark Patton (Spencer/Haley), Danny Hess (Lillard), Gus Salud (Mathews)

A comedy in two acts. The action takes place at the present time in the basement of a beerhall in Table Rock, Iowa.

*Closed Dec. 19, 1982 after 5 performances and 3 previews.

Martha Swope Photos

Right: James Whitmore

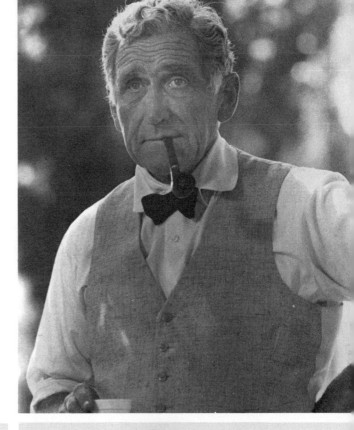

(from top) Mark Bendo, Jeffrey Marcus, John Navin, Scott Simon

James Whitmore, Jeffrey Marcus

ALICE IN WONDERLAND

(VIRGINIA THEATRE) By Lewis Carroll; Adapted for the Stage by Eva LeGallienne and Florida Friebus; Entire Production Conceived and Directed by Miss LeGallienne; Co-Director, John Strasberg; Set, John Lee Beatty; Costumes, Patricia Zipprodt; Lighting, Jennifer Tipton; Puppets, The Puppet People; Music Adapted and Supervised by Jonathan Tunick; Movement, Bambi Linn; Sound, Jack Mann; Musical Conductor, Les Scott; Special Effects, Chic Silber; Presented by Sabra Jones, Anthony D. Marshall in association with WNET/Thirteen; Props, Mel Saltzman; Wardrobe, Nancy Schaefer; Makeup, Fred Patton; Assistant Conductor, James Stenborg; Assistant to the Directors, Peter Arnott; Casting, Johnson-Liff, Andrew Zerman, Shirley Rich; Assistant to the Producers, Susan Fenichell; Production Assistant, John N. Concannon; General Management, McCann & Nugent; Company Manager, Steven Suskin; Press, Solters/Roskin/Friedman, Joshua Ellis, David LeShay, Cindy Valk, Matthew Messinger; Stage Managers, Alan Hall, Ruth E. Rinklin, Skip Harris. Opened Thursday, Dec. 23, 1982.*

CAST

The White Queen	Eva LeGallienne
Alice	Kate Burton
Eagle/Two of Hearts	Rebecca Armen
Five of Spades/Tweedledum	Robert Ott Boyle
March Hare/Front of Horse	Josh Clark
White Rabbit/White Knight	Curt Dawson
Mad Hatter	MacIntyre Dixon
Two of Spades	Geoff Garland
Caterpillar/Sheep	John Heffernan
Gryphon/Old Frog	Edward Hibbert
Singer/Eight of Hearts	Nancy Killmer
Duck/Dormouse/Train Guard	Nicholas Martin
Seven of Spades/Voice of Leg of Mutton	Steve Massa
Small White Rabbit/Four of Hearts	Mary Stuart Masterson
Lory/Seven of Hearts	John Miglietta
Singer/Six of Hearts	Marti Morris
Seven of Clubs/Back of Horse	Cliff Rakerd
Queen of Hearts	Brian Reddy
Mouse/Three of Hearts/Tweedledee	John Remme
Frog Footman/Five of Hearts/Goat	Claude-Albert Saucier
Knave of Hearts	John Seidman
Fish Footman/Voice of Cheshire Cat/Ace of Hearts/ Man in White Paper	Geddeth Smith
Cook/Nine of Hearts	Richard Sterne
Mock Turtle/Dodo	James Valentine
White Chess Queen Alternate	Joan White
Red Queen	Mary Louise Wilson
King of Hearts/Voice of Humpty Dumpty	Richard Woods
Duchess	Edward Zang
Three of Clubs	Skip Harris

ACT I: Alice at Home, The Looking-Glass House, Pool of Tears, Caucus Race, Caterpillar, Duchess, Cheshire Cat, Mad Tea Party, Queen's Croquet Ground, By the Sea, The Trial
ACT II: Red Chess Queen, Railway Carriage, Tweedledum and Tweedledee, White Chess Queen, The Sheep Shop, Humpty Dumpty, White Knight, Alice with the Two Queens, Alice's Door, The Banquet, Alice at Home Again.

*Closed Jan. 9, 1983 after 21 performances and 18 previews.

Martha Swope Photos

Top Left: Kate Burton (center) Below: Eva LeGallienne, Kate Burton, Mary Louise Wilson

Eva LeGallienne, Kate Burton

WHODUNNIT

(BILTMORE THEATRE) By Anthony Shaffer; Director, Michael Kahn; Set, Andrew Jackness; Costumes, Patricia Zipprodt; Lighting, Martin Aronstein; Hairstylist/Make-up, Patrik D. Moreton; Sound, Richard Fitzgerald; Casting, Johnson/Liff; Presented by Douglas Urbanski, Robert A. Buckley, E. Gregg Wallace, Jr.; Dialect Coach, Elizabeth Smith; Wardrobe, Penny Davis; Production Assistants, Jay Kane, Dominique Lowell; General Managers, Robert A. Buckley, Douglas Urbanski; Company Manager, Max Allentuck; Press, Marilynn LeVine, Michael Alpert, Randi Cone, Rebecca Robbins; Stage Managers, Frank Marino, Judith Binus. Opened Thursday, Dec. 30, 1982.*

CAST

Archibald Perkins (the butler)	Gordon Chater
Andreas Capodistriou (oily Levantine)	George Hearn †
Silas Bazeby (family lawyer)	Jerome Dempsey
Rear-Admiral Knatchbull Folliatt	Ronald Drake
Lady Tremurrain (dotty aristocrat)	Barbara Baxley
Lavinia Hargreaves (sweet young thing)	Lauren Thompson
Roger Dashwell (black sheep)	John Glover
Dame Edith Runcible (archeologist)	Hermione Baddeley
Inspector Bowden (Yard detective)	Fred Gwynne
Sergeant	Jeffrey Alan Chandler

STANDBYS AND UNDERSTUDIES: John Hallow (Silas/Folliatt/Inspector), Patricia Gage (Lady Tremurrain/Dame Edith), Robert Nadir (Roger/Sergeant), Johanna Leister (Lavinia)

A mystery in two acts. The action takes place in the library of Orcas Champflower Manor on an evening in the 1930's.

*Closed May 15, 1983 after 157 performances and 19 previews.
†Succeeded by George Gorshin

Martha Swope Photos

**Top: (L) Gordon Chater, Hermione Baddeley
(R) Barbara Baxley, John Glover, Lauren Thompson**

Fred Gwynne, Jeffrey Alan Chandler

Edward Herrmann, Kate Nelligan, Ellen Parker

PLENTY

(PLYMOUTH THEATRE) By David Hare who also directed; Sets, John Gunter; Costumes, Jane Greenwood; Lighting, Arden Fingerhut; Incidental Music, Nick Bicat; Hairstylist, Andrew Reese; A New York Shakespeare Festival Production presented by Joseph Papp; Props, Jan Marasek; Sound, James Limberg; Wardrobe, John A. Guiteras; General Manager, Robert Kamlot; Company Manager, Rheba Flegelman; Production Supervisor, Jason Steven Cohen; Press, Merle Debuskey, Richard Kornberg, Barbara Carroll, Bruce Campbell; Stage Managers, Michael Chambers, Anne King. Opened Thursday, Jan. 6, 1983.*

CAST

Alice Park	Ellen Parker
Susan Traherne	Kate Nelligan
Raymond Brock	Edward Herrmann
Codename Lazar	Ben Masters
Frenchman #1	Ken Meseroll
Leonard Darwin	George N. Martin
Mick	Daniel Gerroll
Louise	Johann Carlo
M. Aung	Conrad Yama
Mme. Aung	Ginny Yang
Dorcas Frey	Madeleine Potter
John Begley	Jeff Allin
Sir Andrew Charleson	Bill Moor
Frenchman #2	Pierre Epstein

STANDBYS AND UNDERSTUDIES: Randy Danson (Alice), Jeff Allin (Codename/Nick), Victor Wong (Aung), Kiya Ann Joyce (Mme. Aung), Elizabeth Norment (Alice/Louise/Dorcas), Tom Klunis (Leonard/Charleson/Frenchman 2), Robert Curtis-Brown (Begley/Frenchman 1)

A drama in 2 acts and 12 scenes. The action takes place in England from 1943 to 1962.

*Closed March 27, 1983 after 92 performances and 11 previews. It was moved from the Public/Newman Theater where it had played 58 performances from Oct. 8 through Nov. 28, 1982. The NY Drama Critics Circle voted it Best Foreign Play of the season.

Martha Swope Photos

Top: George N. Martin, Kate Nelligan, Ellen Parker, Ginny Yang, Edward Herrmann, Conrad Yama

ANGELS FALL

(LONGACRE THEATRE) By Lanford Wilson; Director, Marshall W. Mason; Set, John Lee Beatty; Costumes, Jennifer von Mayrhauser; Lighting, Dennis Parichy; Sound, Chuck London Media/Stewart Werner; Original Music, Norman L. Berman; Presented by Elliot Martin, Circle Repertory Co., Lucille Lortel, The Shubert Organization (Gerald Schoenfeld, Chairman; Bernard B. Jacobs, President), The John F. Kennedy Center (Roger L. Stevens, Chairman); Wardrobe, Barbara Hladsky; Hairstylist, Miriam Nieves; General Managers, Leonard A. Mulhern, Jay Kingwill, Dan Zittel; Press, Jeffrey Richards, C. George Willard, Robert Ganshaw, Ted Killmer, Helen Stern, Richard Humleker; Stage Managers, Fred Reinglas, Ginny Martino. Opened Saturday, Jan. 22, 1983.*

CAST

Niles Harris	Fritz Weaver
Vita Harris	Nancy Snyder
Don Tabaha	Danton Stone
Marion Clay	Tanya Berezin
Salvatore (Zappy) Zappala	Brian Tarantina
Father William Doherty	Barnard Hughes

A drama in two acts. The action takes place at the present time on a late Saturday afternoon in June in a mission in northwest New Mexico.

*Closed Mar. 13, 1983 after 64 performances. It was moved from Off-Broadway's Circle Repertory Theatre where it played 63 performances.

Gerry Goodstein Photos

Danton Stone, Nancy Snyder, Tanya Berezin, Brian Tarantina, Barnard Hughes, Fritz Weaver
Top Right: Fritz Weaver, Barnard Hughes

THE MISANTHROPE

(CIRCLE IN THE SQUARE) By Moliere; English verse translation by Richard Wilbur; Director, Stephen Porter; Set, Marjorie Bradley Kellogg; Costumes, Ann Roth; Lighting, Richard Nelson; Wigs, Peg Schierholz; Presented by Circle in the Square (Theodore Mann, Artistic Director; Paul Libin, Managing Director); Casting, Lynn Kressel; Wardrobe, Millicent Hacker, David Bess; Hairstylist, Eileen Tersago; Props, Frank Jauser; Company Manager, William Conn; Press, Merle Debuskey, David Roggensack; Stage Managers, Michael F. Ritchie, A. Robert Scott. Opened Thursday, Jan. 27, 1983.*

CAST

Philinte, Alceste's friend	Stephen D. Newman
Alceste, in love with Celimene	Brian Bedford †
Oronte, in love with Celimene	David Schramm
Celimene, Alceste's beloved	Mary Beth Hurt
Basque, Celimene's servant	Duffy Hudson
Eliante, Celimene's cousin	Mary Layne
Clitandre, Marquess	Munson Hicks
Acaste, Marquess	George Pentecost
Guard of the Marshalsea	Steve Hendrickson
Arsinoe, friend of Celimene	Carole Shelley
Dubois, Alceste's valet	Stanley Tucci

STANDBYS AND UNDERSTUDIES: Steve Hendrickson (Philinte/Oronte/Clitandre/Basque), Duffy Hudson (Dubois), Stanley Tucci (Alceste/Acaste), A. Robert Scott (Guard), Pamela Lewis (Celimene/Arsinoe/Eliante)

A comedy in two acts. The action takes place in Celimene's house in Paris.

*Closed March 27, 1983 after 69 performances and 23 previews.
†Succeeded by Stephen McHattie

Martha Swope Photos

Right: Mary Beth Hurt, Brian Bedford

Stephen McHattie

Brian Bedford, Mary Beth Hurt, Carole Shelley

A VIEW FROM THE BRIDGE

(AMBASSADOR THEATRE) By Arthur Miller; Director, Arvin Brown; Set, Hugh Landwehr; Costumes, Bill Walker; Lighting, Ronald Wallace; Fights staged by B. H. Barry; Casting, Deborah Brown; Presented by Zev Bufman and Sidney Shlenker; A Long Wharf Theatre Production; Associate Producer, Barbara Livitz; General Management, Theatre Now, William Court Cohen, Edward H. Davis, Norman E. Rothstein, Ralph Roseman, Charlotte Wilcox; Assistant to Director, Michael Urban; Technical Supervisor, Jeremiah J. Harris; Props, Roy Sears; Dialect Consultant, Timothy Monich; Production Assistant, Elizabeth Mundy; Wardrobe, Patricia Britton; Company Manager, Hans Hortig; Press, Fred Nathan, Eileen McMahon, Anne S. Abrams, John Howlett, Charles Cinnamon; Stage Managers, James Harker, Barbara Schneider. Opened Thursday, Feb. 3, 1983.*

CAST

Louis	Stephen Mendillo
Mike	John Shepard
Alfieri	Robert Prosky †1
Eddie	Tony LoBianco
Catherine	Saundra Santiago
Beatrice	Rose Gregorio †2
Marco	Alan Feinstein
Tony	Paul Perri
Rodolpho	James Hayden
First Immigration Officer	Ramon Ramos
Second Immigration Officer	James Vitale
Mr. Lipari	Mitchell Jason
Mrs. Lipari	Rose Arrick
First "Submarine"	Tom Nardini
Second "Submarine"	Joseph Adams

STANDBYS: Michael Baseleon (Eddie), Mitchell Jason (Alfieri), Rose Arrick (Beatrice), Yolanda Lloyd (Catherine), Joseph Adams (Rodolpho), Stephen Mendillo (Marco)

A drama in two acts. The action takes place during the 1950's in the apartment and environs of Eddie Carbone, all in Red Hook, on the Bay seward from Brooklyn Bridge.

*Closed June 12, 1983 after 149 performances and 7 previews.
†Succeeded by: 1. Sam Gray, 2. Tresa Hughes

Martha Swope Photos

Top: Tony LoBianco, Rose Gregorio, Saundra Santiago, James Hayden, Alan Feinstein

Saundra Santiago, Tony LoBianco, James Hayden

35

MERLIN

(MARK HELLINGER THEATRE) Book, Richard Levinson, William Link; Songs and Incidental Music, Elmer Bernstein; Lyrics, Don Black; Magic Illusions, Doug Henning; Director, Ivan Reitman; Choreography, Christopher Chadman, Billy Wilson; Scenery, Robin Wagner; Costumes, Theoni V. Aldredge; Lighting, Tharon Musser; Sound, Abe Jacob; Orchestrations, Larry Wilcox; Musical Direction/Vocal Arrangements, David Spear; Dance Arrangements, Mark Hummel; Magic Consultant, Charles Reynolds; Hairstylist, Ted Azar; Production Supervisor, Jeff Hamlin; Casting, Pulvino & Howard; Produced by Ivan Reitman, Columbia Pictures Stage Productions, Marvin A. Krauss, Manes M. Nederlander; Technical Coordinator, Arthur Siccardi; Sound, Jesse Heimlich; Props, Charles Zuckerman, Alan Steiner; Assistant Conductor, Fred Mangella; Wardrobe, Joseph Busheme, Donald Brassington; Production Assistant, Sherry Cohen; Animals, Rick and Judy Glassey; General Management, Marvin A. Krauss, Gary Gunas, Eric Angelson, Steven C. Callahan, Sue Frost; Press, Merlin Group, Cheryl Sue Dolby, Merle Frimark, Joel W. Dein; Stage Managers, Jeff Lee, Bonnie Panson, B. J. Allen. Opened Sunday, Feb. 13, 1983.*

CAST

Old Merlin/Old Soldier	George Lee Andrews
Young Merlin/Arthur	Christian Slater †1
The Wizard	Edmund Lyndeck
Merlin	Doug Henning
Philomena	Rebecca Wright
The Queen	Chita Rivera
The Queen's Companion	Gregory Mitchell
Prince Fergus	Nathan Lane
Merlin's Vision/Water	Debby Henning
Ariadne	Michelle Nicastro
Acolyte/Manservant	Alan Brasington
Earth	Peggy Parten
Air	Robyn Lee †2
Fire	Spence Ford

ENSEMBLE: Robin Cleaver, Spence Ford, Pat Gorman, Andrea Handler, Debby Henning, Leslie Hicks, Sandy Laufer, Robyn Lee, Peggy Parten, Iris Revson, Claudia Shell, David Asher, Ramon Galindo, Todd Lester, Joe Locarro, Fred C. Mann III, Gregory Mitchell, Andrew Hill Newman, Eric Roach, Robert Tanna, Robert Warners

UNDERSTUDIES: Andrew Hill Newman (Merlin), Sandy Laufer (Queen), Robert Warners (Fergus), Alan Brasington (Wizard/Old Merlin/Old Soldier), David Asher (Wizard/Acolyte/Manservant), Claudia Shell (Philomena), Leslie Hicks (Ariadne), Ron Meier (Young Merlin/Arthur)

MUSICAL NUMBERS: It's about Magic, I Can Make It Happen, Beyond My Wildest Dreams, Something More, The Elements, Fergus' Dilemma, Nobody Will Remember Him, Put a Little Magic in Your Life, He Who Knows the Way, We Haven't Fought a Battle in Years, Satan Rules

A musical in 2 acts and 12 scenes. The action takes place in the time of sorcery.

*Closed Aug. 7, 1983 after 199 performances and 69 previews.
†Succeeded by: 1. Knowl Johnson, 2. Andrea Handler

Peter Cunningham Photos

Top Left: Doug Henning (C) and company

Chita Rivera, Doug Henning

MOOSE MURDERS

(EUGENE O'NEILL THEATRE) By Arthur Bicknell; Director, John Roach; Set, Marjorie Bradley Kellogg; Costumes, John Carver Sullivan; Lighting, Pat Collins; Sound, Chuck London Media/Stewart Werner; Dance Coordinator, Mary Jane Houdina; Stage Violence, Kent Shelton; Casting, Pulvino & Howard; Presented by Force Ten Productions; Associate Producer, Ricka Kanter Fisher; General Management, Theatre Now, William Court Cohen, Edward H. Davis, Norman E. Rothstein, Dorothy Finn, Ralph Roseman; Technical Supervisor, Jeremiah Harris; Props, Laura Koch; Wardrobe, Kathleen Gallagher; Production Assistant, Pierce Bihm; Hairstylist, Ronald DeMann; Press, Betty Lee Hunt, Maria Cristina Pucci, James Sapp, Maurice Turet; Stage Managers, Jerry Bihm, Clifford Schwartz. Opened Tuesday, Feb. 22, 1983.*

CAST

Snooks Keene	June Gable
Howie Keene	Don Potter
Joe Buffalo Dance	Jack Dabdoub
Nurse Dagmar	Lisa McMillan
Hedda Holloway	Holland Taylor †1
Stinky Holloway	Scott Evans
Gay Holloway	Mara Hobel
Lauraine Holloway Fay	Lillie Robertson
Nelson Fay	Nicholas Hormann
Sidney Holloway	Dennis Florzak

UNDERSTUDIES: Suzanne Henry (Snooks/Dagmar/Lauraine/Hedda), Anderson Matthews (Howie/Sidney/Stinky/Joe), Dennis Florzak (Nelson)

A comedy in two acts. The action takes place at the present time in the Wild Moose Lodge during an evening in early fall.

*Closed Feb. 22, 1983 after 1 performance and 13 previews.
†For 2 previews the part was played by Eve Arden

Martha Swope Photos

Top: Mara Hobel, Scott Evans, Holland Taylor, Lillie Robertson

Don Potter, June Gable, Holland Taylor

ON YOUR TOES

(VIRGINIA THEATRE) Book, Richard Rodgers, Lorenz Hart, George Abbott; Music, Richard Rodgers; Lyrics, Lorenz Hart; Director, George Abbott; Original Choreography, George Balanchine; Additional Ballet Choreography, Peter Martins; Musical Numbers Choreographed by Donald Saddler; Design, Zack Brown; Lighting, John McLain; Original Orchestrations, Hans Spialek; Musical Director/Conductor, John Mauceri; Casting, Hughes/Moss; Presented by Alfred de Liagre, Jr., Roger L. Stevens, John Mauceri, Donald R. Seawell, Andre Pastoria; Coordinating Producer, Charlene Harrington; Props, Richard King, Jr.; Soundman, Jan Nebozenko; Wardrobe, Dean Jackson, Rose Ann Moran; Production Associate, Jean Bankier; Production Assistant, Terry Wuthrich; Assistant Musical Director/Conductor, Paul Schwartz; Musical Contractor/Conductor, John Kim Bell; Makeup and Wigs, Charles Elsen, Dennis Bergevin; General Management, Charlene Harrington, C. Edwin Knill; Press, Jeffrey Richards, C. George Willard, Robert Ganshaw, Ted Killmer, Ben Morse, Helen Stern, Richard Humleker; Stage Managers, William Dodds, Amy Pell, Sarah Whitham. Opened Sunday, March 6, 1983.*

CAST

Phil Dolan II/Oscar	Eugene J. Anthony
Lil Dolan/Woman Reporter	Betty Ann Grove
Phil Dolan III/Junior	Philip Arthur Ross
Stage Manager	Dirk Lumbard
Lola	Mary C. Robare
Junior (15 years later)	Lara Teeter
Miss Pinkerton	Michaela K. Hughes
Sidney Cohn	Peter Slutsker
Frankie Frayne	Christine Andreas
Joe McCall	Jerry Mitchell
Vera Baronova	Natalia Makarova †1
Anushka	Tamara Mark
Peggy Porterfield	Dina Merrill †2
Sergei Alexandrovitch	George S. Irving
Konstantine Morrosine	George De La Pena
Stage Doorman	David Gold
Dimitri	Chris Peterson
Ivan	Don Steffy
Louie	George Kmeck

"Princess Zenobia Ballet": Natalia Makarova (Princess Zenobia), George De La Pena (Beggar), George Kmeck (Kringa Khan), Eugene J. Anthony (Ali Shar), David Gold (Ahmud Ben B'Du), Michael Vita (Hank Jay Smith)
"On Your Toes" Ballet: Alexander Filipov, Starr Danias (Ballet Leaders), Dirk Lumbard, Dana Moore (Tap Leaders), Michael Vita (Cop), Dean Badolato (Messenger Boy)
"Slaughter on Tenth Avenue" Ballet: Lara Teeter (Hoofer), Natalia Makarova (Strip Tease Girl), Michael Vita (Big Boss), Jerry Mitchell (Cop)
ENSEMBLE: Melody A. Dye, Michaela K. Hughes, Tamara Mark, Dana Moore, Mary C. Robare, Marcia Lynn Watkins, Leslie Woodies, Sandra Zigars, Dean Badolato, Alexander Filipov, Wade Laboissonniere, Dirk Lumbard, Robert Meadows, Jerry Mitchell, Chris Peterson, Don Steffy, Kirby Tepper, David Gold, George Kmeck
UNDERSTUDIES: Dana Moore (Lil), Dirk Lumbard (Junior/Phil II), Marcia Lynn Watkins (Frankie), Kirby Tepper (Sidney), Starr Danias (Vera), Michaela K. Hughes (Peggy), David Gold (Sergei), Alexander Filipov (Konstantine), Jerry Mitchell (Louie), Steven Ross (Phil III)
MUSICAL NUMBERS: Two a Day for Keith, Questions and Answers, It's Got to Be Love, Too Good for the Average Man, The Seduction, There's a Small Hotel, Princess Zenobia Ballet, The Heart Is Quicker Than the Eye, Glad to Be Unhappy, Quiet Night, On Your Toes, Slaughter on Tenth Avenue

A musical in 2 acts and 12 scenes. The action takes place about 1920.

*Still playing May 31, 1983. The production received 1983 "Tonys" for Best Revival, and Miss Makarova for Best Actress in a Musical. Original production ran for 315 performances at the Imperial Theatre after its opening on April 11, 1936. Tamara Geva and Ray Bolger were starred.
†Succeeded by: 1. Galina Panova, 2. Kitty Carlisle during vacation.

Martha Swope Photos

Top Left: George de la Pena, Natalia Makarova
Below: George S. Irving, Dina Merrill

Christine Andreas, Lara Teeter

SLAB BOYS

(PLAYHOUSE THEATRE) By John Byrne; Director, Robert Allan Ackerman; Scenery, Ray Recht after designs by John Byrne; Lighting, Arden Fingerhut; Costumes, Robert Wojewodski after designs by John Byrne; A Paramount Theatre Productions presentation, in association with Jay D. Kramer, of the Laura Shapiro Kramer and Roberta Weissman production; Assistant to Director, Franco Zavani; Sound, William Dreisbach; Wardrobe, Cheryl Woronoff; Hairstylist and Wigs, Thomas Bracconeri, Charles LoPresto; Language Consultant, Kristin Linklater; Casting/Assistant to Producers, Hank Flacks; Casting, Lois Planco, Ellen Chenoweth; General Manager, Paul B. Berkowsky, Mark Richard; Company Manager, Malcolm Allen; Press, Judy Jacksina, Glenna Freedman, Stephanie Hughley, Susan Chicoine, Marcy Granata, Mari Thompson; Stage Managers, Thomas Kelly, Barrie Moss. Opened Monday, March 7, 1983.*

CAST

George "Spanky" Farrell, slab boy	Sean Penn
Hector McKenzie, slab boy	Jackie Earle Haley
Phil McCann, slab boy	Kevin Bacon
Willie Curry, gaffer	Merwin Goldsmith
Jack Hogg, designer	Brian Benben
Alan Downie, new boy	Val Kilmer
Sadie, the tea lady	Beverly May
Lucille Bentley, sketcher	Madeleine Potter

UNDERSTUDIES: Ron Fassler (Spanky/Hector/Phil/Jack/Alan), Barrie Moss (Sadie/Lucille)

A play in two acts. The action takes place on a Friday in the winter of 1957 in the slab room ... a small paint bespattered hole adjacent to the design studio at A. F. Stobo & Co. Carpet Manufacturers of Elderslie, near Paisley, Scotland.

*Closed April 17, 1983 after 48 performances and 19 previews.

Carol Rosegg/Martha Swope Photos

Top: Val Kilmer, Merwin Goldsmith

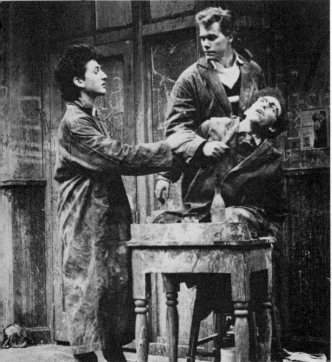

Sean Penn, Kevin Bacon, Jackie Earle Haley

MARCEL MARCEAU

(BELASCO THEATRE) Presented by Ken Myers and The Shubert Organization (Gerald Schoenfeld, Chairman; Bernard B. Jacobs, President) in association with Peter C. Wiese and Ronald A. Wilford; Associate to Producer, Garrett Bowden; Assistant to Producer, Ken Goldsmith; General Management, Ken Myers; Props, Vince Klemmer; Wardrobe, Marianna Torres; Press, Fred Nathan, John Howlett, Eileen McMahon, Anne Abrams, Leo Stern, Bert Fink; Stage Managers, Antoine Casanova, Jean-Pierre Burgard; Management Assistant, James Henry Hulse. Opened Wednesday, March 9, 1983.*
PART I: Style Pantomimes
PART II: Bip Pantomimes
Assistants to Mr. Marceau: Jonathan Lambert, Jean-Jerome Raclot

*Closed April 17, 1983 after 46 performances and 1 preview.

Martha Swope Photos

NOTE:
YVES MONTAND appeared at the Metropolitan Opera House for 7 performances Sept. 7 - 12, 1982. No material submitted.

BETTE MIDLER appeared at Radio City Music Hall for 7 performances March 8 - 14, 1983. No material submitted.

Right: Marcel Marceau as Bip

CHARLES AZNAVOUR

(LUNT-FONTANNE THEATRE) Presented by Ron Delsener, Levon Sayan; Music Director, Aldo Frank; Sound, Robert Kerzman; Mr. Aznavour's wardrobe by Ted Lapidus; Musical Coordinator, Bob Cranshaw; General Management, Marvin A. Krauss, Gary Gunas, Eric M. Angelson, Steven C. Callahan, Susan Sampliner; Press, Solters/Roskin/Friedman, Milly Schoenbaum, Warren Knowlton. Opened Monday, March 14, 1983.*

SONGS

Le Temp, In Your Room, I Didn't See the Time Go By, Etre, Happy Anniversary, In Times to Be, L'Amour Bon Dieu, I Act as If, To Be a Soldier, Nous n'avons pas d'enfant, I'll Be There, Les Comediens, She, Take Me Along, The Happy Days, Mon Ami Mon Judas, And I in My Chair, Isabelle, You've Let Yourself Go, Mon Emouvant Amour, Ave Maria, What Makes a Man, La Boheme, The Old Fashioned Way, Yesterday When I Was Young, You've Got to Learn, La Mama, Mourir d'aimer, Qui, De t'avoir Aimee, Que C'est Triste Venise, Non Je n'ai Rien Oublie, Ils Sont Tombes, The First Dance

A solo performance with one intermission. Background vocalists: Diana Green, Ednah Holt, Carol Steele.

*Closed March 26, 1983 after 14 performances.

Charles Aznavour

BRIGHTON BEACH MEMOIRS

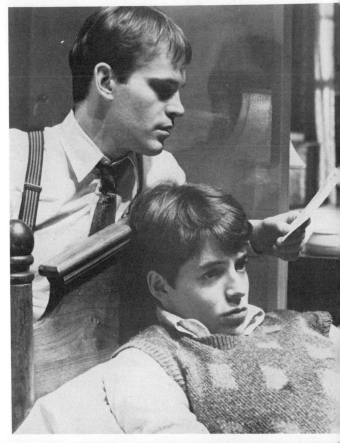

(ALVIN THEATRE) By Neil Simon; Director, Gene Saks; Set, David Mitchell; Costumes, Patricia Zipprodt; Lighting, Tharon Musser; Presented by Emanuel Azenberg, Wayne M. Rogers, Radio City Music Hall Productions in association with Center Theatre Group/Ahmanson; Casting, Marilyn Szatmary, Jane E. Cooper, Hank McCann; Technical Supervisors, Arthur Siccardi, Pete Feller; Props, Jan Marasek; Wardrobe, Nancy Schaefer; Assistant to Producers, Leslie Butler; Assistant to Director, Jane E. Cooper; General Manager, Jose Vega; Company Managers, Maria Anderson, Jane Robinson; Stage Managers, Martin Herzer, Barbara-Mae Phillips; Press, Bill Evans, Sandra Manley. Opened Sunday, March 27, 1983.*

CAST

Eugene	Matthew Broderick †1
Blanche	Joyce Van Patten
Kate	Elizabeth Franz
Laurie	Mandy Ingber †2
Nora	Jodi Thelen
Stanley	Zeljko Ivanek †3
Jack	Peter Michael Goetz

STANDBYS: Donna Haley (Kate/Blanche), Robin Morse (Nora), Timothy Busfield (Eugene/Stanley), Pamela Segall (Laurie), Stefan Gierasch (Jack), J. Patrick Breen (Stanley), Marissa Chibasi (Nora), Theresa Diane (Laurie), Robert Levine (Jack), Jon Cryer/Roger Raines (Eugene)

A comedy in two acts. The action takes place during September 1937 in the home of Jack and Kate Jerome in Brighton Beach, Brooklyn, NY.

*Still playing May 31, 1983. Selected by NY Drama Critics Circle as Best Play of the Season, and Mr. Broderick received a "Tony" Award as Best Supporting Actor in a Play. Mr. Saks also received a "Tony" for Best Director of a Play.
†Succeeded by: 1. Doug McKeon, 2. Theresa Diane, 3. J. Patrick Breen

Jay Thompson Photos

Right: Zeljko Ivanek, Matthew Broderick

Mandy Ingber, Joyce Van Patten, Jodi Thelen, Matthew Broderick, Elizabeth Franz, Peter Michael Goetz, Zeljko Ivanek

K 2

(BROOKS ATKINSON THEATRE) By Patrick Meyers; Director, Terry Schreiber; Set, Ming Cho Lee; Costumes, Noel Borden; Lighting, Allen Lee Hughes; Audio Composition, Herman Chessid; Sound, David Schnirman; Assistant Director, William S. Morris; Presented by Mary K. Frank and Cynthia Wood by arrangement with Saint-Subber; Associate Producers, Shaun Beary, Charles H. Duggan; Production Assistant, Pierce Bihm; Assistant to Director, Irene Meyers; Assistant to Producers, Joanne F. Benson; Soundman, John Cardinale; Props, Val Medina; Wardrobe, Mary P. Eno; Make-up, Ann Belsky; Casting, Mary Colquhoun; Associate Set Designer, Leslie Taylor; General Manager, Victor Samrock; Company Manager, Susan Bell; Stage Managers, Arlene Grayson, Diane Ward; Press, Joe Wolhandler, Kathryn Kempf, Julianne Davidow. Opened Wednesday, March 30, 1983.

CAST

Taylor .... Jeffrey DeMunn
Harold .... Jay Patterson

STANDBY: Michael Tolaydo

A drama performed without intermission. The action takes place on a ledge at 27,000 feet that is 1250 feet below the summit of K2, the world's second highest mountain.

*Closed June 11, 1983 after 85 performances and 10 previews. Ming Cho Lee received a "Tony" Award for Best Scenic Design during the season.

Martha Swope Photos

Jay Patterson, Jeffrey DeMunn

'NIGHT, MOTHER

(GOLDEN THEATRE) By Marsha Norman; Director, Tom Moore; Set and Costumes, Heidi Landesman; Lighting, James F. Ingalls; Presented by Dann Byck, Wendell Cherry, The Shubert Organization (Gerald Schoenfeld, Chairman; Bernard B. Jacobs, President), Frederick M. Zollo; Associate Producer, William P. Suter; Production Coordinator, Mary Nealon; Assistant to Director, Fredda Weiss; Props, Mel Saltzman; Wardrobe, Betty Lee Matelli; Hairstylist, Gerry Leddy; Casting, Mary Colquhoun; General Management, Hunt/Pucci Associates, Elizabeth I. McCann, Nelle Nugent; Company Manager, Sam Pagliaro; Stage Managers, Steven Beckler, Jack Gianino; Press, Betty Lee Hunt, Maria Cristina Pucci, James Sapp, Maurice Turet. Opened Thursday, March 31, 1983.*

CAST

Thelma Cates .... Anne Pitoniak
Jessie Cates .... Kathy Bates
STANDBYS: Helen Harrelson (Thelma), Phyllis Somerville (Jessie)

A drama performed without intermission. The action takes place at the present time in Thelma Cates' relatively new house built way out on a country road.

*Still playing May 31, 1983. Recipient of 1983 Pulitzer Prize for drama.

Richard Feldman Photos

Anne Pitoniak, Kathy Bates

YOU CAN'T TAKE IT WITH YOU

(PLYMOUTH THEATRE) By Moss Hart and George S. Kaufman; Director, Ellis Rabb; Set and Lighting, James Tilton; Costumes, Nancy Potts; Musical Staging, Reed Jones; Presented by Ken Marsolais, Karl Allison, Bryan Bantry; Produced in cooperation with the John F. Kennedy Center; Production Coordinator, Chic Silber; Props, Lawrence G. Barrett, Jr.; Wardrobe, Elonzo Dann; Hairstylist, Ronald Frederick; General Management, Jay Kingwill, Larry Goossen, Susan Sampliner; Stage Managers, Mitchell Erickson, John Handy, William Castleman; Press, Henry Luhrman, Terry M. Lilly, Kevin P. McAnarney, Keith Sherman. Opened Monday, April 4, 1983.*

CAST

Penelope Sycamore	Elizabeth Wilson
Essie	Carol Androsky
Rheba	Rosetta LeNoire
Paul Sycamore	Jack Dodson
Mr. DePinna	Bill McCutcheon
Ed	Christopher Foster
Donald	Arthur French
Martin Vanderhof	Jason Robards[1]
Alice	Maureen Anderman[2]
Henderson	Orrin Reiley
Tony Kirby	Nicolas Surovy
Boris Kolenkhov	James Coco[3]
Gay Wellington	Alice Drummond
Mr. Kirby	Richard Woods
Mrs. Kirby	Meg Mundy[4]
Olga	Colleen Dewhurst
G-Men	Page Johnson, Wayne Elbert, William Castleman

UNDERSTUDIES: William Cain (Martin/Kirby/Paul), William Castleman (G-Men), Wayne Elbert (Donald), Page Johnson (Boris/Henderson/DePinna), Orrin Reiley (Ed/Tony), Frances Helm (Penny/Gay/Mrs. Kirby/Olga), Rosemary Loar (Alice/Essie), Alyce Webb (Rheba).

A comedy in three acts. The action takes place in the home of Martin Vanderhof in New York City.

*Still playing May 31, 1983. Original production opened at the Booth Theatre Dec. 14, 1936 and ran for 837 performances, receiving the Pulitzer Prize.

†Succeeded by: 1. Eddie Albert, 2. Sandy Faison, 3. Ellis Rabb, Rex Robbins, George Rose, 4. Betty Miller

Ken Howard Photos

Jason Robards, Elizabeth Wilson

44

Top: entire cast

THE MAN WHO HAD THREE ARMS

(LYCEUM THEATRE) Written and Directed by Edward Albee; Set, John Jensen; Costumes, John Falabella; Lighting, Jeff Davis; Presented by Allen Klein; Executive Producer, Iris W. Keitel; Associate Producer, Kenneth Salinsky; An ABKCO Theatre Production; Executive Production Assistant, Jeffi Powell; Assistants to Director, Phil Funkenbusch, Glyn O'Malley; Production Assistants, Emily Baratta, Jaijai Jackson; Props, Joe Rogers; Wardrobe, Arlene Konowitz; Visual Effects, Chuck London Media; General Manager, Richard Horner/Leonard Soloway; Stage Managers, James Bernardi, Laura deBuys, Robin Klein; Press, Solters/Roskin/Friedman, Joshua Ellis, David LeShay, Cindy Valk. Opened Tuesday, April 5, 1983.*

CAST

The Man .... William Prince
The Woman .... Patricia Kilgarriff
Himself .... Robert Drivas

STANDBYS: Stephen Markle (Himself), Wyman Pendleton (Man)

A play in two acts. The action takes place at the present time on the stage of a lecture hall.

*Closed April 17, 1983 after 16 performances and 8 previews.

Martha Swope Photos

Robert Drivas (also top right), William Prince

Top: Michael V. Smartt, Henrietta Elizabeth Davis

PORGY AND BESS

(RADIO CITY MUSIC HALL) Music, George Gershwin; Libretto, DuBose Heyward; Lyrics, DuBose Heyward, Ira Gershwin; Based on play "Porgy" by Dorothy and Dubose Heyward; Director, Jack O'Brien; Assistant Director/Production Supervisor, Helaine Head; Choreographer, George Faison; Musical Director, C. William Harwood; Scenery, Douglas W. Schmidt; Costumes, Nancy Potts; Lighting, Gilbert V. Hemsley, Jr.; Associate Conductor, John Miner; Assistant Conductor, Edward Strauss; Musical Preparation, George Darden; Presented by Radio City Music Hall (Bernard Gersten, Executive Producer), and Sherwin M. Goldman; Props, Richard Saltzman; Wardrobe, Leola Edwards; Assistant to Director, Martin Worman; Company Manager, Herbert Scholder; Stage Managers, John Actman, Andre Love, Richert Easley; Press, Gifford/Wallace, Bob Burrichter, Gloria M. Ciaccio, Neil S. Friedman. Opened Thursday, April 7, 1983*

CAST

Jasbo Brown	Edward Strauss
Clara	Priscilla Baskerville, Luvenia Garner
Mingo	Timothy Allen
Jake	Alexander Smalls, James Tyeska
Sportin' Life	Larry Marshall
Robbins	Tyrone Jolivet
Serena	Shirley Baines, Regina McConnell, Wilma A. Shakesnider, Veronica Tyler
Jim	Donald Walter Kase
Peter	Mervin Bertel Wallace
Lily	Y. Yvonne Matthews
Maria	Loretta Holkmann, Gwendolyn Shepherd
Scipio	Akili Prince
Porgy	Robert Mosley, Jr., Michael V. Smartt, Jonathan Sprague, James Tyeska
Crown	Gregg Baker, George Robert Merritt
Bess	Priscilla Baskerville, Henrietta Elizabeth Davis, Naomi Moody, Daisy Newman
Detective	Larry Storch
Policeman	William Moize
Undertaker	Joseph S. Eubanks
Annie	Lou Ann Pickett
Frazier	Raymond H. Bazemore
Strawberry Woman	Denice Woods
Crab Man	Thomas J. Young
Nelson	Everett McCorvey
Coroner	Richert Easley

ENSEMBLE: Loretta Abbott, Timothy Allen, Earl L. Baker, Emerson Battles, Raymond H. Bazemore, Shirley Black-Brown, Roslyn Burroughs, Vertrelle Cameron, Seraiah Carol, Duane Clenton Carter, Dabriah Chapman, Louise Coleman, Janice D. Dixon, Cisco Xavier Drayton, Alberta M. Driver, Joseph S. Eubanks, Karen E. Eubanks, Lori Eubanks, Beno Foster, Jerry Godfrey, Earl Grandison, Milton B. Grayson, Jr., Elvira Green, Lawrence Hamilton, Gurcell Henry, Lisa D. Holkmann, Janice T. Hutson, David-Michael Johnson, Leavata Johnson, Tyrone Jolivet, Dorothy L. Jones, Donald Walter Kase, Roberta Alexandra Laws, Eugene Little, Ann Marie Mackey, Barbara Mahajan, Amelia Marshall, Richard Mason, Y. Yvonne Matthews, Everett McCorvey, John McDaniels, William Moize, Byron Onque, H. William Penn, Marenda Perry, Lou Ann Pickett, Herbert Lee Rawlings, Jr., Roumel Reaux, David Robertson, Lattilia Ronrico, Renee L. Rose, Myles Gregory Savage, Sheryl Shell, Kiki Shepard, Pamela Warrick-Smith, Mervin Bertel Wallace, Cornelius White, Rodney Wing, Denice Woods, Thomas J. Young, and Diallobe Dorsey, Angela Holcomb, Robert Kryser, Jason Little, Noelle Richards, Kevin L. Stroman, Charee Adia Thorpes, Tarik Winston

UNDERSTUDIES: Duane Clenton Carter (Porgy/Crown), Gurcell Henry (Clara), Elvira Green (Maria), Donald Walter Kase, Rodney Wing (Jake), Herbert Lee Rawlings, Jr. (Sportin' Life), David-Michael Johnson (Mingo), John McDaniels (Robbins), Beno Foster (Peter), Leavata Johnson (Annie), Earl Grandison (Frazier), Sheryl Shell (Lily), Y. Yvonne Matthews (Strawberry Woman), Byron Onque (Jim) Myles Gregory Savage (Crab Man), Richert Easley (Detective), William Moize (Nelson)

MUSICAL NUMBERS: Brown Blues, Summertime, A Woman Is a Sometime Thing, Here Come de Honey Man, They Pass by Singin', Oh Little Stars, Gone Gone Gone, Overflow, My Man's Gone Now, Leavin' for the Promise Land, It Takes a Long Pull to Get There, I Got Plenty of Nuttin', Struttin' Style, Buzzard Song, Bess You Is My Woman Now, Oh I Can't Sit Down, I Ain't Got No Shame, It Ain't Necessarily So, What You Want wid Bess, Oh Dr. Jesus, I Loves You Porgy, Oh Heavenly Father, Oh De Lawd Shake de Heavens, Oh Dere's Somebody Knockin' at de Do', A Red Headed Woman, Clara Clara, There's a Boat Dat's Leavin' Soon for New York, Good Mornin' Sistuh!, Oh Where's My Bess, Oh Lawd I'm on My Way

An opera in 2 acts and 9 scenes. The action takes place in the early 1930's in Charleston, S.C.

*Closed May 15, 1983 after 45 performances and 22 previews. Original production opened at the Alvin Theatre on Oct. 10, 1935 and played 124 performances.

Martha Swope Photos

ALL'S WELL THAT ENDS WELL

Philip Franks, John Franklyn-Robbins, Harriet Walter

(MARTIN BECK THEATRE) By William Shakespeare; Director, Trevor Nunn; Sets, John Gunter; U.S. Set in association with John Kasarda; Costumes, Linda Fisher after original designs by Lindy Hemming; Lighting, Beverly Emmons after original designs by Robert Bryan; Music, Guy Woolfenden; Dances, Geraldine Stephenson; Sound, T. Richard Fitzgerald; Musical Director, Donald Johnston; Presented by "The Shubert Organization, Elizabeth I. McCann and Nelle Nugent, ABC Video Enterprises, Roger S. Berlind, Rhoda R. Herrick, Jujamcyn Theaters, Richard G. Wolff, MGM/UA Home Entertainment Group, Mutual Benefit Productions/Karen Crane, by arrangement with the Royal Shakespeare Theatre, Stratford-on-Avon, England; Production Coordinator, Mary T. Nealon; Music Director, Nigel Hess; Assistant Director, Alby James; Sound, Frank Bradley; Props, Mel Saltzman, Terry Diamond; Hair, Fiona Elliott; Wardrobe, Rosalie Lahm, Susan Honey; Assistant to Director, Kate Littlewood; General Management, McCann & Nugent; Company Manager, Steven Suskin; Stage Managers, Janet Beroza, Vikki Heywood, Simon Dodson, Jane Tamlyn; Press, Joshua Ellis, Irene Gandy, David LeShay, Cindy Valk. Opened Wednesday, April 13, 1983.*

CAST

Rossillion:
Countess of Rossillion .... Margaret Tyzack
Bertram, her son .... Philip Franks
Helena, her gentlewoman .... Harriet Walter
Capt. Parolles, Bertram's companion .... Stephen Moore
Rynaldo, countess' steward .... David Lloyd Meredith
Lavache .... Geoffrey Hutchings
Bertram's servant .... John McAndrew
Maids .... Vivienne Argent, Noelyn George, Elizabeth Rider,
Susan Jane Tanner, June Watts

Paris:
King of France .... John Franklyn-Robbins
Lord Lafeu .... Robert Eddison
A Gentleman .... George Raistrick
Capt. Dumaine, the elder .... Peter Land
Capt. Dumaine, the younger .... Simon Templeman
Gentlemen and Suitors .... Tom Hunsinger, Christopher Hurst,
John McAndrew, Gary Sharkey, Graham Turner
Ladies .... Vivienne Argent, Noelyn George, Elizabeth Rider,
Susan Jane Tanner, June Watts

Florence:
Duke of Florence .... John Rogan
Widow Capilet .... Gillian Webb
Diana, her daughter .... Deirdra Morris
Violenta, her neighbor .... Susan Jane Tanner
Mariana .... Elizabeth Rider
Morgan, a soldier .... Roger Allam
Waitresses .... Vivienne Argent, Noelyn George, June Watts
Soldiers ...... Tom Hunsinger, Christopher Hurst, John McAndrew,
Gary Sharkey, Graham Turner

UNDERSTUDIES: Deirdra Morris (Helena), Elizabeth Rider (Diana/-Violenta), Susan Jane Tanner (Widow/Mariana), Gillian Webb (Countess), Roger Allam (Parolles), Tom Hunsinger (Steward), Christopher Hurst (Bertram/2nd Dumaine), John McAndrew (Morgan/Duke of Florence), George Raistrick (King of France), John Rogan (Lafeu), Gary Sharkey (Gentleman/1st Dumaine), Graham Turner (Lavache/Bertram's Servant)

Performed with one intermission.

*Closed May 15, 1983 after 38 performances and 11 previews.

Nobby Clark Photos

Top Left: Philip Franks, Harriet Walter, Margaret Tyzack Below: (center in wheelchair) John Franklyn-Robbins

TEANECK TANZI:
THE VENUS FLYTRAP

(NEDERLANDER THEATRE) By Claire Luckham; Director, Chris Bond; Composer, Chris Monks; Wrestling, Brian Maxine; Scenic Environment/Costumes, Lawrence Miller; Lighting, Arden Fingerhut; Sound, T. Richard Fitzgerald; Casting, Meg Simon/Fran Kumin; Musical Arrangements and Supervision, Martin Silvestri, Jeremy Stone; Presented by Charlene and James Nederlander, Richard Vos, Stewart F. Lane, Kenneth Mark Productions; Executive Producer, Richard Vos; Hairstylist, Steve Atha; Production Supervisor, Jeremiah Harris; Assistant to Producers and Director, Elizabeth Ball; Assistant to Producers, Elizabeth Hermann; Wardrobe, Kathleen Gallagher; General Management, Theatre Now, William Court Cohen, Edward H. Davis, Norman E. Rothstein, Ralph Roseman, Charlotte W. Wilcox; Company Manager, Robb Lady; Stage Managers, Kate Pollock, Paul Schneeberger; Press, Judy Jacksina, Glenna Freedman, Susan Chicoine, Marcy Granata, Mari H. Thompson, Barbara MacNeish, Marc Thibodeau. Opened Wednesday, April 20, 1983.

CAST

The Ref	Andy Kaufman
Tanzi's Mom	Zora Rasmussen
Tanzi's Dad	Clarence Felder
Platinum Sue	Dana Vance
Dean Rebel	Scott Renderer/Thomas G. Waites
Teaneck Tanzi	Caitlin Clarke/Deborah Harry

STANDBYS: Cedering Fox, Christopher Loomis

A comedy in two acts. The action takes place at the present time in a boxing ring.

*Closed April 20, 1983 after 2 performances and 13 previews.

Martha Swope Photos

Top: Thomas G. Waites, Deborah Harry, Caitlin Clarke, Scott Renderer

Deborah Harry, Andy Kaufman, Caitlin Clarke

SHOW BOAT

(URIS THEATRE) Music, Jerome Kern; Book and Lyrics, Oscar Hammerstein II; Based on novel by Edna Ferber; Director, Michael Kahn; Scenery, Herbert Senn, Helen Pond; Costumes, Molly Maginnis; Lighting, Thomas Skelton; Sound, Richard Fitzgerald; Casting, Hughes/Moss; Music Director, John DeMain; Conductor, Jack Everly; Choreography, Dorothy Danner; Presented by James M. Nederlander, John F. Kennedy Center (Roger L. Stevens, Chairman), Denver Center (Donald R. Seawell, Chairman); Executive Producers, Robert A. Buckley, Douglas Urbanski; A Houston Grand Opera Production; Props, Liam Herbert, Walter Wood; Wardrobe, Randy Beth, Colin Ferguson; Assistant Conductor, Michael Battistelli; Hairstylist, Kelvin R. Trahan, Gilbert Lachapelle, Sally Harper, Robert Harper; Assistant to director, Peter Webb; Production Assistant, Ken Arthur; General Managers, Robert A. Buckley, Douglas Urbanski; Company Manager, Martin Cohen; Stage Managers, Warren Crane, Amy Pell, Fred Tyson; Press, Marilynn LeVine, Rebecca Robbins. Opened Sunday, April 24, 1983.*

CAST

Windy	Richard Dix
Steve	Wayne Turnage
Pete	Glenn Martin
Queenie	Karla Burns
Parthy Ann Hawkes	Avril Gentles
Cap'n Andy	Donald O'Connor
Ellie	Paige O'Hara
Frank	Paul Keith
Mahoney/Barker/Jake	Randy Hansen
Julie	Lonette McKee
Gaylord Ravenal	Ron Raines
Vallon/Jim	Jacob Mark Hopkin
Magnolia	Sheryl Woods
Joe	Bruce Hubbard
Backwoodsman/Barker	Lewis White
Jeb/Barker	James Gedge
La Belle Fatima	Lynda Karen
Old Sport/Young Guitarist	Larry Hansen
Landlady	Mary Rocco
Charlie	P. L. Brown
Mother Superior	Linda Milani
Young Kim	Tracy Paul
Lottie	Gloria Parker
Dolly	Dale Kristien
Old Lady on levee	Mary Rocco
Older Kim	Karen Culliver
Radio Announcer's Voice	Hal Douglas

CHORUS: Vanessa Ayers, Joanna Beck, Karen Culliver, Olivia Detante, Kim Fairchild, Cheryl Freeman, Lynda Karen, Dale Kristien, Linda Milani, Gloria Parker, Veronica Rhodes, Mary Rocco, Molly Wassermann, Carrie Wilder, P. L. Brown, Michael-Pierre Dean, Merwin Foard, Joe Garcia, James Gedge, Michael Gray, Larry Hansen, Randy Hansen, Jacob Mark Hopkin, Glenn Martin, Randy Morgan, Dennis Perren, Leonard Piggee, Alton Spencer, Robert Vincent, Lewis White, Wardell Woodard, Swings: Jeane July, Suzanne Ishee, Tom Garrett, Ed Battle

UNDERSTUDIES: Richard Dix (Cap'n Andy), Gloria Parker (Julie), Wayne Turnage (Gaylord), Dale Kristien (Magnolia), Vanessa Ayers (Queenie), Larry Hansen (Frank/Mahoney), Carrie Wilder (Ellie), P.L. Brown (Joe), Lewis White (Vallon/Windy/Jim), Robert Vincent (Steve/-Pete), James Gedge (Backwoodsman/Jake), Linda Milani (Old Lady/-Landlady), Dennis Perren (Charlie), Kim Fairchild (Mother Superior), Tom Garrett (Jeb/Barkers/Guitarist/Old Sport), Suzanne Ishee (Lottie/Older Kim), Joanna Beck (Dolly), Jeane July (La Belle Fatima), Karen Culliver (Young Kim), Lizabeth Pritchett (Parthy)

MUSICAL NUMBERS: Cotton Blossom, Show Boat Parade and Ballyhoo, Only Make Believe, Ol' Man River, Can't Help Lovin' Dat Man, Life upon the Wicked Stage, I Might Fall Back on You, Queenie's Ballyhoo, You Are Love, At the Fair, Why Do I Love You?, Bill, Goodbye My Lady Love, After the Ball, Hey Feller, Finale

A musical in two acts and 15 scenes. The action takes place between 1880 and 1927.

* Closed June 26, 1983 after 73 performances and 5 previews. Original production opened at the Ziegfeld Theatre on Dec. 27, 1927 with Charles Winninger, Helen Morgan, Jules Bledsoe, Howard Marsh, Norma Terris and Edna May Oliver. It ran for 572 performances.

Martha Swope Photos

Top Right: Donald O'Connor (center) Below: Karla Burns (center)

Karla Burns, Lonette McKee

49

TOTAL ABANDON

(BOOTH THEATRE) By Larry Atlas; Director, Jack Hofsiss; Set, David Jenkins; Costumes, Julie Weiss; Lighting, Beverly Emmons; Presented by Elizabeth I. McCann, Nelle Nugent, Ray Larsen, William J. Meloche, Patrick S. Brigham, John Roach; Associate Producers, Marc E. Platt, Sander Jacobs, Tommy DeMaio; Production Coordinator, Mary Nealon; Director's Assistant, David Rodriguez; Props. Mel Saltzman, Thomas J. Boles; Wardrobe, Don Grubler; Production Assistant, Maureen Grady; Casting, Johnson/Liff; Incidental Music, Michael Dansicker; Sound, Louis Shapiro; General Management, McCann & Nugent; Company Manager, Susan Gustafson; Stage Managers, Ruth E. Rinklin, Mark Schorr; Press, Solters/Roskin/Friedman, Joshua Ellis, David LeSahy, Cindy Valk. Opened Thursday, April 28, 1983.*

CAST

Lenny Keller	Richard Dreyfuss
Henry Hirsch	John Heard
Walter Bellmon	George N. Martin
Ben Hammerstein	Clifton James

STANDBYS: Jon Polito, Thomas A. Carlin

A drama in two acts. The action takes place at the present time in a midwest courthouse.

*Closed April 28, 1983 after 1 performance and 7 previews.

Peter Cunningham/Martha Swope Photos

Right: Richard Dreyfuss, John Heard

George N. Martin, John Heard, Richard Dreyfuss (front), Clifton James

MY ONE AND ONLY

(ST. JAMES THEATRE) Music, George Gershwin; Lyrics, Ira Gershwin; Book, Peter Stone, Timothy S. Mayer; Staged and Choreographed by Thommie Walsh and Tommy Tune; Associate Choreographer, Baayork Lee; Associate Director, Phillip Oesterman; Musical and Vocal Direction, Jack Lee; Scenery, Adrianne Lobel; Costumes, Rita Ryack; Lighting, Marcia Madeira; Sound, Otts Munderloh; Musical Concept/Dance Arrangements, Wally Harper; Orchestrations, Michael Gibson; Dance Arrangements, Peter Larson; Casting, Hughes/Moss; Presented by Paramount Theatre Productions, Francine LeFrak, Kenneth-Mark Productions, in association with Jujamcyn Theatres, Tams-Witmark Music Library; Musical Consultant, Michael Feinstein; A King Street Production, Bernard Carragher, Obie Bailey, Bernard Bailey; Produced by Lewis Allen; Associate Producer, Jonathan Farkas; Technical Supervisor, Arthur Siccardi; Props, Paul Biega; Wardrobe, William Campbell; Production Assistant, Tom Santopietro; Assistant to Directors, Lynnette Barkley; Wigs, Paul Huntley; Makeup, Anthony Clavet; Movie Sequence, Kenneth Leigh Hunter; General Management, Joseph P. Harris, Peter T. Kulok, Steven E. Goldstein; Stage Managers, Peter von Mayrhauser, Robert Kellogg, Betty Lynd; Press, Judy Jacksina, Glenna Freedman, Marcy Granata, Susan Chicoine, Mari H. Thompson, John Howlett, Marc Thibodeau, Barbara MacNeish. Opened Sunday, May 1, 1983.*

CAST

New Rhythm Boys	David Jackson, Ronald Dennis, Ken Leigh Rogers
Capt. Billy Buck Chandler	Tommy Tune
Mickey	Denny Dillon
Prince Nicolai Erraclyovitch Tchatchavadze	Bruce McGill
Flounder	Nana Visitor
Sturgeon	Susan Hartley
Minnow	Stephanie Eley
Prawn	Jill Cook
Kipper	Niki Harris
Anchovie	Karen Tamburrelli
Edith Herbert	Twiggy
Rt. Rev. J. D. Montgomery	Roscoe Lee Browne
Reporter	Jill Cook
Mr. Magix	Charles "Honi" Coles
Policeman/Stage Doorman	Paul David Richards
Mrs. O'Malley	Ken Leigh Rogers
Conductor	Adrian Bailey
Achmed	Bruce McGill
Ritz Quartet	Casper Roos, Paul David Richards, Carl Nicholas, Will Blankenship
Dancing Gentlemen	Adrian Bailey, Bar Dell Conner, Ronald Dennis, David Jackson, Alde Lewis, Jr., Bernard Manners, Ken Leigh Rogers

STANDBYS AND UNDERSTUDIES: Ronald Young (Chandler/Prince), Nana Visitor (Edith), Leon Morenzie (Reverend), Jill Cook (Mickey), David Jackson (Magix), Swings: Merilee Magnuson, Melvin Washington

MUSICAL NUMBERS: I Can't Be Bothered Now, Blah Blah Blah, Boy Wanted, Soon, High Hat, Sweet and Low-Down, Just Another Rumba, He Loves and She Loves, 'S Wonderful, Strike Up the Band, In the Swim, What Are We Here For, Nice Work If You Can Get It, My One and Only, Kickin' the Clouds Away, How Long Has This Been Goin' On?, Finale

A musical in 2 acts and 15 scenes. The action takes place during 1927.

*Still playing May 31, 1983. Winner of "Tony" Awards for Best Choreography, Best Actor in a Musical (Tommy Tune), and Best Supporting Actor in a Musical (Charles "Honi" Coles).

Kenn Duncan Photos

Top Right: Twiggy, Tommy Tune

Tommy Tune, Charles "Honi" Coles

PARADE OF STARS PLAYING THE PALACE

PALACE THEATRE Written and Produced by Hildy Parks; Presented by Alexander H. Cohen; Director, Clark Jones; Co-Producer, Roy A. Somlyo; Musical Direction, Elliot Lawrence; Special Musical Staging, Albert Stephenson; Scenery, Robert Randolph; Costumes, Alvin Colt; Lighting, Carl Vitelli, Jr.; Production Supervisor, Robert L. Borod; Makeup, Joe Cranzano; Hairstylist, Joe Tubens; Music Coordinator, Mel Marvin; "Playing the Palace" by John Kander, Fred Ebb; Orchestrations, Tony Zito, Tommy Newsome, Bill Elton; A Brentwood Production; Associate Manager, Seymour Herscher; Associate Producer, Donald Weiner; Production Assistants, Susan Kerber, Victoria Street; Talent Coordinator, Tisha Fein; Assistant to Producers, Colleen Scott, Iva Withers; Technical Supervisor, Arthur Siccardi; Wardrobe, Elonzo Dann; Assistant Choreographer, Richard Haskin; Stage Managers, Christopher A. Cohen, Laurie Somlyo; Press, Sid Garfield, Mike Hall Associates, Solters/Roskin/Friedman. Opened Monday, May 2, 1983.*

PARTICIPATING ARTISTS

Erik Adams and Friends, Eddie Albert as the stagehand, Debbie Allen as Josephine Baker, Edward Asner as a press agent, Lauren Bacall in "Applause" and "Woman of the Year," Harry Belafonte, Milton Berle, George Burns, David Cassidy as George M. Cohan, Dick Cavett as Fred Allen, Carol Channing as Lorelei Lee, Don Correia as Vernon Castle, Michael Davis as juggler, Pam Dawber as Rose Dolly, Sandy Duncan as Irene Castle, Bonnie Franklin in "Applause," Jack Gilford as Charles Dale, Gregory Hines as Bill Robinson, Ann Jillian as Mae West, Larry Kert as Al Jolson, Richard Kiley in "Man of LaMancha," Jack Klugman as Joe Smith, Linda Lavin as Nora Bayes, Michele Lee as The Palace star, Rich Little as Jack Benny, Dorothy Loudon as Fanny Brice, Leonardo Menna as a plate spinner, Lee Meredith as Dr. Kronkite's nurse, Jeanne Moreau as Sarah Bernhardt, Christopher Plummer as "Cyrano," Tony Randall as Frank Fay, Lee Roy Reams as Pat Rooney, Ann Reinking as Jenny Dolly, Dinah Shore as Helen Morgan, Jean Stapleton as the wardrobe mistress, Daniel J. Travanti assisting Milton Berle, Gwen Verdon as "Sweet Charity," Fred Waring and the New Pennsylvanians, James Whitmore as Will Rogers, Shelley Winters as Sophie Tucker, Michael York as Lou Tellegen, The Palace Girls: Anita Ehrier, Darcy Phifer, Paula Lynn, Philomena Nowlin, Julie Parrs, Tina Paul, Debra Schuman, Kimberly Ann Smith, and Michael Leigh Herscher, Paula Laurence, Miller Lide, Arthur Rubin.

*Performed without intermission for one night only as a benefit for the Actors' Fund of America.

Participating Artists: Top Left: Ann Jillian, Milton Berle, Below: George Burns, James Whitmore (*ABC Photos*)
Top opposite page: Sandy Duncan, Don Correia

THE RITZ

(HENRY MILLER THEATRE/XENON) By Terrence McNally; Director, Michael Bavar; Set, Gordon Micunis; Costumes, George Potts; Lighting, Todd Lichtenstein; Choreographer, Robert Speller; Men's Wardrobe, Egon von Furstenberg; Sound, David Schnirman; Music, Man Parrish; Assistant to Director/Production Assistant, Donald Roberts; Presented by Bavar/Culver Productions in association with James R. Cunningham; Production Assistants, Dan Zittel, Pierce Bihm; Casting, Larry Goossen; Sound, David Kobernuss; Wardrobe, Terry Snyder; General Management, Kingwill Office; Company Manager, Leonard A.Mulhern; Stage Managers, T. L. Boston, Arlene Wege; Press, Shirley Herz, Sam Rudy, Peter Cromarty. Opened Monday, May 2, 1983.*

CAST

Abe	Joey Faye
Claude	Don Potter
Gaetano Proclo	Taylor Reed
Chris	Michael Greer
Googie Gomez	Holly Woodlawn
Maurine	Jan Meredith
Michael Brick	Casey Donovan
Tiger	Pi Douglass
Duff	Roland Rodriguez
Carmine Vespucci	Danny Dennis
Vivian Proclo	Dolores Wilson
Crisco	Peter Radon
Sheldon Farenthold	Paige Edwards
Patron in chaps	George Sardi
Patron from Sheridan Square	Tom Terwilliger
Chacha	John Koons
Butch	John Burke

STANDBYS: Tony Hoty, Joyce Mandell

*Closed May 2, 1983 after 1 performance and 14 previews. Original production opened at the Longacre Theatre Jan. 20, 1975 and ran for 398 performances.

Martha Swope Photos

Casey Donovan, Joey Faye

THE CAINE MUTINY
COURT-MARTIAL

(CIRCLE IN THE SQUARE) By Herman Wouk; Director, Arthur Sherman; Set, John Falabella; Costumes, David Murin; Lighting, Richard Nelson; The Hartman Theatre Production is presented by Circle in the Square (Theodore Mann, Artistic Director; Paul Libin, Managing Director) and the John F. Kennedy Center (Roger L. Stevens, Chairman); Casting, Lynn Kressel; Company Manager, William Conn; Technical Adviser, Edwin B. Dexter; Wardrobe, Millicent Hacker; Stage Managers, Michael F. Ritchie, Jace Alexander; Press, Merle Debuskey, David Roggensack. Opened Thursday, May 5, 1983.*

CAST

Lt. Barney Greenwald	John Rubinstein†1
Lt. Stephen Maryk	Jay O. Sanders†2
Stenographer	Tom Paliferro
Orderly	Richard Arbolino
Lt. Cmdr. John Challee	William Atherton
Capt. Blakely	Stephen Joyce
Lt. Cmdr. Philip Francis Queeg	Michael Moriarty†3
Lt. Thomas Keefer	J. Kenneth Campbell
Signalman 3rd Class Junius Urban	Jace Alexander
Lt. (jg) Willis Seward Keith	Jonathan Hogan
Capt. Randolph Southard	Brad Sullivan
Dr. Forrest Lundeen	Leon B. Stevens
Dr. Bird	Geoffrey Horne
Court Members	Clinton Allmon, Warren Ball, Chad Burton, Sam Coppola, Daniel Davin, Oliver Dixon
Caine Officers at the Fairmont	Clinton Allmon, Chad Burton, Sam Coppola

UNDERSTUDIES: Sam Coppola (Southard/Lundeen), Tom Paliferro (Bird), Geoffrey Horne (Queeg), Michael Moriarty (Greenwald), Chad Burton (Blakely), Clinton Allmon (Keefer/Keith), Richard Arbolino (Challee/Urban/Stenographer).

A drama in 2 acts and 3 scenes. The action takes place during February 1945 in the General Court-Martial Room of the Twelfth Naval District, San Francisco, CA. At the end of Act II the scene shifts to a banquet room in the Fairmont Hotel in San Francisco.

*Still playing May 31, 1983. Original production opened at the Plymouth Theatre on Jan. 20, 1954 and ran for 415 performances. Among the cast, were Henry Fonda, Lloyd Nolan, John Hodiak and James Garner.
†Succeeded by: 1. Michael Moriarty, 2. James Widdoes, Joe Namath, 3. Philip Bosco

Martha Swope Photos

John Rubinstein, Michael Moriarty, William Atherton (also at top)

PRIVATE LIVES

(LUNT-FONTANNE THEATRE) By Noel Coward; Director, Milton Katselas; Sets, David Mitchell; Costumes, Theoni V. Aldredge; Lighting, Tharon Musser; Sound, Jack Mann; Additional Music, Stanley Silverman; Casting, Shirley Rich; Hairstylist, Michael Kriston; Presented by The Elizabeth Group (Zev Bufman/Elizabeth Taylor); General Manager, Alexander Morr; Company Manager, Michael Lonergan; Assistant to Director, Rochell Linker; Technical Supervisor, Jeremiah J. Harris; Props, George Green; Wardrobe, Agnes Farrell; Production Assistants, Philip Handberg, Tony Berk; Stage Managers, Patrick Horrigan, Brian Meister; Press, Fred Nathan, Eileen McMahon, Leo Stern, Anne S. Abrams, Chen Sam, Dolph Browning, Adelle Stone, Bert Fink, Charles Cinnamon. Opened Sunday, May 8, 1983.*

CAST

Sybil Chase .... Kathryn Walker
Elyot Chase .... Richard Burton
Victor Prynne .... John Cullum
Amanda Prynne .... Elizabeth Taylor
Louise .... Helena Carroll

STANDBYS: Kathryn Walker (Amanda), John Cullum (Elyot), Judith McGilligan (Sybil), Larry Pine (Victor), Judith McGilligan (Louise)

A comedy in three acts. The action takes place in 1930 on the terrace of a hotel in Deauville on the coast of France, and in Amanda's flat in Paris.

*Closed July 17, 1983 after 63 performances and 12 previews.

Martha Swope Photos

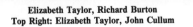

Elizabeth Taylor, Richard Burton
Top Right: Elizabeth Taylor, John Cullum

THE FLYING KARAMAZOV
BROTHERS

(RITZ THEATRE) Presented by Mace Neufeld and Viacom International, Inc.; Associate Producers, Harold Thau, Robert Courson; Setting and Costumes, Robert Fletcher; Lighting, Marc B. Weiss; General Management, Richard Horner, Lynne Stuart; Company Managers, Leonard Soloway, Kerrin K. Clark; Sound, Bob Kerzman; Props, Walter Murphy; Wardrobe, Arlene Konowitz; Stage Managers, Phil Friedman, Amy Richards; Press, Henry Luhrman, Kevin P. McAnarney, Terry M. Lilly, Keith Sherman. Opened Tuesday, May 10, 1983.

CAST

Dmitri .... Paul David Magid
Alyosha .... Randy Nelson
Fyodor .... Timothy Daniel Furst
Smerdyakov .... Sam Williams
Ivan .... Howard Jay Patterson

An "entertainment" in two acts. The action takes place at the present time on the stage of a prestigious Broadway theatre.

*Closed June 19, 1983 after 47 performances and 12 previews.

DANCE A LITTLE CLOSER

MINSKOFF THEATRE Book and Lyrics, Alan Jay Lerner; Music, Charles Strouse; Based on play "Idiot's Delight" by Robert E. Sherwood; Director, Alan Jay Lerner; Musical Staging and Choreography, Billy Wilson; Scenery, David Mitchell; Costumes, Donald Brooks; Lighting, Thomas Skelton; Orchestrations, Jonathan Tunick; Musical Direction, Peter Howard; Dance Music, Glen Kelly; Sound Design, John McClure; Production Supervisor, Stone Widney; Assistant to Producer, Dwight Frye; Hairstylist, Joe Tubens; Presented by Frederick Brisson, Jerome Minskoff, James Nederlander, Kennedy Center (Roger L. Stevens, Chairman); Associate Producer, Paul N. Temple; Technical Supervisor, Jeremiah Harris; Props, Paul Biega; Wardrobe, Jennifer Bryan, Irene Bunis; Assistant Conductor, Les Scott; Assistants to Mr. Lerner, Judy Insel, Ellen Walter; Production Assistants, Marty Erskine, Martin Shelby; Skating staged by Blair Hammond; General Management, Joseph P. Harris, Peter T. Kulok, Steven E. Goldstein, Nancy Simmons; Company Manager, Mitzi Harder; Stage Managers, Alan Hall, Steven Adler, Dianne Trulock; Press, Jeffrey Richards, C. George Willard, Robert Ganshaw, Ben Morse, Richard Humleker, Mary Ann Rubino, Donna DeBlassis. Opened Wednesday, May 11, 1983.*

CAST

Roger Butterfield	Don Chastain
Harry Aikens	Len Cariou

The Delights:

Shirley	Diane Pennington
Bebe	Cheryl Howard
Elaine	Alyson Reed
Johannes Hartog	David Sabin
Contessa Carla Pirianno	Elizabeth Hubbard
Capt. Mueller	Noel Craig
Charles Castleton	Brent Barrett
Edward Dunlop	Jeff Keller
Bellboy/Harry	Philip Mollet
Waiter/Harry's Double/Harry	Brian Sutherland
Rev. Oliver Boyle	I. M. Hobson
Hester Boyle	Joyce Worsley
Heinrich Walter	Joseph Kolinski
Cynthia Brookfield-Bailey	Liz Robertson
Dr. Josef Winkler	George Rose
Cynthia's Double	Robin Stephens
Rink Attendant/Violinist/Harry	James Fatta
Ice Skater	Colleen Ashton

HOTEL GUESTS: Colleen Ashton, Candy Cook, Mary Dale, James Fatta, Philip Mollet, Linda Poser, Robin Stephens, Brian Sutherland, Peter Wandel

STANDBYS AND UNDERSTUDIES: David Sabin (Winkler), Elizabeth Hubbard (Cynthia), Brian Sutherland (Halloway/Charles/Edward), Don Chastain (Harry), Linda Poster (Contessa/Hester), Philip Mollet (Mueller), Colleen Ashton (Elaine), Candy Cook (Shirley), Reuben Singer (Hartog), Joanne Genelle (Bebe), Peter Wandel (Waiter), Swings: Joanne Genelle, Mark Lamanna

MUSICAL NUMBERS: It Never Would've Worked, Happy Happy New Year, No Man Is Worth It, What Are You Going to Do About It?, A Woman Who Thinks I'm Wonderful, Pas de Deux, There's Never Been Anything Like Us, Another Life, Why Can't the World Go and Leave Us Alone?, He Always Comes Home to Me, I Got a New Girl, Dance a Little Closer, There's Always One You Can't Forget, Homesick, Mad, I Don't Know, Auf Wiedersehen, I Never Want to See You Again, On Top of the World

A musical in two acts. The action takes place during "the avoidable future" in the Barclay-Palace Hotel on a hillside in the Austrian Alps.

*Closed May 11, 1983 after 1 performance and 27 previews.

Peter Cunningham Photos

Top Right: Cheryl Howard, Diane Pennington, Alyson Reed, George Rose, Liz Robertson, Len Cariou Below: (foreground) Liz Robertson, Len Cariou, George Rose, Elizabeth Hubbard, Brent Barrett, Jeff Keller

Len Cariou, Liz Robertson

PASSION

(LONGACRE THEATRE) By Peter Nichols; Director, Marshall W. Mason; Set, John Lee Beatty; Costumes, Jennifer von Mayrhauser; Lighting, Ron Wallace; Sound, Chuck London Media/Stewart Werner; Presented by Richmond Crinkley, Eve Skina, Tina Chen, BMP Productions, Martin Markinson, Mike Merrick, John Roach by arrangement with the Royal Shakespeare Theatre of England; Associate Producer, Robert Pesola; Production Associate, Richard Carter; Assistant to Director, Glenna Clay; Production Assistants, Jill Davis, Benjy Levy, Nora Mackey; Props, Val Medina; Wardrobe, Mary Eno; Casting, Mary Colquhoun; General Management, Brent Peek Productions, Scott Green; Company Manager, David Hedges; Stage Managers, Franklin Keysar, Jody Boese; Press, Betty Lee Hunt, Maria Cristina Pucci, James Sapp, Robert W. Larkin. Opened Sunday, May 15, 1983.*

CAST

Kate .... Roxanne Hart
James .... Bob Gunton
Eleanor .... Cathryn Damon
Agnes .... Stephanie Gordon
Jim .... Frank Langella
Nell .... E. Katherine Kerr
and Louis Beachner, Jonathan Bolt, Lisa Emery, Charles Harper, William Snovell, C. B. Toombes

STANDBYS AND UNDERSTUDIES: Jonathan Bolt (James/Jim), Lisa Emery (Kate), Catherine Byers (Agnes/Nell)

A comedy in two acts. The action takes place at the present time in London during autumn.

*Closed Aug. 7, 1983 after 97 performances and 10 previews.

Martha Swope Photos

Left: Roxanne Hart, Frank Langella

Bob Gunton, Cathryn Damon, E. Katherine Kerr, Frank Langella

AGNES OF GOD

By John Pielmeier; Director, Michael Lindsay-Hogg; Set, Eugene Lee; Costumes, Carrie Robbins; Lighting, Roger Morgan; Assistant to Producers, Donna Donaldson, General Assistant, Barbara Hodgen; Wardrobe, Peter FitzGerald; Props, Cheri Herbert; Casting, Hughes/Moss; Hairstylist, Lyn Quiyou; Presented by Kenneth Waissman, Lou Kramer, Paramount Theatre Productions; General Manager, Edward H. Davis; Company Manager, Robb Lady; Assistant to General Manager, Dorothy Finn; Stage Managers, Larry Forde, Mark Rubinsky; Press, Betty Lee Hunt, Maria Cristina Pucci, James Sapp. Opened at the Music Box Theatre on Tuesday, March 30, 1982.

CAST

Dr. Martha Livingstone .... Elizabeth Ashley[1]
Mother Miriam Ruth .... Geraldine Page[2]
Agnes .... Amanda Plummer[3]

UNDERSTUDIES: Susan Riskin (Dr. Livingstone/Mother Ruth), Maryann Plunkett (Agnes)

A drama in two acts. The action takes place in a convent at the present time.

*Closed Sept. 4, 1983 after 599 performances and 12 previews. Miss Plummer received a 1982 "Tony" Award for Best Featured Actress in a Play. For original production, See THEATRE WORLD Vol. 37.
[†]Succeeded by: 1. Diahann Carroll, 2. Susan Riskin during vacation, 3. Carrie Fisher, Mia Dillon during vacation, Maryann Plunkett, Lily Knight

Ken Howard Photos

Top: Geraldine Page, Diahann Carroll, Maryann Plunkett

Geraldine Page, Diahann Carroll

AMADEUS

By Peter Shaffer; Director, Peter Hall; Design, John Bury; Associate Scenic Designer, John David Ridge; Associate Lighting Designer, Beverly Emmons; Music arranged and directed by Harrison Birtwistle; Production Coordinator, Brent Peek; Assistant Director, Giles Block; Wardrobe, Rosalie Lahm; Special Effects, Chick Silber; Production Assistant, Virlana Tkacz; Sound, Jack Mann; Wigs/Hairstylist, Paul Huntley; Presented by the Shubert Organization (Gerald Schoenfeld, Chairman; Bernard B. Jacobs, President), Elizabeth I. McCann, Nelle Nugent, Roger S. Berlind. General Management, McCann & Nugent; Company Manager, Susan Gustafson; Stage Managers, Ellen Raphael, Robert Charles, Richard Jay-Alexander, Mark Torres; Press, Merle Dubuskey, William Schelble. Opened at the Broadhurst Theatre Wednesday, Dec. 17, 1980.*

CAST

Antonio Salieri	Ian McKellen[1]
The Venticelli	Gordon Gould[2], Edward Zang[3]
Salieri's valet	Victor Griffin[4]
Salieri's cook	Haskell Gordon[5]
Joseph II, Emperor of Austria	Nicholas Kepros[6]
Johann Kilian von Strack	Jonathan Moore[7]
Count Orsini-Rosenberg	Patrick Hines[8]
Baron von Swieten	Louis Turenne
Priest	Donald C. Moore[9]
Giuseppe Bonno	Russell Gold[10]
Teresa Salieri	Linda Robbins[11]
Katherina Cavalieri	Michele Farr[12]
Constanze Weber	Jane Seymour[13]
Wolfgang Amadeus Mozart	Tim Curry[14]
Major Domo	Philip Pleasants[15]

VALETS: Ronald Bagden, David Bryant, Benjamin Donenberg, Richard Jay-Alexander[16], Peter Kingsley[17], Bill Roberts[18]
CITIZENS OF VIENNA: Mary A. Dierson[19], Russell Gold[20], Victor Griffin[21], Robert Langdon-Lloyd[22], Mary E. Mastrantonio[23], Donald C. Moore[24], Rene Moreno[25], Philip Pleasants[26], Linda Robbins, Patrick Tull[27]
UNDERSTUDIES: John Thomas Waite (Mozart), Mary A. Dierson (Constanze), Russell Leib (Joseph II/Venticello/Bonno), Fred Melaned (Orsini-Rosenberg/Cook), Richard Lupino (von Strack/van Swieten/Valet), Kristin Rudrud (Teresa/Katherina), Brad O'Hare (Venticello/Major Domo/Valets), David Bryant (Mozart)

A drama in two acts. The action takes place in Vienna in November 1823, and in recall, the decade 1781–1791.
* Closed Oct. 16, 1983 after 1181 performances and 5 previews. Recipient of 1981 Tonys for Best Play, Best Director, Outstanding Actor (Ian McKellen), Outstanding Scenic Design. For original production, see THEATRE WORLD Vol. 37.
† Succeeded by: 1. John Wood, Frank Langella, David Dukes, David Birney, John Horton, Daniel Davis, 2. Michael Connolly, 3. Roy K. Stevens, 4. Time Winters, 5. Donald C. Moore, Haskell Gordon, 6. John Horton, 7. Paul Harding, James Higgins, Jonathan Farwell, 8. Donald C. Moore, 9. Michael McCarty, Patrick Tull, Donald C. Moore, Fred Melamed, 10. Jonathan Moore, Richard Lupino, 11. Tian King, Linda Robbins, 12. Caris Corfman, Michele Farr, Mary Elizabeth Mastrantonio, Mary A. Dierson, Jean McNally, Mary A. Dierson, 13. Caris Corfman, Michele Farr, Suzanne Lederer, Maureen Moore, 14. John Pankow, Dennis Boutsikaris, Mark Hamill, John Thomas Waite, Peter Crook, 15. Russell Leib, 16. Mark Torres, 17. Laurence Overmire, 18. Daniel Watkins, Jonathan Miller, 19. Kristin Rudrud, 20. Jonathan Moore, Richard Lupino, 21. Time Winters, 22. Brad O'Hare, Robert Langdon-Lloyd, Brad O'Hare, 23. Mary A. Dierson, Jean McNally, Mary A. Dierson, 24. Haskell Gordon, 25. John Thomas Waite, 26. Russell Leib, 27. Donald C. Moore, Michael McCarty, Fred Melamed

Martha Swope Photos

Top Right: David Dukes, Suzanne Lederer, John Pankow

David Birney (standing), Mark Hamill

A CHORUS LINE

Conceived, Choreographed and Directed by Michael Bennett; Book, James Kirkwood, Nicholas Dante; Music, Marvin Hamlisch; Lyrics, Edward Kleban; Co-choreographer, Bob Avian; Musical Direction/Vocal Arrangements, Don Pippin; Associate Producer, Bernard Gersten; Setting, Robin Wagner; Costumes, Theoni V. Aldredge; Lighting, Tharon Musser; Sound, Abe Jacobs; Music Coordinator, Robert Thomas; Orchestrations, Bill Byers, Hershy Kay, Jonathan Tunick; Assistant to Choreographers, Baayork Lee; Musical Director, Robert Rogers; Wardrobe, Alyce Gilbert; Production Supervisor, Jason Steven Cohen; Original cast album by Columbia Records; A New York Shakespeare Festival Production; Presented by Joseph Papp in association with Plum Productions; General Manager, Robert Kamlot; Company Manager, Bob MacDonald; Stage Managers, Tom Porter, Wendy Mansfield, Morris Freed, Bradley Jones; Press, Merle Debuskey, William Schelble, Richard Kornberg. Opened at the Shubert Theatre Sunday, October 19, 1975.*

CAST

Roy	Evan Pappas†1
Kristine	Christine Barker
Sheila	Susan Danielle†2
Val	Mitzi Hamilton
Mike	Cary Scott Lowenstein†3
Butch	Roscoe Gilliam
Larry	J. Richard Hart†4
Maggie	Pam Klinger
Richie	Kevin Chinn
Tricia	Diane Fratantoni†5
Tom	James Young†6
Zach	Tim Millett†7
Mark	Danny Herman†8
Cassie	Pamela Sousa
Judy	Melissa Randel
Lois	Catherine Cooper†9
Don	Michael Danek†10
Bebe	Pamela Ann Wilson
Connie	Lily-Lee Wong
Diana	Dorothy Tancredi†11
Al	Jerry Colker†12
Frank	Philip C. Perry†13
Greg	Danny Weathers†14
Bobby	Matt West
Paul	Tommy Aguilar
Vicki	Peggy Parten†15
Ed	Morris Freed
Jarad	Troy Garza
Linda	Tracy Shayne†16
Sam	John Dolf†17
Jenny	Thia Fadel†18
Ralph	Bradley Jones
Hilary	Karen Ziemba

UNDERSTUDIES: Catherine Cooper (Cassie/Sheila/Val), Michael Danek (Zach), Fraser Ellis (Mark/Bobby/Don), Morris Freed (Mark), Laurie Gamache (Kristine/Judy/Cassie), Bradley Jones (Bobby/Greg), Troy Garza (Mike/Mark/Paul/Larry/Al), Roscoe Gilliam (Richie), Brad Jeffries (Don/Zach), Kiel Junius (Maggie/Connie/Val), Frank Kliegel (Don/Zach/Bobby), Evan Pappas (Mark/Al/Paul/Larry), Sam Piperato (Bobby/Larry/Mark), Ann Louise Schaut (Cassie/Sheila/Kristine/Judy), Tracy Shayne (Bebe/Diana/Maggie), Pamela Ann Wilson (Val/Judy), Karen Ziemba (Cassie/Diana/Bebe/Maggie)
MUSICAL NUMBERS: I Hope I Get It, I Can Do That, and. . . ., At the Ballet, Sing!, Hello 12 Hello 13 Hello Love, Nothing, Dance 10 Looks 3, Music and the Mirror, One, Tap Combination, What I Did for Love, Finale

A musical performed without intermission. The action takes place in 1975 during an audition in the theatre.

* Still playing May 31, 1983. Cited as Best Musical by NY Drama Critics Circle, winner of 1976 Pulitzer Prize, 1976 "Tonys" for Best Musical, Best Book, Best Score, Best Direction, Best Lighting, Best Choreography, Best Musical Actress (Donna McKechnie), Best Featured Actor and Actress in a Musical (Sammy Williams, Kelly Bishop), and a Special Theatre World Award was presented to each member of the creative staff and original cast, see THEATRE WORLD Vol. 31.
† Succeeded by: 1. Drew Geraci, Evan Pappas, 2. Jan Leigh Herndon, Jane Summerhays, 3. Scott Wise, Danny Herman, 4. Scott Plank, Brad Jeffries, 5. Karen Curlee, Kiel Junius, 6. Frank Kliegel, 7. Steve Boockvor, 8. Fraser Ellis, Danny Herman, Chris Marshall, 9. Laurie Gamache, 10. Randy Clements, Michael Danek, 11. Diane Fratantoni, Kay Cole, Roxann Caballero, Gay Marshall, Roxann Caballero, Loida Santos, 12. Scott Plank, Buddy Balou, 13. Fraser Ellis, 14. Ronald A. NaVarre, 15. Ann Louise Schaut, 16. Catherine Cooper, 17. Sam Piperato, 18. Tracy Shayne

Martha Swope Photos

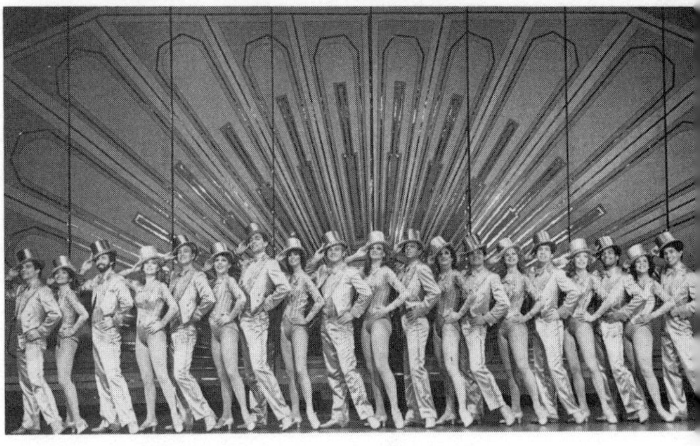

Finale Above: Kevin Chinn Top: Tommy Aguilar, Steve Boockvor, Brad Jeffries, Pamela Sousa, Mitzi Hamilton, Jane Summerhays, Loida Santos

61

DREAMGIRLS

Book and Lyrics, Tom Eyen; Music, Henry Krieger; Direction and Choreography, Michael Bennett; Co-Choreographer, Michael Peters; Scenery, Robin Wagner; Costumes, Theoni V. Aldredge; Lighting, Tharon Musser; Sound, Otts Munderloh; Musical Supervision/Orchestrations, Harold Wheeler; Musical Director, Yolanda Segovia, Paul Gemignani; Vocal Arrangements, Cleavant Derricks; Hairstylist, Ted Azar; Production Supervisor, Jeff Hamlin; Technical Coordinator, Arthur Siccardi; Props, Michael Smanko; Wardrobe, Alyce Gilbert, Stephanie Edwards; Assistant to Choreographers, Geneva Burke; Production Assistant, Charles Suisman; Assistant Conductor, Nick Cerrato; Casting, Olaiya, Johnson/Liff; Original cast album on Geffen Records and Tapes; General Management, Marvin A. Krauss, Eric L. Angelson, Gary Gunas, Steven C. Callahan, Joey Parnes; Stage Managers, Zane Weiner, Frank DiFilia, Jake Bell; Presented by Michael Bennett, Bob Avian, Geffen Records, the Shubert Organization (Gerald Schoenfeld, Chairman; Bernard B. Jacobs, President); Press, Merle Debuskey, Diane Judge. Opened at the Imperial Theatre on Sunday, December 20, 1981.*

CAST

The Stepp Sisters .... Deborah Burrell†1
         Vanessa Bell, Tenita Jordan†2, Brenda Pressley
Charlene .... Cheryl Alexander
Joanne .... Linda Lloyd†3
Marty .... Vondie Curtis-Hall
Curtis Taylor, Jr .... Ben Harney†4
Deena Jones .... Sheryl Lee Ralph
The M. C. .... Larry Stewart
Tiny Joe Dixon/Nightclub Owner .... Joe Lynn
Lorrell Robinson .... Loretta Devine†5
C. C. White .... Obba Babatunde
Effie Melody White .... Jennifer Holliday†6
Little Albert & the Tru-Tones/James Early Band ... Charles Bernard
        Wellington Perkins, Jamie Patterson, Eric Riley
        Charles Randolph-Wright, Frank Mastrocola
James Thunder Early .... Cleavant Derricks†7
Edna Burke .... Sheila Ellis†8
Wayne .... Tony Franklin
Dave and the Sweethearts .... Paul Binotto†9,
        Candy Darling, Carol Logen†10
Frank, press agent .... David Thome†11
Michelle Morris .... Deborah Burrell†1
Mr. Morgan .... Larry Stewart
Film Executives .... Paul Binotto†9, Scott Plank†12,
        Weyman Thompson†13
The Five Tuxedos .... Charles Bernard, Jamie Patterson,
        Charles Randolph-Wright, Eric Riley, Larry Stewart
Les Style .... Cheryl Alexander, Ethel Beatty,
        Mary Denise Bentley, Brenda Pressley

ANNOUNCERS, FANS, REPORTERS, GUESTS, ETC.: Cheryl Alexander, Ethel Beatty, Vanessa Bell, Mary Denise Bentley, Charles Bernard, Candy Darling, Ronald Dunham, Rhetta Hughes, Carol Logen, Joe Lynn, Frank Mastrocola, Julia McGirt, Hal Miller, Jamie Patterson, Wellington Perkins, Richard Poole, Brenda Pressley, Charles Randolph-Wright, Eric Riley, Larry Stewart, Buddy Vest, Swings: Brenda Braxton, Milton Craig Nealy, Allison Williams

UNDERSTUDIES: Ethel Beatty, Terry Burrell (Deena), Julia McGirt, Brenda Pressley (Effie), Cheryl Alexander, Rhetta Hughes (Lorrell), Ethel Beatty, Brenda Pressley (Michelle), Vondie Curtis-Hall (Curtis), Larry Stewart, (James Thunder Early), Wellington Perkins, Tony Franklin (C. C. White), Milton Craig Nealy (Marty), Milton Craig Nealy, Frank Mastrocola (Jerry), Eric Riley (Wayne), Hal Miller (Frank), Milton Craig Nealy, Wellington Perkins (M.C.), Charles Bernard (Tiny Joe)

MUSICAL NUMBERS: I'm Looking for Something, Goin' Downtown, Takin' the Long Way Home, Move, Fake Your Way to the Top, Cadillac Car, Steppin' to the Bad Side, Party, I Want You Baby, Family, Dreamgirls, Press Conference, Only the Beginning, Heavy, It's All Over, And I Am Telling You I'm Not Going, Love Love You Baby, Dreams Medley, I Am Changing, One More Picture Please, When I First Saw You, Got to Be Good Times, Ain't No Party, Quintette, The Rap, I Miss You Old Friend, One Night Only, I'm Somebody, Faith in Myself, Hard to Say Goodbye My Love

A musical in 2 acts and 20 scenes. The action takes place in the early 1960's and 1970's.

*Still playing May 31, 1983. Winner of 1982 "Tonys" for Best Book, Lighting, Choreography, Supporting Actor (Cleavant Derricks), Best Actor and Actress in a Musical (Ben Harney, Jennifer Holliday)
†Succeeded by: 1. Terry Burrell, 2. Rhetta Hughes, 3. Ethel Beatty, 4. Vondie Curtis-Hall during vacation, 5. Cheryl Alexander during vacation, 6. Vanessa Townsell, 7. Hinton Battle during vacation, 8. Julia McGirt, 9. Richard Poole, 10. Carol Logen, 11. Buddy Vest, 12. Hal Miller, 13. Eric Riley

Vanessa Townsell Above: Vondie Curtis-Hall, Obba Babatunde, Cleavant Derricks, Ben Harney, Top: Terry Burrell, Sheryl Lee Ralph, Loretta Devine

Martha Swope Photos

Florence Lacey

EVITA

Lyrics, Tim Rice; Music, Andrew Lloyd Webber; Director, Harold Prince; Choreography, Larry Fuller; Set/Costumes/Projections, Timothy O'Brien, Lazeena Firth; Executive Producers, R. Tyler Gatchell, Jr., Peter Neufeld; Orchestrations, Hershy Kay, Andrew Lloyd Webber; Musical Director, Edward Strauss, Jack Gaughan; Musical Supervisor, Paul Gemignani; Lighting, David Hersey; Sound, Abe Jacob; Original cast album on MCA Records; Presented by Robert Stigwood in association with David Land; General Manager, Howard Haines; Casting, Joanna Merlin; Company Manager, John Caruso; Assistant Conductor, Uel Wade; Props, George Green, Jr.; Wardrobe, Stephanie Cheretun; Hairstylist/Makeup, Richard Allen, Esther Teller; Production Assistant, Wiley Hausam; Stage Managers, George Martin, John Grigas, John-David Wilder, Kenneth W. Urmston; Press, Mary Bryant, Becky Flora, Philip Rinaldi. Opened at the Broadway Theatre on Tuesday, September 25, 1979.*

CAST

Evita	Patti LaPone †1, Terri Klausner†2
Che	Mandy Patinkin†3
Peron	Bob Gunton†4
Peron's Mistress	Jan Ohringer†5
Magaldi	Mark Syers†6
Children	Tammy Amerson, Megan Forste, Colette Sena Heyman, Michael Pastryk, Christopher Wooten, Bradley Kane, Teddy Moran

PEOPLE OF ARGENTINA: Dennis Birchall, Pamela Blake, Susan Cella, Kim Darwin, Patti D'Beck, Al De Cristo, Anny DeGange, Gregg Edelman, Scott Fless, Carole Garcia, Barry Gorbar, David Green, Paul Harman, Barbara Hartman, Lois Hayes, Robert Hendersen, Ken Hilliard, Michael Hayward-Jones, David Horwitz, Robert Kellett, David King, Deborah Lasday, Michael Licata, Robert Logan, Amy Niles, Marcia O'Brien, Ivson Polk, Cassie Rand, Morgan Richardson, Drusilla Ross, Davia Sasks, David Staller, Wilfredo Suarez, Claude Tessier, Leslie Tinnaro, Kenneth W. Urmston.

UNDERSTUDIES: Susan Cella (Evita), Paul Harman (Che), Al DeCristo (Che), David Green (Peron), Michael Licata (Magaldi), Amy Niles (Peron's Mistress)

MUSICAL NUMBERS: A Cinema in Buenos Aires, Requiem for Evita, Oh What a Circus, On This Night of a Thousand Stars, Eva Beware of the City, Buenos Aires, Goodnight and Thank You, The Art of the Possible, Charity Concert, I'd Be Surprisingly Good for You, Another Suitcase in Another Hall, Peron's Latest Flame, A New Argentina, On the Balcony of the Casa Rosada, Don't Cry for Me Argentina, High Flying Adored, Rainbow High, Rainbow Tour, The Actress Hasn't Learned, And the Money Kept Rolling In, Santa Evita, Waltz for Eva and Che, She Is a Diamond, Dice Are Rolling, Eva's Final Broadcast, Montage, Lament

A musical in two acts, based on the life of Eva Peron, second wife of Argentina dictator Juan Peron.

*Closed June 25, 1983 after 1568 performances and 17 previews. Winner of 1980 NY Drama Critics Circle Award for Best Musical, "Tonys" for Best Musical, Best Actress (Patti LuPone), Best Direction, Score, Book, Lighting, and Best Featured Actor in a Musical (Mandy Patinkin). For original production, see THEATRE WORLD Vol. 36.
†Succeeded by: 1. Derin Altay, Loni Ackerman, Florence Lacey, 2. (matinees) Nancy Opel, Pamela Blake, 3. James Stein, Anthony Crivello, Scott Holmes, 4. David Cryer, 5. Cynthia Hunt, 6. James Whitson

Martha Swope Photos

Top Left: Anthony Crivello, Loni Ackerman

FORTY-SECOND STREET

Music, Harry Warren; Lyrics, Al Dubin; Book, Michael Stewart, Mark Bramble, based on novel by Bradford Ropes; Direction and Choreography, Gower Champion; Scenery, Robin Wagner; Costumes, Theoni V. Aldredge; Lighting, Tharon Musser; Musical Direction, Philip Fradkin; Orchestrations, Philip J. Lang; Dance Arrangements, Donald Johnston; Vocal Arrangements, John Lesko; Sound, Richard Fitzgerald; Hairstylist, Ted Azar; Casting, Feuer & Ritzer; Dance Assistants, Karin Baker, Randy Skinner; Presented by David Merrick; Props, Leo Herbert; Wardrobe, Gene Wilson, Kathleen Foster; Assistant Musical Director, Bernie Leighton; Company Manager, Leo K. Cohen; Stage Managers, Steve Zweigbaum, Barry Kearsley, Jane E. Neufeld, Debra Pigliavento; Press, Solters/Roskin/Friedman, Milly Schoenbaum, Warren Knowlton, Josh Ellis, David LeShay, Kevin Patterson. Opened at the Winter Garden Monday, August 25, 1980 and moved to the Majestic Theatre on March 30, 1981.*

CAST

Andy Lee....................................... Danny Carroll
Oscar.. Robert Colston
Mac/Thug/Doctor .... Stan Page
Annie .... Karen Prunczik †1
Maggie Jones.......................... Carole Cook †2
Bert Barry .... Joseph Bova
Billy Lawlor................................ Lee Roy Reams†3
Peggy Sawyer............................... Wanda Richert †4
Lorraine .... Ginny King †5
Phyllis.. Jeri Kansas †6
Julian Marsh .... Jerry Orbach †7
Dorothy Brock .... Tammy Grimes †8
Abner Dillon .... Don Crabtree
Pat Denning........................... James Congdon †9
Thugs .... Stan Page, Ron Schwinn
Doctor .... Stan Page

ENSEMBLE: Doreen Alderman, Dennis Angulo, Carole Banninger, Dennis Batutis, Joel Blum, Mary Cadorette, Pam Cecil, Ronny DeVito, Rob Draper, Brandt Edwards, Sharon Ferrol, Cathy Greco, Kim Morgan Greene, Christine Jacobsen, Jeri Kansas, Jack Karcher, Billye Kersey, Karen Klump, Terri Ann Kundrat, Neva Leigh, Gail Lohla, Shan Martin, Maureen Mellon, Sandra Menhart, Ken Mitchell, Bill Nabel, Don Percassi, Michael Ricardo, Lars Rosager, Linda Sabatelli, Nikki Sahagen, Ron Schwinn, Maryellen Scilla, Yveline Semeria, Robin Stephens
STANDBYS AND UNDERSTUDIES: Sheila Smith/Charlotte Fairchild/Elaine Cancilla (Dorothy/Maggie), Stephen G. Arlen/Steve Elmore (Julian), Mary Cadorette/Nikki Sahagen (Peggy), Joel Blum (Billy), Bill Nable (Bert), Don Percassi (Andy), Stan Page (Abner/Pat), Billye Kersey/Barbara Mandra (Annie), Bernie Leighton (Oscar), Debra Pigliavento/Lorraine Person (Phyllis/Lorraine), Ensemble: Lorraine Person, Yvonne Dutton, Jon Engstrom, Christopher Lucas, Kelli McNally, Lizzie Moran, Debra Pigliavento
MUSICAL NUMBERS: Audition, Young and Healthy, Shadow Waltz, Go Into Your Dance, You're Getting to Be a Habit with Me, Getting Out of Town, Dames, I Know Now, Sunny Side to Every Situation, Lullaby of Broadway, About a Quarter to 9, Shuffle Off to Buffalo, 42nd Street

A musical in 2 acts and 16 scenes. The action takes place during 1933 in New York City and Philadelphia.

*Still playing May 31, 1983. Recipient of 1981 "Tonys" for Best Musical and for Outstanding Choreography. For original production, see THEATRE WORLD Vol. 37.
†Succeeded by: 1. Clare Leach, 2. Charlotte Fairchild, Sheila Smith, Peggy Cass, Carol Swarbrick, Jessica James, 3. Ken Prescott during vacation, 4. Nancy Sinclair, Karen Prunczik, Mary Cadorette, Gail Benedict, Lisa Arlen during vacation, 8. Charlotte Fairchild, Sheila Smith, Millicent Martin, Elizabeth Allen, 9. Stephen G. Arlen, Jered Holmes, Steve Elmore

Martha Swope Photos

Top Right: Lee Roy Reams and chorus

Jerry Orbach, Lisa Brown

JOSEPH AND THE AMAZING TECHNICOLOR DREAMCOAT

Music, Andrew Lloyd Webber; Lyrics, Tim Rice; Direction/Choreography, Tony Tanner; Scenery, Karl Eigsti; Lighting, Barry Arnold; Costumes, Judith Dolan; Sound, Tom Morse; Musical Supervision/Arrangements/Orchestrations, Martin Silvestri, Jeremy Stone; Musical Director, David Friedman; Presented by Zev Bufman, Susan R. Rose, Melvyn Estrin, Sidney Shlenker and Gail Berman by arrangement with Robert Stigwood and David Land; Associate Producers, Thomas Pennini, Jean Luskin, Jerome Edson and the Rose; Original cast album on Chrysalis Records; General Manager, Theatre Now, William Court Cohen, Edward H. Davis, Norman E. Rothstein, Ralph Roseman, Charlotte Wilcox, Alix Morrison; Company Manager, Helen V. Meier; Props, Liam Herbert; Wardrobe, Karen Eifert; Assistant Conductor, Michael Tornick; Assistant to Choreographer, Joni Masella; Wigs, Charles LoPresto; Stage Managers, John Fennessy, Stephen Bourneuf, Jerry Bihm; Press, Fred Nathan, Eileen McMahon, Leo Stern, Anne Abrams, Bert Fink. Opened at the Royale Theatre on Wednesday, January 27, 1982.*

CAST

Narrator	Laurie Beechman †1
Jacob	Gordon Stanley
Reuben	Robert Hyman
Simeon	Kenneth Bryan
Levi	Steve McNaughton †2
Napthali	Charlie Serrano
Issachar	Peter Kapetan †3
Asher	David Asher †4
Dan	James Rich †5
Zebulon	Doug Voet
Gad	Barry Tarallo †6
Benjamin	Philip Carrubba †7
Judah	Stephen Hope
Joseph	Bill Hutton †8
Ismaelites	Tom Carder, David Ardao
Potiphar	David Ardao
Mrs. Potiphar	Randon Lo
Butler	Kenneth Bryan
Baker	Barry Tarallo †9
Pharaoh	Tom Carder

WOMEN'S CHORUS: Karen Bogan, Katharine Buffaloe, Lorraine Barrett, Terry Iten, Randon Lo, Rosalyn Rahn, Dorothy Tancredi, Renee Warren
SWINGS: Stephen Bourneuf, Michael Howell Deane, Terri Homberg, Joni Masella
UNDERSTUDIES: Dorothy Tancredi/Rosalyn Rahn (Narrator), Michael Howell Dean (Jacob), Doug Voet/John Ganzer (Joseph), Kenneth Bryan (Potiphar), James Rich (Pharaoh)
MUSICAL NUMBERS: Prologue, Jacob and Sons, Joseph's Coat, Joseph's Dreams, Poor Poor Joseph, One More Angel in Heaven, Potiphar, Close Every Door, Stone the Crows, Pharaoh's Story, Song of the King, Pharaoh's Dream Explained, Those Canaan Days, The Brothers Came to Egypt, Grovel Grovel, Who's the Thief?, Benjamin Calypso, Joseph All the Time, Jacob in Egypt, Any Dream Will Do, May I Return to the Beginning.

A musical in two acts.

*Closed Sept. 4, 1983 after 747 performances. This production opened Off-Broadway at the Entermedia Theatre on Wednesday, Nov. 18, 1981 and played 77 performances before moving to Broadway's Royale Theatre. †Succeeded by: 1. Sharon Brown, 2. Peter Samuel, 3. Eric Aaron, 4. James Rich, 5. Richard Hilton, 6. John Ganzer, 7. Stephen Bourneuf, 8. Allen Fawcett, Doug Voet, Andy Gibb, Doug Voet, David Cassidy, 9. John Ganzer

Martha Swope Photos

Top Right: Gordon Stanley, David Cassidy and brothers

David Cassidy, Tom Carder

NINE

Laura Kenyon, Liliane Montevecchi, Eileen Barnett, Barbara Stock

Book, Arthur Kopit; Adaptation from the Italian, Mario Fratti; Music and Lyrics, Maury Yeston; Director, Tommy Tune; Scenery, Lawrence Miller; Costumes, William Ivey Long; Lighting, Marcia Madeira; Musical Supervision/Orchestrations, Jonathan Tunick; Sound, Jack Mann; Musical Director, Wally Harper; Musical Conductor, Vincent Fanuele; Choral Composition/Musical Continuity, Maury Yeston; Hairstylist, Michael Gottfried; Dances, Thommie Walsh; Casting, Hughes/Moss; Presented by Michel Stuart, Harvey J. Klaris, Roger S. Berlind, James M. Nederlander, Francine LeFrak, Kenneth D. Greenblatt in association with Shulamith & Michael N. Appell, Jerry Wexler and Michel Kleinman Productions; Associate Producer, Mark Beigelman; Original cast album on Columbia Records; General Management, Marilyn S. Miller, Berenice Weiler, Barbara Carrellas, Marshall B. Purdy, David Jannone; Technical Coordinator, Arthur Siccardi; Props, Michael Durnin; Assistant Conductor, Paul Sullivan; Wardrobe, Jean Steinlein, Sydney Smith; Assistant to Mr. Tune, Priscilla Lopez; Company Captain, Jo Ann Ogawa; Stage Managers, Bruce H. Lumpkin, Kenneth Cox, Nancy Lynch; Press, Judy Jacksina, Glenna Freedman, Marcy Granata, Susan Chicoine, Diane Tomlinson. Opened at the 46th Street Theatre on Sunday, May 9, 1982.*

CAST

Guido Contini	Raul Julia †1
Guido at an early age	Cameron Johann
Luisa	Karen Akers †2
Carla	Anita Morris †3
Claudia	Shelly Burch †4
Guido's Mother	Taina Elg
Liliane La Fleur	Liliane Montevecchi †5
Lina Darling	Laura Kenyon
Stephanie Necrophorus	Stephanie Cotsirilos
Our Lady of the Spa	Kate Dezina
Mama Maddelena, Chief of Chambermaids	Camille Saviola
Saraghina	Kathi Moss
Maria	Jeanie Bowers
Francesca	Kim Criswell †6
Venetian Gondolier	Colleen Dodson
Giulietta	Louise Edeiken
Annabella	Nancy McCall
Diana	Cynthia Meryl †7
Renata	Rita Rehn †8

The Germans:

Gretchen von Krupt	Lulu Downs
Heidi von Sturm	Linda Kerns
Olga von Sturm	Dee Etta Rowe
Ilsa von Hesse	Alaina Warren Zachary
Young Guido's Schoolmates	Evans Allen †9
	Jadrien Steele, Patrick Wilcox

STANDBYS AND UNDERSTUDIES: Cynthia Meryl/Colleen Dodson (Luisa), Clifford David (Guido), Cynthia Meryl/Patrice Pickering (Liliane), Kim Criswell/Colleen Dodson (Claudia), Kim Criswell/Laura Kenyon (Carla), Alaina Warren Zachary/Nancy McCall (Guido's Mother), Colleen Dodson/Patrice Pickering (Our Lady of the Spa), Dorothy Kiara/Patrice Pickering (Lina), Rita Rehn/Laura Kenyon (Stephanie), Camille Saviola/Linda Kerns (Saraghina), Lulu Downs/Alaina Zachary (Chief of Chambermaids), Patrick Wilcox (Young Guido), Leigh Finner/Julie J. Hafner/Dorothy Kiara/Patrice Pickering

MUSICAL NUMBERS: Overture Delle Donne, Spa Music, Not Since Chaplin, Guido's Song, Coda di Guido, The Germans at the Spa, My Husband Makes Movies, A Call from the Vatican, Only with You, Folies Bergeres, Nine, Ti Voglio Bene, Be Italian, The Bells of St. Sebastian, A Man Like You, Unusual Way, Contini Submits, The Grand Canal, Tarantella, Every Girl in Venice, Marcia Di Ragazzi, Recitativo, Amor, Only You, Simple, Be on Your Own, I Can't Make This Movie, Getting Tall

A musical in two acts.

*Still playing May 31, 1983. Recipient of 1982 "Tonys" for Best Musical, Best Score, Best Direction, Best Costumes, Best Featured Actress in a Musical (Liliane Montevecchi).
†Succeeded by: 1. Bert Convy during vacation, Sergio Franchi, 2. Maureen McGovern, Eileen Barnett, 3. Beth McVey for vacation, Wanda Richert, 4. Barbara Stock, 5. Priscilla Lopez for vacation, 6. Beth McVey, 7. Nancy Callman, 8. Lauren Mitchell, Catherine Campbell, 9. Andrew Cassese, Scott Grimes

Kenn Duncan Photos
Top Left: Colleen Dodson, Sergio Franchi, Kate Dezina

OH! CALCUTTA!

Devised by Kenneth Tynan; Conceived and Directed by Jacques Levy; Contributors, Robert Benton, David Newman, Jules Feiffer, Dan Greenberg, Lenore Kandel, John Lennon, Jacques Levy, Leonard Melfi, Sam Shepard, Clovis Trouille, Kenneth Tynan, Sherman Yellen; Music and Lyrics, Robert Dennis, Peter Schickele, Stanley Walden, Jacques Levy; Choreography, Margo Sappington; Musical Director, Stanley Walden; Scenery and Lighting, Harry Silverglat Darrow; Costumes, Kenneth M. Yount; Supervised by James Tilton; Musical Conductor, Norman Bergen; Sound, Sander Hacker; Assistant to Director, Nancy Tribush; Projected Media Design, Gardner Compton; Live Action Film, Ron Merk; Production Assistants, Marcia Edelstein, Andrea Ladik; Assistant Musical Conductor, Dan Carter; Technical Directors, Thomas Healy, Charles Moran; Wardrobe, Melissa Davis, Susan J. Wright, Melissa Davis; Props, James Tilton; Presented by Hillard Elkins, Norman Kean, Robert S. Fishko; Company Managers, Doris J. Buberl, Tobias Beckwith; Stage Managers, Bruce Kagel, Maria DiDia; Press, Les Schecter, Barbara Schwei. Opened June 17, 1969 at the Eden Theatre, and September 24, 1976 at the Edison Theatre.*

CAST

Deborah Bauers	Cheryl Hartley
Nannette Bevelander	David Heisey
Michael A. Clarke	Mary Kilpatrick
Charles E. Gerber	Nick Mangano

MUSICAL NUMBERS AND SKITS: Taking off the Robe, Will Answer All Sincere Replies, Playin', Jack and Jill, The Paintings of Clovis Trouille, Delicious Indignities, Was It Good for You Too?, Suite for Five Letters, One on One, Rock Garden, Spread Your Love Around, Four in Hand, Coming Together Going Together

An "erotic musical" in two acts.

*Still playing May 31, 1983. For original production, see THEATRE WORLD Vol. 33.

Top Left: Nanette Bevelander, Michael A. Clarke, Nick Mangano, Cheryl Hartley, David Heisey, Deborah Bauers, Charles E. Gerber, Mary Kilpatrick

PUMP BOYS AND DINETTES

Conceived and written by the company; Set, Doug Johnson, Christopher Nowak; Costumes, Patricia McGourty; Lighting, Fred Buchholz; Sound, Bill Dreisbach; Production Coordinator, Sherman Warner; Presented by Dodger Productions, Louis Busch Hager, Marilyn Strauss, Kate Studley, Warner Theatre Productions and Max Weitzenhoffer; Original cast album by CBS Records; General Managers, Michael David, Edward Strong, Suzanne Sato; Stage Managers, Mo Donley, Lucia Schliessmann; Press, Betty Lee Hunt, Maria Cristina Pucci, James Sapp, Maurice Turet. Opened at the Princess Theatre, Thursday, February 4, 1982.*

CAST

Jackson	John Foley †1
L. M.	Mark Hardwick †2
Prudie Cupp	Debra Monk †3
Rhetta Cupp	Cass Morgan †4
Eddie	John Schimmel †5
Jim	Jim Wann †6

Understudies: Rhonda Coullet, Erik Frandsen, Michael Sansonia

MUSICAL NUMBERS: Highway 57, Taking It Slow, Serve Yourself, Menu Song, The Best Man, Fisherman's Prayer, Catfish, Mamaw, Be Good or Be Gone, Drinkin' Shoes, Pump Boys, Mona, T.N.D.P.W.A.M., Tips, Sister, Vacation, No Holds Barred, Farmer Tan, Closing Time.

A musical in two acts.

*Closed June 18, 1983 after 573 performances. It opened Off-Broadway on Friday, July 10, 1981 at the Westside Arts Theatre for 20 performances; moved October 31, 1981 to the Colonnades Theatre for 112 performances before its Broadway debut. See THEATRE WORLD Vol. 38.
†Succeeded by: 1. Jimmy Ryan, Malcolm Ruhl, 2. John Lenehan, Mark Hardwick, 3. Rhonda Coullet, Debra Monk, 4. Ronee Blakley, Margaret LaMee, 5. Bruce Samuels, John Schimmel, 6. Loudon Wainwright III, Tom Chapin, John Foley

Gerry Goodstein Photos

Loudon Wainwright, Ronee Blakley

Top: John Schimmel, John Foley, Cass Morgan, Loudon Wainwright, Debra Monk, Mark Hardwick

SULLIVAN STREET PLAYHOUSE Tuesday, May 3, 1960 and still playing May 31, 1983. Lore Noto presents the world's longest running musical:

THE FANTASTICKS with Book and Lyrics by Tom Jones; Music, Harvey Schmidt; Suggested by Edmund Rostand's play "Les Romanesques"; Director, Word Baker; Original Musical Director/Arrangements, Julian Stein; Design, Ed Wittstein; Associate Producers, Sheldon Baron, Dorothy Olim, Jules Field, Robert Alan Gold; Original cast recording by MGM Records; Assistant Producer, Bill Mills; Production Assistant, John Krug; Stage Managers, K. R. Williams, Steve McDonough

CAST

The Narrator/El Gallo	George Lee Andrews†1
The Girl	Marty Morris†2
The Boy	Jeff Knight†3
The Boy's Father	Lore Noto†4
The Girl's Father	Byron Grant†5
The Old Actor	Robert Molnar†6
The Man Who Dies/Indian	James Cook†7
The Mute	Alan Hemingway†8
At the piano	Norman Weiss†9
At the harp	Winifred Starks

MUSICAL NUMBERS: Try to Remember, Much More, Metaphor, Never Say No, It Depends on What You Pay, Soon It's Gonna Rain, Rape Ballet, Happy Ending, This Plum Is Too Ripe, I Can See It, Plant a Radish, Round and Round, They Were You

A Musical in two acts.

†Succeeded by: 1. Sal Provenza, Lance Brodie, Roger Neil, Sal Provenza, 2. Elizabeth Bruzzese, Judith Blazer, Liz Bruzzer, Virginia Gregory, 3. Christopher Seppe, Howard Paul Lawrence, Steve McDonough, 4. David Keiserman, 5. Henry Quinn, Gene Jones, William Tost, Gordon Jones, 6. Bryan Hull, 7. Robert R. Oliver, 8. Glenn Davish, Richard Gervais, Steve McDonough, David Gebel, Peter Reckell, Steve McDonough, Glenn Davish, 9. Jeffrey Klotz

Lou Manna Photo

Sal Provenza, Judith Blazer, Christopher Seppe

PALSSON'S. Opened Friday, January 15, 1982 and still playing May 31, 1983. Michael Chapman presents:

FORBIDDEN BROADWAY a Playkill Production; Concept and Lyrics, Gerard Alessandrini; Associate Producers, Peter Brash, Melissa Burdick; Originally Directed by Michael Chapman; Director, Jeff Martin, Pete Blue; Sound and Lighting, Steven Adler; Executive Producer, Sella Palsson; Stage Manager, Jerry James, Steven Adler; Press, Becky Flora

CAST: Gerard Alessandrini, Bill Carmichael, Nora Mae Lyng, Wendee Winters, Fred Barton, who were succeeded during the year by Chloe Webb, Jason Alexander, Jeff Etjen, Brad Garside, Ann Leslie Morrison, Marilyn Pasekoff, Jan Neuberger, Larry Small

A musical satire in two acts.

Eric Stephen Jacobs Photo

Gerard Alessandrini, Nora Mae Lyng, Fred Barton,
Wendee Winters, Bill Carmichael

CLOUD 9

By Caryl Churchill; Director, Tommy Tune; Set, Lawrence Miller; Costumes, Michel Stuart, Gene London; Lighting, Marcia Madeira; Title Song/Incidental Music, Maury Yeston; Sound, Warren Hogan; Hairstylist, Ethyl Eichelberger, Michael Gottfried; Associate Producer, Mark Beigelman; General Management, Marilyn S. Miller, Berenice Weiler, Barbara Carrellas, Marshall Purdy; Casting, Mary Colquhoun; Wardrobe, Terrence Mintern; Technical Coordinator, Tom Shilhanek; Stage Managers, Murray Gitlin, Michael Morris, Barry Cullison, Steven Stahl; Presented by Michel Stuart and Harvey J. Klaris in association with Michel Kleinman Productions; Press, Judy Jacksina, Glenna Freedman, Diane Tomlinson, Susan Chicoine, Marcy Granata, Marc Thibodeau. Opened at the Theatre de Lys (subsequently re-named Lucille Lortel Theatre) on Monday, May 18, 1981.*

CAST

Act I
Clive .... Jeffrey Jones[†1]
Betty .... Zeljko Ivanek[†2]
Joshua .... Don Amendolia[†3]
Edward .... Concetta Tomei[†4]
Victoria .... Herself
Maud .... Veronica Castang[†5]
Ellen/Mrs. Saunders .... E. Katherine Kerr[†6]
Harry Bagley .... Nicolas Surovy[†7]
Act II
Betty .... E. Katherine Kerr[†6]
Edward .... Jeffrey Jones[†1]
Victoria .... Concetta Tomei[†4]
Martin .... Nicolas Surovy[†7]
Lin .... Veronica Castang[†5]
Cathy .... Don Amendolia[†3]
Gerry .... Zeljko Ivanek[†2]

UNDERSTUDIES: Ron Fassler, John Martinuzzi, Kit Flanagan

A comedy in two acts. The action takes place in Africa in 1880 (Act I) and London in 1980 (Act II) . . . but for the characters it is only 25 years later.

* Closed Sept. 4, 1983 after 971 performances. For original production, see THEATRE WORLD Vol. 37.
† Succeeded by: 1. Ivar Brogger, Stephen Stout, 2. Michael Jeter, John Pankow, Lenny von Dohlen, Bill Sadler, Steven Flynn, 3. Michael Jeter, Ian Trigger, James Lecesne, 4. Katherine Borowitz, Caroline Lagerfelt, Sherry Steiner, Elaine Bromka, 5. Barbara Berg, Caroline Kava, Elizabeth Norment, Kit Flanagan, 6. Catherine Wolf, Cynthia Harris, Cheryl McFadden, 7. Barry Cullison

Peter Cunningham / Martha Swope Photos

Judith Barcroft, Lenny von Dohlen
Top Right: Veronica Castang

THE ACTOR'S NIGHTMARE
and
SISTER MARY IGNATIUS EXPLAINS IT ALL FOR YOU

By Christopher Durang; Director, Jerry Zaks; Sets, Karen Schulz; Costumes, William Ivey Long; Lighting, Paul Gallo; Sound, Aural Fixation; Production Assistants, Lori Steinberg, Lon Scott; Props, Frank Molina; Technical Director, Bob Bertrand; Wardrobe, Daryl Kroken; Casting, John Lyons; Production Managers, William M. Camp, Pat DeRousie, Rachel Chanoff; Presented by Playwrights Horizons (Andre Bishop, Artistic Director; Paul Daniels, Managing Director); Associate Producer, Anne Wilder; Wardrobe, Beckie DeLong; General Manager, Sari E. Weisman; Stage Manager, Esther Cohen; Press, Bob Ullman, Louise Ment. Opened at Playwrights Horizons on Friday, October 16, 1981.*

CAST

"The Actor's Nightmare"
George Spelvin .... Jeff Brooks †1
Meg .... Polly Draper †2
Sarah Siddons .... Elizabeth Franz †3
Dame Ellen Terry...................... Mary Catherine Wright †4
Henry Irving .... Timothy Landfield †5
The action takes place on a stage.

"Sister Mary Ignatius Explains It All for You"
Sister Mary Ignatius......................... Elizabeth Franz †3
Thomas....................................... Mark Stefan †6
Diane Symonds .... Polly Draper †2
Gary Sullavan .... Timothy Landfield †5
Philomena Rostovich .... Mary Catherine Wright †4
Aloysius Benheim .... Jeff Brooks †1
The action takes place in a lecture hall.
UNDERSTUDIES: Brian Keeler, Debra Dean, Kathleen Chalfant, Evan Sandman, Damon Dukakis.

*Still playing May 31, 1983, at Westside Arts Theatre where it moved on February 24, 1982.
†Succeeded by: 1. Christopher Durang during vacation, Brian Keeler, 2. Deborah Rush, Alice Playten, Brenda Currin, 3. Nancy Marchand, Mary Louise Wilson, Lynn Redgrave, 4. Carol Mignini, Cynthia Darlow, Winnie Holzman, 5. Jerry Zaks for vacation, Jeffrey Hayenga, James Eckhouse, 6. Guy-Paris Thompson

Susan Cook Photos

Jerry Zaks, Christopher Durang
Top Right: Guy-Paris Thompson, Mary Louise Wilson

THE DINING ROOM

By A. R. Gurney, Jr.; Director, David Trainer; Set, Loren Sherman; Costumes, Deborah Shaw; Lighting, Frances Aronson; Business Manager, Rory Vanderlick; Production Manager, William M. Camp; Casting, John Lyons; Technical Director, Bob Bertrand; Props, Carol Kalil, Nancy Rifkin; Wardrobe, Susan Gibney; Production Assistants, Tim Claussen, Cathay Brackman, Alice Perlmutter; General Manager, Sari Weisman; Company Manager, Jack Tantleff; Stage Manager, James Long; Press, Bob Ullman, Louise Ment; Presented by Playwrights Horizons (Andre Bishop, Artistic Director; Paul Daniels, Managing Director). Opened at Playwrights Horizons Theatre Thursday, Feb. 11, 1982 and moved April 27, 1982 to the Astor Place Theatre.*

CAST

Lois de Banzie†1　　　　　　　　　　John Shea†4
W. H. Macy†2　　　　　　　　　　　Pippa Pearthree†5
Ann McDonough†3　　　　　　　　　Remak Ramsay†6

A play performed without intermission. The action takes place in a dining room, or rather, many dining rooms, over the course of many years.

* Closed July 17, 1983 after 607 performances, 96 of them at Playwrights Horizons.
† Succeeded by: 1. Debra Mooney, 2. Scott Waara, 3. Cara Duff-MacCormick, Amanda Carlin, 4. Richmond Hoxie, John Getz, Nicholas Hormann, Michael Ayr, 5. Patricia Wettig, Joan Wooters, 6. Charles Kimbrough, Rex Robbins, Frank Hankey

Susan Cook / Gerry Goodstein Photos

Left: (seated) Ann McDonough, Pippa Pearthree, Lois de Banzie, (standing) W. H. Macy, Remak Ramsay, John Shea

Cara Duff-MacCormick, Mark Arnott

OFF-BROADWAY PRODUCTIONS

(WESTSIDE MAINSTAGE) Tuesday, May 11–29, 1982 (20 performances) The Writers Theatre presents:
THE OVERCOAT by Tom Fontana; Adapted from the story by Nikolai Gogol; Director, Linda Laundra; Sets, B. T. Whitehill; Costumes, Clifford Capone; Lighting, Vivien Leone; Sound, Richard Kassel; Choreography, Pamela Hunt; Producers, Linda Laundra, Irene Burns; Stage Manager, Becky Wold.

CAST: Austin Pendleton (Bashmachkin), Jerry Lee (Bagritsky/Thief/-Pallbearer), David Laundra (Chaadaiev/Thief/Pallbearer), Tom Brennan (Zagoskin/Policeman/Commissioner/V.I.P.), Kate Wilkinson (Natalya Danill/Party Guest), Louis Beachner (Petrovich/Guest/Doctor), Donald Berman (Anton Aksakov), Karen Shallo (Anastasia/Masha/Secretaries), Katina Commings (Sophia)
A drama in two acts. The action takes place in or about the 19th Century in St. Petersburg, Russia.

(HAROLD CLURMAN THEATRE) Wednesday, June 2–20, 1982 (29 performances). The Harold Clurman Theatre (Jack Garfein, Artistic Director) presents:
WITH LOVE AND LAUGHTER An evening of varied theatre by 22 authors; Director, Peter Bennett; Set, Harry Feiner; Lighting, Todd Elmer; Production Coordinator, Suzanne Soboloff; Technical Director, Walter Ulasinski; Stage Managers, Anthony Petito, Dayna Clark; Press, Burnham-Callaghan, Lynda Kinney.

CAST: Celeste Holm (The Woman), Wesley Addy (The Man), Gordon Connell (The Other Man)

Performed with one intermission.

(ACTORS REPERTORY THEATRE) Thursday, June 3–20, 1982 (12 performances) Actors Repertory Theatre (Warren Robertson, Artistic Director; Janet Doeden, Artistic Manager) with Lily Turner present:
AFTER YOU'VE GONE by Marjorie Kellogg; Director, Jason Buzas; Set, Don Jensen; Lighting, Steven Helliker; Musical Direction, George Quincy; Costumes, Jane Aire; Choreography, Erica Eigenberg; Technical Director, Leslie Clark Stevens; Stage Managers, Crystal Huntington, Marla R. Kaye; Props, Connie Humphrey, Judith Granite.

CAST: Sylvia Short (Alicia), Lily Lodge (Persie), Barry Ford (Karl)

A drama in five scenes with one intermission. The action takes place at the present time in a hotel room in Kiel, West Germany.

(PERRY STREET THEATRE) Saturday, June 5–27, 1982 (28 performances) Elizabeth I. McCann, Nelle Nugent, Ray Larsen present:
TOTAL ABANDON by Larry Atlas; Director, Jack Hofsiss; Set, David Jenkins; Costumes, Julie Weiss; Lights, Beverly Emmond; General Management, McCann & Nugent; Company Manager, Mary T. Nealon; Stage Managers, Helaine Head, C. Townsend Olcott II; Technical Director, Paul Everett; Wardrobe, Alice Jankowiak; Hairstylist, Leon Gagliardi; Assistant to Director, David Coury; Casting, Johnson/Liff; Sound, Lou Shapiro; Press, Solters/Roskin/Friedman, Joshua Ellis, David LeShay, Cindy Valk

CAST: Jeffrey DeMunn (Lenny Keller), John Heard (Henry Hirsch), W. B. Brydon (Walter Bellmon), Michael Lerner (Ben Hammerstein), Terry O'Quinn (Standby)

A drama in two acts. The action takes place at the present time in a waiting room in a county courthouse.

(AMERICAN RENAISSANCE THEATRE) Tuesday, June 8–26, 1982 (12 performances) Judith Lesley and Sinclair Management present:
THE FURTHER INQUIRY by Ken Kesey; Adapted by Richard Parks, John Higgins; Director, Brandwell Teuscher; Music, Grateful Dead; Set, H. Peet Foster; Lights, Paul Lindsay Butler; Sound, Ken Ross; Costumes, Joseph Rivera; Production Assistant, Stephanie Masters; Stage Managers, John Caywood, Robert Mantione; Press, Fred Hoot, Ken Munzing

CAST: Lois Robbins (Attendant), Maggie Askew (Tooey), Howard Ross (Chest), Luke Sickle (Bailiff), Michael Kolba (Roy Sebern), Erika Petersen (Chloe), Jeremy Slate (Ken Kesey), Jerome Smith (John Page Browning), Lu Leonard (Jane Burton), Suzanne Toren (Gretch), Martin Treat (Hardly Visible), Joel Rooks (Dr. Knot), Brandwell Teuscher (Neal Cassady), Edward Morehouse (Dr. Richy), Judith Lesley (Stark Naked)

A drama in two acts. The action takes place at the present time, more or less, in a courtroom just beyond the imagination, anyplace, USA. The events are historically true; the testimony factual.

Neva Small, Boyd Graham, Mary Testa in "Life Is Not a Doris Day Movie" *(Gerry Goodstein Photo)*

(TOP OF THE GATE/VILLAGE GATE) Thursday, June 10, 1982–July 25, 1982 (54 performances). Reid-Dolph Inc., Stephen O. Reid, Producer, presents:
LIFE IS NOT A DORIS DAY MOVIE with Book and Lyrics by Boyd Graham; Original Music, Stephen Graziano; Director, Norman Rene; Settings, Mike Boak; Costumes, Walker Hicklin; Lighting, Debra J. Kletter; Choreographer, Marcia Milgrom Dodge; Musical Arranger, Elliot Weiss; Musical Director, Jim Cantin; General Manager, Gary Tydings; Stage Managers, Susi Mara, Susan Farwell; Press, Betty Lee Hunt, Maria Cristina Pucci, James Sapp

CAST: Boyd Graham (Lingerie Salesman), Mary Testa (Singing Telegram Lady), Neva Small (Waitress), Olga Merediz (Understudy)
MUSICAL NUMBERS: Waiting for the Bus of Life, Don't Cry for Me, Lament, Oh William Morris, The Fashion Show, The Last Thing That I Want to Do Is Fall in Love, You'll Be Sorry, Tribute, Little Girl-Big Voice, I'm So Fat, The Uh Oh Could It Be That I'm an Oh No Tango, The Right Image, The Last Chance Revue, It's a Doris Day Morning, Influenza, Last Chance Series, Super Wasp, Report on Status, A Man Who Isn't, Geographically Undesirable, Whoa Boy, Junk Food Boogie, Public Service Message, Singer Who Moves Well, Not Mister Right, Pause for Prayer, Cavalcade of Curtain Calls, Think of Me
A musical revue in two acts. The action takes place at the present time at a bus stop on the tip of Manhattan at dawn.

(THEATRE AT STUDIO R) Friday, June 12, 1982– July 5, 1982 (18 performances) C.E.T.W. Theatre Company presents:
ATTENDIN' SKELETONS by James Arlington Jones; Director, Ron Wentz; CAST: Bernita Robinson, Alegreo, Rob Woods, Bill Fort, William Lucas, Kevin Stockton, Les Earl Ford, Ira Belgrade, Brian Douglas, Monique Clark

Lily Lodge, Barry Ford, Sylvia Short in "After You've Gone" *(Dean Powell Photo)*

73

(ENTERMEDIA THEATRE) Monday, June 14, 1982 (1 performance and 10 previews) Dan Fauci, Joseph Scalzo and the Actors Institute in association with Frances T. Hillin, Allen Schoer and Entermedia (Joseph Asaro, Executive Director; David Secter, Creative Director) present:
LOOKING-GLASS by Michael Sutton and Cynthia Mandelberg; Director, David H. Bell; Sets, John Arnone; Lighting, Frances Aronson; Costumes, Jeanne Button; Music, Marc Elliot, David Spangler; General Management, Robert S. Fishko; Company Manager, Nancy Nagel; Stage Managers, Douglas F. Goodman, George Tynan, Catharine Baldwin; Production Supervisor, Gershen Shevett, Wardrobe, Gail Case; Casting, Elissa Myers; Assistants to Producers, Sally Fisher, David Kagan, Torry Robeck; Assistants to General Manager, Susan Dorsey, Margay Witlock; Production Assistants, Barbara Bragg, Josie Good, Twyla Thompson; Magic Consultant, Bill Brunelle; Press, The Merlin Group, Cheryl Sue Dolby, Merle Frimark.

CAST: John Vickery (Charles Lutwidge Dodgson/Lewis Carroll), Nicholas Hormann (Robinson Duckworth), Richard Peterson (William Hayden), Richard Clarke (Rev. Dodgson/Dean Liddell), Robert Machray (Chaplain MacDougal/Josiah Gibbs), Mitchell Steven Tebo (Jenkins/Boy), Tara Kennedy (Alice/Agnes), Tudi Wiggins (Mrs. Liddell), Innes-Fergus McDade (Miss Prickett), Melanie Hague (Young Woman)
UNDERSTUDIES: George Tynan (Charles/Hayden/Duckworth), Innes/Fergus McDade (Mrs. Liddell), Melanie Hague (Miss Prickett), Catherine Baldwin (Alice/Agnes/Young Woman)
A play in two acts. The action takes place in Oxford, London, and in the imagination of Charles Dodgson from 1855 to 1875.

(NAT HORNE MUSICAL THEATRE) Friday, June 18, 1982–July 4, 1982 (19 performances and 9 previews). William Ellis presents:
DIVINE HYSTERIA by Anthony P. Curry; Director, William Ellis; Set, Don Clay; Sound, Sam Agar; Lighting, William Stallings; Costumes, Nina Roth; Production Manager, Nikki Carlino; Production Assistants, Michael Budlow, Michelle Eberts; Stage Managers, Arlene Roseman, Judy Wong; Press, Free Lance Talents, Francine L. Trevens, David Mayhew, Patricia Cooke

CAST: Brenda Thomas (Celeste Robinson), Jay Aubrey Jones (Revealer/Suzie's friend/Father Ahearn/Rag Man), Betty Lester (John's Sister/Housewife/Mrs. Johnston/Mary Jean Loomis/Rich Woman), Barbara Nadel (Millie's friend/Wife/Prisoner/ERA Advocate/Bob's wife/Bum), Phil Di Pietro (Pimp/Father Jimenez/Newstand Owner/Bartender), Michael Varna (Bachelor/husband/Billy's buddy/Emma's husband/bank executive), Kathleen Monteleone (Andrea), Jeffrey Howard Kaufman (Michael), James Bartz (Nick), Althea Lewis (Helen)
A play in two acts. The action takes place at the present time, alternating between a tv newscaster's interviews at various places, and the upper East Side apartment of Michael and Andrea Brandt.

(APPLE CORPS THEATRE) Thursday, June 17, 1982—July 11, 1982 (20 performances). The Apple Corps Theatre (John Raymond, Artistic Director; Neal Arluck, Business Manager) presents:
MURDER ON THE NILE by Agatha Christie; Director, Fred Weiss; Set, Marc Scott; Costumes, Wallace G. Lane; Lighting, Michael Gebhardt; Sound, Elliot Forrest; Props, John P. Chartier; Stage Manager, Cathy Oriol; Press, Aviva Cohen

CAST: Tuttle Andrews (Beadseller/McNaught), Preston Keith Smith (Steward), Suzanne Heitmann (Miss Ffoliot-Ffoulkes), Nancy McDonald (Christina Grant), Robert Coles (Smith), Jane Koenig (Louise), Dan Putnam (Dr. Bessner), Donna Moryn (Kay Mostyn), Frank Latson (Simon Mostyn), Joel Kramer (Canon Pennefather), Lillian Byrd (Jacqueline DeSeverac)
A murder mystery in 3 acts and 4 scenes. The action takes place in 1936 in the observation saloon of the paddle steamer "Lotus" on the Nile between Shellal and Wadi Halfa.

(INTERART THEATRE) Friday, June 25, 1982—August 1, 1982 (39 performances and 16 previews). Interart Theatre (Margot Lewitin, Artistic Director; Sam Sweet, Managing Director) presents:
MERCENARIES by James Yoshimura; Director, Margot Lewitin; Dramaturg, Colette Brooks; Set, Kate Edmunds; Lighting, Ann Wrightson; Costumes, Kate Edmunds, Tom McAlister; Production Manager, Byeager Blackwell; Technical Director, Bruce Hudgens; Stage Managers, Dyana Lee, Susan Haynie, Jeffrey Joseph; Production Assistant, Lisa Kalechstein; Press, Free Lance Talents, Francine L. Trevens, David Mayhew, Patricia Cooke

CAST: Andrew Davis (Spike), Kenneth Ryan (Jimbo), William Winkler (Yogi), Reg E. Cathey (Wells), Roger Brown (Mockis), Anna Deavere Smith (Doctor), L. B. Williams (Guard), Jeffrey Joseph (Attendant)
A drama in 2 acts and 8 scenes. The action takes place at the present time on a small island in the Caribbean during 24 hours.

P. L. Carling, Lillian Byrd in "Murder on the Nile"
(*Austin Trevett Photo*)

(FORTY-SEVENTH STREET THEATRE) Sunday, June 20– 27, 1982 (9 performances and 11 previews). Popcorn Productions present:
A DRIFTER, THE GRIFTER & HEATHER McBRIDE with Music by Bruce Petsche; Book and Lyrics, John Gallagher; Director, Dick Sasso; Musical Staging/Choreography, George Bunt; Musical Direction/Arrangements, Jeremy Harris; Casting, Elizabeth R. Woodman; Scenery and Costumes, Michael Sharp; Lighting, Richard Winkler; Associate Producer, Magee Whelan; General Manager, Frank Scardino; Company Manager, Phil Leach; Stage Managers, Perry Cline, Tracy Danehy; Technical Supervisor, Jeremiah Harris; Production Assistant, Nina Stern; Wardrobe, Davette Pitts; Press, The Merlin Group, Cheryl Sue Dolby, Merle Frimark, Joel W. Dein, Dennis Decker

CAST: Ronald Young (Sky Malinowski), Elizabeth Austin (Heather McBride), William Francis (G. W. Mosely), Dennis Bailey (Bernie Barnardo), Chuck Karel (Luigi O'Hara), Diane Findlay (Goodun Plenty)
MUSICAL NUMBERS: Getaway, Remember the Dream, Love Song, Fat Luigi, Holding the Bag, Just Our Way of Doing Business, Find a Way, Tippity Top, Tiny International Empire, Honesty, I Dream, Skidaddle, Fly with Me, Little Little, Hair Pulling Ballet, Hey Kiddo You Through, Again
A musical comedy in two acts. The action takes place in Greenville, Indiana, a mythical Hoosier village caught in a time warp between the invention of indoor plumbing and the Rolling Stones.

(PROVINCETOWN PLAYHOUSE) Tuesday, June 22, 1982– July 25, 1982 (39 performances and 10 previews). Jenny Besch presents:
JANE AVRIL by Jane Marla Robbins; Director, Albert Takazauckas; Scenery, Peter Harvey; Costumes, David Murin; Lighting, Mal Sturchio; Music, William Schimmel; Dances, Ron Dabney; General Management, Dorothy Olim, Thelma Cooper, Gail Bell; Company Manager, George Elmer; Assistant to Producer, John Huls; Wardrobe, April Briggs; Stage Managers, Robin Kevrick, Arland Russell; Press, Jeffrey Richards, Ben Morse, Robert Ganshaw, Ted Killmer, C. George Willard, Helen Stern

CAST: Jane Marla Robbins (Jane Avril), Kevin O'Connor (Count Henri de Toulouse-Lautrec), Richard Council (Baron Jean-Pierre Dufferin), William Schimmel (Musician)
A play in two acts. The action takes place in Paris during the 1890's in a rehearsal room of the Moulin Rouge, the studio of Toulouse-Lautrec, Jane Avril's apartment, and a sanitorium outside Paris.

Reg E. Cathey (L), Roger Alan Brown (R) in "Mercenaries"
(*Anita Feldman Photo*)

(ACTORS OUTLET) Sunday, June 27– July 3, 1982 (4 performances and 8 previews). Hamilton Richardson presents:
HOME REMEDIES by Paul Minx; Director, David Irving; Set, Tim D'Acquisto, Brian Bomeisler; Costume Coordinator, Jana Eaton; Lighting, William Armstrong; Production Coordinator/Choreographer, Georgianne Walken; Assistant to Producer, John Huls; Production Executive, Susan Berlin; Stage Manager, Ron Jewell; Press, Jeffrey Richards, Robert Ganshaw

CAST: Frances Helm (Betty), Susan Berlin (Millie), Jonathan Farwell (Lou), Meg Kelly (Catherine), Mark Moses (Tom), Scott Valentine (Dan)
   A comedy in two acts. The action takes place at the present time on the evening before Thanksgiving Day, and the following morning.

(UPSTAIRS AT O'NEALS) Wednesday, July 7– August 15, 1982 (39 performances and 3 previews). Walter Willison and Jefrey Silverman in association with Ted Van Antwerp and David Plattner Productions/Theacom Entertainment present:
BROADWAY SCANDALS OF 1928 with Music by Jefrey Silverman; Lyrics and Scenario by Walter Willison; Musical Direction/Arrangements, Jefrey Silverman; Conceived and Directed by Walter Willison; Choreography, Jo Anna Lehmann, Gwen Hillier Lowe; Additional Choreography/Musical Staging, Douglas Norwick; Set, Ron Placzek; Costumes, Robert Turturice; Lighting, Malcolm Sturchio; Hairstylist, Joe Anthony; Makeup, Suki Vazquez; Assistant to Producers, Roberta Silverman; Wardrobe, Cheri Wing; Press, Shirley Herz, Sam Rudy, Peter Cromarty, Alan Hale

CAST: Jefrey Silverman (Tony), Kenny D'Aquila (Joey Staccato), Jo Anna Lehmann (Rusty Parker), Rose Scudder (Roberta Kelley), Jessica James (Texas Guinan) succeeded by Diane J. Findlay, Gwen Hillier Lowe (Trixie Duga) succeeded by Eva Grant, Shelley Bruce (Sandy McGuire), Steve Jerro (Big Phil Castanza), Bill Johnson (Rosie), Walter Willison (Kid Kotten), Understudies: Jo Anna Lehmann, Bill Johnson
MUSICAL NUMBERS: Scandals!, Let's Go Boating, Picture Me with You, Nobody Needs a Man as Bad as That!, Charleston under the Moon, When You Come to the End of Your Rainbow, Happy Jest Bein' with Me, Blowing Bubbles in the Bathtub, I Gotta Hear a Song, A Good Ol' Mammy Song, Things Have Never Been Better, The Man at the Piano, Sodomangamor, I Couldn't Say, Tango, Give a Girl a Break!, Broadway Wedding, Better Bein' Loved, Mazie, Scandals Finale
   A musical revue in two acts.

(PERRY STREET THEATRE) Wednesday, July 14—18, 1982 (7 performances and 8 previews). Victoria Lang and Peter Golden in association with Eugene Albert present:
ALL OF THE ABOVE by Michael Eisenberg; Directed and Staged by Tony Berk; Scenery, Lou Anne Gilleland; Costumes, Carla Kramer; Lighting, Victor En Yu Tan; Musical Direction/Special Piano Arrangements, Ed Eliner; Vocal Direction and Arrangements, Gary Kahn; General Manager, Erik Murkoff; Production Assistant, Gabby Aarons; Technical Director, Ron Burns; Press, Pat Dale, Jim Baldassare

CAST: Ann Morrison, Linda Gelman, Michelan Sisti, Ed Ellner, Understudies: Kelly Coffield, Lennie Del Duca
MUSICAL NUMBERS: A Cry from the Coast, Be My Bland Romantic Lead, Born Again, California Love, Child of a Sweater, Dancin' Shoes, For Alice, Game Show Hosts, It Just Ain't a Party without You, Las Vegas Post-Blitz, Little Rubik's Room, Memories of Kong, Mom Kills Child Comma Self, My Heart's Intact, New Year's Eve at the Computer Center, Pianist's Fingers, School on Saturday Night, Talk to My Machine, The Dictator Who Ran Away, Willy's Prize, Your Show
   A "musical entertainment" performed without intermission.

(SOUTH STREET THEATRE) Wednesday, July 14, 1982—August 29, 1982 (41 performances and 2 previews). Alyce Finell presents:
THE MUSIC KEEPER by Elliot Tiber and Andre Ernotte; Directed by Mr. Ernotte; Set, Karen Schulz; Costumes, Susan Tsu; Lighting, Rachel Budin; Musical Adviser, Mildred Kayden; General Manager, David Lawlor; Stage Managers, Tom Podiak, Kurt Schlesinger; Press, Shirley Herz, Sam Rudy, Peter Cromarty

CAST: Jan Miner (Frau Winifred Wagner, daughter-in-law of composer Richard Wagner), Dennis Bacigalupi (Andrew, the American), Understudy for Andrew, Kurt Schlesinger
   A drama in two acts. The action takes place at dawn on the morning of March 3, 1980 and the following morning. It is a fictional play based in part on information in the public record and in part on the personal experiences of the authors.

Jo Anna Lehmann, Eva Grant, Shelley Bruce, Rose Scudder in "Broadway Scandals of 1928" (*Susan Cook Photo*)

(NEW YORK CITY PARKS) Friday, July 16, 1982—August 1, 1982 (15 performances). Joseph Papp presents the Riverside Shakespeare Company in:
THE COMEDIE OF ERRORS by William Shakespeare; Director, Gloria Skurski; Producer, W. Stuart McDowell; Music, Michael Canick; Costumes, Barbara Weiss; Set, Dorian Vernacchio; Combat Choreography, Scott Leva; Choreography, Beatrix Porter; Assistant Director, Mark Rosenblatt; Stage Managers, Elizabeth Skofield, David Gilman, Julia Ohm; Technical Director, Pat Freni; Press, Merle Debuskey, Richard Kornberg, John Howlett

CAST: Mel Winkler (Solinus), Ronald Lew Harris (Egeon), Connor Smith (Antipholus of Ephesus), Jeff Natter (Antipholus of Syracuse), Andrew Achsen (Dromio of Ephesus), Trip Plymale (Dromio of Syracuse), Ron Litman (Balthazar/Headsman/Nun), Dan Johnson (Angelo), Dan Woods (Merchant), Ann Ducati (Luce/Abbess), Karen Jackson (Adriana), Erin Lanagan (Luciana), Anita Calandrino (Courtesan), Douglas Whitt (Officer), David Gilman (Guard/Citizen), Will Lampe (Guard-/Citizen/Messenger), Julia Ohm (Nun), Michael Canick, David Simons (Musicians)

(ACTORS PLAYHOUSE) Monday, July 19, 1982—August 15, 1982 (29 performances and 19 previews). Dani Ruska and Marina Spinola present:
BROKEN TOYS! with Book, Music and Lyrics by Keith Berger; Director, Carl Haber; Set, Lisa Beck; Costumes, Mara Lonner, Karen Dusenbury; Lighting, Kevin Jones; Musical Arrangements, Lou Forestieri; General Management, David Lawlor; Stage Managers, Alan Preston, Glen M. Santiago; Hairstylist, A. Vernon Keech; Wardrobe, Manuela Crimini, Bernadette Van-dee-Loo; Makeup, Don Mikula, Lynn Smith; Press, Shirley Herz, Sam Rudy, Peter Cromarty

CAST: Debra Greenfield (Melissa), Keith Berger (Rooty Kazooty), Nerida Normal (Kanga), Oona Lind (Big Dolly), Cheryl Lee Stockton (Kandy), Lonnie Lichtenberg (Randy), Daud Svitzer (Golly), Lucille (Pretty Polly), Jhonny Zeitz (3-D Jesus)
MUSICAL NUMBERS: This Life's the Right One for Me, We're on a Shelf in Your Attic, Play with Me, Broken and Bent, Let's Play Let's Say, I Don't Play with Humans, Prayer Song, Johnny Space, Choo Choo Rap, Lady Ride with Me, Not of Her World, Kangaroo Court, I Don't Think I Like This Game, The Temperance Song, So Ya Wanna Be a Toy, I Got That Other Lady's with My Baby Feeling, Ain't Worth a Dime, Rag Doll Rag, Funny Wind-Up Toy, Left Alone to Be, Weird Fun, Wind-Up in New York City
   A musical in two acts. The action takes place in the bedroom and attic of a suburban house.

Dennis Bacigalupi, Jan Miner in "The Music Keeper" (*Carol Rosegg Photo*)

LITTLE SHOP OF HORRORS

(ORPHEUM THEATRE) Book and Lyrics, Howard Ashman; Based on film by Roger Corman; Music, Alan Menken; Director, Howard Ashman; Musical Staging, Edie Cowan; Set, Edward T. Gianfrancesco; Lighting, Craig Evans; Costumes, Sally Lesser; Sound, Otts Munderloh; Puppets, Martin P. Robinson; Vocal Arrangements/Musical Supervision/Musical Direction, Robert Billig; Orchestrations, Robby Merkin; Presented by WPA Theatre (Kyle Renick, Producing Director), David Geffen, Cameron Mackintosh, the Shubert Organization (Gerald Schoenfeld, Chairman; Bernard Jacobs, President); General Management, Albert Poland, Susan L. Falk; Company Manager, Nancy Nagel Gibbs; Stage Managers, Paul Mills Holmes, Peter B. Mumford, Donna Fletcher; Assistant to Director, Constance Grappo; Hairstylists, Leonore Brown, Paul Mills Holmes; Production Assistant, Beth Anne Kushnick; Wardrobe, Kate Amendola, Lynn Hippen, Marcy Elkins, Victor Valentine; Casting, Darlene Kaplan, Albert Tovares; Press, Fred Hoot, Kenneth Munzing, Solters/Roskin/Friedman, Milly Schoenbaum, Kevin Patterson, Warren Knowlton, Bob Larkin. Opened Tuesday, July 27, 1982 and still playing May 31, 1983.*

CAST

Chiffon . . . . Marlene Danielle †1
Crystal . . . . Jennifer Leigh Warren
Ronnette. . . . . Sheila Kay Davis
Mushnik. . . . . Hy Anzell †2
Audrey. . . . . Ellen Greene †3
Seymour. . . . . Lee Wilkof †4
Derelict. . . . . Martin P. Robinson †5
Orin/Bernstein/Snip/Luce/Everyone Else . . . . Franc Luz †6
Audrey II:
 Manipulation . . . . Martin P. Robinson †5
 Voice. . . . . Ron Taylor

UNDERSTUDIES AND STANDBYS: Katherine Meloche (Audrey), Deborah Lynn Sharp (Chiffon/Crystal/Ronnette), Michael Pace (Seymour/Orin/Bernstein/Luce/Everyone Else), Lynn Hippen (Derelict/Audrey II Manipulation)
MUSICAL NUMBERS: Prologue/Little Shop of Horrors, Skid Row, Da-Doo, Grow for Me, Don't It Go to Show Ya Never Know, Somewhere That's Green, Closed for Renovations, Dentist!, Mushnik and Son, Git It!, Now It's Just the Gas, Call Back in the Morning, Suddenly Seymour, Suppertime, The Meek Shall Inherit, Don't Feed the Plants
 A musical in two acts.
 *Received 1983 citation from NY Drama Critics Circle as Best Musical of the season.
 †Succeeded by: 1. Leilani Jones, 2. Fyvush Finkel, 3. Faith Prince, Katherine Meloche, 4. Brad Moranz, 5. Anthony B. Asbury, 6. Robert Frisch

Peter Cunningham Photos

Anthony Asbury, Ron Taylor

Fyvush Finkel, Faith Prince, Brad Moranz
Top: Lee Wilkof, Ellen Greene, Hy Anzell

(SAVOY THEATRE) Wednesday, July 21, 1982—August 14, 1982 (27 performances). Barbara Moore presents:
MANHATTAN RHYTHM conceived and staged by Jon Devlin; Additional Choreography, Jay Norman, Mary Delia Quigley, Harry Bell; Musical Arrangements, Richard Dimino; Costumes, David Toser; Sound, Gary Harris; Lighting, David Adams; Fantasy Creatures, Richard Tautkus; Stage Manager, Mary Delia Quigley; Press, Jeffrey Richards, C. George Willard

CAST: Jon Devlin and His Company: Virginia Clark East, Lyn Gendron, Ann Marie Giambattista, Kim Kuhlman, Diana Laurenson, Linda Paul, Lisa Rudy, Lauren Salerno, Louis Albert, Richard Loreto, Ralph Rodriguez, Steven Van Dyke, Armour Gomez, Teri Hiatt, Karen Quackenbush, Bonnie Sue Taylor
MUSICAL NUMBERS: Love for Sale, Manhattan Rhythm Blues, All Blues, Take Five, Walkin' Sally, One O'Clock Jump, In the Mood, 57th Street, Crossover, Medley, You Can Dance, Star Trek Medley, Star Wars Cantina, Rock 'n' Roll 'n' Rock Medley, Mamabo Cha-Cha, Merengue, Spanish Cape, Tango, Samba, Hey Good Lookin', Lady, 9 to 5, Never Ending Love, Guilty, Physical, Out Here on My Own, Fame, Celebration

(CLASSIC THEATRE) Tuesday, July 27—August 14, 1982 (15 performances). Theatre Fourteen presents:
NEVER SAY DIE by Frank Higgins; Director, Christopher Hanna; Producer, Teresa Elwert; Set, Kevin Hanna; Lighting, David Landau; Costumes, Shelley Norton; Sound, Kim Motter; Stage Manager, Murphy Terrell

CAST: Bill Smitrovich (Moose Corwin), Michael Schwartz (Crystal), Brian Reddy (Scooter), Ann Janowsky (Ann), Shaw Purnell (Susan), Frederick Allen, Patrick O'Connell, Brian Hargrove (Team Members)
A play in two acts. The action takes place at the present time in the visiting baseball team's locker room and in a nearby motel.

(COLONNADES THEATRE) Thursday, July 29—August 1, 1982 (6 performances). Theatre for Actors and Playwrights presents:
VICTIMS OF DUTY by Eugene Ionesco; Translation, Donald Watson; Director, Herman Babad; Scenery, David Moon; Lighting, Randy Becker; Costumes, Michael Massee; Sound, Michael Jay; Executive Producers, Ellen Zisholtz-Herzog, June Oliver; General Manager, Ellen Zisholtz-Herzog; Company Manager, June Oliver; Dramaturg, Rosette C. Lamont; Props, Louise H. Gorham, Elaine Marolakos; Assistant to Producers, Pam Rubinfield; Mask, Erica Babad; Dolls, Cathay Macysyn; Stage Managers, Ann Mathews, David Edelman; Press, David Lipsky

CAST: Beege Barkett (Madeleine), John Marolakos (Choubert), David Edelman (Detective 1), Val Bisoglio (Detective 2/Nicholas)

(WESTSIDE ARTS CENTER/CHERYL CRAWFORD THEATRE) Thursday, August 12—November 7, 1982 (102 performances and 8 previews). Power Productions and Stan Raiff present:
CHARLOTTE SWEET with Libretto by Michael Colby; Music, Gerald Jay Markoe; Director, Edward Stone; Choreography, Dennis Dennehy; Set, Holmes Easley; Costumes, Michele Reisch; Lighting, Jason Kantrowitz; Hair and Makeup, Patrik D. Moreton; Musical Director, Jan Rosenberg; Orchestrations, John McKinney; General Manager, Paul B. Berkowsky, Sheala N. Berkowsky; Company Manager, Lisa Grossman; Stage Managers, Peter Weicker, Tricia Witham; Assistant to Producer, Bonnie Whalen; Production Assistant, Michelle Roberts; Wardrobe, Richard Alfredo; Casting, McCorkle/Sturtevant; Press, Jeffrey Richards, C. George Willard, Bob Ganshaw, Ted Killmer, Helen Stern

CAST: Michael McCormick (Harry Host), Merle Louise (Cecily MacIntosh), Polly Pen (Skitzy Scofield), Nicholas Wyman (Bob Sweet) succeeded by Timothy Landfield, Sandra Wheeler (Katinka Bugaboo) succeeded by Lynn Eldredge, Alan Bradington (Barnaby Bugaboo) succeeded by Jeff Keller, Mara Beckerman (Charlotte Sweet), Christopher Seppe (Ludlow Ladd Grimble), Standbys: Tricia Witham, Connie Coit (Charlotte/Cecily/Katinka/Skitzy), Michael Dantuono
MUSICAL NUMBERS: At the Music Hall, Charlotte Sweet, A Daughter of Valentine's Day, Forever, Liverpool Sunset, Layers of Underwear, Quartet Agonistes, The Circus of Voices, Keep It Low, Bubbles in Me Bonnet, Vegetable Reggie, My Baby and Me, A-Weaving, Your High Note, Katinka, The Darkness, On It Goes, You See in Me a Bobby, A Christmas Buche, The Letter, Dover, Good Things Come, It Could Only Happen in the Theatre, Lonely Canary, Queenly Comments, Surprise Surprise, The Reckoning, Farewell to Auld Lang Syne
A musical in two acts. The action takes place at the turn of the century in England.

Elizabeth Wolynski Photos

Cara Duff-MacCormick, Thomas A. Stewart
in "Journey to Gdansk" (*Steve Shevett Photo*)

(WESTSIDE MAINSTAGE) Tuesday, August 10—28, 1982 (15 performances). The Foothold Project (John Miglietta, Producer) presents:
JOURNEY TO GDANSK four short plays by Jonusz Glowacki; Translated by Halina Filipowicz, Robert Findlay; Director, Kent Paul; Design Consultant, Quentin Thomas; Sound, Terry Alan Smith; Stage Managers, Janet Friedman; Kelly Coffield; General Manager, Abigail Franklin; Production Assistant, Monet Molosk; Press, Fred Nathan, Anne S. Abrams

CAST: "A Walk Before Dawn" with Dave Florek (Man), Chel Chenier (Young Woman), "Tea with Milk" with Cara Duff-MacCormick (Ewa), Thomas A. Stewart (Andrzej), "Journey to Gdansk" with Allan Carlsen (He), April Shawhan (She), "Flashback" with James Carruthers (Man), Allan Carlsen (Writer)
Performed with two intermissions. All the plays take place in Poland in recent years.

(MERCER STREET THEATRE) Thursday, August 19—September 5, 1982 (15 performances). The Facemakers in association with the Fanfare Theatre Ensemble present:
THE IMPORTANCE OF BEING EARNEST by Oscar Wilde; Director, Evan Thompson; Designer, Tom Tippett; Costumes, Jennie Cleaver; Assistant to Mr. Thompson, Margaret Noonan; Stage Managers, Tom Tippett, Bill MacNulty; Wardrobe, Patricia Kannar; General Manager, Max Nadel; Press, Bill Steele, Arthur Clayburgh

CAST: John McGrane (Lane), David H. Hamilton (Algernon), Owen Thompson (John), Quentin Crisp (Lady Bracknell), Anne Burr (Gwendolen), Joan Shepard (Miss Prism), Cecile Callan (Cecily), Evan Thompson (Canon Chasuble), John McGrane (Butler), Bill MacNutly
A comedy in 3 acts. The action takes place during 1895 in mid-summer.

(ACTORS AND DIRECTORS THEATRE) Wednesday, September 8—19, 1982 (14 performances and 7 previews). D. E. Betts, Ned Davis, Michael Saltz present:
INSERTS by Larry Loonin; Adapted from the 1975 screenplay by John Byrum; Set and Lighting, Norman Dodge; Costumes, Andrew B. Marlay; Music, Donna Betts; Film Sequences, Jim Murray; General Manager, Donna E. Betts; Production Manager, David Higlen; Production Assistant, Ward Davis; Sound, Sam Buccio, Fred Galli; Hairstylist, Robert Groves; Wardrobe, Ruth Landau; Stage Managers, Abigail Wright; Press, Burnham-Callaghan, Owen Levy, Lynda Kinney, Jay Schwartz

CAST: Kevin O'Connor (Boy Wonder), Hope Stansbury (Harlene), John Patrick Hurley (Rex), Wendel Meldrum (Cathy Cake), Ed Setrakian (Big Mac), Evan Davis Marlow (David O'Selznick)
A drama in two acts. The action takes place in a Hollywood mansion in the fall of 1930, a year into the Depression.

Merle Louise, Christopher Seppe, Michael McCormick,
Mara Beckerman, Sandra Wheeler in "Charlotte Sweet"
(*Elizabeth Wolynski Photo*)

(RICHARDSON DANCE GALLERY) Thursday, September 9—20, 1982 (12 performances). Bandwagon presents:
ROBIN HOOD with Music by Reginald DeKoven; Lyrics and Libretto, Harry B. Smith; Direction/Choreography, Denny Shearer; Musical Direction/Vocal Arrangements/Orchestrations, Bruce Kirle; Set, Dorian Vernacchio; Costumes, Jean McGavin; Lighting, Rick Pettit; Producer, Jerry Bell; Managing Director, Jon Hutcheson; Stage Managers, Marygrace Tardi, Lisa Michiloff; Props, Margaret Weber; Makeup, Sam Maupin; Assistant to Director, David Vernon; Wardrobe, Joanne Stekler; Production Coordinator, Sandra Starr; Press, Nancy Frederick Sussan

CAST: Lynn Delaney (Schottische), Lessie Burnum (Chaconne), Kate Wylie (Passacaglia), Susan Levin (Rondelay), Ben Levy (Mark-o-the-Mill), David Vernon (Ribbando), Jeffery Brocklin (Subven), Kenny Gannon (Yeoman Frederick), Alfred Gress (Yeoman Habsburg), Jack Gremli (Little John), Lee Lobenhofer (Allan-a-Dale), Randy Gianetti (Will Scarlet), Ron Lee Savin (Friar Tuck), Lynne Kolber (Annabel), Peggy Atkinson (Dame Durden), Roy Alan Wilson (Robert Earl of Huntington/Robin Hood), K. C. Wilson (Sheriff of Nottingham), John Barone (Sir Guy of Gisborne), Carole-Ann Scott (Maid Marian)
MUSICAL NUMBERS: Cavaliers, Come Dream So Bright, Sheriff of Nottingham's Song, Quintet, An Outlaw's Life for Me, A Tinker's Song, When Lads Have Drunk Enough, Serenade, Quartet, The Armorer's Song, When a Maid Weds, Nothing in Life My Love
A musical in 2 acts and 4 scenes.

(28th STREET PLAYHOUSE) Friday, September 10—26, 1982 (12 performances). Judith Carroll presents:
PARTNERS by John L. Kallas; Director, Warren Kliewer; Sets, Ray Recht; Lighting, William J. Plachy; Costumes, Lewis Anthony Wilkes; Choreographer, Vera Lekas; Technical Director, Jeffrey Berzon; Stage Manager, Kathy Uhler; Press, David Mayhew, Fran Pappas, Terry Kokas

CAST: Peter Johl (Nick), Charles McKenna (Lt. Fallon), Reuben Schafer (Morris), Linda Christian-Jones (Ms. Bradley), David Higlen (Marion Yoblick), Bonnie Deroski (Nancy), Bob Harris (Newscaster), Tina Santorineou (Greek Voice)
The first play, "Morris," takes place over a long weekend in Nick's Liberty Diner on Staten Island; The second play, "Nick," takes place a month later in the same diner.

(LION THEATRE) Saturday, September 11—26, 1982 (16 performances). Donald Arsenault presents:
SOAP with Book and Lyrics by David Man; Music, Aaron Egigian; Director, David Man; Set, Rob Hamilton; Lighting, Todd Elmer; Costumes, Elaine Lee; Musical Direction/Vocal Arrangements, Craig Lee; Choreography, Jerri Garner; Technical Director, Kim Novick; Sound, Georgia Harrell; Wardrobe, Jean Wyatt; Production Assistants, Peter Brennan, Patti Lee; Stage Managers, Bo Metzler, Kim Novick; Press, Keith Sherman

CAST: Gwen Strong (Martha), Catherine Schultz (Cibele), Suzanne Blakeslee (Claire), Mark Goetzinger (Howard), Karen Bruhn (Sherri), Todd Robinson (George), Aileen Savage (Debbie), Cindy Benson (Nicki), Joseph Kelly (Ted), James Leach (Eddie)
MUSICAL NUMBERS: Martha by the Pyramids, Born Blonde, Share, I'm the Only One That's Home, Grovel, Red Rover, At the Singles Bar, Early Efforts, The Girl Who Has Everything, The Days of My Lives, The Good Stuff, Weren't We Together, Four Sides of the Coin
A musical in two acts. The action takes place in Los Angeles, CA, during the week of December 10, 1972.

Larry Guardino, James Gleason, Gail Dahms, Harris Laskawy in "Guys in the Truck" (*Carol Rosegg Photo*)

Susan Scherer, Brenda Forbes, Maureen Kenny in "Busybody"

(NAT HORNE MUSICAL THEATRE) Wednesday, September 15—October 9, 1982 (33 performances). Ronan O'Casey and Jay Perry present:
KNUCKLEBONES by Douglas Anderson; Director, Jay Perry; Set, Daniel Proett; Costumes, David Loveless; Lighting, Zack Zanolli; General Manager, Leonard A. Mulhern; Company Manager, Jack Tantleff; Technical Director, Gary Fassler; Props, Gene Kish; Stage Managers, Dan Zittel, Loreda Shuster; Press, Alpert/LeVine

CAST: Christopher Loomis (Eddie Evans), Jean Barker (Adriane Evans), Lollipop (Mathilda), Kathleen Swan (Anne Yoder), Arch Johnson (Jake Svoboda), Understudies: Loreda Shuster (Anne/Adriane), Jonathan Blair (Eddie/Jake), Sweetheart (Mathilda)
A comedy in two acts. The action takes place in a small college town in the Midwest on a Sunday evening in May.

(ATA/SARGENT THEATRE) Thursday, September 16—November 27, 1982 (60 performances and 12 previews). NTC presents:
THE GUYS IN THE TRUCK by Howard Reifsnyder; Director, David Black; Set/Lighting, Kevin Hickson; Sound, George Jacobs; Stage Managers, Dawn Eaton, Suzanne Fossett; Props, Miss Fossett; Press, Burnham-Callaghan

CAST: Harris Laskawy (Al Klein), Lawrence Guardino (Louie DeFalco), Robert Trumbull (Les Hammond), Dan Martin (Charlie Johnson), James Gleason (Harvey Olmstead), Chazz Palminteri (Nick Caruso), Ellen Newman (Emily Klein), Mike Starr (Doug Frischetti), Gary Klar (Broonzy), Gail Dahms (Billie)
A comedy in 2 acts and 4 scenes. The action takes place in a TV remote control truck outside Cleveland Municipal Stadium before and during a football game.

(WESTSIDE MAINSTAGE) Monday, September 20, 1982—October 10, 1982 (16 performances). Jan Bowes, Craig Noble and Gary Werthiem present:
BILLY LIAR by Keith Waterhouse and Willis Hall; Director, Shan Willson; Sets, John C. Jackson; Lighting, Jim Holden; Music, Bill Taradash; Sound, A & J Studio; Production Manager, Jeff Dougherty; Props, Jamie Allen; Costumes, Don Newcomb; Assistant Director, Lisa Barnes; Casting, David Tochterman, Elisse Myers; Stage Manager, David Young; Press, Owen Levy

CAST: Virginia Downing (Florence), Marlena Lustik (Alice Fisher), John Swindells (Geoffrey Fisher), Neal Jones (Billy Fisher), Daniel Ahearn (Arthur), Cindie Lovelace (Barbara), Lydia Leeds (Rita), Donna Bullock (Liz)
A comedy in three acts. The action takes place in a small industrial town to the north of London on a Saturday.

(RIVERWEST THEATRE) Thursday, September 23—October 10, 1982. (12 performances). Riverwest Theatre presents:
BUSYBODY by Jack Popplewell; Director, Michael Bavar; Set, Toby Corbett; Costumes, George Potts; Lighting, Joel Carliglia; Sound, John LaFex; Producers, Nat Habib, June Summers; Technical Director, Christopher Cole; Wardrobe, Kim Alpaugh; Stage Managers, Beth Wilber, Cliff Alpaugh; Press, Nancy Sussan

CAST: Brenda Forbes (Mrs. Piper), Richard Merrell (Richard Marshall), James Gallagher (Det. Goddard), Peter Pagan (Det. Superintendent Baxter), Gretchen Trapp (Claire Marshall), Maureen Kenny (Marian Selby), Omar Lotayef (Robert Westerby), Susan Scherer (Vickie Reynolds), Understudy for Mrs. Piper, Rica Martens
A comedy mystery in 3 acts and 5 scenes. The action takes place in Richard Marshall's private office high up in a block of offices in London in 1934.

(INTAR THEATRE) Thursday, September 23—October 10, 1982 (15 performances). F & C productions presents:
AMERICAN PRINCESS with Book by Leonard Orr, Jed Feuer, David Hurwitz; Music, Jed Feuer; Lyrics, Leonard Orr; Director, Jed Feuer; Choreography/Musical Staging, Daniel Joseph Giagni; Set, Charles McCarry; Costumes, Kenneth M. Yount; Lighting, John Hickey; Musical Director, Sariva Padgug; Orchestrator, Larry Hochman; General Management, Maria DiDia, Jim Fiore, Rosemary Carey; Stage Managers, Carol Klein, Daniel Kanter; Assistant to Director, David Diamond; Sound, T. Richard Fitzgerald; Wardrobe, Cheryl Woronoff; Props, Cornelius Conboy; Press, Bruce Cohen

CAST: Janet Aldrich (Exerciser/Nurse/Joan), Valerie Coorlas (Shirley/-Linda), Jason Kincaid (Instructor/Smack/Guard/Boulevard/Messenger), Florence Levitt (Ruth Waxman), Paul Mack (Dr. Woodruff/Minister/-Messenger/Rabbi/Young Lou), Alison Morgan (Exerciser/Nurse/Beverly), Merilee Magnuson (Exerciser/Nurse/Connie/Victim), Jack Sevier (Louis Waxman), Mary Testa (Amanda Waxman), Mark Yetter (Gorgeous Goy/Guard/Messenger)
MUSICAL NUMBERS: Hail Professor, Hold Your Temper, Lying in My Crib, With That Hand, Yes I'm Here, Breakdown, Amanda, The Perfect Man, Back to Me, Wake Up Late, His Name Is Lou, Family Man, You've Gone Too Far, Mr. and Mrs., That Hand Is Still, Gotta Stop Her, I Think

(PERRY STREET THEATRE) Saturday, September 25,—October 2, 1982 (9 performances and 12 previews). D. Kain Productions presents:
I AM WHO I AM by Royce Ryton; Director, Jaemes Esterly; Setting, Neil Jacob; Costumes, Jaemes Esterly, Janet Eiger; Lighting, Frances Aronson; Associate Producer, Neil Jacob; General Manager, Erik Murkoff; Fight Coordinator, David Farkas; Sound, Dyana Lee; Assistant to Director, Waltrudis Buck; Technical Director, Ron Burns; Stage Managers, Thom Mangan, Uriel Menson; Press, Jeffrey Richards, Robert Ganshaw, C. George Willard, Helen Stern, Ted Killmer

CAST: Jeff Abbott (The Actor), Leslie Lyles (Mrs. Manahan), Lucille Patton (The Actress), Nick Stannard (Inspector), Standbys: Waltrudis Buck, Gregory Chase
A drama in two acts. The action takes place in the 1960's and the 1920's in Germany and the U.S. in an attempt to examine the facts relative to Princess Anastasia of Russia.

(SOUTH STREET THEATER) Sunday, September 26, 1982 (1 performance and 11 previews). June Hunt Mayer presents:
a/k/a TENNESSEE devised by Maxim Mazumdar; Words, Tennessee Williams; Director, Albert Takazauckas; Design, Peter Harvey; Lighting, Mal Sturchio; Executive Producer, Lawrence Goossen; General Manager, Kingwill Office; Company Manager, Susan Sampliner; Production Assistants, John Traub, Diane Mahigan; Technical Director, William Stallings; Stage Managers, William Hare, David Mack; Press, Warren Knowlton

CAST: Maxim Mazumdar, Carrie Nye, J. T. Walsh in facts and fictions of Thomas Lanier Williams taken from his works.

(LAMBS THEATRE) Tuesday, September 28—October 17, 1982 (21 performances and 8 previews). Bruce Levy in association with Leslie Steinweiss (Levy/Steinweiss Productions) presents:
THE PRICE OF GENIUS by Betty Neustat; Director, Sande Shurin; Set, David Potts; Lighting, Richard Nelson; Costumes, Patricia Adshead; Incidental Music, Leslie Steinweiss; General Management, Dorothy Olim, Gail Bell, Thelma Cooper, George Elmer; Sound, Tom Gould; Production Associate, Patrick Hanson; Makeup/Hairstylist, James Takos; Assistant to Director, Patty Bender; Wardrobe, Maria Kaye; Stage Managers, Rick Ralston, James Bernardi; Press, Shirley Herz, Sam Rudy, Peter Cromarty

CAST: Patrizia Norcia (Juana Ines de la Cruz), Fred Velde (Carlos/Prof. Martinez/Cardinal Minelli), Alfred Karl (Viceroy de Mancera), Rae Kraus (Dona Leonor de Mancera), Fred Rivers (Eduardo), Timothy Wahrer (Jose), Sterling Swann (Manuel), Jeremy Brooks (Father Nunez), Bob Cooper (Bishop), Jody Catlin (Anita), Patricia Mertens (Abbess), Understudies: Jody Catlin (Juana), Timothy Wahrer (Manuel), Fred Velde (Father Nunez), Rae Kraus (Abbess)
A drama in two acts. the action takes place in Mexico City from 1666 to 1695.

Marcella Lowery, Lynn Goodwin, Carol Teitel
in "Baseball Wives"

(HAROLD CLURMAN THEATRE) Wednesday, September 29—November 7, 1982 (42 performances and 9 previews). Tom E. Greene III presents:
BASEBALL WIVES by Grubb Graebner; Director, Gloria Maddox; Set and Costumes, John Falabella; Lighting, Jeff Davis; Sound, Gordon Kupperstein; Casting, Margo McKee; General Manager/Associate Producer, Allan Francis; Company Manager, Brian Dunbar; Sound/Wardrobe, Mitchell Lemsky; Stage Managers, David Rubinstein, Gigi Benson-Smith; Press, Shirley Herz, Sam Rudy, Peter Cromarty

CAST: Marcella Lowery (Janelle), Carol Teitel (Doris), Lynn Goodwin (Becky), Understudy: Gigi Benson-Smith
A play in two acts. The action takes place throughout the professional baseball season, from early spring through late fall.

(MARYMOUNT MANHATTAN THEATRE) Tuesday, October 5—10, 1982 (7 performances). John Stark presents:
IN AGONY by Miroslav Krleza; Translated by John Stark and Mihajlo Starcevic; Adapted by Tom Grainger; Director, John Stark; Lighting, Patti Marin, Carolyne Anderson; Costumes, Pat Henry; Stage Managers, John Stark, Aurelia De Felice

CAST: Margret Warnke (Laura), Marshall Borden (Lenbach), Roy Steinberg (Krizovec), Aurelia De Felice (Madeline)
A drama in two acts. The action takes place in 1921 in the reception room and study of Laura's Fashion Salon, Zagreb.

(ACTORS PLAYHOUSE) Wednesday, October 6—10, 1982 (5 performances and 9 previews). The Anthem Company in association with Sari Weisman presents:
ANTHEM FOR DOOMED YOUTH by Michael Adler; Director, Patricia Turney; Set, Don Gardiner, Lee Mills; Lighting, Seth Orbach; General Manager, Sari Weisman; Company Manager, Robert Bertrand; Stage Manager, Janet Friedman; Press, Bob Ullman, Bob Larkin

CAST: Michael Adler
Performed without an intermission. The action takes place in an empty German trench west of the Oise-Sambre Canal in France, near the end of World War I.

J. T. Walsh, Carrie Nye, Maxim Mazumdar
in "a/k/a/ Tennessee" (*Carol Rosegg Photo*)

(ENTERMEDIA THEATRE) Tuesday, October 5—26, 1982 (25 performances and 50 previews). Sid Bernstein, Stanley Bernstein in association with Abe Margolies and Dennis Paget present the Liverpool Everyman Theatre Production of:
LENNON by Bob Eaton; Conceived and Directed by Mr. Eaton; Musical Supervision; Mitch Weissman; Set, Peter David Gould; Lighting, Dennis Parichy; Costumes, Deborah Shaw; Sound, Tom Morse; Casting, Meg Simon/Fran Kumin; General Management, Iron Mountain Productions, Barbara Darwall; Props, Rick Starr; Technical Consultant, Arthur Siccardi; Wardrobe, Jim Hodson; Production Assistant, Sharon Klein; Hairstylist, Juan Rodriguez; Stage Managers, Peter B. Mumford, Gary M. Zabinski; Press, Judy Jacksina, Glenna Freedman, Diane Tomlinson, Susan Chicoine, Leslie Anderson

CAST: Gusti Bogok (Julia/Yoko), Katherine Borowitz (Mimi/Cynthia), Lee Grayson (Jeff/George Harrison/Gerry Marsden/Tony Palma), Vincent Irizarry (Paul McCartney/Tony Tyler), John Jellison (Arthur Ballard/Koschmider/George Martin/Dick Gregory/Elton John/Bob Wonder), David Patrick Kelly (Younger John/Nightclub Manager), Robert LuPone (Older John/Stuart Sutcliffe/Les Chadwick/Brian Epstein), Greg Martyn (Pete Best/Ringo Starr/Harry Nilson/Tony Barrow/Tim Leary), Bill Sadler (Pete Shotton/Alan Williams/Victor Spinetti/Arthur Janov/Andy Peebles), Standbys: Elizabeth Bayer, John Jellison, Joseph Pecorino, Stuart Warmflash, Mitch Weissman
A musical play in two acts about the life of John Lennon.

(TOMI/TERRACE THEATRE) Wednesday, October 6—24, 1982 (15 performances). Theater Opera Music Institute (Tom LoMonaco/Lucy Greene, Artistic Directors) presents:
CORKSCREWS! Sketches and Lyrics, Tony Lang; Music, Arthur Siegel; Direction and Choreography, Miriam Fond; Costumes, Van Broughton Ramsey; Lighting, Margit Allen; General Manager, Paul P. Lapinski; Technical Director, Jeffrey Musmanno; Press, Jim Pyduck

CAST: Tony Aylward, Barbara Barsky, James Hosbein, Gail Oscar
MUSICAL NUMBERS: I'm into Music, Maiden's Prayer, The Daily Grind, Let It All Hang Out, The Betamax Blues, You Have a Friend, Make It Another, The Family That Plays Together, People, Greetings, Psychotic Overtures, The Ballad of Norman, Send Out for Food, She Is Making Norman Antsy, Not Getting Murdered Today, Up the Hill There, I'm Not Queer, Died & Died & Died, I Like Me, The David Somekind Show, What I Need the Most, The Golden Age, Tina and Nina, The Last Minority, Confession, Non-Matriculation, Free Advice, Creative Block, Looking for Love, Finale
A "slightly twisted revue" in two acts.

(ATA/CHERNUCHIN THEATRE) Sunday, October 10—24, 1982 (12 performances). Courage Productions presents:
BUGLES AT DAWN by David Vando; Suggested by Stephen Crane's "The Red Badge of Courage"; Music, Mark Barkan; Lyrics, David Vando; Director, Robert Pesola; Set, David C. Woolard; Costumes, Johnetta Lever; Lighting, David N. Weiss; Musical Director, Stan Free; Choreographer, Jerri Garner; Assistant to Director, Tish Goldberg; Assistant Musical Director, Tim Johnson; Orchestrations, Stan Free; Arrangements, Rolf Barnes; Casting, Alan Coleridge, Barry Shapiro; Stage Manager, John C. Concannon; Press, Tony Staffieri, Steve Karp, Bruce Lynn, Savvy Management

CAST: Joseph Breen (Johnny Fleming), Marcus Neville (Rebel Flagbearer), Jay Devlin (Spirit of Johnny's Father who assumes the guises of The Veteran/Sgt. Ashford/Photographer), Brent Rogers (Recruiter/Chaplain), Edward Crotty (Oscar Redgrave/Captain of 302), Nancy Ringham (Alma/Scarlet), Peggy Atkinson (Johnny's Mother/Battlefield Annie), Luke Lynch (Sgt.), David Nighbert (Bill Burnside), W. Michael Crouch (J.C.), Chuck Stanley (Lt.), Philip Shultz (Pvt. Smith/Gaylord), Mimi Bessette (Cherry/Roseanna), Margaret Benczak (Ruby/Pearl)
MUSICAL NUMBERS: Marching to Victory, Blow Bugles Blow, Take by Giving, More Is Less, The Interlude, Alma's Poem, Covered in the Rear, Sermon, What Is Wrong with Alma, Run, Give Me Love, Picture Perfect, Annie's Song, Dream, Life's Odyssey, Battle Montage, Flag of Death, Finale
A musical play in 2 acts and 13 scenes. The action takes place on the battlefields of the American Civil War and in the mind of Johnny Fleming.

(ACTORS REPERTORY THEATRE) Monday, October 11—24, 1982 (12 performances and 4 previews). Ron Harrington presents:
FOUR TO MAKE TWO by Paul Ruben; Director, Ron Holgate; Set, Jim Chesnutt; Costumes, Lee Entwisle; Lighting, Patti Marin; Production Coordinator, Thomas Shilhanek; Production Assistant, David St. James, Randy Milligan, Jimmy Hale, Jay Klein, James Taylor; Stage Manager, Jan Malthaner, Madora Thomson; Press, Howard Atlee, Barbara Atlee

CAST: Judy Kaye (Virginia McVay), Lauren K. Woods (Robert McVay), Paula Parker (Shelly Butler), Alan Winston (Stephen Gold), William Linton (Harvey le Fleur)
A comedy in 3 acts and 6 scenes. The action takes place at the present time in July and August.

Robert LuPone, Gusti Bogok, David Patrick Kelly in "Lennon" (*Martha Swope Photo*)

Lauren K. Wood, Paula Parker, Judy Kaye, Alan Winson in "4 to Make 2" (*Gerry Goodstein Photo*)

(VAN BUREN) Monday, October 18—November 6, 1982 (12 performances and 6 previews). Tom O'Shea presents:
RATS with Book and Lyrics by Roy Doliner; Music, Vivian Krasner; Staged and Choreographed by Don Swanson; Wardrobe, Jane Driscoll; Costumes, Bronwyn O'Shaughnessy; Musical Director, Vivian Krasner; Press, Patt Dale, Jim Baldassare

CAST: Roy Doliner (Bernie), Yvette Freeman (Yolanda), Gerry Martin (Shirley), George Merritt (Ralph), Ken Ward (Algernon)
MUSICAL NUMBERS: Does Broadway Need Some More Rats?, Acting and Hustling, Rodents, The Night I Bit John Simon, Mr. Sondheim, Never Have a Book, Never Left Home, We Ate the Money, Under the Spotlight, Test Tube Baby, Write about Me, Crastine, The Rat-a-tat Tap, Like Liza Does, I'd Know How to Be Big, Cheese Medley
A musical revue "not based on a book by T. S. Eliot" in two acts.

(WONDERHORSE THEATRE) Thursday, October 14—24, 1982 (12 performances). TRG Repertory Company (Marvin Kahan, Artistic Director; Anita Pintozzi, Associate Producer) presents:
THE GOSPEL ACCORDING TO AL with Theatre Songs by Al Carmines; Director, William Hopkins; Musical Director, James Laev; Set, Peter Harrison; Lighting, Craig Kennedy; Costumes, Vincente Criado; Choreographer, Carmela Guiteras; Props, Mary Jane DiMassi; General Manager, Daniel Clancy; Stage Manager, Ellen Sontag; Press, Jan Greenberg

CAST: Cathleen Axelrod, Georgia Creighton, Paul Farin, Kate Ingram, Tad Ingram
MUSICAL NUMBERS: Sometimes the Sky Is Blue, The Good Old Days, It's a Man's World, My Old Man, A Woman Needs Approval Now and Then, It's Nice to Cuddle in a Threesome, New Boy in Town, Ordinary Thing, Disposable Woman, Cocoa Cola Girl, Montgomery Moon, Dummy Juggler, I'm Peculiar That Way, I Am My Beloved, I Forget and I Remember, Nostalgia, Fifty Years of Making People Laugh, Forgiveness, I'm Innocence, The World Is Yours, God Bless Us All
A celebration of Al Carmines' twenty years in theatre.

(CHERRY LANE THEATRE) Sunday, October 17, 1982 and still playing May 31, 1983. Harold Thau and Wayne Adams in association with Robert Courson, Jay J. Miller, Richard Sturgis present:
TRUE WEST by Sam Shepard; Director, Gary Sinise; Set, Kevin Rigdon, Deb Gohr; Lighting, Kevin Rigdon; Casting, McCorkle Sturtevan; General Management, Proscenium Services (Kevin W. Dowling); Company Manager, Suzanne VanderSanden; Assistant to Producers, Bruce Detrick; Props, Elliot Fox; Wardrobe, Bruce Detrick; Hairstylist, Carlo Collazo; Stage Manager, Larry Bussard; Press, Judy Jacksina, Glenna Freedman, Diane Tomlinson, Susan Chicoine, Marcy Granata

Cast John Malkovich †1 (Lee), Gary Sinise †2 (Austin), Sam Schacht †3 (Saul Kimmer), Margaret Thomson (Mom), Understudies: Joan Kendall, Bruce Lyons, Valerie Charles, Jere Burns
   A drama in two acts. The action takes place at the present time in a Southern California suburb.
†Succeeded by: 1. Bruce Lyons, James Belushi, 2. Richmond Hoxie, Dan Butler, Gary Cole, 3. Peder Melhuse, Bruce A. Jarchow. For original NY production, see THEATRE WORLD Vol. 37

Martha Swope Photos
Right: Gary Sinise, John Malkovich, Sam Schacht

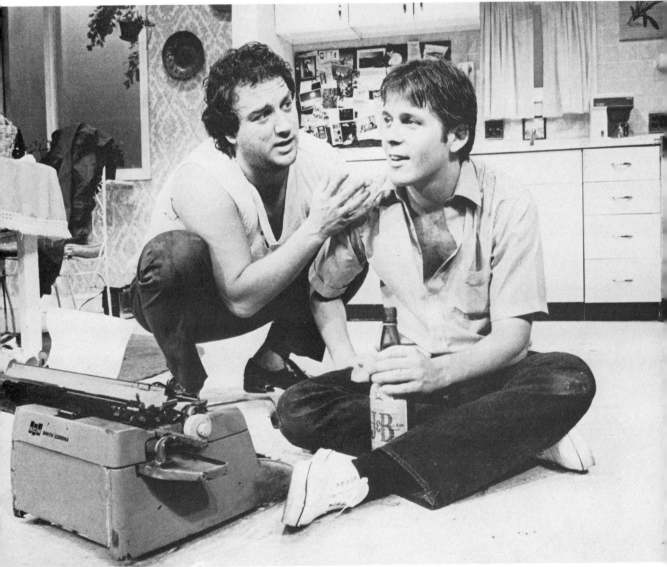

James Belushi, Gary Cole

Joe Sears, Jaston Williams in "Greater Tuna"

(CIRCLE IN THE SQUARE DOWNTOWN) Thursday, October 21, 1982 and still playing May 31, 1982. Karl Allison in association with Bryan Bantry presents:
GREATER TUNA by Jaston Williams, Joe Sears, Ed Howard; Director, Ed Howard; Set, Kevin Rupnik; Costumes, Linda Fisher; Lighting, Judy Rasmuson; Associate Producer, Salisbury Productions; General Management, The Kingwill Office; Company Manager, Susan Sampliner; Assistant to Producers, Gary Davies; Production Associate, Greg Currie; Wardrobe, Greg Currie, August Rothe; Stage Managers, Marjorie Horne, Trip Plymale; Press, Henry Luhrman, Terry M. Lilly, Kevin P. McAnarney

CAST: The Citizens of Tuna, Texas: Mr. Joe Sears†1 plays Thurton Wheelis, Bertha Bumiller, Leonard Childres, Elmer Watkins, Aunt Pearl Burras, R. R. Snavely, Reverend Spikes, Sheriff Givens, Hank Bumiller, Yippy, Mr. Jaston Williams†2 plays Arles Struvie, Harold Dean Lattimer, Peter Fisk, Little Jody Bumiller, Stanley Bumiller, Charlene Bumiller, Chad Hartford, Phinas Blye, Vera Carp, Didi Snavely, Understudy, Trip Plymale.
A comedy in 2 acts and 12 scenes. The action takes place one late-summer day in Tuna, Texas' third-smallest town.
†Succeeded by: 1. Ronn Caroll, Ron Lee Savin, 2. Michael Jeter

(WESTSIDE YMCA) Thursday, October 21—November 14, 1982 (16 performances). American Kaleidoscope (Richard F. Bell, Rebecca Dobson, Joan Rice Franklin) presents:
LIFE WITH FATHER by Howard Lindsay, Russel Crouse; Director, Donald Saddler; Set, Ernest Allen Smith; Costumes, Steven L. Birnbaum; Lighting, Dave McKennan; Technical Director, Michael Bellino; Wardrobe, Varcra Russal; Props, Angelo Musco; Hairstylist, Carmela Mondello; Props, Mitchell Cohen, Mara Quigley; Stage Manager, Alan Mann; Press, Fred Hoot, Joan Rice Franklin, David Mayhew, Richard Dahlia, Janice Gelb

CAST: Rebecca Dobson (Vinnie), Mary Lou Reid (Annie), Ron DeMarco (Clarence), Scott Perrin (John), Kevin Barber (Whitney), Frederick Koehler (Harlan), Tom Crawley (Father), Ellen Humphrey (Margaret), Jayne Chamberlain (Cora), Amanda Naughton (Mary), Ted Tiller (Rev. Lloyd), Debbie Sendax (Delia), Paula Newman (Nora) succeeded by Anne McKenna, Bert Fraser (Dr. Humphreys), Robert Gresh (Dr. Sommers), Marcia-Anne Dovres (Maggie)
A comedy in 3 acts and 6 scenes. The action takes place in the Day home during early summer.

Richard Ryder, Sarah Weeks, Michon Peacock, Douglas Bernstein, Bebe Neuwirth, Randall Edwards in "Upstairs at O'Neal's"
(Peter Cunningham Photo)

(PROVINCETOWN PLAYHOUSE) Wednesday, October 27—December 19, 1982 (62 performaces). The Goodman Theatre, Provincetown Playhouse, David Jiranek, I. Michael Kasser, Marjorie Oberlander, J. P. Pavanelli Ltd. and David Weil present:
EDMOND by David Mamet; Director, Gregory Mosher; Set, Bill Bartelt; Costumes, Marsha Kowal; Lighting, Kevin Rigdon; Fight Choreographer, David Woolley; Associate Producer, Margot Harley; General Manager, David Lawlor; Stage Managers, Ken Porter, Jack Wallace; Press, Shirley Herz, Sam Rudy, Peter Cromarty, Sandra Manley

CAST: Paul Butler (Preacher/Prisoner), Rick Cluchey (Manager/-Leafleteer/Customer/Policeman/Guard), Joyce Hazard (B-Girl/Whore), Laura Innes (Peep Show Girl/Glenna), Bruce Jarchow (Man in Bar/Hotel Clerk/Man in Back/Chaplain), Linda Kimbrough (Edmond's Wife) succeeded by Patti LuPone, Marge Kotlisky (Fortuneteller/Manager/-Woman in subway), Jose Santana (Cardsharp/Guard), Lionel Mark Smith (Shill/Pimp), Colin Stinton (Edmond), Jack Wallace (Bartender/Bystander/Pawnshop Owner/Interrogator)
A drama performed without intermission.

(O'NEAL'S 43rd STREET) Thursday, October 28, 1982—July 2, 1983 (308 performances and 14 previews). Martin Charnin, Michael O'Neal, Patrick O'Neal, Ture Tufvesson present:
UPSTAIRS AT O'NEAL'S conceived and directed by Martin Charnin; Musical Direction/Arrangements, David Krane; Choreographer, Ed Love; Set and Lighting, Ray Recht; Costumes, Zoran; Stage Managers, Edward R. Isser, Neal Klein; Company Manager, Marta Kauffman; Assistant to Director, Heather Hewitt; General Management, R. Tyler Gatchell, Jr., Peter Neufeld; Casting, Peter Cereghetti; Press, Patt Dale, Jim Baldassare

CAST: Douglas Bernstein, Randall Edwards (succeeded by Mary D'Arcy), Bebe Neuwirth, Michon Peacock (succeeded by Carole Schweid), Richard Ryder, Sarah Weeks, Understudies: Kathryn McAteer, Neal Klein, at the pianos: David Krane, Paul Ford
MUSICAL NUMBERS: Upstairs at O'Neal's, Stools, Cancun, Something, I Furnished My One Room Apartment, Little H and Little G, The Ballad of Cy and Beatrice, Signed Peeled Delivered, The Feet, The Soldier and the Washerworker, Table d'Hote, Soap Operetta, Talkin' Morosco Blues, Mommas' Turn, We'll Be Back Right After This Message, All I Can Do Is Cry, Cover Girls, Boy Do We Need It Now, Finale
A satirical revue.

(ACTORS & DIRECTORS THEATRE) Thursday, October 28—November 7, 1982 (12 performances). Theatre Limits, Ltd. (David G. Richenthal, Executive Producer; David M. Fox, Karen Allen, Co-Producers; Robert Bailey, Artistic Director) presents:
LOVE IN THE DARK by Joel Gross; Director, Robert Bailey; Assistant, Regina Miranda; Set, M. Cabot McMullen; Lighting, Gregg Marriner; Costumes, Margo Lasaro; General Manager, Victoria Fahn; Stage Managers, Foy Fred Fish, Janet Callahan; Technical Director, Sam Buccio; Production Assistants, Steve Tager, Jamie DeLorenzo; Casting, Todd Fleischer; Incidental Music, Brian Hurley; Hairstylist, Maru; Press, Jan Greenberg

CAST: Deborah Allison (Gwen Garvey), Howard Korder (Aaron Page), Mel Boudrot (Robert Cade), Julia Curry (Olivia Bedford)
A comedy in 3 acts and 6 scenes. The action takes place at the present time in Olivia Bedford's living room of her apartment on Central Park West in New York City.

(CHAREEVA) Friday, October 29—November 8, 1982 (11 performances and 8 previews). Ed Rubin and Didi Gough present:
THE FRANCES FARMER STORY by Sebastian Stuart; Director, John Albano; Set, Speed Hopkins; Costumes, Gabriel Berry; Lighting, Gerard Bourcier; Assistant Director, Stage Manager, Kate Mennone; General Manager, Ed Rubin; Sound, Dave Schneider; Props, Speed Hopkins; Assistant to Director, Stephen Dym; Makeup/Hairstylist, Eugene Stiegler; Press, Free Lance Talents, Francine L. Trevens, David Mayhew, John Traub

CAST: J. P. Dougherty (Joe Halpern/Judge/Columnist/Sid/Cop/-Rooney/Dr. Beatty/Freddy/Reporter), Elizabeth Hess (Frances Farmer), John Jiler (Clifford Odets/Dr. Freeman/Justice Fraser/Stage Manager/-Sheriff), Penelope Rockwell (Lillian Farmer/Betty/Clara/Lois/Actress), Chris Tanner (Lucky/Jimmy/Guard/Reporter/Cop/Nurse), Mary Lou Wittmer (Sophie Rosenstein/Belle McKenzie/Actress/Adelaide/-Delores/Director/Lady in hat)
A drama in two acts. The action takes place between the years 1931 and 1964.

(47th STREET THEATRE) Thursday, October 28—December 12, 1982 (52 performances and 16 previews). Frank Gero, Mark Gero, Chris Gero in association with Jane Holzer present:
SOME MEN NEED HELP by John Ford Noonan; Director, John Ferraro; Set, Eugene Lee; Lighting, Gregory C. MacPherson; Costumes, Shay Cunliffe; Original Music, Richard Weinstock; Fights, B. H. Barry; Company Manager, Randy Finch; Assistant to Producers, Jason Gero; Stage Managers, Louis D. Pietig, Jonathan Gero; Production Assistants, Dorian Frankel, Robert Galloway; Props, Robert Galloway, Rick Russo; Technical Consultant, Marcus Lopez; Press, Shirley Herz, Sam Rudy, Peter Cromarty

CAST: Treat Williams (Hudley T. Singleton III), Philip Bosco (Gaetano Altobelli)
    A play in 2 acts and 6 scenes. The action takes place at the present time at 77 Huckleberry Drive, Roman Hills, Fairfield County, Connecticut.

(LION THEATRE) Monday, November 1—21, 1982 (12 performances). Red Oak Productions presents:
SOME RAIN by James Edward Luczak; Director, Dale Rose; Set, James Wolk; Costumes, Colleen Muscha; Lighting, Candice Dunn; General Manager, Red Oak Productions; Stage Managers, Jody Laine, Haim Scheininger; Associate Producers, Veronique Devianne, Marc Cornu; Press, Burnham-Callaghan Associates

CAST: Blanche Cholet (Sera), Loren Haynes (Wally), David Dawson (Eddie)
    A drama in 2 acts and 4 scenes. The action takes place during the late summer of 1968 in a trailer and yard in rural Alabama.

(SOUTH STREET THEATRE) Wednesday, November 3,—21, 1982 (17 performances and 3 previews). American Theatre Alliance (Aaron Levin, Artistic Director; Jerold Barnard, Managing Director; Deborah Pope, Associate Artistic Director) presents:
THE WORKROOM (L'ATELIER) by Jean-Claude Grumberg; American version by Daniel A. Stein, Sara O'Connor; Director, Aaron Levin; Set, John Kasarda; Lighting, Robby Monk, Vivien Leone; Costumes, Richard Hornung; Casting, Maureen Snelling; Choreography, Isabel Glasser; Assistant Director, Deborah Rickwald; Dramaturg, Deborah Pope; Wigs, Paul Huntley; Props, Rhonda Goldenberg; Music Adviser, Steven Culbertson; Press, Owen Levy

CAST: Rita Gardner (Helene), Margaret Dulaney (Simone), June Squibb (Gisele), Robin Leary (Marie), Elaine Grollman (Mme. Laurence), Carrie Zivetz (Mimi), Eugene Troobnick (Leon), Frank Maraden (First Presser), Richard Costabile (Machine Operator), Michael Guido (Jean), Ben R. Kelman (Max), Mark Stefan (The Boy)
    A drama in 2 acts and 10 scenes. The action takes place from 1945 to 1952 in a tailoring workroom in Paris.

(WONDERHORSE THEATRE) Wednesday, November 3—21, 1982 (21 performances). Cherubs Guild (Carol Avila, Lesley Starbuck, Hillary Wyler, Producers) in association with Bruce Babbitt, Denny French, Ruth Stoddard Preston, Ned Hall present:
THE TRUTH by Clyde Fitch; Director, James Gordon-Williams; Set, Dan Proett; Lighting, Jo Mayer; Costumes, Lewis Rampino; Technical Director, Bill Blair; Props, David Seatter; Stage Managers, Bruce Babbitt, Tom Moran; Press, Keith Sherman

CAST: Kathleen Noone (Eve Lindon), Ruth Miller (Laura Fraser), David Kroll (Servant), Francesca James (Becky Warder), Warren Burton (Fred Lindon), William Mooney (Tom Warder), Clarke Gordon (Steven Roland), Esther Jenkins (Genevieve Crespigny)
    A comedy in 3 acts and 4 scenes. The action takes place circa 1910 in the Warder residence and in Mrs. Crespigny's flat in Baltimore.

Gavin Reed, Cleavon Little, Christopher Murney in "Two Fish in the Sky" (*Susan Cook/Martha Swope Photo*)

Treat Williams, Philip Bosco in "Some Men Need Help"

(PLAYHOUSE 46) Thursday, November 4—20, 1982 (6 performances and 10 previews). The Lotus Theatre Group presents:
THREE 'LOST' PLAYS OF EUGENE O'NEILL directed by Michael Fields; Producer, Bill Kalmenson; Sets, Stephen Caldwell; Lights, Whitney Quesenbery; Costumes, C. J. Simpson; Sound, Tom Gould; Production Supervisor, James Lockhart; Technical Director, Peter Feuche; Props, Ed Ramage; Production Assistant, Elvira Rohr; Stage Manager, Howard P. Lev; Press, Max Eisen, Madelon Rosen

CAST: "A Wife for Life": P. L. Carling (Older Man), Bill Kalmenson (Jack), Frank Nastasi (Old Pete), "The Movie Man": William Gaynor Dovey (Henry Rogers) succeeded by Bill Kalmenson, Bill Kalmenson (Al Devlin) succeeded by Frank Norris, Frank Norris (Sentry) succeeded by Dan Leventritt, Rosemary Sykes (Anita Fernandez), P. L. Carling (Luis Virella), Frank Nastasi (Pancho Gomez), "The Web": Rosemary Sykes (Rose Thomas), Bill Kalmenson (Steve), William Gaynor Dovey (Tim Moran), P. L. Carling (1st Detective), Frank Nastasi (2nd Detective), Frank Norris (Policeman)
    Performed with one intermission.

(THEATRE AT ST. PETER'S CHURCH) Sunday, November 7—14, 1982 (16 performances and 13 previews). The Phoenix Theatre (T. Edward Hambleton, Managing Director; Steven Robman, Artistic Director; Harold Sogard, General Manager) for its thirtieth anniversary season presents:
TWO FISH IN THE SKY by Michael Hastings; Director, Steven Robman; Set, Wynn P. Thomas; Costumes, Robert Wojewodski; Lighting, Arden Fingerhut; Sound, David Rapkin; Casting, Mary Colquhoun; Dialect Consultant, Timothy Monich; Company Manager, Donna Lieberman; Stage Manager, Loretta Robertson; Production Assistant, Chris Fielder; Props, Jacob Frank; Assistant to Director, Robin Saex; Wardrobe, Ronn Tombaugh; Press, Susan L. Schulman, Keith Sherman

CAST: Gavin Reed (Raymond Borrall), Cleavon Little (Meadowlark Rachel Warner), Christopher Murney (Gerald Radinski), Laura Esterman (Irene Connor), Lynnie Godfrey (Edna Walter), Michael Tucker (Elliott Brucknell)
    A comedy in two acts. The action takes place at the present time in the Brixton section of London and at Gatwick Airport.

(MEZZANINE THEATRE) Monday, November 8—21, 1982 (13 performances and 5 previews). The Going Steady Company presents:
GOING STEADY and Other Fables of the Heart by E. Eugene Baldwin; Director, William E. Hunt; Set, Rick Dennis; Lighting, William J. Plachy; Costumes, Jimm Halliday; Sound, George Jacobs; Assistant to Director, Vincent Bartz; Production Assistant, Gay Isaacs; Title Song by E Eugene Baldwin and performed by Blue with the D. Gordon Band; Press, Free Lance Talents, Francine L. Trevens, David Mayhew, Amy Rothlein

CAST: Mark Lotito (Jimmy), Annette Compton (Jude), Jody Awad (Barrett), Tom Zurich (Golden)
    A play in 2 acts and 3 scenes. The action takes place at the present time in Jimmy-Jude's Bar and Restaurant in Alton, Illinois.

(INTAR THEATRE) Wednesday, November 10—21, 1982 (14 performances and 10 previews). Norman Borisoff and Helen Berg in association with Yale Wexler present:
NIGHT FISHING IN BEVERLY HILLS by Louis C. Adelman; Director, Cash Baxter; Set, James Morgan; Costumes, Dean H. Reiter; Lighting, Mary Jo Dondlinger; General Manager, Karen Etcoff; Technical Director, John P. Reed; Stage Managers, Pamela Edington, Ann Gentry; Press, Max Eisen, Jerry Arrow

CAST: John Arch-Carter (Miako), Brett Somers (Marcia Henry), Michael Beckett (Marvin J. Quartz), James Pritchett (Mike Henry), Jake Turner (Tex Arkanian), William Swan (Alvin), Ann Gentry (Angie)
A comedy in two acts. The action takes place at the present time on the patio of a lush home in Beverly Hills, California.

(NO SMOKING PLAYHOUSE) Friday, November 12—28, 1982 (11 performances and 5 previews). Jayar Productions and Lee Andrews present:
A PRELUDE TO HAMLET by Samuel Sussman; Director, Walter A. Kotrba; Set and Lighting, John Figola; Costumes, Sheya Lederman; Fight Choreography, Peter Nels, Steven Randall; Stage Manager, Pete Herman, Mark Roger; Wardrobe, Joan Green; Press, Max Eisen, Madelon Rosen

CAST: Dunsten J. McCormack (Everard), Richard Tabor (Demetrius), Drew Tillotson (Lucius), Amy Stoller (Ophelia), Bill Rowley (Polonius), Robert Stephen Ryan (Erick), Vincent Harta (Horvendile), Maureen Baskerville (Gertrude), Jonathan Epstein (Claudius), Randy Kovitz (Fortinbras), Jeanette Topar (Cassandra), Paul Duke (Roderick), Michael Onida (Nestor), Understudies: Paul Duke (Fortinbras), Drew Tillotson (Roderick), Bob Robinson (Polonius/Nestor)
A play in 3 acts and 4 scenes. The action takes place in the palace of Elsinore in Denmark.

(RICHARD ALLEN CENTER) Tuesday, November 16—December 5, 1982 (20 performances and 6 previews) The Richard Allen Center (Hazel J. Bryant, producer) presents:
RHINESTONE by Bill Gunn; Music, Sam Waymon; Lyrics, Bill Gunn, Sam Waymon; Director, Bill Gunn; Musical Director, Sam Waymon; Choreographer, George Faison; Arranger, Charles Coleman; Set, Peter Harvey; Lighting, William H. Grant III; Costumes, Scott Barrie; Associate Producer, Shirley J. Radcliffe; Assistant Producer, Toney Blue; Casting, Glenn Johnson; Technical Director, P. Eugene Wood; Stage Managers, Janice C. Lane, Timothy Ferguson; Wardrobe, Tony Wilkes; Props, Lisa L. Watson; Press, Les Schecter, Barbara Schwei, Tim Fisher

CAST: Joe Seneca (Dod's Father/Headwaiter), Joe Morton (Sam Dodd), Jackee Harry (Chicago Woman/Sara/Maid), Pauletta Pearson (Miss Grab-It-All/Florence Yates/Maid), Peter Jay Fernandez (Ira/Chicago Man/Waiter), Donald Greenhill (Chicago Man/Sonny/Waiter), Novella Nelson (Cleola Dodd), Michael Wager (Carl "Cubby" Steinbeck), Annette Hunt (Busybody/Mrs. Scaglioni), Peter Naylor (Sol Rayburn), John D. McNally (Byron Weiner), Lawrence Kletter (Brooks Nori)
MUSICAL NUMBERS: Black Narcissus, Money Was Made to Spend, I'll See You in Jail Old Pal, Miss Grab-It-All, Cleola's Menu, Blue Skies, Our Brazilian Friends, Rhinestone, They'll Never Know You, Palm Gardens, Freedom Is My Name, Doin' the Low Low Down, Give Us Men, This Love, You Shouldn't Wonder, We Both Agree
A musical in 3 acts and 6 scenes. The action takes place at the present time.

(XENON) Wednesday, November 17—27, 1982 (7 performances). The New York Lyric Opera Company (Donald W. Johnston, General Director) presents:
THE CORONATION OF POPPEA by Claudio Monteverdi; Conceived and Directed by John Haber; Conductor/Music Realized by Michael Ward; New English Version, John Haber, Michael Ward: Assistant Conductor, Stuart Diamond; Assistant Musical Director, Mitchell Glickman; Design, Manuel Lutgenhorst; Costumes, Penelope Wehrli; Sound, Charles Bugbee III; General Management, DiDia/Fiore; Company Manager, Blenn Mure; Stage Managers, Rita Calabro, Susi Mara; Technical Director, William Stallings; Press, Patt Dale, Jim Baldassare

CAST: Rosyln Burrough (Goddess of Fortune), Heather B. Withers (Goddess of Virtue), Richie Abanes (God of Love), Louis Tucker (Ottone), David Cahn (1st Soldier/Student/Lucano), Michael Mandell (2nd Soldier), Carolyn Dennis (Poppea), David Weatherspoon (Nero), Julie Kurnitz (Arnalta), Judith Thiergaard (Ottavia), John Mack Ousley (Seneca), Kate Phelan (Drusilla)
An opera in 2 acts and 14 scenes.

Joe Morton, Novella Nelson,
Michael Wager in "Rhinestone"

(WEST PARK PRESBYTERIAN CHURCH) Friday, November 19,—December 12, 1983 (20 performances). The Riverside Shakespeare Company (W. Stuart McDowell, Artistic Director; Gloria Skurski, Executive Director) presents:
RICHARD III by William Shakespeare; Director, John Clingerman; Music, Joseph Church; Set, Thomas Newman; Lighting, Richard Lund; Costumes, Randolf Pearson; Combat Director, Joel Leffert; Props, Alex Polner; Assistant Director, Cash Tilton; Stage Managers, Mary Ellen Allison, Sondra R. Katz; Production Coordinator, Daniel T. Johnson; Technical Director, Laura Mraz; Props, Thomas Harty; Wardrobe, Judith Barr, Keri Mallo, Arlene Roseman; Production Assistant, Scott Weir; Press, Gloria Skurski, Sally Ferguson
CAST: J. Kenneth Campbell (King Richard III), Stockman Barner (Archbishop/Oxford), Elton Beckett (Buckingham), Franklin Brown (Scrivener/Tressel/Brandon), Jeffrey Charles-Reese (Lord Mayor/Guard-/Citizen), Kevin Daly (Dorset/Messenger), Ann Ducati (Duchess of York), Richard Hoyt-Miller (Hastings), Andrew Hubatsek (Prince Edward/Page/Messenger), Charles Kocher (Edward IV/Catesby), George O. Kolombatovich (Duke of York/Messenger), Robert Chessie Lake (Tyrrel/Norfolk/Halberdier), Richard Lee (Duke of Clarence), Russell Leander (Halberd/Ratcliffe), Mary Lowry (Lady Anne), Robert McFarland (Lord Stanley), Mary McTigue (Old Queen Margaret), Richard Marshall (Guard/Murderer/Citizen), Damon O'Hare (Rivers/Alderman/Soldier), Scott Parson (Murderer/Priest/Richmond), Tom Reidy (Grey/Alderman/Christopher Urswick), Maggie Scott (Elizabeth), Nestor Serrano (Brakenbury/Citizen)
Performed with two intermissions. The action takes place in and around London during the last quarter of the 15th Century.

(ACTORS REPERTORY THEATRE) Saturday, November 20—29, 1982 (12 performances and 2 previews) Actors Repertory Theatre with Jean Alexander presents:
THE MEN'S ROOM by Jess Gregg; Director, Warren Robertson; Set, Bonnie Arquilla; Lighting, David Arrow; Costumes, Carol VanValkenburg; Sound, Stuart Schwartz; Music Consultant, Dickson Hughes; Stage Managers, Carol Lang, Garwood; Press, Howard Atlee, Barbara Atlee

CAST: "Escape from Deep Hammock during the Hurricane of '52": Lewis VanBergen (Society), Frankie Faison (Bruh), Jim Lynch (Cappy), Jim Gara (Daddy Creel), Burt Young (Smitty); "The Organ Recital at the New Grand": Burt Young (Dr. Pinkney), Frankie Faison (Bominishus), James Gara (Brother Dawson); "The Men's Room": Burt Young (Bobby Terry), Lewis VanBergen (Mario), Frankie Faison (Ham Shandy), Jim Lynch (Loonie), James Gara (Old Man)
Three one-act plays performed with two intermissions.

Frankie Faison, Bert Young
in "The Men's Room" (*Bill Biggart Photo*)

(PERRY STREET THEATRE) Tuesday, November 23, 1982 (1 performance and 8 previews). Vince Rhomberg in association with Patrick J. Campbell, David Larkin and P. D. Mazza present:
PENELOPE by J. Radloff; Director, Vince Rhomberg; Set, Cecelia Gilchriest; Costumes, Karen Matthews; Lighting, Vivien Leone; General Manager, Michael Thomas Lord; Production Manager, Beth Prevor; Sound, Stephen Dailey; Hairstylist, Linda Wager, Antonio Soddu; Wardrobe, Steve Williams; Stage Managers, Beth Prevor, Patrick J. Campbell; Press, Burnham-Callaghan, Lynda Kinney, Jay Schwartz

CAST: Joy Franz (Penelope Richards), Robert Walsh (Parker Chandler), Mike Champagne (Porter Jeffers), David Snizek (Preston Lawson), Paul O'Connor (Patrick)
   A comedy in three acts. The action takes place during Christmas 1934 in Penelope Richards' beach house on Cape Cod.

(THEATRE GUINEVERE) Wednesday, December 1—26, 1982 (25 performances and 1 preview). Pendragon Productions (A. Arthur Altman, Jean Altman, Producers) presents:
PRIMAL TIME by William Fay Smith; Director, Lee Bloomrosen; Set, Robert Alan Harper; Lighting and Sound, Brenda M. Veltre, Carmen Rudy Veltre; Costumes, P. Chelsea Harriman; General Manager, Kate Harper; Stage Manager, Penny Landau; Press, Mark Goldstaub

CAST: Harley Venton (Adam), Peter E. Green (Mark), Leona Cyphers (Moon Beam the Chimp), Kenneth Gildin (David), Rose Stockton (Moon Beam), Joyce Cohen (Sheila), Peter Murphy (Donald), Selma Rosenblatt (Mrs. Bagelman), Richard Marr (Mr. Bagelman/Mr. Williams)
   A comedy in 2 acts and 17 scenes.

(INTAR THEATRE) Wednesday, December 1—18, 1982 (16 performances). Jacquie Littlefield and John V. N. Philip present:
KNIGHTS ERRANT by John Hunt; with collaboration of Martin Kaplan; Director, Geoffrey Shlaes; Set, Vicki Paul; Costumes, John Falabella; Lighting, David F. Segal; Consultant, Richard Horner Associates; Stage Managers, Mark Baltazar, Mary Beth Able; Production Assistant, Jessica Liebman; Press, Shirley Herz, Sam Rudy, Peter Cromarty, Sandra Manley

CAST: Richard M. Davidson (Herb Jaffe), Frances Barnes (Pat Nixon), J. D. Clarke (Vern Sawyer), Harry Spillman (Richard Nixon), Eddie Jones (Whitaker Chambers), James DeMarse (Alger Hiss), Tudi Wiggins (Priscilla Hiss)
   A play in two acts. The action takes place some years after Nixon's resignation in his "Western White House," "La Casa Pacifica."

(ACTORS OUTLET) Thursday, December 2—19, 1982 (20 performances). Legal Eagle Productions (Alice Van Leer, Producer) presents:
JUSTICE by Terry Curtis Fox; Director, Dale Rose; Set and Costumes, David C. Woolard; Lights, David Weiss; Stage Manager, T. Newell Kring; Technical Director, Jeff Berzon; Press, Becky Flora

CAST: Antonia Banewicz (Cathy Hart), Michael Fischetti (John Fidello), Willard Morgan (Roger Ackerman), Paul Mullins (Daniel Kalen), Raphael Nash (Cleland Jones), Tracey Phelphs (Barbara Walters), Rikki Ricard (Voice of Roseanne DeVito), T. A. Taylor (Philip Skylar)
   A comedy in two acts.

(UNITARIAN CHURCH OF ALL SOULS) Thursday, December 3—18, 1982 (12 performances). The All Souls Players present:
THE BUTTERFINGERS ANGEL, MARY & JOSEPH, HEROD THE NOT, & THE SLAUGHTER OF 12 HIT CAROLS IN A PEAR TREE by William Gibson; Director, Henry Levinson; Producers, Marie Landa, Peter Sauerbrey, Pat Sheffield; Set/Costumes, Charles W. Roeder; Lighting, Mark H. Weingartner; Stage Managers, Ira Stoller, Margaret Willard; Musical Direction, Wendell Kindberg; Props, Wendy Northup

CAST: Robert Aberdeen (The Angel), Sarah Barab (Donkey/Village Child), Stefan Desalle (Sheep/Village Child), Talbott Dowst (Lout/King/Soldier), Marcia Iris Feldman (Village Woman/Court Lady), Mark Ferrera (Lout/King/Soldier), Peter Francis (Lout/King/Soldier), Julie Hand (Girl/Innkeeper's Daughter), Ayanna Hendricks (Cow/Child), Fran Hendricks (Woman/Court Lady), Anthony John Lizzul (Herod/Man in Grey/Courier), Terri Orth-Pallavicini (Mary), Herman Petras (Joseph), Geraldine Singer (Tree)
   A play in two acts.

(s.n.a.f.u.) Sunday, December 5—26, 1982 (8 performances).
ETIQUETTE with Book and Lyrics by William M. Hoffman; Music and Lyrics, John Braden; Director, John Vaccaro; Additional Lyrics, Emily Post; Musical Director, Bruce W. Goyle; Costumes, Gabriel Berry; Lighting, Russell Krum; Press, Howard Atlee, Barbara Atlee

CAST: Joseph Addeo, Michael Arian, Donald Arrington, Billy Barnes, Cindy Benson, Gretel Cummings, Jerry Cunliffe, Marcia McClain, Molly Regan, Camille Tibaldeo
   A musical revue with manners.

Harley Venton, Kenneth Gildin, Peter E. Green
in "Primal Time"

(LION THEATRE) Monday, December 6—12, 1982 (7 performances and 12 previews). Lucille Lortel and Haila Stoddard in association with Jerry Keller and Noel Silverman present:
MARVELOUS GRAY by Diane Kagan; Director, Burry Fredrik; Set/Lighting/Sound, Meryl Joseph; Costumes, Sigrid Insull; Associate Producer, Vincent Curcio; General Manager, David Lawlor; Technical Director, Larry Petersen; Production Assistant, Kate Redway; Assistant Manager, Helen L. Nickerson; Stage Manager, David Hyslop; Press, Shirley Herz, Sandra Manley

CAST: Diane Kagan (Tamara Gray), Brent Spiner (Electrician), Dave Florek (Light Man), Edward Seamon (Sound Man), Mark Hofmaier (Director), Roger Morden (Alan Stafford), Bill Hoag (Videographer)
   A play performed without intermission.

INTAR STAGE TWO Friday, December 9, 1982—January 2, 1983 (16 performances). INTAR Hispanic American Theatre (Max Ferra, Artistic Director) presents:
EXILES with Book and Lyrics by Ana Maria Simo; Music, Elliot Sokolov, Louis Milgrom; Director, Maria Irene Fornes; Set, Carlos Almada, Paulette Crowther; Costumes, Gabriel Berry; Lighting, Edward M. Greenberg; Film, Hugh Lavergne; Managing Director, Dennis Ferguson-Acosta; General Administrator, Janet L. Murphy; Technical Director, Tony Fitsch; Production Assistants, Rene R. Aloma, Leonora Rodriguez; Stage Manager, Gail A. Burns; Casting, The Little Co.; Press, Bruce Cohen, Jose Rivas
CAST: Nicole Baptiste (Elsa), Jose Febus (Orla), Maria Garcia (Paule), Anita Keal (Adelaida), Karen Ludwig (Olga), Jose Antonio Maldonado (Emilio), Rebecca Schull (Ana A.)
MUSICAL NUMBERS: Hurricane of Revolution, Did I See You?, If I Resigned, Do You See This Card?, Because I Wanted, Got Your Letter, Memory Is an Art, It's Love What Else?, Hold Me Paule, Icebergs Collide, A Sleeping Black Panther
   A mixed media musical without intermission.

Edward Seamon, Diane Kagan in "Marvelous Gray"

(NEW VIC THEATRE) Friday, December 17, 1982—January 9, 1983 (15 performances). Stonewall Repertory Theater (Michael Pritchard, Executive Producer; Evan Senreich, Artistic Director; Billy Cunningham, Associate Producer) presents:
LORD ALFRED'S LOVER written and directed by Eric Bentley; Set, Robert Edmonds; Lighting, Pat Dignan; Costumes, Richard Hieronymus; Pianists, Charles Clifton, Jerome Clegg; Stage Managers, Neal Fox, Kevin Wakefield-Cristy
CAST: Christopher Consani (Charles Parker/Lockwood/Lord Roseberry), Quentin Crisp (Lord Alfred Douglas in 1945), Matthew Conlon (Young Lord Alfred "Bosie" Douglas), Callan Egan (Queensberry/Sir Edward Clarke), Michael Gnat (Freddy Wood/Cliburn), Suzanne Hall (Constance Wilde/Jane Cotter), Mitchell Sugarman (Robbie Ross), Nicholas Haylett (Plainclothesman/Allen/Carson/Adrian Hope), Maxim Mazumdar (Oscar Wilde), David Officer (Arthur Marling)

(WONDERHORSE THEATRE) Friday, December 10—19, 1982 (9 performances and 3 previews). Henry Street Settlement's New Federal Theatre (Woodie King, Jr., Producer) and Chelsea Theater Center (Robert Kalfin, Artistic Director; Joseph V. Melillo, Producing Director) present:
THE UPPER DEPTHS by David Steven Rappoport; Director, Robert Kalfin; Costumes, Judy Dearing; Set, Bob Edmonds; Lighting, John Tomlinson, Sandy Ross; Sound, Gary Harris; Technical Director, Llewellyn Harrison; Casting, Raymond Benkoczy; Assistant to Director, Steven Rosenbaum; Production Assistants, Phil Peratore, Steven Powell; Props, Marcia Simon; Wardrobe, Cathy Latch; Fight Consultant, Neil Rosenberg; Stage Managers, Ray Benkoczy, Marcia Simon; Press, Warren Knowlton

CAST: Rikke Borge (Laurette), Marilyn Chris (Hilda), Meg Guttman (Fannie), Elizabeth Longo (Consuela), Bill Mooney (Gilmer), Steven Gary Simon (Daniel)
A "tragifarce" in 3 acts and 24 scenes. The action takes place in 1973.

(NO SMOKING PLAYHOUSE) Friday, December 10—16, 1982 (6 performances and 6 previews). Robert McKay presents:
THE COARSE ACTING SHOW by Michael Green; Director, Charles Suisman; Set, Larry Fulton; Costumes, Eileen Sieff; Lighting, Bruce A. Kraemer; Sound, Daryl Bornstein; Technical Director, Charles Collum/Stage Combat, Dan Butler; Stage Managers, Steven Kelley, Nancy Hussar; Press, Shirley Herz, Sam Rudy, Peter Cromarty

CAST: Dan Butler (D'Arcy/Bronchio/Schoolmaster), Victor D'Altorio (Inspector/Frederigo/He), Bill Lopatto (James/Friar/Piles), Brian Anthony Nelson (Vicar/Mud/Grot/Lute Player/Messenger/Bolio/Capt. Sodov), Susan Plaksin (Prompt/Attendant/Veruka), Carolyn Porter (Mrs. D'Arcy/Nurse Dracula), Philip Shultz (Major/Testiculo/Stationmaster), Nealla Spano (Cook/Soldier/She/Basha), Deborah Stenard (Delia/Cube of Sugar/Gnasha), Timothy Wahrer (Hubert D'Arcy/Dronio/Footrotski), Nona Waldeck (Solider/Babushka/Understudy)
A comedy in two acts and four scenes: Streuth, All's Well That Ends as You Like It, Last Call for Breakfast, The Cherry Sisters.

(SOUTH STREET THEATRE) Saturday, December 11, 1982—January 2, 1983 (25 performances). The South Street Theatre presents the Vienna Theater production of:
THE WORLD OF RUTH DRAPER adapted by Alan Levy from "The Art of Ruth Draper" by Morton Dauwen Zabel; Director, Franz Schafranek; Production Supervisor/Assistant Director, Adele Ziminski; Music Director, James Logan Cramer; Set and Costumes, Tamare; Press, Burnham-Callaghan, Lynda Kinney

CAST: Ruth Brinkmann, Eugene Hartzell (Narrator)
A one-woman show about the art of the legendary American monologist, Ruth Draper. (No photos available)

(V. A. SMITH'S CHAPEL THEATRE) Wednesday, December 15, 1982—January 4, 1983 (13 performances). Kozo Theatre Development Corporation (James A. Simpson, Artistic Director) presents:
THE 36 DRAMATIC SITUATIONS by Paavo Hall; Based on work of Georges Polti; Director James Simpson; Set, Debbie Huff; Lighting, David Prittie; Costumes, Karen Hummel; Musical Direction, Mike Nolan; Press, Susan Bloch & Company, Adrian Bryan-Brown, Ron Jewell

CAST: Stephen Burks, Keith Druhl, Jody Gelb, Roger Middleton, Ron Orbach, Angela Pietropinto, Bern Sundstedt, Karen Tull. The cast played 101 characters.

(PERRY STREET THEATRE) Monday, December 13, 1982—January 1, 1983 (35 performances and 10 previews). Thomas C. Anderson, Jr., and Triskaidek Productions present:
A CHRISTMAS CAROL adapted by Orson Bean from Charles Dickens' novel; Director, Christopher Catt; Set, Johnienne Papandreas; Costumes, Lindsay W. Davis; Lighting, Curt Ostermann; Casting, Mary Jo Slater; Choreographer, Mary Corsaro; Sound/Special Effects, Peter Kallish; Musical Director, Bonita Labossiere; General Manager, Thomas C. Anderson, Jr.; Production Assistant, Janie Gavin; Props, Susan Andrews; Stage Manager, J. Barry Lewis; Press, Judy Jacksina, Glenna Freedman

CAST: Orson Bean (Scrooge), Michael Champagne (Bob Cratchit/Dick Williams), Mitchell Greenberg (1st Businessman/1st Gravedigger/Ghost of Past/Poulterer/Shopper), Debbie Hines (Fan/Belinda/Daughter of Man), Knowl Johnson (Tiny Tim), Sherman Lloyd (Marley/Ghost of Present/Debtor), Albie Polinsky (Peter/Son of Man/Turkey Boy), Jay E. Raphael (Charity Collector/Gravedigger/Fop), Mary Stout (Mrs. Cratchit/Mrs. Fezziwigg), A. C. Weary (Fred/Gravedigger/Young Scrooge/Ghost of Future), Kim Zimmer (Sally/Martha Cratchit/Niece/Debtor's Daughter/Lady of the Night)
Performed without intermission. The action takes place in London during Christmas of 1843.

Martha Swope Photo

Top Left: Dan Butler, Deborah Stenard in "The Coarse Acting Show"
(*Carol Rosegg Photo*)

Orson Bean, Knowl Johnson in "A Christmas Carol"
(*Martha Swope Photo*)

(WESTSIDE MAINSTAGE) Wednesday, December 15—30, 1982 (16 performances).* Actors Producing Company (Joan Montgomery, Executive Producer) presents:
NOT-SO-NEW FACES OF '82 conceived and directed by Stuart Ross; Music, Lyrics and Sketches by Brenda Bergman, Lynne Bernfield, Michael Colby, Michael Feingold, Mark Hampton, Gerald Markoe, Alan Menken, Jim Morgan, Scott Oakley, Bob Ost, Ronald Reagan, Jim Ricketts, Terry Rieser, Scott Robertson, Stuart Ross, Paul Ruben, Schreier/Roth, William Shakespeare, Paul Trueblood, David Zippel, and the cast; Musical Director, Jonny Bowden; Choreography, Edmond Kresley; Assistant Director, Linda Stine; Set, Jim Stewart; Lighting, Jeffrey McRoberts; Musical Assistant, Thomas Textort; Associate Producer, Joanne Zippel; Production Manager, Tom Textort; Special Consultant, Brenda Bergman; Stage Managers, Anne Singer, Patrick O'Connor; Press, George B. Goldey

CAST: Nancy Ringham, Scott Robertson, Carole Schweid, Mary Testa, William Thomas, Jr., Margery Cohen, and George Bohn
SKETCHES AND MUSICAL NUMBERS: Not-So-New Faces, Schizophrenia 101A, Ask the Doctor, Summer's Breeze, Nobody Knows That It's Me, Night of the Living Preppies, Hollywood Has Got Her, Mom I've Got Something to Tell You, The Boyfriend, Christmas Tree, P.M. With Lufa, Princess Di, The News, Edie, E.T., Portman Kick, Cell of the Well-to-Do, Rosie, The Dancer and the Dance, Amyl, Your Back, French Tickler, Special Guest Spot, Last Call, Dueling Neurotics, Baby You Give Good Heart, New Face in Town, Friends Like You
   "An evening of wanton mischief and songs" in two acts.
*Re-opened at the Century Cafe for 16 additional performances (Thursday, March 17–April 16, 1983) with Barry Preston, Nancy Ringham, Mary Testa and William Thomas, Jr.

Nancy Ringham, Mary Testa, William Thomas, Jr., Barry Preston in "Not-So-New Faces of '82" (*Linda Alaniz Photo*)

(LAMBS THEATRE) Monday, December 20, 1982—May 1, 1983 (152 performances and 4 previews). Gene Persson in association with Paula D. Hughes, Martin Markinson, Donald Tick and United Media Productions (Robert Roy Metz, President) presents:
SNOOPY based on the comic strip "Peanuts" by Charles M. Schulz; Book, Charles M. Schulz Creative Associates, Warren Lockhart, Arthur Whitelaw, Michael L. Grace; Music, Larry Grossman; Lyrics, Hal Hackady; Director, Arthur Whitelaw; Choreography, Marc Breaux; Set and Costumes, David Graden; Lighting, Ken Billington; Musical Direction/Additional Orchestrations, Ronald Melrose; Associate Producer, Miranda Smith; Production Associate, Mary C. Miller; General Manager, James Walsh; Wardrobe, Maria Kaye; Stage Managers, Melissa Davis, Marc Schlackman; Press, Jeffrey Richards, C. George Willard, Robert Ganshaw, Ted Killmer, Helen Stern, Richard Humleker

CAST: Terry Kirwin (Charlie Brown), Stephen Fenning (Linus), Deborah Graham (Sally Brown), Kay Cole (Lucy), Vicki Lewis (Peppermint Patty) succeeded by Lorna Luft, David Garrison (Snoopy) succeeded by Jason Graae, Cathy Cahn (Woodstock), Standbys: Nina Hennessey, Jason Graae
MUSICAL NUMBERS: The World according to Snoopy, Snoopy's Song, Woodstock's Theme, Edgar Allan Poe, Mother's Day, I Know Now, Vigil, Clouds, Where Did That Little Dog Go?, Dime a Dozen, Daisy Hill, Bunnies, The Great Writer, Poor Sweet Baby, Don't Be Anything Less Than Everything You Can Be, The Big Bow-Wow, Just One Person, Bows
   A musical in two acts.

Lorna Luft, Kay Cole, Terry Kirwin, Stephen Fenning, Deborah Graham, Cathy Cain in "Snoopy" (*Peter Cunningham Photo*)

(WESTSIDE ARTS CENTER/CHERYL CRAWFORD THEATRE) Wednesday, December 22, 1982 and still playing May 31, 1983. Frank Gero, Mark Gero, Chris Gero, Jason Gero, Della Koenig present:
EXTREMITIES by William Mastrosimone; Director, Robert Allan Ackerman; Set, Marjorie Bradley Kellogg; Lighting, Arden Fingerhut; Costumes, Robert Wojewodski; Action Sequences, B. H. Barry; Sound, Scott Lehrer; General Management, Randy Finch, Gero Communications; Company Manager, Kim Sellon; Assistant to Director, Franco Zavani; Production Assistants, Dorian Frankel, Elissa Leonard; Props, David Smith; Stage Managers, Louis D. Pietig, Jonathan Gero; Press, Solters-/Roskin/Friedman, Milly Schoenbaum, Warren Knowlton, Kevin Patterson

CAST: Susan Sarandon†1 (Marjorie), James Russo†2 (Raul), Ellen Barkin†3 (Terry), Deborah Hedwall†4 (Patricia)
   A drama in two acts. The action takes place at the present time between Trenton and Princeton, NJ, where the cornfield meets the highway.

†Succeeded by: 1. Karen Allen, Farrah Fawcett, 2. Michael Dinelli during illness, Thomas G. Waites, 3. Glenn E. Headly, Priscilla Lopez, Lorna Luft, 4. Joyce Reehling Christopher

James Hamilton/Martha Swope Photos

Deborah Hedwall, Susan Sarandon, James Russo in "Extremities" (*James Hamilton Photo*)

(ST. CLEMENT'S THEATRE) Tuesday, December 28, 1982—March 5, 1983. Moved to Douglas Fairbanks Theatre Thursday, March 17, 1983 where it closed May 8, 1983 after 113 performances and 23 previews. Edward Miller presents:

POPPIE NONGENA based on the novel by Elsa Joubert; Adapted for the stage by Sandra Kotze and Elsa Joubert; Director, Hilary Blecher; Set, Jon Ringbom; Lighting, William Armstrong; Costumes, Shura Cohen; Original songs/Arrangements for traditional songs, Sophie Mgcina; General Management, Dorothy Olim, Gail Bell, Thelma Cooper; Company Manager, George Elmer; Assistant to Producer, Cynthia Coffey; Technical Director, William B. Stallings; Stage Managers, Meyer Baron, Sara Gormley Plass; Press, Monina von Opel, Jeffrey Richards, Ben Morse, Robert Ganshaw

CAST: Thuli Dumakude (Poppie), Sophie Mgcina (Her Grandmother/Her Mother), Seth Sibanda (Her Brother Mosie), Tsepo Mokone (Her Brother Plank), Fana Kekana (Her Brother Jakkie/Preacher), Selaelo Maredi (Her Uncle/Suitor/Her Husband), Maggie Soboil (Mrs. Constantia/Mrs. Relief/Mrs. Swanepoel/Narrator), Alex Wipf (Policeman/Pass Official/Doctor/Mr. Green)

A drama in two acts. The action takes place in South Africa over the past 40 years.

Lowell Williams, Fana Kekana, Thuli Dumakude in "Poppie Nongena" (*Bert Andrews Photo*)

(HAROLD CLURMAN THEATRE) Tuesday, December 28, 1982—January 2, 1983 (5 performances and 3 previews). A. Joseph Tandet presents:

THE LITTLE PRINCE from the book by Antoine De Saint Exupery; Adapted by Ada Janik; Director, Maggie L. Harrer; Set and Costumes, Sara Denning; Lighting, Bridget Beier; General Managers, David Lawlor/Helen Nickerson; Stage Manager, Ruth E. Kramer; Press, Free Lance Talents, Francine L. Trevens, David Mayhew, Matthew Daniels

CAST: Charles Coleman (The Little Prince), Andre DeShields (King/Snake), J. P. Dougherty (Tippler/Businessman/Switchman), Elisa Fiorillo (The Rose), Kathy Morath (Flower/Rose/Water Spirit), Thelma Nevitt (Boa Constrictor/Flower/Rose/Water Spirit), William Parry (Aviator), Douglas Thom (The Fox)

A musical in 2 acts and 4 scenes. The action takes place somewhere on the Sahara Desert, on the Prince's planet, and on various parts of the planet earth.

(NO SMOKING PLAYHOUSE) Wednesday, January 5—16, 1983 (12 performances and 6 previews). The Netherlands-America Community Association presents:

PICTURES AT AN EXHIBITION by Anny Tangelder; Translated by James Brockway; Music, Modest Mussorgsky; Director, Charles Baird; Piano, Jacqueline Smit; Sound, George Jacobs; Lighting, Dominick Balletta; Costumes, Tanya Duncan; Stage Manager, Malik

CAST: Ron Berliner (Boy), Bill Galarno (Andre), Joyce Hainley (Madeleine), Vincent Hank (Peasant), Lenore Harris (Tonie), Paul Hart (Nikolay Alexandrovitch), Stephan Hart (Papa Gascon), Anita Lobel (Sofia Alexeyvna), Janet Morrison (Jeanne), Russell Ochocki (Gnome), Duke Potter (Jacob Israelovitch), Mari Reeves (Girl), Marina Stefan (Tamara Sergeyva), Jeremy Stuart (Pjotr Petrovich), Victor Talmadge (Sergey Nikolayovitch), Michael Twain (Avram Simonivitch)

A play in 2 acts and 18 scenes. The action takes place in Western and Eastern Europe during the 19th and 20th centuries, this world and the next.

(AMERICAN THEATRE OF ACTORS) Thursday, January 6—29, 1983 (19 performances). Flair Theatrical Productions presents:

SKYLINE with Book and Music by Sonny Casella; Directors, Dennis Dennehy, Sonny Casella; Choreography, Dennis Dennehy; Set, M. Cabot McMullen; Lighting, Curt Osterman; Costumes, Margo LaZaro; Sound, Tom Morse; Production Manager, E. Pixley Lewis; Wardrobe, Michael Marotta; Stage Managers, Stacey Fleischer, Linda Pilz; Press, John Springer, Gary Springer

CAST: Lawrence Clayton (Lucky), Carole-Ann Scott (Amy), Clark Sterling (Bill), Fern Radov (Olga), Stanley Ramsey (Fred), Jeffrey Shafer (Michael), Pi Douglass (Kevin), Wendy Laws (Kansas), Amelia Marshall (Cassie), Shannon Lee Jones (Shannon), Michael Piatkowski (Leo), Arthur D'Alessio (Chico), Bambi Jordan (Singing Messenger), and Michael Biondi, Cheri Butcher, Rhonda Click, Danielle P. Conell, Tom Dudash, John Gibson, Pixley Lewis, Daniel May, Erica Paulson, Mercedes Perez, Beverly Poltrack, Donna M. Pompei, Jack Rich, Danielle Striker, Charles Lavont Williams

A musical in two acts. The action takes place at the present time in the Skyline Cafe on Columbus Avenue in New York City.

(LION THEATRE) Saturday, January 8—22, 1983 (13 performances). The Broadway and Wall Company (Steve Axelrod, Michael Hardstark, Producers) presents:

SUNDAY AFTERNOON by Marshall Borden; Director, Michael Hardstark; Set, John Tingley; Lighting, Patrick Dearborn; Company Manager, Dan Zittel; Costume Coordinator, Maura Clifford; Sound, A. Aaron Stahl; Special Effects, Anthony Mazzarino; Casting, Nani-Saperstein; Stage Managers, James Gandia, Fred Nicholson; General Manager, Leonard Mulhern; Press, Jeffrey Richards, C. George Willard, Robert Ganshaw, Helen Stern, Ted Killmer

CAST: Steve Axelrod (Jack Resinsky), Kathleen McKiernan (Linda Resinsky) succeeded by Peggy Walton-Walker, Gina Battist (Jackie Resinsky), Fred Keeler (Ernie), Ed Easton (Jerry), Lawrence Guardino (Artie), George J. Peters (Alfred), Willie C. Carpenter (Chuck)

A comedy-drama in two acts. The action takes place at the present time in the home of Jack Resinsky on a Sunday afternoon in Queens, New York.

(KING COLE ROOM) Monday, January 24, 1983—The St. Regis-Sheraton presents:

SOME ENCHANTED EVENING The songs of Rodgers and Hammerstein performed with one intermission. Executive Producer, Jerry Kravat; Director, Jeffrey B. Moss; Musical Direction, Larry Hochman; Choreography, Barbara Siman Strouse; Stage Manager, Bill Kavanagh; Costumes, George Bergeron; Press, Henry Luhrman Associates

CAST: Laurie Beechman, Ernestine Jackson, Lisby Larson succeeded by Barbara Heumann, Russ Thacker, Martin Vidnovic

Shannon Lee Jones, Wendy Laws, Stanley Ramsey, Amelia Marshall, Jeffrey Shafer in "Skyline" (*John McMullen Photo*)

(WEST SIDE YMCA) Thursday, January 27—February 20, 1983 (16 performances). American Kaleidoscope Theatre, Richard F. Bell, Rebecca Dobson, Joan Rice Franklin, Artistic Directors in association with the West Side Y Arts Center presents:
THE CARPENTERS by Steve Tesich; Director, Cliff Goodwin; Set and Costumes, Daniel Michaelson; Lighting, John Hickey; Technical Director, John Enea; Props, Bill Moser; Company Manager, Allison Post; Production Manager, George Ivolin; Stage Managers, Bill McComb, Dana Giddings; Press, Fred Hoot, David Mayhew

CAST: Jack R. Marks (Father), Laurinda Barrett (Mother), Peter Filiaci (Waldo), Eloise Watt (Sissy), Mark French (Mark)
   A dark comedy without intermission. The action takes place at the present time.

(WESTSIDE MAINSTAGE) Monday, January 31—February 13, 1983 (13 performances and 3 previews). Rene Savich and Lyle Ruppenthal in association with Steven Zuckerman present:
PUNCHY by Daniel Landon; Director, Peter Pope; Set, Vicki Paul; Lighting, Scott Pinkney; Costumes, Sam Fleming; Sound, John North; General Manager, Rene Savich; Assistant to Producers, Laura Rankin; Casting, Elizabeth R. Woodman; Stage Managers, Brian Mertes, Peter Palazzo; Press, Joe Wolhandler, Kathryn Kempf

CAST: Deborah McDowell (Alice Dupree), Claude Vincent (Tommy Franco), Bernard Barrow (Eddie Dukes), Dan Lauria (Donny Dukes), Craig Sheffer (Billy Dukes), Ed O'Ross (Johnny Black Bear), Priscilla Manning (Sally), Norman Jacob (Tony)
   A drama in two acts. The action takes place on a hot night of June 1976 in a dressing room in Sunnyside Garden, an old arena in Sunnyside, Queens, NY.

(HAROLD CLURMAN THEATRE) Wednesday, February 2—27, 1983 (15 performances and 23 previews). Jack Garfein (Artistic Director) by arrangement with Jack Lawrence presents:
HANNAH by Israel Eliraz; Music, Mark Kopytman; Directed and Choreographed by Anna Sokolow; Design, Wolfgang Roth; Costumes, Ruth Morley; Lighting, Edward Effron; Company Manager, Melinda Atwood; Assistant Director, Mark Hough; Casting, David Tochterman; Wardrobe, Ellen Bryson; Production Assistants, Gail Gerber, Julie Shevach; Stage Managers, Tom W. Picard, Annette Holloway; Press, Shirley Herz, Sam Rudy, Peter Cromarty

CAST: Blanche Baker (Hannah), Lois Smith (Mother), Stephen Lang (Interrogator), Steve Pesola (Brother), David Sharpe, Joel Kaufman (Soldiers), Kibbutz Members/Hungarian Citizens/Soldiers/Guests/Prisoners: Amanda Kercher, Leah Kreutzer, Andrew Krichels, Jim May, Lorry May, Stuart Smith, Brian Taylor, Susan Thomasson, Understudies: Debra Griboff (Hannah), Lorry May (Mother), Stuart Smith (Brother/Interrogator), Swing, Lorry May
   A drama performed without intermission. The action takes place between 1937 and 1944.

(DON'T TELL MAMA) Wednesday, February 2—26, 1983 (16 performances). Re-opened Tuesday, March 29, 1983 at Sardi's Club Room and closed April 30, 1983 after 47 performances.
IT'S BETTER WITH A BAND with Lyrics by David Zippel; Music, Wally Harper, Doug Katsaros, Rob LaRocco, Alan Menken, Jimmy Roberts, Jonathan Sheffer, Bryon Sommers, Pamela Stanley; Director/Staging, Joseph Leonard; Musical Director, Rob LaRocco; Production Coordinator, Faye Greenberg; Design, Cindi Waas; Lighting, John Hastings; Technical Director, Annette DeMeo; Producers, Roger Alan Gindi, Joseph Hartney; Stage Managers, Perry Cline, Trey Hunt; Press, Free Lance Talents, Francine L. Trevens, Matthew Daniels

CAST: Catherine Cox, Nancy LaMott, Jenifer Lewis, Patrick Quinn (succeeded by Scott Bakula)
MUSICAL NUMBERS: It's Better with a Band, The Camel Song, You'll Never See Me Run, Loud Is Good, The Ingenue, What I Like Is You, God's Gift to Women, Why Don't We Run Away, Make Me a Star/Movie Queen, Until Tomorrow, I Can't Remember Living without Loving You, Horsin' Around, Forget It, I Reach for a Star, Time on Our Side, I Was Born to Be a Slide Trombone, Another Mr. Right, I'm Singin' a Song for Myself
   A musical revue performed without intermission.

(SARGENT THEATRE) Friday, February 4—26, 1983 (17 performances). StageArts Theatre Company (Nell Robinson, Ruth Ann Norris, Artistic Directors), formerly Actors and Directors Theater, presents:
MAN OVERBOARD by Jerry Polner; Director, Ronald Roston; Set, Ernest Allen Smith; Lighting, Cheryl Thacker; Costumes, Jeffrey L. Ullman; Press, Shirley Herz, Sam Rudy, Peter Cromarty

CAST: Sharon Chatten, Michael Kaufman, Sam McMurray
   A comedy about love, friendship, and safe boating in Pittsburgh, PA.

Ed O'Ross, Dan Lauria, Norman Jacob in "Punchy"
(Matthew J. Franjola Photo)

(THEATRE 22) Thursday, February 10—27, 1983 (12 performances). Moonlight Productions presents:
TALES FROM THE VERMONT WOODS by Sharon Linnea; Director, Robert Owens Scott; Costumes, Isis Mussenden; Music, Skip Kennon; Lighting, Craig Kennedy; Stage Managers, Debbie Higgins, Robert Stuart; Press, Michelle Rapkin

CAST: Chel Chenier (Cindy Logan), Paul Duke (Bryan Dane), Charles Dinstuhl (William Stacey), Elizabeth Lage (Erin Stacey), Jayne Heller (Rose Chaplain), Jack Schmidt (Albert Casey)
   A play in two acts. The action takes place during early autumn in the woods outside a Vermont resort.

(RIVERWEST THEATRE) Thursday, February 10—27, 1983 (16 performances). C. H. S. Productions and E. & S. Torn Productions in association with Riverwest Management Corp. present:
IS PARIS FLAMING? (Paris en Folie) by Alain Marcel; Translated by Mort Shuman; Director/Choreographer, Fred Weiss; Musical Director, Betty Longnecker Thomas; Set, Toby Corbett; Lighting, Donald Edmund Thomas; Costumes, Michel Dussarrat; Technical Director, Christopher Cole; Assistant Musical Director, Lawrence Yurman; Costume Coordinator, Cynthia Taub; Additional Costumes, Bob Thompson; Creative Consultant, Alain Marcel; Puppets, Catherine Policella; Producers, Nat Habib, June Summers, Susan Torn; Wardrobe, John Curtis Hay, Joanie Nelson; Production Assistant, Elliott Goliger; Stage Managers, Penny Marks, Jeffrey Holt Gardner

CAST: David L. Carson, Larry Goodsight, Steven Joseph
   A musical revue in 2 acts and 20 scenes.

(NAT HORNE MUSICAL THEATRE) Friday, February 18—March 6, 1983 (14 performances and 14 previews). Fernando Haro Productions present:
GETTING MAMA MARRIED by Stephen Levi; Director, Emiliano Haro; Set and Lighting, Robert Alan Harper; General Manager, Kate Harper; Sound, Carmen Rudy Veltre; Costumes, Sharon Smith; Stage Managers, Doug Fogel, Michael Stephens; Press, Free Lance Talents, Francine L. Trevens, Amy Carr, Matthew Daniels

CAST: Jeanette Topar (Julie Garrett), Annie Kravat (Ann Finnery), Mark Weston (Ed Finnery), Fernando Haro (Mr. Apollo), Ed Breen (Jack Stanton), Understudy: Marilyn Alex
   A comedy in three acts. The action takes place at the present time in Ann Finnery's one-bedroom apartment in Santa Monica, California.

Stephen Lang, Blanche Baker, Lois Smith
in "Hannah" *(Martha Swope Photo)*

(WONDERHORSE THEATER) Wednesday, February 23—March 6, 1983 (12 performances). Crossroads Theatre Productions (Diane Wicks, Artistic Director) presents:
A PEARL OF GREAT PRICE by Elizabeth Hansen; Director, Elizabeth King; Set and Lighting, Kevin Allen; Costumers, Wendy Stuart; Assistant Director, Maureen Moore; Technical Director, Joseph E. Tully; Production Manager, Diane Wicks; Stage Managers, Lue Morgan Douthit, Michael Cohen; Press, Sandra Manley

CAST: Patti Specht (Diane Taylor), Diane Dunn (Louise Taylor Gifford), Leslie Lachlan (Elaine Taylor), Rick Weber (Ezra K. Gifford)
    A play in 2 acts and 5 scenes. The action takes place at the present time in Salt Lake City, Utah.

(PLAYHOUSE 91) Opened Thursday, February 24, 1983 and still playing May 31, 1983. John A. McQuiggan, Ethel Watt in association with Brent Peek Productions present the Long Wharf Theatre Production of:
QUARTERMAINE'S TERMS by Simon Gray; Director, Kenneth Frankel; Set, David Jenkins; Costumes, Bill Walker; Lighting, Pat Collins; Production Associate, Scott Green; Company Manager, Claire Calkins; Assistant to Director, Robin Saex; Props, Jean Spence; Wardrobe, Barbara Perkins, Katherine Bel Geddes; Casting, Deborah Brown, Michael Lane; Stage Managers, George Darveris, Robin Herskowitz; Press, Betty Lee Hunt, Maria Cristina Pucci, James Sapp, Maurice Turet

CAST: Remak Ramsay (St. John Quartermaine) succeeded by Lee Richardson, Caroline Lagerfelt (Anita Manchip) succeeded by Caitlin Clarke, Kelsey Grammer (Mark Sackling) succeeded by John Christopher Jones, Roy Poole (Eddie Loomis), Anthony Heald (Derek Meadle), John Cunningham (Henry Windscape) succeeded by John Ryland, Dana Ivey (Melanie Garth)
    A drama in 2 acts and 5 scenes. The action takes place over a period of three years during the early 1960's in the Staff Room of the Cull-Loomis School of English for Foreigners in Cambridge, England.

Milton Berle, Lee Wallace in "Goodnight, Grandpa"
(*Martha Swope Photo*)

(UNITARIAN CHURCH OF ALL SOULS) Friday, February 25—March 20, 1983 (14 performances). The All Souls Players presents:
KISS ME, KATE with Book by Sam and Bella Spewack; Music and Lyrics, Cole Porter; Director, Jeffery K. Neill; Musical Director, Wendell Kindberg; Associate Musical Director, Joyce Hitchcock; Sets, Craig Shepherd; Costumes, Susan L. Soetaert; Lighting, Peter Van der Meulen; Producers, Tran William Rhodes, Pat Sheffield, Howard Van der Meulen; Assistant to Director, Suzanne Kaszynski; Stage Managers, Ruth E. Kramer, Cassandra Conyers

CAST: Harry Bennett (Fred/Petruchio), James Lawson (Harry/Baptista) succeeded by Tran William Rhodes, Kathee Kendall (Lois/Bianca), Michael E. Busch (Ralph/Gregory), Melliss Kenworthy (Lilli/Katharine), Brian O'Halloran (Paul), Melissa Bailey (Hattie), Pamela D. Chabora (Chorus/Nurse), Joe Aronica (2nd Gangster), Norb Joerder (Bill/Lucentio), Carol Leigh Stevens (Cab Driver), Michael Alan Gregory (Hortensio/Doorman/Truck Driver), Jon Dover (Chorus/Swing), Jerry Kappes (Harrison), Marianne Kenney (Chorus/Nurse), Michael Levy (Chorus/Nathaniel/1st Messenger), Scott McLennan (Chorus/Philip/Messenger), Drew Taylor (Gremio/Doctor/Chauffeur), Jeffrey J. Wilkins (1st Gangster)
    A musical in two acts. The action takes place in and around Ford's Theatre in Baltimore, MD, in late June.

(LION THEATRE) Monday, February 28—March 13, 1983 (16 performances). Dorothy Serdenis presents;
WIVES by Lynda Myles; Director, Stan Salfas; Set and Lighting, Richard B. Williams; Costumes, Danajean Cicerchi; Press, Free Lance Talents, Francine Trevens, Amy Carr

CAST: David Greenan, Carla Hayes, Lucy Martin, Kelly Monaghan, Nita Novy, Lou Vuolo

(ENTERMEDIA THEATRE) Wednesday, March 2—6, 1983 (6 performances and 14 previews). Walin Productions in association with Arthur Albert presents:

GOODNIGHT, GRANDPA by Walter Landau; Director, Jack Garfein; Set, David Potts; Costumes, Robert Wojewodski; Lighting, Todd Elmer; Associate Producer/ General Manager, Paul B. Berkowsky; Company Manager, Stephen Arnold; Wardrobe, Toni Baer Reed; Props, Sharon Seymour; Assistant to Director, Nina Schulman; Stage Managers, William Hare, Bill Kalmenson; Press, Jeffrey Richards, C. George Willard, Ben Morse, Robert Ganshaw, Ted Killmer, Helen Stern

CAST: Lorry Goldman (Sam), Laurie Heineman (Joan), Milton Berle (Isaac), Lee Wallace (Morris), Maxine Taylor-Morris (Fanny), Martin Haber (Sol), Jean Barker (Bertha), Estelle Kemler (Mrs. Solomon), P. Jay Sidney (Mr. Wilson), Understudies: Bill Kalmenson (Sam), Daniel Pollack (Isaac/Morris/Sol/Wilson)
    A play in 2 acts and 6 scenes. The action takes place today and in the past.

(GENE FRANKEL THEATRE) Monday, March 7—28, 1983 (12 performances and 14 previews). Southhill Productions presents:
UNEASY LIES by Andrew Glaze; Director, Susann Brinkley; Costumes, Jeff Wolz; Lighting, Bernadette Englart; Sound, Peter Glaze; Set Consultant, Salvator A. Lupo; Press, Free Lance Talents, Francine L. Trevens, Amy Carr

CAST: Adriana Keathley (Jackie), Lois Meredith (Erna)

(CHERNUCHIN THEATRE) Friday, March 11—26, 1983 (15 performances and 2 previews). Carl Schaeffer in association with D-H Productions and Gayle Greene presents:
RETURNINGS by Richie Allan; Director, Dan Held; Sets, Tony Castrigno; Costumes, Karen Hummel; Lighting, Greg Chabay; Technical Director, Bern Gautier; Sound, Dan Welsh; Stage Manager, Joe Erdey; Press, Free Lance Talents, Francine L. Trevens, Amy Carr, Matthew Daniels

CAST: Richie Allan (Ed Hochman), James Handy (Tom Reilly), Sylvia O'Brien (Mrs. Reilly), Sam Gray (Morris Hochman), Martha Greenhouse (Jennie Hochman), Gayle Greene (Mary Haggerty), Joseph Jamrog (Simpson), Earl Hammond (Brendan Reilly)
    A drama in 2 acts. The action takes place at the present time in the South Bronx during early autumn.

Top Left: Anthony Heald, Remak Ramsay, Dana Ivey, Kelsey Grammer, John Cunningham, Roy Poole, Caroline Lagerfelt in "Quartermaine's Terms" (*Bill Carter Photo*)

(TOP OF THE GATE) Sunday, March 13—April 10, 1983 (43 performances). Leonard Finger, Howard J. Burnett, Terry Spiegel present:
A BUNDLE OF NERVES with Music by Brian Lasser; Lyrics, Geoff Leon, Edward Dunn; Director, Arthur Faria; Set and Lighting, Barry Arnold; Costumes, David Toser; Sound, Tom Morse; Musical and Vocal Arrangements, Steven Margoshes; Musical Director, Clay Fullum; General Managers, Leonard A. Mulhern, Dan Zittel; Company Manager, Jean Rocco; Production Assistant, Ted Williams; Assistant to Producers, Maggi Burnett; Wardrobe, Terry Snyder; Stage Manager, Joseph DePauw; Press, Henry Luhrman, Terry M. Lilly, Kevin P. McAnarney, Keith Sherman, Bill Miller

CAST: Gary Beach, Carolyn Casanave, Ray Gill, Vicki Lewis, Karen Mason
MUSICAL NUMBERS: A Bundle of Nerves, The News, I Eat, She Smiled at Me, Boogey Man, Flying, Old Enough to Know Better, Studs, That's What'll Happen to Me, I Don't Know How to Have Sex, The Fatality Hop, Waiting, After Dinner Drinks, Slice of Life, What Do You Do, Connie, I'm Afraid, That Sound
A musical revue in two acts.

(WONDERHORSE THEATRE) Thursday, March 17—April 3, 1983 (16 performances). TRG Repertory Company presents:
GRUNTS by Joshua Brand; Director, Marvin Kahan; Set, Peter Harrison; Lights, Craig Kennedy; Costumes, Rosalie Contino; Press, Jan Greenberg

CAST: Shelly Desai (Paz), Mac Randall (Don), Tony McGrath (Red), Ron Ryan, Mart McChesney
A play in two acts. The action takes place at the present time on a Hollywood sound stage.

(RICHARD ALLEN CENTER) Friday, March 11—April 10, 1983 (28). J. Mc Productions and Don Hampton present:

CHANGING PALETTES by Seth Bornstein; Director, Edward Medina; Set, Donald Beckman; Costumes, Lorraine Calvert; Lighting, Scott Pinkney; Sound, John North; Assistant Director, Celeste Clark; Props, Jeff Lucchese; Technical Director, Donna Catanzaro; Stage Managers, Gabriel Reyes, Robert Herrig, Scott Bloom; Press, Freelance Talents, Francine Trevens, Amy Carr

CAST: Kathryn Eames (Merita), Bruce Pitzer (Mark), Joffre McClung (Lisa), Michael Countryman (Robert), Jane Hamilton (Jeanette)
A play in 2 acts and 4 scenes. The action takes place at the present time in Merita's apartment, Dixie Bell Motel in Hickory Hill NC, and Jeanette's trailer home.

(PARK ROYAL THEATRE) Saturday, March 19—April 10, 1983 (16 performances). Russ Banham in association with Dolphin Head Productions, Christopher Knight, Kin Shriner present:
RED ROVER RED ROVER by Oliver Hailey; Director, Tony Napoli; Set and Lighting, Bennet Averyt; Costumes, Susan Hum; Technical Director, Jeff Musmanno; Props, Terry Banham; Wardrobe, Mary Lou Rios; Stage Managers, Vincent A. Feraudo, John M. Flood; Press, Howard Atlee, Barbara Atlee

CAST: Phyllis Newman (Nell), Ron Harper (Eddie), Bryan Clark (Joe), Michael Kirby (Harris), Jill Larson (Leigh), Helen Gallagher (Vic), Understudies: John Flood (Joe), Michael Kirby (Eddie), Russ Banham (Harris), Karen McLaughlin (Vic/Nell/Leigh)
A drama in two acts. The action takes place at the present time in the home of Vic and Joe.

(THEATRE AT ST. PETER'S CHURCH) Wednesday, March 23—June 26, 1983 (110 performances and 14 previews). Alison Clarkson, Stephen Graham, Joan Stein and the Shubert Organization (Gerald Schoenfeld, Chairman; Bernard B. Jacobs, President) present:
THE MIDDLE AGES by A. R. Gurney, Jr.; Director, David Trainer; Set, John Lee Beatty; Costumes, David Murin; Lights, Frances Aronson; Sound, Paul Garrity; Stage Managers, M. A. Howard, Connie Coit; General Management, Albert Poland, Susan L. Falk; Company Manager, Erik Murkoff; Wardrobe, Tom Hansen; Casting, Mary Colquhoun; Hairstylist, David Lawrence; Press, David Powers

CAST: Jack Gilpin (Barney), Ann McDonough (Eleanor), Andre Gregory (Charles) succeeded by Donald Barton, Jo Henderson (Myra)
A comedy in two acts. The action takes place in the trophy room of a men's club in a large city over a span of time from the mid-1940's to the late 1970's.

Vicki Lewis, Karen Mason, Carolyn Casanave, Ray Gill, Gary Beach in "A Bundle of Nerves"

(PERRY STREET THEATRE) Thursday, March 24—April 10, 1983 (20 performances). J. R. Frank presents:
WATER MUSIC by Norman Lock; Director, William E. Hunt; Set, Rick Dennis; Lighting, William J. Plachy; Costumes, Jimm Halliday; Sound, George Jacobs; Stage Managers, Geraldine Teagarden, Victoria St. George, Michelle Lockhart; Press, Betty Lee Hunt, Maria Cristina Pucci, James Sapp

CAST: Haru Aki (Mary/Bathing Beauty), Jimmy Butts (Charlie Gruber), Marjorie Gayle Edwards (Manicurist/Bathing Beauty), Peter Flint (Walt-/Policeman/Movie Director), Julio Guasp (Eduardo), James E. Mosiej (George), Pat Squire (Shirley), Victoria St. George (Saleswoman/Bathing Beauty), Len Stranger (Joe), Linda Watkins (Eleanor Williams), Christopher Yarrow (Steve), Eric Karner (Webelo), Michelle Lockhart (Script Girl), Chuck Kates (Carpenter)
A comedy in 2 acts and 5 scenes. The action takes place during July of the present time in Joe and Shirley's small, rundown private home in a "turning" section of Queens, New York City.

(HAROLD CLURMAN THEATRE) Wednesday, March 30—April 2, 1983 (4 performances). Joseph L. Runner presents:
FROM BROOKS WITH LOVE with Book and Lyrics by Wayne Sheridan; Music, George Koch, Russ Taylor; Director, William Michael Maher; Set, Tom Barnes; Costumes, Carol H. Buele; Lighting, Paul Sullivan; Musical Arrangements/Musical Director, Jim Fradrich; Musical numbers Staged and Choreographed by Robin Reseen; General Manager, Herbert J. Sheridan; Stage Managers, Ruth E. Kramer, Janet Bliss; Press, David Lipsky

CAST: Ralph Anthony (Jerry Wakefield), Gillian Walke (Lynn Pennington), Fred Bishop (Brendan Adams), Gwen Arment (Marjorie Morgan), Richard Sabellico (Rocco Sanducci), Geraldine Hanning (Countess), Ken Seiter (Alan Perkins), Peter Blaxill (Harold Nettleton), Understudies: Janet Bliss, Ken Seiter
MUSICAL NUMBERS: The Main Floor, I'll Be Someone Today, Brendan's Dream, Shopping, Marjorie's Dream, Love Is a Feeling, The Service, The Customer's Nightmare, Security, Showbiz, Eggs, Rocco's Dream, It's Nice, Unemployment, A New Kind of Husband, Let's Go, Lynn's Dream, Will They Remember, We'd Like to Go Back, Jerry's Dream, Move Over You Guys
A musical in 2 acts and 16 scenes. The action takes place at the present time (8:59 A.M. to 5:30 P.M.) on July 3rd on the main floor and in the employee's lounge of one of New York's exclusive clothiers.

Jack Gilpin, Jo Henderson, Andre Gregory, Ann McDonough in "The Middle Ages"
(Gerry Goodstein Photo)

91

(ACTOR'S PLAYHOUSE) Thursday, March 31—May 22, 1983 (63 performances and 18 previews). William Alan presents:
THE OTHER SIDE OF THE SWAMP by Royce Ryton; Director, Lawrence Hardy; Set, Jan S. Utstein; Costumes, George Potts; Lighting, Bruce Kahle; General Manager, Penny M. Landau; Associate Producer, Jeff Eisenberg; Props, Jeff Younger; Stage Manager, Charles Y. Doyle; Press, Free Lance Talents, Francine L. Trevens, Amy Carr, Ann Edwards

CAST: Alexander Wilson (Terence Jenkins), David Schmitt (Leslie Brown)
A play in 2 acts and 9 scenes. The action takes place in the sitting room of Terry's flat in Kensington, London, from 1977 to 1981.

(LA MAMA) Friday, April 1—17, 1983 (17 performances). Ellen Stewart's La Mama E.T.C. (Wesley Jansby, Artistic Director) in association with STEPA presents:
BARNUM'S LAST LIFE by Richard Ploetz; Director, Paul Lazarus; Set, Keith Gonzales; Costumes, Karen Hummel; Lighting, Rick Butler; Sound, Tim Roberts; Stage Managers, Lori M. Doyle, Jill Frizsell, Wendy Chapin; General Manager, Stephen Nisbet; Production Coordinator, Susan B. Smythe; Assistant to Director, Mary Sullivan; Casting, David Rubin; Associate Producer, Stephen Nisbet; Press, Max Eisen, Madelon Rosen

CAST: Harris Yulin (P. T. Barnum), Brent Collins (Admiral Dott), Sharita Hunt (Joice Heth), Daniel Leventritt (Joseph White), Paul LaGreca (Young Bailey), Don Plumley (Old Bailey), Thomas Ikeda/Du-Yee Chang (Wing-Fats)
A play without intermission. The action takes place in the attic of P. T. Barnum's American Museum on Lower Broadway in New York City.

(CHERNUCHIN THEATRE) Thursday, April 7—23, 1983 (16 performances). StageArts Theater Company (Nell Robinson and Ruth Ann Norris, Artistic Directors) presents:
ROYAL BOB by Richard Stockton; Director, Ronald Roston; Set, Ernest Allen Smith; Costumes, Jeffrey Ullman; Lighting, Robert F. Strohmeier; Technical Director, Dickson Lane; Stage Managers, Richard Hauenstein, Dennis Cameron; Press, Shirley Herz, Sam Rudy, Peter Cromarty

CAST: Brian Evers (Ebon Ingersoll), Larry Bryggman (Robert Ingersoll), Thomas Barbour (Rev. John Ingersoll), Janet Zarish (Eva Parker Ingersoll), Thomas A. Carlin (Judge Palmer) succeeded by Allen Swift, Alan Leach (Vestryman Sanhope/A Man)
A drama in 2 acts and 4 scenes. The action takes place in Peoria, Illinois from 1857 to 1868.

(MIRROR THEATRE) Sunday, April 10—24, 1983 (15 performances and 3 previews). Mirror Theatre presents:
JOAN OF LORRAINE by Maxwell Anderson; Director, John Strasberg; Assistant Director, Susan Fenichell; Fight Coordinator, Paxti Martin; Stage Managers, Robert Pross, Robert Watson; Wigs, Paul Huntley; General Management, Richard Horner, Lynne Stuart, Kerrin Clark, Roger Sherman; Press, Owen Levy

CAST: William Hardy (Jimmy Masters/Director/Inquisitor), Robert Watson (Al/Stage Manager), Elaine Rinehart (Tessie/Assistant Stage Manager/Aurore), Virginia Daly (Marie/Costumer), Tobin Wheeler (Garder/Jean de Metz/Executioner), Charles Regan (Kipner/Jacques d'Arc/Archbishop of Rheims/Cauchon/Bishop of Beauvais), Ralph Roberts (Elling/Durand Laxart/La Hire), Sabra Jones (Mary Grey/Joan), Henry Marsden (Dollner/Pierre d'Arc), Lee Allen (Cordwell/Jean d'Arc), Gisli Jonsson (Quirke/St. Michael/Courcelles), Isabel Garcia-Lorca (Miss Reeves/St. Catherine), Rawn Harding (Miss Sadler/St. Margaret), Joel Anderson (Sheppard/Alain Chartier/Dunois), Will Patton (Ward/Dauphin), Jim Knobeloch (Jeffson/Tremoille), Matt O'Toole (Champlain/Father Massieu)
A drama in 2 acts and 15 scenes. The action takes place with a contemporary acting company in rehearsal for a play about the Joan of Arc legend.

(NAT HORNE THEATRE) Wednesday, April 20—May 15, 1983 (28 performances and 5 previews). The New American Theater Company (Stephanie Wein, Paul Elman, Matthew Campion) presents:
WAITING FOR LEFTY and TILL THE DAY I DIE two one-act plays by Clifford Odets; Director, Dominic DeFazio; Sets, Roger Benischek; Lighting, Craig Kennedy; Costumes, Carla Kramer; Sound, Tom Gould; Makeup/Hairstylist, Tom Brumberger; General Manager, Stephanie Wein; Production Stage Managers, Howard P. Lev, Laurie B. Clark; Wardrobe, Carol Wood; Props, Norma Vaucrosson; Press, Betty Lee Hunt, Maria Cristina Pucci, James Sapp

CAST: "Till the Day I Die": Paul Elman (Carl Tausig), Michael Iannucci (Baum), Randy Rocca (Ernst Tausig), Jacqueline Jacobus (Tilly), Lisa Trafficante (Zelda/Prisoner), Sully Boyar (Det. Popper), Jackson Baroden (Edsel/Julius), Don Stark (Martin/Arno), Matthew Campion (Capt. Schlegel), Michael Ornstein (Adolph), James Fry (Zeltner/Detective), Edward Hodson (Peltz), Ted Zurkowski (Weiner), Curt Owens (Fritz), Lee Shepherd (Max), Leonard Donato (Hassel), Robert Heller (Maj. Duhring), Julie Ariola (Hedvig Duhring), David Matthau (Secretary) (Stieglitz)
"Waiting for Lefty": Sully Boyar (Fatt), Randy Rocca (Henchman), Jackson Baroden (Joe), Julie Ariola (Edna), Robert Heller (Fayette), Matthew Campion (Miller), Jacqueline Jacobus (Florrie), Michael Iannucci (Irv), Don Stark (Sid), Michael Ornstein (Clayton), James Fry (Reilly), Harry Davis (Dr. Barnes), David Matthau (Dr. Benjamin), Paul Elman (Agate Keller), Union Members: Leonard Donato, Edward Hodson, Curt Owens, Lee Sheherd, Ted Zurkowski

(PROVINCETOWN PLAYHOUSE) Thursday, April 21—June 5, 1983 (49 performances and 13 previews). Rosita Sarnoff, Anne Wilder, Joseph L. Butt, Doug Cole present:
WIN/LOSE/DRAW by Mary Gallagher and Ara Watson; Director, Amy Saltz; Sets, Louis Nelson; Costumes, Ruth Morley; Lighting, David F. Segal; Associate Producers, Joseph K. Fisher, Betsy Rosenfield; Sound, Bob Kerzman; Casting, Donna Issacson; General Managers, David Lawlor, Helen L. Nickerson; Stage Manager, Peter Weicker; Props, Susan Wright Podiak; Wigs, Paul Huntley; Press, Shirley Herz, Sam Rudy, Peter Cromarty

CAST: "Little Miss Fresno" by Ara Watson and Mary Gallagher: Christine Estabrook (Ginger Khabaki), Lynn Milgrim (Doris Nettles). The action takes place at a fair ground in Fresno, CA.
"Final Placement" by Ara Watson: Lynn Milgrim (Mary Hanson), Christine Estabrook (Luellen James). The action takes place in a child welfare office in Tulsa, OK.
"Chocolate Cake" by Mary Gallagher: Christine Estabrook (Annmarie Fitzer), Lynn Milgrim (Delia Baron). The action takes place in a motel room in Western Massachusetts. Understudies: Jeanne Michels, Jeannie Cullens

Top Right: David Schmitt, Alexander Wilson in "The Other Side of the Swamp" (*Anita Feldman/Shevett Photo*)

Right: Christine Estabrook, Lynn Milgrim in "Win/Lose/Draw" (*Carol Rosegg Photo*)

(VANDAM THEATRE) Tuesday, May 3—June 20, 1983 (55 performances and 15 previews). Stevie Phillips in association with Universal Pictures presents:
WILD LIFE four one-act plays by Shel Silverstein; Director, Art Wolff; Settings, Marjorie Bradley Kellogg; Costumes, Franne Lee; Lighting, Arden Fingerhut; Sound, Bruce Ellman; General Management, Kingwill Office, Jay Kingwill, Larry Goossen; Production Coordinator, Joe Cacaci; Associate Producer, Bonnie Champion; Assistant to Producer, Laurie Basch; Company Manager, Margay Whitlock; Props, David Smith; Wardrobe, Pallas Romaguera; Production Assistant, Richard Theologus; Stage Managers, David S. Felder, Jody Gelb; Press, Jeffrey Richards, C. George Willard, Robert Ganshaw, Ben Morse, Richard Humleker, Mary Ann Rubino

CAST: "Non-Stop": Robert Trebor (Edgar), Raynor Scheine (Bobby), "I'm Good to My Doggies": Henderson Forsythe (Louis Benjamin Hinkle), W. H. Macy (Arthur Pitler), "Charades": Conard Fowkes (Irving Seltz), Howard Sherman (Les), Jody Gelb (Cynthia), W. H. Macy (Peter), Robert Trebor (Al), Julie Hagerty (Mimi), "The Lady of the Tiger Show": Christopher Murney (Elliot Cushman), Howard Sherman (Tucker Pym), Conard Fowkes (Kenny Crane), Henderson Forsythe (Bishop Cooley), Jody Gelb (Lavinia Tremaine), Julie Hagerty (Florence Haskins), Raynor Scheine (Lamar Darfield)

(DRAMATIS PERSONAE THEATRE) Sunday, May 1—June 26, 1983 (25 performances)
RUN JACOB, RUN! by and with Zwi Kanar and Ted Davis. An autobiographical drama about a Jewish child growing up in Poland during the holocaust.

(PERRY STREET THEATRE) Tuesday, April 26—May 8, 1983 (14 performances). The British Council presents the Actors Touring Company of London in repertory productions of:
THE PROVOKED WIFE by Sir John Vanbrugh; Director, John Retallack; Music, Chris Barnes; Costumes, Jean Turnbull; Lighting/Stage Manager, Justin Savage; Production, Eric Starch; Press, Howard Atlee, Barbara Atlee

CAST: Russell Enoch (Sir John Brute), Valerie Braddell (Lady Brute), Christine Bishop (Bellinda), Susan Colverd (Lady Fancyfull), Raymond Sawyer (Heartfree), Jack Ellis (Constant), Chris Barnes (Rasor/Treble/Lord Rake/Justice)
QUIXOTE from Cervantes; Adapted and Written by Richard Curtis, John Retallack; Director, John Retallack; Music Scored by Susan Biggs; Musical Direction, Susan Biggs, Chris Barnes; Design, Poppy Mitchell, Janet Newton; Company Manager, Justin Savage; Production Manager, Michael Diamond

CAST: Russell Enoch (Don Quixote), Raymond Sawyer (Sanson Carrasco/Gregorio), Chris Barnes (Sancho Panza), Jack Ellis (Innkeeper/Cardenio/Narrator/Duke), Valerie Braddell (Innkeeper's Wife/Dorothea/Niece/Altisadora), Christine Bishop (Teresa Panza/Maritornes/Duchess), Susan Biggs (Musician)

(OHIO THEATRE) Wednesday, May 4-22, 1983 (15 performances). Staret Productions (Michael Parva, Artistic Director; Victoria Lanman, Producing/Managing Director; Kerry Edwards, Associate Producing Director) presents:
BODY PARTS by Paul Selig; Director, Jennifer McCray; Set, Jim Cozby; Lighting, Heather Carson; Costumes, D. V. Thompson; Sound, Sam Buccio; Choreography, David Fredericks; Stage Managers, Bruce T. Paddock, Sanja Kabalin

CAST: Frederick Allen (Toddy-O), David Combs (Hardy), Helen Hanft (Ida), Kevin Sessums (Baby), Lynnie Godfrey (Miss Bethesda), Winnie Holzman (Jackie), Kevin McGuire (Curtis), Jerry Pavlon (Dom)
A drama in two acts. The action takes place during winter in the recent past in and around the Male World, a porno house on Eighth Avenue in New York City.

(HAROLD CLURMAN THEATRE) Wednesday, May 4—22, 1983 (24 performances). The Fool's Theatre Company, Oxford, England, in association with the Harold Clurman Theatre (Jack Garfein, Artistic Director) presents:
UNSPEAKABLE ACTS by David Gibson; Director, Nigel Warrington; Design, Lee Dean; Lighting, Paul Armstrong; Wardrobe, Kimberly A. Gheen; Executive Producer, Robert Dawson Scott; Stage Manager, William Hare; Press, Fred Hoot, David Mayhew

CAST: David Gibson

Raynor Scheine, Christopher Murney in "Wild Life" (*Peter Cunningham Photo*)

(WEST SIDE Y) Monday, May 9—29, 1983 (13 performances and 4 previews). American Kaleidoscope (Rebecca Dobson, Joan Rice Franklin, Artistic Directors) in association with the West Side Y Arts Center presents:
STEEL ON STEEL by Brandon Cole; Director, Richard Bell; Set, Ernest Allen Smith; Costumes, Lynn P. Hoffman; Lighting, Dennis Size; Sound, Daryl Bornstein; General Manager, George Ivolin; Company Manager/Assistant Director, Allison Post; Production Assistant, Arthur Bryant; Props, James DeLorenzo; Stage Managers, Clark Taylor, Carolyn Caldwell; Press, Fred Hoot, David Mayhew

CAST: John Turturro (Niccollo "Mac" Vittelli), Michael Badalucco (Vico "Vic" Vitelli), Jeff Braun (Gus), Stephen Burks (Leon Parish), Donald Berman (Bruno "Bernie" Vitelli), Susan Pellegrino (Jenny), Joel Stevens (Philip Gold)
A drama in 3 acts and 13 scenes. The action takes place between 1954 and 1960.

(NEW YORK THEATRE ENSEMBLE) Wednesday, May 18—29, 1983 (14 performances and 2 previews). N.Y.T.E. presents a Chepshow Mansions Ltd. (Will MacAdam, Artistic Director) production of:
FROZEN ASSETS by Barrie Keeffe; Director, Will MacAdam; Set, Michael Boyer; Lighting, Denise Yaney; Producing Director, Beverly Severino; Stage Manager, Randy Norton; Press, Free Lance Talents, Francine L. Trevens, Terry Dobris

CAST: Steven Kollmorgen (Al), Sharon Laughlin (Joan), William Preston (Sammy), Vicki Shelton (Pam), Michael Sinclair (Screw/Lord Plaistow), Allan Stevens (Priest/Peter), Richard Voigts (Henry), Chip Bolcik (Ronnie), Tobias Haller (Buddy), Mark Hamilton (Frank/Dave), Myvanwy Jenn (Aunt Connie/Edna)
A play in 2 acts and 16 scenes. The action takes place during "not quite Christmas" in the East End of London and the countryside.

Susan Pellegrino, John Turturro in "Steel on Steel" (*Peter Marschark Photo*)

(back) Kelle Kipp, Jeff McCracken, John Leonard, (front)
Holland Taylor, Keith Charles in "Breakfast with Les
and Bess"

(BALDWIN THEATRE) Wednesday, May 11—29, 1983 (12 performances). Baldwin Manhattan Lights Theatre (Anita Sorel, Artistic Director; Carol Mennie, Executive Director) presents:
A FAMILY COMEDY by Robert Cessna; Director, Jamie Brown; Set, Michael DeSouza; Lighting, Robert Dorfman; Casting, Judy Henderson; Costumes, Elaine Saussotte; Stage Managers, Eric Kramer, Cindy Weissler; Production Assistants, Mathias Holzman, Larry Wald; Props, Michael Jarahian; Wardrobe, T. Hammond; Press, Sydney Ramey, Dick Rizzo

CAST: James DeMarse (Arthur), Duane F. Mazey (David), Mary Fogarty (Gladys), Mark Neely (Donnie), Richard Merrell (Frank), Nicholas Saunders (Paul)
   A play on 3 acts and 5 scenes. The action takes place at the present time in a split-level apartment on the ground floor of a small west side townhouse in New York City.

(PLAYERS THEATRE) Thursday, May 12—June 5, 1983 (37 performances). Howard J. Burnett and Morton Wolkowitz present:
MY ASTONISHING SELF devised by Michael Voysey from the writings of George Bernard Shaw; Set and Lighting, Victor Capecce; Stage Manager, Larry Bussard; Press, Henry Luhrman, Terry M. Lilly, Kevin P. McAnarney, Keith Sherman

CAST: Donal Donnelly as George Bernard Shaw

(FIRST CITY) Sunday, May 15—June 26, 1983 (49 performances and 13 previews). Pat Productions presents:
JACQUES BREL IS ALIVE AND WELL AND LIVING IN PARIS with Music by Jacques Brel, Francois Rauber, Gerard Jouannest, Jean Corti; Production Conception, English Lyrics, Additional Material by Eric Blau and Mort Shuman; Based on Brel's lyrics and commentary; Director, Eric Blau; Scenery and Costumes, Don Jensen; Lighting and Sound, Steve Helliker; General Manager, Lily Turner; Stage Managers, Steve Helliker, Joseph Neal; Press, M. J. Boyer

CAST: Leon Bibb, Betty Rhodes, Joseph Neal, Jacqueline Reilly, Alternates: Margery Cohen, J. T. Cromwell
MUSICAL NUMBERS: Marathon, Alone, Madeleine, I Loved, Mathilde, Bachelor's Dance, Timid Frieda, My Death, Girls and Dog, Jackie, The Statue, Desperate Ones, Sons of, Amsterdam, The Bulls, Old Folks, Marieke, Brussels, Fannette, Funeral Tango, Middle Class, You're Not Alone, Next, Carousel, If We Only Have Love
   Performed with one intermission.

(SPACE AT CITY CENTER) Thursday, May 17—June 18, 1983 (35 performances and 11 previews). Lawrence N. Dykun, Michael J. Needham, Robert L. Sachter present:
JEEVES TAKES CHARGE by P. G. Wodehouse; Conceived and Adapted by Edward Duke; Director, Gillian Lynne; Design, Carl Toms; Lighting, Craig Miller; Costumes, Una-Mary Parker; Choreography, Susan Holderness; Company Manager, Andrea Ladik; Wardrobe, Scott Wiscamb; Props, Howard Munford, Teresa Buckley; Stage Manager, Cosmo P. Hanson; Press, Judy Jacksina, Glenna Freedman, Marcy Granata, Susan Chicoine, Mari H. Thompson, John Howlett

CAST: Edward Duke
   Performed in two acts four scenes with a prologue. The action takes place in 1925.

(LAMBS THEATRE) Thursday, May 19, 1983 and still playing May 31, 1983. Howard J. Burnett, David E. Jones, Steven K. Goldberg present the Hudson Guild Theatre (David Kerry Heefner, Producing Director) production of:
BREAKFAST WITH LES AND BESS by Lee Kalcheim; Director, Barnet Kellman; Set, Dean Tschetter; Lighting, Ian Calderon; Costumes, Timothy Dunleavy; Sound, Michael Jay; General Management, Maria DiDia, Jim Fiore, Rosemary Carey; Assistant Director, Donna Jacobson; Assistant to Producers, Maggi Burnett; Production Assistant, Laura Kravets; Wardrobe, Christina Ringelstein; Stage Managers, Andrea Naier, Jay Lowman; Press, Henry Luhrman, Keith Sherman, Terry M. Lilley, Kevin P. McArnarney

CAST: Holland Taylor (Bess Dischinger), Keith Charles (Les Dischinger), Kelle Kipp (Shelby Dischinger), Jeff McCracken (Roger Everson) succeeded by Tom Nolan, John Leonard (David Dischinger), Daniel Ziskie (Nate Moody/Announcer) succeeded by Jay Lowman, Understudies: Daniel Ziskie (Les), Tudi Wiggins (Bess), Laura Kravets (Shelby), Jay Lowman (Roger/Nate/David)
   A comedy in 2 acts and 3 scenes. The action takes place in 1961 in the living room of Les and Bess Dischinger, on Central Park South in New York City.

(CSC THEATRE) Thursday, May 19—June 12, 1983 (20 performances). The Independent Eye (Conrad Bishop, Artistic Director) presents:
MEDEA/SACRAMENT adapted, directed and performed by Conrad Bishop and Elizabeth Fuller

(APPLE CORPS THEATRE) Sunday, May 22—29, 1983 (12 performances). Apple Corps Theatre (John Raymond, Artistic Director) presents:
ABOUT IRIS BERMAN by Arnold Rabin; Director, John Raymond; Set, Rick Dennis; Costumes, Marie Hilgemann; Lighting, Wayne S. Lawrence; Sound, Mark Laiosa; Stage Manager, Skip Corris; Press, Aviva Cohen

CAST: Estelle Kemler (Celia Davidson), Michael Marcus (Manny Berman), Jean Barker (Esther Berman), Kathryn C. Sparer (Iris Berman), Gary Richards (Paul Riceman)
   A family drama in 2 acts and 4 scenes. The action takes place at the present time in the Berman house and in Howard's apartment.

(WONDERHORSE THEATRE) Wednesday, May 25—June 12, 1983 (16 performances). Cherubs Guild presents:
IN RESIDENCE by Harvey Zuckerman; Director, Gail Kellstrom; Producers, Carol Avila, Laura Balboni, Lesley Starbuck, Hillary Wyler; Lighting, Jo Mayer; Paintings, Joann Flaherty; Set, Edmond Ramage; Costumes, Martha Hally; Stage Manager, David Malvin; Props, Georganne Rogers; Press, Bruce Cohen

CAST: Rebecca Taylor (Isabelle), John Genke (Ralph), Martha Kearns (Lena), Dean Kyburz (Dan)
   A comedy in 2 acts and 4 scenes. The action takes place at the present time on the second floor parlor of a brownstone on East 68th Street in New York City.

Edward Duke in "Jeeves Takes Charge"

OFF BROADWAY SERIES

AMAS REPERTORY THEATRE

Rosetta LeNoire, Founder/Artistic Director
Fourteenth Season

Administrator/Business Manager, Gary Halcott; Administrator, Jerry Lapidus; Stage Managers, Jim Griffith, Kuan Mangle

Thursday, October 28,—November 21, 1982 (16 performances).

LOUISIANA SUMMER with Book by Robert and Bradley Wexler; Lyrics, Robert Wexler; Music, Rocky Stone; Director, Robert Stark; Choreographer, Keith Rozie; Musical Director/Vocal, Dance and Instrumental Arrangements, Lea Richardson; Assistant Musical Director/Dance Arrangements, Darryl M. Waters; Set, Tom Barnes; Lighting, Ronald L. McIntyre; Costumes, Eiko Yamaguchi; Technical Director, Adam Hart; Animal Designer, Susan McClain-Moore; Puppet Consultant, John Lovelady; Stage Managers, Jim Griffith, Kuan Mangle, Darren McGill; Assistant to Director, Andrea Gordon; Press, Howard Atlee, Barbara Atlee
CAST: Sonia Bailey (Dossie), Hal Blankenship (Boswell/Loup-Garou), Jeff Reade (Charlie/Willie), R. Michael Dayton (Grandpa Paul/Olidon), Robin Dunn (Rosalind/Voodoo Queen), Steve Fickinger (Luke), Douglass D. Frazier (Willard), Margaret Goodman (Dodie), Tracy O'Neil Heffernan (Dot), Wendy Kimball (Narrator/Older Bradley), Hans Krown (Bobby/Squeak), Garrick Lavon (Floyd/Egret), Lani Marrell (Alice), Kimberly Mucci (Bradley), Raphael Nash (James Lee/Voodoo King), Don Oliver (Louisiana Jack), Cynthia I. Pearson (Older Dossie), Kevin Ramsey (Freddie/Papa Gator), Ann Talman (Josette), Tug Wilson (Luke), Raymond Skip Zipf (Lloyd/Egret), Understudies: Alan Paul Michaels, Andrea Gordon
MUSICAL NUMBERS: Prologue, Cutting in the Cane, Silent Summer Nights, Pictures in the Sky, Busy Days, Country Harmony, Go Your Way with the Lord, Train Song, Cane Cutter's Ballet, Voodoo Dance, Lullaby of Night, Alligator Romp, Josette's Theme, Louisiana Summer, Louisiana Cajun Man, Loup's Lament, Black Annie, My Friend, Epilogue

A musical in 2 acts and 18 scenes with a prologue and epilogue. The action takes place in 1947 and 1954 in Paradise, Louisiana, and in the swamps and bayous between Paradise and New Orleans.

Thursday, February 24—March 20, 1982 (17 performances)

MISS WATERS, TO YOU with Book by Loften Mitchell; Based on a concept by Rosetta LeNoire; Music from Miss Waters' repertoire; Director, Billie Allen; Musical Direction/Arrangements/Special Material, Luther Henderson; Choreography, Keith Henderson; Set, Tom Barnes; Lighting, Gregg Marriner; Costumes, Jeff Mazor; Technical Director, Adam Hart; Assistant to Director, Ronald L. McIntyre; Stage Managers, Jim Griffith, Kuan Mangle, Darren McGill; Hats, Breelun Daniels; Assistant Choreographer, Robin Dunn

(front) Kimberly Mucci, Sonia Bailey, (back) Kevin Ramsey, Hans Krown, Cynthia Pearson in "Louisiana Summer" (*JWL Photo*)

CAST: Jeff Bates (Duke Ellington/Walt Maxton), Donna Brown (Pearl Wright), Keith David (Earl Dancer/Narrator), Robin Dunn (Young Lady), Douglas Frazier (Buddy/Bartender), Yolanda Graves (Maggie Hill), Lucille Harley (Momweez/Understudy), Luther Henderson (Fletcher Henderson), Mary Louise (Ethel Waters), Ronald Mann (Milton Starr/Irving Berlin), Devron Minion (Nugent/Man/Young Man), Denise Morgan (Bessie Smith/Young Woman), Stanley Ramsey (Sporty-O-Tee/Eddie Matthews), Melodee Savage (Jo Hill), Angela Sprouse (Sally Anderson), Leon Summers, Jr. (Cab Calloway/Braxton), Carole Sylvan (Vi/Woman), Ed Taylor (Joe/Bob White/Professor), Lee Winston (Charles Bailey, Jr./Gumm)

A musical in 2 acts and 23 scenes. The action takes place in various cities, theatres and clubs in the life and travels of Ethel Waters from 1917 to 1960.

Thursday, April 21—May 15, 1983 (15 performances)

OPENING NIGHT with Book, Music and Lyrics by Corliss Taylor-Dunn and Sandra Reaves-Phillips; Director, William Michael Maher; Musical Director/Arranger, Grenoldo; Choreographer, Mabel Robinson; Set, Larry Fulton; Lighting, Gregg Marriner; Costumes, Judy Dearing; Stage Managers, Jim Griffith, Kuan Mangle, Terrance J. Hart; Technical Director, Bill Covington; Wardrobe, Cindy Boyle; Conductor/Pianist, Louis Small
CAST: Julia Collins (Jill/Preacher/Secretary), Leslie Dockery (Pepper/Young Mother/Heavenly Choir), Adam Hart (Askind/Musician/Rabbi), Eddie Jordan (Vodnoff/Joe/Policeman), Kashka (Satin/Ted/Preacher/Ambassador), Amy Lachinsky (Roz/Hooker/Choir), Larry Lowe (Steve/Artist/Choir), Becky Woodley (Dutchess/Bag Lady), Bob McAndrew (Sid/Choir), Adjora Faith McMillan (Leslie), Marishka Shanice Phillips (Young Sarai/Denise/Skar), Chauncey Roberts (Hilary/Hustler), Michael Anthony Roberts (Lucivious/Carl/Student), Avery Sommers (Sarai), Dan Strayhorn (Errol), Sandra Courtney Williams (Young Leslie/Kim/Hooker)
MUSICAL NUMBERS: Mr. Playwright, I Don't Have a Name, Mommy Says, You're My Friend, New Beginnings, Song of Praise, Hanging Around, Get Thee Behind Me, New York City Cock Roach Blues, We're Almost There, How Many Rainbows, The Man I Want to Be, Take a Chance, Cause a Sensation, Nobody's Blues, Keep Holding On, I Love the Dance, If We Can't Lick 'Em Join 'Em, Opening Night, Let Me Show You a New Way to Love

A musical in 2 acts and 19 scenes. The action takes place at the present time in New York City.

Stanley Ramsey, Mary Louise, Donna Brown, Toi Cordy
in "Miss Waters, to You" (*JWL Photo*)

95

AMERICAN JEWISH THEATRE

Stanley Brechner, Artistic Director
Third Season

Business Manager, Sheila M. Lippman; Production Supervisor, Stewart Schneck; Resident Director, Dan Held; Technical Director, Richard Wright; Press, Norman Golden, Kathy Hurley; Executive Director, Dr. Reynold Levy; Associate Executive Director, Sidney I. Zachter
(92nd STREET YM-YWCA) Saturday, October 23—31, 1982
THE TENTH MAN by Paddy Chayefsky; Director, Dan Held; Set, Tony Castrigno; Lighting, Helen Gatling; Costumes, Karen Hummel; Production Supervisor, Stewart Schneck; Stage Manager, Jennifer Borge
CAST: Albert S. Bennett (Sexton), Ed Breen (Policeman), Arthur Burns (Arthur), Bill Hugh Collins (Kessler Brother), Sol Frieder (Hirschman), Norman Golden (Alper), Victor Jacoby (Zitorsky), Milton Lansky (Schlissel), Lydia Leeds (Evelyn), Lou Miranda (Foreman), Victor Ritz (Harris), Joel Rooks (Rabbi), Robert Vogel (Kessler Brother)

A drama in 3 acts and 4 scenes. The action takes place during one day in the winter of 1959 in a small orthodox Synagogue in Mineola, Long Island, NY.

Saturday, November 6—December 19, 1982
DAVID AND PAULA by Howard Fast; Director, Stanley Brechner; Set, Keith Gonzales; Lighting, Martha Gibson; Costumes, Kathleen Blake; Stage Manager, Lori Hirschman
CAST: David Margulies (David), Veronica Castang (Paula)

A drama in 2 acts and 14 scenes. The action takes place in Tel Aviv and New York City from 1917 to 1948.

Saturday, January 8—February 20, 1983
THE MAN IN THE GLASS BOOTH by Robert Shaw; Director, Dan Held; Set, Tony Castrigno; Lighting, Gregory Chabay; Costumes, Karen Hummel; Technical Director, Larry Springer; Stage Managers, Debra A. Acquavella, Tracy Crum
CAST: Frank Anderson (Steiger/Tzelniker), Win Atkins (Flowerman/Judge), Arthur Burns (Charlie Cohn), Marvin A. Chatinover (Dr. Kessel/Prosecutor), Jesse Emmett (Durer/Landau), Norman Golden (Rudin/Marowski), Mark Henderson (Jack/Guard), Max Jacobs (Presiding Judge), Vera Lockwood (Mrs. Rosen), Bennes Mardenn (Judge), David Perrine (Sam/Guard), Beatrice Pons (Mrs. Lehmann), Tamara Reed (Mrs. Levi), Albert Sinkys (Goldman)

A drama in 2 acts and 4 scenes. The action takes place in New York City and Israel during 1964–1965.

Milton Lansky, Norman Golden, Victor Jacoby
in "The Tenth Man"

Saturday, March 12—April 24, 1983
THE RISE OF DAVID LEVINSKY with Book and Lyrics by Isaiah Sheffer; Based on novel by Abraham Cahan; Music, Bobby Paul; Director, Sue Lawless; Set, Kenneth Foy; Costumes, Richard Hornung; Lighting, Phil Monat; Musical Direction, John Franceschina; Choreography, Bick Goss; Assistant to Director, France Burke; Stage Managers, Tracy Crum, Charlie Johnston; Technical Director, Larry Springer
CAST: Lawrence Asher (Gitelson), Robert Ott Boyle (Chaikin), Eva Charney (Matilda/Ruchel/Gussie), Clarke Evans (Huntington/Shlank/Mannheimer), Norman Golden (Reb Shmerl/Mr. Diamond), Mickey Hartnett (Neighbor/Sadie/Customer)
MUSICAL NUMBERS: Who Is This Man, Learning, Five Hundred Pages, Letter Fantasy; Grand Street, In America, The Boarder, Transformation, Sharp, Two of a Kind, Hard Times, Credit Face, Five Hundred Garments, Ready Made, The Garment, Welcome to the Merry-Go-Round, Just Like Me, The Shopping Waltz, Bittersweet, Survival of the Fittest, I'll Love Again, Build a Union, After All

A musical in two acts.

Saturday, May 14—June 30, 1983
TWO FOR THE SEESAW by William Gibson; Director, Dan Held; Set, Tony Castrigno; Costumes, Karen Hummel; Lighting, Gregory Chabay; Stage Managers, Debra A. Acquavella, Meg Knowles
CAST: Art Burns (Jerry Ryan), Marilyn Sokol (Gittel Mosca)

A drama in 3 acts and 9 scenes. The action takes place between fall and spring of 1957–58 in two rooms (Jerry's and Gittel's) in New York City.

Marilyn Sokol, Art Burns
in "Two for the Seesaw"

(*Gerry Goodstein Photo*)

AMERICAN PLACE THEATRE

Wynn Handman, Director
Nineteenth Season

(AMERICAN PLACE THEATRE SUBPLOT) Monday, June 14–30, 1982 (8 performances) American Place Theatre (Wynn Handman, Director; Julia Miles, Associate Director) presents:
A CROWD OF TWO: Created and performed by Lisa Loomer and Rita Nachtmann; Director, Miriam Fond; Assistant Director, Patrick McCord; Production Manager, Carl Zutz; Stage Manager, Cheryl Singleton; Press, Jeffrey Richards, Ted Killmer

CAST OF COMIC CHARACTERS: WASP Rap, Mercedes the Tea Room Hostess, Miss Subways of 1982, Playing for Company, Princess Sha Na Na, Reincarnated, What's My Beef?, Miss Champaign County Fair, Jasmine, Talking to Grandma, Bag Rap

(AMERICAN PLACE THEATRE SUBPLOT) Wednesday, September 22—October 17, 1982 (23 performances and 1 preview). The American Humorists Series presents:
THE STAGE THAT WALKS by and with Bruce D. Schwartz; Lighting, Christine Wopat; Production Manager, Carl Zutz; Stage Manager, Cheryl Singleton; Production Assistant, Melvin Yaemans; Technical Director, Earl Vedder; Press, Jeffrey Richards, Bob Ganshaw

CAST: Bruce D. Schwartz performing The Rat of Huge Proportions, Victorian Songs and Dances, Mary of Scotland, The Farmer's Cursed Wife, The Dance of Possession, Pierrot and the Butterfly or The Suicide Attempt

(AMERICAN PLACE THEATRE) Saturday, October 23, 1982—January 23, 1983 (97 performances). Moved Saturday, January 29, 1983 to Town Hall, and closed February 26, 1983 after 30 additional performances. American Place Theatre presents:
DO LORD REMEMBER ME by James DeJongh; Director, Regge Life; Set, Julie Taymor; Lighting, Sandra L. Ross; Costumes, Judy Dearing; Technical Director, Nina Stern; Production Assistant, Sarah McThay; Stage Managers, Nancy Harrington, Dwight R. B. Cook; Press, Jeffrey Richards, Robert Ganshaw

CAST: Frances Foster, Ebony Jo-Ann, Lou Myers, Charles H. Patterson, Glynn Turman
A memory play inspired by, and derived from actual words and songs of former slaves in Virginia as described to interviewers in a 1936 WPA Federal Writers Project.

Frances Foster, Lou Myers, Charles H. Patterson, Ebony Jo-Ann, Glynn Turman in "Do Lord Remember Me"

(AMERICAN PLACE THEATRE) Wednesday, January 26—February 13, 1983, (18 performances). The Women's Project (Julia Miles, Director) presents:
LITTLE VICTORIES by Lavonne Mueller; Director, Bryna Wortman; Set, William M. Barclay; Lighting, Phil Monat; Costumes, Mimi Maxmen; Music, Clay Fullum; Sound, Regina M. Mullen; Technical Director, Nina Stern; Wardrobe, Winsome McKoy; Stage Managers, Renee F. Lutz, John Griesemer; Press, Jeffrey Richards, Robert Ganshaw

CAST: Caroline Kava (Susan B. Anthony), Linda Hunt (Joan of Arc), Terrence Markovich (Marshal/Capt. Battau), Bill Cwikowski (Hotel Owner/Tailor/Bar Dog), Jimmy Smits (Capt. Lavour/Ben Caleb), John Griesemer (Double Ugly/Archer/Limpy Bob), Randy Spence (Voices of Judge/Cardinal)
A drama in two acts. The action takes place in the American West and Medieval France during the last half of the 1800's and 1429.

(AMERICAN PLACE THEATRE) Thursday, February 24—March 13, 1983 (16 performances and 5 previews). The American Place Theatre and Playwrights Horizons present:
BUCK by Ronald Ribman; Director, Elinor Renfield; Set, John Arnone; Lighting, Frances Aronson; Costumes, David C. Woolard; Sound, Paul Garrity; Fights, Robert Aberdeen; Casting, Judy Courtney, John Lyons; Stage Managers, Jay Adler, Charles Kindl; Production Assistant, Blake Malouf; Assistant to Director, David Warren; Props, C. J. Simpson; Technical Adviser, Marc Schubin; Wardrobe, Kathy Newmann; Press, Jeffrey Richards Associates, Robert Ganshaw

CAST: Jack Davidson (Frank), Morgan Freeman (Fred Milly), Richard Leighton (Heegan), Joseph Leon (Nathan), Madeleine LeRoux (Madame/Woman with hat), Michael Lipton (Salesman), Priscilla Lopez (Joy-/Shirley), Bernie Passeltiner (Mr. Lollipop/Milton Berman), Alan Rosenberg (Buck Halloran), Robert Silver (Charlie Corvanni), Jimmy Smits (Vincent/Vendor), Ted Sod (Goglas/Mr. Hawaiian Shirt), Stagehands: Mitchell Gossett, Nick Iacovino, Charles Kindl, Michael Linden, Kenneth Lodge, Richard Mandel, Michael O'Boyll, Jason O'Malley, David Sennett
A "dark comedy" in 2 acts and 5 scenes. The action takes place at the present time in a cable TV studio, a department store, and a bar.

Priscilla Lopez, Alan Rosenberg in "Buck"
(*Martha Holmes Photo*)

(AMERICAN PLACE THEATRE) Tuesday, April 19—May 1, 1983 (16 performances). The American Place Theatre presents The Acting Company (John Houseman, Producing Artistic Director; Margot Harley, Executive Producer; Michael Kahn, Alan Schneider, Artistic Directors) in repertory productions of:
PERICLES by William Shakespeare; Director, Toby Robertson; Set, Franco Colavecchia; Costumes, Judith Dolan; Lights, Dennis Parichy; Musical Director, Jim Cummings; Music, Carl Davis, Jim Cummings; Choreography, Devorah Fong; Associate Director, Morton Milder; Stage Managers, Giles F. Colahan, Michael S. Mantel; Wardrobe, Marcia Ellen Cohen; Props, David Byron Fish; Press, Fred Nathan, Anne Abrams

CAST: J. Andrew McGrath (Gower), David Manis (Antiochus), Tom Hewitt (Pericles), Michael Manuelian (Thaliard/Leonine), Libby Colahan (Helicanus/Lychorida/Diana), John Stehlin (Cleon), Margaret Reed (Dionyza/Boult), Jack Kenny (Fisherman/Pandar), David O. Harum (Fisherman/Lysimachus), Ray Virta (Fisherman/Philemon/Philoten), Richard S. Iglewski (Simonides), Ronna Kress (Thaisa/Marina), Philip Goodwin (Cerimon). The action takes place at the present time on the Mediterranean Seaboard in two acts.

TARTUFFE by Moliere; Translated by Richard Wilbur; Director, Brian Murray; Set, Michael Yeargan; Costumes, Jane Greenwood; Lighting, Gregory C. MacPherson; Composer/Musical Director, Catherine MacDonald; Assistant to Director, Morton Milder

CAST: Libby Colahan (Mme. Pernelle), Richard S. Iglewski (Orgon), Megan Gallagher (Elmire), John Stehlin (Damis), Margaret Reed (Mariane), Ray Virta (Valere), J. Andrew McGrath (Cleante), Philip Goodwin (Tartuffe), Lynn Chausow (Dorine), Jack Kenny (M. Loyal), Michael Manuelian (Police Officer), Ronna Kress (Flipote), David O. Harum (Laurent), David Manis (Servant). The action takes place in Orgon's home in Paris and performed in two acts.
PLAY AND OTHER PLAYS by Samuel Beckett; Director, Alan Schneider; Sets, Mark Fitzgibbons; Costumes, John David Ridge; Lights, Dennis Parichy; Director's Assistant, Christopher Hanna

CAST: "Play": Libby Colahan (W1), Jack Kenny (M), Megan Gallagher (W2)
"Krapp's Last Tape": Richard S. Iglewski
"Come and Go": Margaret Reed (Flo), Libby Colahan (Vi), Megan Gallagher (Ru)

(AMERICAN PLACE THEATRE) Monday, May 9—29, 1983 (29 performances and 3 previews). The Acting Company (John Houseman, Producing Artistic Director; Margot Harley, Executive Producer; Michael Kahn, Alan Schneider, Artistic Directors) presents its alumni in:
THE CRADLE WILL ROCK by Marc Blitzstein; Director, John Houseman; Set, Mark Fitzgibbons; Costumes, Judith Dolan; Lighting, Dennis Parichy; Musical Direction, Michael Barrett; Stage Managers, Don Judge, Kathleen B. Boyette; Assistant Director, Christopher Markle; Musical Staging Consultant, Denny Shearer; Associate Musical Director, Charles Berigan; Assistant to Director, Joan Houseman; Technical Director, J. Austin; Wigs, Charles LoPresto; Press, Fred Nathan, Anne Abrams, Eileen McMahon, Leo Stern, Bert Fink

CAST: John Houseman (Prologue), Casey Biggs (Cop/Gus Polock), Daniel Corcoran (Steve/Prof. Scoot/Reporter), Gerald Gutierrez (Yasha), James Harper (Rev. Salvation/Prof. Trixie), Laura Hicks (Sadie Polock/Reporter), Patti LuPone (Moll/Sister Mister), Randle Mell (Dauber/Larry Foreman), Brian Reddy (Prof. Mamie/Harry Druggist), Tom Robbins (Gent/Editor Daily), Mary Lou Rosato (Mrs. Mister), Susan Rosenstock (Reporter), David Schramm (Mr. Mister), Charles Shaw-Robinson (Dr. Specialist/Bugs), Henry Stram (Dick/Junior Mister), Paul Walker (Pres. Prexy), Michele-Denise Woods (Ella Hammer).
A drama with music in 2 acts and 10 scenes. The action takes place in Steeltown, U.S.A., on the night of a union drive

(c)Randle Mell, Patti LuPone in "The Cradle
Will Rock" (*Martha Swope Photo*)

(clockwise from left) Etain O'Malley,
Elizabeth Perry, Donna Davis, Mary Hamill in
"A Difficult Borning"

AMERICAN RENAISSANCE THEATER

Robert Elston, Artistic Director; Associate Director, Elizabeth Perry; Artistic Adviser, Susan Reed; Sets and Lighting, Dale Jordan; Business Administrator, Susan Egert; Technical Director, Ernie Schenk; Press, David Lipsky
(AMERICAN RENAISSANCE THEATER) Tuesday, July 6—30, 1982 (20 performances)
A DIFFICULT BORNING the words of Sylvia Plath; Created by The New York Tea Party (Janet Gardner, Kayla Kazahn Zalk, Margo Berdeshevsky, Mary Hammill, Etain O'Malley, Elizabeth Perry); Director, Anita Khanzadian; Stage Manager, Jaclyn Barnhart-Ferraro.
CAST: Donna Davis, Mary Hamill, Etain O'Malley, Elizabeth Perry
Wednesday, September 8—October 3, 1982 (20 performances)
UNDER MILK WOOD by Dylan Thomas; Director, Susan Reed; Set, Ernie Schenk; Stage Manager, Hal Coon
CAST: Roger Baron, Jim Boerlin, Robert Crest, Merriman Gatch (succeeded by Sharon Alpert), David Greenan, Stacy Lidell, Sally Moffet, Susan Reed
Wednesday, October 13,—November 7, 1982 (20 performances)
PORTRAIT OF A MAN by Robert Elston; Selections from the works of Fry, Rosten, Roethke, Stevenson, Ives, Sosenko, Daniels, Stanislavsky, Arlen/Capote, Dickenson/Williams, Masters, Weill/Gershwin, Berryman, Kern/Harbach, Thurber, Sexton, Kern/Gershwin, Bredeman, Rolland, Williams, Van Gogh, Hopkins, Porter, Cavafy, Burton, Weill/Brecht; Director, Anita Khanzadian; Musical Director, Erica Kaplan; Set, Ernie Schenk; Lighting, David Shepherd; Stage Manager, Jaclyn Ferraro
CAST: Robert Elston
Wednesday, November 17,—December 12, 1982 (20 performances)
I'M OKAY BUT YOU KEEP SCREWING ME UP! with Sketches by Robert John Keiber, Sel Epstein, Robert Elston; Music, Danny Lanning; Director, Barry Kleinbort; Set, Victoria Nourafchan; Lighting, Gary Fassler; Costumes, Karen Nash; Stage Manager, Hal Coon
CAST: Claiborne Cary, Robert John Keiber, Terry Markovich, Gretchen Oehler, Susan Reed, Francis Reilly
MUSICAL NUMBERS AND SKETCHES: The Elevator, Co-oping in New York, Sin-a-card, Caring, Dr. Neizer, He and She, The Lewis Longacre Show, Cloudy Fair, The Book Club, Restaurant, Bicentennial Sex, Auditions for Bellevue, Mother and Daughter, Hell's Deli, Homage a'Molnar, Trading, Ducks, I'm Okay!
A comedy revue in 2 acts and 19 scenes.
Wednesday, March 2—27, 1983 (20 performances)
THE GOOD DOCTOR by Neil Simon; Adapted from and suggested by stories of Anton Chekhov; Director, Bill Herndon; Assistant to Director, David Greenan; Set, Ernie Schenk; Costumes, Karen Nash; Lighting, Gary Fassler
CAST: Molly Adams, Roy Barnitt, Davis Hall, Stephanie Satie, Jeff Scott
Wednesday, April 27,—May 22, 1983 (20 performances)
PAS DE DEUX by Pascal Vrebos; Sets, Ernie Schenk; Costumes, Karen Nash; Lights, Gary Fassler; Stage Manager, Kathy Zoumis. "Entre-Chats" translated by John Van Burek; Director, Robert Elston; Performed by Eunice Anderson, Andrea Weber. "Polycarpe Reincarnate" translated by Robert Hammond; Director, Janet Sarno; Performed by Dulcie Arnold, Victor Truro

AMISTAD WORLD THEATRE

Samuel P. Barton, Artistic Director
Shirley Fishman, Managing Director
(N.E.T.W.O.R.K.) Thursday, September 23,—October 24, 1982 (20 performances). Amistad World Theatre presents:
BLUES FOR MR. CHARLIE by James Baldwin; Director, Samuel P. Barton; Music and Lyrics, Cornelia J. Post; Set, Samuel P. Barton; Lighting, William J. Plachy; Costumes, Neil Cooper; Sound, Our House Productions; Technical Director, David Lough; Music Directors, Cornelia J. Post, Lucy Holstedt; Stage Managers, Richard Schiff, Susan Goodman; Press, Shirley Fishman
CAST: Herb Downer (Meridian), Keith F. Williams (Jimmy), Joseph Wigfall, Jr. (Arthur), Carlos Gerald (Ken), Kim Yancey (Juanita), Walter Allen Bennett (Lorenzo), Raymond Anthony Thomas (Pete), Betty Vaughn (Mother Henry), Sims Wueth (Lyle), Sharon Dennis (Jo), Robert Hancock (Parnell), Jeffrey Joseph (Richard), Lee Roy Giles (Papa D), Lynn Archer (Hazel), Joan Fallows (Lillian), Katey Doherty (Susan), David Lough (Ralph), Rick Washburn (Ellis), James Doherty (Rev. Phelps), Stanley Harrison (The State), Randy Frazier (Counsel for Bereaved), Cornelia J. Post (Rachel), Arline Williams (Elizabeth), Sharon Douglas (Pauline)
A drama in 3 acts with a prologue. The action takes place in Plaguetown, U.S.A. in the 1960's and in the past memories of the characters
Friday, November 5—28, 1982 (12 performances)
SWAP by Frank Shiras; Director, Samuel P. Barton; Set, Mr. Barton; Music, Cornelia J. Post; Lighting/Technical Director, David Lough; Stage Managers, Claire A. Dorsey, Gordon Skinner; Press, Shirley Fishman
CAST: Walter Allen Bennett (Finn), Betty Vaughn (Luve), Marissa Rivera (Ginger), Kim Yancey (Sibyl), Rick Washburn (Hadley)
A comedy in two acts. The action takes place in a Skid-Row hotel room.
(AMERICAN THEATRE OF ACTORS/ANNEX) Thursday, April 21, —May 8, 1983 (12 performances)
STRICTLY FORBIDDEN by Jorge Diaz/SARAH AND THE SAX by Lewis John Carlino; Director, Carlos Carrasco; Composer/Musical Arranger, Felix Mendez; Composers, Manuel Morel, Richard Cohen; Lyrics, Carlos Carrasco; Costumes, Marilyn Smith; Lighting, David Lough; Props, Douglas Scruggs; Choreographer, Paula Kalustian; Dialogue Coach, Rochelle Newman; Stage Manager, Claire A. Dorsey; Press, Shirley Fishman
CAST: 'Strictly Forbidden': Donna Bailey (The Lady), Hugo Halbrich (The Gentleman), Felipe Gorostiza (Epifanio), Felix Pitre (Placido); "Sarah and the Sax": Walter Allen Bennett (The Sax), Lois Raebeck (Sarah)

Lois Raebeck, Walter Allen Bennett in "Sarah and the Sax"
(*Austin Trevett Photo*)

ARK THEATRE COMPANY

Fifth Season
Directors, Donald Marcus, Lisa Milligan, Bruce Daniel; Literary Manager, Melissa Whitcraft; Press, Jeffrey Richards, Ted Killmer; Chairman of the Board, John P. Engel
(ARK THEATRE) Thursday, November 11—21, 1982
FINDING DONIS ANNE by Hal Corley; Director, Rebecca Guy; Set, Loy Arcenas; Costumes, Gail Brassard; Lighting, Jo Mayer; Sound, Daryl Bornstein; Stage Managers, Jeanne Oster, Anne Singer; Casting, Donna Isaacson; Technical Director, Walter Williams; Assistant to Producers, Sheryl Kaller; Wardrobe, Pam Peterson
CAST: Melodie Somers (Rachel), Albert Macklin (Darryl), Marilyn Byrd (Donis Anne), Mel Winkler (Luther), Peggy Schoditsch (Claire)
A drama in two acts. The action takes place during the last week of August 1969 just outside Richmond, VA, and in and around Washington, DC. Donis Anne speaks from 1982.
Thursday, February 10—27, 1983 (15 performances)

LUMIERE by Donald Marcus; Director, Irene Lewis; Set, Kevin Rupnik; Lighting, James F. Ingalls; Costumes, Richard Hornung; Sound, Daryl Bornstein; Stage Managers, Rebecca Linn, Virginia Jones; Technical Director, Carl Zutz; Associate Producer, Ken Schwenker; Portrait, Janet Secreti; Casting, Stanley Soble, Jim Mulkin
CAST: Concetta Tomei (Berthe), Kate Wilkinson (Madame Morisot), Denise DeLong (Mirella), J. T. Walsh (Edouard), William Converse-Roberts (Eugene)
A drama in 2 acts and 6 scenes. The action takes place in a garden studio behind the Morisot family's home in Paris circa 1870.

(No photos submitted)

Jeffrey Joseph, Kim Yancey, Robert Hancock in "Blues for Mr. Charlie"
(*Austin Trevett Photo*)

99

CIRCLE REPERTORY COMPANY

Marshall W. Mason, Artistic Director
Fourteenth Season

Managing Director, Richard Frankel; Executive Assistant to Managing Director, Carol True Palmer; Business Manager, Glynn Lowrey; Associate Artistic Director, Tony Giordano; Dramaturg, John Bishop; Casting Director, John Bard Manulis; Assistant to Mr. Mason, Glenna Clay; Production Manager, Michael Spellman; Stage Managers, Jody Boese, Fred Reinglas, Ginny Martino, Mark Lorenzen; Wardrobe, Miriam Nieves, Alice Connorton, Nina Schulman; Technical Director, Mark Henry; Props, Ginger Andrews; Fight Consultant, Peter Nets; Press, Richard Frankel, Reva Cooper.
Saturday, June 26— July 4, 1982 (41 performances)

A THINK PIECE by Jules Feiffer; Director, Caymichael Patten; Set, Kert Lundell; Costumes, Denise Romano; Lighting, Dennis Parichy; Sound, Chuck London Media/Stewart Werner; Stage Manager, Ginny Martino

CAST: Debra Mooney (Betty), Katherine Cortez (Pam), Andrew Duncan (Gordon), Ann Sachs (Mandy), Tenney Walsh (Ginny), Samantha Atkins (Lulu), Patches (Zero), Sara Saltus (Understudy)
  A play in three acts. The action takes place at the present time in the Castle's apartment in Manhattan in the East Eighties.

(CIRCLE REPERTORY THEATRE) Tuesday, August 3—September 2, 1982 (27 performances). Circle Repertory (Marshall W. Mason, Artistic Director) presents:
JOHNNY GOT HIS GUN by Dalton Trumbo; Adapted for the stage by Bradley Rand Smith; Director, Elinor Renfield; Set, Kert Lundell; Sound, Chuck London Media; Lights, Mal Sturchio; Costumes, Miriam Nieves; Assistant Director, Jonathan Hogan; Offstage Voices, Jonathan Bolt, Roger Chapman; "Amazing Grace" sung by Shami Chaikin; Production Manager, Ginn Martino; Stage Managers, Ann Bridgers, Jody Boese, Fred Reinglas, Adam Guettel; Technical Director, Mark S. Henry; Original Music, Adam Guettel; Press, Reva Cooper

CAST: Jeff Daniels (Joe Bonham)
  Performed without intermission. The action takes place in 1918 in the mind of Joe Bonham.

(CIRCLE REPERTORY THEATRE) Saturday, October 16,—November 28, 1982 (52 performances and 11 previews) Circle Repertory (Marshall W. Mason Artistic Director; Acting Artistic Directors, B. Rodney Marriott, Tanya Berezin) presents:
ANGELS FALL by Lanford Wilson; Director, Marshall W. Mason; Set, John Lee Beatty; Costumes, Jennifer von Mayrhauser; Lights, Dennis Parichy; Sound, Chuck London Media/Stewart Werner; Original Music, Norman L. Berman; Stage Manager, Fred Reinglas; Press, Richard Frankel, Reva Cooper

CAST: Fritz Weaver (Niles Harris), Nancy Snyder (Vita Harris), Danton Stone (Don Tabaha), Tanya Berezin (Marion Clay), Brian Tarantina (Salvatore (Zappy) Zappala, Barnard Hughes (Father William Doherty)
  A drama in two acts. The action takes place on a late Saturday afternoon in June of the present time in a mission in northwest New Mexico.

Josef Sommer, Tom Aldredge in "Black Angel"
(*Gerry Goodstein Photo*)

(CIRCLE REPERTORY THEATRE) Saturday, December 18, 1982—January 9, 1983(32 performances). Circle Repertory (Marshall W. Mason, Artistic Director) presents:
BLACK ANGEL by Michael Cristofer; Director, Gordon Davidson; Set and Costumes, Sally Jacobs; Lighting, John Gleason; Sound, Chuck London Media/Stewart Werner; Fights, Peter Nels; Stage Manager, Jody Boese; Press, Reva Cooper

CAST: Josef Sommer (Martin Engel), Mary McDonnell (Simone Engel), Burke Pearson (Claude), Tom Aldredge (Louis Puget), Jonathan Bolt (August Moreault), Jimmy Ray Weeks (Andy Raines/M.P./1st Hooded Man), Robert LuPone (Bob Hawkins/M.P./3rd Hooded Man), Lou Liberatore (M.P./2nd Hooded Man), Hooded Men: Evan A. Georges, William Snovell, Randell Spence
  A drama in two acts.

(CIRCLE REPERTORY THEATRE) Saturday, January 29—February 20, 1983. (36 performances). Circle Repertory Company (Marshall W. Mason, Artistic Director) presents:
WHAT I DID LAST SUMMER by A. R. Gurney, Jr.; Production Supervisor, B. Rodney Marriott; Set, John Lee Beatty; Costumes, Jennifer von Mayrhauser; Lighting, Craig Miller; Sound, Chuck London Media/Stewart Werner; Production Manager, Alex Baker; Props, G. Fred Null; Wardrobe, Nina Stachenfeld; Stage Managers, Suzanne Fry, Alexander Egan; Press, Reva Cooper

CAST: Ben Siegler (Charlie), Robert Joy (Ted) succeeded by Bruce McCarty, Debra Mooney (Grace), Christine Estabrook (Elsie), Ann McDonough (Bonny), Jacqueline Brookes (Anna Trumbull)
  A drama in two acts. The action takes place during the summer of 1945 in a summer colony on the Canadian shore of Lake Erie, near Buffalo, NY.

(CIRCLE REPERTORY THEATRE) Sunday, March 13—April 3, 1983 (39 performances). Circle Repertory Company presents:
DOMESTIC ISSUES by Corinne Jacker; Director, Eve Merriam; Set, David Potts; Costumes, Joan E. Weiss; Lighting, Dennis Parichy; Sound, Chuck London Media/Stewart Werner; Production Manager, Alex Baker; Fights, Tony Simotes; Stage Manager, Jody Boese; Press, Reva Cooper

CAST: Michael Ayr (Stephen Porter), Joyce Reehling Christopher (Susan Porter), Caroline Kava (Ellen Porter), Glynnis O'Connor (Nancy Graham), James Pickens, Jr. (George Allison), Robert Stattel (Larry Porter)
  A drama in two acts. The action takes place in Larry Porter's house in a Chicago suburb, during September of this year.

Ben Siegler, Jacqueline Brookes in "What I Did Last Summer"
(*Gerry Goodstein Photo*)

(CIRCLE REPERTORY THEATRE) Sunday, April 17—May 1, 1983 (20 performances). The Foundation of the Dramatists Guild and Circle Repertory Company present:

THE YOUNG PLAYWRIGHTS FESTIVAL with Sets by John Arnone: Costumes, Patricia McGourty; Lighting, Mal Sturchio; Sound, Chuck London Media/Stewart Werner; Original Music, Richard Weinstock; Artistic Director, Gerald Chapman; Managing Director, Peggy Hansen; Production Supervisor, B. Rodney Marriott

A NEW APPROACH TO HUMAN SACRIFICE by Peter Getty; Director, Garland Wright; Dramaturg, Wendy Wasserstein. **CAST:** Deborah Rush (Mrs. Wall), Christopher Durang (Michael), Edward Power (Mr. Wall), Blanche Baker (Susan), Greg Germann (Alvin), Brendan Murphy (Bobby)

I'M TIRED AND I WANT TO GO TO BED by David Torbett; Director, Gerald Chapman; Dramaturg, Michael Weller. **CAST:** Novella Nelson (Narrator), Greg Germann (Jerome), Jean DeBaer (Mother), Edward Power (Father)

THIRD STREET by Richard Colman; Director, Michael Bennett; Dramaturg, Michael Weller. **CAST:** Keith Gordon (Ron), Robert Alan Morrow (John), Brian Tarantina (Frank)

THE BIRTHDAY PRESENT by Charlie Schulman; Director, John Ferraro; Dramaturg, A. R. Gurney, Jr. **CAST:** Christopher Durang (Wallace), Jean DeBaer (Mary), Deborah Rush (Sheila), Bill Moor (Henry), Burke Pearson (Hopp), Kim Beaty (Lucy), Novella Nelson (Newscaster), Edward Power (Joe Flanagan), Brian Tarantina (TV Host)

(CIRCLE REPERTORY THEATRE) Wednesday, May 18, 1983 and still playing May 31, 1983. Circle Repertory Company (Marshall W. Mason, Artistic Director) presents the Magic Theatre of San Francisco's production of:

FOOL FOR LOVE by Sam Shepard; Director, Mr. Shepard; Set, Andy Stacklin; Costumes, Ardyss L. Golden; Lighting, Kurt Landisman; Sound, J. A. Deane; Associate Director, Julie Hebert; Lighting Supervisor, Mal Sturchio; Production Manager, Alex Baker; Stage Managers, Suzanne Fry, Jody Boese, Fred Reinglas; Press, Reva Cooper

CAST: Kathy Whitton Baker (May), Ed Harris (Eddie) succeeded by Will Patton, Dennis Ludlow (Martin) succeeded by Stephen Mendillo, Will Marchetti (Old Man) succeeded by John Nesci, Tom Aldredge

A drama performed without intermission. The action takes place at the present time in a motel room on the edge of the Mojave Desert.

Keith Gordon, Rob Morrow, Brian Tarantina in "Third Street" (*Gerry Goodstein Photo*)

Kathy Baker, Ed Harris in "Fool For Love" (*Gerry Goodstein Photo*)

CSC/CLASSIC STAGE COMPANY

Christopher Martin, Artistic Director
October 31, 1982—May 8, 1983
Sixteenth Season

Associate Director/Dramaturg, Karen Sunde; Assistant Artistic Director, Craig Kinzer; Managing Director, Dan J. Martin; Business Manager, Claudia Lee; Press, Krista M. Altok; Technical Director, Michael Meyer; Costumes, Miriam Nieves; Lighting, Rick Butler; Administrative Assistant, Seth J. Goldberg; Production Assistant, Bonnie Edgcomb; Stage Manager, Christine Michael; Resident Composer, Noble Shropshire; Press, Will Maitland Weiss
COMPANY: Christopher Martin, Karen Sunde, Ginger Grace, Thomas Lenz, Howard Lucas, Barry Mulholland, Mary Eileen O'Donnell, Noble Shropshire, Gary Sloan, Tom Spackman, Tom Spiller, Amy Warner, Walter Williamson
PRODUCTIONS (in repertory): *Faust Part One, Faust Part Two* by Johann Wolfgang von Goethe adapted by Philip Wayne, directed and designed by Christopher Martin; *Ghost Sonata* by August Strindberg, directed by Christopher Martin and Karen Sunde; *Wild Oats* by John O'Keefe, directed by Christopher Martin; *Balloon* by Karen Sunde, directed by Ms. Sunde and Mr. Martin; *Danton's Death* by Georg Buechner and directed by Mr. Martin.

Gerry Goodstein Photos

Gary Sloan, Tom Spackman, Christopher Martin in "Faust"
(*Gerry Goodstein Photo*)

Julie Garfield, Stefano Loverso in "Modern Ladies of Guanabacoa" (*Carol Rosegg Photo*)

ENSEMBLE STUDIO THEATRE

Curt Dempster, Artistic Director
Eleventh Season

Managing Director, David S. Rosenak; Literary Manager, Pamela Berlin; Stage Manager, Teresa Elwert; Technical Director, Barnard Baker; Production Coordinator, Lori Gale Hirschman; Associate Producer/Workshop Coordinator, Spence Halperin; Business Manager, Joyce Farra; Assistant to Artistic Director, Lori Steinberg; Press, Shirley Herz, Sam Rudy, Peter Cromarty
   Friday, November 12—December 5, 1982 (24 performances)
WELCOME TO THE MOON by John Patrick Shanley; Director, Douglas Aibel; Set, Evelyn Sakash; Costumes, Deborah Shaw; Lighting, Mal Sturchio; Musical Director, Barry Koron; Sound, Bruce Ellman
CAST: Robert Joy, John Henry Kurtz, Michael Albert Mantel, Anne O'Sullivan, James Ryan, June Stein
PROGRAM: The Red Coat, Let Us Go Out into the Starry Night, Out West, The Bull Made of Stars, Jimmy and the Doll, Down and Out, A Lonely Impulse of Delight, Ahoy!, October, Among Monuments and Devils, Welcome to the Moon
   Performed without intermission.
   Friday, January 14—February 13, 1983 (32 performances)
MODERN LADIES OF GUANABACOA by Eduardo Machado; Director, James Hammerstein; Set/Lighting, Bennet Averyt; Costumes, Deborah Shaw; Sound, Bruce Ellman; Music, Rick Vartorella; Stage Manager, Lisa DiFranza
CAST: Ellen Barber (Manuela), Larry Bryggman (Arturo), Julie Garfield (Adelita), Robert Hallak (Miguel), Tresa Hughes (Maria Josefa), Stefano Loverso (Mario), Susan Merson (Dolores), John Rothman (Ernesto), Jose Santana (Oscar)
   A drama in two acts. The action takes place in Guanabacoa, Cuba in 1928 and 1931.
   Sunday, March 6—April 10, 1983 (36 performances)
THE HOUSE OF RAMON IGLESIA by Jose Rivera; Director, Jack Gelber; Set, Brian Martin; Costumes, Deborah Shaw; Lighting, Cheryl Thacker; Stage Manager, Virginia Addison, Anne Marie Hopson; Technical Director, Richard Meyer; Props, Nan Siegmund
CAST: Roberto Badillo (Julio), Norman Briski (Ramon), Giancarlo Esposito (Javier), Michael Fischetti (Calla), Lisa Maurer (Caroline), Lionel Pina, Jr. (Charlie), Carla Pinza (Dolores)
   A drama in two acts. The action takes place in February 1980 in a house in Holbrook, NY.

102

THE CLASSIC THEATRE

Maurice Edwards, Artistic Director

Executive Director, Nicholas John Stathis; Production Director, Robert Anthony

(CLASSIC THEATRE) Friday, June 11—27, 1982 (12 performances)
THE DREAM KEEPER SPEAKS based on the poems of the late Langston Hughes; Director, Ernest Parham; Design, Donald L. Brooks; Lighting, Blaise Dupuy; Stage Manager, Rudyard Heady
CAST: John S. Patterson
  Performed with one intermission.
  Friday, September 23,—October 17, 1982 (16 performances)

HAMLET by William Shakespeare; Director, Shane Kilpatrick; Assistant Director, Set and Costumes, Fotini Dimou; Lighting, David Landau; Fencing, Anthony Passantino; Executive Assistant, Tina Vanessa Smith; Stage Manager, Lawrence Berrick; Producer, Nicholas John Stathis
CAST: David Erdiakoff (Hamlet), Richard Maxwell (Claudius), Linda Lehr (Gertrude), Michael Sutton (Polonius), Joe Maruzzo (Laertes), Holly Hawkins (Ophelia/Player Queen), Tom Moran (Horatio), Joseph Walsh (Rosencrantz), Andy Ciccarelli (Guildenstern), Wayne Rodda (Ghost), Robert Frederick (Player King/Osric), Eleni Lambros (Player Queen/Ophelia), Marshall Taylor (Marcellus), Norman Clark (Fortinbras/Grave Digger), Robert Tekampe (Cornelius/1st Grave Digger), Loren Bass (Francisco/Player/Lucianus/Messenger/Norwegian Captain), Nicholas Haylett (Voltemand/Reynaldo/English Ambassador), Jack Koenig (Bernardo/Gentleman/Priest)
  Thursday, October 28,—November 21, 1982 (16 performances)

LOVE AFFAIRS AND WEDDING BELLS by Johann Nestroy; Translated by Max Knight and Joseph Fabry; Director, Maurice Edwards; Set, Kevin Allen; Costumes, Susan Sudert; Lighting, David Landau; Music, Mordechai Sheinkman; Stage Manager, Neal Fox
CAST: Murray Moston (Herr von Lard), Mary Munger (Fritzi), Laura Perrotta (Ulrike), Eve Collyer (Lucis Thistle), Steven Lysohir (Ferdinand Buchner), John High (Marquis Francois de Vincelli), Scott Klavan (Alfred), Robert Anthony (Moon), David Berry (Innkeeper), Patricia Guinan (Innkeeper's Wife), Nili Yelin (Philippina), Peter Fortune (Kling/Snail), Barry Kulick (George/Policeman), Gregory Rangel (Heinrich/Policeman), Jane Snyder (Musician)
  A comedy of errors in 3 acts and 5 scenes. The action takes place during mid-19th Century in Austria.
  Thursday, December 2—19, 1982 (12 performances). The Classic Theatre in association with The East Lynne Company (Warren Kliewer, Artistic Director) presents:
A FESTIVAL OF AMERICAN PLAYS directed by Warren Kliewer. Concert readings of six plays once popular on the 19th Century American stage.
SHAKESPEARE IN LOVE by Richard Penn Smith; with J. C. Hoyt (Shakespeare), Laura Livingston (Anna), Michele LaRue (Clarence).
DAVY CROCKETT or Be Sure You're Right Then Go Ahead by Frank Murdoch; with Thomas L. Rindge (Narrator/Big Dan/Parson), Rob Neukirch (Davy Crockett), Jack Deisler (Oscar Crampton), David Higlen (Neil Crampton), Richard Stack (Maj. Roysten), Christian Deisler (Bob), Paula Gerhardt (Eleanor Vaughn), Shirley Bodtke (Dame Crockett).
TORTESA, THE USURER by Nathaniel Parker Willis; with James Collins (Narrator/Duke of Florence), John Genke (Tortesa), Jonathan Chappell (Count de Falcone), Jody Hingle (Zippa), William J. Daprato (Tomaso), Drew Keil (Angelo), Elizabeth Ann Reavey (Isabella de Falcone). **THE IMPOSSIBLE** by William Dean Howells; with Don Atkinson (Clarence Fountain), Linda Christian-Jones (Lucy Fountain), Michael T. Folie (Jules). **THE NIGHT BEFORE CHRISTMAS: A MORALITY** by William Dean Howells; with Don Atkinson (Clarence Fountain), Linda Christian-Jones (Lucy Fountain), Robert Hull (Frank Watkins), Lis Adams (Maggie), Maureen Donnelly (Minnie), Michael T. Folie (Hazard), Jonathan Ward (Jim), Danielle DuClos (Susy), Jimmy Wolf (Benny). **BRIDE ROSES** by William Dean Howells; with Reuben Schafer (Mr. Eichenlaub), Maureen Donnelly (The Lady), Robert Hull (Young Man), Lis Adams (Second Lady)
  Thursday, January 20,—February 13, 1983 (16 performances)
A SLIGHT ACHE/THE DWARFS by Harold Pinter; Director, Robert Anthony; Sets, Kevin Allen; Costumes, Jennifer Cook; Lighting, Pat Dignan; Stage Manager, John Goldstein
CAST: *A Slight Ache* with Jonathan Chappell (Edward), Dina Paisner (Flora), Warrington Winters (Matchseller). *The Dwarfs* with Craig Pinder (Len), Robert Chamberlain (Pete), Barry Kulick (Mark)
  Thursday, March 17,—April 10, 1983 (16 performances)

Top Right: John Patterson in "The Dreamkeeper Speaks" Below: Andy Ciccarelli, Joseph Walsh, David Erdiakoff in "Hamlet"

THE KNIGHT OF THE BURNING PESTLE by Francis Beaumont; Adapted and Directed by Ron Daley; Set, Bob Phillips; Lighting, Lisa Grossman; Production Manager, Lysbeth Hopper; Assistant Director, Marisa Cardinale; Music, Deena Kaye; Stage Manager, John Goldstein; Technical Director, Edmond Ramage
CAST: Edmond Ramage (Prologue), Amy Simon (Stage Manager), Stephen Root (Venturewell), Craig Purinton (Jasper Merrythought), Nancy Hammill (Luce Venturewell), Richard Abernethy (Humphrey), Laurie Oudin (Mistress Merrythought), Peter Smith (Michael Merrythought), Vince Nieman (Charles Merrythought), Rose Riggins (Musician)
  Thursday, April 28,—May 22, 1983 (16 performances)
THE FATHER by August Strindberg; Adapted by William Kramer; Director, Jerry Roth; Costumes, Claire MacDonald; Stage Manager, John Goldstein; Set, Bertha Rogers; Lighting, David H. Tasso; Assistant Stage Manager, Jodi Shaw; Special Makeup, Juliana Criss
CAST: John High (Captain), Chet Carlin (Pastor), Fritz Feick (Nojd), Patricia Mertens (Laura), Brent Shaphren (Doctor), Emmy Meyer (Margret), Danae Torn (Bertha)

EQUITY LIBRARY THEATRE

George Wojtasik, Managing Director
Fortieth Season

Production Director, Lynn Montgomery; Business Manager, Claude H. Maluenda; Officer Manager/Informals Producer, Julie Ellen Prusinowski; Development Directors, Caroline Muller, Barbara B. Johnson; Production Coordinator/Informals Producer, Stephanie Brown; Theatre Manager, Patrick J. Casey; Technical Director, Richard H. Malone, Michael Yarborough; Costumer, Ken Brown; Staff Assistant Musical Director, Nelson C. Huber; Sound, Hal Schuler; Press, Lewis Harmon.

(MASTER THEATRE) Thursday, September 23—October 10, 1982 (22 performances)
NOT NOW, DARLING by Ray Cooney and John Chapman; Director, William Koch; Set, Larry Fulton; Costumes, Barbara Blackwood; Lighting, Bruce A! Kraemer; Props, Paul Dana Naish; Wardrobe, Harriet Ross-Smith; Stage Managers, Lori M. Doyle, Katrina D. Jeffries.

CAST: Robert Lydiard (Arnold Crouch), Alynne Amkraut (Miss Tipdale), Ava Tulchin (Miss Whittington), Eliza Miller (Mrs. Frencham), Frederick Walters (Gilbert Bodley), Richard Portnow (Harry McMichael), Jane Culley (Janie McMichael), Regis Bowman (Mr. Frencham), Rusty Riegelman (Sue Lawson), Marilyn Alex (Made Bodley), Harry Bennett (Lawson), Standby for Rusty, Ava Tulchin
A comedy in two acts. The action takes place at the present time in the fourth floor salon of Bodley, Bodley & Crouch, an exclusive London firm of furriers, on a day in late September.

(MASTER THEATRE) Thursday, October 18—November 21, 1982 (30 performances)
NEW FACES OF 1952 originally produced by Leonard Sillman; Direction and Choreography, Joseph Patton; Co-Choreographer, Wende Pollock; Musical Director, Stephen Bates; Set, Rob Hamilton; Lighting, Phil Monat; Costumes, Julie Schwolow; Stage Managers, Renee F. Lutz, Ruth E. Kramer, Clark Taylor; Props, Thomas Harty; Wardrobe, Harriet Ross-Smith; Assistant Musical Director, Ken Uy; Press, Lewis Harmon.

CAST: Randy Brenner, Suzanne Dawson, Jack Doyle, Michael Ehlers, Lillian Graff, Anna Marie Gutierrez, Philip William McKinley, Roxann Parker, Michele Pigliavento, Alan Safier, Denise Schafer (succeeded by Eartha Kitt), Staci Sweeden, Michael Waldron
MUSICAL NUMBERS AND SKITS: Opening, Lucky Pierre, Guess Who I Saw Today, Restoration Piece, Love Is a Simple Thing, April in Fairbanks, Nanty Puts Her Hair Up, Oedipus Goes South, Time for Tea, Bal Petit Bal, Of Fathers and Sons, Three for the Road, The Pitch, Don't Fall Asleep, After Canasta What?, Lizzie Borden, I'm in Love with Miss Logan, Trip of the Month, Hark the Extra Marital Lark, Penny Candy, Boston Beguine, Whither America? (Another Revival?) or The Energy Contained in a Glass of Water Would Drive an Ocean Liner?, Monotonous, The Great American Opera, Finale
A revue in two acts.

Victoria Gabrielle Platt, Marcia Savella, Richard Voigts
in "Happy Birthday, Wanda June" (*Gary Wheeler Photo*)

Robert Lydiard, Rusty Riegelman, Alynne Amkraut
in "Not Now, Darling" (*Gary Wheeler Photo*)

(ELT/MASTER THEATRE) Thursday, December 2—19, 1982 (21 performances). Equity Library Theatre presents:
WHO'LL SAVE THE PLOWBOY? by Frank D. Gilroy; Director, Stephen Jarrett; Set, Allan Trumpler; Costumes, Arnold S. Levine; Lighting, Whitney Quesenbery; Stage Managers, David K. Black, Penny Marks; Wardrobe, Ali Davis; Hairstylist, Scott A. Mortimer; Press, Lewis Harmon

CAST: Suzanne Toren (Helen Cobb), Hardy Rawls (Albert Cobb), Michael Rothhaar (Larry Doyle), Emmett O'Sullivan-Moore (Doctor), Martha Miller (Mrs. Doyle), Jon Mindell (The Man), Kirk Caliendo (Joey Pike)
A play in 2 acts and 3 scenes. The action takes place in New York City two days before Christmas of 1959.

(ELT/MASTER THEATRE) Thursday, January 6—30, 1983 (30 performances). Equity Library Theatre presents:
THE ROBBER BRIDEGROOM adapted from the novella by Eudora Welty; Book and Lyrics, Alfred Uhry; Music, Robert Waldman; Director/Choreographer, Richard Casper; Musical Director, Keith Thompson; Set, Christian Thee; Costumes, Barbara Weiss; Lighting, Andrew Taines; Assistant to Director, Sari Ketter; Production Assistant, Scott Phillips; Wardrobe, Pamela Marlatt; Stage Managers, Trey Hunt, Mary E. Lawson, Pierce Bihm; Press, Lewis Harmon

CAST: Stephen Crain (Jamie Lockhart), Michael McCarty (Clemment Musgrove), Libby Garten (Rosamund), Carolyn Marlow (Salome), Patrick Richwood (Goat), Sean McGuirk (Little Harp), Paul Jackel (Big Harp), Michael Edwin (Innkeeper), Lynne V. Lamberis (Innkeeper's Wife), Ann-Ngaire Martin (Raven), Melinda Gilb (Goat's Mother), Jennifer Butt (Airie), Stephen Schmidt (Ship's Captain), Tony Gilbert (Preacher), and Jennifer Butt, Willy Falk, Steve Fickinger, Karen Longwell, Carmen Rupe
MUSICAL NUMBERS: Once Upon the Natchez Trace, Two Heads, Steal with Style, Rosamund's Dream, The Pricklepear Bloom, Nothin' Up, Deeper in the Woods, Riches, Love Stolen, Poor Tied Up Darlin', Goodbye Salome, Sleepy Man, Where Oh Where
A musical in two acts. The action takes place in and around Rodney, Mississippi in 1983 and 1795.

(ELT/MASTER THEATRE) Thursday, February 10—27, 1983 (22 performances). Equity Library Theatre presents:
HAPPY BIRTHDAY, WANDA JUNE by Kurt Vonnegut, Jr.; Director, Elowyn Castle; Set, Joe Mobilia; Costumes, Margie Peterson; Lighting, Mark Weingartner; Stage Manager, Penny Landau; Press, Lewis Harmon

CAST: David Adamson (Harold Ryan), Ward Asquith (Looseleaf Harper), Mark Ballou (Paul Ryan), Joyce Cohen (Penelope Ryan), James Mathers (Herb Shuttle), Dale Place (Dr. Woodly), Victoria Gabrielle Platt (Wanda June), Marcia Savella (Mildred), Richard Voigts (Siegfried von Konigswald)
A comedy in two acts. The action takes place in the Ryan apartment in a large city at the present time.

(ELT/MASTER THEATRE) Thursday, March 10—April 3, 1983 (30 performances). Equity Library Theatre presents:
WHERE'S CHARLEY? based on "Charley's Aunt" by Brandon Thomas; Book, George Abbott; Words and Music, Frank Loesser; Directed and Staged by Dennis Grimaldi; Choreography, Donald Mark; Musical Director, Jerald B. Stone; Set, Leo Meyer; Lighting, Steven T. Howell; Costumes, Colleen Muscha; Additional Choreography, Dennis Grimaldi; Dialect Coach, Dean Button; Props, Paul Dana Naish; Wardrobe, Leslie Meeker; Stage Managers, Nancy Kohlbeck, Susan Whelan, Nancy Rifkind, David Lober; Press, Lewis Harmon.

CAST: Charles Abbott (Charley), Jon Brothers (Humboldt/Ensemble), Austin Colyer (Spettigue), Byron Conner (Reggie/Ensemble), Clayton Davis (Jack), Carolyn DeLany (Patricia/Ensemble), Annette Hunt (Donna Lucia), Michael Irwin (Freddie/Ensemble), Chris Kahler (Gwen/Ensemble), Kelby Kirk (Twombley/Ensemble), Marin Mazzie (Kitty), William McClary (Wilkinson/Photographer/Ensemble), Nancy Miller (Gloria/Ensemble), Kevin Moore (Kenneth/Ensemble), Don Moran (Brassett), Jennifer S. Myers (Betty/Ensemble), Linda Paul (Rae/Ensemble), Erica Paulson (Ruth/Ensemble), Virginia Seidel (Amy), Jeffrey Shafer (Evelyn/Ensemble), Frank Torren (Sir Francis Chesney).
MUSICAL NUMBERS: The Years Before Us, Better Get Out of Here, The New Ashmolean Marching Society, My Darling, Make a Miracle, Serenade with Asides, Lovelier than Ever, The Woman in His Room, Pernambuco, Where's Charley?, Once in Love with Amy, The Gossips, At the Red Rose Cotillion, Finale
  A musical in 2 acts and 9 scenes.

(ELT/MASTER THEATRE) Thursday, April 14—May 1, 1983 (22 performances). Equity Library Theatre presents:
THE CHANGELING by Thomas Middleton and William Rowley; Director, Thomas Edward West; Set, Roger Benischek; Costumes, Martha Hally; Lighting, Richard Dorfman; Makeup Effects, Michael Laudati; Sound, Hal Schuler; Madmen's Masque, John Ford; Masque Choreography, Beth Kurtz; Stage Managers, D. Kyria Krezel, Marianne Cane, Virginia Jones; Production Assistant, Stacy M. Long; Hairstylist, Scott A. Mortimer; Press, Lewis Harmon.

CAST: John Armstrong (Vermandero), Lisa Bansavage (Beatrice), Alan Brooks (Alsemero), Jesse Caldwell (Tomaso de Piracquo), Joseph Costa (DeFlores), Ken Costigan (Alibius), Christopher Cull (Franciscus), Brenda Denmark (Grilla), Larry Filiaci (Pedro/Pelias), Myra Morris (Diaphanta), Kim Ivan Motter (Alonzo), Christopher S. Nelson (Jasperino), Patricia O'Donnell (Isabella), William L. Schwarber (Rhetias), Robert Trebor (Lollio), Gershon Tucker (Antonio).
  A Jacobean revenge tragedy in 2 acts and 12 scenes. The action takes place in the city of Alicante, Spain.

ELT/MASTER THEATRE Thursday, May 12—June 5, 1983 (30 performances). Equity Library Theatre (George Wojtasik, Managing Director) presents:
PROMISES, PROMISES by Neil Simon; Music, Burt Bacharach; Lyrics, Hal David; Based on Screenplay of "The Apartment" by Billy Wilder and I. A. L. Diamond; Director, Alan Fox; Choreography, Derek Wolshonak; Musical Direction, Bob Goldstone; Set, Bruce Monroe; Lighting, Fred Jason Hancock; Costumes, Van Broughton Ramsey; Props, Lisa Rosen; Wardrobe, Terry Eccles; Assistant to Director, Lisa Salomon; Assistant Choreographer, Tim Millett; Stage Managers, Vincent A. Feraudo, Cornelia Twitchell; Technical Director, Richard H. Malone; Press, Lewis Harmon. For original Broadway production, see THEATRE WORLD Vol. 25.

CAST: Kathleen Conry (Ms. Olson), C. J. Critt (Marge), Leslie Feagan (Dobitch), Paul F. Hewitt (Eichelberger), Larry Hirschhorn (Dr. Dreyfuss), Beth Leavel (Fran), Gordon Lockwood (Chuck), Tom McBride (Karl), Chris Reisner (Ginger), Lew Resseguie (Sheldrake), Peter J. Saputo (Vanderhof), Ron Wisniski (Mr. Kirkeby), Vocalists: Victoria Casella, Jessica Houston, Debora Stanton, Ensemble: Ralph Cole, Jr., David Merrill, John Milne, Lorena Palacios, Elyssa Paternoster, Alan Pratt, Mimi Quillin, Chris Reisner, Ralph Rodriguez, Tara Tyrrell
MUSICAL NUMBERS: Half as Big as Life, Grapes of Roth, Upstairs, You'll Think of Someone, It's Our Little Secret, She Likes Basketball, Knowing When to Leave, Where Can You Take a Girl, Wanting Things, Turkey Lurkey Time, A Fact Can Be a Beautiful Thing, Whoever You Are I Love You, Christmas Day, A Young Pretty Girl Like You, I'll Never Fall in Love Again, Promises Promises
  A musical in 2 acts and 15 scenes.

Top Right: Austin Colyer, Charles Abbott in "Where's Charley?"
Below: Elyssa Paternoster, Gordon Lockwood, C. J. Critt in
"Promises, Promises" *(Gary Wheeler Photos)*

EQUITY LIBRARY THEATRE INFORMALS

Stephanie Brown, Julie Ellen Prusinowski, Producers

(BRUNO WALTER AUDITORIUM/LINCOLN CENTER) Each production presented for three performances. Sept. 20—22, 1982: "Taking in the Grave Outdoors" by Ted Enik; Director, Kip Rosser; Lighting, Paul Gallo; with Jeffrey Bingham, Brian Kosnik, Terrence Markovich, Susan Blummaert, Jill Tomarken. Oct. 18—20, 1982: "My Early Years" by Charles Leipart; Director, Pat McCorkle; with Alice Elliott, Tom Toner. Nov. 22—24, 1982: "Nobody's Perfect" with book by Ron Sproat; Music, Earl Rose; Lyrics, Frank Evans; Director, J. Barry Lewis; Musical Director, Denise Puricelli; Stage Manager, Richard Valentine; with Mitchell Bonta, Jennifer Butt, Andy Gale, James Harder, Janet Koenig, Nevil Martyn, Doug McQueen, Marilyn Pasekoff, Charlie Schwartz, Barry Simpson, Peggy Stamper, Pattie Tierce, Joe S. Wyatt. Dec. 13—15, 1982: "Dreamboats" by Irene Wagner; Director, Lise Liepmann; with David Carson, Edwin Gur, Davis Hall, Avery Hart, Paul Mantell, Dale Place, Doug Popper, Ken Rubenfeld. Jan. 17—19, 1983: "Lead Us Not into Penn Station" by Maura Swanson; Director, Darlene Kaplan; with Jo Dedato Clark, Warren David Keith, Alice Elizabeth Pearl. Feb. 14—16, 1983: "Loose Joints" a musical revue with lyrics and sketches by Jim Morgan; Music, Alan Cove, Bob Lindner, Ed Linderman, Davia Sacks, Donald Seigal, Madeline Stone, Paul Trueblood; Director, Bill Gile; Choreography, George Bunt; Musical Director, Patrick Brady; Stage Manager, Todd Fleischer; with Sara Kreiger, Barbara Marineau, Diana Szlosberg, William Thomas, Jr., Eric Weitz. March 14—16, 1983: "Sharing" by James Van Maanen; Director, Stuart Ross; with John Patrick Hurley, Gene Lindsey, Tom Gerard, David Wirth. Apr. 25—27, 1983: "Independent Study" by Don Rifkin; Director, Duane Sidden; with Neil Alexander, Elf Fairservis, Brian Keeler, Julia Murray. May 9—11, 1983: Two One-act Plays directed by Julie Cesari; Music, Quinn Richards; Stage Manager, Stephen Powell; "Medusa in the Suburbs" by David Steven Rappoport with Frances Ford, Richard Tanner; "Le Petit Mort" by Stephen Essex with Ann Chapin, Lou Bonacki. June 6—8, 1983: "Rivertrip" by Rita Deanin Abbey; Adapted and Directed by Joshua Abbey; Choreography, Robert Dixon; Music, Kathleen Kernell; Lighting, Jack Jacobs; Stage Manager, Paul Harris; Producers, Rebecca Kreinen, Stephanie Brown; with Joffrey Spaulding, Aaron Abbey, Yve Eiholzer, Debra Flobery, Jackie Leigh, Lanyard Williams, Kathleen Kernell, Barbara Held

HENRY STREET SETTLEMENT'S NEW FEDERAL THEATRE

Woodie King, Jr., Steven Tennen, Producers
Thirteenth Season

(LOUIS ABRONS ARTS FOR LIVING CENTER) Thursday, June 3—20, 1982 (12 performances).
LOVE by Carolyn M. Rodgers; Conceived and Directed by Shauneille Perry; Costumes, Judy Dearing; Set, Robert Edmonds; Lighting, Sandra Ross; Dance Consultant, John Parks; Musical Consultant, Leone Thomas; Production Coordinator, Dwight R. B. Cook; Production Manager, Robert Edmonds; Technical Director, Bonnie L. Becker; Props, Sam Singleton; Wardrobe, Leona Heyward; Stage Manager, Fai Walker; Press, Warren Knowlton
CAST: Judy Dearing, Yvette Hawkins, Andre Robinson, Jr., Leone Thomas
The poems of Carolyn M. Rodgers presented in two parts: Love, the People.
Thursday, July 15—August 1, 1982.
JAZZ SET by Ron Milner; Director, Norman Riley; Music, Max Roach; Costumes, Judy Dearing; Set, Robert Edmonds; Lighting, Shirley Prendergast; Stage Manager, Richard Douglass; Assistant to Director/Understudy, Andre Worthy; Press, Warren Knowlton, Kojo Ade
CAST: S. Epatha Merkerson (Pianist), William Kennedy (Bassist), E. L. James (Drummer), Rony Clanton (Tenor), Mansoor Najee-Ullah (Alto), Nick Smith (Trumpet)
(HARRY DeJUR PLAYHOUSE) Friday, November 26—December 19, 1982 (7 performances and 7 previews)
PORTRAIT OF JENNIE adapted by Enid Futterman and Dennis Rosa from the novel by Robert Nathan; Music, Howard Marren; Lyrics, Enid Futterman; Direction and Choreography, Dennis Rosa; Musical Direction/Vocal Arrangements, Uel Wade; Orchestrations, William D. Brohn; Musical Continuity, Howard Marren, Uel Wade; Costumes, Charles Schoonmaker; Set, Michael H. Yeargan; Lighting, Jeff Davis; Projection, Wendall K. Harrington; Sound, David Congdon; Stage Manager, Richard Douglass; Production Assistants, Andre Worthy, Misty Owens; Casting, Barbara Sacharow; Assistant to Choreographer, John Caleb; Technical Director, Janice A. Matteucci; Wardrobe, Windsome McKoy; Production Manager, Robert Edmonds; Press, Warren Knowlton
CAST: Stratton Walling (Eben as an old man), Brent Barrett (Eben as a young man), Maggie O'Connell (Jennie as a little girl), Paul Milikin (Mr. Mathews), Jean Barker (Miss Spinney), Karyn Lynn Dale (Jennie as a young girl), David Wohl (Gus), Brian Phipps (Mr. Moore), John-Bedford Lloyd (Arne), Donna Bullock (Jennie as a young woman), Chorus: Marcia Brushingham, Nancy Cameron, Ann Deblinger, Marion Hunter, Marilyn O'Connell, Patricia Roark, Greg Anderson, John Caleb, Bob Freschi, Bobby Grayson, Robert W. Laur, James van Treuren, Martin van Treauren, Bob Wrenn
MUSICAL NUMBERS: Prologue, Winter of the Mind, Where I Come From, Hammerstein's Music Hall, My City, Wish, Alhambra Nights, Secrets, Portrait of Jennie, A Green Place, Remember Today, Paris, Time Stands Still in Truro, I Love You, Epilogue
A musical in two acts with a prologue and epilogue. The action takes place at the present time in the Metropolitan Museum of Art in New York City, and in 1938 in New York and in Truro.
HARRY DeJUR PLAYHOUSE Sunday, January 23—February 6, 1983 (12 performances).
ADAM with Book by June Tansey; Music and Lyrics, Richard Ahlert; Director, Don Evans; Choreography/Musical Staging, Dianne McIntyre; Costumes, Judy Dearing; Set, Llewellyn Harrison; Lighting, Shirley Prendergast; Choral/Dance Arrangements, Annie Joe Edwards; Sound, Michael Melziner; Orchestration/Solo Arrangements, Neal Tate; Produced by special arrangement with Gloria Turner and Don McGlone Stage Managers, C. Harrison Avery, Jr., Leigh Abernathy; Props, Andre Worthy; Press, Warren Knowlton, Max Eisen, Madelon Rosen
CAST: Jeff Bates (Charley/Reporter/Maitre D'), Frederick Beals (Congressman Mudd), Bill Boss (Congressman Gilgo), Richard Chiffy (Reporter), Dawn Davis (Sally/Louise/Southern Bell), Randy Flood (Don Marshall), Reuben Green (Adam Clayton Powell, Jr.), Suzanne Hall (Socialite), Hugh Harrell (Adam Clayton Powell, Sr.), Jackee Harry (Rachel Watts), Rosetta Evonne Jefferson (Serena Crawford), James Keels (Congressman Shanklin), S. Epatha Merkerson (Addie Carmichael), Kevin M. Ramsey (Charley/Bellboy/Young Militant/Clerk), Deborah Smith (Annie/Barmaid), Raymond Stough (Sam Bradbury), Robin M. Wilson (Mme. Rochais/Miss Lee), Kevin Anthony Wynn (Photographer/Young Brad)

Top Right: Judy Dearing, Andre Robinson, Jr., Yvette Hawkins in "Carolyn Rodgers' Love" Below: Minnie Gentry, Barbara Smith, Otis Young-Smith in "Trio" (_Bert Andrews Photos_)

MUSICAL NUMBERS: Prologue, Walk Just a Few Feet, The Strike, Operator, Prettiest Politician, Give Me the Power, 125th Street, L'Amour Dangereux, The Best Is None Too Good for Me, When I'm Your Woman, I'd Like to Propose a Bill, He Should Have Been Mine, He's Gotta Go, Mr. Harlem, Gilgo Shanklin & Mudd, We Got Grounds, Good Ole Boys, Lament and Argument, I Never Thought I'd See the Day, Let's Do It for Adam, Did I Get Too Far Away from You, In Bimini, We Kept the Faith, Look Who's Coming to Harlem
A musical in 2 acts and 32 scenes, celebrating the late Adam Clayton Powell, Jr.
HARRY DeJUR PLAYHOUSE Friday. March 18—April 17, 1983 (24 performances)
CHAMPEEEN! with Book, Music, Lyrics and Direction by Melvin Van Peebles; Musical Director, Bob Carten; Choreography, Louis Johnson; Set, Chris Thomas, Bob Edmonds; Lighting, Shirley Prendergast; Costumes, Quay Truitt; Sound, Louis Gonzalez; Stage Manager/Assistant to Mr. Van Peebles, Nate Barnett; Production Manager, Llewellyn Harrison; Production Coordinator, Bill Harris; Assistant Stage Managers, Frank Echols, Elizabeth Omilami; Hairstylist, Teddy Jenkins; Production Assistant, Megan Van Peebles; Props, Tim Ferguson; Technical Director, Janice Matteucci; Press, Warren Knowlton
CAST: Sandra Reaves-Phillips (Bessie Smith), Ruth Brown (Lilly), David Connell (Old Man), Lawrence Vincent (Referee), Ted Ross (Jack Gee), Ensemble: Louis Albert, Gary Easterling, Denise Elliott, John Forges, Herbert Kerr, Meachie Jones, Marcia James, Nanette LaChance, John D. McNally, DeNessa Tobin, Mario Van Peebles, Carolyn Webb, Charles Lavont Williams
MUSICAL NUMBERS: You Had Me Anyhow, Like a Dream, Home Ballet, Come to Mama, Opportunity, Knockout, The World's a Stage, Gimme a Pigfoot, Home, Tain't Nobody's Bizness If I Do, Ole Raggedy Song, Greasy Lightnin', Knockout
A musical in two acts based on the life of Bessie Smith.
HARRY DeJUR PLAYHOUSE Thursday, April 28—May 15, 1983 (12 performances).
TRIO by Bill Harris (three one-act plays); Director, Nathan George; Set, Llewellyn Harrison; Costumes, Vicki Jones; Sound, Sande Knighton; Lighting, DeWarren Moses; Executive Assistant, Barbara Tate; Chief Operating Officer, Michael Frey; Stage Managers, Imani, Pete Williams; Press, Warren Knowlton
CAST: Otis Young-Smith (Lewis), Gregory Jackson/Adetobi (#2), Daniel Carter (Saxophonist), Minnie Gentry (Preacher Woman), LeeRoy Giles (Rev. Sweet), Myra Anderson (Sister), Ellis Williams (Alphonse), Barbara Smith (Sheila), Obaka Adedunyo (Frank), S. Epatha Merkerson (Rula)
Performed with one intermission.

HUDSON GUILD THEATRE

David Kerry Heefner, Producing Director

(HUDSON GUILD THEATRE) Wednesday, October 20—November 7, 1982 (22 performances and 6 previews). Hudson Guild Theatre presents: HOOTERS by Ted Tally; Director, David Kerry Heefner; Associate Director, Daniel Swee; Set, Paul Kelly; Costumes, Joan E. Weiss; Lighting, Paul Wonsek; Production Assistants, Nancy L. Rifkind, Dana Handler; Props, Mariann Blaine; Stage Manager, Brian A. Kaufman; Production Manager/Technical Director, Edward R. F. Matthews; Press, Jeffrey Richards, Robert Ganshaw, Ted Killmer, Helen Stern, C. George Willard

CAST: Griffin Dunne (Clint) succeeded by Mark Rowen, Paul McCrane (Ricky), Susan Greenhill (Rhonda), Polly Draper (Cheryl)
A comedy in 2 acts and 12 scenes. The action takes place on a late-summer weekend in 1972 in a motel on Cape Cod and the beach nearby.

(HUDSON GUILD THEATRE) Tuesday, November 23—January 9, 1983 (14 performances and 28 previews). Re-opened at Lambs Theatre Thursday, May 19, and still playing May 31, 1983.
BREAKFAST WITH LES AND BESS by Lee Kalcheim; Director, Barnet Kellman; Set, Dean Tschetter; Costumes, Timothy Dunleavy; Lighting, Ian Calderon; Sound, Michael Jay; Associate Director, Daniel Swee; Marketing Director, John B. Fisher; Assistant Director, Donna Jacobson; Production Assistant, Laura Kravets; Props, Evie Ratner; Stage Manager, Brian A. Kaufman; Press, Jeffrey Richards, Ted Killmer

CAST: Amy Wright (Shelby Dischinger), Tom Nolan (Roger Everson), Holland Taylor (Bess), Keith Charles (Les), John Leonard (David Dischinger), Daniel Ziskie (Nate Moody/Announcer)
A comedy in 2 acts and 3 scenes. The action takes place during 1961 in the living room of Les and Bess Dischinger on Central Park South of New York City.

(HUDSON GUILD THEATRE) Wednesday, February 2—27, 1983 (15 performances and 13 previews). Hudson Guild Theatre presents:
BLOOD RELATIONS by Sharon Pollock; Director, David Kerry Heefner; Set, Ron Placzek; Costumes, Mariann Verheyen; Lighting, Paul Wonsek; Production Assistants, Bob Hallman, Sonja Lanzener; Dance Consultant, John Montgomery; Hairstylist, Frank Paul; Props, David Lober; Wardrobe, Susan Slagle; Stage Manager, Brian A. Kaufman; Press, Jeffrey Richards, Ted Killmer

CAST: Marti Maraden (Actress/Lizzie Borden), Jennifer Sternberg, (Miss Lizzie/Bridget), Adrian Sparks (The Defense/Dr. Patrick), Gerald J. Quimby (Harry Wingate), Kathleen Chalfant (Emma Borden), Sloane Shelton (Abigail Borden), Maurice Copeland (Andrew Borden)
A drama in two acts. The action takes place during the fall of 1902 and the summer of 1892 in the Borden house in Fall River, Massachusetts.

(HUDSON GUILD THEATRE) Sunday, April 10—May 1, 1983 (27 performances). Hudson Guild Theatre (David Kerry Heefner, Producing Director) presents:
SUS by Barrie Keeffe; Director, Geoffrey Sherman; Set and Lighting, Paul Wonsek; Costumes, Barbara Hladsky; Stage Manager, Brian A. Kaufman; Production Assistant, Michele Hinrichs; Press, Jeffrey Richards, Robert Ganshaw, Ben Morse

CAST: David Leary (Karn), John Curless (Wilby), Terry Alexander (Delroy)
A drama in 3 scenes, performed without intermission. The action takes place on Election Night of 1979 in a police station interrogation room in England.

Jack Aaron, Harvey Pierce in "Taking Steam"

Jennifer Sternberg, Marti Maraden in "Blood Relations" (*Charles Marinaro Photo*)

JEWISH REPERTORY THEATRE

Ron Avni, Artistic Director
Ninth Season

(EMANU-EL MIDTOWN YM-YWHA) Wednesday, October 12—November 7, 1982 (24 performances)
AFTER THE FALL by Arthur Miller; Director, William Shroder; Set, Jeffrey Schneider; Lighting, Phil Monat; Costumes, Karen Hummel; Stage Manager, Meryl Schaffer
CAST: Katherine Barry, Robin Bartlett, Rikke Borge, Krista Dien, Nancy Franklin, Eric Kohner, Vivienne Lenk, Michael Marcus, Kelly Monaghan, Peggy Moss, Garrison Phillips, Michael William Schwartz, Martin Shakar
Sunday, December 4, 1982—January 2, 1983 (20 performances)
FRIENDS TOO NUMEROUS TO MENTION by Neil Cohen, Joel Cohen; Director, Allen Coulter; Set, Geoffrey Hall; Costumes, Gayle Goldberg; Lighting, Naomi Berger; Stage Manager, Lawrence Rosenthal
Saturday, February 5—March 6, 1983 (23 performances)
IVANOV by Anton Chekhov; Director, Anthony McKay; Set, Mike Boyer; Costumes, Laura Drawbaugh; Lighting, Dan Kinsley; Original Music, David Sudaley; Stage Managers, Patrick D'Antonio, Lori Bloustein
CAST: Steven Amico, Donald Berman, Cecile Callan, Roger DeKoven, Henry Fonte, Martha Greenhouse, Viola Harris, Wilbur E. Henry, Ray Ivey, Daren Kelly, Marcia Jean Kurtz, William LeMassena, Lilene Mansell, Michael Albert Mantel, Anne Schwartz, Susan Thompson
Saturday, April 2—May 1, 1983 (23 performances)
TAKING STEAM by Kenneth Klonsky and Brian Shein; Director, Edward M. Cohen; Set, Adalberto Ortiz; Costumes, Melissa Binder; Lights, Dan Kinsley; Sound, John Morrison; Stage Managers, Thomas Quigley, Ben Steven
Saturday, May 28—June 26, 1983 (23 performances)
MY HEART IS IN THE EAST a musical inspired by the life and times of 12th Century Spanish poet, Judah Halevy; Book, Linda Kline; Music, Raphael Crystal; Lyrics, Richard Engquist; Director, Ran Avni; Sets, Jeffrey Schneider; Costumes, Karen Hummel; Lighting, Phil Monat; Choreographer, Wende Pollock; Sound, John Morrison; Stage Manager, Frank Heller

Adam Newman Photos

MANHATTAN PUNCH LINE

Steve Kaplan, Artistic Director
Fifth Season

Executive Director, Mitch McGuire; Producing Directors, Jerry Heymann, Richard Erickson; General Manager, Mark Richard; Production Supervisor, James T. Slater; Production Assistants, Arthur Brown, Ahmet Gillbey, George Litter, Henry Petty; Press, Jeffrey Richards, C. George Willard, Robert Ganshaw, Ted Killmer, Helen Stern, Richard Humleker (ACTORS & DIRECTORS THEATRE) Thursday, November 18—December 5, 1982. (15 performances). Manhattan Punch Line presents:
IT'S ONLY A PLAY by Terrence McNally; Director, Paul Benedict; Set, Bob Phillips; Costumes, Judianna Makovsky; Lighting, Ruth Roberts; Sound, Aural Fixation; Props, Christopher Santee; Assistant to Director, Mary Irwin; Stage Managers, Pamela Singer, Tony Berk.
CAST: Reg E. Cathey (Gus), Frances Cuka (Julia Budder), Paul Guilfoyle (Frank Finger), Ken Kliban (Ira Drew), Jill Larson (Virginia Noyes), Richard Leighton (James Wicker), Harriet Rogers (Emma), Michael Sacks (Peter Austin)
   A comedy in two acts. The action takes place at the present time in a bedroom in Julia Budder's townhouse in New York City.
   Thursday, December 16—29, 1982 (16 performances)
THE BUTTER AND EGG MAN by George S. Kaufman; Director, Steve Kaplan; Production Consultant, Anne Kaufman Sheiks; Set, William Barclay; Costumes, Karen Hummel; Lighting, Richard Dorfman; Music, The Savannah Sheiks; Props, Allan Benjamin; Assistant Director, James Weissenbach; Stage Manager, Jane MacPherson
CAST: Doug Baldwin (Bernie Simpson), Mary Boucher (Fanny Lehman), Kelly Connell (Oscar Fritchie), Tom Costello (Lehman), Therese Hanley (Peggy Marlowe), James Hawthorne (Cecil Denham), Terry Layman (Peter Jones), Neal Alan Lerner (Waiter), Valerie Mahaffey (Jane Weston), Robert McFarland (A. J. Patterson), Mitch McGuire (Mac), Kathrin King Segal (Kitty), Louise Shaffer (Mary Maxwell)
   A comedy in 3 acts and 4 scenes. The action takes place in the office of Lehmac Productions in New York City, and in a hotel room in Syracuse, NY.
   Thursday, February 3—27, 1983 (20 performances).
WITHOUT WILLIE by Barrie Cockburn; Director, Jerry Heymann; Set, John Wright Stevens; Lighting, Gregory MacPherson; Costumes, Oleksa; Sound, Gary Harris; Production Coordinator, Steven Shaw; General Manager, Terry Hodge Taylor; Associate Producer, Randall Robbins; Stage Manager, Laurie B. Clark
CAST: Lamis Beasley Faris (Fatma), Joan Lorring (Hertha), Loris Sallahian (Abdul), John Milligan (Roxy), David Khouri (Prince Yusuf)
   A comedy in three acts. The action takes place in a fictitious kingdom in Arabic North Africa on a Monday, Thursday and Friday of the present time.
   Thursday, April 14—May 1, 1983 (15 performances and 4 previews)
COMEDIANS by Trevor Griffiths; Director, Munson Hicks; Set, Rob Hamilton; Lighting, Betsy Adams; Costumes, Michelle Reisch; Stage Managers, Sheryl A. Kaller, Victoria Ruskin; Props, Lisa Graham; Casting, Simon Kunin
CAST: Gladys Fleischman (Caretaker), Tim Choate (Gethin Price), Tony Noll (Phil Murray), Tom Costello (George McBrain), Stefan Weyte (Sammy Samuels), Sam McMurray (Mick Connor), Alan North (Eddie Waters), Arthur Erickson (Ged Murray), Joseph Daly (Bert Challenor), Harsh Nayyar (Patel)
   A play in three acts. The action takes place at the present time in a secondary school, and in a workingman's club in Manchester, England.

Reg E. Cathey, Michael Sacks, Richard Leighton, Jill Larson, Frances Cuka in "It's Only a Play" (*Peter Cunningham Photo*)

MANHATTAN THEATRE CLUB

Lynne Meadow, Artistic Director
Barry Grove, Managing Director
Eleventh Season

(MANHATTAN THEATRE CLUB/DOWNSTAGE) Monday, June 7, 1982—July 10, 1982 (40 performances). Manhattan Theatre Club (Lynne Meadow, Artistic Director; Barry Grove, Managing Director) presents:
THE SINGULAR LIFE OF ALBERT NOBBS by Simone Benmussa; From a short story by George Moore; Translated by Barbara Wright; Directed and Designed by Miss Benmussa; Scenic Supervisor, Ron Placzek; Lighting Supervisor, Mal Sturchio; Associate Artistic Director, Douglas Hughes; General Manager, Connie L. Alexis; Assistant to Director, Liz Diamond; Production Assistant, Sally Mellis; Wig, Paul Huntley; Stage Managers, Amy Schecter, D. King Rodger; Production Manager, Peter Glazer; Technical Director, Brian Lago; Press, Patricia Cox, Bob Burrichter, Marina Sheriff.

CAST: Lucinda Childs (Hubert Page), Glenn Close (Albert Nobbs), Lynn Johnson (2nd Chambermaid), Anna Levine (Kitty Maccan), Patricia O'Connell (Mrs. Baker), Pippa Pearthree (Helen Dawes), Keliher Walsh (1st Chambermaid), David Warrilow (George Moore's Voice), D. King Rodger (Alec's Voice), Jamey Sheridan (Joe Mackin's Voice)
   A drama performed without intermission. The action takes place during the 1860's in a hotel in Ireland.

(MTC/DOWNSTAGE) Tuesday, September 21—November 7, 1982. (56 performances). Manhattan Theatre Club (Lynne Meadow, Artistic Director; Barry Grove, Managing Director) presents the Actors Theatre of Louisville production of:
TALKING WITH by Jane Martin; Director, Jon Jory; Set, Tony Straiges; Costumes, Jess Goldstein; Lighting, Pat Collins; Stage Managers, Elizabeth Ives, David K. Rodger; Sound, Mollysue Wedding; Tattoos, Jess Goldstein, Ellen Oshins; Press, Patricia Cox, Eliza Gaynor

CAST: Act I: "Fifteen Minutes" performed by Laura Hicks, "Scraps" performed by Penelope Allen, "Clear Glass Marbles" performed by Sally Faye Reit, "Audition" performed by Ellen Tobie, "Rodeo" performed by Margo Martindale, "Twirler" performed by Lisa Goodman, Act II: "Lamps" performed by Anne Pitoniak, "Handler" performed by Susan Cash, "Dragons" performed by Lee Anne Fahey, "French Fries" performed by Theresa Merritt, "Marks" performed by Lynn Milgrim

(MTC/UPSTAGE) Tuesday, October 12—November 14, 1982 (40 performances). Manhattan Theatre Club presents:
STANDING ON MY KNEES by John Olive; Director, Robert Falls; Costumes, Nan Cibula; Set, David Emmons; Lighting, William Mintzer; Associate Artistic Director, Douglas Hughes; Stage Managers, Johnna Murray, Alice Jankowiak; General Manager, Connie L. Alexis; Press, Patricia Cox, Eliza Gaynor, Marina Sheriff

CAST: Pamela Reed (Catherine), Tresa Hughes (Joanne), Jean DeBaer (Alice), Robert Neches (Robert)
   A drama in two acts.

Lucinda Childs, Glenn Close in "The Singular Life of Albert Nobbs"
(*Gerry Goodstein Photo*)

(MTC/CABARET) Tuesday, November 9—21, 1982 (16 performances). Manhattan Theatre Club (Lynne Meadows, Artistic Director; Barry Grove, Managing Director) presents:
DON'T START ME TALKIN' OR I'LL TELL EVERYTHING I KNOW: Sayings from the Life and Writings of Junebug Jabbo Jones by John O'Neal with Ron Castine and Glenda Lindsay; Director, Steven Kent; Based on a production directed by Curtis L. King; Technical Coordinator, Ruth Kreshka; Press, Patricia Cox, Marina Sheriff

CAST: John O'Neal in a one-man performance of folklore and anecdote.

(MTC/DOWNSTAGE) Tuesday, November 30, 1982—January 9, 1983 (64 performances). Manhattan Theatre Club presents:
THREE SISTERS by Anton Chekhov; New English version by Jean-Claude Van Itallie; Director, Lynne Meadow; Set, Santo Loquasto; Costumes, Dunya Ramicova; Lighting, Pat Collins; Music, Jonathan Sheffer; Sound, Chuck London Media/Stewart Werner; Stage Managers, Patrick Horrigan, Wendy Chapin; Assistant to Director, Michael Bush; Wardrobe, Ginger Travis Page; Wigs, Paul Huntley; Press, Patricia Cox, Marina Sheriff

CAST: Lisa Banes (Olga), Dianne Wiest (Masha), Mia Dillon (Irina), Jeff Daniels (Andrei), Christine Ebersole (Natasha), Baxter Harris (Fyodor), Sam Waterston (Alexander Vershinin), Bob Balaban (Baron Nicolai Tuzenbach), Stephen McHattie (Vasily Solyony), Jack Gilford (Ivan Romanic Chebutykin), Brian Hargrove (Alexei Fedotik), Gene O'Neill (Vladimir Rode), Jerome Collamore (Messenger), Margaret Barker (Anfisa), Rosemary Quinn (Maid), Standbys: George Bamford (Solyony/Fedotik/Rode), James Burge (Kulygin/Vershinin), Sheila Coonan (Anfisa/Maid), Brian Hargrove (Tuzenbach), Gene O'Neill (Andrei), Rosemary Quinn (Olga/Masha), Denise Stephenson (Irina/Natasha), John Straub (Chebutykin/Feraport)
A drama in 4 acts performed with two intermissions. The action takes place in a provincial Russian town.

(MTC/UPSTAGE) Thursday, December 30, 1982—February 20, 1983 (72 performances). Manhattan Theatre Club (Lynne Meadow, Artistic Director; Barry Grove, Managing Director) presents:
SKIRMISHES by Catherine Hayes; Director, Sharon Ott; Set, Kate Edmunds; Costumes, Susan Hilferty; Lighting, Dennis Parichy; Dialect Coach, Timothy Monich; Stage Managers, Barbara Abel, Daniel Kanter; Press, Patricia Cox, Marina Sheriff

CAST: Suzanne Bertish (Jean), Fran Brill (Rita), Hope Cameron (Mother)
Performed without intermission. The action takes place at the present time in England.

(MTC/DOWNSTAGE) Tuesday, January 25—March 6, 1983 (48 performances). Manhattan Theatre Club presents:
SUMMER by Edward Bond; Director, Douglas Hughes; Set, Tony Straiges; Costumes, Linda Fisher; Lighting, Pat Collins; Music, Paul Sullivan; Sound, Chuck London Media/Stewart Werner; General Manager, Connie L. Alexis; Stage Manager, John Beven; Press, Patricia Cox, Marina Sheriff

CAST: David Pierce (David), Frances Sternhagen (Xenia), Caitlin Clarke (Ann), Betty Miller (Marthe), Tom Brennan (Heinrich Hemmel), Standbys: John Clarkson (Hemmel), Jean Matthiessen (Xenia/Marthe), Denise Stephenson (Ann)
A drama in 3 acts and 7 scenes. The action takes place at the present time on the terrace of a cliff house facing the sea in Eastern Europe.

(MTC/UPSTAGE) Tuesday, March 8—April 10, 1983 (40 performances). Manhattan Theatre Club presents:
TRIPLE FEATURE with Sets by Pat Woodbridge; Costumes, Jess Goldstein; Lighting, Ann Wrightson; Wardrobe, Susan Andrews; Stage Managers, David K. Rodger, Dan B. Sedgwick, Chris Fielder; Press, Patricia Cox, Marina Sheriff

CAST: "Slacks and Tops: by Harry Kondoleon; Director, Douglas Hughes; with Sasha von Scherler (Wanda), Amy Wright (Connie), Dan B. Sedgwick (Todd), Eddie Jones (Edwin), Jessica Rene Carroll (Ginger). "Half a Lifetime" by Stephen Metcalfe; Director, Dann Florek; with James Rebhorn (Tobias), Peter Zapp (Spalding), John Goodman (Winninger), J. T. Walsh (Winter). "The Groves of Academe" by Mark Stein; Director, Steven Schachter; with Terrance O'Quinn (Bill Groves), Neal Jones (Paul Morris)
Three one-act plays presented with two intermissions.

(MTC/DOWNSTAGE) Sunday, April 10—May 1, 1983 (48 performances). Manhattan Theatre Club presents:
ELBA by Vaughn McBride; Director, Tom Bullard; Set, Kate Edmunds; Costumes, Patricia McGourty; Lighting, Dennis Parichy; Sound, Chuck London Media/Stewart Werner; Stage Managers, Susie Cordon, James Dawson; Assistant to Director, Liz Wright; Production Assistant, Lauren Schneider; Wardrobe, James Latus; Press, Patricia Cox, Marina Sheriff

CAST: James Whitmore (Don), Audra Lindley (Flo), Frank Hamilton (Young Roy Eames), Ann Wedgeworth (Harley), Barbara Sohmers (Lete), Standbys: Helen Jean Arthur (Flo), Nesbitt Blaisdell (Don/Young Roy Eames)
A play in two acts. The action takes place during the summer of the early 1960's in the main room of a small ranch house in Elba, Idaho.

(MTC/UPSTAGE) Tuesday, April 26—May 29, 1983 (40 performances). Manhattan Theatre Club presents:
EARLY WARNINGS by Jean-Claude van Itallie; Director, Steven Kent; Set, David Potts; Costumes, Gwen Fabricant; Lighting, Dennis Parichy; Sound, Bill Dreisbach, Don Preston; Stage Managers, Ruth Kreshka, Patrick D'Antonio; Press, Patricia Cox, Marina Sheriff

CAST: "Bag Lady": Shami Chaikin (Clara);
"Sunset Freeway": Rosemary Quinn (Judy);
"Final Orders": Colin Stinton (Angus McGrath), Evan Handler (Mike Patterson). Presented with two intermissions.

(MTC/DOWNSTAGE) Friday, May 20—June 26, 1983 (37 performances). Manhattan Theatre Club (Lynne Meadow, Artistic Director) presents:
ON THE SWING SHIFT with Music by Michael Dansicker; Lyrics, Sarah Schlesinger; Set, Tony Straiges; Costumes, Jess Goldstein; Lighting, Arden Fingerhut; Sound, Chuck London Media/Stewart Werner; Arrangements and Musical Supervision, Michael Dansicker; Musical Director, Janet Glazener; Choreography, Janie Sell; Production Supervised by Martin Charnin; Stage Managers, David K. Rodger, Mindy K. Farbrother; Press, Patricia Cox, Marina Sheriff

CAST: Kay Cole (Vera), Valerie Perri (Dot), Ann-Ngaire Martin (Maise), Standbys: Christine Anderson, Kimberly Kish
MUSICAL NUMBERS: Morning, Row 10 Aisle 6 Bench 114, We Got a Job to Do, There's a War Going On, Bond Sequence, Killing Time, When Tomorrow Comes, I'm Someone Now, Something to Do Tonight, Night on the Town, Chorale, Evening
Performed without an intermission.

Fran Brill, Suzanne Bertish in "Skirmishes" Above: Mia Dillon, Lisa Banes, Dianne Wiest in "Three Sisters" (*Gerry Goodstein Photo*)

THE MEAT & POTATOES COMPANY

Neal Weaver, Artistic Director
Seventh Season

Administrative Director, Marilys Ernst; Treasurer, Elliott Landen; Costumer, Carol Van Valkenburg; Administrative Assistant, Diane Lane; Photographer, Herbert Fogelson; Lighting, David L. Arrow
(ALVINA KRAUSE THEATRE) Friday, July 1—August 1, 1982 (20 performances). The Meat and Potatoes Company presents:
THE UNEXPECTED GUEST by Agatha Christie; Director, Neal Weaver; Assistant Director, Jay Berman; Lighting, Terry H. Wells; Stage Managers, Press, Diane Lane, Mary Colgan
CASE: Jay Berman (Richard Warwick), Tom Crawley (Julian Farrar), Edward Hyland (Michael Starkwedder), Barbara Leto (Laura Warwick), Dale Merchant (Jan Warwick), Tessa M. Mills (Mrs. Warwick), Richard Payne (Sgt. Cadwallader), Joel Parsons (Insp. Thomas), Steve Rapella (Henry Angell), Jeanne Schlegel (Miss Bennett)
   Thursday, September 2—October 2, 1982 (20 performances)
'TIS PITY SHE'S A WHORE by John Ford; Director, Neal Weaver; Set, Bonnie Arquilla; Choreographer, Jane E. Dwyer; Fight Choreography, Neil Samuels; Stage Managers, Bernita Robinson, Ivelisse Diaz
CAST: Robert Barbalato (Servant/Officer), Jonathan Cantor (Servant-/Guest/Banditti), John P. Connolly (Vasques) succeeded by Steve Lovett, James Cimino (Poggio), Rick Copeland (Giovanni), Leslie Den Dooven (Annabella), Jean Gennis (Philotus), Steve Kollmorgen (Grimaldi/Banditti), Elliott Landen (Florio), Ben Lemon (Soranzo), Jinx Lindenauer (Putana), Mark McGovern (Cardinal), Paul Meacham (Richardetto), Kevin Osborne (Bergetto/Banditti), Henry J. Quinn (Friar Bonaventure), Stanley Sayer (Donado), Kathryn C. Sparer (Hippolyta)
   Thursday, October 14—November 14, 1982 (20 performances)
A PLACE ON THE MAGDALENA FLATS by Preston Jones; Director, Jon Teta; Set, Bonnie Arquilla; Stage Manager, Garwood; Incidental Music, Michael Ferraro
CAST: Toni Genfan Brown (Wanda), Bob Donahoe (Booger), Bill Fears (Carl Grey), Jeanne Morrissey (Charlene), Scott Renderer (Frank), Armando Rivas (George Sandoval), Valerie Shaldene (Mary Helen Kilgore), Jennifer Sullivan (Patsy Jo Boatright)
   Wednesday, November 24—December 19, 1982 (20 performances)
A SCRAP OF PAPER by Victorien Sardou; English version by Leonie Gilmour; Direction/Set, Neal Weaver; Stage Managers, Joanna Allen, Cathy Heusel, Bill Johnson, Caitlin Kelly, Ken Natter
CAST: Leslie Den Dooven (Clarisse), Bob Donahoe (Busonier), Judith Greentree (Mme. Solange), Bill Johnson (Henri), David Kampman (M. Vanhove), Caitlin Kelly (Caludine), Casey Kizziah (Prosper Block), Steve Lovett (Paul), Lenore Manzella (Colomba/Mme. Thirion), Denise McCarthy (Martha), Ken Natter (Hercule/Servant), Donald Pace (M. Thirion), Terry Price (Suzanne)
   Thursday, January 13—February 13, 1983 (20 performances)
CANDIDA: by George Bernard Shaw; Direction/Set, Neal Weaver; Stage Manager, Tom Vaccaro
CAST: Robert Caccomo (Lexy Mill), Jayne Chamberlin (Prossy), Robin Lawson (Manes Morrell), Bradford Minkoss (Marchbanks), Elissa Napolin (Candida), Donald Pace (Burgess)
   Thursday, February 24—March 27, 1983 (20 performances)
THE PLAYBOY OF THE WESTERN WORLD by J. M. Synge; Director, Herbert DuVal; Set, Toru Shimakawa; Costumes, Madeleine Doran-McEvoy, Barbara Gerard; Props, Joanna Allen, Cathy Heusel; Dance Consultants, Alice McInerney, Elissa Napolin; Stage Manager, Tom Vaccaro
CAST: Patricia Kalember (Pegeen Mike), Warren Sweeney (Shawn Keogh), James Harder (Michael James), Donald Pace (Philly Cullen), David Emge (Jimmy Farrell), Alexander MacDonald (Christopher Mahon), Leslie Lyles (Widow Quinn), Barbara Callander (Sara Tansey), Sue Ellen Hunter (Susan Brady), Elizabeth Harder (Honor Blake), Frank Vohs (Old Mahon)
   Thursday, April 7—May 8, 1983 (20 performances)
SHE STOOPS TO CONQUER by Oliver Goldsmith; Director, Casey Kizziah; Stage Manager, Penny Weinberger
CAST: David Barbee (Diggory), Frances Ford (Mrs. Hardcastle), Jonathan Fuller (Tony Lumpkin), Darian Harris (Kate Hardcastle), Christopher Holloway (Jeremy), Barbara Leto (Constance), Joseph O'Brien (Sir Charles), Joel Parsons (Hardcastle), Patricia Powers (Maid), Douglas Werner (Hastings), Scott Winters (Charles Marlow), Joseph O'Brien (Sir Charles), Christopher Holloway (Jeremy)
   Saturday, April 9—10, 1983 (2 performances)

Top Right: Elissa Napolin, Bradford Minkoff in "Candida" Below: Scott
   Renderer, Valerie Shaldene in "A Place on the Magdalena Flats"

BENCHLEY BESIDE HIMSELF conceived, adapted and performed by Donald Pace in two acts. Stage Manager, Charlie St. John
   Sunday, May 1—4, 1983 (4 performances)
IRREVOCABLY YOURS from the letters and lyrics of Edna St. Vincent Millay; Arranged and performed by Elissa Napolin; Music Coordinator, Donald Pace; Stage Managers, Penny Weinberger, Kevin Osborne
   Thursday, May 19—June 19, 1983 (20 performances)
TIGER AT THE GATES by Jean Giraudoux; Adapted by Christopher Fry; Director, Neal Weaver; Set, Jim Gilmartin; Lighting, Janet Herzenberg; Stage Managers, Joseph Scott, Elliott Landen, Becca Bean, Jeff Buckland
CAST: Stephen Bess (Priam's Guard), Stephanie Beswick (Lady-in-waiting/Iris), Richard Bourg (Ulysses), Rick Copeland (Troilus), Leslie Den Dooven (Andromache), Derek Edward-Evans (Hector), Raymond Farraday (Abneos), Mitchell Gossett (Olpides/Hector's Guard) succeeded by Joseph Scott, Elliott Landen (Mathematician), Barbara Leto (Cassandra), Michael Levine (Old Man/Top Man), Dunsten J. McCormack (Paris), Tessa Mills (Hecuba), Ken Natter (Busiris), Donald Pace (Demokos), Jack Poggi (Priam), Aleaze Schaap-Rios (Laundry Maid), Jeanette Topar (Polyxene), Frank Rand (Ajax), Lynn Weaver (Helen)

Herbert Fogelson Photos

NEGRO ENSEMBLE COMPANY

Douglas Turner Ward, Artistic Director
Sixteenth Season

Managing Director, Leon B. Denmark; Administrative Manager, William Edwards; Production Manager, Karen Johnson-Vundia; Technical Director, Rodney J. Lucas; Production Supervisor, Clinton Turner Davis; Stage Managers, Janice C. Lane, Edward Deshae; Press, Howard Atlee, Barbara Atlee

(WESTSIDE ARTS CENTER/CHERYL CRAWFORD THEATRE)
Thursday, June 3, 1982–July 18, 1982 (56 performances). The Negro Ensemble Company (Douglas Turner Ward, Artistic Director; Leon B. Denmark, Managing Director) presents:
ABERCROMBIE APOCALYPSE by Paul Carter Harrison; Director, Clinton Turner Davis; Set, Wynn Thomas; Costumes, Myrna Colley-Lee; Lighting, Shirley Prendergast; Sound, Gary Harris; Production Manager, Susan E. Watson; Stage Managers, Femi Sarah Heggie, Chester A. Sims; Technical Director, Rodney J. Lucas; Props, Lisa L. Watson; Wardrobe, Vicki Jones; Press, Howard Atlee, Ellen Levene, Barbara Atlee, Jerry Mickey

CAST: Graham Brown (Culpepper), Timothy B. Lynch (Jude), Barbara Montgomery (Bethesda)

A drama in two acts. The action takes place at the present time on the Abercrombie Estate.

(THEATRE FOUR) Friday, January 28—February 20, 1983. (29 performances and 16 previews). NEC presents:
SONS AND FATHERS OF SONS by Ray Aranha; Director, Walter Dallas; Set, Wynn Thomas; Costumes, Vicki Jones; Lighting, William H. Grant III; Sound, Gary Harris; Costume Supervisor, Judy Dearing; Stage Manager, Horacena J. Taylor

CAST: Olivia Virgil Harper (Sister 2), Sarallen (Sister 1), Ethel Ayler (Sister 3), Eugene Lee (Clyde), Howard Baines (Emmitt), Graham Brown (Fred T. Blachley/Johnny), Robert Gossett (Bubba/Bruce), Phylicia Ayers-Allen (Vickie/Melanie)

A drama in two acts. The action takes place around 1943 in a rural Southern town in Mississippi, around 1953 in the same town, and around 1960 in an all-Black university in Tallahassee, Florida.

Eugene Lee, Graham Brown in "Sons and Fathers of Sons"
(Bert Andrews Photo)

Douglas Turner Ward in "About Heaven and Earth"
(Bert Andrews Photo)

(THEATRE FOUR) Tuesday, April 12—May 1, 1983 (33 performances)
ABOUT HEAVEN AND EARTH (3 one-act plays) Director, Douglas Turner Ward; Production Assistant, Lisa Watson; Stage Manager, Femi Sarah Heggie; Management, Dorothy Olim Associates; Press, Howard Atlee, Barbara Atlee

CAST: "The Redeemer" by Douglas Turner Ward; with Naomi Riseman (Old Lady), Curt Williams (Rabbi), L. Scott Caldwell (Black Woman), Kathleen Forbes (Feminist), David Davies (White Revolutionary), Eugene Lee (Black Man). The Action takes place at Easter in Anywhere U.S.A. "Nightline" by Julie Jensen; with Naomi Riseman (Sarah), L. Scott Caldwell (Raimy), Eugene Lee (Ogilvy), Curt Williams (Driver). The action takes place at the present time on a Greyhound bus. "Tigus" by Ali Wadud; with Douglas Turner Ward as Tigus. The action takes place at the present time in Harlem.

(THEATRE FOUR) Tuesday, May 17—June 5, 1983 (32 performances). The Negro Ensemble Company (Douglas Turner Ward, Artistic Director) presents:
MANHATTAN MADE ME by Gus Edwards; Director, Douglas Turner Ward; Set and Costumes, Felix E. Cochren; Lights, Sylvester N. Weaver, Jr.; Sound, Bernard Hall; Stage Managers, Ed DeShae, Jesse Wooden, Jr.; Production Assistant, Lisa Watson; Props, Win Anderson; Press, Howard Atlee, Barbara Atlee

CAST: Eugene Lee (Barry Anderson), Kathleen Forbes (Claire McKenzie), Robert Gossett (Duncan), David Davies (Alan McKenzie)

A drama in two acts. The action takes place in Claire's apartment in New York City.

NEW YORK THEATRE STUDIO

Richard V. Romagnoli, Artistic Director
Sixth Season

Managing Director, Cheryl Faraone; Artistic Associate, Susan Sharkey; Administrative Director, Sally Burnett; Director Special Projects, Deborah Ensign; Press, Patt Dale, Jim Baldassare

(AMDA STUDIO ONE) Sunday, Janary 30—February 20, 1983 (20 performances). New York Theatre Studio presents:
OUR LORD OF LYNCHVILLE by Snoo Wilson; Director, Richard V. Romagnoli; Sets, Gerard P. Bourcier; Costumes, Karen Matthews; Sound, Ron Annas; Lighting, John Hickey; Production Manager, Moss Hassell; Stage Managers, Sally Burnett, Tom Stamp, Donna Rossler; Dialect Consultant, Timothy Monich; Technical Director, Bill Wells; Press, Patt Dale, Jim Baldassare

CAST: Leon Russom (Dr. Windfall), K. C. Kelly (Ed), Megan Bagot (Candy), Debra Jo Rupp (Charlene), Don Perkins (Pa), Ned Eisenberg (Pete), Tom Stamp (Charlie), Gisele Richardson (Lazy Susan), Tom Carder (Announcer)
A "surreal comedy" in 2 acts and 5 scenes. The action takes place at the present time in Lynchville, a mythical city in Virginia.

(AMDA STUDIO ONE) Sunday, February 27—March 20, 1983 (20 performances). New York Theatre Studio (Richard V. Romagnoli, Artistic Director; Cheryl Faraone, Managing Director) presents:
LOVING RENO by Snoo Wilson; Director, Dorothy Lyman; Set, Gerard P. Bourcier; Costumes, Timothy Dunleavy; Sound, Tommy Hawk; Lighting, John Hickey; Production Manager, Moss Hassell; Technical Director, Bill Wells; Wardrobe, Mark Finley; Hairstylist, Richard Greene; Stage Managers, Sherry Cohen, Paula Cohen, Devon O'Brien; Press, Patt Dale, Jim Baldassare

CAST: Robin Strasser (Margarita), Mark Blum (Johnson) succeeded by Leon Russom, Manuel Sebastian (Reno), Kim Delaney (Dory), Robin Roosa (Adrienne), Shami Chaikin (Marie), Understudy: Devon O'Brien (Margarita/Dory)
A play in two acts. The action takes place at the present time in an aircraft waiting room in a private airport in Florida.

(AMDA STUDIO ONE) Wednesday, March 30—April 17, 1983 (20 performances). New York Theatre Studio (Richard V. Romagnoli, Artistic Director) presents:
THE QUILLING OF PRUE by Mary Kojis; Director, Cheryl Faraone; Original Music/Musical Director, James Petosa; Set, Loy Arcenas; Costumes, James Delaney Collum; Sound, Tommy Hawk; Lighting, John Hickey; Stage Managers, Moss Hassell, Michael Verbil; Assistant Director, Sally Burnett; Technical Director, Bill Wells; Wardrobe, Mark R. Finley; Props, Wendy Pepper; Movement Consultant, Grant Stewart; Press, Patt Dale, Jim Baldassare

CAST: Robert LuPone/Philip LeStrange (Rev. Prue Dimmes), Timothy Wahrer (Duncan Albright), Megan Bagot (Frances Dimmes), Mary Jay (Mother Dimmes), Sally Burnett (Priestess/Bride), Timothy Jenkins (Rev. Firmin St. Cloud/Novice Master), Understudy: Tom Stamp
A drama in two acts. The action takes place in a seminary, the Dimmes and Albright homes, an art gallery, and Frances' apartment.

(AMDA STUDIO ONE) Sunday, May 8—June 5, 1983 (24 performances). The New York Theatre Studio presents:
MARY BARNES by David Edgar; Based on "Mary Barnes; Two Accounts of a Journey through Madness" by Mary Barnes and Joseph Berke; Director, Gideon Y. Schein; Set, Richard Hoover; Costumes, Pamela Scofield; Sound, Tommy Hawk, Jesse Plumley; Production Manager, Moss Hassell; Casting, David Tochterman; Stage Managers, Nicholas Dunn, Deborah Ensign, Cheryl Butler; Technical Director, Bill Wells; Dialect Consultant, Stanley Tucci; Wardrobe, Mark R. Finley; Press, Patt Dale, Jim Baldassare

CAST: Dennis Bailey (Zimmerman), William Brenner (Simon), Lance Davis (Eddie), Laura Esterman (Mary Barnes), Monique Fowler (Angie), James Hurdle (Hugo), Martin LaPlatney (Douglas), Bruce MacVittie (Keith), Ted McAdams (Angie's Brother), Deirdre O'Connell (Beth), Margo Skinner (Brenda), Angela Thornton (Angie's Mother), John Tillotson (Laurence), Understudy: Tom Stamp
A drama in two acts. The action takes place in a large old house in East London, beginning in 1965.

Top Right: Demetra Karras, Robert LuPone in "The Quilling of Prue"
Below: Martin LaPlatney, Laura Esterman, Lance Davis in "Mary Barnes" (*Martha Swope Photos*)

OPEN SPACE THEATRE EXPERIMENT

Lynn Michaels, Artistic Director
Eleventh Season

Administrator, Harry Baum; Administrative Assistant, Donna Herman; Technical Directors, Rick Shannin, Ken Young; Press, Jeffrey Richards Associates
(OPEN SPACE THEATRE) Thursday, October 14,—November 14, 1982 (20 performances)
THE TWO-CHARACTER PLAY by Tennessee Williams; Director, Tom Brennan; Set, Bob Phillips; Costumes, Sigrid Insull; Lighting, Greg MacPherson
CAST: Austin Pendleton, Barbara eda-Young
Monday, April 11—24, 1983 (12 performances and 6 previews)
IN THE COUNTRY by Griselda Gambaro; Translated and adapted by Susana Meyer, Francoise Kourilsky; Director, Francoise Kourilsky; Set, Beth Kuhn; Lighting, Gregory MacPherson; Costumes, Deborah Van Wetering; Original Music, Michael Sirotta; Sound, Phil Lee; Stage Manager, Crystal Huntington
CAST: Colette Berge (Emma), James Eckhouse (Frank), Adam LeFevre (Man), Daniel Ziskie (Martin), Emmanuel Dom (Frank's Man), Tom Radigan (Frank's Man), Eric Hall (Piano Tuner)
Performed without intermission. The action takes place at the present time in the country.
Wednesday, May 18,—June 5, 1983 (15 performances)
UPSIDE DOWN ON THE HANDLEBARS by Leslie Weiner; Director, Salem Ludwig; Set, Bob Phillips; Lighting, Richard Dorfman; Costumes, Barbara Weiss; Stage Managers, Crystal Huntington, Eric Hall; Production Assistants, Paul Dimeo, David Butler
CAST: Douglass Watson (Ben Gerard), Jacqueline Knapp (Sarah Zaleski), Robert Heller (Warren Blumenfeld), Leslie Lyles (Nicola Gerard), Ken Chapin (Arthur Berry), Rick Weatherwax (Gus Williams), Tom Amick (Herb Gerard)
A drama in two acts. The action takes place February through May of the early 1980's in and about the central New Jersey city of Plainview, in Ben's office, Nicola's office, and the Gerard living room.
Thursday, May 12—29, 1983 (12 performances)
THE RUFFIAN ON THE STAIR by Joe Orton; Director, Rosemary Hay; Costumes, Karla Barker; Lighting, John Jay; Set, Robert Thayer; Stage Manager, Garl Arthur
CAST: Leon Russom (Mike), Laura Copland (Joyce), Rudi Caporaso (Wilson)
A play performed without intermission.

PAN ASIAN REPERTORY THEATRE

Tisa Chang, Artistic Director
Sixth Season

Administrative Director, Susan Socolowski; Development, Connie Kelly, Kasumi Shiraishi; Press, Shirley Herz, Sam Rudy, Peter Cromarty
(PAN ASIAN REPERTORY THEATRE) Tuesday, November 30,—December 26, 1982 (28 performances)
YELLOW FEVER by R. A. Shiomi; Story conceived by Marc Hayashi; Director, Raul Aranas; Set, Christopher Stapleton; Costumes, Lillian Pan; Lighting, Dawn Chiang; Technical Director, Henry Stevens; Sound, Alvin Lum; Stage Managers, Eddas Bennett, Jon Nakagawa
CAST: Donald Li (Sam Shikaze), Carol Honda (Rosie), James Jenner (Goldberg), Henry Yuk (Chuck Chan), Freda Foh Shen (Nancy Wing), Jeffrey Spolan (Sgt. Mackenzie), Ernest Abuba (Capt. Kenji Kadota), James Jenner (Supt. Jameson)
A mystery-comedy in two acts. The action takes place on Powell Street in Vancouver, British Columbia, during March in the 1970's.
Thursday, March 17,—April 9, 1983 (24 performances)
TEAHOUSE by Lao She; Translated by Ying Rocheng, John Howard-Gibbon; Director, Tisa Chang; Set, Atsushi Moriyasu; Lighting, Victor En Yu Tan; Costumes, Eiko Yamaguchi; Hair and Beard Design, Christine Cooper; Technical Director, Jeff Berzon; Stage Managers, Eddas Bennett, Anne Anda; Press, Sam Rudy
CAST: Mel D. Gionson, Toshi Toda, Michelle Shibamura, Natsuko Ohama, Sandy Hom, Bea Soong, Koji Okamura, Kazuki Takase, Ernest Abuba, Michael G. Chin, Lester J. N. Mau, Tom Matsusaka, Ron Nakahara, Edmund Eng, Ron Yamamoto, Donald Li, Lynette Chun, Michael G. Chin, Mao Zhao, Kazuki Takase, Henry Yuk, Alvin Lum, Glen Athaide, William Hao, Christen Villamor, Matt Nichols
A drama in three acts. The action takes place in Beijing, Yutai Teahouse in 1898, 1918 and 1948.
Friday, April 15,—May 1, 1983 (20 performances)
A MIDSUMMER NIGHT'S DREAM by William Shakespeare; Chinese translation, Liang Shi Chiu; Director, Tisa Chang; Set, Atsushi Moriyasu; Costumes, Julie Schwolow; Lighting, Karen Wenderoff; Stage Manager, Jon Nakagawa; Press, Sam Rudy
CAST: Elizabeth Sung (Hermia), Koji Okamura (Lysander), Mel D. Gionson (Demetrius), Tina Chen (Helena), Sandy Hom (Peter Quince), Ron Yamamoto (Francis Flute), Lester J.N. Mao (Egeus/Snout), Ron Nakahara (Nick Bottom), Yung Yung Tsuai (Puck), Lu Yu (Theseus/Oberon), Jodi Long (Hippolyta/Titania), William Hao (Philostrate/Snug)
The action takes place during the Chou Dynasty (1000 B.C.) in Changan, ancient capital of China.

Donald Li, Carol Honda, Freda Foh Shen, Henry Yuk in "Yellow Fever"
(*Carol Rosegg Photo*)

THE PRODUCTION COMPANY

Norman Rene, Artistic Director
Sixth Season

Managing Director, Abigail Franklin; Company Manager, Margi Rountree; Executive Assistant, Andrew Shearer; President, Ricka Kanter Fisher; Press, Fred Nathan, Anne Abrams
(PRODUCTION COMPANY THEATRE) Wednesday, January 12—29, 1983 (23 performances). Moved Thursday, March 3, 1983 to Actors & Directors Theatre with producers Richard Horner, Lynne Stuart, Hinks Shimberg, Philip M. Getter, Louis F. Burke. Closed March 27, 1983 after 31 performances.
BLOOD MOON by Nicholas Kazan; Director, Allen R. Belknap; Set, Michael Hotopp, Paul dePass; Costumes, Amanda J. Klein; Lighting, Debra J. Kletter; Choreography, Dan Walsh; Technical Directors, Jeff Berzon, Peter Bendevski; Props, Bonnie Saltzman; Production Assistants, David Beris, Sandford Stokes; Stage Manager, Jan Malthaner; Press, Fred Nathan, Anne Abrams, Henry Luhrman, Kevin P. McAnarney, Terry M. Lilly, Keith Sherman
CAST: Dana Delany (Manya), David Canary (Alan), Nicholas Saunders (Gregory)
A drama in two acts. The action takes place at the present time on the Sunday after Thanksgiving, and a year later on the Sunday before Christmas.
Sunday, January 9—30, 1983 (19 performances)
THE GILDED CAGE conceived and directed by James Milton; Musical Director/Arrangements, Polly Pen; Choreography, Marcia Milgrom Dodge; Costumes, Amanda J. Klein; Lighting, Debra J. Kletter; Technical Directors, Jeff Berzon, Peter Bendevski; Production Assistant, Mireya Hepner; Stage Manager, Jeanne Oster
CAST: Marianne Tatum (Evelyn Nesbit), Tom McKinney (Stanford White), Robert Stillman (Harry K. Thaw), Paula Sweeney (Mimi), Susan Blommaert (Lulu), Marilyn Firment (Kitty), Polly Pen (Pinkie)
MUSICAL NUMBERS: There's a Broken Heart for Every Light on Broadway, Always Do as People Say You Should, You Naughty Man, Little Birdies Learning How to Fly, Put on Your Tatta Little Girlie, Bird in a Gilded Cage, Take Back Your Gold, A Good Cigar Is a Smoke, Nobody, She Was One of the Early Birds, Je Ne Sais Pa Pa, She Is More to Be Pitied Than Censured, Sawing a Woman in Half, In the Baggage Car Ahead, Waitin' for the Evenin' Mail, Kiss a Lonely Wife, Absinthe Frappe
(THEATRE GUINEVERE) Wednesday, March 9,—April 3, 1983 (24 performances)
JAZZ POETS AT THE GROTTO conceived and directed by Greg McCaslin; Musical Direction/Arrangements, Elliot Weiss; Movement, Katherine Laub; Set Dressing, Michael G. Smith; Costumes, Debra Stein; Lighting, Debra J. Kletter; Stage Manager, David Hansen
CAST: John Korkes (Saul), Ruthe Staples, Michael Butler (Bob), Judith Ivey (Joyce), Randy Denson (Diane), John Pankow (Gregory), John Shearin (Jack)

Polly Pen, Marianne Tatum in "The Gilded Cage"
(*Anita Photo*)

PLAYWRIGHTS HORIZONS

Andre Bishop, Artistic Director
Twelfth Season

Managing Director, Paul Daniels; Business Manager, Rory Vanderlick; Musical Theatre Program Director, Ira Weitzman; Casting Director, John Lyons; Technical Director, Bob Bertrand; Assistant Production Manager/Wardrobe, Rachel Chanoff; Director of Development, Cynthia Gold; Assistant to Mr. Bishop, Hillary Nelson; Assistant to Mr. Daniels, Mary Kay Hamalainen; Press, Bob Ullman, Louise Ment

HERRINGBONE with Book by Tom Cone; Music by Skip Kennon; Lyrics by Ellen Fitzhugh; Based on play by Tom Cone; Director, Ben Levit; Musical Numbers Staged by Theodore Pappas; Set, Christopher Nowak; Costumes, Karen Matthews; Lights, Frances Aronson; Production Manager, William Camp; Production Assistant, Risa Schwartz

CAST: Skip Kennon (Thumbs DuBois), David Rounds (Herringbone/Arthur/Louise/Grandmother/George/Lawyer/Nathan Mosely/Howard/Lou/Dot)
MUSICAL NUMBERS: Herringbone, Not President Please, Uncle Billy, God Said, Little Mister Tippy Toes, George, The Cheap Exit, What's a Body to Do?, The Chicken and the Frog, Lily Pad Tango, A Mother, Lullabye, Tulip Print Waltz, Ten Years, 3/4 for Three
A musical in two acts.

(DOUGLAS FAIRBANKS THEATER) Tuesday, June 22, 1982—March 13, 1983 (329 performances and 15 previews). Playwrights Horizons (Andre Bishop, Artistic Director; Paul Daniels, Managing Director) presents:
GENIUSES by Jonathan Reynolds; Director, Gerald Gutierrez; Set, Andrew Jackness; Costumes, Ann Emonts; Lighting, James F. Ingalls; Sound, Scott Lehrer; Fights, B. H. Barry; Special Effects, Esquire Jauchem, Gregory Meeh; Associate Producers, Anne G. Wilder, Edith K. Ehrman; General Manager, Sari Weisman; Company Manager, Andy Cohn; Casting, John Lyons; Wardrobe, Christina Ringelstein; Production Assistants, Deborah Gavito, Gabelle Aarons, William L. McMullen; Assistant to Director, Jennifer McCray; Stage Manager, Gerald B. Nobles; Press, Bob Ullman, Robert W. Larkin

CAST: Peter Evans (Jocko Pyle), Joanne Camp (Skye Bullene) succeeded by Christine Ebersole, Linda Lee Johnson, Morgan Fairchild, and Joanne Camp, Thomas Ikeda (Winston Legazpi), David Rasche (Eugene Winter) succeeded by Tom Ligon and James Eckhouse, Kurt Knudson (Bart Keely), David Garrison (Milo McGee McGarr) succeeded by Jay O. Sanders, UNDERSTUDIES: Linda Lee Johnson (Skye), Stephen Ahern (Jocko/Eugene/Bart/Milo), Lester Mau (Winston)
A Comedy in 3 acts. The action takes place at the present time in a village 200 miles north of Manila, the Philippines.

(PLAYWRIGHTS HORIZONS) Thursday, December 16—17, 1982 (2 performances and 30 previews). Playwrights Horizons (Andre Bishop, Artistic Director; Paul S. Daniels, Managing Director) presents:
THE RISE AND RISE OF DANIEL ROCKET by Peter Parnell; Director, Gerald Gutierrez; Set, Andrew Jackness; Costumes, Ann Emonts; Lighting, James F. Ingalls; Sound, Scott Lehrer; Incidental Music, Robert Waldman; Production Assistants, Mireya Hepner, Eitan Weinreich; Director's Assistants, Jennifer McCray, David Warren; Props, Gay Smerek; Wardrobe, Jordan Simon; Special Effects, Robert Aberdeen; Production Manager, Pat DeRousie; Stage Manger, Jay Adler; Press, Bob Ullman, Louise Ment

CAST: Thomas Hulce (Daniel Rocket/"Snood"), Tom Robbins (Jeffrey), Scott Waara (Roger), James Eckhouse (Steven), Jack Gilpin (Richard), Shelley Rogers (Penny), Kathryn C. Sparer (Claudia), Jane Jones (Judy), Ann McDonough (Alice), Jane Connell (Mrs. Rice)
A play in 2 acts and 15 scenes. Twenty years pass between the two acts.

Jane Hickley, Clement Fowler, Natalija Nogulich, Peter Evans in
"Transfiguration of Benno Blimpie"
(Bert Andrews Photo)

David Rounds in "Herringbone"
(Gerry Goodstein Photo)

(PLAYWRIGHTS HORIZONS MAINSTAGE) Wednesday, February 9—March 27, 1983 (28 performances)
AMERICA KICKS UP ITS HEELS with Music and Lyrics by William Finn; Book, Charles Rubin; Directors, Mary Kyte, Ben Levit; Choreography, Mary Kyte; Set and Costumes, Santo Loquasto; Lighting, Frances Aronson; Musical Theatre Program Director, Ira Weitzman; Musical Direction/Orchestrations, Michael Starobin; Assistants to Directors, Susan Rosenstock, Barry Bovshow; Production Assistants, Avishay Greenfield, Gay Smerek, Mireya Hepner, Deena Merlen; Props, William Squier; Wardrobe, D. V. Thompson; Hairstylist, Ethyl Eichelberger; Stage Managers, Johnna Murray, Arturo E. Porazzi, Robin Boudreau; Press, Bob Ullman, Louise Ment

CAST: Robin Boudreau (Thyra), Robert Dorfman (Julie), Peggy Hewett (Mrs. Roosevelt), I. M. Hobson (Polly), Rodney Hudson (Harlan), Alexandra Korey (Zoe), Dick Latessa (Boris), Patti LuPone (Cleo), Lenora Nemetz (Hennie)
MUSICAL NUMBERS: All of Us Are Niggers, Put It Together, Eleanor Roosevelt (A Discussion of Soup), A Better World, Cutting Hair, Red Faces at the Kremlin, America Kick Up Your Heels, Push and Pull, All Fall Down, The Depression Is Over, I Don't Want to Be Fired Again, Happiest Moment of My Life, Ask Me No Question, Pull It Together, Sex Stories in Hard Times, Nobody's Ever Gonna Step on Me, Why, It was Fun, My Day Has Come, Papa Says
A musical in two acts. The action takes place at the present time.

(PLAYWRIGHTS HORIZONS) Wednesday, March 9—April 17, 1983 (49 performances). Playwrights Horizons (Andre Bishop, Artistic Director) presents:
THE TRANSFIGURATION OF BENNO BLIMPIE by Albert Innaurato; Director, Mr. Innaurato; Set, Jeffrey Beecroft; Costumes, D. V. Thompson; Lighting, Loren Sherman; Music, Noa Ain; Stage Managers, Rita Calabro, Jane Hickey; Production Assistant, Randi Kelly; Assistant to Director, Roberta Harkavy; Props, Ned Pollack; Wardrobe, Randi Kelly; Press, Bob Ullman, Louise Ment

CAST: Peter Evans (Benno), Clement Fowler (Old Man), Natalija Nogulich (Mother), Jane Hickey (Girl), Jay Thomas (Father)
A drama performed without intermission.

NEW YORK SHAKESPEARE FESTIVAL PUBLIC THEATER

Joseph Papp, Producer
Sixteenth Season

(PUBLIC/MARTINSON HALL) Thursday, July 8—29, 1982; Thursday, September 9—25, 1982 (13 performances). Joseph Papp presents: **ERIC BOGOSIAN** performing two solo pieces, "Men Inside" and "Voices of America." Production Supervisor, Jason Steven Cohen; Lighting, Terry Christgau; Sound, Peter Scherer

(PUBLIC/NEWMAN THEATRE) Thursday, July 29—September 5, 1982 (45 performances and 9 previews). Joseph Papp presents: **THE DEATH OF VON RICHTHOFEN AS WITNESSED FROM EARTH** by Des McAnuff; Composed and Directed by Mr. McAnuff; Choreography, Jennifer Muller; Set, Douglas W. Schmidt; Costumes, Patricia McGourty; Lighting, Richard Nelson; Sound, Bill Dreisbach; Sound Effects, James LeBrecht; Musical Director, Michael S. Roth; Vocal arrangements, Michael Starobin, Michael S. Roth, Des McAnuff; Production Supervisor, Jason Steven Cohen; General Manager, Robert Kamlot; Stage Managers, Fredric H. Orner, Loretta Robertson; Dialect Coach, Elizabeth Smith; Assistant to Mr. McAnuff, Page Burkholder; Production Assistant, Craig Shipler; Hairstylist, Andrew Reese; Props, John Masterson, Evan Canary; Wardrobe, Judith Chew; Press, Merle Debuskey, Richard Kornberg, Bruce Campbell

CAST: Robert Westenberg (R. Raymond Barker), Marek Norman (N.C.O. Secull), Robert Joy (Robert Buie), Mark Linn-Baker (William Evans), Brent Barrett (Wolfram von Richthofen), John Vickery (Manfred von Richthofen, the Red Dragon), Jeffrey Jones (Karl Bodenschatz), Sigrid Wurschmidt (Violinist), Susan Berman (Lutanist), Peggy Harmon (Flautist), Mark Petrakis (German Lance Corporal), Bob Gunton (Hermann Goering), Michael Brian, Eric Elice, Davis Gaines, Karl Heist, Tad Ingram, Ken Land, Martha Wingate (Flying Circus), Understudies: Karl Heist (Buie), Tad Ingram (Goering/Lance Cpl.), Eric Elice (Wolfram), Michael Brian (Evans), Ken Land (Bodenschatz), Davis Gaines (Barker), Robert Westenberg (Manfred), Martha Wingate (Women), Tommy Breslin (Secull), David Jordan (Swing)
MUSICAL NUMBERS: All I Wanted Was a Cup of Tea, Our Red Knight, Good Luck, Speed, Sweet Eternity, Take What You Can, If I Have the Will, I've Got a Girl, England the U.K., Save the Last Dance, Here We Are, Congratulations, Stand Up for the Fatherland, Sitting in the Garden, It's All Right God, Four White Horses, 1918, Dear Icarus, Sarah, I Don't Ask about Tomorrow, April Twenty-One, The Skies Have Gone Dry
A play with songs in two acts. The action takes place in 1918 on the afternoon and evening of April 20 and the morning of April 21, in the West, No Man's Land, the East.

(PUBLIC/OTHER STAGE) Tuesday, August 10—29, 1982 (21 performances). Joseph Papp presents in repertory Michael Moriarty and the Potter's Field Players in:
UNCLE VANYA by Anton Chekhov; Translated by Ann Dunnigan; Director, Peter von Berg; Sets, Jesse Rosenthal; Lighting, Allen Lee Hughes; Costumes, Elena Pellicciaro; Producing Director, Tulis McCall; Stage Managers, Anne Marie Hobson, Colin Garrey; Props, Steve Stevens, Richard Holland; Wardrobe, Debra Hosmer; Sound, James Maxson, Kenn Dovel; Artistic Director, Dennis Moore; General Manager, Pat Yellen; Original Music, Joseph Rescigno

CAST: Louise Campbell (Marina), Michael Moriarty (Astrov), Colin Garrey (Vanya), Charles Duval (Serabryakov Alexander Vladimirovich), Nancy-Elizabeth Kammer (Sonya), James Maxson (Waffles), Anna Galiena (Elena Andreyevna), Muriel Mason (Vany's Mother), Michael Sullivan (Workman)
WHAT EVERYWOMAN KNOWS written and performed by Tulis McCall in collaboration with Nancy-Elizabeth Kammer and Michael T. Gregoric

(PUBLIC/NEWMAN THEATER) Thursday, October 21,—November 28, 1982 (45 performances and 13 previews). Joseph Papp presents: **PLENTY** by David Hare; Director, Mr.Hare; Set, John Gunter; Lighting, Arden Fingerhut; Costumes, Jane Greenwood; Incidental Music, Nick Bicat; General Manager, Robert Kamlot; Production Supervisor, Jason Steven Cohen; Wardrobe, Judy Chew; Props, John Masterson; Stage Managers, Michael Chambers, Anne King; Press, Merle Debuskey, John Howlett, Richard Kornberg

CAST: Ellen Parker (Alice), Kate Nelligan (Susan), Edward Herrmann (Raymond), Kelsey Grammer (Codename Lazar), Philippe Benichou (Frenchman 1), George Martin (Darwin), Daniel Gerroll (Mick), Johann Carlo (Louise), Conrad Yama (M. Aung), Ginny Yang (Mme. Aung), Madeleine Potter (Dorcas), Stephen Mellor (Begley), Bill Moor (Sir Andrew Charleson), Dominic Chianese (Frenchman 2)
A drama in 2 acts and 12 scenes. The action takes place between 1943 and 1962.

Mark Linn-Baker, Robert Joy, John Vickery, Robert Westenberg in "The Death of von Richthofen . . . " (*Martha Swope Photo*)

(PUBLIC/ANSPACHER THEATER) Thursday, December 2, 1982—January 16, 1983 (37 performances and 8 previews). Joseph Papp presents: **HAMLET** by William Shakespeare; Director, Joseph Papp; Set, Robert Yodice; Lighting, Ralph K. Holmes; Music, Allen Shawn; Costumes, Theoni V. Aldredge; Fight Sequences, B. H. Barry; Hair and Wigs, Vincent Tucker; Stage Managers, Fredric H. Orner, Jane Hubbard; Production Assistant, Janet Callahan; Props, John Doyle; Wardrobe, Hannah Murray; Movement, John Lone; General Manager, Robert Kamlot; Production Supervisor, Jason Steven Cohen; Press, Merle Debuskey, Richard Kornberg, Barbara Carroll, Bruce Campbell

CAST: Ralph Byers (Guildenstern), James Cromwell (Horatio), Brian Delate (Switzer/Messenger), Bob Gunton (Claudius), George Hall (Polonius/Old Gravedigger), George Hamlin (Ghost), Annette Helde (Lady-in-waiting/Player), Ric Lavin (Voltemand/Priest), Rich Lieberman (Rosencrantz), Stephen McNaughton (Francisco/Cornelius/Sailor), Pippa Pearthree (Ophelia), Brett Porter (Switzer/Norweigian Captain), Raphael Sbarge (Reynaldo/Player), Jamey Sheridan (Bernardo/Fortinbras), Rocco Sisto (Osric), Jimmy Smits (Switzer/Messenger), Diane Venora (Hamlet), J. T. Walsh (Marcellus/Player/English Ambassador), Robert Westenberg (Laertes), Kathleen Widdoes (Gertrude), Daniel P. Wirth (Switzer/Messenger), Pamela Payton-Wright (Alternate for Hamlet)
A drama performed with one intermission.

(PUBLIC/LuESTHER HALL) Tuesday, December 7—26, 1982 (19 performances). Joseph Papp presents: **NECESSARY ENDS** by Marvin Cohen; Director, James Milton; Set, Jim Clayburgh; Costumes, Amanda J. Klein; Lighting, John Gisondi; Music, Robert Dennis; Production Supervisor, Jason Steven Cohen; General Manager, Robert Kamlot; Props, Tom Perry; Wardrobe, Saidha Nelson; Stage Managers, G. Roger Abell, Evan Canary; Press, Merle Debuskey, Richard Kornberg, Barbara Carroll, Bruce Campbell

CAST: Alma Cuervo (Girlfriend of Burt), Larry Pine (Boyfriend of Georgia/Friend of Jasper), Bill Sadler (Jasper/Boyfriend of Ginger/Friend of Burt), Gretchen Van Ryper (Ginger/Girlfriend of Jasper)
A comedy in two acts.

Pippa Pearthree, Diane Venora in "Hamlet" (*Martha Swope Photo*)

(PUBLIC/NEWMAN THEATER) Tuesday, December 28, 1982—January 30, 1983 (40 performances and 6 previews). Joseph Papp presents the Royal Court Theatre Production of:
TOP GIRLS by Caryl Churchill; Director, Max Stafford-Clark; Sets, Peter Hartwell; Costumes, Pam Tait; Lighting, Robin Myerscough-Walker; Production Manager, Alison Ritchie; Assistant to Director, Simon Curtis; Sound, Patrick Bridgeman; Props, John Masterson; Wardrobe, Dawn Johnson; General Manager, Robert Kamlot; Production Supervisor, Jason Steven Cohen; Stage Managers, Julie Davies, Susan Green; Press, Merle Debuskey, Richard Kornberg, Barbara Carroll, Bruce Campbell

CAST: Gwen Taylor (Marlene), Lou Wakefield (Waitress/Kit/Shona), Deborah Findlay (Isabella Bird/Joyce/Mrs. Kidd), Lindsay Duncan (Lady Nijo/Win), Carole Hayman (Dull Gret/Angie), Selina Cadell (Pope Joan/Louise), Lesley Manville (Patient Griselda/Nell/Jeanine)
A play in 2 acts and 5 scenes. The action takes place in a restaurant, Top Girls Employment Agency in London, Joyce's backyard in Suffolk, and Joyce's kitchen.

(PUBLIC/NEWMAN THEATER) Thursday, February 24—May 29, 1983 (89 performances and 20 previews). Joseph Papp presents:
TOP GIRLS by Caryl Churchill; Director, Max Stafford-Clark; Scenery, Peter Hartwell; Costumes, Pam Tait; Lighting, Robin Myerscough-Walker; Dialect Coach, Daniel Gerroll; Makeup/Hairstylist, J. Roy Helland; Sound, Vanessa Witt; Props, Patrick Bridgeman; Props, John Masterson; Wardrobe, Dawn Johnson; Production Supervisor, Jason Steven Cohen; General Manager, Robert Kamlot; Company Manager, Robert Reilly; Stage Managers, Jane Hubbard, G. Roger Abell; Press, Merle Debuskey, Richard Kornberg, Barbara Carroll, Bruce Campbell

CAST: Lise Hilboldt (Marlene) succeeded by Polly Draper, Donna Bullock (Waitress/Jeanine/Win), Sara Botsford (Isabella Bird/Joyce/Nell), Freda Foh Shen (Lady Nijo/Mrs. Kidd), Kathryn Grody (Dull Gret/Angie), Linda Hunt (Pope Joan/Louise) succeeded by Elaine Hausman, Valerie Mahaffey (Patient Griselda/Kit/Shona), Understudies: Elaine Hausman (Gret/Angie/Pop/Louise), Sherie Berk (Griselda/Kit/Shona/-Waitress/Jeanine/Win), Fredi Olster (Marlene/Nijo/Mrs. Kidd), Dale Hodges (Isabella/Joyce/Nell
A play in 2 acts and 5 scenes.

(PUBLIC/OTHER STAGE) Sunday, January 16—30, 1983 (9 performances and 11 previews). Joseph Papp presents the New York Shakespeare Festival/Mabou Mines production of:
COMPANY by Samuel Beckett; Directors, Honora Fergusson, Frederick Neumann; Assistant to Directors, Rita Tiplitz; Set, Gerald Marks, Lighting, Craig Miller; Music, Philip Glass; Stage Managers, L. B. Dallas, Sabrina Hamilton; Production Supervisor, Jason Steven Cohen; General Manager, Robert Kamlot; Press, Merle Debuskey, Richard Kornberg, Barbara Carroll, Bruce Campbell

CAST: Frederick Neumann (The Performer), Honora Fergusson (She)

(PUBLIC/LuESTHER HALL) Tuesday, February 22—April 17, 1983 (64 performances). Joseph Papp presents a New York Shakespeare Festival/Mabou Mines production of:
COLD HARBOR conceived and directed by Bill Raymond and Dale Worsley; Text, Dale Worsley with excerpts from the memoirs of Ulysses S. Grant and Julia Dent Grant; Tableaux, Greg Mehrten; Music, Philip Glass; Set, Linda Hartinian; Costumes, Greg Mehrten; Sound, L. B. Dallas; Projections, Stephanie Rudolph; Exhibits, David Hardy; Technical Director/Stage Manager, David Hardy; Assistant Stage Manager, David Earl Williams; Music performed by Michael Riesman; Press, Merle Debuskey, Richard Kornberg, Barbara Carroll, Bruce Campbell

CAST: Bill Raymond (Ulysses S. Grant), Greg Mehrten, B-St. John Schofield, Julia's Voice by Ellen McElduff, Joe Stackell (The Double), Tableau: Meg Eginton, Peter Levine, Jesse Kitten, Joe Stackell, Kevin Kuhlke

(PUBLIC/LuESTHER HALL) Wednesday, April 27—May 15, 1983 (22 performances). Joseph Papp presents a New York Shakespeare Festival/-Mabou Mines Production of:
HAJJ by Ruth Maleczech, Craig Jones, Lee Breuer, Julie Archer; A performance poem conceived in collaboration; Video, Craig Jones; Direction, Lee Breuer; Set and Lighting, Julie Archer; Music, Chris Abajian; Makeup, Linda Hartinian; Taped Performances by Phil Schenk (Father), Lute Ramblin (Child); Technical Director, David Hardy; Props, Migdalia Cruz; Production Supervisor, Jason Steven Cohen; General Manager, Robert Kamlot; Press, Merle Debuskey, Richard Kornberg, Barbara Carroll, Bruce Campbell

Carole Hayman, Lindsay Duncan, Lou Wakefield, Gwen Taylor, Selina Cadell, Lesley Manville, Deborah Findlay in "Top Girls" (British cast) (*Martha Swope Photo*)

(PUBLIC/OTHER STAGE) Tuesday, May 3—June 26, 1983 (48 performances and 14 previews). Joseph Papp presents:
EGYPTOLOGY (My Head Was a Sledgehammer) with Text, Staging, Scenery and Musical Scoring by Richard Foreman; Associate Scenic Design, Nancy Winters; Lighting, Spencer Mosse; Costumes, Patricia McGourty; Sound, Daniel M. Schreier; Production Supervisor, Jason Steven Cohen; General Manager, Robert Kamlot; Stage Managers, Michael Chambers, Anne Marie Hobson; Props, Mark Burns Sweeney; Hairstylist-/Makeup, Lisa Fahrner; Wardrobe, Karen Nowack; Press, Merle Debuskey, Richard Kornberg, Barbara Carroll, Bruce Campbell

CAST: Seth Allen (Man in the bar), Raymond Barry (Strong Man #1), Gretel Cummings (Tall Whore), William Duff-Griffin (Egyptian Gentleman), Cynthia Gillette (Thin Blonde Whore/Nurse Ebastian), Kate Manheim (Lady Aviator), Frank Maraden (Louis XIV), George McGrath (The Dog/Egyptian), Christine Morris (Whore Who Roller Skates), Lola Pashalinski (Plump Whore/Nurse Who Menaces), Understudies; Wanda Bimson, Claire Lewis, Frank Dahill, Jere Burns

Kathryn Grody, Sara Botsford, Lise Hilboldt, Valerie Mahaffey, Linda Hunt, Donna Bullock, Freda Foh Shen in "Top Girls" (*Martha Swope Photo*)

(PUBLIC/MARTINSON HALL) Wednesday, May 4—May 29, 1983 (31 performances and 22 previews). Joseph Papp presents:
BURIED INSIDE EXTRA by Thomas Babe; Director, Joseph Papp; Set, Mike Boak; Lighting, Ralph K. Holmes; Costumes, Theoni V. Aldredge; Production Supervisor, Jason Steven Cohen; Production Assistant, Nancy Kohlbeck; Assistant to Director, Morgan Jenness; Hairstylist, Marlies Vallant; General Manager, Robert Kamlot: Company Manager, Robert Reilly; Props, Tom Perry; Wardrobe, Dawn Johnson, Stage Managers, Susan Green, Stephen McCorkle; Press Merle Debuskey, Richard Kornberg, Barbara Carroll, Bruce Campbell

CAST: Hal Holbrook (Jake K. Bowsky), Dixie Carter (Liz Conlon), Vincent Gardenia (Wild Bob Culhane), William Converse-Roberts (Don Kane), Sandy Dennis (Sophia Bowsky), Understudies: Linda Selman, William H. Andrews
    A drama in two acts.

(PUBLIC/LuESTHER HALL) Tuesday, May 24—July 3, 1983 (43 performances and 5 previews). Joseph Papp presents London's Joint Stock Theatre Group's production of:
FEN by Caryl Churchill; Director, Les Waters; Design, Annie Smart; Lighting, Tom Donnellan; Associate Producer, Jason Steven Cohen; General Manager, Robert Kamlot; Stage Managers, Alan Day, Ingrid Haskal, Ginny Martino; Original Music, Ilona Sekacz; Wardrobe, Bruce Brumage; Press, Merle Debuskey, Richard Kornberg, Barbara Carroll, Bruce Campbell

CAST: Linda Bassett (Shirley/Shona/Miss Cade/Margaret), Amelda Brown (Boy/Angela/Deb/Mrs. Finch), Cecily Hobbs (Japanese Businessman/Nell/May/Mavis), Tricia Kelly (Mrs. Hassett/Becky/Alice/Ivy), Jennie Stoller (Val/Woman Working in the field), Bernard Strother (Wilson/Frank/Tewson/Geoffrey)
    Performed without intermission.

Sandy Dennis, Hal Holbrook, Dixie Carter in "Buried Inside Extra" Left Center: Tricia Kelly, Cecily Hobbs, Linda Bassett, Amelda Brown (rear) in "Fen" (*Martha Swope Photos*)

Brian Bovell, Victor Romero Evans in "Welcome Back Jack-O"

QUAIGH THEATRE

Will Lieberson, Artistic Director
Eighth Season

Managing Director, Peggy Ward; Development Director, Iris Posner; Press, Max Eisen, Maria Somma
    Sunday, August 1—13, 1982 (7 performances)
BIRDBATH composed by Kenneth Lieberson; Based on play by Leonard Melfi; Text adapted by Martin Rogers; Director, John Margulis; Assistant Director/Stage Manager, Stephen Catron; Stage Manager, Rita Tiplitz
CAST: Martha Ihde (Velma Sparrow), Michael Kutner (Frankie Basta)
    Saturday, October 23,—November 14, 1982 (20 performances)
THE CLOSED DOOR by Graham Reid; Director, Dennis Lieberson; Set/Lighting, Linda Tate; Associate Designer, Sharon Stover; Stage Managers, Lysbeth Hopper, Marisa Cardinale
CAST: Michael O'Sullivan (Victor Donnelly), Sarah Venable (Doreen Donnelly), Noel Lawlor (Spud), Ron Berliner (Soapy), Tom Sminkey (John "Slabber" McCoy), James Pyduck (Gunner), Sally Parrish (Mrs. Courtney), Jack Poggi (Patterson), Naomi Riseman (Mrs. McCoy)
    A drama in two acts. The action takes place in the Donnelly living room and other locales in Belfast during autumn of the recent past.
    Tuesday, April 19,—May 8, 1983 (18 performances)
THE VENTRILOQUIST with Book by Steven Otfinoski; Music and Lyrics, Eddie Garson; Director, Will Lieberson; Musical Director/Vocal Arrangements/Orchestrations, Rick Lewis; Choreographer, Dan Walsh; Set, Bob Phillips; Costumes, Mary Ellen Bosche; Lighting, John C. Merriman; Stage Managers, Linda Pilz, Shari Goldstein, Nancy Rutter; Producer, Claudia Genteel
CAST: Frank Anderson (Manfred), Scott Bylund (Dale Hammond), Chico Chico (Cheeky), Michele Franks (Naomi), Eddie Garson (Jackie Jordan), Annie Heller (Flo), Eric Kornfeld (Jimmie Sharp), Barbara Mappus (Lanta LaRue), Barbara Nicoll (Bertha), Russell Ochocki (Freddie), Herbert Rubens (Ten Percent Joe)
MUSICAL NUMBERS: The Ventriloquist, There She Goes, The Agent's Song, Hello World, Rehearsing, Love, You Did I Didn't, Someday, Opera Bit, How Far Will You Go, Thirty Days, The Kid Don't Wanna Talk, Just Because He's Made of Wood, Zelda Farquad, Zyzzle, I'm the Ventriloquist He's the Dummy
    Thursday, May 17—29, 1983 (16 performances)
WELCOME HOME JACKO by Mustapha Matura; Director, Charlie Hanson; Costumes, Gemma Jackson; Stage Management, Melvyn Jones, Dennis Lieberson; A Theatre Royal (London) production
CAST: Gary Beadle (Fret), Chris Tummings (Dole), Brian Bovell (Zippy), Victor Romero Evans (Marcus), Maggie Shevlin (Sandy), Shope Shodeinde (Gail), Malcolm Frederick (Jacko)

ROUNDABOUT THEATRE

Gene Feist, Producing Director
Seventeenth Season

Managing Director, Todd Haimes; Business Manager, Patricia A. Yost; Executive Assistant to Mr. Feist, Erica Evans; Technical Director/Producing Manager, Eddie Feldman; Casting, Cindy Leiter; Stage Managers, M. R. Jacobs, Kurt Wagemann; Composer/Musical Director, Philip Campanella; Production Assistant, Mark Herko; Press, Susan Bloch & Co., Adrian Bryan-Brown, Ellen Zeisler, Ron Jewell

(ROUNDABOUT STAGE ONE) Thursday, July 8—September 19, 1982 (87 performances). Roundabout Theatre Company (Gene Feist/Michael Fried) present:
THE FOX by Allan Miller; Adapted from the novella by D. H. Lawrence; Director, Allan Miller; Set, Roger Mooney; Lighting, Ronald Wallace; Costumes, A. Christina Giannini; Sound, Philip Campanella; Stage Manager, M. R. Jacobs

CAST: Jenny O'Hara (Nelli March), Mary Layne (Jill Banford), Anthony Heald (Henry Grenfel)
A drama in two acts. The action takes place on the old Bailey Farm in England in November of 1918.

(RAFT THEATRE) Wednesday, July 14, 1982—August 1, 1982 (48 performances). Roundabout Theatre presents:
THE LEARNED LADIES by Moliere; English verse translation, Richard Wilbur; Director, Norman Ayrton; Set, Roger Mooney; Costumes, John David Ridge; Lighting, David F. Segal; Sound, Philip Campanella; Wigs/Hairstyles, Paul Huntley; Stage Managers, Howard Kolins, George Holmes; Company Manager, Lisa Grossman; Wardrobe, Richard Hieronymus; Props, John N. Concannon

CAST: Philip Bosco (Chrysale), Rosemary Murphy (Philaminte), Jennifer Harmon (Armande), Cynthia Dozier (Henriette), Carol Teitel (Belise), Robert Stattel (Ariste), Randle Mell (Clitandre), Richard Kavanaugh (Trissotin), Gordon Chater (Vadius), Ann MacMillan (Martine), Thomas Delaney (Lepine), George Holmes (Julien), Servants: Bonita Beach, Paul Booth, Marcia Cross
A comedy in two acts. The action takes place in 1672 in Chrysale's house in Paris.

Top Right: Mary Layne, Jenny O'Hara, Anthony Heald in "The Fox"
Below: cast of "The Holly and the Ivy" (*Martha Swope Photos*)

(SUSAN BLOCH THEATRE) Thursday, November 18, 1982—March 13, 1983 (199 performances). Roundabout Theatre Company (Gene Feist, Producing Director) presents:
THE HOLLY AND THE IVY by Wynyard Browne; Director, Lindsay Anderson; Set, Roger Mooney; Lighting, Ronald Wallace; Costumes, A. Christina Giannini; Sound, Philip Campanella; Stage Manager, Kurt Wagemann; Props, Jean Andres; Technical Director, Eddie R. Feldman; Press, Adrian Bryan-Brown, Ron Jewell, Ellen Zeisler

CAST: Gwyllum Evans (Rev. Martin Gregory), Jennifer Harmon (Jenny), Pamela Brook (Margaret), Frank Grimes (Mick), Betty Low (Aunt Lydia), Helen Lloyd Breed (Aunt Bridget), Thomas Ruisinger (Richard Wyndham), Gerald Walker (David Paterson)
A drama in 3 acts. The action takes place during Christmas 1948 in the living room of a vicarage in Norfolk, England.

(STAGE ONE) Thursday, January 20—March 12, 1983 (96 performances). Roundabout Theatre Company (Gene Feist, Producing Director) presents:
THE ENTERTAINER by John Osborne; Director, William Gaskill; Set, Michael Sharp; Costumes, A. Christina Giannini; Lighting, Barry Arnold; Music, John Addison; Choreography, David Vaughan; Projections, Patrick Burns; Props, Chris Mealy; Stage Managers, Patrick J. O'Leary, Roger Kent Brechner; Press, Susan Bloch & Company, Adrian Bryan-Brown, Ron Jewell, Ellen Zeisler

CAST: Humphrey Davis (Billy Rice), Ellen Tobie (Jean Rice), Nicol Williamson (Archie Rice), Frances Cuka (Phoebe Rice), Keith Reddin (Frank Rice), Richard M. Davidson (Brother Bill Rice), John Curless (Graham Dodd), David Brunetti (Conductor), Elizabeth Owens (Gorgeous Gladys), Understudies: Richard M. Davidson (Archie), Elizabeth Owens (Phoebe/Jean), David Burnetti (Frank/Graham), John Curless (Bill)
A drama in 2 acts and 12 scenes. The action takes place during 1956.

Nicol Williamson, Keith Reddin, Frances Cuka, Ellen Tobie
in "The Entertainer"
(*Martha Swope Photo*)

(ROUNDABOUT/SUSAN BLOCH THEATRE) Thursday, April 21—September 11, 1983 (199 performances). Roundabout Theatre Company (Gene Feist, Producing Director; Todd Haimes, Managing Director) presents:
WINNERS/HOW HE LIED TO HER HUSBAND directed by Nye Heron; Sets, Roger Mooney; Costumes, Richard Hieronymus; Lighting, Pat Kelly; Sound, Philip Campanella; Technical Director/Production Manager, Eddie R. Feldman; Stage Manager, Kurt Wagemann; Press, Susan Bloch Co., Adrian Bryan-Brown, Ron Jewell, Ellen Zeisler

CAST: "Winners" by Brian Friel: Bernie McInerney (Man) succeeded by William Shust, Kate Burton (Mag) succeeded by Mary Sullivan, Jeanne Ruskin (Woman) succeeded by Tandy Cronyn, Sally Dunn, Michael Butler (Joe)
"How He Lied to Her Husband" by George Bernard Shaw: Michael Butler (He), Jeanne Ruskin (She) succeeded by Tandy Cronyn, Sally Dunn, Bernie McInerney (Her Husband) succeeded by William Shust

(ROUNDABOUT STAGE ONE) Thursday, April 28—June 12, 1983 (88 performances). Roundabout Theatre Company in association with Yale R. Wexler presents:
DUET FOR ONE by Tom Kempinski; Director, Jeffrey Hayden; Set, Michael Sharp; Costumes, Jessica Hahn; Lighting, Judy Rasmuson; Sound, Philip Campanella; Production Assistant, Bruce Babbitt; Stage Manager, Robert Townsend; Press, Susan Bloch Co., Adrian Bryan-Brown, Ron Jewell, Ellen Zeisler

CAST: Eva Marie Saint (Stephanie Abrahams), Milton Selzer (Dr. Alfred Feldmann)
   A drama in two acts. The action takes place at the present time in the consulting room of Dr. Feldman.

Eva Marie Saint, Milton Selzer in "Duet for One" (*Martha Swope Photo*)

Cast of "Winterplay"
(*Susan Cook Photo*)

Michael Butler, Kate Burton in "Winners"
(*Martha Swope Photo*)

SECOND STAGE

Robyn Goodman/Carole Rothman, Artistic Directors
Fourth Season

Associate Director, Drew Farber; Dramaturg, Kim Powers; Management, Pentacle, Mara Greenberg, Ivan Sygoda; Casting, Meg Simon/Fran Kumin; Production Supervisor, Kim Novick; Press, Richard Kornberg

(SOUTH STREET THEATRE) Tuesday, January 25—February 27, 1983 (18 performances and 12 previews). The Second Stage presents:
PAINTING CHURCHES by Tina Howe; Director, Carole Rothman; Set, Heidi Landesman; Lighting, Frances Aronson; Costumes, Nan Cibula; Sound, Gary Harris; Hairstylist, Antonio Soddu; Technical Director, Dale Harris; Props, Janet Callahan; Wardrobe, Rita Robbins; Stage Managers, Loretta Robertson, Nancy Kohlbeck, Marisa Cardinale

CAST: Marian Seldes (Fanny Church), Donald Moffat (Gardner Church), Frances Conroy (Mags Church)
   A drama in 2 acts and 5 scenes. The action takes place "a few years ago" in the Beacon Hill section of Boston, Massachusetts.

(SOUTH STREET THEATRE) Tuesday, March 22—April 2, 1983 (20 performances) The Second Stage presents:
SOMETHING DIFFERENT by Carl Reiner; Director, Michael Kahn; Casting, Meg Simon/Frank Kumin; Production Supervisor, Kim Novick; Set, Jim Clayburgh; Lighting, Victor En Yu Tan; Costumes, Mariann Verheyen; Sound, Gary Harris; Hairstylist, Antonio Soddu; Assistant Director, Peter Webb; Technical Director, Dale Harris; Wardrobe, Rita Robbins; Props, Janet Callahan; Stage Managers, Janet Friedman, Susanne Jul; Press, Richard Kornberg

CAST: Andrew Duncan (Bud Nemerov), Robyn Goodman (Beth Nemerov), Norman Parker (Phil Caponetti), Wendy Wolfe (Mrs. Kupferman), Audree Rae (Rose Keller), Ellen March (Ida Schwartz), Theresa Merritt (Sarah Goldfine)
   A comedy in 2 acts and 4 scenes. The action takes place in the den of the Nemerov suburban home.

(SOUTH STREET THEATRE) Tuesday, May 10—28, 1983 (16 performances). The Second Stage (Robyn Goodman, Carole Rothman, Artistic Directors) presents:
WINTERPLAY by Adele Edling Shank; Director, Harris Yulin; Set, Douglas Stein; Lighting, William Armstrong; Sound, Gary Harris; Hairstylist, Antonio Soddu; Production Supervisor, Kim Novick; Casting, Meg Simon/Fran Kumin; Technical Director, Phil Miller; Wardrobe, Rita Robbins; Props, William Squier; Associate Director, Drew Farber; Press, Richard Kornberg

CAST: James Olson (James), Carlin Glynn (Louise), Geoffrey Sharp (Josh), Ann Talman (Anne), Judith Roberts (Gem), Reed Birney (Jonathan), Robert Dorfman (Michael), Cristine Rose (Jenny)
   A drama in two acts. The action takes place last Christmas in suburban California.

SOHO REPERTORY THEATRE

Eighth Season

Artistic Directors, Jerry Engelbach, Marlene Swartz; Production Manager, Brian Chavanne; Managing Director, Frank Simon; Dramaturge, Victor Gluck; Stage Manager, Deborah A. Friedman

Thursday, October 21,—November 14, 1982 (20 performances)
THE SILVER TASSIE by Sean O'Casey; Music by author and from traditional sources; Director, Carey Perloff; Set, Louanne Gilleland; Costumes, Kalina Ivanov; Lighting, Mary Jo Dondlinger; Musical Director/Pianist, Catherine Reid; Technical Director, Brad Sizemore
CAST: Ralph Drischell (Sylvester Heegan), Jonathan Chappell (Simon Norton/Corporal), Angela Workman (Susie Monican), Janni Brenn (Mrs. Foran), Joi Staton (Mrs. Heegan), Dustin Evans (Teddy Foran), Victor Talmadge (Harry Heegan), Simon Sachs (Barney Bagnal), Ellen Maxted (Jessie Taite), Joe White (Croucher/Forby Maxwell)

A tragicomedy in four acts with one intermission.

Thursday, January 27,—February 27, 1983 (27 performances)
FANSHEN by David Hare; Director, Michael Bloom; Set, Raymond Kluga; Costumes, Steven L. Birnbaum; Lighting, David Noling; Sound, Steven Brant; Fight Director, Ellen Saland; Props, Stephanie Rowden; Stage Manager, Vincent A. Feraudo
CAST: Sharita Hunt (Ch'ung-lai's Wife), Time Winters (Cheng K'uan), Tom Sminkey (T'ien-ming), Ryn Hodes (Hu Hsueh-chen), Patrizia Norcia (Fa-liang), Fredric Mao (Shen Chiang-ho), Dustin Evans (Man-hsi), Robertson Dean (Yu-lai), Shelly Desai (Tui-chin)

New York premiere of play in two parts, based on book by William Hinton.

Thursday, March 10,—April 3, 1983 (20 performances)
KID TWIST by Len Jenkin; Director, Tony Barsha; Set, Dorian Vernacchio; Costumes, Elena Pellicciaro; Lighting, Chaim Gitter; Sound, Kathleen King
CAST: Jean Bambury (Shade), Mark Margolis (Sarge), Anthony Risoli (Puggy/Rabbi/D.A.), Andrew Clark (Big Sid/Babe Ruth/Warden/Santa), Brian Delate (Jake/Capt. Pruss), Richard Bright (Abe Reles), Kathryn Beckwith (Goldie), Richard Council (Babyface), Michael Brody (Joker), Judson Camp (Reporter), Ray Xifo (Finkle), Diane Cypkin (Shirley Reles)

A play in two acts about the life and time of Abe Reles, alias Kid Twist.

Thursday, April 28,—May 22, 1983 (20 performances)
RAPE UPON RAPE by Henry Fielding; Director, Anthony Bowles; Set, Raymond Kluga; Costumes, Gene K. Lakin; Lighting, David Noling; Stage Manager, Pamela Edington; "Drinking Song" written and arranged by Anthony Bowles; Technical Director, Tracy Martin; Casting, Joel Goldman
CAST: Andrew Barnicle (Capt. Constant/Porer), Suzanne Ford (Hilaret), Marilyn Redfield (Cloris/Mrs. Staff/Isabella), Alan Zampese (Politic), George Maguire (Dabble/Quill/Worthy), Jim Denton (Faithful/Watch/Drawer), Steve Sterner (Sotmore), Richard Behren (Ramble/Fireball), Ward Asquith (Constable Staff), Victor Caroli (Justice Squeezum), Ann MacMillan (Mrs. Squeezum)

American premiere of an 18th Century political farce in 10 scenes and 2 acts.
(NEW VIC THEATRE) Thursday, December 9, 1982—January 9, 1983 (12 performances). Stonewall Repertory Theater (Evan Senreich, Artistic Director; Michael Pritchard, Executive Producer; Billy Cunningham, Associate Producer) presents:
THE LOVERS' PLAY by Philip Blackwell; Director, Randy Buck; Set, Robert Edmonds; Sound, Bob Katz; Lighting, Pat Dignan; Stage Managers, Tom Vaccaro, Garwood
CAST: Robert Bell (Michael), Peter Oliver-Norman (Robert), Rafael Fuentes (Attendant)

A play in two acts

Suzanne Ford, Steve Sterner, Victor Caroli, Andrew Barnicle in "Rape upon Rape" (*Joseph Schuyler Photo*)

TEN TEN REP

Courtney Tucker, Gary P. Martin, Producing Directors
Third Season

(PARK AVENUE CHRISTIAN CHURCH) Saturday, June 12—27, 1982 (12 performances)
THE FREEDOM OF THE CITY by Brian Friel; Director, Ron Daley; Set, Bob Phillips; Lighting, Lisa Grossman; Costumes, Susan Cox; Music Director, Deena Kaye; Stage Manager, Lysbeth Hopper
CAST: Todd Waring (Skinner), Patty O'Brien (Lily), Courtney Tucker (Michael), Wendy Northup (Cameraperson), Ernest R. Davies (Judge), Jack Mahoney (Constable), Richard Abernethy (Dr. Dobbs), Brett Cochrane (Soldier 1), Doug Lewis (Soldier 2), Craig Purinton (Liam O'Kelly), Jim Lyness (Balladeer), Callan Egan (Priest), Rodney W. Clark (Brigadier), Gary F. Martin (Dr. Winbourne), Philip Wentworth (Prof. Cuppley)

Friday, October 8—24, 1982 (12 performances)
TWILIGHT CANTATA by Bradley Rand Smith; Director, David Saint; Set, Bill Motyka; Lighting, Jeffrey McRoberts; Costumes, Joan Weis; Assistant Director, Martha Kearns; Production Assistant, Stephen Hicks
CAST: Ellyn Williams (Karen), Mollie Collison (Jeanie), Patrick James Clarke (Peter), Victor Slezak (Lyle), Mary Doyle (Millie), Sam Stoneburner (Ed), Martha Schlamme (Caroline)

Friday, December 3—19, 1982 (12 performances)
PERIOD OF ADJUSTMENT by Tennessee Williams; Director, Thomas Edward West; Set, Toru Shimakawa; Lighting, Debra Dumas; Costumes, Martha Hally; Stage Manager, Kathe Mull; Props, Wanda Ortiz
CAST: David Mack (Ralph Bates), Alana West (Isabel Haverstick), Courtney Tucker (George Haverstick), Ritch Brinkley (Mr. McGillicuddy), Jayne Heller (Mrs. McGillicuddy), Robert Stuart (Police Officer), Mary Ed Porter (Dorothea Bates), Barbara Callander (Susie)

Tuesday, May 24,—June 8, 1983 (11 performances)
AS YOU LIKE IT by William Shakespeare; Director, Robert W. Smith; Set, Alan E. Muraoka; Costumes, Greg Barnes; Lighting, Larry Opitz; Musical Score, Ron Herder; Sound, Ray Hopper; Stage Managers, Kathleen Marsters, Diana Kain; Technical Director, David Yergan
CAST: Hunt Block (Orlando), Tom Sleeth (Adam), Peter Bergman (Oliver), Cynthia Altmann (Dennis), Raphael Nash (Charles), Annette Helde (Rosalind), Sally Dunn (Celia), William Denis (Touchstone), Todd Waring (Le Beau/Jacues), Malachy Cleary (Forest Lord), Roger Hatch (Forest Lord), Dan Mirro (Forest Lord), Barry Ford (Duke Frederick), Jodi Lynne McClintock (Hisperia), George Hamlin (Duke Senior), Mark Barchelder (Amiens), Lee Sloan (Corin), Emmett Smith (Silvius), Terry Finn (Audrey), Courtney Tucker (Sir Oliver Martext/Jaques de Boys), Largo Woodruff (Phebe), Dennis Drake (William), Irma Larrison (Hymen)

David Mack, Mary Ed Porter
in "Period of Adjustment"

VINEYARD THEATRE

Barbara Zinn, Artistic Director
Second Season

Administrative Director, Susan Wilder; Literary Manager, Douglas Aibel; Technical Director, Don Coleman; Music Directors, Hanna Tennen, Elliot Weiss; Art Director, Helen Burdon Price; Press, Free Lance Talents, Francine L. Trevens, David Mayhew

VINEYARD THEATRE Friday, October 8—31, 1982 (13 performances and 3 previews)
ROCKAWAY by John Patrick Shanley; Director, June Stein; Set, Evelyn Sakash; Lights, Mal Sturchio; Costumes, Michele Reisch; Stage Managers, Carol Lang, Susan Aronoff
CAST: Orson Bean (John Caroon), MacIntyre Dixon (Blackie Caroon), John Fiedler (Dr. Welch), Elizabeth Lawrence (Maud), Lela Ivey (Oona Caroon), Keith Reddin (Tommy Caroon), Linda Selman (Kathleen Caroon), Hall Hunsinger (Raymond Durmond)
A comedy in 2 acts and 3 scenes. The action takes place in June of 1957 in Rockaway Beach, Queens, NY.

Friday, November 19,—December 5, 1982 (12 performances)
MIRANDA AND THE DARK YOUNG MAN with Music by Elie Siegmeister; Libretto, Edward Eager; Director, Joseph A. LoSchiavo; Conductor, Scott Thompson; Sets, Sally Locke; Lights, Ron McIntyre; Costumes, Gail Brassard; Stage Manager, Julie Moseley
CAST: Marla Welker (Miranda), Gary Giardina (Father), Glenn Billingsley (Dark Young Man), Eileen Schauler (Aunt Nan), Jim Beers (Fair Young Man), Middle Aged Man (Robert E. Miller)
SUNDAY EXCURSION with Music by Alec Wilder; Libretto, Arnold Sundgaard; Other credits same as preceding listing
CAST: Cynthia Reynolds (Alice), Laura Campbell (Veronica), David Kellett (Hillary), Timothy LaFontaine (Marvin), Wilbur Lewis (Tim)

Friday, January 7—30, 1983 (16 performances)
DADDIES by Douglas Gower; Set, William John Aupperlee; Director, Douglas Aibel; Lighting, David Bergstein; Sound, Brad Phillips; Production Coordinator, Leslie B. Goldstein; Technical Director, Kate Mennone; Stage Managers, Leslie B. Goldstein, Lawrence Rajotte
CAST: Richmond Hoxie (George Ross), Frank Girardeau (Carl Cooper)
A play in two acts. The action takes place at the present time during Christmas Eve

Friday, February 18—27, 1983 (16 performances)
LIVING QUARTERS by Brian Friel; Director, Susan Einhorn; Set, Ursula Belden; Costumes, Muriel Stockdale; Lighting, Toni Goldin; Stage Managers, Laura Heller, Kathy Neufeld; Technical Director, Kate Mennone; Wardrobe, Linda Melloy; Production Assistants, Lisa Immarco, Terri Klestzick; Press, Bruce Cohen
CAST: Ralph Williams (Sir), John Braden (Commandant Frank Butler), Anne O'Sullivan (Tina Butler), Robin Butler (Helen Kelly), Laura Gardner (Miriam Donnelly), Michael Butler (Ben Butler), Vince O'Brien (Father Tom Carty), Tony Pasquilini (Charlie Donnelly), Keliher Walsh (Anna)
A drama in two acts. The action takes place at the present time in Ireland.

WPA THEATRE

Kyle Renick, Artistic Director
Sixth Season

Managing Director, Wendy Bustard; Literary Adviser/Casting Director, Darlene Kaplan; Technical Directors, Ross Wilmeth, Lynn Fiorenzano; Production Manager, Julia Barclay; Press, Fred Hoot, David Mayhew

(WPA THEATRE) Thursday, October 28—November 21, 1982 (23 performances)
BACK TO BACK by Al Brown; Director, Douglas Johnson; Setting, Edward T. Gianfrancesco; Lighting, Craig Evans; Costumes, Don Newcomb; Sound, Michael Kartzmer; Stage Manager, Mary Fran Loftus; Props, Julia Barclay; Production Assistant, Andree Devine
CAST: Eugene Lee (Verville), Keith Gordon (Hughes)
A drama in two acts. The action takes place during November of 1966 in Dong Ha, an artillery base on the edge of the demilitarized zone in South Vietnam.

(WPA THEATRE) Thursday, January 27—February 27, 1983 (25 performances). WPA Theatre (Kyle Renick, Artistic Director) presents:
A DIFFERENT MOON by Ara Watson; Director, Sam Blackwell; Setting, Jim Steere; Lighting, Craig Evans; Costumes, Don Newcomb; Sound, Michael Kartzmer; Assistant to Mr. Blackwell, Julia Barclay; Props, Leah Menken; Stage Manager, Mary Fran Loftus; Press, Fred Hoot, David Mayhew, Christopher Kimble
CAST: Christopher Cooper (Tyler Biars), Zina Jasper (Ruth Biars), Betsy Aidem (Jean Biars), Linda Lee Johnson (Sarah Johnson)
A drama in two acts. The action takes place during the summer of 1951 in Masefield, Arkansas.

Elizabeth Lawrence, John Fiedler, Orson Bean, Linda Selman in "Rockaway" (*Gerry Goodstein Photo*)

(WPA THEATRE) Thursday, March 31—April 24, 1983 (22 performances and 3 previews). WPA Theatre (Kyle Renick, Artistic Director) presents:
VIEUX CARRE by Tennessee Williams; Director, Stephen Zuckerman; Set, James Fenhagen; Lighting, Charles Cosler; Costumes, Mimi Maxmen; Sound, Aural Fixation; Incidental Music, Alan Menken; Assistant to Director, Julia Barclay; Wigs, Ethyl Eichelberger; Technical Directors, Ross A. Wilmeth, John Paul Rock; Stage Managers, Mary Fran Loftus, Sharon Stover; Press, Fred Hoot, David Mayhew
CAST: Jacqueline Brookes (Mrs. Wire), Louise Stubbs (Nursie), Mark Soper (The Writer), Anne Twomey (Jane), Tom Klunis (Nightingale), Alex Stuhl (Blake/Policeman/Orderly), Elaine Swann (Mary Maude), Anna Minot (Miss Carrie), John Bedford-Lloyd (Tye), Jeff Garrett (Photographer/Orderly), Brian Hargrove (Sky)
A drama in two acts. The action takes place during the period between the winter of 1938 and the spring of 1939 in a rooming house in the French Quarter of New Orleans, Louisiana.

(WPA THEATRE) Thursday, May 5—June 5, 1983 (25 performances). WPA Theatre (Kyle Renick, Artistic Director) presents:
ASIAN SHADE by Larry Ketron; Director, Dann Florek; Set, Ross A. Wilmeth; Lighting, Phil Monat; Costumes, Don Newcomb; Incidental Music, Denny McCormick; Assistant to Director, Julia Barclay; Stage Managers, R. Nelson Barbee, Sharon Stover; Press, Fred Hoot, David Mayhew
CAST: Mark Benninghofen (Ernie), Lenny Von Dohlen (Tom), Tom Brennan (Neal), Marissa Chibas (Casey), Dianne Neil (Jean), J. Smith-Cameron (Kaylene)
A play in 2 acts and 10 scenes. The action takes place during June 1967 and a year later.

Anne Twomey, John Bedford-Lloyd, Mark Soper in "Vieux Carre"
(*Gerry Goodstein Photo*)

YORK THEATRE COMPANY
Janet Hayes Walker, Producing Director
Fourteenth Season

(CHURCH OF THE HEAVENLY REST) Saturday, November 20—December 5, 1982 (20 performances). The York Theatre Company presents:
THE WISTERIA TREES by Joshua Logan; Newly revised by Mr. Logan; Based on "The Cherry Orchard" by Anton Chekhov; Director, Peter Phillips; Set, James Morgan; Lighting, Mary Jo Dondlinger; Costumes, Sydney Brooks; Production Manager, Molly Grose; Technical Director, Chip Latimer; Stage Managers, Mark Schorr, Jean Davis; Casting, Terry Lorden; Sound, Hal Schuller; Wardrobe, Robert Swasey; Press, Susan L. Schulman, Keith Sherman

CAST Dianne Kirksey (Dolly May), Susan Pellegrino (Martha), David Little (Yancy Loper), Hubert Kelly, Jr. (Henry Arthur Henry), Heather Lupton (Antoinette), Avon Long (Scott), Carrie Nye (Lucy Ransdell), Lil Henderson (Cassie), Louis Edmonds (Gavin Leon Andrea), J. R. Horne (Bowman Witherspoon), Mac Randall (Jacques), Chad Restum (Peter Whitfield), Robert Earl Jones (The Stranger), Children: Nell Benjamin, Trelan Holder, Trevor Holder, Zohar Massey, Nathaniel McIlvain, Tahanna Wolcott, Zadikim Ysrael
A drama in 3 acts and 4 scenes. The action takes place during 1905 in the children's parlor and part of the gallery surrounding the big house on Wisteria Plantation.

(CHURCH OF THE HEAVENLY REST) Thursday, January 13—30, 1983 (15 performances and 1 preview). The York Theatre Company (Janet Hayes Walker, Producing Director) presents:
THE BOY'S OWN STORY by Peter Flannery; Director, Richard Seyd; Set, James Morgan; Lighting, Mary Jo Dondlinger; Technical Director, Sally Smith; Production Manager, Molly Grose; Presented in association with Bruce Michael and Neil Fleckman; Stage Managers, Mark Rhodes, Jean T. Davis; Press, Keith Sherman

CAST: Jim Piddock in a solo performance. The action takes place on a remote playing field in a public park on a Sunday morning in Stratton England, at the present time.

(CHURCH OF THE HEAVENLY REST) Saturday and Sunday, March 5—6, 1983 (2 performances). The York Theatre Company presents:
TO HEAVEN IN A SWING written and performed by Katharine Houghton; Director, Ken Jenkins; Presented in association with First Folium Productions.

Avon Long, Carrie Nye
in "The Wisteria Trees"

(CHURCH OF THE HEAVENLY REST) Thursday, March 31—April 17, 1983 (20 performances). The York Theatre Company (Janet Hayes Walker, Producing Director) presents:
COLETTE COLLAGE with Book and Lyrics by Tom Jones; Music, Harvey Schmidt; Director, Fran Soeder; Set, James Morgan; Lighting, Mary Jo Dondlinger; Costumes, Sigrid Insull; Production Manager, Molly Grose; Technical Directors, Deborah Alix Martin, Sally Smith; Choreography, Janet Watson; Musical Director, Eric Stern; Stage Managers, Peter J. Taylor, Jean Davis, Steven Benson; Props, Jonathan Blum; Wigs, David H. Lawrence; Wardrobe, Robert Swasey; Press, Keith Sherman

CAST: Steven F. Hall (Maurice), George Hall (Jacques), Joanne Beretta (Sido), Timothy Jerome (Willy), Jana Robbins (Colette), Howard Pinhasik (Captain/Ensemble), Mayla McKeehan (Aimee/Ensemble), Terry Baughan (Ida/Ensemble), Tim Ewing (Cheri/Ensemble), Dan Shaheen (Dr. Dutrate/Ensemble/Stage Manager), Susan J. Baum (Nita/Fluff/Ensemble)
MUSICAL NUMBERS: Opening, Somewhere, Come to Life, A Simple Country Wedding, Do It for Willy, Woman of the World, There's Another World, Why Can't I Walk Through That Door?, The Music Hall, Dream of Egypt, Love Is Not a Sentiment Worthy of Respect, Autumn Love, Riviera Nights, Oo-La-La, Something for the Summer, Madame Colette, You Could Hurt Me, Be My Lady, Earthly Paradise, Growing Older, Joy
A musical in two acts based on the life of the French writer Colette.

(CHURCH OF THE HEAVENLY REST) Tuesday, May 10—20, 1983 (12 performances). The York Theatre Co. (Janet Hayes Walker, Producing Director) presents:
A MIDSUMMER NIGHT'S DREAM by William Shakespeare; Director, Janet Hayes Walker; Set, James Morgan; Costumes, Holly Hynes; Lighting, Michael Baumgarten; Music, Richard Aven; Choreographer, Martha Hirschman; Technical Director, Deborah Alix Martin; Stage Managers, Jean Davis, Molly Grose; Sound, David Oberon; Wardrobe, Robert Swasey; Press, Keith Sherman

CAST: Lisa Barnes (Mernia), Amy Beatie (Cobweb), John Bergstrom (Theseus), Kermit Brown (Peter Quince), Roger Cox (Snug/Lion), Carrie Drosnes (Peaseblossom), Scott Ellis (Puck), Elmore James (Philostrate), Kurt Johnson (Oberon), Julia Kay (Moth), Laurie Klatscher (Helena), Gregory Lehane (Flute), Dyllan McGee (Mustardseed), Thomas Nahrwold (Lysander), John Newton (Bottom), Viveca Parker (Titania), Julie Ramaker (Hippolyta), Tom Ramsay (Starveling/Moon), Scott Rhyne (Demetrius), Frederick Walters (Egeus), Ralph David Westfall (Snout/-Wall)
A comedy performed in two acts. The action takes place in Athens and a wood nearby.

Joanna Beretta, Jana Robbins
in "Colette Collage"

ALBERT EINSTEIN: THE PRACTICAL BOHEMIAN

Written by Ed Metzger, Laya Gelff; Director/Producer, Laya Gelff; Artistic Coordinator, Sully Boyar; Presented by MC Square Productions; Tour began during November 1982 and continued through May of 1983.

CAST
ED METZGER

A solo performance portraying the character and ideas of Albert Einstein in two acts: The Years in Europe, The Years in America.

Right: Ed Metzger as Einstein

Entire cast of "Amadeus"

Peter Crook, Daniel Davis, Tanya Pushkine in "Amadeus"

AMADEUS

By Peter Shaffer; Director, Roger Williams; Production, Peter Hall; Design, John Bury; Associate Scenic Designer, Ursula Belden; Associate Costume Designer, John David Ridge; Associate Lighting Designer, Beverly Emmons; Music Directed and Arranged by Harrison Birtwistle; Presented by Tom Mallow in association with James Janek; Associate Producer/General Manager, James Janek; Assistants to Producers, Jay Brooks, George MacPherson, Jan Mallow; Company Manager, Daryl Dodson; Stage Managers, Charles Collins, Alice Dewey, William Campbell; Production Supervisor, Ellen Raphael; Props, Robert Michael; Wardrobe, Al Costa, Jude Timlin; Assistant to Director, Richard Jay-Alexander; Production Assistants, Susan O'Brien, Brian Callanan; Casting, Johnson/Liff; Sound, Jack Mann; Wigs and Hairstylist, Paul Huntley; Press, Max Eisen, Maria Somma. Opened at the Masonic Temple, Scranton, PA, on Friday, October 8, 1982, and still touring May 31, 1983. For original Broadway production, see THEATRE WORLD Vol. 37.

CAST

Antonio Salieri	Daniel Davis
Venticelli	Ronald Sopyla, W. P. Dremak
Salieri's valet	Stuart Rudin
Salieri's cook	Donald L. Norris
Joseph II, Emperor of Austria	Philip Pleasants
Johann Kilian von Strack	Jonathan Farwell
Count Orsini-Rosenberg	Charles Rule
Baron van Swieten	Keith Perry
Priest	Fred Melamed
Giuseppe Bonno	Kevin Sullivan
Teresa Salieri, wife of Salieri	Bonnie Bowers
Katherina Cavalieri, Salieri's pupil	Mary Jo Salerno
Constanze Weber, wife of Mozart	Tanya Pushkine
Wolfgang Amadeus Mozart	Peter Crook
Major Domo	Ron Keith
Valets	Peter Kingsley, Walker Hicklin, Peter Toran, William Campbell, Paul Maisano, Arnie Burton

CITIZENS OF VIENNA: Arnie Burton, Bonnie Bowers, William Campbell, W. P. Dremak, Jonathan Farwell, Walker Hicklin, Jill Jones, Ron Keith, Peter Kingsley, Paul Maisano, Donald L. Norris, Keith Perry, Philip Pleasants, Stuart Rudin, Charles Rule, Mary Jo Salerno, Ronald Sopyla, Kevin Sullivan, Peter Toran.
UNDERSTUDIES: Jonathan Farwell (Salieri), Peter Kingsley (Mozart), Mary Jo Salerno (Constanze), Ron Keith (Joseph II/Venticelli), Walter Hicklin (Bonno/Venticelli), Kevin Sullivan (von Strack/van Sweiten/Valet), Fred Melamed (Count/Cook), Jill Jones (Teresa/Katherina), William Campbell (Major Domo)

A drama in two acts. The action takes place in Vienna in November 1823 and, in recall, the decade 1781–1791.

Martha Swope Photos

BARNUM

Music, Cy Coleman; Lyrics, Michael Stewart; Book, Mark Bramble; Directed and Staged by Joe Layton; Design, David Mitchell; Costumes, Theoni V. Aldredge; Lighting, Craig Miller; Sound, Otts Munderloh; Orchestrations, Michael Gibson; Vocal and Dance Arrangements, Cy Coleman; Musical Director, Ross Allen; Presented by Tom Mallow and The Muny of St. Louis in association with James Janek; Associate Producer/General Manager, James Janek; Assistant to Producers, Jay Brooks, George MacPherson, Jan Mallow; Company Manager, Alan Ross Kosher; Stage Managers, Harold Goldfaden, Steve Wappel, Carol Schuberg; Props, Bill Pomeroy, Devin Query; Wardrobe, Fred Lloyd, Francis Obidowski; Hairstylist, Meg Davis; Production Assistants, Susan O'Brien, Brian Callanan; Assistant Musical Director, Jeff Conrad; Press, Barbara Glenn, Maria Somma. Opened at the Palace Theatre, Columbus, OH, on Thursday, August 5, 1982 and still touring May 31, 1983. For original Broadway production, see THEATRE WORLD Vol. 36.

CAST

Phineas Taylor Barnum	Harvey Evans
Chairy Barnum	Jan Pessano
Ringmaster/Julius Goldschmidt/James A. Bailey	Kelly Walters
Chester Lyman/Wilton	R. Robert Melvin
Joice Heth	Robin Kersey
Amos Scudder/Edgar Templeton	Gordon Weiss
Acrobat Extraordinaire	Malcolm Perry
Lady Plate Balancer	Mary Ellen Richardson
Lady Juggler/Susan B. Anthony	Susan Dawn Carson
Baton Twirler	Darlene Cory
Chief Bricklayer	Skip Lackey
White-faced Clown	Robert D. Newell
Sherwood Stratton/One-Man Band/Humbert Morrissey	Charles Edward Hall
Mrs. Sherwood Stratton	Diane Abrams
Tom Thumb	Leonard John Crofoot
Jenny Lind	Kathleen Marsh
Lady Aerialist	Kathy Lynn
Juggler Extraordinaire	Fred Feldt
Pianists	Kristen Blodgette, David Rhodes

UNDERSTUDIES: Kelly Walters (Barnum), Susan Dawn Carson (Chairy), Mary Ellen Richardson (Jenny), Charles Edward Hall (Chester/Amos), Fred Feldt (Ringmaster/Stratton/Bailey), Malcolm Perry (Goldschmidt/Morrissey), Kathy Lynn (Mrs. Stratton), Carol Schuberg (Susan B. Anthony), Diane Abrams (Tom Thumb/Joice Heth), Robert D. Newell (Wilton), Skip Lackey (Clown), Cee Lewis (Band/Bricklayer/Templeton), Swing: Carol Schuberg, Cee Lewis

MUSICAL NUMBERS: There Is a Sucker Born Ev'ry Minute, Thank God I'm Old, The Colors of My Life, One Brick at a Time, Museum Song, I Like Your Style, Bigger Isn't Better, Love Makes Such Fools of Us All, Out There, Come Follow the Band, Black and White, The Prince of Humbug, Join the Circus

A musical in two acts.

Martha Swope Photos

Harvey Evans, Jan Pessano in "Barnum"

DANCIN'

Conceived, Directed and Choreographed by Bob Fosse; Recreated by Gail Benedict; Scenery, Peter Larkin; Costumes, Willa Kim; Lighting, Jules Fisher; Sound, Abe Jacob; Music Arranged by Gordon Lowry Harrell; Orchestrations, Ralph Burns, Michael Gibson; Musical Director, Randy Booth; Music and Lyrics by Ralph Burns, George M. Cohan, Neil Diamond, Jerry Leiber & Mike Stoller, Bob Haggart, Ray Bauduc, Gil Rodin & Bob Crosby, Johnny Mercer & Harry Warren, Louis Prima, John Philip Sousa, Barry Mann & Cynthia Weil, Felix Powell & George Asaf, Sigmund Romberg & Oscar Hammerstein II, Cat Stevens, Jerry Jeff Walker; Presented by Tom Mallow in association with James Janek; General Manager, S. Krause, Luis Montero, Barbara McKinley; Props, Alan Alexander; Wardrobe, Tina Ryan, Margaret Danz; Production Assistant, Brian Callanan; Associate Musical Director, Steve Guttman; Hairstylist, Romaine Greene; Wigs/Makeup, Rhonda Esposito; Press, Max Eisen, Irene Gandy. Opened in the Performing Arts Center, Milwaukee, WI, Tuesday, July 29, 1980 and still touring May 21, 1983. For original Broadway production, see THEATRE WORLD Vol. 34.

CAST

Quin Baird, Brian Bullard, Maggie Caponio, Stephanie Conlow, Andre De La Roche, Germaine Edwards, Karen E. Fraction, Keith Keen, Joseph Konicki, Diana Laurenson, Kevin McCready, Barbara McKinley, Kim Noor, Joanie O'Neill, Stanley Perryman, Garrison Rochelle, Alison Sherve, Linda Smith

MUSICAL NUMBERS: Hot August Night, Crunchy Granola Suite, Mr. Bojangles, Percussion, I Wanna Be a Dancin' Man, Big Noise from Winnetka, I've Got Them Feelin' Too Good Today Blues, Was Dog a Doughnut, Sing Sing Sing, Here You Come Again, Yankee Doodle Dandy, Gary Owen, Stouthearted Men, Under the Double Eagle, Dixie, Rally Round the Flag, Pack Up Your Troubles, Stars and Stripes Forever, Yankee Doodle Disco, Dancin'

Martha Swope Photos

"Dancin'"

A CHORUS LINE

Conceived, Directed and Choreographed by Michael Bennett; Book, James Kirkwood, Nicholas Dante; Music, Marvin Hamlisch; Lyrics, Edward Kleban; Set, Robin Wagner; Costumes, Theoni V. Aldredge; Lighting, Tharon Musser; Sound, Abe Jacobs; Orchestrations, Bill Byers, Hershy Kay, Jonathan Tunick; Vocal Arrangements, Don Pippin; Music Coordinator, Robert Thomas; Associate Producer, Bernard Gersten; Music, Director, Sherman Frank; Joseph Papp presents the New York Shakespeare Festival Production in association with Plum Production; Co-Choreographer, Bob Avian; General Managers, Laurel Ann Wilson, Jennifer Hadley, Robert Kamlot; Production Supervisor, Jason Steven Cohen; Company Manager, Noel Gilmore; Associate Conductor, Howard Levitsky; Wardrobe, Alyce Gilbert, David Barnard; Props, William Barnard, Jr.; Sound, Otts Munderloh; Stage Managers, Bud Coffey, J. Marvin Crosland, Christopher Gregory; Press, Merle Debuskey, Bill Wilson, Richard Kornberg, Barbara Carroll, William Schelble. Closed at the Shubert Theatre, Chicago, IL., on May 29, 1983. For original Broadway production see Theatre World Vol. 31.

CAST: John Addis (Larry), Robert Amirante (Greg), Karis Christensen (Roy), Lisa Clarson (Sheila), Randy Clements (Don), Mary Lou Crivello (Diana), John Dolf (Mike), Lois Englund (Val), Helen Frank (Bebe), Laurie Gamache (Kristine), Lauren Goler (Rhoda), Christopher Gregory (Kevin), J. Richard Hart (Tom), Eivind Harum (Zach), Michael Ian-Lerner (Frank), Angelique Ilo (Cassie), Ron Kurowski (Bobby), Robin Lyon (Maggie), Wayne Meledandri (Paul), Kari Nicolaisen (Tricia), Evan Pappas (Al), Reggie A. Phoenix (Butch), Laureen Valuch Piper (Vickie), Tommy Re (Joe), Sachi Shimizu (Connie), J. Thomas Smith (Mark), Kimberly Dawn Smith (Lois), Woodrow Thompson (Richie), Leigh Webster (Cynthia), Joanna Zercher (Judy)

MUSICAL NUMBERS: See Broadway Calendar, page 61

Martha Swope Photos

A CHORUS LINE

General Managers, Laurel Ann Wilson, Janet Brown; Stage Managers, Jake Bell, Carmen Albanese, Christopher Gregory; Company Managers, Alexander Holt, Jennifer Hadley; Sound, David Gottwald; Props, John Selig; Wardrobe, Alyce Gilbert, Marilyn Knotts; Press, Merle Debuskey, David Roggensack, William Schelble; For additional credits see preceding listing. Closed Oct. 3, 1982 in Pittsburgh, PA.

CAST: John Addis (Larry), Kevin Blair (Mike), Karis Christensen (Tom), Mary Lou Crivello (Diana), Fraser Ellis (Mark), Sheryll Fager-Jones (Sheila), Willy Falk (Paul), Raymond Flowers (Richie), Helen Frank (Bebe), Mary Ann Hay (Lois), Frank Kliegel (Don), Frank Kosik (Al), Philip Mollet (Roy), Phineas Newborn III (Butch), Kari Nicolaisen (Tricia), Scott Pearson (Zach), Laureen Valuch Piper (Val), Joseph Rich (Greg), Jim T. Ruttman (Bobby), Ann Louise Schaut (Cassie), Cilda Shaur (Cassie), Sachi Shimizu (Connie), Seth Walsh (Frank), Leigh Webster (Judy), Kathy Flynn-McGrath (Kristine), Karen Ziemba (Maggie)

MUSICAL NUMBERS: See Broadway Calendar, page 61

DREAMGIRLS

Book and Lyrics, Tom Eyen; Music, Henry Krieger; Direction and Choreography, Michael Bennett; Co-Choreographer, Michael Peters; Set, Robin Wagner; Costumes, Theoni V. Aldredge; Lighting, Tharon Musser; Sound Otts Munderloh; Musical Supervision/Orchestrations, Harold Wheeler; Musical Director, Yolanda Segovia; Vocal Arrangements, Cleavant Derricks; Hairstylist, Ted Azar; General Management, Marvin A. Krauss, Eric L. Angelson, Gary Gunas, Steven C. Callahan, Joey Parnes; Company Manager, Drew Murphy; Stage Managers, Jeff Hamlin, Jacqueline Yancey, David Blackwell; Technical Coordinator, Arthur Siccardi; Props, Al Steiner, Greg Martin; Wardrobe, Alyce Gilbert, Dan Lomax, Sally Smith; Assistant to Choreographers, Geneva Burke; Associate Costume Designer, Frank Krenz; Production Assistant, Rob Morrow; Casting, Johnson/Liff, Olaiya; Press, Merle Debuskey, Diane Judge, Judi Davidson, Tim Choy, Ellen Friedberg; Presented by Michael Bennett, Bob Avian, David Geffen and the Shubert Organization (Gerald Schoenfeld, Chairman; Bernard B. Jacobs, President). Opened at the Shubert Theatre, Los Angeles, CA, Sunday, March 20, 1983 and still playing May 31, 1983. For original Broadway production, see THEATRE WORLD, Vol. 38.

CAST

The Stepp Sisters	Deborah Burrell, Tyra T. Ferrell, LueCinda RamSeur, Johnnie Teamer
Charlene	Betty K. Bynum
Joanne	Susan Beaubian
Marty	Weyman Thompson
Curtis Taylor, Jr	Larry Riley
Deena Jones	Linda Leilani Brown
M.C./Mr. Morgan	Ron Richardson
Tiny Joe Dixon/Nightclub Owner	Roy L. Jones
Lorrell Robinson	Arnetia Walker
C. C. White	Lawrence Clayton
Effie Melody White	Jennifer Holliday
Little Albert and the Tru-Tones	Rudy Huston, Abe Clark, Vincent M. Cole, Thomas Scott Gordon, Gordon J. Owens
James Thunder Early	Clinton Derricks-Carroll
Edna Burke	Edwina Lewis
James Early Band	Abe Clark, Vincent M. Cole, Rudy Huston, Gordon J. Owens, Stephen Terrell
Wayne	Maurice Felder
Dave and the Sweethearts	Ray Benson, Delyse Lively, Candi Milo
Frank, press agent	Tim Cassidy
Michelle Morris	Deborah Burrell
Five Tuxedos	Abe Clark, Vincent M. Cole, Thomas Scott Gordon, Gordon J. Owens, Ron Richardson
Les Style	Susan Beaubian, Betty K. Bynum, Candi Milo, Johnnie Teamer
Film Executives	Ray Benson, Donn Simione, Abe Clark

FANS, REPORTERS, PARTY GUESTS, ETC.: Susan Beaubian, Ray Benson, Betty Clark, Tim Cassidy, Abe Clark, Lawrence Clayton, Vincent M. Cole, Tyra T. Ferrell, Thomas Scott Gordon, Rudy Huston, Roy L. Jones, Edwina Lewis, Delyse Lively, Candi Milo, Gordon Owens, LueCinda RamSeur, Ron Richardson, Angel Rogers, Donn Simione, Johnnie Teamer, Stephen Terrell, Kristi Tucker, Derryl Yeager, Swings: Sharon Brooks, Helen Castillo, Phillip Gilmore
UNDERSTUDIES: Lillias White (Effie), Deborah Burrell (Deena), Susan Beaubian (Lorrell), LueCinda RamSeur (Michelle), Weyman Thompson (Curtis), Ron Richardson (James Thunder Early/Marty/Jerry)
MUSICAL NUMBERS: I'm Looking for Something, Goin' Downtown, Taking the Long Way Home, Move, Fake Your Way to the Top, Cadillac Car, Steppin' to the Bad Side, Party Party, I Want You Baby, Family, Dreamgirls, Press Conference, Only the Beginning, Heavy, It's All Over, And I Am Telling You I'm Not Going, Love Love You Baby, I Am Changing, One More Picture Please, When I First Saw You, Got to be Good Times, Ain't No Party, I Meant You No Harm, Quintette, The Rap, I Miss You Old Friend, One Night Only, I'm Somebody, Faith in Myself, Hard to Say Goodbye My Love

A musical in 2 acts and 20 scenes. The action takes place during the early 1960's and the early 1970's.

Martha Swope Photos

Top Right: Arnetia Walker, Linda Leilani Brown, Lawrence Clayton, Larry Riley, Jennifer Holliday in "Dreamgirls" (*Martha Swope Photo*)

FORBIDDEN BROADWAY

Concept and Lyrics, Gerard Alessandrini; Director, Gerard Alessandrini; Costumes, Chet Ferris; General Manager, Norman Maibaum; Presented by Playkill Productions (Peter Brash, Melissa Burdick); Executive Producer, Sella Palsson; Stage Manager, Jeff Peters; Assistant to General Manager, Diahnne Hill; Press, Becky Flora, Ed Cassidy, John Watson. Opened at The Comedy Store, Los Angeles, CA, Tuesday, April 26, 1983 and still playing May 31, 1983. For original NY production, see THEATRE WORLD Vol. 38.

CAST

Gerard Alessandrini

Fred Barton	Dee Hoty
Bill Carmichael	Chloe Webb

A musical satire in two acts.

Henry Grossman Photos

Gerard Alessandrini, Dee Hoty, Bill Carmichael, Chloe Webb, Fred Barton in "Forbidden Broadway" (*Henry Grossman Photo*)

Derin Altay, R. Michael Baker in "Evita"

EVITA

Lyrics, Tim Rice; Music, Andrew Lloyd Webber; Director, Harold Prince; Choreography, Larry Fuller; General Manager, Howard Haines; Sets/Costumes/Projections, Timothy O'Brien, Tazeena Firth; Lighting, David Hersey; Sound, Abe Jacob; Assistant to Mr. Prince, Ruth Mitchell; Original cast album on MCA Records; Presented by Robert Stigwood in association with David Land; Executive Producers, R. Tyler Gatchell, Jr., Peter Neufeld; Musical Director, Pamela Phillips; Assistant Musical Director, Keith Phillips; Props, George Green, Jr.; Wardrobe, Adelaide Laurino; Hairstylist/Makeup, Richard Allen, Jay Braddick Hirt; Production Assistants, Charles Christensen, Patrick Fitzpatrick; Stage Managers, Thomas M. Guerra, Richard Evans, Jayne Turner; Company Manager, James Jensen; Press, Mary Bryant, Philip Rinaldi, Becky Flora. Opened Sunday, Jan. 13, 1980 at Shubert Theatre, Los Angeles, CA, and closed March 27, 1983 in Minneapolis Orpheum Theatre. For original Broadway production, see THEATRE WORLD Vol. 36.

CAST

Eva .... Derin Altay
matinees: Joy Lober
Che .... R. Michael Baker
Peron .... Robb Alton
Peron's Mistress .... Jill Geddes
Magaldi .... David Dannehl

PEOPLE OF ARGENTINA: David James Cain, Mary Anne Dunroe, John Eskola, Elaine Freedman, William Gilinsky, Paul Harman, James Harms, Lois Hayes, Didi Hitt, Rudy Hogenmiller, Michelle C. Kelly, Mark Lazore, James A. Linduska, Joy Lober, Michael Lofton, Charles Lubeck, Giselle Montanez, Alison Morgan, Sha Newman, Bryan Nicholas, Susan Lubeck Oken, Candice Prior, William Ryall, Bruce Senesac, Laura Soltis, Heidi Stallings, Cheryl Stern, Bruce Taylor, Madeline Weston, Doug Okerson

MUSICAL NUMBERS: July 26, 1952, Requiem for Evita, Oh What a Circus, On This Night of a Thousand Stars, Eva Beware of the City, Buenos Aires, Goodnight and Thank You, The Art of the Possible, Charity Concert, I'd Be Surprisingly Good for You, Another Suitcase in Another Hall, Peron's Latest Flame, A New Argentina, On the Balcony of the Casa Rosada, Don't Cry for Me Argentina, High Flying Adored, Rainbow High, Rainbow Tour, The Actress Hasn't Learned, And the Money Kept Rolling In, Santa Evita, Waltz for Eva and Che, She Is a Diamond, Dice Are Rolling, Eva's Final Broadcast, Montage, Lament

EVITA

Musical Supervisor, Paul Gemignani; Musical Director, Kevin Farrell; Company Manager, Robert Ossenfort; Stage Managers, Frank Marino, Arturo E. Porazzi; Assistant Musical Director, Tim Stella; Press, Mary Bryant, Philip Rinaldi, Jon Essex. Opened in Masonic Temple, Detroit, MI, Sunday, Feb. 28, 1982 and still touring May 31, 1983.

CAST

Eva .... Florence Lacey†1
matinees: Patricia Hemenway†2
Che .... Tim Bowman
Peron .... John Leslie Wolfe
Peron's Mistress .... Patricia Ludd
Magaldi .... Vincent Pirillo

PEOPLE OF ARGENTINA: Marianna Allen, R. Michael Baker, Scott Bodie, John McCool Bowers, Laurie Crochet, Mark Dovey, Diane Duncan, Lynn East, Mark East, Mark East IV, Donna Marie Elio, Kerry Finn, Joanna Glushak, Thomas Scott Gordon, Curtis Gregory, Michael Hansen, Patricia Hemenway, Ken Miller, Jeff Mooring, Marily Morreale, Ron Rusthoven, Lynn Sterling, Robert Torres, Kathy Vestuto, Sam Viverito, Kenneth H. Waller, Don Wonder

MUSICAL NUMBERS: See preceding listing.

†Succeeded by: 1. Patricia Hemenway, 2. Donna Marie Elio

Martha Swope Photos

Above: Tim Bowman

John Leslie Wolfe, Patricia Hemenway in "Evita"

42nd STREET

Music, Harry Warren; Lyrics, Al Dubin; Book, Michael Stewart, Mark Bramble; Based on novel by Bradford Ropes; Director, Lucia Victor after the original by Gower Champion; Choreography by Gower Champion, reproduced by Karin Baker, Randy Skinner; Scenery, Robin Wagner; Costumes, Theoni V. Aldredge; Lighting, Tharon Musser; Musical Director, Stephen Bates; Orchestrations, Philip J. Lang; Musical Coordination, Philip Fradkin; Vocal Arrangements, John Lesko; Dance Arrangements, Donald Johnston; Hairstylist, Anne Sampogna; Sound, Richard Fitzgerald; Casting, Feuer & Ritzer; Presented by David Merrick; General Manager, Leo K. Cohen; Company Manager, John Corkill; Stage Managers, John Brigleb, Douglas F. Goodman, William Kirk, Trudi Green; Props, Leo Herbert; Wardrobe, Gene Wilson, Kathleen Foster, Maria Maldonado; Assistant to the Producer, Bonnie Warschauer; Press, Solters/Roskin/Friedman. Opened in Chicago, IL, at the Lyric Opera House, on Saturday, January 1, 1983 and still touring May 31, 1983. For original Broadway production, see THEATRE WORLD Vol. 37.

CAST

Andy Lee	Leo Muller
Oscar	Chuck Hunnicutt
Mac/Doctor/Thug	Igors Gavon
Annie	Cathleen McGowen
Maggie Jones	Bibi Osterwald
Bert Barry	William Linton
Billy Lawlor	Jim Walton
Peggy Sawyer	Nancy Sinclair†1
Lorraine	Sandra Yarish
Phyllis	Bonnie Patrick
Julian Marsh	Ron Holgate
Dorothy Brock	Elizabeth Allen†2
Abner Dillon	Brooks Morton
Pat Denning	Randy Phillips
Thug	Al Micacchion

ENSEMBLE: David Askler, Kevin Backstrom, Bobby Clark, Marietta Clark, Jeffrey Cornell, Kelly Crafton, Debbie DeBiase, Deanna Dys, Barbara Early, Judy Ehrlich, Mark Frawley, Russell Giesenschlag, Eileen Grace, Terri Griffin, Suzie Jary, Cathy Jones, Frank Kosik, Michael Lee, Patricia Lockery, Bobby Longbottom, Susan Banks McGonegle, Al Micacchion, Bonnie Patrick, Marc Pluf, Russell Rhodes, Richard Ruth, Anne Rutter, John Salvatore, Jeanna Schweppe, Karen Sorensen, Susanne Leslie Sullivan, Nikki Summerford, Vickie Taylor, Cynthia Thole, Evelyn Watson, Sandra Yarish
STANDBYS AND UNDERSTUDIES: Kelly Britt (Dorothy/Maggie), Randy Phillips (Julian), Vickie Taylor (Peggy), Russell Rhodes (Billy), Bobby Clark (Bert), Marc Pluf (Andy), Igors Gavon (Abner/Pat), Sandra Yarish (Annie), Patricia Jepsen, Anne Rutter (Phyllis/Lorraine), Al Micacchion (Mac/Thug/Doctor), Ensemble: Paul Del Vecchio, Trudi Green, Patricia Jepsen, Lynn Marlowe, Tony Parise, Brenda Pipik.

A musical in 2 acts and 13 scenes. The action takes place during 1933 in New York City and Philadelphia.
†Succeeded by: 1. Karen Prunczik, Nancy Sinclair, 2. Millicent Martin

Jennifer Girard Photos

Nancy Sinclair and chorus in "42nd Street"

GEORGIA BROWN AND FRIENDS

The Hillard Elkins Production presented by James M. Nederlander and Laizer Productions; Director, Stanley Dorfman; Conceived and Written by Georgia Brown; Music Director/Arrangements, Steven Cagan; Additional Arrangements, Stanley Myers; Design, Peter David Gould; Costumes, Ruth Morley; Lighting, David F. Segal; Associate Producers, Stanley Schneider, Barbara Platoff, Marcelle Garfield; Sound, Thomas Morse; General Manager, Iron Mountain Productions, Jane E. Cooper; Technical Supervision, Theatrical Services, Arthur Siccardi, Pete Feller; Music Coordinator, Earl Shendell; Assistant to Producers, Ilyanne Dana Morden; Company Manager, Jose Vega; Stage Managers, Charles Blackwell, Jacqueline Crampton, John Elkins; Press, Brocato & Kelman, Solters/-Roskin/Friedman, Josh Ellis, David LeShay, Cindy Valk. Opened at the Curran Theatre in San Francisco, CA, on Wednesday, September 1, 1982 and closed there on September 18, 1982.

CAST

GEORGIA BROWN

MUSICAL NUMBERS: As Long as He Needs Me, The Eagle and Me, Getting Married Today, Going to the Country, I'm Still Here, Is That All There Is?, Jew's Whore, Job Application, Johnny I Hardly Knew You, Ali Ali, Spanish Lament, Lost in the Stars, Mack the Knife, Mad about the Boy, Madame Song, My Father, Pirate Jenny, Raisins and Almonds, Sweet Georgia Brown, Victorian Medley, Waters of March, Who Do You Have to Fuck to Get into the Movies?

A solo performance by Miss Brown who traces the various phases in her life and career.

Vera Anderson Photos

Georgia Brown

HELLO, DOLLY!

Book, Michael Stewart; Music and Lyrics, Jerry Herman; Based on play "The Merchant of Yonkers" by Thornton Wilder; Director, Lucia Victor; Original Choreography by Gower Champion re-created by Terry Lacy; Musical Conductor, Terry La Bolt; Production Supervisor, Jerry Herman; Sets, Oliver Smith; Costumes, Freddy Wittop; Lighting, Martin Aronstein; Musical Director/Dance Music Arrangements, Peter Howard; Costumes re-created by Gail Cooper-Hecht; Sound, Peter J. Fitzgerald; Casting, Mark Reiner; Presented by James M. Nederlander and Fred Walker in conjunction with Charles Lowe Productions; General Management, Theatre Now, William Court Cohen, Edward H. Davis, Norman E. Rothstein, Ralph Roseman, Charlotte Wilcox; Company Manager, Marion Finkler; Production Supervisor, Jeremiah J. Harris; Stage Managers, Pat Tolson, Charles Reif, David Hansen; Wardrobe, Roy Young; Props, Chet Perry; Production Assistant, Bruce Voss; Press, Solters/Roskin/Friedman, Kevin Patterson, Matthew Messinger. Opened at Auditorium Theatre, Rochester, NY, on Monday, April 11, 1983 and still touring May 31, 1983. For original Broadway production, see THEATRE WORLD Volume 20.

CAST

Mrs. Dolly Gallagher Levi	Carol Channing
Ernestina	P. J. Nelson
Ambrose	Michael C. Booker
Horse	Melanie Hodges, Ann Nieman
Horace Vandergelder	Tom Batten
Ermengarde	Jane Dorian
Cornelius Hackl	Davis Gaines
Barnaby Tucker	Gary Wright
Minnie Fay	K. T. Baumann
Irene Molloy	Elizabeth Hansen
Mrs. Rose	Barbara Ann Thompson
Court Clerk	Michael Duran
Rudolph/Judge	Robert L. Hultman

TOWNSPEOPLE: Carolyn DeLany, Kim Farmer, Melanie Hodges, Shannon Lee Jones, Joan Nielsen, Ann Nieman, Jill R. Mackie, Pamela Scott, Connie Beth Speight, Barbara Ann Thompsom, Mary Jo Todaro, Joe Cutaia, Dick Dufour, Michael Duran, Mark Edward, David Lee Kistner, Michael Lackey, David Larson, Kevin Ligon, Ray McFarland, Mark Pennington, Tom Schumacher, Michael Serrechia, Mike Smiley, Garrett Walters, Larry Wray; Swings: Valerie Wright, Terry Lacy

MUSICAL NUMBERS: I Put My Hand In, It Takes a Woman, Put on Your Sunday Clothes, Ribbons Down My Back, Motherhood, Dancing, Before the Parade Passes By, Elegance, Waiters Gallop, Hello Dolly!, Polka Contest, It Only Takes a Moment, So Long Dearie, Finale

A musical in 2 acts and 15 scenes.

Carol Channing (center) in "Hello, Dolly!"

THE KING AND I

Music, Richard Rodgers; Book and Lyrics, Oscar Hammerstein 2nd; Based on novel "Anna and the King of Siam" by Margaret Landon; Sets, John Jay Moore; Costumes, Stanley Simmons; Lighting, Ruth Roberts; Sound, Jack Shearing; Musical Director, Lawrence Brown; Production Supervisor, Conwell Worthington II; Hairstylist, Bobby Abbott; Producer-Director, Mitch Leigh; Jerome Robbins Choreography re-produced by Rebecca West; Executive Producer, Milton Herson; Associate Producer, Manny Kladitis; Company Manager, Louise M. Bayer; Stage Managers, Nikos Kafkalis, Jon R. Hand, Kenneth L. Peck; Props, Nelson F. D'Aloia; Wardrobe, Mary Beth Regan; Hairstylists, Burt Pitcher, Patricia M. LaRocco; Musical Coordinator, Martin Grupp; Assistant to Mr. Leigh, Susan Reed; Press, John Prescott. Opened Feb. 15, 1981 at the Warner Theatre, Washington, DC, and closed at the Fox Theatre, San Diego, CA, June 5, 1983. For original Broadway production, see THEATRE WORLD Vol. 7.

CAST

The King	Yul Brynner
Anna Leonowens	Kate Hunter Brown
Lady Thiang	Hye-Young Choi
The Kralahome	Michael Kermoyan
Lun Tha	Sal Provenza
Tuptim	Patricia Anne Welch
Sir Edward Ramsey	Edward Crotty
Captain Orton	Morton Banks
Prince Chulalongkorn	Kevan Weber
Louis Leonowens	Anthony Rapp
Eliza	Marie Takazawa
The Interpreter	Jae Woo Lee
Simon	Rebecca West
Angel/Fan Dancer	Patricia Weber
Princess Ying Yaowalak	Yvette Laura Martin
Topsy	Sandy Sueoka
Uncle Thomas	Hope Sogawa
Little Eva/Lead Royal Dancer	Evelina Deocares

ENSEMBLE: Alis Elaine Anderson, Aulani, Evelina Deocares, Deborah Harada, Janet Jordan, Cho-Young Kim, Nina Lam, Nancy Latuja, Makalina, Denisa Reyes, Frances Roth, Hope Sogawa, Maggie Stewart, Sandy Sueoka, Cornel Chan, Paul Charles, Kaipo Daniels, Ron Stefan Davis, Raul Gallyot, Thomas Heath, George Mars, Darnell E. Scott, Eric Chan, Timothy Duong, Mark Manasseri, Kathy Nghiem

MUSICAL NUMBERS: I Whistle a Happy Tune, My Lord and Master, Hello Young Lovers, March of the Siamese Children, A Puzzlement, Royal Bankok Academy, Getting to Know You, We Kiss in a Shadow, Shall I Tell You What I Think of You?, Something Wonderful, Western People Funny, I Have Dreamed, The Small House of Uncle Thomas, Song of King, Shall We Dance

A musical in two acts. The action takes place in and around the King's Palace in Bangkok in the 1860's.

Yul Brynner, Kate Hunter Brown in "The King and I"

LENA HORNE: THE LADY AND HER MUSIC

Musical Direction, Harold Wheeler; Set, David Gropman; Costumes, Stanley Simmons; Lighting, Thomas Skelton; Musical Conductor, Coleridge T. Perkinson; Musical Consultant, Luther Henderson; Hairstylist, Phyllis Della; Miss Horne's wardrobe, Giorgio Sant'Angelo; Production Stage by Arthur Faria; Production Assistant, Brenda Braxton; Assistant Conductor, Linda Twine; Recorded by Qwest Records; Presented by James M. Nederlander, Michael Frazier, Fred Walker in association with Sherman Snee and Jack Lawrence. Opened Saturday, September 11, 1982 at Golden Gate Theatre, San Francisco, CA., and still touring May 31, 1983.
LENA'S TRIO: Grady Tate (Drums), Steve Bargonetti (Guitar), Bob Cranshaw (Bass)
MUSICAL NUMBERS: Life Goes On, I'm Going to Sit Right Down, Stormy Weather, As Long as I Live, Push de Button, Fly, I'm Glad There Is You, That's What Miracles Are All About, From This Moment On, Just One of Those Things, Love, A Lady Must Live, Where or When, Surrey with the Fringe on Top, Can't Help Lovin' Dat Man of Mine, Copper Colored Gal of Mine, Deed I Do, I Got a Name, If You Believe, Lady with a Fan, Raisin' the Rent, Watch What Happens, I Want to Be Happy, Better Than Anything

Performed with one intermission.

Martha Swope Photos

Lena Horne

Charles Michael Wright, James Earl Jones, Delroy Lindo

MASTER HAROLD ... and the boys

By Athol Fugard; Director, Mr. Fugard; Set, Jane Clark; Costumes, Sheila McLamb; Lighting, David Noling; Stage Movement, Wesley Fata; General Management, Marvin A. Krauss Associates; Company Manager, Bruce Birkenhead; Props, Patrick Harmeson; Wardrobe, Patti Brundage; Assistant to Mr. Fugard, Gordon Gray; Casting, Meg Simon/Fran Cumin; Presented by Marvin A. Krauss and Irving Siders; Stage Managers, Thomas P. Carr, Lisa Hogarty; Press, Bill Evans, Sandra Manley. Opened Wednesday, March 2, 1983 at the Wilbur Theatre, Boston, MA, and still touring May 31, 1983. For original Broadway production, see THEATRE WORLD Vol. 38.

CAST

Sam .... James Earl Jones
Willie .... Delroy Lindo
Hally .... Charles Michael Wright
STANDBYS: Sullivan Walker (Sam/Willie), John Bowman (Hally)

A drama performed without intermission. The action takes place in the St. Georges Park Tea Room on a wet and windy afternoon in Port Elizabeth, South Africa in 1950.

Martha Swope Photos

NATIONAL SHAKESPEARE COMPANY

TWENTIETH YEAR

Dedicated to the late Philip Meister, Co-Founder and Artistic Director. Managing Director, Elaine Sulka; Scenic and Lighting Designer, Chris Thomas; Costume Designer, Barbara Forbes; Original Music, Clive Smith, John Franceschina; Tour Directors, William Weir, Anthony Ridley; General Manager, Deborah Teller; Production Manager, Pat Kennerly; Casting, Elaine Sulka; Company Manager, Douglas Mackaye Harrington; Stage Manager, Louis J. Fischer; Technical Director, James Deschenes; Stage Combat Choreography, Mykael O'Sruitheain; Choreography, Joan Evans; Assistant to Company, Lysbeth Hopper. On tour from September 1982 through May 1983.

PRODUCTIONS & CASTS

AS YOU LIKE IT directed by James Tripp, with Louis J. Fischer (Adam-/Audrey), James Deschenes (Orlando), Michael Perez (Oliver/Martex/-Forester), Russell Wilson (Dennis/Amiens/William), Douglas Mackaye Harrington (Charles/Duke Senior), Pat Kennerly (LeBeau/Silvius/Forester), Jean Tafler (Rosalind), Sharon A. Frei (Celia), Ivan Sandoval (Touchstone), Alfred Casas (Duke/Jacques/Corin), Mykael O'Sruitheain (Jacques), Denise Simone (Phoebe)

KING LEAR directed by Gene Frankel, with Michael Perez (Edmund), Douglas Mackaye Harrington (Kent), Alfred Casas (Earl of Gloucester), Mykael O'Sruitheain (Lear), James Deschenes (Cornwall), Pat Kennerly (Albany), Ivan Sandoval (King of France/Oswald), Jean Tafler (Goneril), Sharon A. Frei (Regan), Denise Simone (Cordelia), Russell Wilson (Edgar), Louis J. Fischer (Fool)

A MIDSUMMER NIGHT'S DREAM directed by Sue Lawless and B. J. Whiting, with Ivan Sandoval (Puck/Philostrate), Michael Perez (Theseus/Oberon), Jean Tafler (Hippolyta/Titania), Alfred Casas (Egeus/-Quince/Moth), James Deschenes (Demetrius), Russell Wilson (Lysander), Denise Simone (Hermia), Sharon A. Frei (Helena), Louis J. Fischer (Bottom), Mykael O'Sruitheain (Flute/Mustard Seed), Douglas Mackaye Harrington (Snout/Cobweb), Pat Kennerly (Snug/Peasblossom)

Sharon A. Frei, Jean Tafler Photos

"As You Like It"

PETER PAN

Based on play by James M. Barrie; Lyrics, Carolyn Leigh; Music, Moose Charlap; Additional Lyrics, Betty Comden, Adolph Green; Additional Music, Jule Styne; Original production conceived, directed and choreographed by Jerome Robbins; Orchestrations, Ralph Burns; Entire production directed and choreographed by Ron Field; Musical Supervision, Jack Lee; Flying by Foy; Scenery, Michael Hotopp, Paul dePass; Costumes, Bill Hargate; Lighting, Thomas Skelton; Sound, Richard Fitzgerald; Musical Direction, Glen Clugston; Casting, Hughes/Moss; Dance Arrangements, Wally Harper, Dorothea Freitag; Presented by Zev Bufman, James M. Nederlander, Lewis Friedman in association with Spencer Tandy and Jack Molthen; Associate Producers, Richard Martini, Richard Grayson; An Edgewood Organization Production; General Managers, Theatre Now, William Court Cohen, Edward H. Davis, Norman E. Rothstein, Ralph Roseman; Company Manager, L. Liberatore; Assistant Director, David Rubinstein; Stage Managers, Christopher "Kit" Bond, Gregory Nicholas, Allen McMullen; Hairstylist, Robert Abbott; Props, Sam Bagarella; Wardrobe, Donna Peck, Rebecca Denson; Associate Conductor, Stephen Hinnenkamp; Press, Harry Davies, Gurtman & Murtha, Isa Goldberg; A Kolmar-Luth Entertainment. Opened Tuesday, June 15, 1982 in Providence, RI, and closed July 17, 1983 in San Antonio, TX.

CAST

Wendy/Jane	Ann Marie Lee
John	Christopher Wooten
Liza/Shadow	Anne McVey
Michael	Johnny Morgal
Nana/Smee	Andy Hostettler
Mrs. Darling	Lola Fisher
Mr. Darling/Capt. Hook	Rip Taylor
Peter Pan	Karyn Cole
Ostrich	C. J. McCaffrey
Tootles	Dodd Wooten
Nibs	Jason Moreland
Slightly	Michael Emery, Jr.
Curly/Crocodile	Michelan Sisti
Noodler	J. C. Sheets
Crocodile	Jim Wolfe
Tiger Lily	Evelyn Ante
Starkey	Anthony Mastrorilli
Cecco	Tim Salce
Jukes	Edward Magel
Mullins	Maic More
Wendy (Grown up)	Missy Whitchurch

INDIANS, PIRATES: Joel Ferrell, C. J. McCaffrey, Anthony Mastrorilli, James Boyd Parker, Tim Salce, J. C. Sheets, Ronald Stafford, Jim Wolfe

STANDBYS AND UNDERSTUDIES: Missy Whitchurch (Peter Pan), Andi Henig (Wendy/Lost Boys), Edward Magel (Capt. Hook/Mr. Darling), Anne McVey (Mrs. Darling/Wendy (grown)/Tiger Lily), J. C. Sheets (Nana/Smee), Michael Emery (John), Jason Moreland (Michael)

MUSICAL NUMBERS: Tender Shepherd, I Gotta Crow, Neverland, I'm Flying, Morning in Neverland, Pirate March, A Princely Scheme, Indians, Wendy, Another Princely Scheme, I Won't Grow Up, Mysterious Lady, Ugg-a-Wugg, Distant Melody, Hook's Waltz, The Battle.

A musical in 2 acts and 8 scenes.

Gerry Goodstein Photos

Rip Taylor, Karyn Cole in "Peter Pan"

PUMP BOYS AND DINETTES

Conceived and written by John Foley, Mark Hardwick, Debra Monk, Cass Morgan, John Schimmel and Jim Wann; Scenery, Doug Johnson, Christopher Nowak; Costumes, Patricia McGourty; Lighting, Richard Nelson; Sound, Otts Munderloh; Musical Supervision, John Miller; Staging, Patrick Tovatt; Presented by Dodger Productions, Louis Busch Hager, Marilyn Strauss, Kate Studley, Warner Theatre Productions and Max Weitzenhoffer in association with Nederlander Theatricals; Original cast album by CBS Records; General Management, Alexander Morr & Associates/Dodger Productions; Band Leader/Conductor, George Clinton; Company Manager, Paul Holland; Stage Managers, B. J. Allen, Lynn Utzinger; Casting, Meg Simon/Fran Kumin; Press, Hunt/Pucci, James Sapp, Jon Essex. Opened in Detroit, MI, at the Fisher Theatre on Friday, October 29, 1982 and closed there December 5, 1982. For original NY production, see THEATRE WORLD Vol. 38.

CAST

Jim	Tom Chapin
Rhetta Cupp	Maria Muldaur
Eddie	Gary Bristol
L.M.	George Clinton
Prudie Cupp	Shawn Colvin
Jackson	Richard Perrin

MUSICAL NUMBERS: Highway 57, Taking It Slow, Serve Yourself, Menu Song, The Best Man, Fisherman's Prayer, Catfish, Mamaw, Be Good or Be Gone, Drinkin' Shoes, Pump Boys, Mona, T.N.D.P.W.A.M., Tips, Sister, Vacation, No Holds Barred, Farmer Tan, Closing Time

Gerry Goodstein Photos

SUGAR BABIES

Conceived by Ralph G. Allen and Harry Rigby; Book, Ralph G. Allen; Based on traditional material; Music, Jimmy McHugh; Lyrics, Dorothy Fields, Al Dubin; Additional Music and Lyrics, Arthur Malvin; Staged and Choreographed by Ernest O. Flatt; Sketches directed by Rudy Tronto; Entire production supervised by Ernest O. Flatt; Scenery/Costumes, Raoul Pene du Bois; Lighting, Gilbert V. Hemsley, Jr.; Vocal Arrangements, Arthur Malvin, Hugh Martin and Ralph Blane; Music Director, Larry Blank; Orchestrations, Dick Hyman; Dance Music Arranged by Arnold Gross; Presented by Terry Allen Kramer and Harry Rigby in association with Columbia Pictures; Associate Producers, Frank Montalvo, Thomas Walton Associates; General Management, Alan Wasser; Company Managers, Louise K. Bendall, Stanley D. Silver; Stage Managers, Jay Jacobson, Robert Bennett, Kay Vance, Bill Braden; Assistant to Producers, David Campbell; Assistant Choreographer, Eddie Pfeiffer; Associate Conductor, Jon Olson; Wardrobe, Irene Ferrari; Hairstylists, Stephen LoVullo, Howard Leonard; Press, Henry Luhrman, Bill Miller, Terry M. Lilly, Kevin P. McAnarney. Opened at the Arie Crown Theatre, Chicago, IL, on Monday, November 8, 1982 and still touring May 31, 1983. For original Broadway production, see THEATRE WORLD Vol. 36.

CAST

Mickey	Mickey Rooney
Jay	Jay Stuart
Lori	Lori Street[1]
Mike	Mickey Deems
Maxie	Maxie Furman
Milton	Milton Frome
Ann	Ann Miller[2]
Ronn	Ronn Lucas[3]
Michael	Michael Allen Davis[4]
Gaiety Quartet	Jonathan Aronson, David Brownlee,
	Eddie Pruett, Michael Radigan, Keith Ellinger (alternate)

SUGAR BABIES: Carol Ann Basch, Carole Cotter, Kimberly Dean, Candy Durkin succeeded by Robin Manus, Yvonne Dutton, Chris Elia, Debbie Gornay, Julia Hannibal, Katherine Hopkins, Jane Lanier, Faye Fujisaki Mar succeeded by Kris Mooney, Melanie Montana, Tracy Poulter succeeded by Jill Deerey, Rose Scudder succeeded by Sarah Grove, Gwen Hillier Lowe (Alternate)
STANDBYS AND UNDERSTUDIES: Toni Kaye (Ann), Julia Hannibal (Ann), Mickey Deems (Mickey), Gwen Hillier Lowe/Rose Scudder (Ann), Jonathan Aronson (Mike), Bill Braden/Milton Frome/Maxie Furman (Mike), Mickey Deems/Maxie Furman/Eddie Pruett (Milton), Mickey Deems/Milton Frome (Maxie), Julia Hannibal (Lori), Milton Frome/Michael Radigan (Milton)
SKITS AND MUSICAL NUMBERS: Overture, A Good Old Burlesque Show, Let Me Be Your Sugar Baby, I Want a Girl, In Louisiana, I Feel a Song Comin' On, Goin' Back to New Orleans, Broken Arms Hotel, Sally, Scenes from Domestic Life, Don't Blame Me, Monkey Business, Orientale, Little Red Schoolhouse, Ronn Lucas, Mme. Rentz and Her All Female Minstrels, Down at the Gaiety Burlesque, Mr. Banjo Man, Candy Butcher, I'm Keepin' Myself Available for You, Exactly Like You, Court of Last Retort, I'm in the Mood for Love, Presenting Mme. Alla Gazaza, Cuban Love Song, Cautionary Tales, I Can't Give You Anything But Love Baby, I'm Shootin' High, When You and I Were Young Maggie Blues, On the Sunny Side of the Street, Michael Allen Davis, You Can't Blame Uncle Sammy

A musical in 2 acts and 24 scenes.
[†]Succeeded by: 1. Gail Dahms, 2. Carol Lawrence during Miss Miller's recovery from a foot injury (March 14-May 15, 1983), 3. Senor Wences during absence, 4. James Marcel, Frank Olivier

Martha Swope Photos

Left: Ann Miller, Mickey Rooney in "Sugar Babies" Above: George Clinton, Shawn Colvin, Maria Muldaur, Tom Chapin, (kneeling) Gary Bristol, Richard Perrin in "Pump Boys and Dinettes"

TINTYPES

Conceived by Mary Kyte with Mel Marvin and Gary Pearle; Director, Jerry Zaks; Musical/Vocal Arrangements, Mel Marvin; Orchestration/Vocal Arrangements, John McKinney; Musical Staging, Derek Wolshonak; Set, David Weller; Costumes, Carl Heastand; Musical Director, Andrew Howard; Lighting, Robert Strohmeier; Presented by Gordon Crowe; Tour Direction, Bruce Michael/Neil Fleckman Associates; Company Manager, James Awe; Sound, Weisbergsound; Wardrobe, Juki Halek; Assistant to Producer, Kathleen Wade; Stage Managers, Ed Preston, Mindy K. Farbrother; Press, Bill Watters. Opened at Page Auditorium, Durham, NC, on Wednesday, September 29, 1982 and closed at Dixon Hall, New Orleans, LA, on March 16, 1983. For original Broadway production, see THEATRE WORLD, Vol. 37.

CAST

Charlie	Stuart Zagnit
T. R.	Ronald A. Wisniski
Susannah	Janet Powell
Anna	Patrice Munsel
Emma	Robin Taylor

STANDBYS: Mimi Wyatt (Anna/Emma), Deborah Moldow (Anna), Mark Madama (T. R./Charlie)
MUSICAL NUMBERS: Arrivals, Ingenuity and Inventions, TR, Wheels, The Factory, Anna Held, Outside Looking In, Fitting In, Panama, The Ladies, Rich and Poor, Vaudeville, Finale

Presented in two acts.

ZORBA

Book, Joseph Stein; Based on novel by Nikos Kazantzakis; Music, John Kander; Lyrics, Fred Ebb; Director, Michael Cacoyannis; Choreography, Graciela Daniele; Scenery, David Chapman; Costumes, Hal George; Lighting, Marc B. Weiss; Sound, T. Richard Fitzgerald; Hairstylist-/Makeup, Steve Atha; Musical Director, Paul Gemignani; Orchestrations, Don Walker; Dance Arrangements, Thomas Fay; Conductor, Randolph Mauldin; Presented by Barry and Fran Weissler, Kenneth-Mark Productions (Kenneth D. Greenblatt/Mark S. Schwartz); Associate Producer, Alecia Parker; General Manager, National Artists Management; Company Managers, Robert H. Wallner/Kathryn Frawley; Stage Managers, Peter Lawrence, Jim Woolley, James Lockhart; Production Assistants, Peter Feuche, Trevor Brown; Assistant to Director, Jane Kessler Bassin; Props, George A. Wagner, Jr.; Wardrobe, Frank Green, Kathleen Melcher; Hair and Wigs, Robert Cybula, Carmel A. Vargyas; Casting, Howard Feuer/Jeremy Ritzer; Press, Fred Nathan, Anne Abrams, Eileen McMahon, Leo Stern, Judi Davidson, Bert Fink. Opened in the Forest Theatre, Philadelphia, PA, Tuesday, January 25, 1983 and still touring May 31, 1983. For original Broadway production, see THEATRE WORLD Vol. 25.

CAST

Konstandi/Turkish Dancer/Russian Admiral	Frank De Sal
Thanassai/French Admiral/Monk	John Mineo
Athena/Crow	Suzanne Costallos
Niko	Robert Westenberg
Despo/Crow	Panchali Null
Zorba	Anthony Quinn
The Woman	Debbie Shapiro
Marsalias/Monk	Rob Marshall
Mavrodani	Charles Karel
Manolakas	Michael Dantuono
Marika/Crow	Angelina Fioredellisi
Katina	Susan Terry
Vassilakas	Chip Cornelius
Marinakos/Monk	Peter Marinos
Mimiko	Aurelio Padron
Katapolis/Monk	Peter Kevoian
Yorgo/Italian Admiral	Richard Warren Pugh
Constable	Raphael La Manna
Sophia/Crow	Theresa Rakov
Pavli	Thomas David
Priest/English Admiral	Paul Straney
Anagnosti	Tim Flavin
Maria/Cafe Whore	Karen Giombetti
Madame Hortense	Lila Kedrova
The Widow	Taro Meyer

STANDBYS AND UNDERSTUDIES: Charles Karel/James Lockhart (Zorba), Suzanne Costallos (Hortense), Theresa Rakov (The Woman), Michael Dantuono (Niko), Susan Terry (The Widow), James Lockhart (Mavrodani), John Mineo (Mimiko), Chip Cornelius (Manolakas), Swings: Jim Litten, Tori Brenno
MUSICAL NUMBERS: Life Is, The First Time, The Top of the Hill, No Boom Boom, Vive La Difference, Mine Song, The Butterfly, Goodbye Canavaro, Grandpapa, Only Love, The Bend of the Road, Yassou, Woman, Why Can't I Speak, That's a Beginning, Easter Dance, Miners' Dance, The Crow, Happy Birthday, I Am Free

A musical in 2 acts and 15 scenes.

Martha Swope Photos

Left: Lila Kedrova, Anthony Quinn in "Zorba" Above: Patrice Munsel, Ron Wisniski in "Tintypes"

PROFESSIONAL RESIDENT COMPANIES

ACTORS THEATRE OF LOUISVILLE

Louisville, Kentucky
Nineteenth Season

Producing Director, Jon Jory; Administrative Directors, Alexander Speer, Marilee Hebert-Slater; Sets, Paul Owen, Grady Larkins, Loren Sherman; Costumes, Karen Gerson; Lighting, Jeff Hill, Karl Haas; Sound, Richard L. Sirois, Mollysue Wedding; Props, Sam Garst, Sandra Strawn; Directors, Steven D. Albrezzi, Thomas Bullard, Larry Deckel, Robert Falls, Ray Fry, Susan Gregg, Norris Houghton, Elizabeth Ives, Ken Jenkins, Jon Jory, James Kramer, Emily Mann, Frazier W. Marsh, Vaughn McBride, Adale O'Brien, Theodore Shank, Robert Spera, Dierk Torsek, Russell Treyz; Fight Director, Steve Rankin; Production Manager, Frazier Marsh; Stage Managers, Steven D. Albrezzi, Susanna M. Banks, Wendy Chapin, Richard A. Cunningham, Bob Hornung, Elizabeth Ives, Peter Jack, George Kimmel, Barbara A. Lutz, Kevin Mangan, Frazier Marsh, Fredric H. Orner, L. Susan Rowland, Craig Weindling; Literary Managers, Julie Beckett Crutcher, Bill Thomas; Assistant to Mr. Jory, Corey Beth Madden; Press, Jenan Dorman, Mina S. Davis

RESIDENT COMPANY: Andy Backer, Leo Burmester, Peggy Cowles, Dawn Didawick, Lee Anne Fahey, Ray Fry, Daniel Jenkins, Ken Jenkins, Susan Kingsley, Bruce Kuhn, Frederic Major, Vaughn McBride, William McNulty, Randle Mell, William Mesnik, Adale O'Brien, K. Lype O'Dell, Steve Rankin, Sally Faye Reit, Fred Sanders, Dierk Torsek, Patrick Tovatt, John C. Vennema

GUEST ARTISTS: Patricia Arnell, Helen-Jean Arthur, Marco Barricelli, Peter Bartlett, Larry Block, Reed Birney, Kent Broadhurst, Dan Butler, Cynthia Carle, Patricia Charbonneau, Nora Chester, Kirtan Coan, Gilbert Cole, Paul Collins, Mary Diveny, Dennis Dixie, Beth Dixon, Ellen Fiske, Ben Gotlieb, Reuben Green, Robin Groves, Murphy Guyer, Georgine Hall, Gary Leon Hill, Patricia Hodges, Laura Hughes, Holly Hunter, Laura Innes, J. S. Johnson, Jessie K. Jones, Jen Jones, Kerstin Kilgo, George Kimmel, Joyce Krempel, Johanna Liester, Margo Martindale, Mary McDonnell, Nancy Mette, Isabell Monk, Jay Oney, John Pielmeier, Polly Pen, Gordana Rashovich, Cristine Rose, Robert Schenkkan, David Schramm, Mary Seward-McKeon, John Short, Carol Shoupe-Sanders, Bill Smitrovich, Connor Steffens, Robert Stoeckle, Dale Soules, Fritz Sperberg, George Sutton, Hal Tenny, John Anthony Weaver

PRODUCTIONS: Julius Caesar by William Shakespeare, A Christmas Carol by Charles Dickens and adapted by Barbara Field, The Gift of the Magi by O. Henry and adapted by Peter Ekstrom, Murder at the Vicarage by Agatha Christie, Misalliance by George Bernard Shaw, Mass Appeal by Bill C. Davis, The Hasty Heart by John Patrick, Key Exchange by Kevin Wade, Wuthering Heights by Randolph Carter adapted from Emily Bronte's novel

1982 SHORTS FESTIVAL: I Love You I Love You Not by Wendy Kesselman, The Cameo by Ray Fry, In the Bag by Lezley Havard, Bartok as Dog by Patrick Tovatt, The Happy Worker by Stephen Feinberg, Partners by Dave Higgins, Good Old Boy by Vaughn McBride, A Tantalizing by William Mastrosimone, The Value of Names by Jeffrey Sweet, The Habitual Acceptance of the Near Enough by Kent Broadhurst, Flight Lines by Barbara Schneider, I Want to Be an Indian by William Borden, Coup by Jane Martin, Clucks by Jane Martin, Mine by David Epstein, The Art of Self Defense by Trish Johnson, Nice People Dancing to Good Country Music by Lee Blessing

FESTIVAL OF NEW AMERICAN PLAYS: Eden Court by Murphy Guyer, A Weekend Near Madison by Kathleen Tolan, Neutral Countries by Barbara Field, Courage by John Pielmeier, Food from Trash by Gary Leon Hill, In a Northern Landscape by Timothy Mason, Sand Castles by Adele Edling Shank, Thanksgiving by James McLure

David S. Talbott Photos

Top Left: Bill Smitrovich, Kent Broadhurst in "Food from Trash"

**Mary McDonnell, William Mesnik, Randle Mell (back)
in "A Weekend Near Madison"**

A CONTEMPORARY THEATRE

Seattle, Washington
Eighteenth Season

Producing Director, Gregory A. Falls; Producing Manager, Phillip Schermer; Administrative Manager, Susan Trapnell Moritz; Press, Michael Eagan, Jr.

DA with Allen Nause (Charlie Now), R. A. Farrell (Oliver), Ursula Meyer (Yellow Peril), James Hildebrandt (Da), Lyn Tyrrell (Mother), Kathryn Mesney (Mrs. Prynne), Bill O'Leary (Charlie Then), Rick Tutor (Drumm)
FRIDAYS with John Gilbert (Holly), Andrew Johns (George), Ursula Meyer (Kay), R. A. Farrell (Chuck), Lyn Terrell (Virginia), Allen Nause (Douglas), Kathryn Mesney (Gail)
WAITING FOR THE PARADE with Suzy Hunt (Catherine), Mara Scott-Wood (Janet), Lyn Terrell (Margaret), Ursula Meyer (Eve), Kathryn Mesney (Marta)
THE GIN GAME with Julie Follansbee (Fonsia Dorsey), Ben Tone (Weller Martin)
A CHRISTMAS CAROL with John Gilbert, David Pichette, R. A. Farrell, Bill ter Kuile, David Colacci, Daniel Mahar, Kevin Field, Amy Steltz, Jane Ryan, Noah Marks, Michael Flynn, Ursula Meyer, Christopher Marks, Barbara Morin, Linda Alper, Vern Taylor
ALI BABA AND THE FORTY THIEVES by Gregory A. Falls. *World Premiere* with Mark Drusch, Michael Flynn, David Hunter Koch, Ursula Meyer, Jane Ryan, Edward Sampson
THE GREEKS with John Aylward, Demetra Pittman, Toni Cross, Vincent D'Augelli, Stuart Anderson Duckworth, Mitchell Edmonds, R. A. Farrell, Katherine Ferrand, Michael Flynn, Patricia Hamilton, Harriet Harris, Christine Healy, Christopher Marks, Noah Marks, Kathryn Mesney, Ursula Meyer, Allen Nause, David Pichette, Rod Pilloud, Curt Simmons, Cameron Sisk, Faye B. Summers

Chris Bennion Photos

Faye B. Summers, R. A. Farrell, Vincent D'Augelli, Curt Simmons, Cameron Sisk, Harriet Harris, Toni Cross in "The Greeks"

ALASKA REPERTORY THEATRE

Anchorage/Fairbanks, Alaska
Seventh Season

Artistic Director, Robert J. Farley; Producing Director, Paul V. Brown; Managing Director, Mark Somers; General Manager, Dan Dixon; Production Manager, Bennett E. Taber; Associate Artistic Directors, John Going, Walton Jones; Technical Director, Gary C. Field; Coordinator, Hugh Hall; Development, Vince Walker; Stage Managers, Ann Mathews, Carol Chiavetta, Pamela Guion, James Sparky Woodard; Marketing, Jane Bradbury; President, Loren H. Lounsbury; Sets, Oliver Smith, William Schroder, Ron Placzek; Costumes, Christine Andrews, Kurt Wilhelm, Randy Barcelo; Lights, Victor En Yu Tan, Spencer Mosse, Pat Collins; Sound, Stephen Bennett

TUKAK TEATRET presented as statewide tour; Reidar Nilsson, Artistic Director; Manager, Ole Jorgensen. **CAST:** Agga, Anda, Makka Kleist, Maariu, Mooqqu, Qisu
NIGHTINGALE by Charles Strouse; Director, Meridee Stein; Musical/-Vocal Director, Joseph Church. **CAST:** Steve Steiner, Marina Arakelian, Lada Boder, Kim Brown, Amanda Chase, Adam Davidson, Debra DeHass, Davian Delise, Doreen Delise, Liz DeVivo, Gerard Dure, Michael Feigin, Justine Fitzgerald, Kim Gambino, Karl Gaskin, Anne Marie Gerard, Jenny Golden, Samaria Graham, Helena Green, Mika Hadani, Bebo Haddad, Erika Honda, Rena Kliot, Michelle League, Kathleen Manousos, Stacey McClendon, Caitlin Murray, Edie Ogando, Wendy Rockman, Philip Rodriguez, Candace Sassman, Ben Schwartz, Wayne Spector, Ian Wagreich, Steven Ward
TWO FOR THE ROAD directed by Robert J. Farley. **CAST:** Dana Hart, Jane Lind
MAJOR BARBARA by George Bernard Shaw; Director, John Going. **CAST:** Elizabeth Parrish, James Maxwell, Arlene Lencioni, Elizabeth McGovern, Ivar Brogger, Guy Paul, Peter Murphy, Emery Battis, Jennie Ventriss, Gary McGurk, Elizabeth Burr, Nesbitt Blaisdell, Ken Olin, Vanya Frank, Tom Bradley
AIN'T MISBEHAVIN' directed by Murray Horwitz; Musical Director, J. Leonard Oxley; Dance Director, Connie Gould. **CAST:** Debra Byrd, Andre DeShields, Adriane Lenox, Ken Prymus, Understudies: Ellia English, Miles McMillan, George Bell, Jackie Lowe

Chris Arend Photos

Elizabeth McGovern, Ivar Brogger in "Major Barbara"

ALLEY THEATRE

Houston, Texas
Thirty-sixth Season

Artistic Director, Pat Brown; Press, Bob Feingold, John Eaton; Business Manager, Bill Halbert; Managing Director, Tom Spray; Production Manager, Bettye Fitzpatrick; Casting, George Anderson; Stage Managers, Florine Sissy Pulley, Janice Heidke; Design, Michael Olich; Company Manager, Chuck Lutke; Sets, John Bos; Lighting, Jonathan Duff; Set/Lights, Matthew Grant; Sets/Costumes, Michael Olich; Costumes, John Carver Sullivan; Technical Directors, Joseph M. Kaplor, Bryan Wingo; Props, Sandra Lee Cottone; Sound, Tony Johnson.

TALLEY'S FOLLY by Lanford Wilson; Director, Beth Sanford; Stage Manager, Janice Heidke. CAST: Ron Rifkin (Matt Friedman), Holly Villaire (Sally Talley)

THE UNEXPECTED GUEST by Agatha Christie; Director, John Vreeke; Original Music, Stephen Houtz. CAST: Andrew Smoot (Richard), Robin Moseley (Laura), Michael LaGue (Michael), Patricia Kilgarriff (Miss Bennett), Dan LaRocque (Jan), Lillian Evans (Mrs. Warwick), Robert Graham (Henry), James Belcher (Sgt. Cadwallader), Bob Burrus (Insp. Thomas), Jim McQueen (Julian)

GREATER TUNA written and performed by Jaston Williams and Joe Sears; Written and directed by Ed Howard.

SCENES FROM AMERICAN LIFE by A. R. Gurney; Director, Beth Sanford. CAST: Mary Barry, Laurie Daniels, Daydrie Hague, Dee Hennigan, Richard Hill, Jeff Laite, Norman Moses, David Radford, Larry Schneider, Jordan Thaler, Laurel White

PRIVATE WARS by James McLure; Director, Michael LaGue. CAST: Michael LaGue (Woodruff), John Woodson (Silvio), William Johnson (Natwick)

PINOCCHIO: EVVIVA! a World Premiere with Book by Vance G. Ormes; Based on original story by Carlo Collodi; Music and Lyrics, Stephen Houtz; Staging, Vance G. Ormes; Musical Direction, Stephen Houtz; Masks, Lynne Mackey. CAST: Brenda Williams (Pulcinella), Danny Alford (Capitano), Teresa Heck (Pantalone), Dede Lowe (Isabella), Sarah Brown (Colombina), Scott Roser (Pedrolino), Tom Flynn (Arlecchino), Cynthia Lammel (Beltrame), Steve Cassling (Pine Log/Pinocchio)

HOME by Samm-Art Williams; Director, Horacena J. Taylor. CAST: Samuel L. Jackson (Cephus), Elain Graham (Woman #1/Pattie Mae Wells), S. Epatha Merkerson (Woman #2)

CLOSE TIES by Elizabeth Diggs; Director, Pat Brown. CAST: Ruth Nelson (Josephine), James E. Brodhead (Watson), Lillian Evans (Bess), Dede Lowe (Connie), Robin Moseley (Anna), Cynthia Lammel (Evelyn), David McCracken (Thayer), Ira Bienstock (Dan LaRocque)

THE PRINCE AND THE PAUPER a World Premiere by Charlotte E. Chorpenning; Adapted and Directed by John Vreeke; Original Music, Tony Johnson; Based on story by Mark Twain. CAST: Jeff Laite (Narrator/Miles), Richard Hill (Prince Edward), David Radford (Tom Canty), William Johnson (Hertford/Canty), Mary Barry (Lady Catherine/Mrs. Canty), Jordan Thaler (St. John/Hugo), Norman Moses (Henry VIII/King of Thieves), Laurie Daniels (Princess Elizabeth/Black Bess), Dee Hennigan (Lady Jane Grey/Bet), Larry Schneider (Page/Will), Stuart Litchfield (Archbishop/Father Andrew), David McCracken (Duelist/Street Man), Sean Hennigan (Guard/Sheriff), John Strano (Guard/Hodge), David Gould (Messenger/Yokel), Laurel White (Server/Margery), Meg McSweeney (Courtier/Bet's Mother), Sheri Tyrrell Brogdon (Courtier/Street Woman)

THE RIVALS by Richard Brinsley Sheridan; Director, John Going. CAST: Bob Burrus (Thomas), Timothy Arrington (Fag), Daydrie Hague (Lydia), Robin Moseley (Lucy), Glynis Bell (Julia), Jeannette Clift (Mrs. Malaprop), Robert Graham (Sir Anthony), John Cagan (Capt. Jack), Michael LaGue (Bob), Dan LaRocque (Faulkland), Jim McQueen (Sir Lucius), James Belcher (David), and Laurie Daniels, David Gould, Dee Hennigan, Stuart Litchfield, Norman Moses, Laurel White, Mary Barry, Larry Schneider, Sean Hennigan, David McCracken, Richard Hill, Jeff Laite, David Radford, John Strano

FIFTH OF JULY by Lanford Wilson; Director, Neil Havens. CAST: John Woodson (Kenneth), William Johnson (Jed), Brandon Smith (John), Lynn Humphrey (Gwen), Dede Lowe (June), Cynthia Lammel (Shirley), Bettye Fitzpatrick (Sally), Jordan Thaler (Weston)

NUTS by Tom Topor; Director, Charles Abbott. CAST: John Strano (Giordano), Rutherford Cravens (Aaron), Jim McQueen (Franklin), Cynthia Lammel (Recorder), Jean Proctor (Rose), Bob Burrus (Arthur), Dale Helward (Dr. Rosenthal), Robert Graham (Judge Murdoch), Robin Moseley (Claudia)

FAMILY BUSINESS by Dick Goldberg; Director, George Anderson. CAST: Timothy Arrington (Isaiah), Dan LaRocque (Jerry), Michael LaGue (Norman), James Belcher (Bobby), John Woodson (Phil), Larry Schneider (Young Man)

THE VISIT by Friedrich Duerrenmatt; Adapted by Maurice Valency; Director, Beth Sanford. CAST: Ruth Ford (Claire Zachanassian), and Jim McQueen, Dan LaRocque, John Strano, Sean Hennigan, Timothy Arrington, Jeff Laite, Bruce Hall, Bettye Fitzpatrick, John Cagan, Laurie Daniels, Dale Helward, Brandon Smith, Robert Graham, Philip Fisher, Bob Burrus, J. Shane McClure, James Belcher, Norman Moses, Richard Hill, William Johnson, Robin Moseley, Cynthia Lammel, Joe Finkelstein, Laurel White, Dee Hennigan, Daydrie Hague, Jordan Thaler, Dede Lowe, Meg McSweeney, Stuart Litchfield, Larry Schneider, David McCracken, David Radford

HOW I GOT THAT STORY by Amlin Gray; Director, Pat Brown. CAST: John Woodson (The Reporter), Michael LaGue (The Historical Event)

THE DINING ROOM by A. R. Gurney, Jr.; Director, Beth Sanford. CAST: Laurie Daniels, Lillian Evans, Bettye Fitzpatrick, Robert Graham, Dan LaRocque, Jim McQueen

HOLY GHOSTS by Romulus Linney; Directed by Mr. Linney. CAST: Cynthia Lammel (Nancy), Brandon Smith (Coleman), Timothy Arrington (Rogers), Blue Deckert (Obediah), David Radford (Virgil), John Woodson (Orin), James Belcher (Howard), Laurel White (Lorena), Jo Alessandro Marks (Mrs. Wall), Dede Lowe (Muriel), William Johnson (Billy), Bob Burrus (Rev. Buckhorn), Michael LaGue (Carl), Robin Moseley (Bonnie), Richard Hill (Cancer Man)

TAKING STEPS by Alan Ayckbourn; Director, Robert Graham. CAST: Holly Villaire (Elizabeth), Jim McQueen (Mark), John Cagan (Tristram), Jim Bernhard (Roland), Rutherford Cravens (Leslie), Mary Barry (Kitty)

Carl Davis Photos

Top Right: **Ruth Ford, Dan LaRocque** in "The Visit" Below: **Lillian Evans, Robert Graham, Laurie Daniels, Jim McQueen, Bettye Fitzpatrick, Bruce Hall** in "The Dining Room"

ALLIANCE THEATRE COMPANY

Atlanta, Georgia

Artistic Director, Fred Chappell; Resident Director, Kent Stephens; Administrative Director, Edith Love; Sets, Mark Morton; Costumes, Thom Coates, Susan Hirschfeld; Lighting, Michael Stauffer, Bill Duncan; Production Manager, Billings Lapierre; Stage Managers, Gretchen Van Horne, Pat Waldorf, Dale Lawrence, Kathy Richardson; Press, Mark Arnold, Kim Resnik, Brock Haley.

WATERGATE, A MUSICAL with book/music/lyrics by Tommy Oliver and Edward J. Lasko; A World Premiere; Director, Edward J. Lasko. **CAST:** Gene Barry, Betty Claire Barry, Jan Maris, Betsy Banks Harper, Clay Newton, Chick Durrett Smith, Kay Daphne, Adrian Elder, John Purcell, Nancy Farrar, Richard Fagan, Jon Menick, Al Hamacher, Terri Kayser, Victoria Tabaka, Frank Kosik, Joey Farr, Ken Ellis, Judy Anne Nelson, James Stovall, Ed Herlihy, John Steele.
COTTON PATCH GOSPEL by Tom Key and Russell Treyz; Music/Lyrics, Harry Chapin. **CAST:** Tom Key, Dan Fox, Jim Lauderdale, Jeff Pinkham, Steven J. Riddle.
ANOTHER PART OF THE FOREST by Lillian Hellman; Director, Fred Chappell. **CAST:** Michele Farr, Richard Fagan, Mary Nell Santacroce, Georgia Allen, Eddie Lee, Gary Reineke, Bill Nunn, Al Hamacher, Larry Larson, Suzanne Calvert, David Wasman, Jim Peck, Marianne Hammock.
THE EMPEROR'S NEW CLOTHES by Larry Shue; Director, Kent Stephens. **CAST:** James Stovall, Dana Laughlin, Alan Kilpatrick, J. Alexander Gilliam, Chris Wiggins, Jon Kohler, Jihad Babarunde, Denise Burse-Mickelbury.
CHEKHOV IN YALTA by John Driver, Jeffrey Haddow. **CAST:** Michele Farr, Alan Mixon, Al Hamacher, Richard Fagan, Brenda Bynum, Judy Langford, Eddie Lee, David Wasman, Lon Waitmen, Yetta Levitt, Gary Reineke.
MAME by Jerome Lawrence and Robert E. Lee; Music and Lyrics, Jerry Herman; Director, Russell Treyz; Musical Director, Michael Fauss; Choreographer, Mary Jane Houdina. **CAST:** Benji Wilhoite, Jan Maris, Ginny Parker, Judy Langford, John Adair, Adrian Elder, Thomas Y. Shim, Jon Menick, Patrick McCann, Wayne Lancaster, Ron Culbreth, Clay Newton, Brent Black, Roberta Illg, Ken Ellis, Marc Clement, Ellen Heard, Victoria Tabaka, Stanton Cunningham, Kay McClelland, Karen DiBianco, Zack Finch, Chick Durrett-Smith, Terri Kayser, Cathy Larson, Tambra Smith.
THE PIRATES OF PENZANCE by W. S. Gilbert, Arthur Sullivan; Adapted by Charles Abbott; Director, Kent Stephens; Musical Director, Michael Fauss; Choreography, Patrick McCann. **CAST:** Jon Kohler, Jay Scovill, Robert Schultz, Jeroy Hannah, Wade Benson, Gigi Weinrich, Tambra Smith, Dana Laughlin, Roberta Illg, Sean McGinity, Calvin Smith.
MY SISTER IN THIS HOUSE by Wendy Kesselman; Director, Bob Wright. **CAST:** Chondra Wolle, Cathy Larson, Muriel Moore, Kathy Sterlin Caden.
FIFTH OF JULY by Lanford Wilson; Director, Kent Stephens. **CAST:** Eric Conger, Don Spalding, John Martinuzzi, Julia Murray, Linda Stephens, Suzanne Calvert, Betty Leighton, Seth Steiger.
IMMORALITY PLAY by James Yaffe; World Premiere; Director, David McKenna. **CAST:** Jim Peck, Mary Nell Santacroce, Bea Swanson, Stephen Hamilton, Larry Larson.
A LITTLE NIGHT MUSIC with Book by Hugh Wheeler; Music/Lyrics, Stephen Sondheim; Director, Fred Chappell; Choreographer, Lee Harper; Musical Director, Michael Fauss. **CAST:** Clay Newton, Susan Russell, Jan Maris, Ken Ellis, Amanda Beason, Cathy Larson, Betty Leighton, Don Spalding, Larry Solowitz, Suzanne Sloan, Jess Richards, Kay McClelland, Linda Stephens, Sharon Caplan, Dennis Smith, Roy Alan Wilson, Lynn Fitzpatrick, Jude Wido.
HOME by Samm-Art Williams; Director, Walter Dallas. **CAST:** Iris Little-Roberts, Sharlene Ross, Bill Nunn.
TWELFTH NIGHT by William Shakespeare; Director, Kent Stephens. **CAST:** Lane Davies, Marc Reeves, Larry Larson, Al Hamacher, Don Spalding, Larry Solowitz, Skip Foster, Eddie Lee, Brooks Baldwin, Gordon Paddison, Francois De La Giroday, Michele Farr, Frances McDormand, Marianne Hammock, Deborah Anderson, Della Cole, John Courtney.
EDUCATING RITA by Willy Russell; Adapted by Ntozake Shange; Director, Fred Chappell. **CAST:** David Canary, Lynne Thigpen.

Charles Rafshoon Photos

Top Right: Iris Little-Roberts, Bill Nunn in "Home"

AMERICAN MIME THEATRE

New York, NY
Thirtieth Year

Founder/Director, Paul J. Curtis; Administrator, Jean Barbour; Counsel, Joel S. Charleston.

COMPANY: Jean Barbour, Charles Barney, Joseph Citta, Paul Curtis, Dale Fuller, Kevin Kaloostian, Erica Sarzin, Mr. Bones.
REPERTOIRE: Dream, The Lovers, The Scarecrow, Hurly-Burly, Evolution, Sludge, Six, Unitaur.

Jess Richards, Linda Stephens in "A Little Night Music"

AMERICAN CONSERVATORY THEATRE

San Francisco, California
Seventeenth Season

General Director, William Ball; Conservatory Director, Allen Fletcher; Managing Director, Benjamin Moore; Executive Producer, James B. McKenzie; Production Manager, John Brown; Technical Coordinator, Eric Shortt; Production Coordinator, Alice Smith; Sets, Ralph Funicello, Richard Seger; Lighting, Joseph Appelt, Dirk Epperson, Robert Peterson, Duane Schuler, Greg Sullivan; Costumes, Michael Casey; Stage Managers, James Haire, Eugene Barcone, James L. Burke, Karen Van Zandt; Costumes and Wigs, Lani Abbott, Rick Echols; Props, Oliver C. Olsen; Wardrobe, Donald Long-Hurst; Business Manager, Carole Hewitt; Press, Marne Davis Kellogg, Kirsten Mickelwaite

COMPANY: Annette Bening, Joseph Bird, Raye Birk, Mimi Carr, Joan Croydeon, George Deloy, Barbara Dirickson, Peter Donat, Gina Ferrall, James Edmondson, Lawrence Hecht, John Noah Hertzler, Nancy Houfek, Elizabeth Huddle, Janice Hutchins, Anne Lawder, Deborah May, Dakin Matthews, William McKereghan, Anne McNaughton, DeAnn Mears, Mark Murphey, Delores Mitchell, Sharon Newman, Thomas Patrick O'-Brien, Frank Ottiwell, William Paterson, Ray Reinhardt, Randall Richard, Jeremy Roberts, Frank Savino, Sally Smythe, Harold Surratt, Deborah Sussel, Francine Tacker, Carol Teitel, Sydney Walker, Marrian Walters, J. Steven White, Bruce Williams, Laura Ann Worthen, D. Paul Yeuell. Directors: William Ball, Eugene Barcone, Helen Burns, James Edmondson, Allen Fletcher, Edward Hastings, Michael Langham, Dakin Matthews, Tom Moore, Ken Ruta, Laird Williamson
PRODUCTIONS: The Gin Game by D. L. Coburn, Dear Liar by Jerome Kilty, The Chalk Garden by Enid Bagnold, A Christmas Carol by Charles Dickens, Uncle Vanya by Anton Chekhov, Loot by Joe Orton, Morning's at Seven by Paul Osborn, The Holdup by Marsha Norman

Larry Merkle Photos

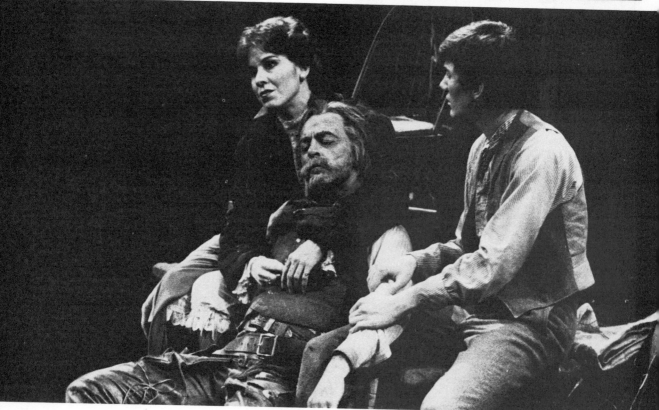

Barbara Dirickson, Peter Donat, Tom O'Brien in "The Holdup"
Top: Deborah May, Dakin Matthews in "Uncle Vanya"

138

AMERICAN REPERTORY THEATRE

Cambridge, Massachusetts
Fourth Season

Artistic Director, Robert Brustein; Managing Director, Robert J. Orchard; Literary Director, Jonathan Marks; Production Manager, Jonathan Miller; Marketing Director, Jeanne Brodeur; Press, Jan Geidt; Technical Director, Donald R. Soule; Production Coordinator, Thomas C. Behrens; Stage Managers, John Grant-Phillips, Abbie Katz, Anthony Rudie

THREE SISTERS By Anton Chekhov; Director, Andrei Serban; New version by Jean-Claude van Itallie; Set/Costumes/Lighting, Beni Montresor; Original Music, Richard Peaslee. CAST: John Bottoms, Thomas Derrah, Alvin Epstein, Cheryl Giannini, Richard Grusin, Cherry Jones, Karen MacDonald, Marianne Owen, Anne Pitoniak, Tony Shalhoub, Richard Spore, Mark Driscoll, Jamie Hanes, Deborah Phillips, Robin Driscoll
'NIGHT, MOTHER (World Premiere) by Marsha Norman; Director, Tom Moore; Set/Costumes, Heidi Landesman; Lighting, James F. Ingalls. CAST: Kathy Bates, Anne Pitoniak
WAITING FOR GODOT by Samuel Beckett; Director, Andrei Belgrader; Set, Tony Straiges; Costumes, Kevin Rupnik; Lighting, James F. Ingalls. CAST: John Bottoms, Mark Linn-Baker, Tony Shalhoub, Richard Spore, Seth Goldstein
THE BOYS FROM SYRACUSE based on "The Comedy of Errors" by William Shakespeare; Music, Richard Rodgers; Lyrics, Lorenz Hart; Book, George Abbott; Production conceived and directed by Alvin Epstein; Choreography, Kathryn Posin; Music Director, Paul Schierhorn; Conductor, Tom Lynch; Costumes, Nancy Thun. CAST: John Bottoms, Thomas Derrah, Jeremy Geidt, Cherry Jones, Susan Larson, Karen MacDonald, Jonathan Marks, Harry S. Murphy, Marianne Owen, Stephen Rowe, Paul Shierhorn, Tony Shalhoub, Richard Spore, Shirley Wilber, Glenn J. Cohen, Bill Foeller, Martha Hackett, Mari Hageman, Maria Moessen, Kathleen Mulligan, Joan Storey, Alison Taylor
THE SCHOOL FOR SCANDAL by Richard Brinsley Sheridan; Director, Jonathan Miller; Set, Patrick Robertson; Costumes, Rosemary Vercoe; Lighting, Jennifer Tipton. CAST: John Bottoms, Thomas Derrah, Alvin Epstein, Jeremy Geidt, Cherry Jones, Karen MacDonald, Jonathan Marks, Harry S. Murphy, Marianne Owen, Stephen Rowe, Tony Shalhoub, Richard Spore, Shirley Wilber, Michael Allio, Mark Driscoll, Bill Foeller, Maggie Topkis, Nick Wyse, Jerome Kilty
A.R.T. AT THE PUDDING SERIES:
BABY WITH THE BATH WATER (World Premiere) by Christopher Durang; Director, Mark Linn-Baker; Set, Don Soule; Costumes, Liz Perlman; Lighting, Thom Palm; Sound, Randolph Head. CAST: Cherry Jones, Karen MacDonald, Marianne Owen, Stephen Rowe, Tony Shalhoub
FOOTBALLS and ROCKABY by Samuel Beckett; Director, John Grant-Phillips; Set, Don Soule; Costumes, Lynn Jeffrey; Lighting, Thom Palm. CAST: Karen MacDonald, Marianne Owen
HUGHIE by Eugene O'Neill; Director, Bill Foeller; Set, Don Soule; Lighting, Thom Palm; Costumes, Lynn Jeffrey. CAST: John Bottoms, Richard Spore

Richard Feldman Photos

Thomas Derrah (L), Alvin Epstein, Cherry Jones, Cheryl Giannini in "Three Sisters" with A.R.T. resident company

ARIZONA THEATRE COMPANY

Tucson/Phoenix, Arizona

Artistic Director, Gary Gisselman; Associate Artistic Director, Jon R. Cranney; Managing Director, David R. Hawkanson; Press, Sharon Griggins, Julie C. Devane; Development, Barbara R. Levy; Sets, Peter A. Davis, Jack Barkla, Don Yunker; Lighting, Kent Dorsey, Don Darnutzer, Michael Vennerstrom; Costumes, Sally Cleveland, Gene Davis Buck, David Kay Mickelsen, Bobbi Culbert, Jared Aswegan

WHAT THE BUTLER SAW by Joe Orton; Director, Gary Gisselman. CAST: Tony DeBruno (Dr. Prentice), Liz Georges (Geraldine), Lillian Garrett (Mrs. Prentice), Arnie Krauss (Nicholas), Benjamin Stewart (Dr. Rance), Oliver Cliff (Sgt. Match)
A CHRISTMAS CAROL by Charles Dickens; Director, Jon R. Cranney. CAST: Ken Bahn, Ann Carlson-Brown, Kitty Carroll, Oliver Cliff, Tony DeBruno, Harold Dixon, Mattie Figueroa, Allyson Gannon, Lillian Garrett, Liz Georges, Michael Goodsite, Claudine Gooter, Bill Guise, Claire Harlan, Thomas Harris, Henry Hank Kendrick, Arnie Krauss, Diane Landis, Scott Levin, Leonard Meenach, Philip Rosenberg, Benjamin Stewart, Matt Tashiro, Danny Taylor, Jack van Natter, Jak Zodiak
JOURNEY'S END by R. C. Sherriff; Director, Jon R. Cranney. CAST: Henry Kendrick (Capt. Hardy), John-Frederick Jones (Lt. Osborne), Tony DeBruno (Pvt. Mason), Douglas Anderson (Lance-Cpl. Braughton), Cameron Smith (2nd Lt. Raleigh), John Jellison (Capt. Stanhope), Troy Evans (2nd Lt. Trotter), Michael Ellison (2nd Lt. Hibbert), Benjamin Stewart (Sgt.-Major), Oliver Cliff (Colonel), Mark Ruch (German Soldier)
MASS APPEAL by Bill C. David; Director, Jay Broad. CAST: Charles White (Father Tim Farley), Casey Biggs (Mark Dolson)
UNCLE VANYA by Anton Chekhov; Director, Gary Gisselman. CAST: Roberta Streicher (Marina), Ken Ruta (Dr. Astrov), Benjamin Stewart (Uncle Vanya), Paul Ballantyne (Serebriakov), Oliver Cliff (Telyegin), Jahnna Beecham (Sonia), Katherine Ferrand (Yelena), Dee Maaske (Maria), Hank Kendrick (Workman/Watchman)
A FUNNY THING HAPPENED ON THE WAY TO THE FORUM by Bert Shevelove, Larry Gelbart; Music and Lyrics, Stephen Sondheim; Director, Gary Gisselman. CAST: Benjamin Stewart (Prologus/Actor), Oliver Cliff (Senex/Old Man), Ruth Kobart (Domina), Cameron Smith (Hero), Michael Ellison (Hysterium), Benjamin Stewart (Pseudolus), Paul Ballantyne (Erronius), Armen Dirtadian (Miles Gloriosus), Paul C. Thomas (Lycus), Ann Carlson Brown (Tintinabula), Tenaj Davis (Panacea), Della Davidson (Cymbelina), Ruth Ashton-Blake (Vibrata), Karen McIntyre (Gymnasia), Kitty Carroll (Philia), Proteans: Carl Craig, John Parra, Dave Coffman

Tim Fuller Photos

Richard Howard, Glenda Young, J. Patrick Martin, Judy Leavell in "The Dining Room" (A.T.C.)

ARENA STAGE

Washington, D.C.
Fifteenth Season

Producing Director, Zelda Fichandler; Executive Director, Thomas C. Fichandler; Associate Producing Director, Douglas C. Wager; Administrative Director, JoAnn M. Overholt; Press, Richard Bryant; Development Director, Elspeth Udvarhelyi; Production Coordinator, Guy Bergquist; Technical Director, David M. Glenn; Literary Manager, John Glore; Stage Directors, David Chambers, Zelda Fichandler, Gilbert Moses, James Nicola, Gary Pearle, Horacena J. Taylor, Douglas C. Wager, Garland Wright; Sets, John Arnone, Zack Brown, Felix E. Cochren, Karl Eigsti, Ming Cho Lee, Tony Straiges; Costumes, Ann Hould-Ward, Alvin B. Perry, Mary Ann Powell, Marjorie Slaiman; Lighting, Frances Aronson, Arden Fingerhut, William H. Grant III, Allen Lee Hughes, Hugh Lester, William Mintzer, Nancy Schertler; Choreographer, Theodore Pappas; Musical Directors, Robert Fisher, Mel Marvin, John McKinney; Stage Managers, Tom Aberger, Jay Beckner, Rita Calabro, Peter Dowling, Femi Sarah Heggie, Maxine Krasowski, Susan Proctor

COMPANY: Stanley Anderson, Richard Bauer, Terrence Currier, Kevin Donovan, Mark Hammer, Charles Janasz, Christina Moore, Joe Palmieri, Halo Wines
GUEST ARTISTS: Dion Anderson, Ivy Austin, Hans Bachmann, Daniel Benzali, Paul Binotto, Laura Bradford, Jenny Brown, Britt Burr, Robert Burr, Nancy Cameron, Ron Canada, Marilyn Caskey, Philip Casnoff, Claudine Cassan, Jonathan S. Cerullo, Frances Chaney, Jerry Christakos, Michael Cone, Caris Corfman, David Cromwell, Regina David, Joseph Dellger, Dan Desmond, Andrew Dodge, Franchelle Stewart Dorn, Tracy Flint, Constance Fowlkes, Peter Francis-James, Jim Fyfe, Joey Ginza, Michael Govan, Elain Graham, Dorothea Hammond, Michael Heintzman, Laura Hicks, Christopher Hux, Samuel L. Jackson, Richard Jaynes, John Jellison, Marcy Jellison, Linda Lee Johnson, Michael J. Johnson, Darryl Jones, Skip LaPlante, Katherine Leask, Victor Love, Joan MacIntosh, Frank Maraden, Christopher McHale, S. Epatha Merkerson, John Edward Mueller, Douglas Nelson, Deborah Offner, Julie Osburn, Teresa Payne, Seth Resnik, Nanette Savard, John Seitz, Donald Sheehan, J. Fred Shiffman, Michael T. Skinker, Yeardley Smith, Barbara Sohmers, Cary Anne Spear, Alexander Spencer, Dan Strickler, Margaret Strickett, Henry Strozier, Olga Talyn, Kevin Tighe, David Toney, Bree Andra Wagner, Kirby Lynn Wagner, William Whitaker, Stephen White, Dorothy Yaness, Paul Zawadsky, Stephen Zazanis
PRODUCTIONS: Home by Samm-Art Williams; Cymbeline by William Shakespeare; The Imaginary Invalid by Moliere; Geniuses by Jonathan Reynolds; Buried Child by Sam Shepard; Candide based on Voltaire with music by Leonard Bernstein, book by Hugh Wheeler, lyrics by Richard Wilbur with Stephen Sondheim and John Latouche; Still Life by Emily Mann; *U.S. Premieres* of On the Razzle by Tom Stoppard from Johann Nestroy's play; Screenplay by Istvan Orkeny, adapted by Gitta Honegger with Zelda Fichandler
SPECIAL EVENTS: Banjo Dancing *or* the 48th Annual Squitters Mountain Song Dance Folklore Convention ... and How I Lost, The Flying Karamazov Brothers, Monteith and Rand, The Play Lab

George de Vincent, Joan Marcus Photos

Top Right: Christina Moore, Stanley Anderson, Kevin Tighe, Kevin Donovan, Henry Strozier, Halo Wines in "Buried Child"

Christina Moore, Stanley Anderson in "On the Razzle"

Richard Bauer in "The Imaginary Invalid"

140

ASOLO STATE THEATER

Sarasota, Florida
Twenty-third Season

Executive Director, Richard G. Fallon; Managing Director, David S. Levenson; Artistic Adviser, Stuart Vaughan; Artistic Director, John Ulmer; Press, Edith N. Anson; Musical Director, John Franceschina; Choreographer/Director, Jim Hoskins; Sets, Sam Bagarella, Gordon Micunis, John Ezell, John Doepp; Costumes, Catherine King, Sally Kos Harrison, Vicki S. Holden, Ellis Tillman; Lighting, Martin Petlock; Stage Managers, Marian Wallace, Stephanie Moss, John J. Toia, Dolly Meenan, Patricia Halpop; Technical Director, Victor Meyrich; Guest Stage Directors, Jonathan Bolt, Norris Houghton, Isa Thomas

RESIDENT COMPANY: Dion Chesse, Joseph Culliton, John Fitzgibbon, Mary Francina Golden, David S. Howard, Douglas Jones, Kenneth Kay, Robert Murch, Bette Oliver, Moultrie Patten, Karl Redcoff, Isa Thomas, W. Francis Walters, Stephen Daley, Cynthia Dozier, Arthur Hanket, Richard Hoyt-Miller, Rory Kelly, Gretchen Lord, Innes-Fergus McDade, Victor Slezak, Bradford Wallace, Colleen Smith Wallnau
CONSERVATORY COMPANY: Laurence Daggett, Ray Frewen, Leo Garcia, Richard Grubbs, Jay Keye, Graves Keily, Philip Lombardo, Vicki March, Carol McCann, Mark Mikesell, Jane Rosinski, Sharon Taylor, Carlos Valdes-Dapena, Kevin Brief, Phillip Douglas, Suzanne Grodner, Kelly Hazen, Randy Hyten, Paul Kassel, Tom Kendall, Keith LaPan, Jerry Plourde, Brant Pope, Wendy Scharfman, Leslie J. Smith, Lizbeth Trepel, Kevin Brief, Philip Cass, Diance C. Compton, Joan Crowe, Ricardo Dominiquez, Paul J. Ellis, Neil Lee Friedman, Colleen B. Kane, Tim O'Neal Lorah, Patrick Manley, Holly Methfessel, Cynthia Newman, Pam T. Taylor, William L. Thomas, Andrew Watts, Jack Willis
PRODUCTIONS: The All Night Strut!, Charley's Aunt, The Male Animal, The Girl of the Golden West, The Dining Room, A View from the Bridge, Misalliance, Man with a Load of Mischief

Gary W. Sweetman Photos

"A View from the Bridge"
Top Right: "The Girl of the Golden West"

141

BARTER THEATRE

Abingdon/Fairfax, Virginia
Fiftieth Season

Artistic Director/Producer, Rex Partington; Business Manager, Pearl Hayter; Press, Lou Flanigan; Stage Managers, Don Buschmann, Debra Acquavella, Champe Leary; Directors, Paul Berman, Ken Costigan, Thomas Gruenewald, Pamela Hunt, Rex Partington, Dorothy Marie Robinson; Sets, Bennet Averyt, Daniel H. Ettinger, John C. Larrance, Lynn Pecktal; Costumes, Georgia Baker, Barbara Forbes, Sigrid Insull; Lighting, Charles Beatty, Daniel H. Ettinger, Al Oster, Tony Partington, Christopher H. Shaw.

YOU CAN'T TAKE IT WITH YOU by George S. Kaufman, Moss Hart; with Florence Anglin, Paul Bement, Ross Bickell, Ken Costigan, Harry Ellerbe, Tom Gerhardt, Edward Gero, Cleo Holladay, George Hosmer, Cynthia Judge, Ben Kapen, Damien Leake, Arlene Lencioni, Alta McKay, Alec Murphy, Amelia Penland, Diane Reynolds, Claude-Albert Saucier
HEDDA GABLER by Henrik Ibsen; with Eunice Anderson, Ross Bickell, Marlene Bryan, Edward Gero, Dorothy Holland, George Hosmer, Paula Mann, John Michalski, Joan Strueber
THE MATCHMAKER by Thornton Wilder; with Lee Alexander, Eunice Anderson, Ross Bickell, Marlene Bryan, Catherine Flye, Edward Gero, Gerry Goodman, Cleo Holladay, George Hosmer, Kate Kelly, Dixie Partington, Rex Partington, Tony Partington, John Shepard, Michael Tierney, Linda Gillin, Joan Grant, W. Eric Maeder, John Michalski, Mary Shelley
TINTYPES conceived by Mary Kyte with Mel Marvin, Gary Pearle; with Don Bradford, Randy Brenner, Audrey Heffernan, Barbara Niles, Vanessa Shaw
I OUGHT TO BE IN PICTURES by Neil Simon; with Ross Bickell, Catherine Coray, Cleo Holladay
THE MOUSETRAP by Agatha Christie; with Cynthia Barnett, Jason Culp, Cleo Holladay, Drew Keil, Sherman Lloyd, Michael P. O'Brien, Alexandra O'Karma, Ian Stuart, Colin Bruce, Marlene Bryan, Bob Horen, Charles Hudson, Paul Mackley, Alexandra O'Karma, Susan Pellegrino, Sara Herrnstadt, Kevin Spacey

Bill Adams, Dave Grace Photos

(front) Audrey Heffernan, Randy Brenner (back) Don Bradford, Barbara Niles, Vanessa Shaw in "Tintypes" (Barter Theatre)

Charles C. Welch, Will Osborne in "Mass Appeal" (Caldwell Playhouse)

CALDWELL PLAYHOUSE

Boca Raton, Florida
Third Season

Artistic/Managing Director, Michael Hall; Sets, Frank Bennett, Marion Kolsby; Costumes, Bridget Bartlett, Frank Bennett; Lighting, Craig R. Ferraro, Joyce Fleming; Press, Patricia Burdett; Stage Manager, Linda Van Horn

ONCE UPON A MATTRESS with Susan Hatfield, Patrick Maguire, Dan Shaheen, Michael Coerver, Maria Fazio, Joseph H. Reed, John Ordway, Martie Dearmin, Dennis Fury, Jim Bumgardner, Carolyn Bowes, Barbara Lafier, Heidi White, George McCulloch
MASS APPEAL with Charles C. Welch, Will Osborne
EVEN IN LAUGHTER (World Premiere) by Lee and Marilyn Nestor; with Grant Walden, John Gardiner, Pat Nesbit, Will Osborne, Barbara Bradshaw, Rebecca Nestor
THE BARRETTS OF WIMPOLE STREET with Barbara Bradshaw, Grant Walden, Will Osborne, Pat Nesbit, Kay Brady, Gary Nathanson, John Gardiner, Erin Brady, Fritz Bronner, Kenneth Kay, Andrea Hirschler, Jack Hrkach, Luke Yankee, Jim Bumgardner
LIGHT UP THE SKY with Gary Nathanson, Barbara Bradshaw, John Gardiner, Mara Landi, Will Osborne, Naomi Davis, Kay Brady, Jack Hrkach, Jim Bumgardner, Kenneth Kay, J. Robert Dietz
MISALLIANCE with Max Gulack, June Prud'homme, Diana Sloszberg, Kenneth Garner, Geoffrey Wade, Caroline McGee, Doug Fogel, John Bjostad, Colin Leslie Fox

Joyce Brock, Mike Bady Photos

CAPITAL REPERTORY COMPANY

Albany, New York
October 30, 1982—April 17, 1983

Producing Directors, Bruce Bouchard, Peter H. Clough; General Manager, Martha E. Gottlieb; Press, Hilde Schuster; Literary Manager, Paula Cizmar; Administrative Assistant, Sandi Potenski; Technical Director, David Yergan; Stage Manager, Mary E. Quinn; Costumes, Lloyd Waiwaiole, Heidi Hollmann, Cinthia Waas, Barbara Forbes; Sets, Dale F. Jordan, Neil Prince, Robert Thayer, Ray Recht, Leslie Taylor; Lighting, Lary Opitz, Dale F. Jordan, Mark DiQuinzio, Mal Sturchio

SEA MARKS by Gardner McKay; Director, Gloria Muzio Thayer; with Marylou DiFilippo, Richard Zobel
TARTUFFE by Moliere; Translated by Richard Wilbur; with Marion McKendree, Alan Zampese, Kathleen Masterson, Michael J. Hume, Laralu Smith, Chris Ceraso, Michael Arkin, James Goodwin Rice, Susanne Marley, Joe Geoco, William Counter, Claire Goulet Wagner
TRUE WEST by Sam Shepard; Director, Pamela Berlin; with James Goodwin Rice, Lanny Flaherty, Alan Zampese, Miriam Layn
THE MOUND BUILDERS by Lanford Wilson; Director, Peter H. Clough; with James Goodwin Rice, Christie Virtue, Amy Dick, Chris Fracchiolla, Michael J. Hume, Kathleen Masterson, Susanne Marley
HOMESTEADERS (World Premiere) by Nina Shengold; Director, June Stein; with Keith Langsdale, Jamey Sheridan, Shelley Wyant, Jane Jones, Terri VandenBosch
THE SKIN OF OUR TEETH by Thornton Wilder; Director, Michael J. Hume; with Michael Arkin, Ann Stoney, Joan Kendall, William J. Coulter, Chris Fracchiolla, Deborah Van Nostrand, Richard Zobel, Art Kempf, Leonard Tucker, Philip Soltanoff, Leigh Nelson, Pat Devane, Pat Titterton, Claire Goulet Wagner, Joseph Burby, Shelley Wyant

Top Right: "Homesteaders"

CENTER STAGE

Baltimore, Maryland
Fourth Season

Artistic Director, Stan Wojewodski, Jr.; Managing Director, Peter W. Culman; Associate Artistic Director, Jackson Phippin; Dramaturg, Warren MacIsaac; Sets/Artistic Associate, Hugh Landwehr; Press, Patrick John Lombard; Stage Managers, Amanda Mengden, Nancy Kay Uffner; Technical Director, Jeff Muskovin; Props, Meg Aeby; Assistant Managing Director, Victoria Nolan; Business Manager, Ellen H. Mullan

LAST LOOKS (World Premiere) by Grace McKeaney; Director, Jackson Phippin; Costumes, Linda Fisher; Lighting, Judy Rasmuson; Sound, Lewis Erskine. **CAST:** Emery Battis, Gloria Cromwell, Chris Weatherhead, Graham Beckel, Lucinda Jenney, Sarah Chodoff, Josh MacFarland, John Procaccino
THE MISER by Moliere; Adapted by Miles Malleson; Director, Stan Wojewodski, Jr.; Costumes, Dona Granata; Lighting, Craig Miller. **CAST:** James McDonnell, Patricia Kalember, Tony Soper, Bill McCutcheon, Jeff Natter, Daniel Szelag, Tana Nicken, John Madden Towey, Bill Chappelle, Kimberley L. Lynne, Joanne Manley
DIVISION STREET by Steve Tesich; Director, Stan Wojewodski, Jr.; Set, Richard R. Goodwin; Costumes, Del W. Risberg; Lighting, Bonnie Ann Brown. **CAST:** Keith Langsdale, Paulene Myers, Victor Argo, Carolyn Hurlburt, Billy Padgett, Sarah Chodoff, John Madden Towey, Gerald Gilmore
WINGS by Arthur Kopit; Director, Stan Wojewodski, Jr.; Costumes, Dona Granata; Lighting, Ann G. Wrightson; Sound/Music, Bruce Odland; Sound, Bill Ballou. **CAST:** Bette Henritze, Phyllis Somerville, Daniel Szelag, Joanne Manley, Vivienne Shub, Christopher McCann, Irving Engleman, Beth Vaughan
THE WOMAN (U.S. Premiere) by Edward Bond; Director, Jackson Phippin; Set, Hugh Landwehr; Costumes, Dona Granata, Walter Pickette; Lighting, Arden Fingerhut; Music, Stuart Smith; Sound, Janet Kalas; Movement, Elizabeth Walton; Fight Direction, Tony Soper **CAST:** Peter Burnell, Jennifer Harmon, Emery Battis, Anderson Matthews, Tony Soper, J. S. Johnson, Wil Love, Timothy Boisvert, Lance Lewman, Beatrice Manley, Rodney W. Clark, Tania Myren, Lisa Ellen Abrams, Daniel Szelag, Vivienne Shub, Susan Beverly, Shirley Harris, Joanne Manley, Kate Phelan, Lorraine Toussaint, Alice Adler, Stevan Arbona, Michael Buster, Scott Elliott, Julian Fleisher, Nancy Franklin, Adam Gish, William Jensen, Rosemary Knower, Zachary Knower, Thomas Kopache, Victor Love, J. Daniel McDonald, Andrew MacHenry, Walt MacPherson, Tonia Michaels, Kevin O'Rourke, Joshua Roffman, Lonnie Shapiro, Bernard Solano
LOVE'S LABOR'S LOST by William Shakespeare; Director, Stan Wojewodski, Jr.; Set, Ed Wittstein; Costumes, Robert Wojewodski; Lighting, Craig Miller; Music, Claude White. **CAST:** Peter Burnell, Boyd Gaines, Timothy Boisvert, Kevin O'Rourke, Anderson Matthews, Lance Lewman, Pamela Brook, Lorraine Toussaint, Kate Phelan, Joanne Manley, Daniel Szelag, Victor Love, Rodney W. Clark, Emery Battis, Wil Love, J. S. Johnson, Susan Beverly, Michael Buster

Barry Holniker Photos

Peter Burnell, Boyd Gaines in "Love's Labor's Lost"

CENTER THEATRE GROUP
AHMANSON THEATRE

Los Angeles, California
Sixteenth Season

Artistic Director, Robert Fryer; Managing Director, Michael Grossman; Associate Artistic Director, James H. Hansen; Press/Production Associate, Michelle McGrath; Press, Rick Miramontez, Robert Pinger, Mona Kim; Management Associate, Tom Jordan; Executive Associate, Joyce Zaccaro; Administrative Assistant, Constance Von Briesen; Production Administrator, Ralph Beaumont; Technical Director, Robert Routolo; Props, Steve Rapollo; Sound, William Hennigh; Wardrobe, Eddie Dodds

A LITTLE FAMILY BUSINESS (*American Premiere*) by Barillet and Gredy; Adapted by Jay Presson Allen; Director, Martin Charnin; Set, David Gropman; Costumes, Theoni V. Aldredge; Lighting, Richard Nelson. **CAST:** Angela Lansbury (Lillian), John McMartin (Ben), Sally Stark (Nadine), Anthony Shaw (Scott), Tracy Brooks Swope (Connie), Theodore Sorel (Sal), Tony Cummings (Marco), Hallie Foote (Sophia), Gordon Rigsby (Vinnie), Donald E. Fischer (Joe) (See Broadway Calendar for New York Production)

BRIGHTON BEACH MEMOIRS (*World Premiere*) by Neil Simon; Director, Gene Saks; Set, David Mitchell; Costumes, Patricia Zipprodt; Lighting, Tharon Musser; Assistant to Director, Jane E. Cooper. **CAST:** Matthew Broderick (Eugene), Joyce Van Patten (Blanche), Elizabeth Franz (Kate), Mandy Ingber (Laurie), Jodi Thelen (Nora), Zeljko Ivanek (Stanley), Peter Michael Goetz (Jack) (See Broadway Calendar for New York Production)

HAY FEVER BY Noel Coward; Director, Tom Moore; Set, Richard Seger; Costumes, Robert Blackman; Lighting, Martin Aronstein. **CAST:** Celeste Holm (Judith Bliss), Michael Allinson (David Bliss), Laurie Kennedy (Sorel Bliss), Courtney Burr (Simon Bliss), Patricia Elliott (Myra Arundel), Paddy Croft (Clara), Nicholas Hammond (Sandy Tyrrell), Charles Kimbrough (Richard Greatham), Melora Marshall (Jackie Coryton)

CRIMES OF THE HEART by Beth Henley; Director, Melvin Bernhardt; Set, John Lee Beatty; Costumes, Patricia McGourty; Lighting, Dennis Parichy; Company Manager, James Gerald; Stage Managers, Rick Ralston, Gregory Johnson. **CAST:** Lizbeth Mackay (Lenny MaGrath), Sharon Ullrick (Chick Boyle), Raymond Baker (Doc Porter), Mary Beth Hurt (Meg MaGrath), Mia Dillon (Babe Botrelle), Peter MacNicol (Barnette Lloyd), Understudies: Jane Fleiss (Babe/Meg), Margery Shaw (Lenny/Chick), Harley Venton (Doc/Barnette)

(For original Broadway production see THEATRE WORLD Vol. 38)

Jay Thompson, Martha Swope Photos

Lizbeth Mackay, Mary Beth Hurt, Mia Dillon in "Crimes of the Heart"

Celeste Holm, Michael Allinson, Laurie Kennedy, Courtney Burr, Paddy Croft, Nicholas Hammond,
Melora Marshall, Patricia Elliott, Charles Kimbrough in "Hay Fever"

CENTER THEATRE GROUP
MARK TAPER FORUM

Los Angeles, California
Sixteenth Season

Artistic Director/Producer, Gordon Davidson; Managing Director, William P. Wingate; Acting Artistic Director, Kenneth Brecher; Producing Director, Madeline Puzo; Press, Nancy Hereford, Karen Kruzich, Guy Giarrizzo; Literary Manager, Russell Vandenbroucke; Lighting, Tharon Musser; Production Coordinator, Frank Bayer; Stage Managers, Clinton Turner Davis, Linda Intaschi, Mary Michele Miner, Michael F. Wolf, Lin Hensley, Carol Horner, Jonathan Barlow Lee, James T. McDermott, Toby Simpkins, Tami Toon, Richard Winnie; Technical Director, Robert Routolo; Production Administrator, Don Winton

A SOLDIER'S PLAY by Charles Fuller; Director, Douglas Turner Ward; Set, Michael Devine; Costumes, Judy Dearing; Lighting, Martin Aronstein; Sound, Regge Life. **CAST:** Adolph Caesar (Tech/Sgt. Vernon Waters), David Ackroyd (Capt. Charles Taylor), Bill Overton (Cpl. Bernard Cobb), Denzel Washington (Pfc. Melvin Peterson), Jesse D. Goins (Cpl. Ellis), Charles Weldon (Pvt. Louis Henson), Earl Billings (Pvt. James Wilkie), Kene Holliday (Pvt. Tony Smalls), Robert Hooks (Capt. Richard Davenport), Larry Riley (Pvt. C. J. Memphis), Cotter Smith (Lt. Byrd), Philip Reeves (Capt. Wilcox).
(For original New York production, see THEATRE WORLD Vol. 38)
METAMORPHOSIS (*American Premiere*) by Franz Kafka; Adapted and Directed by Steven Berkoff; Set, Thomas A. Walsh; Costumes, Terence Tam Soon; Lighting, Marilyn Rennagel; Assistant to Director, John Frank Levey. **CAST:** Brad Davis (Gregor), Pat McNamara (Mr. Samsa), Annabella Price (Greta), Ebbe Roe Smith (Chief Clerk/Lodger), Priscilla Smith (Mrs. Samsa), Gregg Johnson (Musician).
ACCIDENTAL DEATH OF AN ANARCHIST (*American Premiere*) by Dario Fo; Adapted by John Lahr; Director, Mel Shapiro; Set, David Jenkins; Costumes, Marianna Elliott; Lighting, Marilyn Rennagel; Presented by arrangement with Alexander H. Cohen. **CAST:** John Carpenter (Det. Bertozzo), Tony Azito (Patrolman), Ned Beatty (Fool), Paul E. Richards (Insp. Pissani), Andrew Bloch (Massimo), Tom Toner (Chief), Sue Kiel (Maria Feletti). The action takes place at the present time in a police station in Milan, Italy.

Pat McNamara, Priscilla Smith, Anabella Price, Brad Davis in "Metamorphosis"

GROWN UPS by Jules Feiffer; Director, John Madden; Set, Tom Lynch; Costumes, Dunya Ramicova; Lighting, Paul Gallo; Assistant Director, John Frank Levey. **CAST:** Nan Martin (Helen), Harold Gould (Jack), Mimi Kennedy (Marilyn), Bob Dishy (Jake), Cheryl Giannini (Louise), Jennie Dundas (Edie), Understudies: Nicole Eggert (Edie), Edith Fields (Helen), Ben Kapen (Jack), Lance Rosen (Jake), Kate Skinner (Marilyn/-Louise)
(For original Broadway production, see THEATRE WORLD Vol. 38)
A MONTH IN THE COUNTRY by Ivan Turgenev; Adapted by Willis Bell; Director, Tom Moore; Set, Ralph Funicello; Costumes, Robert Blackman; Lighting, Martin Aronstein; Music, Larry Delinger; Production Coordinator, Frank Bayer. **CAST:** David Byrd (Schaaf), Irene Tedrow (Anna Semyonovna), Paddi Edwards (Lizaveta), Paul Shenar (Mihail Alexandrovich Rakitin), Michael Learned (Natalya), Remy Auberjonois (Kolya), Thomas Harrison (Alexei Nikolaich Belyaev), Douglas Blair (Marvei), Raye Birk (Dr. Shpigelsky), Laurie Walters (Vera), Lawrence Pressman (Arkady Sergeich Islaev), Melora Marshall (Katya), Wortham Krimmer (Krimenskov), Ford Rainey (Afanasy Ivanovich Bolshintsov)
RICHARD III by William Shakespeare; Director, Diana Maddox; Set, Ralph Funicello; Costumes, Peter J. Hall; Lighting, Martin Aronstein; Music, Conrad Susa; Battles/Dueling, Christopher Tanner; Production Coordinator, Frank Bayer. **CAST:** Paul Shenar (Voice of King's Herald), Vaughn Armstrong (Edward IV), Sally Kemp (Queen Elizabeth), L. Walters (Prince of Wales), Adam Carl (Duke of York), James R. Winker (Duke of Clarence), Rene Auberjonois (Duke of Gloucester), Elizabeth Hoffman (Duchess of York), Wortham Krimmer (Marquess of Dorset), Gary Dontzig (Lord Rivers), Lawrence Pressman (Duke of Buckingham), David Sage (Lord Hastings), Tom Rosqui (Lord Stanley), James Horan (Earl of Richmond), Thomas Harrison (Sir William Catesby), Jay Louden (Sir Richard Ratcliffe), Lawrence Lott (Lord Lovel), Melora Marshall (Lady Anne Neville), Paddi Edwards (Queen Margaret), Dudley Knight (Sir Robert Brakenbury), David Prather (Squire Tressel), Charles Gregory (Squire Berkeley), John Vargas (Friar Penker), Michael R. Lueders (Friar Shaw), Douglas Blair, James Horan, Lawrence Lott (Friars), Lawrence Lott (Murderer #1), Tony Plana (Murderer #2), Charles Berendt (Lord Mayor of London), Douglas Blair (Master Hampton), Ford Rainey (Archbishop of York), James R. Winker (Archbishop of Canterbury), Charles Gregory (Stanley's Messenger), Ford Rainey (Duke of Norfolk), Vaughn Armstrong (Sir James Tyrrel), Tony Plana (Earl of Surrey), Michael R. Lueders (Sir Christopher Urswick), David Sage (Earl of Oxford), Douglas Blair (Sir Walter Herbert), Dudley Knight (Sir James Blunt), James R. Winker (Sir William Brandon)

Jay Thompson Photos

Paul Shenar, Michael Learned in "Richard III"

145

CLARENCE BROWN COMPANY

Knoxville, Tennessee

Honorary Chairman, Clarence Brown; Artistic Director, Wandalie Henshaw; Managing Director, Bashie Curfman; Associate Directors, Thomas Cooke, Albert J. Harris; Design, Robert Cothran; Costumes, Marianne Custer, Bill Black; Sets, Robert Cothran, Leonard Harman; Lighting, L. J. DeCuir, Leonard Harman; Technical Director, Robert Field; Press, Robert Hutchens; Company Manager, Nancy Walther; Stage Managers, Sarah Byler, Phebe A. Day, Chris Deatherage

DOCTOR FAUSTUS by Christopher Marlowe; Director, Wandalie Henshaw. **CAST:** Jeffery Brocklin, Thomas Brooks, Charles Michael Howard, Leonard Kelly-Young, John Krich, Jim Stubbs, Ian Thomson, K. C. Wilson
JULIUS CAESAR by William Shakespeare; Director, Thomas P. Cooke. **CAST:** Richard Bowden, Michel Cullen, Marian Hampton, Wandalie Henshaw, Charles Michael Howard, Don Jones, Leonard Kelly-Young, Jonathan A. Lutz, Harvey M. Miller, Mark Sandlin, Jim Stubbs, Ian Thomson
THE IMPORTANCE OF BEING EARNEST by Oscar Wilde; Director, Albert J. Harris. **CAST:** Thomas Brooks, Amanda Carlin, Jay Doyle, Richard Gilliam, Wandalie Henshaw, Don Jones, Wesley Stevens, Patrick Tull, Lynn Watson

Marc Engel Photos

Amanda Carlin, Lynn Watson in "The Importance of Being Earnest" (Clarence Brown Company)

James J. Lawless as Clarence Darrow (Cricket Theatre)

THE CRICKET THEATRE

Minneapolis, Minnesota

Artistic Director, Lou Salerni; Managing Director, Rossi Snipper; Assistant Managing Director, Eric Athman; Assistant Technical Director, Gary Baird; Development Director, Sara Burstein; Production Coordinator/Technical Director, Bob Davis; Associate Artistic Director, Sean Michael Dowse; Press, Glenn Skov, Pamela Hendrick, Betsy Husting; Props, Amy Shaff; Stage Managers, Brian Rehr, Lawrence S. Wechsler; Sets and Costumes, Vera Polovka Mednikov; Lighting, Michael Vennerstrom

CLARENCE DARROW by David W. Rintels; Director, Lou Salerni; Lighting, Lisa Johnson. **CAST:** James J. Lawless
THE DANCE AND THE RAILROAD by David Henry Hwang; Director/Choreographer/Composer, John Lone. **CAST:** John Lone, Tzi Ma
TERRA NOVA by Ted Tally; Director, Lou Salerni; Sound, Bob Jorissen. **CAST:** James J. Lawless, Allen Hamilton, Allison Giglio, Frederick Winship, J. Patrick Martin, Stephen D'Ambrose, James Cada
BILLY BISHOP GOES TO WAR by John Gray, Eric Peterson; Director, James J. Lawless; Musical Director, David Colacci. **CAST:** Christopher Bloch, David Colacci
AMERICAN BUFFALO by David Mamet; Director, Lou Salerni; Costumes, Christopher Beesley; Sound, Nancy Hart. **CAST:** Robert Breuler, Frederick Winship, Joe Horvath
THE CONSTANT WIFE by W. Somerset Maugham; Director, Nicholas Kepros; Set/Costumes, Jerry R. Williams. **CAST:** Barbara Davidson, Alan Woodward, Mari Rovang, Shirley Venard Diercks, Camille D'Ambrose, Janet Burrows, Ross Bickell, Nathaniel Fuller, Peter Thoemke

Pat Boemer Photos

CLEVELAND PLAY HOUSE

Cleveland, Ohio
Sixty-seventh Season

Director, Richard Oberlin; Managing Director, Janet Wade; Business Manager, Nelson Isekeit; Assistant to Director, William Roudebush; Consulting dramaturg, Peter Sander; Administrative Assistant, Angela Pohlman; Press, Nanci C. Shanley, Rita Buchanan, Corinne L. Bomba, David Budin; Series Coordinator, Jane Dugan; Directors, Paul Lee, Evie McElroy, William Rhys, William Roudebush, Woodie King, Jr., Michael Maggio, Harper Jane McAdoo, Thomas Riccio, Dennis Zacek; Designers, Richard Gould, James Irwin, Estelle Painter, Gary Eckhart; Music Director/Consultant, David Gooding; Production Manager, James Irwin; Stage Managers, Michael Stanley, Jack Doulin, Deborah A. Gosney, Richard Oberlin, Jim Hassert, Megan M. Murphy, Mark Pellegrino; Production Assistant, Paul Wells; Props, James A. Guy, Sue Ellen Frank, Jon Trzaska; Wardrobe, Estelle Painter, Frances Blau, Barbara Brock

COMPANY: Norm Berman, Sharon Bicknell, John Buck, Jr., Allan Byrne, Gregory M. Del Torto, Paul A. Floriano, Richard Halverson, James P. Kisicki, Anthony Kittrell, Lisa Kittrell, Allen Leatherman, Paul Lee, Morgan Lund, Evie McElroy, Kelly C. Morgan, Marcus Naylor, Richard Oberlin, Thomas S. Oleniacz, Tracee Patterson, Alden Redgrave, Carolyn Reed, William Rhys, William Roudebush, William Straempek, Wayne S. Turney, Cassandra Wolfe
GUEST ARTISTS: Catherine Albers, Ray Aranha, Cliff Bemis, Graham Brown, Jill Hayman, Providence Hollander, Ron Newell, Robert D. Phillips, Si Osborne, Theresa Piteo, Carol Schultz, Dudley Swetland, Dan Westbrook, Yvetta
PRODUCTIONS: Appear and Show Cause (*World Premiere*) by Stephen Taylor, The Middle Ages by A. R. Gurney, Jr., Fifth of July by Lanford Wilson, Black Coffee by Agatha Christie, A Christmas Carol by Charles Dickens and adapted by Doris Baizley, Tomfoolery adapted by Cameron Mackintosh and Robin Ray from the songs of Tom Lehrer, Sea Marks by Gardner McKay, A Tale of Two Cities (*World Premiere*) adapted by Mark Fitzgibbons from Charles Dickens' novel, Key Exchange by Kevin Wade, Ten Times Table (*American Premiere*) by Alan Ayckbourn, The Robber Bridegroom by Alfred Uhry and Robert Waldman, The Potsdam Quartet by David Pinner

Mike Edwards, Tena Richards, Rick Cicigoi Photos

Catherine Albers, Dudley Swetland in "Fifth of July" Top Right: Evie McElroy, James P. Kisicki in "A Tale of Two Cities"

147

COCONUT GROVE PLAYHOUSE

Coconut Grove, Florida
Sixth Season

(Formerly Players State Theatre) Artistic Director, Jose Ferrer; Managing Director, G. David Black; General Manager, Barry J. W. Steinman; Marketing, Jacques Valery; Development, Ilene Zweig; Press, Susan Westfall
THE DRESSER by Ronald Harwood; Director, Douglas Seale; Set, David Trimble; Lighting, David Goodman; Costumes, Claire Gatrell; Stage Manager, Rafael V. Blanco. **CAST:** Jose Ferrer (Sir), Michael Tolaydo (Norman), Brenda Curtis (Her Ladyship), Betty Leighton (Madge), Sarah Burke (Irene), William Preston (Geoffrey), John Bergstrom (Oxenby), Jerry Hotchkiss (Knight/Albany), Tom Buckland (Knight/Gentleman), Ronald Shelley (Glouster), Jim Puig (Kent)
FIFTH OF JULY by Lanford Wilson; Director, Kent Stephens; Set/Lighting, Kenneth N. Kurtz; Costumes, Ellis Tillman; Stage Managers, Debbie Ann Thompson, Lee Geisel. **CAST:** Eric Conger (Ken), Don Spaulding (Jed), John Martinuzzi (John), Julia Murray (Gwen), Linda Stephens (June), Suzanne Calvert (Shirley), Betty Leighton (Sally), Seth Steiger (Weston)
A COUPLA WHITE CHICKS SITTING AROUND TALKING by John Ford Noonan; Director, James Riley, Set, H. Paul Mazer; Costumes, Steve Lambert; Lighting, Pat Simmons; Stage Managers, Rafael V. Blanco, Alexandra Canfield Fuller. **CAST:** Megan McTavish (Maude Mix), Annie Stafford (Hannah Mae Bindler)
FALLEN ANGELS by Noel Coward; Director, Frith Banbury; Set/Costumes, David Trimble; Lighting, Stephen Welsh; Audio, Ken Libutti; Stage Managers, Debbie Ann Thompson, Lee Geisel. **CAST:** Tudi Wiggins (Julia), Ronald Shelley (Fred), Lillian Graff (Saunders), Peter Haig (Willy), Peggy Cosgrave (Jane), Alfredo Alvarez-Calderon (Mauricio)
A DESTINY WITH HALF MOON STREET (*World Premiere*) by Paul Zindel; Director, Jose Ferrer; Set, David Trimble; Costumes, Steve Lambert; Lighting, Stephen Welsh; Audio, Ken Libutti; Stage Managers, Alexandra Canfield Fuller, Rafael V. Blanco. **CAST:** Rafael Ferrer (Harold), Danny Aiello (Floyd), Sondra Barrett (Mrs. Dipardi), Lenny Pass, Martin Patrick Tobin (Hospital Attendants), Anne Meacham (Nurse Boyd), Brian Backer (Chris Boyd), Douglas Weiser (Joey), Lenny Pass (Richie), Martin Patrick Tobin (Leroy), Randy Bass, Alan Curelop, Scott Stuart
WITNESS FOR THE PROSECUTION by Agatha Christie; Director, Douglas Seale; Set, Kenneth Kurtz; Costumes, Barbara Forbes; Lighting, Stephen Welsh; Stage Managers, Debbie Ann Thompson, Lee Geisel. **CAST:** Sarah Burke (Miss Brogan-Moore), Ronald Shelley (Carter), John Milligan (Mayhew), Daren Kelly (Leonard), James Valentine (Sir Wilfred), Richard Liberty (Det. Insp. Hearne), O. Randbass (Detective), Jennifer Sternberg (Romaine), Jerry Hotchkiss (Wainwright), Peter Haig (Myers), Blanche Richards (Stenographer), Aaron Rose (Barrister), A. D. Cover (Dr. Wyatt), Martha Farrar (Janet), Darcy Shean (Other Woman)
PEPPERPOT by Susan Westfall; Director, Tony Wagner; Set, Marsha Hardy; Costumes, Ellis Tillman; Music/Lyrics, Roberto Lozano; Stage Manager, Ross Michaels. **CAST:** Irene D'Auria (Lily), Leslie Duncan (Velma), Jose A. Fong (Roberto), David Anthony Said (Kenny), Sonia Barriel (Woman)

Henry Friedman, Ray Fisher Photos

Top Right: Michael Tolaydo, Jose Ferrer in "The Dresser" Right: Danny Aiello, Douglas Weiser, Martin Patrick Tobin, Rafael Ferrer, Brian Backer in "A Destiny with Half Moon Street"

CROSSROADS THEATRE COMPANY

New Brunswick, New Jersey
September 10, 1982—May 15, 1983

Artistic Director/Founder, Lee Richardson; Executive Director/Founder, Rick Khan; Stage Directors, Rick Khan, Harold Scott, Lee Richardson, Samuel Barton; Sets, Bill Motyka, Dan Proett, Brian Martin; Lighting, Shirley Prendergast, Bob Scheeler, Gary Fassler; Costumes, Judy Dearing; Stage Manager, Kenneth Johnson

MEETINGS BY MUSTAPHA MUTURA with Lee Richardson, Janet League, Dana Hollowell
THE STY OF THE BLIND PIG by Phillip Hayes Dean. **CAST:** Minnie Gentry, Marge Eliot, Thom Brimm, Carl Gordon
RAISIN by Judd Woldin, Robert Britton, Robert Nemiroff, Charlotte Zaltzberg. **CAST:** Sandra Reaves-Phillips, Mel Johnson, Jr., Donna Ingram-Young, Vanessa Shaw, George Antony Bell, Cyril Johnson
TO BE YOUNG, GIFTED AND BLACK by Lorraine Hansberry and adapted by Robert Nemiroff. **CAST:** Gisela Caldwell, Rosanna Carter, Jeanne Johnson, Cynthia Martels, Brenda Thomas, Carl Wallnau, Mel Winkler
THE BLOOD KNOT by Athol Fugard. **CAST:** Daniel Ahearn, Basil Wallace
THE TRIALS AND TRIBULATIONS OF STAGGERLEE BOOKER T. BROWN (*World Premiere*) by Don Evans. **CAST:** Geoffrey Ewing, Wilhelmina Rochester, Reuben Green, Cynthia Martells, Bingo Johnson, Damien Leake, Neil Ross

Harry Rubel Photos

Gisela Caldwell, Carl Wallnau, Cynthia Martells, Jeanne Johnson, Rosanna Carter in "To Be Young, Gifted and Black" (Crossroads Theatre Co.)

Virginia McKinney, Jillian Raye, Kaki Hopkins (seated) in "Angel and Dragon" (Dallas Theater Center)

DALLAS THEATER CENTER

Dallas, Texas

Artistic Director, Mary Sue Jones; General Manager, Albert Milano; Production Manager, Robert Duffy; Dramaturge, Glenn Allen Smith; Casting, Judith Davis; Technical Directors, Paul Munger, Zak Herring; Costumes, Ann Stephens; Stage Manager, Paul Munger; Props, Arthur Olaisen, Susan McDaniel Hill; Hair and Wig Stylist, Renee LeCuyer; Lighting, David Edwards; Sound, John Vigna; Press, Nancy Akers; Development, David R. Woolf; Assistant to General Manager, Andre Christopher Gaupp

RESIDENT COMPANY: Sally Askins, Randy Bonifay, Victor Bravo, Judith Davis, Robert Duffy, John Figlmiller, Robyn Flatt, Andrew Christopher Gaupp, Tim Haynes, Russell Henderson, Zak Herring, Kenneth Hill, Susan McDaniel Hill, Mary Lou Hoyle, Ken Hudson, Mary Sue Jones, Deborah Kinghorn, Jeffrey Kinghorn, Eleanor Lindsay, John Logan, Ronni Lopez, Peter Lynch, Stella McCord, Carol Miles, Lynne Moon, Randy Moore, Nancy Munger, Paul Munger, Arthur Olaisen, Synthia Rogers, Ann Stephens, Lynn Trammel, Dennis Vincent, Gene Wolande
GUEST ARTISTS: Norma Moore, Cliff Stephens, Jeanne Cairns, Gloria Hocking, Paul Winfield, James Hurdle, Jenny Pichanick, Christopher Councill, Candy Buckley, Gary Moody, Marcee Smith, Lou Williford, Jack Gwillim
PRODUCTIONS: The Gin Game by D. L. Coburn, The Three Musketeers by Alexandre Dumas and Adapted by Peter Raby (Director, David Pursley; Fight Choreography, David Boushey), A Murder Is Announced by Agatha Christie, A Lesson from Aloes by Athol Fugard, The Threepenny Opera by Bertolt Brecht and Kurt Weill (Director, Ivan Rider; Musical Director, Raymond Allen), The Dresser by Ronald Harwood, Talley's Folly by Lanford Wilson, Embarcadero Fugue by Tom Strelich, and *World Premieres* of Topeka Scuffle by Paul Munger, The Pride of the Brittons by Kenneth Robbins, Angel and Dragon by Sally Netzel

Linda Blase, Andy Hanson Photos

DELAWARE THEATRE COMPANY

Wilmington, Delaware
Fourth Season

Artistic Director, Cleveland Morris; Managing Director, Raymond Bonnard; Associate Director, Peter DeLaurier; Business Manager, Ray Barto; Designers, Howard P. Beals, Jr., Peter Reader, Teri Beals; Stage Manager, Linda Harris; Press, Thomas Hischak

TINTYPES directed by Derek Wolshonak; Musical Director, Judy Brown; Lighting, Dennis Size. **CAST:** Dorothy Brooks, Richard Doran, Allan Stevens, Susan Victor, Mary Yarbrough
A LESSON FROM ALOES by Athol Fugard; Director, Bill Thompson; Set, Robert McBroom. **CAST:** James Doerr, Bonita Beach, William Hall, Jr.
TALLEY'S FOLLY by Lanford Wilson; Director, Peter DeLaurier. **CAST:** Charles Antalosky, Ceal Phelan
THE PHILOCTETES by Sophocles; Director, Cleveland Morris; Set, Thomas Schraeder; Costumes, Barbara Forbes. **CAST:** David Baffone, Jarlath Conroy, Peter DeLaurier, Robert Graham, Jack Koenig, William Verderber, Tom Sleeth
GRAND'S FINALE (*World Premiere*) by Casey Kelly; Director, Cleveland Morris. **CAST:** Mary Cooper, Dallas Greer, Drucie McDaniel, Carole Monferdini, Ceal Phelan, Dick Seltzer

Richard Carter Photos

Top: Ceal Phelan, Mary Cooper, Drucie McDaniel in "Grand's Finale"

Charles Antalosky, Ceal Phelan in "Talley's Folly"

150

DENVER CENTER THEATRE COMPANY

Denver, Colorado
Fourth Season

Artistic Director, Edward Payson Call; Associate Artistic Director, Peter Hackett; Managing Director, Gully Stanford; Production Manager, Danny Ionazzi; Stage Managers, Diane F. DiVita, Ken Heer, Jane Page; Business Manager, Madeline Kwok-Dodd; Company Manager, Mary Nelson; Literary Manager, Larry Eilenberg; Press, Penelope Nelson, Andrew Eiseman, Peter Epperson, Annette Griswold

COMPANY: Gregg Almquist, Stephen M. Ayers, Dixie Baker, Kevin Bartlett, Marjorie Berman, Duane Black, Mick Bolger, Charlotte Booker, Michael Butler, Mark Capri, Kay Casperson, Emily Chatfield, David Connell, Shelley Crandall, Peter Davison, Red Denious, Jeff Dinmore, Mary Esterling, Ken Fenwick, Julian Gamble, Reno Goodale, Jon Held, Bill Higham, Ingrid Hillhouse, Audre Johnston, Glenna Kelly, Jason Kenny, Tim Laboria, Dorothy Lancaster, Darrie Lawrence, Judy Leavell, Pirie MacDonald, Michael Maes, Michael McClure, Mark McCoin, Gary Montgomery, Margery Murray, William Myers, James Newcomb, William Newman, Caitlin O'Connell, Carolyn Odell, Brenda Brock Rogers, Raymond Ross, Diane Salinger, Walter Schoen, Ruth Seeber, Keith Ashley Sellon, Bruce K. Sevy, Jane Shepard, Georgia Southcotte, Michael Brennan Starr, Miles Stasica, Mary Stribling, Kezia Tenenbaum, Hal Terrance, Arnold E. Turner, W. Francis Walters, Jerry Webb, Jack Welch
QUILTERS (*World Premiere*) by Molly Newman and Barbara Damashek; Director, Barbara Damashek; Set/Costumes, Christina Haatainen; Lighting, Allen Lee Hughes; Music/Lyrics, Barbara Damashek
THE TEMPEST by William Shakespeare; Director, Edward Payson Call; Set, Robert Blackman; Costumes, Lowell Detweiler; Lighting, Kent Dorsey; Music/Sound, Bruce Odland
THE HOSTAGE by Brendan Behan; Director, Donovan Marley; Set/Costumes, Robert Blackman; Lighting, Greg Sullivan; Musical Direction, Bruce K. Sevy; Choreography, John Broome
ARMS AND THE MAN by George Bernard Shaw; Director, Edward Hastings; Set, Peter A. Davis; Costumes, Robert Fletcher; Lighting, Kent Dorsey; Sound, Bruce Odland
OF MICE AND MEN by John Steinbeck; Director, Richard Owen Geer; Set/Costumes, Robert Blackman; Sound, G. Thomas Clark; Lighting, Greg Sullivan

Georgia Southcotte in "Quilters"

THE THREE SISTERS by Anton Chekhov; Translated by Tyrone Guthrie, Claude Kipnis; Director, Edward Payson Call; Set, Peter A. Davis; Costumes, Christina Haatainen; Music/Sound, Bruce Odland; Lighting, Dawn Chiang
THE TAMING OF THE SHREW by William Shakespeare; Director, Barbara Damashek; Set, Peter A. Davis; Costumes, Lowell Detweiler; Lighting, Allen Lee Hughes; Composer, Barbara Damashek; Musical Direction, Bruce Odland
RUNESTONE HILL by Laura Shamas; Director, Jane Page; Set/Costumes/Lights, Rodney J. Smith. CAST: Frank Collison, Glenna Kelly, Brenda Brock Rogers, Keith Ashley Sellon, Greg Ward, Llewellyn Wells
JIM BRIDGER'S FRONTIER TALES AND SURVIVAL LORE WITH MUSIC BY JOHNNY TWOSNAKE by Willard Simms; Director, Dan Hiester; Set/Costumes, Joe Dodd; Lighting, Don Gilmore; Music, Steve Montano. CAST: Steve Montano, Hal Terrance
A BEAUTIFUL WORLD by David Jones; Director, Dan Hiester; Set/Costumes, Joe Dodd; Lighting, Don Gilmore; Sound, David Jones. CAST: Frank Collison, Craig Stout, Hal Terrance, Robert Wells, Vince Zaffiro
RUNAWAY TRUCK RAMP by Paul Redford; Direction/Lyrics, Paul Redford; Composer/Musical Director, Barbara Damashek, Bruce K. Sevy; Lighting, Jim McBride; Pianist, Bruce K. Sevy. CAST: Julian Gamble, Darrie Lawrence, Caitlin O'Connell, Jane Shepard, W. Francis Walters
WAITING FOR LEFTY by Clifford Odets; Director, Walter Schoen; Set/Lighting, Don Gilmore, Jon Waber; Costumes, Laura Love. CAST: Steve Ayers, Kevin Bartlett, John Bennett, Mick Bolger, Dwayne Carrington, Jeff Dinmore, Ken Fenwick, James Frazier, Paul Frellick, Glenna Kelly, Jason Kenny, David Kristin, Regina Krueger, Michael Mancuso, Gary Mazzu, Joe McDonald, Gary Montgomery, Jeanne Paulsen, Larry Paulsen, Paul Redford, Chris Rock, Norm Silver, Eric Small, Ted Stevens, Hal Terrance, Peter Van Dyke, John Waber, W. Francis Walters

Nicholas DeSciose Photos

Pirie MacDonald (center) in "The Tempest"

DETROIT REPERTORY THEATRE

Detroit, Michigan
November 4, 1982—June 26, 1983

Artistic Director, Bruce E. Millan; Executive Producer, Robert Williams; Manager, Monica Deeter; Directors, Dee Andrus, Barbara Busby, Bruce E. Millan, Ruth Palmer; Stage Managers, William Boswell, Barbara Busby; Sets, Patrick Czeski, Bruce E. Millan; Lighting, Marylynn Kacir, Steven Dambach, Kenneth R. Hewitt, Jr.; Costumes, Anne Saunders, Anne-Kristine Flones Czeski

HOLY GHOSTS by Romulus Linney. **CAST:** Charlotte Nelson, Willie Hodge, Mack Palmer, Ellis Foster, Anthony Lucas, Ken Earl, Robert Williams, LeDene Barron, Milfordean Luster, Fran L. Washington, Michael Joseph, Booker Hinton, Robert Skrok, Dee Andrus, Darius L. Dudley
TWO BY SOUTH: PRECIOUS BLOOD/RATTLESNAKE IN A COOLER by Frank South. **CAST:** Paul E. Scheier, Fran L. Washington, Council Cargle, Dee Andrus, Monica Sobieraj, William Boswell, Darius L. Dudley
TWO PIECES OF SILVER: BELDER AND THE BLOOM/THE FISHERMAN AND HIS WIFE by Bruce E. Millan. **CAST:** Milfordean Luster, Wilton Hurtt, Jim Sterner, Dee Andrus, Monica Deeter, Gary Steward-Jones, Robert K. Douglas, Paulette Brockington, Barbara Busby, Darius L. Dudley, Mack Palmer, Fran L. Washington, Reuben Yabuku, William Boswell
THE MAN WHO KILLED THE BUDDHA by Martin Epstein. **CAST:** Wilton Hurtt, William Paul Unger, Reuben Yabuku, Peggy J. Woods, Jim Sterner, William Boswell, James Cowans, Monica Deeter, Lea Charisse Woods, Darius L. Dudley

Bruce E. Millan Photos

Willie Hodge, Mack Palmer, Dee Andrus, Ellis Foster, Booker Hinton in "Holy Ghosts" Top Left: Barbara Busby, Darius L. Dudley, Reuben Yabuku, Gary Steward-Jones in "Two Pieces of Silver"

FOLGER THEATRE

Washington, D.C.
Thirteenth Season

Artistic Producer, John Neville-Andrews; Managing Director, Mary Ann de Barbieri; Production Manager, Elizabeth Hamilton; Technical Director, Tom Whittington; Costumes, Bary Allen Odom; Sets, Russell Metheny, Hugh McKay, Lewis Folden, Hugh Lester; Stage Managers, Kevin Kinley, Patricia Noto; Press, Lisa Ponak

COMPANY: Gail Arias, Mario Arrambide, Jim Beard, David DiGiannantonio, Floyd King, Mikel Lambert, Paul Norwood, John Reese, Thomas Schall, Kerry Waters, John Wojda, Craig Paul Wroe

GUEST ARTISTS: Richard Bauer, Chip Bolcik, Chris Casady, James Davis, Connie Geis, Kathryn Kelly, Irwin Ziff, Tina Chancey, Ann Monoyios, Ross Allen, Lucinda Hitchcock Cone, Davey Marlin-Jones, Kristen Beard, Lucy Brightman, Brian Petchey, Diana Rose, Sherry Skinker, Giles Havergal, Jeff Holbrook, David Jones, Gwendolyn Lewis, Donna Sacco, Vivienne Shub, Peter Webster, John Wylie

PRODUCTIONS: The Merchant of Venice by William Shakespeare directed by John Neville-Andrews, A Medieval Christmas Pageant directed by Ross Allen, She Stoops to Conquer by Oliver Goldsmith directed by Davey Marlin-Jones, *U.S. Premiere* of Marriage a La Mode by John Dryden adapted by Giles Havergal, All's Well That Ends Well by William Shakespeare directed by John Neville-Andrews

Valerie Hanlon, Don Vafiades Photos

Top: Gwendolyn Lewis, Paul Norwood, David Jones, Jeff Holbrook, Mario Arrambide in "All's Well That Ends Well"

Mikel Lambert, Paul Norwood, Brian Petchey in "Marriage a la Mode"

153

GeVa THEATRE

Rochester, New York

Producing Director, Howard J. Millman; General Manager, Timothy C. Norland; Marketing, Adele Fico; Development, Bonnie Gisel; Membership, Annette Brenna; Assistant to Producing Director, Cherrie Barbour; Technical Director, Michael Powers; Props, Nick Fici; Stage Managers, James Stephen Sulanowski, Catherine Norberg; Costumes, Pamela Scofield
A HISTORY OF THE AMERICAN FILM by Christopher Durang; Director, Howard J. Millman; Set, David Emmons; Lighting, Walter R. Uhrman; Costumes, Pamela Scofield; Choreography, Jim Hoskins; Musical Direction, Mark Goodman. **CAST:** Monique Morgan, William Pitts, Alison Fraser, Matthew Kimbrough, Barbara Redmond, Frederick Walters, Saylor Creswell, Lance Roberts, Lois Diane Hicks, Devora Millman, Brian Coughlin, Lon Salzman, Gary Grana, John Quinn, Caroline Kaiser
THE GIN GAME by D. L. Coburn; Director, Stephen Rothman; Sets/Lighting, Bennet Averyt; Costumes, Mary-Anne Aston; Sound, Mark Hendren, Jon Gottlieb; **CAST:** Arthur Peterson, Norma Ransom
TARTUFFE ALIAS "THE PREACHER" an adaptation of Moliere's comedy by Eberle Thomas and Robert Strane; Director, Eberle Thomas; Sets, Rick Pike; Lighting, Walter R. Uhrman; Costumes, Pamela Scofield; Score, John Franceschina. **CAST:** Jay Bell, Kathleen Klein, Saylor Creswell, Monique Morgan, Joyce Sullivan, Philip LeStrange, Daniel Ahearn, Anna Deavere Smith, John Sterling Arnold, Lancer Boyd, John Quinn, Lon Salzman, Brian Coughlin
MASS APPEAL by Bill C. Davis; Director, Gus Kaikkonen; Set, Bob Barnett; Lighting, William Armstrong; Costumes, Henri Ewaskio. **CAST:** Gerald Richards, Todd Waring
ALMS FOR THE MIDDLE CLASS by Stuart Hample; Director, William Ludel; Set, John Kasarda; Lighting, Jeffrey Beecroft; Costumes, Pamela Scofield. **CAST:** Robert Downey, Laura Esterman, Steven Gilborn, Kerstin Kilgo, Fritz Sperberg
AH, WILDERNESS! by Eugene O'Neill; Director, Thomas Gruenewald; Set, William Barclay; Lighting, Phil Monat; Costumes, Pamela Scofield. **CAST:** John Peakes, Carmen Decker, Bill Pullman, Daniel Tamm, Gerald Richards, Valerie von Volz, Saylor Creswell, Denise Bessette, Devora Millman, Frederick Nuernberg, Marcia Nowik, Larry Torrella, Lawrence Woodhouse, Jessica Stone, Scott Brodows

George Kamper Photos

Matthew Kimbrough, Barbara Redmond in "A History of the American Film"
Top Right: Arthur Peterson, Norma Ransom in "The Gin Game"

GOODMAN THEATRE

Chicago, Illinois

Artistic Director, Gregory Mosher; Managing Director, Roche Schulfer; Associate Directors, David Mamet, Richard Nelson, Jennifer Tipton; General Manager, Barbara Janowitz; Development, Marie O'Connor; Press, Carol Ball, Barbara Fordney; Production Manager, Phil Eickhoff; Stage Managers, Joseph Drummond, Chuck Henry; Sound, Michael Schweppe; **THE MAN WHO HAD THREE ARMS** by Edward Albee directed by the playwright; Set, John Jensen; Costumes, Barbara A. Bell; Lighting, F. Mitchell Dana; Stage Manager, Joseph Drummond. **CAST:** Robert Drivas, Patricia Kilgarriff, Wyman Pendleton
A CHRISTMAS CAROL by Charles Dickens; Adapted by Barbara Field; Director, Tony Mockus; Sets, Joseph Nieminski; Costumes, James Edmund Brady; Light, Robert Christen; Choreography, Gus Giordano; Stage Manager, Chuck Henry. **CAST:** Annabel Armour, Mary Best, Donald Brearly, Belinda Bremner, Del Close, Ralph Concepcion, Darci Dunbar, Dawn Dunbar, Joseph Buzaldo, Richard Gilbert-Hill, Heather Gray, Tricia Grennan, Tim Halligan, Geoffrey Herden, Dennis Kennedy, Michael A. Krawic, Lauren Leeder, Tony Lincoln, Robby Medina, David Mink, Tony Mockus, Jr., Roger Mueller, Mark Nelson, William J. Norris, John Ostrander, Elizabeth Perkins, Vernon R. Schwartz, Mary Pat Sullivan, Robert Thompson, Jamie Wild
THE COMEDY OF ERRORS by William Shakespeare; Director, Robert Woodruff; Set, David Gropman; Costumes, Susan Hilferty; Lighting, Paul Gallo; Music Composed and Directed by Doug Wieselman; Stage Manager, Joseph Drummond. **CAST:** Bud Chase, Avner Eisenberg, Laurel Cronin, Chas Elstner, Christopher Fisher, Timothy Daniel Furst, Charles Edward Glover, Gina Leishman, Paul Magid, Randy Nelson, Wendy Parkman, Howard Jay Patterson, Jeffery Raz, Santana, Sophie Schwab, Douglas Wieselman, Samuel Ross Williams, Alec Willows
THE DINING ROOM by A. R. Gurney, Jr.; Director, Michael Maggio; Set, Joseph Nieminski; Costumes, Marsha Kowal; Lighting, Robert Christen; Stage Manager, Chuck Henry. **CAST:** Joseph Guzaldo, Cordis Heard, B. J. Jones, Linda Kimbrough, Pamela Nyberg, Rob Riley

**Patricia Kilgarriff, Robert Drivas, Wyman Pendleton
in "The Man Who Had Three Arms"**

RED RIVER (*U.S. Premiere*) by Pierre Laville; Adapted by David Mamet; Set, Karen Schulz; Costumes, Susan Hilferty; Lighting, Paul Gallo; Music, William Harper; Choreography, Charles Vernon; Director, Robert Woodruff; Stage Manager, Joseph Drummond. **CAST:** Roy Brocksmith, Rebecca Cole, Jane MacIver, Christopher McCann, Mary McDonnell, D. W. Moffett, Mike Nussbaum, Alan Ruck, Lionel Mark Smith, John Spencer, Caryn West
A SOLDIER'S PLAY by Charles Fuller; Director, Douglas Turner Ward; Set, Felix E. Cochren; Costumes, Judy Deering; Lighting, Allen Lee Hughes; Sound, Regge Life; Stage Manager, Edward DeShae. **CAST:** Adolph Caesar, David Davies, Eugene Lee, Denzel Washington, James Pickens, Jr., Samuel L. Jackson, Steven A. Jones, John Dewey Carter, Charles Brown, David Allen Grier, Dan Lutzky, Stephen Zettler
THE BECKETT PROJECT by Samuel Beckett; Directors, Alan Schneider, Rich Cluchey; Lighting/Sets, Kevin Rigdon, Rocky Greenberg; Costumes, Teresita Garcia Suro; Stage Manager, Chuck Henry. **CAST:** Helen Gary Bishop, Rick Cluchey, David Warrilow
JUNGLE COUP (*World Premiere*) by Richard Nelson; Director, David Chambers; Set, Kevin Rigdon; Costumes, Marsha Kowal; Lights, Jennifer Tipton; Stage Manager, Cathryn Bulicek. **CAST:** Seth Allen, Mike Nussbaum, Jack Wallace
GARDENIA by John Guare; Director, Gregory Mosher; Set, David Emmons, Gregory Mosher; Costumes, Nan Cibula; Lighting, Kevin Rigdon; Stage Manager, Tom Biscotto. **CAST:** Gary Cole, Patrick Harkness, Elizabeth Perkins, David Perry, William L. Petersen, Richard Seer, Jack Wallace
THE DISAPPEARANCE OF THE JEWS by David Mamet/- **GORILLA** by Shel Silverstein/**HOT LINE** by Elaine May; Directors, Gregory Mosher, Art Wolff; Sets, Franne Lee; Stage Managers, Tom Biscotto, Chuck Henry. **CAST:** Del Close, Peter Falk, Paul Guilfoyle, Tim Halligan, Joe Mantegna, Elaine May, Susan Orrick, Norman Parker, Ron Silver

**Gary Cole, Elizabeth Perkins in "Gardenia"
Right Center: "The Dining Room"**

GUTHRIE THEATER

Minneapolis, Minnesota
Twentieth Season

Artistic Director, Liviu Ciulei; Managing Director, Donald Schoenbaum; Associate Artistic Director, Garland Wright; Dramaturg, Richard Nelson; Directors, Liviu Ciulei, Gary Gissleman, Christopher Markle, Andrei Serban, Harold Stone, Garland Wright; Sets, Jack Barkla, Adrianne Lobel, Santo Loquasto, Beni Montresor, Michael Yeargan; Costumes, Jared Aswegan, Lawrence Casey, Jack Edwards, Ann Hould-Ward, Santo Loquasto, Beni Montresor; Lighting, William Armstrong, Craig Miller, Paul Scharfenberger, Duane Schuler, Jennifer Tipton; Sound, Bob Jorssen, Bruce Margolis, Terry Tilley; Stage Managers, Sharon Ewald, Peg Guilfoyle, Bill Gregg, Charlie Otte, Barbara Wiener; Choreographers, Maria Cheng, Loyce Houlton, Randolyn Zinn; Composers, Fiorenzo Carpi, Richard Peaslee

COMPANY: Seth Allen, Fred Applegate, Walter Atamaniuk, Gerry Bamman, Gary Basaraba, Catherine Burns, Yolanda Childress, Caitlin Clarke, Robert Dorfman, Denise Ellis, Dillon Evans, Ellen Finholt, Gloria Foster, Richard Frank, Kate Fuglei, June Gibbons, Gail Grate, Jossie de Guzman, James Harper, Delphi Harrington, Munson Hicks, Richard Howard, Jacqueline Knapp, Linda Kozlowski, Colin Lane, Wendy Lawless, John Lewin, Peter M. Lucas, Greg Martyn, Steven McCloskey, Bill McIntyre, Peter McRobbie, Isabell Monk, Bill Moor, Annie Murray, Frederick Neumann, Kristine Nielsen, Richard Ooms, Charlie Otte, Robert Pastene, Warren Pincus, Gary Rayppy, Cristine Rose, Malcolm Rothman, Ken Ruta, Richard Sale, Jane Schneider, Danny Sewell, Fruud Smith, Cherie Sprosty, Henry Stram, Louella St. Ville, Eugene Troobnick, Jack Walsh, David Warrilow, Dona Werner, Claudia Wilkens

PRODUCTIONS: Summer Vacation Madness (U.S. Premiere) by Carlo Goldoni, Requiem for a Nun by William Faulkner, Room Service by Murray and Boretz, The Marriage of Figaro by Beaumarchais adapted by Richard Nelson, Heartbreak House by George Bernard Shaw, A Christmas Carol by Charles Dickens adapted by Barbara Field, Entertaining Mr. Sloane by Joe Orton, Peer Gynt by Henrik Ibsen translated by Rolf Fjelde

Joe Giannetti Photos

**Caitlin Clarke, Dona Werner, Kristine Nielsen
in "Summer Vacation Madness"**

Top: (L) Greg Martyn, Jossie de Guzman in "Peer Gynt"

HARTFORD STAGE COMPANY

Hartford, Connecticut

Artistic Director, Mark Lamos; Managing Director, William Stewart; Associate Artistic Director/Literary Manager, Mary B. Robinson; Production Manager, Dorothy Maffei; Press, Natalie D. Crotty; General Manager, William Monroe; Technical Director, Clayton Austin, Costumer, Martha Christian

ON BORROWED TIME by Paul Osborn; Director, Tony Giordano; Set, Karen Schulz, Costumes, David Murin; Lighting, Paul Gallo. **CAST:** C. B. Barnes, William Swetland, Leora Dana, Ralph Williams, Laura Hughes, Brendon DeSimone, Sloane Shelton, F. Allan Tibbetts, Mark O'Donnell, Maurice Copeland, Clark Rogers, Don Plumley
THE GREAT MAGOO by Ben Hecht, Gene Fowler; Director, Mark Lamos; Set, Tony Straiges; Costumes, Linda Fisher; Lighting, Arden Fingerhut; Musical Consultant/Arranger, Mel Marvin; Wigs, Paul Huntley. **CAST:** Ruth Jaroslow, David A. Butler, Christine Estabrook, Merwin Goldsmith, Robert Machray, Janelle Winston, Sam McMurray, Roberta Prescott, Steve Carter, Ben Siegler, Sandy Faison, Bonnie Peterson, Ana Maria Allessi, Jean Marie Conway, Robert Blumenfeld, Ed Garfield, Ralph Williams, Bill Corsair, Graham Bruce, Roger S. G. Wilks, Chuck Andrus, Daniel May, Albert Geetter, Michael O'Hare, Chadwick Brown
THE PORTAGE TO SAN CRISTOBAL OF A. H. (*U.S. Premiere*) adapted for the stage by Christopher Hampton from the novel by George Steiner; Director, Mark Lamos; Set, John Conklin; Costumes, Merrily Murray-Walsh; Lighting, Pat Collins; Sound, David Budries. **CAST:** Alan Mixon, Mark Zeller, Robert Blumenfeld, Ian Stuart, Mordecai Lawner, Dennis Bacigalupi, Mark Wayne Nelson, Talbott Dowst, John Cullum, Robert Blackburn, Thomas Carson, Jerry Allan Jones, Robert Machray, Carla Dean, Michael O'Hare, Ann-Sara Matthews
DOG EAT DOG (*World Premiere*) by Mary Gallagher; Director, Mary B. Robinson; Set, Andrew Jackness; Costumes, Nan Cibula; Lighting, Robert Jared. **CAST:** Susan Pellegrino, Lewis Arlt, Peter Boyden, Robert Nichols, Jeanne Michels, Denise DeSimone, Justin McGlamery, Kayden Will, Lynn Cohen, Jane Connell, Vic Polizos
THE MISANTHROPE by Moliere; Director, Mark Lamos; Set, Kevin Rupnik; Costumes, Dunya Ramicova; Lighting, Pat Collins; Wigs, Paul Huntley. **CAST:** Nicholas Woodeson, Ivar Brogger, Will Lyman, Tandy Cronyn, David H. Lawrence, Olivia Virgil Harper, Christopher Britton, Davis Hall, Mark Wayne Nelson, Pamela Payton-Wright, David Brisbin
THE GLASS MENAGERIE by Tennessee Williams; Director, George Keathley; Set/Costumes, Santo Loquasto; Lighting, James F. Ingalls; Wigs, Paul Huntley. **CAST:** Jan Miner, Laura Hughes, Kevin Geer, Eric Roberts

Lanny Nagler Photos

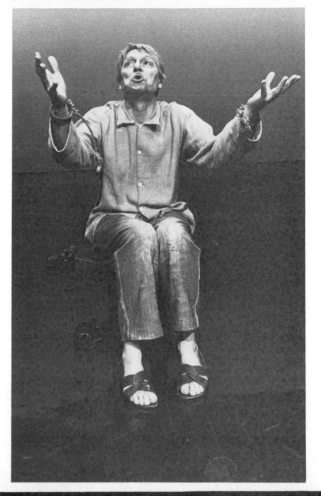

Christopher Britton, Ivar Brogger, Tandy Cronyn, Olivia Virgil Harper, Davis Hall in "The Misanthrope"
Top Right: John Cullum in "The Portage to San Cristobal of A. H."

HUNTINGTON THEATRE COMPANY

Boston, Massachusetts
First Season

Producing Director, Peter Altman; Artistic Adviser, Zelda Fichandler; Managing Director, Michael Moso; Production Manager, Roger Meeker; Press, Marty Jones, John Bentz; Technical Director, Jim Ray; Sets, Franco Colavecchia, James Leonard Joy, Richard Isackes, Hugh Landwehr; Costumes, Rachel Kurland, Mariann Verheyen, Ann Wallace, Michaele Hite; Lighting, William Mintzer, Jeff Davis, Roger Meeker; Stage Managers, Peggy Peterson, Tom Aberger, Kate Hancock.

NIGHT AND DAY by Tom Stoppard; Director, Toby Robertson. **CAST:** Caroline Lagerfelt, Jack Ryland, Edmond Genest, Milledge Mosley, William Cain, David Fuller, Kim Sullivan, Max Deitch

THE DINING ROOM by A. R. Gurney, Jr.; Director, Thomas Gruenewald. **CAST:** Denise Bessette, Lynn Bowman, Peter Davies, Douglas Jones, Tanny McDonald, Robert Stattel

TRANSLATIONS by Brian Friel; Director, Jacques Cartier. **CAST:** Jack Aranson, Ray Dooley, Raymond Hardie, Linda Kozlowski, Richard Seer, Eric Tull, Kathleen Melvin, Richard Mathews, Sara Bradley, Derek Murcott

TIME AND THE CONWAYS by J. B. Priestley; Director, Elinor Renfield. **CAST:** Pauline Flanagan, Margaret Whitton, Ralph Byers, Pamela Lewis, Karen Sederholm, Monica Merryman, Edward Hibbert, Cynthia Mace, John Carroll, Jarlath Conroy

THE TAMING OF THE SHREW by William Shakespeare; Director, Toby Robertson. **CAST:** David Purdham, Laura Gardner, Anna Levine, George Hall, Richard Seer, Jack Kenny, Adam Redfield, Eric Tull, Jeffrey Eiche, Richard Poe, Robert Shampain, Michael Adler, Mark Chamberlin, Elton Cormier, Mark McConnell, Joseph Muzikar, Tyrone Power, Deborah LaCoy

Gerry Goodstein Photos

Cynthia Mace, Edward Hibbert, Margaret Whitton in "Time and the Conways"
Top Right: Richard Seer, Anna Levine in "The Taming of the Shrew"

LONG WHARF THEATRE

New Haven, Connecticut
Eighteenth Season

Artistic Director, Arvin Brown; Executive Director, M. Edgar Rosenblum; Press, Marta Mellinger, Marilaine Dyer; Stage Managers, George Darveris, James Harker, Anne Keefe, Franklin Keysar, Robin Kevrick, Peggy Peterson

OPEN ADMISSIONS (*World Premiere*) by Shirley Lauro; Director Arvin Brown; Set, Marjorie Bradley Kellogg; Costumes, Ann Roth, Gary Jones; Lighting, Ronald Wallace. **CAST:** Paul Gleason, Roberta Maxwell, Mary Alice, Calvin Levels, Wendy Ann Finnegan, Pamela Potillo, Paula Fritz, Thomas Calabro, Evan H. Miranda, Ntombi Peters, Tarah Roberts

HOLIDAY by Philip Barry; Director, John Pasquin; Set, Steven Rubin; Costumes, Bill Walker; Lighting, Ronald Wallace. **CAST:** Jill Eikenberry, William Barry, Robert Koon, Richard Jenkins, Joanne Camp, Dana Cashman, David Pierce, William Swetland, Clayton Berry, Peggy Cosgrave, Jonathan Hadary, Sofia Landon

ANOTHER COUNTRY (*American Premiere*) by Julian Mitchell; Director, John Tillinger; Set, Marjorie Bradley Kellogg; Costumes, Bill Walker; Lighting, Pat Collins; Dialect Consultant, Elizabeth Smith. **CAST:** Peter Gallagher, Peter MacNicol, Tait Rupert, Albert Macklin, Owen Thompson, Tyrone Power, Mark Moses, Rob Gomes, Robert Byron Allen, Edmond Genest

THE GUARDSMAN by Ferenc Molnar; Director, Harris Yulin; Set, John Conklin; Costumes, Jane Greenwood; Lighting, Jamie Gallagher. **CAST:** Richard Jordan, Maria Tucci, Paul Benedict, Jane Cronin, Lisa Goodman, Henry Thomas, Robert Koon, Pater Haller, Sarah Peterson

PAL JOEY by Rodgers and Hart; Book, John O'Hara; Director, Kenneth Frankel; Set, John Conklin; Costumes, Robert Wojewodski; Lighting, Judy Rasmuson; Musical Director, Tom Fay; Choreography, Dan Siretta. **CAST:** Philip Casnoff, Will McIntyre, Tammy Silva, Louisa Flaningam, Penelope Richards, Dorothy Stanley, Susan Danielle, David Monzione, Mayme Paul, Michele Rogers, Rick Pessagno, Gary Kirsch, Brad Witsger, Betsy Joslyn, Joyce Ebert, Tom Offt, Frank Kopyc, D'Jamin Bartlett, Lou Criscuolo, Charles W. Noel, Harrison Eldredge, Meg Gianotti, Karen Hageman, David Houde, Andy Rage, Maury Rosenberg, Nancy Wolfe

Joyce Ebert, John Tillinger in "The Cherry Orchard"

Stockard Channing, Kevin Geer in "The Lady and the Clarinet"

THE CHERRY ORCHARD by Anton Chekhov; Director, Arvin Brown; Set, John Jensen; Costumes, William Walker; Lighting, Judy Rasmuson. **CAST:** Tom Atkins, Betsy Joslyn, Brent Spiner, Stephanie Zimbalist, Joyce Ebert, Fran Brill, John Tillinger, Pippa Scott, Michael Egan, Wally Kurth, Morris Carnovsky, Mark Blum, Tony Taddei, Alan Bergreen, Rob Koon, Andrea Iovino, Nicolette Vannais, Katherine Frankfurt

TWO BY A. M. (*World Premiere*) by Arthur Miller; Director, Mr. Miller; Set, Hugh Landwehr; Costumes, Bill Walker; Lighting, Ronald Wallace; Original Music, Stanley Silverman. **CAST:** Charles Cioffi, Christine Lahti

QUARTERMAINE'S TERMS (*American Premiere*) by Simon Gray; Director, Kenneth Frankel; Set, David Jenkins; Costumes, Bill Walker; Lighting, Pat Collins; Dialect Consultant, Timothy Monich. **CAST:** Remak Ramsay, Caroline Lagerfelt, Kelsey Grammer, Roy Poole, Anthony Heald, John Cunningham, Dana Ivey

THE LADY AND THE CLARINET by Michael Cristofer; Director, Gordon Davidson; Set, Michael Yeargan; Costumes, Jane Greenwood; Lighting, Paul Gallo; Original Music, Stanley Silverman. **CAST:** David Singer, Stockard Channing, Kevin Geer, Michael Brandon, Edmond Genest

FREE AND CLEAR (*World Premiere*) by Robert Anderson; Director, Arvin Brown; Set, Karl Eigsti; Costumes, Bill Walker; Lighting, Ronald Wallace. **CAST:** James Naughton, David Marshall Grant, William Swetland, Phyllis Thaxter

William B. Carter Photos

159

LOS ANGELES ACTORS THEATRE

Los Angeles, California

Producing/Artistic Director, Bill Bushnell; Producer, Diane White; Consulting Director, Alan Mandell; Associate Producer/Dramaturge, Adam Leipzig; General Manager, Stephen Richard; Production Manager, John York; Lighting, Barbara Ling; Costumer, Michele Jo Blanche; Stage Managers, Chaz McEwan, Don Hill, Christina M. Frank; Assistant to Mr. Bushnell, Diane Tucker; Production Associate, Kathleen Brass; Press, Constance Harvey, John C. Mahoney, Richard S. Bailey, Roger Martinez; Administrative Associate, Lori Zimmerman.

THE SUN ALWAYS SHINES FOR THE COOL by Miguel Pinero; Director, Jaime Sanchez; Set/Lighting, Barbara Ling; Costumes, Karen Miller; Choreography, Jerry Grimes; Musical Director, John F. York; Stage Manager, Kyria Krezel. CAST: Christine Avila, Earl Billings, Tanya Boyd, Henry Celis, Dena Lesser, Alma Martinez, Jack O'Leary, Rudy Ramos, Jaime Sanchez, J. W. Smith, Jaime Tirelli, Marilyn Tokuda, Gary Wood
FESTIVAL OF ONE-ACTS (*World Premieres*) "Island" by Joseph Scott Kierland, with Benny Baker, Carl Ballantine, Amzie Strickland; "The Removal" by Charles Marowitz, with Ian Abercrombie, Alan Mandell, Terence Pushman, Kate Williamson; "Triplet" by Kitty Johnson, with Janet Carroll, Pamela Segall, Diane Tyler; "Internal Examination" by Carla Tomaso, with Mary McCusker, Barbara Tarbuck; "Only Kidding" by Jim Geoghan, with Joseph DiReda, Clark Niederjohn
FAMILIAR FACES/MIXED FEELINGS (*English Language Premiere*) by Botho Stauss; Director, Fred Haines; Translation, Fred Haines. CAST: Christine Avila, Channing Chase, Martin Ferrero, Lelia Goldoni, Barbara Lindsay, Frank McCarthy, Franklyn Seales, Kurtwood Smith

Esther Rolle, Davis Roberts in "Dame Lorraine"
(*Demetrios Demetropoulos Photo*)

Barbara Babcock, Stefan Gierasch in "Park Your Car
in the Harvard Yard"

THESE MEN (*U.S. Premiere*) by Mayo Simon; Director, Bill Bushnell. CAST: Sally Kirkland, Patti Johns
HOUSEGUEST (*U.S. Premiere*) by Mario Diament; Director, Jaime Jaimes. CAST: Martin Ferrero, Robin Ginsburg, Roger Kern
GANDHIJI by Rose Leiman Goldenberg; Director, Marilyn Coleman. CAST: Artie Cornelius, Anthony Greene, Valerie Mamches, Nelson Mashita, Mark Ringer, Roger Robinson, Glen Towery, Patti Yasutake
THE WIDOW'S BLIND DATE by Israel Horovitz; Director, Bill Bushnell. CAST: Patricia Mattick, Frank McCarthy, Charles Parks
ARTAUD AT RODEZ by Charles Marowitz who directed. CAST: Paul Ainsley, Tom Everett, Neil Flanagan, Joseph Hindy, John Sinclair, Robert Symonds, Barbara Tarbuck, Jane Windsor
FEMALE PARTS(One-woman plays) by Franca Rame, Dario Fo; Directors, Adam Leipzig, Lee Rose; Translated by Margaret Knuzle, Adam Leipzig. CAST: Rhoda Gemignani, Marian Mercer
DAME LORRAINE by Steve Carter; Director, Edmund J. Cambridge. CAST: Thom Christopher, Denise Nicholas-Hill, Davis Roberts, Esther Rolle, Emily Yancy, Tonkins M. Anderson, Tijuana Layne, Leland P. Smith, Gamy L. Taylor, Myrna White
THE QUANNAPOWITT QUARTET by Israel Horovitz; Director, Alan Mandell; Set/Costumes/Lights, Fred Chuang. CAST: "Hopscotch" with Gretchen Corbett, Andrew Rubin; "The 75th" with Frances Bay, Ford Rainey; "Stage Directions" with Rene Assa, Bea Silvern, Helen Duffy; "Spared" with Alan Oppenheimer
THE PRIMARY ENGLISH CLASS by Israel Horovitz; Director, Ray Whelan; Set/Lighting, Russell Pyle; Costumes, Marianna Elliott. CAST: Zachary Berger, Karen Huie, Anthony Ponzini, Carol Potter, David Hunt Stafford, Kenneth Tigar, Marilyn Tokuda, Michel Voletti; Alternate Cast: George Dickerson, Adrian Drake, Noreen Hennessy, Lori Rika Inano, Milt Jamin, Casey Kramer, Vincent Marino, Patty Toy

McCARTER THEATRE COMPANY

Princeton, New Jersey

Artistic Director, Nagle Jackson; Managing Director, Alison Harris; Associate Artistic Director, Robert Lanchester; Sets, Daniel Boylen; Costumes, Susan Rheaume; Lighting, Richard Moore; Production Manager, John Herochik; Stage Managers, Jeanne Anich, Jacques Desnoyers, Peter C. Cook, Francis X. Kuhn, Cynthia J. Tillotson; Technical Director, David R. York; Assistant Production Manager, Susan Smith; Wardrobe, Ann-Marie Arcery; Props, Daniel Sliwinski; Business Manager, Timothy Shields; Assistant to Directors, Heidi Holtz-Eakin; Press, Linda S. Kinsey, Veronica Ann Brady

BLITHE SPIRIT by Noel Coward; Director, William Woodman. **CAST:** Penelope Reed (Edith), Marion Lines (Ruth), Paul Shenar (Charles), Robert Lanchester (Dr. Bradman), Jane Moore (Mrs. Bradman), Anna Russell (Madame Arcati), Christine Baranski (Elivira)
HAMLET by William Shakespeare; Director, Nagle Jackson. **CAST:** Harry Hamlin (Hamlet), James S. Horton (Bernardo), Paul Donahoe (Francisco/Prologue), Darryl Croxton (Horatio), Francis P. Bilancio (Marcellus), Robert Lanchester (Ghost/Gravedigger), Neil Vipond (Claudius), Jill Tanner (Getrude), Jay Doyle (Polonius), Gary Roberts (Laertes), Stacy Ray (Ophelia), Mark Kincaid (Osric), Greg Thornton (Rosencrantz), Gerald Lancaster (Guildenstern), Herb Foster (Player King), Penelope Reed (Player Queen), Jared Reed (Boy), Herbert McAneny (Priest), Lesley Schisgall (Lady), Dale M. Ducko

Harry Hamlin as Hamlet

Right: Mercedes Ruehl, David Obrien in "The Three Sisters"

A CHRISTMAS CAROL adapted and directed by Nagel Jackson; Associate Director, Francis X. Kuhn. **CAST:** Herb Foster (Scrooge), Jonathan Holub (Tiny Tim), Gerald Lancaster (Cratchitt), Darryl Croxton, Michael Plunkett, Greg Thornton, Robin Chadwick, Penelope Reed, Lawrence Holofcener, Bruce Somerville, Stacy Ray, Jay Doyle, Paul Donahoe, Francis P. Bilancio, Leslie Geraci, Dana Litvak, Scott Seymour, Jill Tanner (Mrs. Cratchitt), Cynthia J. Babler, Robert Weed, Kimberly Bell, Eddie Hughes, Rona Binenbaum, Stacy Ray, Penelope Reed, Robin Chadwick, Jay Doyle, Bruce Somerville, Moses Rosenblum, Scott Seymour, Dana Litvak
THE DAY THEY SHOT JOHN LENNON by James McLure; Director, Robert Lanchester. **CAST:** Mercedes Ruehl (Fran), Ann Adams (Sally), Greg Thornton (Kevin), Clifford Fetters (Mike), Damien Leake (Larry), Karl Light (Morris), Tony Campisi (Silvio), Gregory Grove (Gately), Gary Roberts (Brian)
AT THIS EVENING'S PERFORMANCE written and directed by Nagle Jackson. **CAST:** Stacy Ray (Saskia), Robin Chadwick (Oskar), Stephen Oates Smith (Piers), Raye Birk (Gunther Posnik), Penelope Reed (Hippolyta Posnik), Steven Moses (Valdez), Jay Doyle (Pankoff)
THE THREE SISTERS by Anton Chekhov; Director, Nagle Jackson. **CAST:** Penelope Reed (Olga), Stacy Ray (Irina), Mercedes Ruehl (Masha), Robert Lanchester (Baron Nikolay), Jay Doyle (Ivan), Bruce Somerville (Solyony), Anne Sheldon (Anfisa), Dion M. Chesse (Feraponta), David O'Brien (Alexandr), Greg Thornton (Andrey), Anthony DeFonte (Fyodor), Leslie Geraci (Natalya), Steven Oates Smith (Alexey), Stephen Oates Smith (Vladimir), Leslie Dance, Grace Zandarski (Servants)
A DELICATE BALANCE by Edward Albee; Director, Paul Weidner. **CAST:** Nancy Marchand (Agnes), Paul Sparer (Tobias), Barbara Cason (Claire), Myra Carter (Edna), Karl Light (Harry), Elaine Bromka (Julia)

Cliff Moore Photos

Paul Shenar, Christine Baranski in "Blithe Spirit"

161

MEADOW BROOK THEATRE

Rochester, Michigan

General/Artistic Director, Terence Kilburn; Assistant to Mr. Kilburn, Frank F. Bollinger; Directors, Terence Kilburn, Arif Hasnain, Charles Nolte, Judith Haskell; Sets, Peter W. Hicks, Barry Griffith; Lighting, Barry Griffith, Reid G. Johnson, Daniel M. Jaffe, Deatra Smith; Stage Managers, Terry W. Carpenter, Thomas Spence; Technical Director, Barry Griffith; Costume Coordinator, Mary Lynn Crum; Wardrobe, Renee Sinclair; Props, Mary Chmelko

MACBETH: Andrew Barnicle, Sara Morrison, Richard Bradshaw, Linda Gehringer, Matthew Gray, Richard Hilger, J. C. Howe, Henson Keys, Phillip Locker, Wil Love, Jane MacIver, Thomas Mahard, Lisa McMillan, David Wayne Parker, Glen Allen Pruett, David Regal, Carl Schurr, Thomas Spence, Dennis Wrosch

THE ROYAL FAMILY: Burniece Avery, Andrew Barnicle, Sara Morrison, Terry W. Carpenter, Henson Keys, William LeMassena, Phillip Locker, Jane Lowry, Jane MacIver, Marian Primont, Carl Schurr, Eric Tavaris, Wil Love

A CHRISTMAS CAROL: Grace Aiello, Raphael Aiello, Judi Ammar, Andrew Barnicle, Eric Bruggemann, Mary Bruin, George Bufford, Booth Colman, Joshua Dawson, Jan Elliott, Thom Haneline, Henson Keys, Phillip Locker, Wil Love, Luke Huber, Jane MacIver, Sara Morrison, Graham Pollock, Carl Schurr, Jane Shaffmaster, Terrence Sherman, Kevin Siles, Rebecca Watts

TALLEY'S FOLLY: Deanna Dunagan, David Regal

THE CHILDREN'S HOUR: Grace Aiello, Judi Ammar, Jeanne Arnold, Linda Boyd, Bethany Carpenter, Linda Gehringer, Naomi Hatfield, Meghan Heffernan, Jayne Houdyshell, Phillip Locker, Anne-Catharine O'Connell, Jennifer Roberts, Katherine Thorpe

MORNING'S AT SEVEN: Roslyn Alexander, Jeanne Arnold, Mary Benson, Harry Ellerbe, Thom Haneline, Jayne Houdyshell, Phillip Pruneau, John Roberts, Maureen Steindler

THE UNEXPECTED GUEST: Barbara Barringer, Richard Blumenfeld, Peter Brandon, Mary Pat Gleason, George Gitto, Thom Haneline, Naomi Hatfield, Phillip Locker, Tom Mahard

THE FANTASTICKS: Keith David, Hugh L. Hurd, Norman Matlock, Eddie Robinson, Tamara Tunie, Jaison Walker, Von H. Washington, Robert LeVoyd-Wright

Richard Hunt Photos

Jaison Walker, Tamara Tunie, Eddie Robinson in "The Fantasticks"

Top: Cast of "Morning's at Seven"

MERRIMACK REGIONAL THEATRE

Lowell, Massachusetts

Producing Director, Daniel L. Schay; Business Manager, Doris Hubert; Producing Director, D. Douglas O'Dell; Company Manager, Patricia McAlpine; Technical Director, John F. McHugh; Stage Managers, Thomas Clewell, Patricia Frey; Wardrobe, Amanda Aldridge; Props, Victoria Stangroom, Susan Christiansen; Sound, Sheila Comai

DA by Hugh Leonard; Director, Terence Lamude; Set, Duke Durfee; Costumes, Barbara Forbes; Lighting, David Sparky Lockner. **CAST:** John Finn (Charlie), Richard Abernethy (Oliver), Frances Helm (Mother), Michael James Stratford (Young Charlie), Larry Swansen (Drumm), Ann Crumb (Mary Tate), Sarah Melici (Mrs. Prynne)
THE SEVEN YEAR ITCH by George Axelrod; Director, Larry Carpenter; Set, Dennis Bradford; Costumes, Amanda Aldridge; Lighting, John Gisondi; Sound, Philip Campanella. **CAST:** Mart Hulswit (Richard), Eda Roth (Helen), Mark Mullaney (Ricky), Lisa Erikson (Miss Morris), Pamela Demoulas (Elaine), Megan R. Angell (Marie), Eli Marder (The Girl), Jerry Gershman (Dr. Brubaker), Will Lyman (Tom)
TALLEY'S FOLLY by Lanford Wilson; Director, Josephine R. Abady; Set, David Potts; Costumes, Amanda Aldridge; Lighting, Ann G. Wrightson. **CAST:** Richard Portnow (Matt), Shelley Rogers (Sally Talley)
VERONICA'S ROOM by Ira Levin; Director, Robert W. Tolan; Set/Lighting, David Lockner; Costumes, Joellen Bendall. **CAST:** Aideen O'Kelly (The Woman), Thomas Ruisinger (The Man), Ann-Sara Matthews (Young Woman), Richard Sale (Young Man)
TINTYPES by Mary Kyte, Mel Marvin, Gary Pearle; Director, Jim Peskin; Set, Matthew Bliss; Costumes, Amanda Aldridge; Lighting, David Lockner; Musical Director, Rusty Magee; Musical Staging, Lois Hoffman. **CAST:** Steve Liebman (T. R.), Michele Mais (Susannah), Maureen McNamara (Anna), Polly Pen (Emma), David Pevsner (Charlie)

Jo Anne B. Weisman Photos

Ann Crumb, James Hilbrandt (back), Michael James Stratford in "Da" (Merrimack Theatre)

Eric Hill, Jose Santana in "The Government Man" (Milwaukee Repertory Theatre)

MILWAUKEE REPERTORY THEATER

Milwaukee, Wisconsin

Artistic Director, John Dillon; Managing Director, Sara O'Connor; Business Manager, Peggy Haessler Rose; Directors, Sharon Ott, Nick Faust, Rob Goodman, Richard Cottrell, Tetsuo Arakawa; Production Manager, Gregory S. Murphy; Stage Managers, Robert Goodman, Robin Rumpf, Cassandra McFatridge; Sets, Laura Maurer, Tim Thomas, Christopher M. Idoine, David Jenkins, Hugh Landwehr, Bil Mikulewicz; Costumes, Elizabeth Covey, Sam Fleming, Colleen Muscha, Patricia M. Risser, Kurt Wilhelm, Katherine E. Duckert, Mary Piering, Gayle M. Strege; Lighting, Rachel Budin, Dawn Chiang, Dan J. Kotlowitz, Spencer Mosse, Dan Brovarney; Wardrobe, Carol Jean Horaitis; Assistant Production Manager, Deborah Simon; Props, Sandy Struth; Music Directors, Edmund Assaly, Michael Kaminski; Composers, Mark Van Hecke, William Stancil, Larry Delinger; Press, Susan Medak, Phil Orkin, Cheryl Jones

COMPANY: Eric Hill, Ellen Lauren, Daniel Mooney, James Pickering, Rose Pickering, Larry Shue, Victor Raider-Wexler, Kenneth Albers, Laurence Ballard, Jahnna Beecham, Raoul Breton, Alan Brooks, Erma Campbell, Michael Paul Chan, Maury Cooper, Albert Corbin, Montgomery Davis, Julie Follansbee, Abel Franco, Richard Gustin, Ernest Harada, Suzanna Hay, Malcolm Hillgartner, Mimi Honce, Megan Hunt, Kiya Ann Joyce, Darrie Lawrence, Frederick Mao, Harriet Medin, William Ontiveros, Dennis Parlato, Peggity Price, Marion Primont, Rosemary Prinz, Peter Rybolt, Jose Santana, Jeanne Schlagel, Joan Shangold, Peter Silbert, Emmett O'Sullivan-Moore, Patricia Turney, Millie Vega, Isiah Whitlock, Jr., Virginia Wing, Keone Young
PRODUCTIONS: Miss Lulu Bett by Zona Gale, Buried Child by Sam Shepard, The Glass Menagerie by Tennessee Williams, The Foreigner by Larry Shue (*World Premiere*), Uncle Vanya by Anton Chekhov, The Government Man by Felipe Santander and translated by Joe Rosenberg (*English-language Premiere*), The Eighties or Last Love by Tom Cole, The Pentecost by William Stancil (*World Premiere*), The Fuhrer Is Still Alive (*American Premiere*)

Mark Avery Photos

NASSAU REPERTORY THEATRE

New Hyde Park, New York

Artistic Director, Clinton J. Atkinson; Managing Director, Kenneth E. Hahn; Production Coordinator, Sally Cohen; Technical Director, John Pender; Development, Ruby Balter; Press, Joel Dein, Cheryl Dolby, The Merlin Group; Lighting, John Hickey; Costumes, Barbara Weiss, Joan Weiss, Muriel Stockdale, Heidi Hollmann, Fran Rosenthal; Sets, Joseph Forbes, Daniel Ettinger, Ronald Placzek; Stage Managers, J. Barry Lewis, Tom Mangan, David Lansky

GIGI by Anita Loos; Based on novel by Colette. **CAST:** Dori Arnold (Gigi), Tarina Lewis (Mme. Alvarez), Janie Kelly (Andree), Richard Tabor (Gaston), Jerome Collamore (Victor), Ann Shropshire (Alicia), Lippy Lyman (Sidonie)

ROCKET TO THE MOON by Clifford Odets. **CAST:** Joe Ponazecki (Ben Stark), Pamela Burrell (Belle Stark), Katherine Carlson (Cleo Singer), Arland Russell (Phil Cooper), Tom Brennan (Prince), Joel Leffery (Frenchy), Steve Weiser (Willie Wax)

CHARLEY'S AUNT by Brandon Thomas. **CAST:** David Jordan (Jack), William Sevedge Jr. (Brassett), Ben Lemon (Charley), Lee Sloan (Lord Babberly), Alison Courtney Holt (Kitty), Catherine Kent (Amy), George Gitto (Sol. Sir Francis Chesney), George Cavey (Stephen), Celia Howard (Donna Lucia), Bridget Crumpler (Ella)

GHOSTS by Henrik Ibsen, translated by William Archer. **CAST:** P. J. Barry (Engstrand), Peggy Harmon (Regina), John Carroll (Manders), Katherine Jay-Carroll (Mrs. Alving), Ben Lemon (Oswald)

BUS STOP by William Inge. **CAST:** Kathleen Kellaigh (Elma), Pamela Burrell (Grace), David Adamson (Will), Jill Hill (Cherie), Robert Barend (Dr. Lyman), Kirk Condyles (Carl), Donald Reeves (Virgil), Matt McCoy (Bo)

Cathy Blaivas Photos

Pamela Burrell, Joe Ponazecki in "Rocket to the Moon"
(Nassau Repertory Theatre)

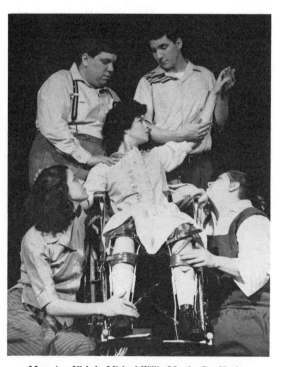

Mary Ann Nichols, Michael Willis, Marsha Gay Harden,
Buzz Roddy, Lynnie Raybuck in "And They Dance Real Slow
in Jackson"

NEW PLAYWRIGHTS' THEATRE

Washington, D.C.

Founder/Artistic Director, Harry M. Bagdasian; Managing Director, Todd Bethel; Literary Manager/Dramaturge, Lloyd Rose; Press, Michael Shoop; Development, Shelley Marston Clark; Production Manager, Tom Moseman; Technical Directors, Jim Katen, Neil Wilson; Sets, Lewis Folden, Jim Hobbs, Russell Metheny; Lighting, Richard Moore, Jim Katen, Lewis Folden, Jim Hobbs; Costumes, Mary Claire Gromet, Mary Ann Powell, Jane Phalen; Props, Deborah Glassberg; Stage Managers, Susan Munson, Jim Taylor, Ron Goodman, Jim Wilder, Larry Redmond; Directors, Jim Nicola, Fred Lee, Tom Evans, Harry M. Bagdasian, Lloyd Rose

PRODUCTIONS (*All World Premieres*) **AND CASTS**
THE NEW NEW IMPROVED BRIDE OF SIROCCO by Tim Grundmann. **CAST:** Chuck Tobin, Yeardley Smith, Caron Tate, Diana Ridge, Steven LeBlanc

BLOOD RELATIONS by Michael Wright. **CAST:** Steven Dawn, Jim Fyfe, Robin Deck, Vic Gialanella

OUT OF THE REACH OF CHILDREN with Book/Music/Lyrics by Cornelia Ravenal; Musical Direction, Ed Rejuney; Orchestrations, Marc T. Johnson. **CAST:** Melissa Berman, Caron Tate, Bev Sheehan, Gretchen Weihe, Veanne Cox

AND THEY DANCE REAL SLOW IN JACKSON by Jim Leonard, Jr. **CAST:** Marsha Gay Harden, Dion Anderson, Barbara Evans, Michael Willis, Buzz Roddy, Lynnie Raybuck, Mary Ann Nichols

STOPOVER ON WHITNEY STREET by Peter Perhonis. **CAST:** Seymour Horowitz, Barbara Rappaport, Buzz Roddy, Sam Baum, Peggy Pridemore

BURRHEAD by Deborah Pryor. **CAST:** Marsha Gay Harden, Dale Stein, Dave Sitler, Lynnie Raybuck, Connie Fowlkes, T. G. Finkbinder, T. J. Edwards, Prudence Barry

Doc Dougherty Photos

NORTH LIGHT REPERTORY

Evanston, Illinois
Seventh Season

Artistic Director, Eric Steiner; Managing Director, Jeffrey Bentley; Associate Artistic Director, Mary F. Monroe; Marketing, Eileen Gill; Press, Ellie Meindl; Stage Managers, James K. Tinsley, Mary Murphy Kenny; Sets/Costumes, Nan Zabriskie; Lighting, Dawn Hollingsworth

WHO'S AFRAID OF VIRGINIA WOOLF? by Edward Albee; Director, Eric Steiner; Set, Nels Anderson; Costumes, Kate Bergh. **CAST:** Megan McTavish, Jack McLaughlin-Gray, Laurie Metcalf, Rick Snyder
FILTHY RICH by George Walker; Director, Robert Woodruff; Set, Michael Merritt; Lights, Robert Shook; Costumes, Jordan Ross. **CAST:** P. J. Barry, Michael Grodenchik, Diane D'Aquila, Maria Ricossa, Ron Parady, Brooks Gardner
DUET FOR ONE by Tom Kempinski; Director, Jeffrey Hayden; Set, David Emmons; Costumes, Jessica Hahn. **CAST:** Eva Marie Saint, Milton Selzer
CHILDREN by A. R. Gurney, Jr.; Director, Mary F. Monroe; Set, Robert Barnett. **CAST:** Fern Persons, Allison Giglio, Peter Syvertsen, Elizabeth Smith
THE IMPROMPTU OF OUTREMENT by Michel Trembley; Director, Eric Steiner; Set, Shawn Kerwin. **CAST:** Pauline Brailsford, Diane D'Aquila, Laurel Cronin, Allison Giglio
THE EARLY MALE YEARS by John McNamara; Director, Mary F. Monroe. **CAST:** Ed Henzel, James Sudik, Johnny Heller, Debra Engle, Pam Gay
DOUGLAS by Robert Litz; Director, David Rotenberg; Performed by Glenn Mazen
DEMOLITION JOB by Gordon Graham; Director, Edward Stern. **CAST:** Joe Lauck, Robert Browning, Jeff Ginsberg

Ebright and Lascher Photos

Debra Engle, Johnny Heller in "The Early Male Years"
(North Light Repertory)

Shaun Cassidy, Milo O'Shea in "Mass Appeal"
(Paper Mill Playhouse)

PAPER MILL PLAYHOUSE

Millburn, New Jersey

Executive Producer, Angelo Del Rossi; General Manager, Wade Miller; Administrative Director, James Thesing

ROBERT AND ELIZABETH directed by Robert Johanson. **CAST:** Leigh Beery, Mark Jacoby, Ron Randell
YOU CAN'T TAKE IT WITH YOU by Moss Hart, George S. Kaufman; Director, Ellis Rabb. **CAST:** Jason Robards, Colleen Dewhurst, George Rose, Elizabeth Wilson
MASS APPEAL by Bill C. Davis; Director, Geraldine Fitzgerald. **CAST:** Milo O'Shea, Shaun Cassidy
SUITE IN TWO KEYS directed by Richard Barr. **CAST:** Gwyda DonHowe, Barry Nelson, Elaine Stritch
THE NEW MOON directed by Robert Johanson. **CAST:** Judith McCauley, Richard White, Norman A. Large, Christopher Hewett
MAN OF LA MANCHA directed by Rudy Tronto. Starring Jerome Hines and Bernice Massi

Terence A. Gili

165

PENNSYLVANIA STAGE COMPANY

Allentown, Pennsylvania

Producing Director, Gregory S. Hurst; General Manager, Gary C. Porto; Stage Directors, Stephen Rothman, Gregory S. Hurst, Susan Kerner, Ken Jenkins, Pamela K. Pepper; Sets, Curtis Dretsch, David Potts, Raymond C. Recht, William Schroder, Robert Thayer; Costumes, Mary-Anne Aston, Bernard Johnson, David Toser, Colleen Muscha; Lights, Curtis Dretsch, Syd Bennett, Todd Lichtenstein, Mark Hendren; Stage Managers, Peter S. Del Vecho, Dennis Blackledge; Press, Sharon P. Bernstein

BORN YESTERDAY by Garson Kanin; Director, Stephen Rothman. **CAST:** Shelley Hack, Michael O. Smith, Fritz Sperberg, Kelly Fitzpatric, Rick Riker, Mary Hara, Dennis Patella, Estelle Kemler, Christopher Hoke, Anne Allgood, Liz Silon, Daniel Roebuck, Margaret Snow, David Smith, Edward Polgardy

BLITHE SPIRIT by Noel Coward; Director, Ken Jenkins. **CAST:** Lesley Vogel, Beth Dixon, Edward Conery, David O. Petersen, Judith Tillman, Joyce Worsley, Gwyn Gillis

DESIRE UNDER THE ELMS by Eugene O'Neill; Director, Gregory S. Hurst. **CAST:** Arch Johnson, Douglas R. Nielsen, Rand Bridges, Richard McWilliams, Susan Greenhill, Margaret Snow, Ian Gallihue, Christopher Hoke, Anne Allgood

MASS APPEAL by Bill C. Davis; Director, Pamela K. Pepper. **CAST:** James Maxwell, Malachy McCourt

SHIM SHAM (*World Premiere*) by Eric Blau; Music/Lyrics, Johnny Brandon; Director, Gregory S. Hurst, Choreography, Bick Goss, Henry LeTang; Musical Direction, Thom Bridwell. **CAST:** Hinton Battle, Wayne McCarthy, Arnetia Walker, Joanna Lehman, Kim Morgan, Luther Fontaine, Bernard Marsh, Jan Mickens, Leah Louise Bass, Keith Curran, David Arthur, Anne Allgood, Christopher Hoke, Margaret Snow

READY OR NOT (*World Premiere*) by Casey Kelly; Director, Susan Kerner. **CAST:** Donna Davis, Lynnie Greene, Fran Stevens, William Van Hunter

Gregory M. Fota Photos

Arch Johnson, Susan Greenhill in "Desire under the Elms"

Top: Hinton Battle, Arnetia Walker in "Shim Sham"

PHILADELPHIA DRAMA GUILD

Philadelphia, Pennsylvania

Artistic/Managing Director, Gergory Poggi; Development/Planning Director, Tom Sherman; Business Manager, Mark Bernstein; Marketing, Barbara Konik; Press, Mary P. Packwood; Sets, Roger Mooney, Eldon Elder, John Falabella, Karen Schulz, John Jensen; Costumes, John David Ridge, Jess Goldstein, Frankie Fehr, David Murin; Lighting, Dennis Parichy, William Armstrong, Ann Wrightson; Stage Managers, John Toia, Mark Ramont; Project Coordinator, Steven Schachter

THE KEEPER (*World Premiere*) by Karolyn Nelke; Director, Steven Schachter. **CAST:** Stuart Germain, Richard Frank, I. M. Hobson, Valerie Mahaffey, Dwight Schultz, Eunice Anderson, Patricia Elliott
THE DIARY OF ANNE FRANK by Frances Goodrich, Albert Hackett; Director, William Woodman. **CAST:** Barbara Caruso, Marissa Chibas, John Dukakis, Pierre Epstein, Ron Faber, George Guidall, Jan Leslie Harding, Conrad L. Osborne, Marilyn Sokol, Christine Wiedeman
TALLEY'S FOLLY by Lanford Wilson; Director, Charles I. Karchmer. **CAST:** Jerry Zaks, Robin Groves
DAUGHTERS by John Morgan Evans; Director, Tony Giordano. **CAST:** Jenny O'Hara, Vera Lockwood, Kathleen Doyle, Yudie Bank, Roxann Caballero
ALL MY SONS by Arthur Miller; Director, William Woodman. **CAST:** Dan Frazer, Edward Seamon, Tony Pasqualini, Lilene Mansell, Sarah Felder, Court Miller, Lenka Peterson, Kristin Griffith, Adrian Sparks, Morgan Land, Judd Serotta

Kenneth Kauffman Photos

Patricia Elliott, Dwight Schultz, Valerie Mahaffey in "The Keeper"
(Philadelphia Drama Guild)
Left: Kathleen Doyle, Vera Lockwood, Roxann
Caballero, Jenny O'Hara in "Daughters"

PORTLAND STAGE COMPANY

Portland, Maine

Producing Director, Barbara Rosoff; General Manager, Patricia Egan; Press/Development, Lindsay Hancock; Assistant to Ms. Rosoff, Lynn Polan; Technical Director, Tim Pickens; Props, Joan Sand; Stage Manager, Mark Kindschi; Lighting, Arden Fingerhut; Sets, Marjorie Kellogg, Patricia Woodbridge

GETTING OUT by Marsha Norman; Director, Barbara Rosoff. **CAST:** Rebecca Nelson, Cynthia Mace, William Hall, Jr., JD. Swain, Rodman Neumann, David LaGraffe, Anna Minot, Margaretmary McCann, Martin Jones, Eric Michels, J. E. Freeman, Rheatha Forster
THE DINING ROOM by A. R. Gurney, Jr.; Director, Lynn Polan. **CAST:** Mona Stiles, James Selby, James Seymour, Shaw Purnell, Cynthia Barnett, Richard Maynard
GARDENIA by John Guare; Director, Barbara Rosoff. **CAST:** Keliher Walsh, Michael Landrum, Richard Maynard, Thomas A. Stewart, Frank Geracci, Chris Bride
A LESSON FROM ALOES by Athol Fugard; Director, Arden Fingernut. **CAST:** Tad Ingram, William Hall, Jr., Susan Stevens
HOW I GOT THAT STORY by Amlin Gray; Director, Louis Rackoff. **CAST:** Stephen C. Bradbury, Stanley Flood
ECCO! by Gerry Bamman (*World Premiere*); Director, Barbara Rosoff. **CAST:** Robert Burns, Conan McCarthy, Sofia Landon, Dexter Witherell, Susan Botti, Paul Walker, Etain O'Malley, Peter Dane, Sandra T. Colby, Stephen C. Bradbury, Michael Hughes

Dean Abramson Photos

Shaw Purnell, Mona Stiles, James Seymour, Richard Maynard
in "The Dining Room" (Portland Stage Company)

REPERTORY THEATRE OF ST. LOUIS

St. Louis, Missouri

(Formerly Loretto-Hilton Repertory Theatre) Artistic Director, Wallace Chappell; Managing Director, Steven Woolf; Associate Artistic Director, Jan Eliasberg; Development, Anne B. DesRosiers, Barbara Harris; Assistant Managing Director, Jane E. Bryan; Press, Connie Romine, Sharon Salomon, Doyle Reynolds, Karen Schneider; Technical Director, Max DeVolder, Peggy J. DePuy; Company Manager, Joyce Volker Ruebel; Stage Managers, Glenn Dunn, Rachael Lindhart; Sets, Carolyn L. Ross, Tim Jozwick, Richard Tolkkuhn; Props, John Roslevich, Jr., Michael Ganio; Costumes, Dorothy L. Marshall; Wardrobe, Janice TenBroek, John J. Olivastro; Lighting, Peter E. Sargent.

TARTUFFE by Moliere; Director, Philip Kerr; Adapted by Miles Malleson; Set/Costumes, John Carver Sullivan; Stage Manager, T. R. Martin. **CAST:** Brendan Burke, Joan Croydon, Patrick Farrelly, Sarah-Jane Gwillim, Arthur Hanket, John Christopher Jones, Joneal Joplin, Chris Limber, Doyle Reynolds, Susan Saunders, William Wright, Susie Wall

A TALE OF TWO CITIES (*World Premiere*) by Charles Dickens; Adapted and Directed by Wallace Chappell. **CAST:** Brendan Burke, Alan Clarey, Stephen A. Cowan, Craig Dudley, Patrick Farrelly, Skip Foster, Sarah-Jane Gwillim, Joneal Joplin, Philip Kerr, Susan Leigh, Chris Limber, James Paul, Judith Roberts, Wayne Salomon, Gray Stephens, and Alex M. Adams, Aaron Bass, Beth Baur, Ron Bohmer, Ryan Bollman, Patti Marie Butler, Jeffrey Carpenter, Diane Carr, Roscoe Carroll, Amy Caton-Ford, Mark Colson, Rhea Anne Cook, Mitti Crosier, Robert Dorn, Diane DuMar, Amy Endres, Thomas Estler, Tyne Firmin, Catherine Fitzgerald, Kate Gengo, Christa Germanson, Jeffrey Gimble, Kathryn Graves, Pamela Gray, Bethany Hanson, Mae Haskins, Sarah Holden, Dan La-Force, Maggie Lerian, Kevin Leslie, Jeff Lewis, Kathy McGowan, Nancy Sue Magarill, Joel Manatt, Mark Daniel Marderosian, Ruth Ann Martin, Walter E. Marts, Jennifer Mates, Paula Newsome, Steve O'Connell, Kathleen O'Rourke, Greg Parmley, Stacey Parke, John Phelan, Lisa Raziq, Cindy Reading, Gigi Repetti, Nancy V. Reynen, Lisa Rigdon, James Riordan, Maria L. Ross, Nada Salib, Judith Scott, Gia Shukair, Patrick Siler, Robert Standley, Brian Stansifer, Haley B. Sweet, Peggy Taphorn, Lisa Tejero, Tiffany Thomas, Elaine Wadsworth, Charles White, Tanya White, David P. Whitehead, Kelly Williams, Suzanne Williams, Kate Yust, Pam Zoth

Craig Dudley as Charles Darnay in "A Tale of Two Cities"

Leonard Frey, Julie Harris in "Under the Ilex"

A CHRISTMAS TAPESTRY based on farces by Anton Chekhov; Adapted and Directed by Jan Eliasberg; Music, Janes Mobberley. **CAST:** Skip Foster, Jeff Ginsberg, Bradley Mott, Jim Reardon, Richard Wharton

PRESENT LAUGHTER by Noel Coward; Director, Philip Kerr; Set, John Roslevich, Jr. **CAST:** Brendan Burke, Christa Germanson, Sarah-Jane Gwillim, Ruby Holbrook, Julia Jonathan, John Christopher Jones, Joneal Joplin, Philip Kerr, Sharon Laughlin, James Paul, Enid Rodgers

HEDDA GABLER by Henrik Ibsen; Translated by Rolf Fjelde; Director, Jan Eliasberg; Assistant Director, Milton R. Zoth. **CAST:** Katherine Borowitz, Martin Donegan, Julia Jonathan, John Christopher Jones, Martha Miller, Donna Snow, Richard Wharton

UNDER THE ILEX (*World Premiere*) by Clyde Talmage: Director, Charles Nelson Reilly; Associate Director, Timothy Helgeson; Set, Marjorie Bradley Kellogg; Costumes, Noel Taylor; Lighting, Max DeVolder; Stage Manager, Glenn Dunn. **CAST:** Leonard Frey, Julie Harris

SORE THROATS (*U.S. Premiere*) by Howard Brenton; Director, Jan Eliasberg; Set, Tim Jozwick; Costumes, Gail A. Crellin; Lighting, Max DeVolder; Stage Manager, Rachael Lindhart; Fight Director, Gray Stephens. **CAST:** David Little, Joan MacIntosh, Denise Stephenson

Scott Dine Photos

168

SEATTLE REPERTORY THEATRE

Seattle, Washington

Artistic Director, Daniel Sullivan; Producing Director, Peter Donnelly; Associate Artistic Director, Robert Egan; Technical Production Director, Robert Scales; Production Manager, Vito Zingarelli; Costume Coordinator, Sally Roberts; Business Manager, Marene Wilkinson; Press, Marta Mellinger, Marnie Andrews; Marketing, Jerry Sando; Development, Frank Self

ROMEO AND JULIET by William Shakespeare; Director, Daniel Sullivan; Set, Robert Dahlstrom; Costumes, Robert Blackman; Lighting, Robert Dahlstrom; Music, Kenneth Benshoof; Sound, Michael Holten; Fight Choreography, David Boushey; Stage Manager, Marc Rush. **CAST:** Daniel Mahar (Barber/Friar John/Father), Sheri Lee Miller (Rosalind), J V Bradley (Sampson), Bill terKuile (Gregory), Edward Sampson (Apothecary), David Boushey (Abram), James Brousseau (Balthasar), Jeffrey Hutchinson (Benvolio), Ron King (Tybalt), Brian Faker (Tybalt's Friend), Ted D'Arms (Capulet), Marjorie Lovett (Lady Capulet), Robert Loper (Montague), Anne O'Connell (Lady Montague), Lachlan Macleay (Capt. of Guard), Frank Corrado (Escalus), Nathan Haas (Paris), Tuck Milligan (Romeo), Lou Hetler (Peter), Florence Stanley (Nurse), Amy Irving (Juliet), Lance Davis (Mercutio) Clayton Corzatte (Friar Laurence)
THE FRONT PAGE by Ben Hecht, Charles MacArthur; Director, Daniel Sullivan; Set, Ralph Funicello; Costumes, Robert Wojewodski; Lighting, James F. Ingalls; Stage Manager, Mary Hunter. **CAST:** Barry M. Press (Wilson), Glen Mazen (Endicott), Paul Hostetler (Murphy), John Aylward (McCue), Richard Riehle (Schwartz), Allen Nause (Kruger), Michael Santo (Bensinger), Robert Lopez (Woodenshoes), Frank Corrado (Diamond Louis), Denis Arndt (Hildy Johnson), Jill Klein (Jennie), Lori Larsen (Mollie), Tobias Andersen (Sheriff), Katherine Ferrand (Peggy), Eve Roberts (Mrs. Grant), Ted D'Arms (Mayor), Clayton Corzatte (Pincus), Jeffrey Hutchinson (Earl), Tom Toner (Burns), Lachlan Macleay (Carl/Tony), Michael Smith (Frank), Roderick Aird (Policeman)
DEATH OF A SALESMAN by Arthur Miller; Director, Allen Fletcher; Set, Scott Weldin; Costumes, Sally Richardson; Lighting, James Sale; Sound, Michael Holten; Original Music, Paige Wheeler; Stage Manager, Mary Hunter. **CAST:** Edward Binns (Willy Loman), Mary Doyle (Linda), John Procaccino (Happy), Mark Jenkins (Biff), Gibby Brand (Bernard), Jill Klein (Woman), Robert Ellenstein (Charley), Paul Hostetler (Uncle Ben), John Aylward (Howard Wagner), Kathleen Worley (Jenny), Michael Santo/Lachlan Macleay (Stanley), Mara Scott-Wood (Miss Forsythe), Sheri Lee Miller (Letta), Lachlan Macleay/Nick Flynn (Waiter)

Tuck Milligan, Amy Irving, Clayton Corzatte in "Romeo and Juliet"

TAKING STEPS by Alan Ayckbourn; Director, Daniel Sullivan; Set, Robert Dahlstrom; Costumes, Robert Wojewodski; Dance Consultant, Adam Miller; Stage Managers, Marc Rush, Michael Paul. **CAST:** Brenda Wehle (Elizabeth), Shaun Austin-Olsen (Mark), Brad O'Hara (Tristram), Ted D'Arms (Roland), Michael Santo (Leslie), Susan Cash (Kitty)
TRANSLATIONS by Brian Friel; Director, Robert Egan; Set, Kate Edmunds; Sound, Michael Holten; Dialect Consultant, Nancy Lane; Stage Manager, Mary Hunter. **CAST:** Sean G. Griffin (Manus), Deirdre O'Connell (Sarah), James Hilbrandt (Jimmy Jack), Marek Johnson (Maire), Brian Martin (Doalty), Susan Cash (Bridget), Anthony Mockus (Hugh), Josh Clark (Owen), Ted D'Arms (Capt. Lancy) Peter Webster (Lt. Yolland)
THE VINEGAR TREE by Paul Osborn; Director, Daniel Sullivan; Set, Hugh Landwehr; Costumes, Kurt Wilhelm; Lighting, James F. Ingalls; Sound, Michael Holten; Stage Manager, Marc Rush; Assistant Director, Roberta Levitow. **CAST:** David White (Augustus), Woody Eney (Max), Lori Larsen (Winifred), John Boylan (Louis), Ludi Claire (Laura), Eva Bennett-Gordon (Leone), Nathan Haas (Geoffrey)

Greg Gilbert Photos

David White, Ludi Claire in "The Vinegar Tree"
Right Center: "Translations"

SOUTH COAST REPERTORY

Costa Mesa, California

Producing Artistic Director, David Emmes; Artistic Director, Martin Benson; General Manager, Timothy Brennan; Development, Barbara Grady; Literary Manager, Jerry Patch; Marketing, Paula Bond; Press, John Mouledoux, Michael Bigelow Dixon; Company Manager, Leo Collin; Production Manager, Paul Hammond; Lighting, Rom Ruzika; Props, Michael Beech; Stage Managers, Julie Haber, Richard Heeger, Bonnie Lorenger; Directors, Jules Aaron, Martin Benson, David Emmes, John-David Keller, Richard Russell Ramos, Lee Sankowich, Lee Shallat; Sets, Michael Devine, Mark Donnelly, Cliff Faulkner, Keith Hein, Dwight Richard Odle, Thomas A. Walsh; Lighting, Richard Devin, Kent Dorsey, John Ivo Gilles, Cameron Harvey, Paulie Jenkins, Donna Ruzika, Tom Ruzika, Greg Sullivan; Costumes, Carol Brolaski, Barbara Cox, Merrily Murray-Walsh, Dwight Richard Odle, Tom Rasmussen, Kim Simons, Skipper Skeoch

ALL IN FAVOUR SAID NO! (*U.S. Premiere*) by Bernard Farrell. **CAST:** Tom Rosqui (Gilbert), Paul Rudd (Christy), Steven Breese (Dave), Jeffrey Combs (Liam), Patricia Fraser (Miss Temple), Mary Beth Evans (Sally), Hal Landon, Jr. (Mike), Kendall McLean (Dee), Richard Doyle (Eddie), Kristen Lowman (Una), Anni Long (Joan), John-David Keller (Ronnie)
THE DIVINERS by Jim Leonard, Jr. **CAST:** Don Tuche (Basil), John Walcutt (Dewey), Jeffrey Combs (Buddy), Joe McNeely (Melvin), Rita Rene Stevens (Luella), Emily Heebner (Jennie Mae), Thomas R. Oglesby (C.C.), Wayne Grace (Ferris), Martha McFarland (Norma), Sylvia Meredith (Goldie), Patti Johns (Darlene)
A CHRISTMAS CAROL by Charles Dickens; Adapted by Jerry Patch. **CAST:** Hal Landon, Jr. (Scrooge), John Ellington (Cratchit), Noreen Hennessy (Mrs. Cratchit), Michele Wallen, Samantha Chagollan, Elizabeth Lockie, Robert Dominguez, Charlie Cummins (Tiny Tim), Richard Doyle, Martha McFarland, Don Tuche, Ron Michaelson, Chris Murphy, Chad Tilner, Joann DiSano, Art Koustik, Howard Shangraw, Anni Long, James LeGros, Wayne Alexander, Sam Hamann, Rian Rasmussen, Frank Minano, Lisa deKruif, Gretchen McClintock, Peter Koebler
BOY MEETS GIRL by Bella and Samuel Spewack. **CAST:** Kristoffer Tabori (Robert), Hal Landon, Jr. (Larry), James Staley (J. Carlyle), Richard Doyle (Rosetti), Anni Long (Miss Crews), William Bogert (C. F.), Diane dePriest (Peggy), Wayne Alexander (Rodney), Ron Boussom (Green), John Ellington (Slade), Kristen Lowman (Susie), Joann DiSano (Nurse), James LeGros (Elevator Operator), Sam Hamann (Young Man/-Patient), Art Koustik (Cutter/Thompson)
BETRAYAL by Harold Pinter. **CAST:** Thomas R. Oglesby (Jerry), Cecelia Riddett (Emma), Dan Kern (Robert), Art Koustik (Waiter)

Paul Rudd, Reid Shelton in "Major Barbara"

THE IMAGINARY INVALID by Moliere; Adapted by Donald Frame. **CAST:** Raye Birk (Argan), Jane Murray (Toinette), Kristen Lowman (Angelique), Irene Roseen (Beline), John-Frederick Jones (DeBonnefoi), Wayne Alexander (Cleante), Robert Machray (Dr. Diafoirus), John Ellington (Dr. Thomas Diafoirus), Michelle Wall (Louison), Wayne Grace (Beralde), Ron Boussom (Fleurant), John-David Keller (Dr. Purgon), Kathie Cain, Sam Hamann, James LeGros
MAJOR BARBARA by George Bernard Shaw. **CAST:** Patricia Fraser (Britomart), Jeffrey Combs (Stephen), Kathleen Lloyd (Barbara), Kristen Lowman (Sarah), Reid Shelton (Andrew), Marilyn Fox (Jenny), Ron Boussom (Bill), Art Koustik (Morrison/Bilton), Paul Rudd (Adolphus), John Ellington (Charles), Martha McFarland (Rummy), Richard Doyle (Snobby), John-David Keller (Peter), Anni Long (Mrs. Baines)

WORLD PREMIERES:
BROTHERS by George Sibbald. **CAST:** Joe Pantoliano (Tommy MacMillan), Jonathan Terry (James MacMillan), George Murdock (Jim MacMillan), Dennis Franz (Earl MacMillan), David Ralphe (Harry (MacMillan))
SHE ALSO DANCES by Kenneth Arnold. **CAST:** Marc Vahanian (Ted), Patti Johns (Lucy)
CLOSELY RELATED by Bruce MacDonald. **CAST:** Lycia Naff (Melissa), Stephen Keep (Alan), Penelope Windust (Allison), Kaz Garas (Tim), Brad Cowgill (Christian), Laura Campbell (Myrna)
GOODBYE FREDDY by Elizabeth Diggs. **CAST:** Andrew Prine (Hank), Pamela Dunlap (Kate), Charles Parks (Paul), Joan Welles (Alice), Timothy Shelton (Andy), Susan Barnes (Nessa)
APRIL SNOW by Romulus Linney. **CAST:** Jordan Charney (Gordon Tate), Scott Hylands (Lucien Field), K Callan (Grady Gunn), Brad Cowgill (Bill Evans), Rhonda Aldrich (Millicent Beck)
BITS & BYTES by Michael Bigelow Dixon and Jerry Patch; Music, Diane King. **CAST:** James LeGros (Morton B. Norton), Deborah Nishimura (Bits), Sam Hamann (Bytes), Laura Leyva (Happy), Robert Crow (Mr. Chips)

Ron M. Stone Photos

Andrew Prine, Pamela Dunlap in "Goodbye Freddy"

STAGEWEST

West Springfield, Massachusetts

Producing Director, Stephen E. Hays; Production Manager, Ken Denison; Stage Managers, Kaz J. Reed, Juliet O. Campbell; Company Manager, Tony Elliot; Production Assistant, Kristyne Taylor; Casting, McCorkle/-Sturtevant; Technical Directors, Joseph W. Long, Jim Brewczynski; Designers, Jeffrey Struckman, David Johnson; Props, Ken Larson; Wardrobe, Carla Froberg; Press, Tara K. Becker, Sheldon Wolf, David C. Maguire; Business Manager, Val Pori; Producing Associate, Julie Monahan; Project Manager/Lighting/Sound, Paul J. Horton

THE CRUCIFER OF BLOOD by Paul Giovanni; Director, Ted Weiant; Costumes, John Carver Sullivan; Lighting, Ned Hallick. **CAST:** Bruce Vavrina (Maj. Ross), Michael Parva (Capt. St. Claire), Stephen Rool (Jonathan), Richard Abernathy (Durga/Insp. Lestrad), Larry Singer (Wali/Birdy), Bruce Mohat (Mohammed/Mordecai), Gregory Salata (Sherlock Holmes), John Doolittle (Watson), Kimberly Farr (Irene), Clarence Brown (Louis Rogers/Tonga), Amy Anson, Linda Crough, John Raposa, Bill Whitman
MASS APPEAL by Bill C. Davis; Director, Gregory Abels; Costumes, Georgia Carney. **CAST:** Larry Keith (Father Tim Farley), Steven Culp (Mark Dolson)
SIDE BY SIDE BY SONDHEIM with Music and Lyrics by Stephen Sondheim, Leonard Bernstein, Mary Rodgers, Richard Rodgers, Jule Styne; Continuity, Ned Sherin; Musical Director/Additional Musical Arrangements, J. T. Smith; Director, Wayne Bryan. **CAST:** Michael Magnusen, Henrietta Valor, Anna Marie Guttierrez, Stephen E. Hays (Narrator)
THE BELLE OF AMHERST by William Luce; Compiled by Timothy Helgeson; Director, Donald Hicken; Lighting, Margaret Lee; Costumes, Jan Morrison. **CAST:** Tana Hicken (Emily Dickinson)
HOME by Samm-Art Williams; Director, Woodie King, Jr.; Set, Jeffrey A. Fiala; Costumes, Rebecca Senske. **CAST:** Elizabeth Van Dyke (Woman #1/Pattie Mae Wells), Nadyne Cassandra (Woman #2), Samm-Art Williams (Cephus Miles)
A STREETCAR NAMED DESIRE by Tennessee Williams; Director, Timothy Near; Sound, Paul J. Horton; Set/Lighting, Paul Wonsek. **CAST:** Erika Petersen, (Blanche), John Homa (Stanley), Elizabeth Hess (Stella), Kim Staunton (Neighbor/Flower Vendor/Nurse), Elizabeth Flynn-Jones (Eunice), Matthew Kimbrough (Mitch), Timothy Meyers (Steve Hubbell), Joe Zaloom (Pablo Gonzales), Steve Carter (Young Collector), David O. Petersen (Doctor), Amelia Hays (Little Girl)
CHAPTER TWO by Neil Simon; Director, Stephen E. Hays; Lighting, Margaret Lee; Costumes, Deborah Shaw. **CAST:** Rudy Hornish (George), John LaGioia (Leo), Jody Catlin (Jennie), Annette Miller (Faye)

Bob Welsh, Jr. Photos

Top Right: John Homa, Erika Petersen in
"A Streetcar Named Desire"

Larry Keith, Steven Culp in "Mass Appeal"

STUDIO ARENA THEATRE

Buffalo, New York
Eighteenth Season

Artistic Director, David Frank; Managing Director, Michael P. Pitek III; Associate Managing Director, Carol A. Kolis; Associate Director/-Dramaturge, Kathryn Long; Stage Managers, Beverly J. Andreozzi, Margaret Stuart-Ramsey; Production Coordinator, Brett Thomas; Technical Directors, Brett Thomas, Bruce Rogers; Wardrobe, Gail Evans; Props, Carroll Ann Simon, Jennifer Lang; Sound, Rick Menke; Marketing, J. Dennis Rich; Sets, Robert Morgan, Gary C. Eckhart, J. Robin Modereger, Thomas Michael Cariello, Paul Wonsek, Grady Larkins; Costumes, Robert Morgan, Donna Langman, Judy Dearing, Catherine B. Reich, Janice I. Lines; Lighting, Robert Jared, Robby Monk, Michael Orris Watson, Shirley Prendergast, Paul Wonsek, Brett Thomas; Press, Blossom Cohan

SHE STOOPS TO CONQUER by Oliver Goldsmith; Director, David Frank. **CAST:** Lenka Peterson, Clement Fowler, Sam Tsoutsouvas, Wanda Bimson, Ellen Fiske, James Maxwell, Warren David Keith, Carl Kowalkowski, Walter Barrett, Gerald Halter, Ken Telesco, Elise Pearlman, Evan Parry, Timothy Meyers

TRUE WEST by Sam Shepard; Director, Kathryn Long. **CAST:** James Maxwell, Keith Jochim, Richard Fitzpatrick, Timothy Meyers, Helen Harrelson

WITNESS FOR THE PROSECUTION by Agatha Christie; Director, David Frank. **CAST:** Cindy Rosenthal, David Fendrick, Jim Oyster, William McGlinn, John Clarkson, David Hyde-Lamb, William C. Rickard, Holly Barron, Walter Barrett, Sean G. Griffin, Timothy Joyce, Robert J. Paul, George Scheitinger, Robert G. Toone, Michael Mirand, Tess Spangler, Brian LaTulip, Mary Fogarty, Carl Kowalkowski, Kate K. S. Olena

A RAISIN IN THE SUN by Lorraine Hansberry; Director, Harold Scott. **CAST:** L. Scott Caldwell, Keith Mixon, Herb Downer, Kim Yancey, Theresa Merritt, Lou Ferguson, Melcourt Poux, Jr., Stephen McKinley Henderson, Sean G. Griffin, Ron O. J. Parson, Eugene Key

WEAPONS OF HAPPINESS (*American Premiere*) by Howard Brenton; Director, Geoffrey Sherman. **CAST:** Robert Burr, Carl Schurr, Evan Handler, David Bottrell, Brett Porter, Tara Lowenstern, Nona Waldeck, Dermot McNamara, Diana Van Fossen, John Rainer, Doug Stender, Robert Spencer, Earle Edgerton, Shaun McLaughlin, Jim Zelanis, Brian LaTulip, Brian DeMarco, Richard Hummert, Gerald Halter, Matthew Darnell, William C. Rickard

IN THE SWEET BYE AND BYE (*World Premiere*) by Donald Driver; Director, John Henry Davis. **CAST:** Addison Powell, Mary Carver, Scotty Bloch, Alma Cuervo, Carl Schurr, Robert Spencer, Gerald Halter

ABSURD PERSON SINGULAR by Alan Ayckbourne; Director, David Frank. **CAST:** Nancy Mette, Robert Spencer, John Rainer, le Clanche du Rand, Cynthia Carle, Carl Schurr

Irene Haupt Photos

Alma Cuervo, Carl Schurr, Addison Powell, Mary Carver, Scotty Bloch in "In the Sweet Bye and Bye" Top Left: L. Scott Caldwell, Theresa Merritt, Kim Yancey, Herb Downer in "A Raisin in the Sun"

172

TRINITY SQUARE REPERTORY COMPANY

Providence, Rhode Island
Twentieth Season

Director, Adrian Hall; Managing Director, E. Timothy Langan; Assistant to Mr. Hall, Marion Simon; General Manager, Michael Ducharme; Musical Director, Richard Cumming; Press, Scotti DeDonato; Sets, Eugene Lee, Robert D. Soule; Lighting, Eugene Lee, John F. Custer; Costumes, William Lane; Technical Director, Richard Rogers; Props, Cheryl Ottaviano; Stage Managers, Maureen F. Gibson, Carroll L. Cartwright III, Mary O'Leary; Stage Directors, Adrian Hall, Philip Minor, Henry Velez, Peter Gerety, David Wheeler, Sharon Jenkins

COMPANY: Bonnie Black, Robert Black, Barbara Blossom, Dan Butler, Lori Cardille, James Carruthers, Timothy Crowe, Richard Cumming, Timothy Daly, Maurice Dolbier, David Eliet, Richard Ferrone, Anne Gerety, Peter Gerety, Tom Griffin, Ed Hall, Ann Hamilton, Lura Bane Howes, Whip Hubley, Richard Jenkins, Keith Jochim, David C. Jones, Richard Kavanaugh, Drew Keil, David Kennett, Richard Kneeland, Becca Lish, Howard London, Jean Marsh, Derek Meader, Barbara Meek, Philip Minor, Barbara Orson, Bonnie Strickman, Ford Rainey, Charles Scovil, Anne Scurria, James Seymour, Margo Skinner, David P. B. Stephens, Patricia Thomas, Amy Van Nostrand, Daniel Von Bargen, Howard Walters, Rose Weaver, Christopher Wells
PRODUCTIONS: Tintypes, The Crucifer of Blood, 13 Rue de L'Amour, The Dresser, Translations, A Christmas Carol, The Front Page, The Tempest, Pygmalion, and *World Premieres* of The Web by Martha Boesing, Letters from Prison by Jack Henry Abbott

Constance Brown Photos

Top: **Ed Hall, Jean Marsh, Richard Kavanaugh, Howard London**
in **"Pygmalion"**

Richard Kneeland, Ford Rainey, Barbara Orson in "The Dresser"

173

THEATRE THREE

Dallas, Texas

Founder/Artistic Director, Norma Young; Executive Producer/Director, Jac Alder; Associate Producer/Sets, Charles Howard; Associate Director, Laurence O'Dwyer; Costumes, Patty Greer McGarity; Lighting, Shari Melde; Stage Manager, Jimmy Mullen; Press, Shannon Williams
CLOSE OF PLAY by Simon Gray; Director, Norma Young. **CAST:** Cheryl Black, Sharon Bunn, Jeanne Cairns, Michael Dendy, Joel Donelson, Hugh Feagin, Laurence O'Dwyer, Jenny Pichanick
BILLY BISHOP GOES TO WAR by John Gray; Director, Jac Alder. **CAST:** Robert Burke, Michael Deep
REJOICE, DANG IT, REJOICE! (*World Premiere*) by Paul Crume; Revised by Laurence O'Dwyer, Jerry Haynes; Director, Laurence O'Dwyer. **CAST:** Jerry Haynes
SWEENEY TODD by Stephen Sondheim; Director, Jack Eddleman. **CAST:** Judy Blue, Sharon Bunn, Jeanne Cairns, Mark Guerett, John Hanby, Ken Hornbeck, R. Andrew Martinsen, Ken Miller, Laurence O'Dwyer, Gary Taggart, Joan Marie Zimmerman, Thomas Zinn
SHE STOOPS TO CONQUER by Oliver Goldsmith; Director, Norma Young. **CAST:** Louis B. Allgeier, Esther M. Benson, Cheryl Black, John Brook, Teresa Cook, Ken Hornbeck, Bill Jenkins, Paul Lazar, Steve Lovett, R. Andrew Martinsen, John Cannon Nichols, Laurence O'Dwyer, Stephanie Rascoe, Gary Taggart
MORNING'S AT SEVEN by Paul Osborn; Director, Charles Howard. **CAST:** Jac Alder, Esther Benson, Dwain Fail, Anna Heins, Tom Matts, Lillian Prather, Warren Watson, Ouida White, Norma Young
THE QUALITY OF MERCY by David Hall; Director, Jimmy Mullen. **CAST:** Sa'Mi Chester, Stephanie Dunnam, Erin Jeanne Evans, Hugh Feagin, Gray Palmer, Everett SiFuentes, Peggy Townsley
THE CRASHING OF MOSES FLYING-BY by Adam LeFevre; Director, Laurence O'Dwyer. **CAST:** Ned C. Butikofer, Vince Davis, Douglas Parker, Karen Ruth Radcliffe, Vicki Sparks
TRUE WEST by Sam Shepard; Director, Laurence O'Dwyer. **CAST:** Dov Fahrer, Paul Lazar, Thurman Moss, Norma Young
MAN AND SUPERMAN by George Bernard Shaw; Director, Jac Alder. **CAST:** Louis B. Allgeier, Esther Benson, Carol Cleaver, Stephanie Dunnam, Dwain Fail, Laura Ferri, Michael Harrington, R. Andrew Martinsen, Tom Matts, Laurence O'Dwyer, Gray Palmer, Stephanie Rascoe, Gary Severen, Dustye Winniford

Andy Hanson Photos

Gary Taggert, Sharon Bunn in "Sweeney Todd" (Theatre Three)

VIRGINIA MUSEUM THEATRE

Richmond, Virginia
Twenty-eighth Season

Artistic Director, Tom Markus; Managing Director, Ira Schlosser; Business Manager, Edward W. Rucker; Company Manager, Phil Crosby; Press, Don Dale, David Griffith; Directors, Terry Burgler, Alfred Drake, Woodie King, Jr., Darwin Knight, Tom Markus; Sets, Neil Bierbower, Charles Caldwell, C. Jane Epperson, Susan Senita, Joseph A. Varga; Costumes, Bronwyn Jones Caldwell, Julie D. Keen, Rebecca Senske, Susan Tsu; Lighting, F. Mitchell Dana, Richard Devin, Lynne M. Hartman, Richard Moore, Kevin Rigdon; Stage Managers, Doug Flinchum, Andy Wiesnet; Musical Directors, Manford Abrahamson, Sand Lawn

THE PLAY'S THE THING by Ferenc Molnar; Adapted by P. G. Wodehouse. **CAST:** Humbert Allen Astredo, Dan Bedard, James Braden, William Denis, Robert Foley, David Hawes, Carole Monferdini, Clint Terrill, Eric Zwemer
HOME by Samm-Art Williams. **CAST:** Nadyne Cassandra Spratt, Elizabeth Van Dyke, Samm-Art Williams
A CHRISTMAS CAROL by Charles Dickens; Adapted by Tom Markus. **CAST:** Bev Appleton, Nancy Boykin, Susan Brandner, Donald Christopher, Judith Drake, Lucien Douglas, Christy Michelle Fairman, Robert Foley, Tracy O'Neil Heffernan, Maj-Lis Jalkio, Daniel Timothy Johnson, Adrien Rieder, Todd Rodriguez, Emily Skinner, Rob Storrs, Andrew Umberger, John Winn III, Curry Worsham, Nan Wray
THE LION IN WINTER by James Goldman. **CAST:** Terry Burgler, Maury Erickson, Patricia Falkenhain, Robert Gerringer, Sherry Skinker, Todd Taylor, Eric Zwemer
THE GIN GAME by D. L. Coburn. **CAST:** Patricia Falkenhain, Robert Gerringer
BILLY BISHOP GOES TO WAR by John Gray and Eric Peterson. **CAST:** Dan Hamilton, Manford Abrahamson
DAMES AT SEA with Book and Lyrics by George Haimsohn, Robin Miller; Music, Jim Wise. **CAST:** Tim Barber, N. A. Klein, Lora Jeanne Martens, Kim Morgan, Todd Taylor, Barbara Walsh
A STRETCH OF THE IMAGINATION (*American Premiere*) by Jack Hibberd. **CAST:** William Denis
THE HIDING PLACE (*WORLD PREMIERE*) by Alfred Drake. **CAST:** Norman Barrs, Charles Baxter, Kim Beaty, Charles Brown, Lucien Douglas, Alfred Drake, Marion Lines, Tom McDermott, Dana Mills, Andrew Umberger, Rudolph Willrich
HAVEN'T A CLUE (*World Premiere*) by Douglas Watson. **CAST:** Terry Burgler, Laura Copland, Henson Keys, Ian Stuart, Randolph Walker

Charles Brown, Norman Barrs, Kim Beaty, Marion Lines, Dana Mills, Tom McDermott, Alfred Drake, Lucien Douglas in "The Hiding Place" (Virginia Museum Theatre)

VIRGINIA STAGE COMPANY

Norfolk, Virginia
Fourth Season

Producing Director, Robert Tolan; Artistic Director, Charles Towers; Managing Director/General Manager, Randy Adams; Development, Patricia Rhodes; Marketing/Press, Tempy Cornelius-Fisk; Business Manager, Cathy Jones; Designer/Production Manager, Joe Ragey; Costumes, Carrie Curtis; Stage Managers, J. P. Elins, John Kingsbury, Ann S. Ostermayer

TALLEY'S FOLLY by Lanford Wilson; Director, Michael Hankins; Lighting, Ted Bartenstein. **CAST:** Joel Swetow (Matt), Innes Fergus-McDade (Sally)
THE CRUCIBLE by Arthur Miller; Director, Robert Tolan. **CAST:** Paul Meacham (Rev. Parris), Yolande Bavan (Tituba), Ruth Kidder (Abigail), Denise Elkins (Susanna), Marty Terry (Mrs. Putnam), G. F. Rowe (Thomas), Dee Myers (Mercy), Ashley Izard (Mary), Nancy Lynn Allen (Betty), John Hertzler (John Proctor), Fiona Hale (Rebecca), John Milligan (Giles), DeVeren Bookwalter (Rev. Hale), Innes Fergus-McDade (Elizabeth), Carl Balon (Francis), David Lively (Ezekiel), David Drummond (Marshal), Charles Terry (Judge), Robert Lewis Karlin (Deputy Governor Danforth), Robin Westphal (Ruth/Sarah Good), Jim Harlow (Hopkins), Guards: Chris Christman, Daryl Donley, Mark Heffernan
A CHRISTMAS CAROL by Charles Dickens; Director, Michael Hankins; Sets, Duke Durfee. **CAST:** Nancy Lynn Allen, Yolande Bavan, DeVeren Bookwalter (Scrooge), Cathy Butler, Chris Christman, John Daman (Tiny Tim), Daryl Donley, David Drummond, Denise Elkins, Fiona Hale, James Harlow, Mark Heffernan, John Hertzler, Ashley Izard, Robert Lewis Karlin, Ruth Kidder, David Lively (Cratchit), Peter Lockamy, James Luse, Innes Fergus-McDade (Mrs. Cratchit), Paul Meacham, John Milligan, Dee Myers, David Paterson, Robin Westphal
VANITIES by Jack Heifner; Director, Robert Tolan; Set, Neil Peter Jampolis. **CAST:** Pamela Beth Harris (Joanne), Susan Ronn (Kath), Kim Ameen (Mary)

World Premieres:
HIGH ROLLING by Robert Litz; Director, Michael Hankins; Set, Joe Ragey; Costumes, Carrie Curtis; Lighting, Ted Bartenstein. **CAST:** John Newton (T. Allen Madison), Jeff Abbott (Thomas Madison), Ruth Miller (Agnes McCaslin-Madison), Ashley Izard (Katherine McCaslin), Rex Ellis (Imbawbe/Sonny/Senator)
TIOVIVO by Mary G. St. Cloud; Director, Robert Tolan; Set, Joe Ragey; Costumes, Anne-Marie Wright; Lighting, Ted Bartenstein. **CAST:** Ruth Miller (Louisa), Luke Sickle (Patch), Robin Westphal (Ronnie), Jeff Abbot (Ray), Ashley Izard (Vikki), Anne Biggs (Helga), David Lively (Howie), Rex Ellis (Krack), Nancy Lynn Allen (Mayra)
HAZARD CO. WONDER by Bruce Peyton; Director, Michael Hankins; Set, Joe Ragey; Costumes, Carrie Curtis; Lighting, Ted Bartenstein. **CAST:** Jeff Abbott (Cletis), Ashley Izard (Jo-Etta), David Drummond (Christy), G. F. Rowe (Baylor), David Lively (Tyler), John Newton (W. T.), Mark Heffernan (Hog), Ruth Miller (Sudie), Luke Sickle (Harley), Anne Biggs (Elvira), Dee Myers (Beulah), Denise Elkins (Bertha), Stephen Brown (Old Man), Townspeople: Chris Christman, Mark Heffernan, Nancy Lynn Allen, Robin Westphal

Bob Ander, Susan Best Photos

G. F. Rowe, DeVeren Bookwalter, Marty Terry, Ruth Kidder, Paul Meacham, Yolande Bavan (kneeling) in "The Crucible" (Virginia Stage Company)

WHOLE THEATRE COMPANY

Montclair, New Jersey

Producer/Director, Arnold Mittelman; Artistic Director, Olympia Dukakis; Managing Director, Patricia K. Quinn; Press/Marketing, Helen Stein; Stage Manager, Tom Brubaker; Sets, Paul Dorphley, Raymond C. Recht, Loren Sherman, Jack Chandler; Costumes, Galen M. Logsdon, Joseph G. Aulisi, Ann Emonts, Sigrid Insull; Lighting, Loren Sherman, David Noling, Carol Rubinstein, David F. Segal, John I. Tissot; Directors, Arnold Mittelman, Olympia Dukakis, Austin Pendleton, Tony Stevens; Musical Director, Philip Campanella

A TOUCH OF THE POET by Eugene O'Neill. **CAST:** Quincy Long, Eddie Jones, Judith Delgado, Olympia Dukakis, Louis Zorich, John L. Bryan, Thomas Gilpin, Rod Houts, Maggie Abeckerly, Apollo Dukakis
ALL DRESSED UP (*World Premiere*) by Leslie Eberhard and David Levy. **CAST:** Dolores Gray, Michael Tartel
UNCLE VANYA by Anton Chekhov. **CAST:** Grace Grote, George Sperdakos, Austin Pendleton, Louis Zorich, Apollo Dukakis, Katina Commings, Judith Delgado, Maggie Abeckerly, Thomas Gilpin, Jack Keller
ANGEL STREET by Patrick Hamilton. **CAST:** Barbara eda-Young, Stephen Joyce, Moira Harris, Harriet Rogers, Louis Beachner, Jack Keller, Frank Capasso
ALONE TOGETHER (*World Premiere*) by Lawrence Roman. **CAST:** William Mooney, Marilyn Chris, Joseph Siravo, Bill Randolph, Alexandra Gersten, David Stocker

Robert Faulkner Photos

Olympia Dukakis, Judith Delgado, Louis Zorich in "A Touch of the Poet" (Whole Theatre)

Above: Austin Pendleton, Apollo Dukakis in "Uncle Vanya"

YALE REPERTORY THEATRE

New Haven, Connecticut
Seventeenth Season

Artistic Director, Lloyd Richards; Managing Director, Benjamin Mordecai; Literary Managers, Michael Cadden, Barbara Davenport, Joel Schecter; Press, Rosalind Heinz; Set Adviser, Ming Cho Lee; Costume Adviser, Jane Greenwood; Lighting Adviser, Jennifer Tipton; Movement, Wesley Fata

A DOLL'S HOUSE by Henrik Ibsen; Director, Lloyd Richards; Set, G. W. Mercier; Costumes, Dunya Ramicova; Lighting, William B. Warfel; Dramaturge, Sasha Zeif. CAST: Lisa Banes, John Glover, Earle Hyman, Richard Jenkins, Barbara Lester, Barbara Somerville, Dianne Wiest
HELLO AND GOODBYE by Athol Fugard; Director, Tony Giordano; Set, Philipp Jung; Costumes, Donna Zakowski; Lighting, Robert M. Wierzel; Dramaturge, Shelly Berc. CAST: Jenny O'Hara, Warren Manzi
THE PHILANDERER by George Bernard Shaw; Director, David Hammond; Set, Christopher H. Barreca; Costumes, Connie Singer; Lighting, Stephen Strawbridge; Dramaturge, Michael X. Zelenak. CAST: Brooke Adams, Roy Cooper, Tandy Cronyn, Dann Florek, William Kux, Sabrina LeBeauf, Addison Powell, Christopher Walken
MUCH ADO ABOUT NOTHING by William Shakespeare; Director, Walton Jones; Set, Joel Fontaine; Costumes, G. W. Mercier; Lighting, Peter Maradudin; Dramaturge, Philippa Keil. CAST: Marshall Bordon, Julie Boyd, Bill Buell, Patrick James Clarke, Maury Cooper, Jon DeVries, Mia Dillon, Rick Grove, Paul Guilfoyle, John Harnagle, Roxanne Hart, William Kux, Moultrie Patten, Wyman Pendleton, Marcell Rosenblatt, Bill Sadler, Marilyn Sommer, Matt Sussman
A TOUCH OF THE POET by Eugene O'Neill; Director, Lloyd Richards; Set, Wing Lee; Costumes, Philipp Jung; Lighting, Jennifer Tipton; Dramaturge, Rassami Paoluengtong. CAST Barbara Caruso, Bryan Clark, Rex Everhart, Julie Fulton, George Grizzard, Katharine Houghton, Jack R. Marks, Ron McLarty, John Remme, David Thornton
ABOUT FACE (American Premiere) by Dario Fo; Director, Andrei Belgrader; Set, Ricardo Morin; Costumes, Connie Singer; Lighting, Stephen Strawbridge; Dramaturge, Kenneth Schlesinger; Translation by Charles Mann, Dale McAdoo. CAST: Dylan Baker, William Duell, Joe Grifasi, Andreas Katsulas, Warren Keith, Keith Reddin, Patricia Richardson, Karen Shallo, Patterson Skipper, David Thornton, George Griggs, Craig Shapiro

World Premieres of:
ASTOPOVO by Leon Katz; Director, Lawrence Kornfeld; Set, Michael Yeargan; Costumes, Catherine Zuber; Lighting, William B. Warfel; Dramaturge, Richard Davis. CAST: Christian Clemenson, Charles S. Dutton, Rick Grove, Joycelyn Johnson, Andreas Katsulas, Leon Katz, Lauren Klein, William Kux, Jan Miner, Joel Rooks, Reno Roop, Marilyn Sommer, John Turturro
COYOTE UGLY by Lynn Siefert; Director, Christian Angermann; Set, Robert M. Wierzel; Costumes, Richard Mays; Lighting, Andrew Carter; Dramaturge, Michael Evenden. CAST: Dorothy Holland, Mark Metcalf, Edward Seamon, Barbara Somerville, Sallyanne Tackus
PLAYING IN LOCAL BANDS by Nancy Fales Garrett; Director, William Ludel; Set, Michael Yeargan; Costumes, Ricardo Morin; Lighting, Laurence F. Schwartz; Dramaturge, Sasha Zeif. CAST: Julie Boyd, John Harnagle, Lauren Klein, Michael Murphy, Seret Scott

William B. Carter Photos

Christopher Walken, Brooke Adams in "The Philanderer" Top: Roxanne Hart, Jon DeVries in "Much Ado about Nothing"

ANNUAL SHAKESPEARE FESTIVALS

AMERICAN PLAYERS THEATRE

Spring Green, Wisconsin
Third Season

Artistic Director, Randall Duk Kim; Managing Director, Charles J. Bright; Resident Director, Anne Occhiogrosso; Directors, Mik Derks, Fred Ollerman; Stage Managers, Diane DiVita, Melinda Degucz; Sets, Sam Kirkpatrick; Costumes, Budd Hill, Nanalee Raphael; Lighting, Dennis A. Gorke, Elizabeth Green; Props, Harlan Ferstl; Composer/Musical Director, Tim Schirmer; Movement, Jerry Gardner; Press, Jean Louise Sassor

COMPANY: John Aden, Pamela Carol-Blake, David Cecsarini, A. D. Cover, Lee Elmer Ernst, Janis Flax, Timothy Alan Gregory, Steven Helmeke, Lucas G. Hendrickson, Jonathan Herold, James Hulin, Jeffery Lowell Jackson, Terry Kerr, Peter Kettler, Randall Duk Kim, Alexis Lauren, Marie Mathay, Peter Adam Menken, Alexandra Mitchell, Mark Nelson, Si Osborne, Nina Polan, Arleigh Richards, William Schlaht, Theodore Swetz, Peter Syvertsen, Eloise Watt, George A. Wilson
PRODUCTIONS: The Taming of the Shrew, Romeo and Juliet, The Comedy of Errors, A Midsummer Night's Dream, The Two Gentlemen of Verona, Titus Andronicus

Robert Wood Photos

Alexandra Mitchell, Alexis Lauren, Randall Duk Kim in "The Taming of the Shrew" (American Players Theatre)

Christopher Walken as Hamlet (American Shakespeare Theatre)

AMERICAN SHAKESPEARE THEATRE

Stratford, Connecticut

Artistic Director, Peter Coe; Executive Directors, Richard Horner, Lynne Stuart; Deputy Executive Director, Roger Sherman; Press, Richard P. Pheneger; Company Manager, Robert G. Sheftic; Stage Managers, Elliott Woodruff, Consuelo Mira; Production Assistant, Mark D'Alessio; Props, Mario Fedeli; Wardrobe, Mildred Patria

HENRY IV PART I by William Shakespeare; Director, Peter Coe; Sets and Costumes, David Chapman; Deputy Executive Director, Roger Sherman; Hairstylist, Rick Echols; Fights, B. H. Barry; Lighting, Marc B. Weiss; Deputy Executive Director, Roger Sherman
CAST: Michael Allinson (Henry IV), Roy Dotrice (Falstaff), Chris Sarandon (Hal, Prince of Wales), Christopher Walken (Henry Percy), Mary Wickes (Mistress Quickly), Norman Allen (Nym/Sir Richard Vernon), Edward Atienza (Thomas Percy/Owen Glendower), Patrick Clear (Lord John/Traveller), Sophie Gilmartin (Attendant), Peter Johl (Earl of Westmoreland/Sheriff), Stephen Lang (Ned Poins/Earl of Douglas), Joel Leffert (Soldier), John Messenger (Henry Percy), Scott Rhyne (Soldier), Gary Roberts (Soldier), Brian Rose (Bardolph), David Sabin (Sir Walter Blunt/-Traveller), Diana Stagner (Taverner), Richard Sterne (Exton/Edmund Mortimer), Ellen Tobie (Lady Percy), Karen Trott (Lady Mortimer/Doll Tearsheet), John Wojda (Soldier), Understudies; Michael Guido, Sylvia Short
HAMLET by William Shakespeare; Director, Peter Coe; Sets/Costumes, David Chapman; Lighting, Marc B. Weiss; Music, Joe Griffiths; Deputy Executive Director, Roger Sherman
CAST: Michael Allinson (Ghost/Player King), Anne Baxter (Queen Gertrude), Roy Dotrice (Polonius/1st Gravedigger), Fred Gwynne (King Claudius) Chris Sarandon (Laertes), Christopher Walken (Hamlet), Norman Allen (Lucianus/Francisco/2nd Gravedigger), Lisabeth Bartlett (Ophelia), Chet Carlin (Osric), Patrick Clear (Fortinbras/Queen Mime), Sophie Gilmartin (Harpist), Michael Guido (Guildenstern), Stephen Lang (Horatio), Joel Leffert (1st Soldier), Matt Mulhern (2nd Soldier), Scott Rhyne (3rd Soldier), Gary Roberts (4th Soldier), Brian Rose (King Mime/Bernardo/Priest), David Sabin (Prologue/Marcellus/Captain), Sylvia Short (Understudy), Fritz Sperberg (Rosencrantz), Karen Trott (Player Queen), John Wojda (5th Soldier)

Martha Swope Photos

CAMDEN SHAKESPEARE COMPANY

Camden, New Jersey
Fifth Season

Artistic Director, Casey Kizziah; Managing Director, Mary Rindfleisch; Press, Alexa Fogel, Katrinka Wilder; Directors, William James Kelly, Rosa Parfrey, James Tripp, Kevin Gardner; Stage Manager, Charles Scott; Sets, Thomas Harty; Costumes, Ellen McCartney; Lighting/Technical Director, Vincent Boucher; Fight Choreographer, Stephen White; Musicans/Composers, Sanchie Bobrow, Throop Wilder

COMPANY: Dylan Baker, Richard Boddy, Steve Callaway, Alison Edwards, Kevin Gardner, Nancy Hammill, Thomas Harty, Marceline Hugot, Casey Kizziah, Michael McGuinness, Kenneth Metivier, Joseph Menino, Anthony Moore, Gregg Ostrin, Michael Perez, Dustyn Taylor, Lois Tibbetts, Kim Waltman, Karen Elain Wells, John Wise
PRODUCTIONS: Romeo and Juliet by William Shakespeare, Our Town by Thornton Wilder, As You Like It by William Shakespeare, Beauty and the Beast adapted by Kevin Gardner

BA Southers Photos

Right Center: Dylan Baker, Nancy Hammill as Romeo and Juliet

"As You Like It" (Camden Shakespeare Co.)

CHAMPLAIN SHAKESPEARE FESTIVAL

Burlington, Vermont
July 7—August 14, 1982
Twenty-fifth Season

Artistic Director, Jem Graves; Managing Director, Heidi Racht; Technical Director, Roger Y. Edes; Press, Dorothy Walker; Composer, Jameson Allen; Company Manager, Ken Alsleben; Sets, Gary C. Eckhart, Marc Rubinstein; Costumes, Carol J. Blanchard, Patrick Rocheleau; Lighting, Rick Dean; Music Director, Valerie Sue Jones; Props, Mark Nash, Amy Calter; Sound, Christopher Archer; Stage Manager, Amy London; Fight Coach, Chris Pino; Festival Stage Designer, W. M. Schenk
COMPANY: Lewan Alexander, Jameson Allen, Ken Alsleben, Jon Beaupre, Carol J. Blanchard, Michael Breen, Simon Brooking, Sarah W. Bull, Amy Calter, Kathleen Cavanagh, Joanne Clark, Steven Culp, Richard Dean, Dawn Defuria, Antone Jose Dias, Sandra Dias, Diane Dreux, Gary C. Eckhart, Roger Y. Edes, Terri Fluker, Michael L. Forrest, Jem Graves, Marcia Grund, Veronique Hovde, Brenda Jimmo, Valerie Sue Jones, Donna Kalil, Mike Kunes, Kelly C. Morgan, Mark D. Nash, Rusty Laushman, Amy London, Holly Methfessel, Eric Ness, Chris Pinto, David Poirier, Heidi Racht, Louie Racht, Paul Reese, Mike Richards, Janet Scarlata, W. M. Schenk, David Stern, Rebecca Sullivan, Jim Tabakin, Joseph Totaro, Dorothy Walker
PRODUCTIONS: Much Ado about Nothing by William Shakespeare; Director, Joseph Totaro. Hay Fever by Noel Coward; Director, Jem Graves. Coriolanus by William Shakespeare; Director, Jon Beaupre

Heidi Racht Photos

"Coriolanus" (Champlain Shakespeare Festival)

GREAT LAKES SHAKESPEARE FESTIVAL

Cleveland, Ohio
Twenty-first Season

Producing Director, Vincent Dowling; Managing Director, Mary Bill; Chairman of the Board, William C. Fine; President, Natalie Epstein; Design/Associate Director, John Ezell; Press, Maureen Hrehocik, Robin Hubbard; Casting, Richard Pagano; Musical Director, Daniel Hathaway; Costumes, Mary-Anne Aston, Paul Costelloe, Gene Lakin, Lewis D. Rampino; Lighting, Kirk Bookman, Toni Goldin, Roger Morgan; Sound, Joseph Martin; Stage Managers, Andrew Feigin, Peter Muste, Anthony Berg, Kevin Haslinger, Sharon Rush; Technical Coordinator, Robert Scales; Production Manager, Olwen O'Herlihy; Assistant to Mr. Dowling, John Love; Technical Director, John Sadler; Wardrobe, Barbara Brock; Props, Mary K. Stone; Dramaturg, John M. Gulley
COMPANY: Leta Anderson, Tom Blair, Barry Boys, Madylon Branstetter, Bob Breuler, Richard C. Brown, John Q. Bruce, Helena Carroll, Gale Fury Childs, Bairbre Dowling, Robert Elliott, Larry Gates, Maurice Good, John Greenleaf, Frank Grimes, Michael Haney, Jill Holden, Jeannine Hutchings, Bernard Kates, Michael John McGann, Colm Meaney, Aideen O'Kelly, David Purdham, Clive Rosengren, Nicola Sheara, Reuben Silver, Maggie Thatcher, Michael Thompson, Dan Westbrook, Sara Woods, William Youmans, Gay Marshall
PRODUCTIONS: As You Like It, The Playboy of the Western World, Piaf La Vie L'Amour (a musical premiere), The Life and Adventures of Nicholas Nickleby

Mike Edwards Photos

David Purdham, Sara Woods (seated), Maggie Thatcher
in "Nicholas Nickleby" (Great Lakes Festival)

Morgan Freeman, Valerie Mahaffey in "Othello" (Dallas Festival)

SHAKESPEARE FESTIVAL OF DALLAS

Dallas, Texas
Ninth Season

Founder/Producer, Robert Glenn; Managing Director, Phillip Glenn; Development Director, John Davis; Press, Jeannine Kadane; Consulting Artistic Director, Kenneth Frankel; Production Manager, Francis X. Kuhn; Stage Managers, Carol Anne Clark, Montgomery Kuklenski, Susie Charlton, Chip Washabaugh; Technical Director, Chris Rusch; Wardrobe, Carla Parker; Props, David Newell; Sound, Jerry Worden; Production Assistant, David Hoover; Sets, James Wolk; Lighting, James Paccone; Costumes, Sheila Hargett, Colleen Muscha; Music, Bruce Coughlin; Fight Choreography, Jim Hancock; Choreographer, Fern N. Tresvan
ALL'S WELL THAT ENDS WELL by William Shakespeare; Directed by Jason Buzas. CAST: Margaret Loft (Countess of Rossillion), Milton Blankenship (Bertram), Robert Blackburn (Lafew), Niki Flacks (Helena), Jonathan Hadary (Parolles), John Swindells (King of France), Nicholas Bakay, Douglas Parker (Dumaine Brothers), David Edwards, Dan Foster, Bill Jenkins, Jim McLellan (Soldiers), John Rainone (Lavatch), Karen Carver (Isbel), Carter Reardon (Rynaldo), Nelson Coates, Bill Jenkins, Jim McLellan (Lords), Judy Nunn (Maudlin), Morgan Freeman (Duke of Florence), Gail Cronauer (Widow Capilet), Valerie Mahaffey (Diana), Pam Dougherty (Mariana), Andrew Barach (Italian Man), Michael Ross (King's Attendant), Townspeople: Karen Carver, Nelson Coates, David Edwards, Dan Foster, Bill Jenkins, Jim McLellan, Judy Nunn
OTHELLO by William Shakespeare; Director, Dale AJ Rose. CAST: Douglas Parker (Roderigo), Mark Blum (Iago), Robert Blackburn (Brabantio), Morgan Freeman (Othello), Milton Blankenship (Cassio), John Swindells (Duke of Venice), Carter Reardon (Gratiano), Jonathan Hadary (Lodovico), Bill Jenkins (Senator of Venice), Valerie Mahaffey (Desdemona), Nicholas Bakay (Montano), Gail Cronauer (Emilia), Pam Dougherty (Bianca), Servants and Soldiers: Nelson Coates, David Edwards, Dan Foster, Bill Jenkins, Jim McLellan, John Rainone, Karen Carver, Doran Rochell, Judy Nunn

Tom Geddie Photos

NEW JERSEY SHAKESPEARE FESTIVAL

Madison, New Jersey
Eighteenth Season

Artistic Director, Paul Barry; Producing Director, Ellen Barry; Stage Manager, Jon P. Ogden, Richard Dorfman; Sets, Ann E. Gumpper, Jeff Wisor; Costumes, Heidi Hollmann, Alice S. Hughes, Barbara C. Inglehart, Susan Konvit; Lighting, Richard Dorfman, Eric Anthony; Musical Director, Deborah Martin; Press, Debra Waxman; Business Manager, Donna M. Gearhardt; Technical Directors, David Arnold, Tony Cocchiara; Props, Tony Cocchiara; Directors, Paul Barry, Christopher Martin

COMPANY: John Abajian, Frank Bara, Ellen Barry, Paul Barry, John Barrett, Peter Burnell, Lynn Cohen, Robert Colston, J. C. Hoyt, Patrick Husted, Bertina Johnson, Dane Knell, Robin Leary, Odysseus Llowell, Virginia Mattis, Nita Novy, John O'Hurley, Don Perkins, Graham Pollock, Margery Shaw, Gary Sloan, Geddeth Smith, Tom Spackman, Annie Stafford, Ron Steelman, Zeke Zaccaro,

Lisa Angelocci, Scott Barton, Jeff Becker, Norman Blumenstaadt, Alan Brown, Nancy-Anna Bull, Jorin Burr, Brenda Lynn Bynum, Lindsay Cobb, Jeanne E. Collins, Michael Currie, Mark Daneri, Jay DeCesare, Anni Dewey, Lisa Edelstein, Margaret Emory, Cornelia Evans, Lamis Faris, Marjorie P. Feenan, Beth Anna Ferguson, Linda Jean Frank, David Goewey, Stu Goldman, Michael S. Haupt, Philip Hillery, Shelley Hoffman, Chet Hood, Richard Jenkins, Stacy Kelnar, Robert A. Klein, Sandy Laub, Martin Lerner, Leslie Ann Loeb, Linda Lovitch, Marily Magana, Penny Marks, Michael S. Monroe, Barbara Murray, Lewis Musser, Anita Namar, Bill Nickerson, Susan B. Pascucci, Tonia L. Payne, John Pietrowski, Robert Quinn, Tim Quinn, Mark Randall, Diane Rieck, Kenneth Rosenberg, Julie Rosner, Van Santvoord, Jonathan Sherman, Valerie Sherwood, Elaine Smith, Bruce Steves, Elizabeth Towson, Nancy Van Winkle, David von Salis, Veronica Vidovsky, David Waggett, Pam Welch, Virginia White, Donn Youngstrom

PRODUCTIONS: Twelfth Night/Timon of Athens by William Shakespeare, Wild Oats by John O'Keefe, Our Town by Thornton Wilder, Cat on a Hot Tin Roof by Tennessee Williams, Fifth of July by Lanford Wilson

Jerry Dalia Photos

Annie Stafford, Paul Barry, Robin Leary in "Timon of Athens"
(N. J. Festival)

NEW YORK SHAKESPEARE FESTIVAL

Joseph Papp, Producer
Delacorte Theatre/Central Park
Twenty-seventh Season

Friday, June 25, 1982—July 23, 1982 (25 performances)
DON JUAN by Moliere; Director, Richard Foreman; Translation by Donald M. Frame; Scenery, Richard Foreman; Associate Set Designer, Nancy Winters; Costumes, Patricia Zipprodt; Lighting, Spencer Mosse; Sound, Daniel M. Schreier; Stage Managers, Michael Chambers, Susan Green; Production Assistants, Anne Marie Kuehling, Lisa Ann Wilson; Wigs, Charles Lo Presto; Production Supervisor, Jason Steven Cohen; General Manager, Robert Kamlot; Production Manager, Andrew Mihok; Technical Director, Sebastian Schulherr, Mervyn Haines, Jr.; Props, Joe Toland, Pat Robertson; Wardrobe, Dawn Johnson; Press, Merle Debuskey, John Howlett, Richard Kornberg

CAST: Roy Brocksmith (Sganarelle), Burke Pearson (Gusman), John Seitz (Don Juan), Pamela Payton-Wright (Dona Elvire), Margaret Whitton (Charlotte), Clarence Felder (Pierrot), Deborah Offner (Mathurine), William Duff-Griffin (La Ramee), Christopher McCann (Poor Man), Frank Maraden (Don Carlos), Andreas Katsulas (Don Alonse), George McGrath (Statue), Marcell Rosenblatt (La Violette), Wanda Bimson (Ragotin/Spectre), James Cahill (Don Louis), Ensemble: Jere Burns, Frank Dahill, Kate Falk, Cynthia Gillette, Katherine Gowan, Yolanda Hawkins, Timothy Jeffryes, Ric Lavin, Melissa Leon, Kelly McGillis, Christine Morris, Thomas Q. Morris, Susan Murray, Laurence Overmire, Alex Paul, Ken Scherer, Penelope Smith, Jack Stehlin, Darrell Stern

UNDERSTUDIES: Christopher McCann (Don Juan), Burke Pearson (Sganarelle), Kelly McGillis (Dona Elvire), Jere Burns (Don Carlo), Frank Dahill (Statue/Alonse), Ric Lavin (Don Louis), Thomas Q. Morris (Pierrot/Dimanche), Melissa Leo (Mathurine), Christine Morris (Charlotte), Alex Paul (La Ramee), Jack Stehlin (Poor Man), Penelope Smith (Violette), Katherine Gowan (Ragotin/Spirit), William Duff-Griffin (Gusman)

Tuesday, August 3, 1982—September 3, 1982 (29 performances)
A MIDSUMMER NIGHT'S DREAM by William Shakespeare; Director, James Lapine; Choreography, Graciela Daniele; Scenery, Heidi Landesman; Costumes, Randy Barcelo; Lighting, Frances Aronson; Music, Allen Shawn; Magic Effects, Ricky Jay; Wigs, Charles Lo Presto; Production Supervisor, Jason Steven Cohen; Stage Managers, D. W. Koehler, Johnna Murray; Director's Assistants, Anne Cattaneo, Rosemary Hay; Landscape Consultants, Diana Balmori/Cesar Pelli Associates; Production Assistant, Sarah Golden; Technical Director, Sebastian Schulherr; General Manager, Robert Kamlot; Props, Pat Robertson; Wardrobe, Hannah Murray; Press, Merle Debuskey, John Howlett, Richard Kornberg

CAST: Ricky Jay (Philostrate), Diane Venora (Hippolyta), James Hurdle (Theseus), Ralph Drischell (Egeus), Deborah Rush (Hermia), Rick Lieberman (Demetrius), Kevin Conroy (Lysander), Christine Baranski (Helena), Steve Vinovich (Quince), Jeffrey DeMunn (Bottom), Paul Bates (Flute), J. Patrick O'Brien (Starveling), Andreas Katsulas (Snout), Peter Crook (Snug), Marcell Rosenblatt (Puck), William Hurt (Oberon), Michele Shay (Titania), Attendants to the Duke: Caroline McGee, David Logan-Morrow, Marcie Shaw, Prologue: Paul Kreshka, Roshi Handwerger, Cheryl McFadden, Tina Paul, Caroline McGee, David Logan-Morrow, Tim Flavin, Marcie Shaw, Fairies: Tessa Capodice, Tim Falvin, Leah Carla Gordone, Roshi Handwerger, Paul Kreshka, Emmanuel Lewis, Cheryl McFadden, Nicky Paraiso, Tina Paul, Angela Pietropinto, Rosemary Richert

Martha Swope/Susan Cook Photos

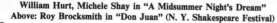

William Hurt, Michele Shay in "A Midsummer Night's Dream"
Above: Roy Brocksmith in "Don Juan" (N. Y. Shakespeare Festival)

OLD GLOBE THEATRE

San Diego, California
Thirty-third Season

Executive Director, Craig Noel; Artistic Director, Jack O'Brien; Managing Director, Thomas Hall; Press, Bill Eaton

THE MISER by Moliere; Director, Joseph Hardy; Set/Costumes, Steven Rubin; Lighting, Kent Dorsey; Composer, Conrad Susa; Stage Manager, Kent Conrad. CAST: Victor Garber (Valere), Deborah Fallender (Elise), Gary Dontzig (Cleante), John Tucky (Servant), Paxton Whitehead (Harpagon), Bill Geisslinger (LaFleche), Tom Mitchell (Master Simon), Erica Yohn (Frosine), Tom Lacy (Jacques), Sands Hall (Mariane), John Tucky (Commissioner), Gregg Bartell (Clerk), Larry Drake (Anselm).

THE TEMPEST by William Shakespeare; Director, Jack O'Brien; Set, Douglas W. Schmidt; Costumes, Sam Kirkpatrick; Lighting, David F. Segal; Composer, Bob James; Stage Manager, Douglas Pagliotti. CAST: Robert Strane (Alonso), Joe Vincent (Sebastian), Ellis Rabb (Prospero), David Graf (Antonio), Francisco Lagueruela (Ferdinand), G. Wood (Gonzalo), Michael Masterson (Adrian), J. Kenneth Campbell (Caliban), Don Knight (Trinculo) succeeded by Drew Eshelman, Jonathan McMurtry (Stephano), Jeff Harry Woolf (Boatswain), Monique Fowler (Miranda), Christopher Brown (Ariel), Susan Marshall (Iris), Theresa DePaolo (Ceres), Susan Hegarty (Juno), Martin Burns, David Flaxman, Deborah Mathews, William Quiett, Julieanna Rumsey, Ron Salvador.

BILLY BISHOP GOES TO WAR by John Gray; Director, Craig Noel; Set, Mark Donnelly; Costumes, Dianne Holly; Lighting, Robert Peterson; Stage Manager, Maria Carrera. CAST: Harry Groener (Billy Bishop) succeeded by David Ogden Stiers, David Colacci (Pianist).

THE IMPORTANCE OF BEING EARNEST by Oscar Wilde; Director, Tom Moore; Set, Richard Seger; Costumes, Robert Morgan; Lights, David D. Segal; Composer, Conrad Susa; Stage Manager, Kent Conrad. CAST: Harry Groener (Algernon) succeeded by Donald Corren, Jonathan McMurtry (Lane), Victor Garber (John), Ellis Rabb (Lady Bracknell), Barbara Dirickson (Gwendoline), Kate Wilkinson (Miss Prism), Sands Hall (Cecily), Tom Lacy (Rev. Chasuble).

THE TAMING OF THE SHREW by William Shakespeare; Director, Joseph Hardy; Sets/Costumes, Steven Rubin; Composer, Conrad Susa; Lighting, Kent Dorsey; Sound, Roger Gans; Stage Manager, Douglas Pagliotti. Robert Strane (Baptista), Larry Drake (Vincentio), Francisco Lagueruela (Lucentio), Tony Musante (Petruchio), Drew Eshelman (Gremio), Bill Beisslinger (Hortensio), Joe Vincent (Tranio), Gary Dontzig (Biondello), Christopher Brown (Grumio), Ron Salvador (Curtis), David Graf (Pedant), Amanda McBroom (Katherine), Deborah (Bianca), Susan Marshall (Widow), Jeff Harry Woolf (Tailor), Gregg Bartell (Haberdasher), Martin Burns, Theresa Depaolo, David Flaxman, Susan Hegarty, Michael C. Masterson, Deborah Mathews, Tom Mitchell, William Quiett, Julieanne Rumsey, John Tucky, Cory Fayman, Cam Schiff, Fannie Davis.

THE GIN GAME by D. L. Coburn; Director, Jack O'Brien; Set, Richard Seger; Costumes, Robert Morgan; Lights, Robert Peterson; Stage Manager, Anne Marie Salazar; Sound, Michael Winston. CAST: Eve Roberts (Fonsia Dorsey), G. Wood (Weller Martin).

Victor Garber, Kate Wilkinson, Tom Lacy, Ellis Rabb (seated), Harry Groener, Sands Hall in "The Importance of Being Earnest"

AS YOU LIKE IT by William Shakespeare; Director, Craig Noel; Set, Richard Hay; Costumes, Deborah Dryden; Lighting, John McLain; Composer, Conrad Susa; Sound, Roger Gans; Stage Manager, Douglas Pagliotti. CAST: Peter Donat (Duke, Senior), G. Wood (Duke Fredrick), Francisco Lagueruela (Amiens), Ellis Rabb (Jacques), Michael Lueders (LeBeau), Larry Drake (Charles), Joe Vincent (Oliver), George Deloy (Orlando), John Eames (Adam), Arnie Burton (Dennis), James R. Winker (Touchstone), Eric Christmas (Martext), Jonathan McMurtry (Corin), Craig Zehms (Silvius), Phil Meyer (William), Deborah May (Rosalind), Melora Marshall (Celia), Adrienne Alexander (Phebe), Susan Hegarty (Audrey), Martin Gerrish, Victor Love, Bill Ritchie, Jeff Woolf.

SORROWS OF STEPHEN by Peter Parnell; Director, Andrew J. Traister; Set, Kent Dorsey; Costumes, Mary Gibson; Lighting, Robert Peterson; Stage Managers, Kent Conrad, Maria Carrera. CAST: Bruce Davison (Stephen), Barbara Dirickson (Christine), William Geisslinger (William), Theresa DePaolo (Liz), Deena Gornick (Ginny), Jeannetta Arnette (Waitress/Sophia), Jonathan Miller (Bum/Howard), Derrick Harrison Hurd (Man at the opera), Susan Marshall (Woman at the opera), James Tyrone Wallace (Desk Clerk).

YANKEE WIVES (*World Premiere*) by David Rimmer; Director, Jack O'Brien; Set, Steven Rubin; Costumes, Ann Roth; Lighting, Craig Miller; Sound, Roger Gans; Stage Manager, Kent Conrad. CAST: Ronnie Claire Edwards (Sally Hite), Barbara Anderson (Pam Monday), Connie Antonelli (Ronnie Roberts), Alice Playten (Ronnie Roberts), Joan Pringle (Marceline Davis), Annette O'Toole (Wyla Lee), Jonathan McMurtry (Bob Dolan), Bill Geisslinger (Scamper Frizetti).

OH, COWARD! a musical revue devised by Roderick Cook from the works of Noel Coward; Director, G. Wood; Set, Mark Donnelly; Costumes, Ann Roth; Lighting, Ken Dorsey; Musical Director, Terry O'Donnell; Choreography Assistant, Derrick Harrison Hurd; Stage Manager, Douglas Pagliotti. CAST: Ann Mitchell, Joe Vincent, G. Wood, Susan Hegarty, Phil Meyer.

MISALLIANCE by George Bernard Shaw; Director, Paxton Whitehead; Set, Mark Donnelly; Costumes, Robert Morgan; Lighting, Robert Peterson; Sound, Roger Gans; Stage Manager, Douglas Pagliotti. CAST: Gary Dontzig (Junior), Jonathan Miller (Bentley), Kristin Griffith (Hypatia), Neva Patterson (Mrs. Tarleton), Murray Matheson (Lord Summerhays), G. Wood (John Tarleton), Gregory Itzin (Percival), Tandy Cronyn (Lina), Steven Peterman (Gunner).

MOBY DICK REHEARSED by Orson Welles; Director, David McClendon; Set, Kent Dorsey; Costumes, Sally Cleveland; Lighting, John B. Forbes; Music, Les Williams; Sound, Roger Gans; Stage Manager, Kent Conrad. CAST: Phil Meyer (Stage Manager), Francisco Lagueruela (Ishmael), Don Knight (Peleg), Susan Hegarty (Actress), Jeff Harry Woolf (Elija), Bill Geisslinger (Starbuck), Larry Drake (Stubb), Richard Rossi (Flask), Christopher Lewis Wylie (Pip), Ricardo Pitts-Wiley (Queequeg), Jonathan McMurtry (Ahab).

Tony Musante, Amanda McBroom in "The Taming of the Shrew"

OREGON SHAKESPEARE FESTIVAL

Ashland, Oregon
Forty-seventh Season

Artistic Director, Jerry Turner; Executive Director, William W. Patton; Choreographer, Judith Kennedy; Costumes, Martha Burke, Candice Cain, Jeannie Davidson, Deborah M. Dryden, Warren Travis, Mariann Verheyen, Carole Wheeldon; Fight Choreographer, Christopher Villa; Lighting, Peter W. Allen, Robert Peterson, Richard Riddell, James Sale; Music Director/Composer, Todd Barton; Sets, William Bloodgood, Karen Gjelsteen, Richard L. Hay; Production Manager, Pat Patton; Technical Directors, Tom Knapp, LeHook; Wardrobe, Lynn M. Ramey; Wigmaker/Hairdresser, Ranny Byer; Props, Paul-James Martin, Kevin Boog; Sound, Douglas K. Faerber; Stage Managers, Peter W. Allen, Kirk M. Boyd, David W. Brock, Lee Alan Byron, Mary Steinmetz; General Manager, Paul E. Nicholson; Press, Margaret Rubin, Sally K. White, William Bingham
COMPANY: Denis Arndt, Wayne Ballantyne, Gayle Bellows, Gloria Biegler, Michael Cadigan, James Carpenter, Gary A. Christianson, Phyllis Courtney, Philip Davidson, Richard Elmore, James Finnegan, Stefan Fischer, Tina Marie Goff, Bruce T. Gooch, Luther Hanson, Joyce Harris, William Keeler, Michael Kevin, Barry Kraft, Priscilla Hake Lauris, David M. LoVine, Helen Machin-Smith, Kyle MacLachlan, Daniel Mayes, Ivars Mikelson, Mark D. Murphey, Karen Norris, Paul Vincent O'Connor, Steven Patterson, JoAnn Johnson Patton, Shirley Patton, Jeanne Paulsen, Richard Poe, Sam Pond, Ted Roisum, Craig Rovere, Robert Sicular, Nelsen Beim Spickard, Randall Stuart, Joan Stuart-Morris, Mary Ellen Thomas, Mary Turner, Cal Winn, Weldon L. Carmichael, Mara Carrion, Robert Chase, Lee C. Crider, Evan Davidson, Carol Ernest, Walt Fadden, David Harrer, Sherril Kannasto, Bruce Marrs, Knut Jarl Norass, Bradford O'Neil, Kimberly Patton, Pat Patton III, Margaret Rubin, Matt Schwartz, Eric Stone, Mark Teeters, Douglas White, Douglas Zalud-Mackie, Marguerite Zalud-Mackie, Dancers: James Giancarlo, Robert F. Hoggard, Tammy K. Lorr, Kristin Patton, Clydine Scales, Thomas A. Scales, Wayne Wagner, Sonja Wold
PRODUCTIONS: *The Comedy of Errors* by William Shakespeare; Director, Julian Lopez-Morillas; Set, Richard L. Hay; Costumes, Warren Travis; Lighting, Richard Riddell. *Romeo and Juliet* by William Shakespeare; Director, Dennis Bigelow; Set, William Bloodgood; Costumes, Jeannie Davidson; Lighting, Richard Riddell. *Henry V* by William Shakespeare; Director, Pat Patton; Set, Richard L. Hay; Costumes, Mariann Verheyen; Lighting, Richard Riddell. *Julius Caesar* by William Shakespeare; Director, Jerry Turner; Set, Richard L. Hay; Costumes, Jeannie Davidson; Lighting, James Sale; Music, Todd Barton; Sound, Douglas K. Faerber. *Blithe Spirit* by Noel Coward; Director, Pat Patton; Set, William Bloodgood; Costumes, Jeannie Davidson; Lighting, Robert Peterson. *Spokesong* by Stewart Parker; Director, Denis Arndt; Set, William Bloodgood; Costumes, Deborah M. Dryden; Lighting, Robert Peterson; Music, Jimmy Kennedy; Lyrics, Stewart Parker; Arranged by Todd Barton. *The Matchmaker* by Thornton Wilder; Director, Rod Alexander; Set, William Bloodgood; Costumes, Jeannie Davidson; Lighting, James Sale; Music, Todd Barton. *Inherit the Wind* by Jerome Lawrence and Robert E. Lee; Director, Dennis Bigelow; Set, Richard L. Hay; Costumes, Martha Burke; Lighting, Robert Peterson; Music, Todd Barton. *Wings* by Arthur Kopit; Director, James Moll; Set, William Bloodgood; Costumes, Carole Wheeldon; Lighting, James Sale; Music, Todd Barton; Sound, Douglas K. Faerber *HOLD ME!* by Jules Feiffer; Director, Paul Barnes; Set, Karen Gjelsteen; Costumes, Candice Cain; Lighting, Peter W. Allen. *The Father* by August Strindberg; Director, Jerry Turner; Set, Richard L. Hay; Costumes, Jeannie Davidson; Lighting, James Sale

Hank Krantzler Photos

"Romeo and Juliet" (Oregon Shakespeare Festival)

Natsuko Ohama, Kaia Calhoun, Gregory Uel Cole in "Macbeth" (Shakespeare & Company)

SHAKESPEARE & COMPANY

Lenox, Massachusetts
Fifth Season

Artistic Director, Tina Packer; Associate Director, Dennis Krausnick; Movement, John Broome; Fights and tumbling, B. H. Barry; Sets/Lighting/Technical Director, Bill Ballou; Costumes, Kiki Smith; Assistant Designer, Janet Kalas; Stage Managers, J. P. Elins, Rich Meyer, Ann Ostermayer; Managing Director, Walter Perner, Jr.; Business Manager, Ann Olson; Press, Judy Salsbury, Carmel Ross, Deborah Duncan, Sue Osthoff, Tamara S. Peters, Stephanie Copeland
TWELFTH NIGHT by William Shakespeare; Director, Tina Packer; Music, Bruce Odland. CAST: Gregory Uel Cole (Orsino), Dan Moran (Curio), Carlos Carrasco (Valentine), Virginia Ness (Viola), Tony Simotes (Sea Captain), Larry Block (Sir Toby), Kristin Linklater (Maria), Kevin Coleman (Sir Andrew), John Hadden (Feste), Kaia Calhoun (Olivia), Rocco Sisto (Malvolio), Timothy Saukiavicus (Antonio), Gregory Johnson (Sebastian), James Newcomb (Fabian), Jonathan Croy (1st Officer), Ken Klineman (2nd Officer), David Coffin, Judianna Lunseth (Musicians)
MACBETH by William Shakespeare; Director, Tina Packer; Special Text Analysis, Neil Freeman. CAST: Kaia Calhoun (Witch/Gentlewoman), Carlos Carrasco (Captain/Seyton), Gregory Uel Cole (Porter/Murderer/-Witch), Maury Cooper (Duncan), Jonathan Croy (English Doctor/Angus), John Hadden (Malcolm), Gregory Johnson (Donalbain/Caithness), Kent Klineman (Messenger/Servant), Thomas Kopache (Macduff), Peter McRobbie (Old Man/Siward), James Newcomb (Murderer/Young Siward), Dan Moran (Murderer/Scotch Doctor), Virginia Ness (Lady Macduff), Natsuko Ohama (1st Witch), Leon Russom (Banquo), Timothy Saukiavicus (Macbeth), Tony Simotes (Ross), Rocco Sisto (Lennox), Lorraine Toussaint (Lady Macbeth)
EDITH WHARTON: AN INTIMATE PORTRAIT by Karen Shreefter; Director, Tina Packer; Props, Charles Bayrer. CAST: Kristin Linklater (Edith Wharton), Virginia Dwyer (Anna Bahlman)
THE COMEDY OF ERRORS by William Shakespeare; Director, Kevin Coleman; Assistant Director, Normi Noel; Set, Janet Kalas; Costumes, Govane Nadig, Bill Ballou; Voice, Zoe Alexander; Movement, Susan Dibble. CAST: Michael Mathis (Solinus), Courtenay Bernard Vance (Egeon), John C. Talbot (Antipholus of Syracuse), Walton Wilson (Antipholus of Ephesus), Jason Brown (Cromio of Syracuse), Stevenson Carlebach (Dromio of Ephesus), Hamish McIntosh (Balthasar), Tyrone Harris (Angelo), Reginold Hobbs (Merchant), James Ellis Martin (Merchant), Anthony F. Chase (Dr. Pinch), Evy Daniell (Emilia), Kimberly Scott (Adriana), Kimberleigh Burroughs (Luciana), Evy Daniell (Luce/Nell), Katherine Udall (Courtesan), Ron Yamamoto (Jailer), Hamish McIntosh, Headsmen; Anthony F. Chase, Reginald Hobbs, Attendants: Courtenay Bernard Vance, Michael Mathis, Reginald Hobbs, Hamish McIntosh

Hilary Scott, Martha Swope Photos

STRATFORD FESTIVAL
Stratford, Ontario, Canada
Thirtieth Season

Artistic Director, John Hirsch; Executive Director, Gerry Eldred; Executive Producer, John Hayes; General Manager, Gary Thomas; Press, Mary Joliffe, John Uren, Anne Selby, Elaine Lomenzo; Director of Production, Richard C. Dennison; Literary Manager, Michal Schonberg; Production Manager, Dwight Griffin; Technical Directors, Ken McKay, Gie Roberts; Company Manager, Harvey Chusid; Stage Managers, Paul Shaw, Vincent Berns, Michael Benoit, Laurie Freeman, Mary Hunter, Nora Polley, Michael Shamata; Directors, Robert Beard, Brian Bedford, Richard Cottrell, Peter Froehlich, Derek Goldby, John Hirsch, Michael Langham, Brian Macdonald, Guy Sprung; Designers, Susan Benson, Patrick Clark, Debra Hanson, Desmone Heeley, Ming Cho Lee, Barbara Matis, Douglas McLean, Tanya Moiseiwitsch, John Pennoyer, Christina Poddubiuk, Phillip Silver, David Walker; Lighting, Michael J. Whitfield, Beverly Emmons, Harry Frehner, Steven Hawkins; Composers, Berthold Carriere, Stanley Silverman

COMPANY: David Agro, Shaun Austin-Olsen, Marie Baron, Brian Bedford, Richard Binsley, Mervyn Blake, Simon Bradbury, James Bradford, Douglas Campbell, Graeme Campbell, Helen Carey, Len Cariou, Aggie Cekuta, Nick Colicos, Paul Craig, Timothy Cruickshank, Richard Curnock, Ian Deakin, Katia de Pena, Elise Dewsberry, Keith Dinicol, Margot Dionne, Curzon Dobell, John Dolan, Peter Donaldson, Eric Donkin, Maurice E. Evans, Donald Ewer, Colm Feore, Sharry Flett, Colin Fox, Glori Gage, Pat Galloway, Chris Gibson, Lewis Gordon, Allison Grant, Tammy Grimes, Amelia Hall, Mary Haney, Sheila Haney, Deryck E. Hazel, Max Helpmann, Raymond Hunt, Henry Ingram, Christina James, John Jarvis, Debora Joy, Joel Kenyon, Avo Kittask, Beverly Kreller, Robert Lachance, Elizabeth Leigh-Milne, Richard March, Ted Marshall, Biff McGuire, Loreena McKennitt, Richard McMillan, Jack Medley, Jim Mezon, Dale Mieske, Richard Monette, Tony Nardi, William Needles, Irene Neufeld, Anita Noel-Antscherl, Nicholas Pennel, Miles Potter, Karl Pruner, Paul Punyi, Kelly Robinson, Astrid Roch, Robert Rooney, Elizabeth Rukavina, Stephen Russell, Gidon Saks, Carole Shelley, Michael Shepherd, Michael Simpson, Karen Skidmore, Scott Smith, Gerald Smuin, Martin Spencer, Reid Spencer, Allen Stewart-Coates, Jean Stilwell, Heather Suttie, R. H. Thomson, Marcia Tratt, Kate Trotter, Craig Walker, Joan Warren, Tim Whelan, Ian White, Karen Wood, Susan Wright, Peter Zednik, Lee J. Campbell, Nicky Gaudagni, Thomas Hauff, David Huband, Kieron Jecchinis, Eric Keenleyside, Charmion King, Paul Massie, Diego Matamoros, Seana McKenna, John Novak, Fiona Reid, Joseph Shaw, Nicholas Simons, Cheryl Swartz, William Vickers

PRODUCTIONS: Julius Caesar, The Merry Wives of Windsor, The Tempest, A Midsummer Night's Dream, and All's Well That Ends Well by William Shakespeare, Arms and the Man by George Bernard Shaw, The Mikado by Gilbert and Sullivan, Translations by Brian Friel, Mary Stuart by Friedrich Schiller, Blithe Spirit by Noel Coward, Damien by Aldyth Morris, A Variable Passion compiled by Nicholas Pennell

Robert C. Ragsdale Photos

Carole Shelley, Brian Bedford in "Blithe Spirit" Top Right: Jim Mezon, Len Cariou, Sharry Flett in "The Tempest"

Len Cariou, Simon Bradbury, Nicholas Pennell in "Julius Caesar"

PULITZER PRIZE PRODUCTIONS

1918–Why Marry? **1919**–No award, **1920**–Beyond the Horizon, **1921**–Miss Lulu Bett, **1922**–Anna Christie, **1923**–Icebound, **1924**–Hell-Bent fer Heaven, **1925**–They Knew What They Wanted, **1926**–Craig's Wife, **1927**–In Abraham's Bosom, **1928**–Strange Interlude, **1929**–Street Scene, **1930**–The Green Pastures, **1931**–Alison's House, **1932**–Of Thee I Sing, **1933**–Both Your Houses, **1934**–Men in White, **1935**–The Old Maid, **1936**–Idiot's Delight, **1937**–You Can't Take It with You, **1938**–Our Town, **1939**–Abe Lincoln in Illinois, **1940**–The Time of Your Life, **1941**–There Shall Be No Night, **1942**–No award, **1943**–The Skin of Our Teeth, **1944**–No award, **1945**–Harvey, **1946**–State of the Union, **1947**–No award, **1948**–A Streetcar Named Desire, **1949**–Death of a Salesman, **1950**–South Pacific, **1951**–No award, **1952**–The Shrike, **1953**–Picnic, **1954**–The Teahouse of the August Moon, **1955**–Cat on a Hot Tin Roof, **1956**–The Diary of Anne Frank, **1957**–Long Day's Journey into Night, **1958**–Look Homeward, Angel, **1959**–J.B., **1960**–Fiorello!, **1961**–All the Way Home, **1962**–How to Succeed in Business without Really Trying, **1963**–No award, **1964**–No award, **1965**–The Subject Was Roses, **1966**–No award, **1967**–A Delicate Balance, **1968**–No award, **1969**–The Great White Hope, 1776, **1970**–The Effect of Gamma Rays on Man-in-the-Moon Marigolds, Borstal Boy, Company, **1971**–Home, Follies, The House of Blue Leaves, **1972**–That Championship Season, **1974**–No award, **1975**–Seascape, **1976**–A Chorus Line, **1977**–The Shadow Box, **1978**–The Gin Game, **1979**–Buried Child, **1980**–Talley's Folly, **1981**–Crimes of the Heart, **1982**–A Soldier's Play, **1983**–'night, Mother

NEW YORK DRAMA CRITICS CIRCLE AWARDS

1936–Winterset, **1937**–High Tor, **1938**–Of Mice and Men, Shadow and Substance, **1939**–The White Steed, **1940**–The Time of Your Life, **1941**–Watch on the Rhine, The Corn is Green, **1942**–Blithe Spirit, **1943**–The Patriots, **1944**–Jacobowsky and the Colonel, **1945**–The Glass Menagerie, **1946**–Carousel, **1947**–All My Sons, No Exit, Brigadoon, **1948**–A Streetcar Named Desire, The Winslow Boy, **1949**–Death of a Salesman, The Madwoman of Chaillot, South Pacific, **1950**–The Member of the Wedding, The Cocktail Party, The Consul, **1951**–Darkness at Noon, The Lady's Not for Burning, Guys and Dolls, **1952**–I Am a Camera, Venus Observed, Pal Joey, **1953**–Picnic, The Love of Four Colonels, Wonderful Town, **1954**–Teahouse of the August Moon, Ondine, The Golden Apple, **1955**–Cat on a Hot Tin Roof, Witness for the Prosecution, The Saint of Bleecker Street, **1956**–The Diary of Anne Frank, Tiger at the Gates, My Fair Lady, **1957**–Long Day's Journey into Night, The Most Happy Fella, **1958**–Look Homeward Angel, Look Back in Anger, The Music Man, **1959**–A Raisin in the Sun, The Visit, La Plume de Ma Tante, **1960**–Toys in the Attic, Five Finger Exercise, Fiorello! **1961**–All the Way Home, A Taste of Honey, Carnival, **1962**–Night of the Iguana, A Man for All Seasons, How to Succeed in Business without Really Trying, **1963**–Who's Afraid of Virginia Woolf?, **1964**–Luther, Hello Dolly!, **1965**–The Subject Was Roses, Fiddler on the Roof, **1966**–The Persecution and Assassination of Marat as Performed by the Inmates of the Asylum of Charenton under the Direction of the Marquis de Sade, Man of La Mancha, **1967**–The Homecoming, Cabaret, **1968**–Rosencrantz and Guildenstern Are Dead, Your Own Thing, **1969**–The Great White Hope, 1776, **1970**–The Effect of Gamma Rays on Man-in-the-Moon Marigolds, Borstal Boy, Company, **1971**–Home, Follies, The House of Blue Leaves, **1972**–That Championship Season, Two Gentlemen of Verona, **1973**–The Hot l Baltimore, The Changing Room, A Little Night Music, **1974**–The Contractor, Short Eyes, Candide, **1975**–Equus, The Taking of Miss Janie, A Chorus Line, **1976**–Travesties, Streamers, Pacific Overtures, **1977**–Otherwise Engaged, American Buffalo, Annie, **1978**–Da, Ain't Misbehavin', **1979**–The Elephant Man, Sweeney Todd, **1980**–Talley's Folly, Evita, Betrayal, **1981**–Crimes of the Heart, A Lesson from Aloes, Special Citations to Lena Horne, "The Pirates of Penzance, **1982**–The Life and Adventures of Nicholas Nickleby, A Soldier's Play, (no musical honored), **1983**–Brighton Beach Memoirs, Plenty, Little Shop of Horrors

AMERICAN THEATRE WING ANTOINETTE PERRY (TONY) AWARD PRODUCTIONS

1948–Mister Roberts, **1949**–Death of a Salesman, Kiss Me, Kate, **1950**–The Cocktail Party, South Pacific, **1951**–The Rose Tattoo, Guys and Dolls, **1952**–The Fourposter, The King and I, **1953**–The Crucible, Wonderful Town, **1954**–The Teahouse of the August Moon, Kismet, **1955**–The Desperate Hours, The Pajama Game, **1956**–The Diary of Anne Frank, Damn Yankees, **1957**–Long Day's Journey into Night, My Fair Lady, **1958**–Sunrise at Campobello, The Music Man, **1959**–J.B., Redhead, **1960**–The Miracle Worker, Fiorello! tied with The Sound of Music, **1961**–Becket, Bye Bye Birdie, **1962**–A Man for All Seasons, How to Succeed in Business without Really Trying, **1963**–Who's Afraid of Virginia Woolf?, A Funny Thing Happened on the Way to the Forum, **1964**–Luther, Hello Dolly!, **1965**–The Subject Was Roses, Fiddler on the Roof, **1966**–The Persecution and Assassination of Marat as Performed by the Inmates of the Asylum of Charenton under the Direction of the Marquis de Sade, Man of La Mancha, **1967**–The Homecoming, Cabaret, **1968**–Rosencrantz and Guildenstern Are Dead, Hallelujah Baby!, **1969**–The Great White Hope, 1776, **1970**–Borstal Boy, Applause, **1971**–Sleuth, Company, **1972**–Sticks and Bones, Two Gentlemen of Verona, **1973**–That Championship Season, A Little Night Music, **1974**–The River Niger, Raisin, **1975**–Equus, The Wiz, **1976**–Travesties, A Chorus Line, **1977**–The Shadow Box, Annie, **1978**–Da, Ain't Misbehavin', Dracula, **1979**–The Elephant Man, Sweeney Todd, **1980**–Children of a Lesser God, Evita, Morning's at Seven, **1981**–Amadeus, 42nd Street, The Pirates of Penzance, **1982**–The Life and Adventures of Nicholas Nickleby, Nine, Othello **1983**–Torch Song Trilogy, Cats, On Your Toes

1983 THEATRE WORLD AWARD WINNERS

KAREN ALLEN
of "Monday after the Miracle"

MATTHEW BRODERICK
of "Brighton Beach Memoirs"

HARVEY FIERSTEIN
of "Torch Song Trilogy"

SUZANNE BERTISH
of "Skirmishes"

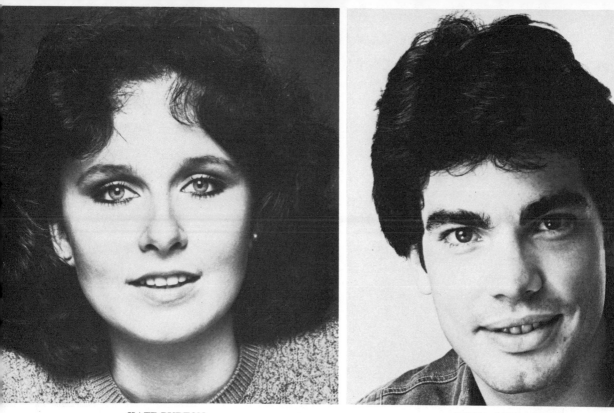

KATE BURTON
of "Winners"

PETER GALLAGHER
of "A Doll's Life"

JOANNE CAMP
of "Geniuses"

NATALIA MAKAROVA
of "On Your Toes"

ANNE PITONIAK
of "'night, Mother"

JAMES RUSSO
of "Extremities"

BRIAN TARANTINA
of "Angels Fall"

LINDA THORSON
of "Steaming"

THEATRE WORLD AWARDS presentations, Thursday, June 9, 1983. Top: Richard Burton, John Cullum, Maureen Stapleton, James MacArthur, Dorothy Loudon, Ben Vereen; Walter Willison, Jason Robards, Eva Marie Saint, Richard Kiley, Zoe Caldwell, David Birney; Below: Bill Boggs, Jason Robards; David Birney, Karen Allen; Peter Gallagher; Ben Vereen, Anne Pitoniak, James MacArthur; Third Row: Ben Vereen, Joanne Camp; Kate Burton, Richard Burton; Eva Marie Saint, James Russo; Jason Robards, Matthew Broderick; Bottom Row: Natalia Makarova, Clive Barnes; Francine LeFrak for Suzanne Bertish; Zoe Caldwell, Brian Tarantina; Harvey Fierstein, Dorothy Loudon

Van Williams, J. M. Viade Photos

Top: Richard Burton, John Cullum, Maureen Stapleton; Jason Robards, Eva Marie Saint, Richard Kiley; Zoe Caldwell, David Birney; Below: Ken Page, Juliette Koka; Liliane Montevecchi, Lee Roy Reams; Juliet Mills, Maxwell Caulfield; Melba Moore, Ben Vereen; Third Row: Patricia Elliott, Jess Richards; Fritz Weaver, Brian Tarantina, Barnard Hughes; Kim Black, Mary Ann Niles, Walter Willison, Jo Anna Lehmann; Bottom Row: Matthew Broderick, Harvey Fierstein; Dorothy Loudon, George Grizzard; Joan Bennett, Maureen Stapleton; Gregory Hines, Laurie Beechman

Van Williams Photos

Betty Comden   Richard Gere   Blythe Danner   Larry Hagman   Julie Harris   Burt Lancaster

PREVIOUS THEATRE WORLD AWARD WINNERS

1944–45: Betty Comden, Richard Davis, Richard Hart, Judy Holliday Charles Lang, Bambi Linn, John Lund, Donald Murphy, Nancy Noland, Margaret Phillips, John Raitt
1945–46: Barbara Bel Geddes, Marlon Brando, Bill Callahan, Wendell Corey, Paul Douglas, Mary James, Burt Lancaster, Patricia Marshall, Beatrice Pearson
1946–47: Keith Andes, Marion Bell, Peter Cookson, Ann Crowley, Ellen Hanley, John Jordan, George Keane, Dorothea MacFarland, James Mitchell, Patricia Neal, David Wayne
1947–48: Valerie Bettis, Edward Bryce, Whitfield Connor, Mark Dawson, June Lockhart, Estelle Loring, Peggy Maley, Ralph Meeker, Meg Mundy, Douglass Watson, James Whitmore, Patrice Wymore
1948–49: Tod Andrews, Doe Avedon, Jean Carson, Carol Channing, Richard Derr, Julie Harris, Mary McCarty, Allyn Ann McLerie, Cameron Mitchell, Gene Nelson, Byron Palmer, Bob Scheerer
1949–50: Nancy Andrews, Phil Arthur, Barbara Brady, Lydia Clarke, Priscilla Gillette, Don Hanmer, Marcia Henderson, Charlton Heston, Rick Jason, Grace Kelly, Charles Nolte, Roger Price.
1950–51: Barbara Ashley, Isabel Bigley, Martin Brooks, Richard Burton, Pat Crowley, James Daly, Cloris Leachman, Russell Nype, Jack Palance, William Smothers, Maureen Stapleton, Marcia Van Dyke, Eli Wallach
1951–52: Tony Bavaar, Patricia Benoit, Peter Conlow, Virginia de Luce, Ronny Graham, Audrey Hepburn, Diana Herbert, Conrad Janis, Dick Kallman, Charles Proctor, Eric Sinclair, Kim Stanley, Marian Winters, Helen Wood
1952–53: Edie Adams, Rosemary Harris, Eileen Heckart, Peter Kelley, John Kerr, Richard Kiley, Gloria Marlowe, Penelope Munday, Paul Newman, Sheree North, Geraldine Page, John Stewart, Ray Stricklyn, Gwen Verdon
1953–54: Orson Bean, Harry Belafonte, James Dean, Joan Diener, Ben Gazzara, Carol Haney, Jonathan Lucas, Kay Medford, Scott Merrill, Elizabeth Montgomery, Leo Penn, Eva Marie Saint
1954–55: Julie Andrews, Jacqueline Brookes, Shirl Conway, Barbara Cook, David Daniels, Mary Fickett, Page Johnson, Loretta Leversee, Jack Lord, Dennis Patrick, Anthony Perkins, Christopher Plummer
1955–56: Diane Cilento, Dick Davalos, Anthony Franciosa, Andy Griffith, Laurence Harvey, David Hedison, Earle Hyman, Susan Johnson, John Michael King, Jayne Mansfield, Sara Marshall, Gaby Rodgers, Susan Strasberg, Fritz Weaver
1956–57: Peggy Cass, Sydney Chaplin, Sylvia Daneel, Bradford Dillman, Peter Donat, George Grizzard, Carol Lynley, Peter Palmer, Jason Robards, Cliff Robertson, Pippa Scott, Inga Swenson
1957–58: Anne Bancroft, Warren Berlinger, Colleen Dewhurst, Richard Easton, Tim Everett, Eddie Hodges, Joan Hovis, Carol Lawrence, Jacqueline McKeever, Wynne Miller, Robert Morse, George C. Scott
1958–59: Lou Antonio, Ina Balin, Richard Cross, Tammy Grimes, Larry Hagman, Dolores Hart, Roger Mollien, France Nuyen, Susan Oliver, Ben Piazza, Paul Roebling, William Shatner, Pat Suzuki, Rip Torn
1959–60: Warren Beatty, Eileen Brennan, Carol Burnett, Patty Duke, Jane Fonda, Anita Gillette, Elisa Loti, Donald Madden, George Maharis, John McMartin, Lauri Peters, Dick Van Dyke
1960–61: Joyce Bulifant, Dennis Cooney, Sandy Dennis, Nancy Dussault, Robert Goulet, Joan Hackett, June Harding, Ron Husmann, James MacArthur, Bruce Yarnell
1961–62: Elizabeth Ashley, Keith Baxter, Peter Fonda, Don Galloway, Sean Garrison, Barbara Harris, James Earl Jones, Janet Margolin, Karen Morrow, Robert Redford, John Stride, Brenda Vaccaro
1962–63: Alan Arkin, Stuart Damon, Melinda Dillon, Robert Drivas, Bob Gentry, Dorothy Loudon, Brandon Maggart, Julienne Marie, Liza Minnelli, Estelle Parsons. Diana Sands, Swen Swenson
1963–64: Alan Alda, Gloria Bleezarde, Imelda De Martin, Claude Giraud, Ketty Lester, Barbara Loden, Lawrence Pressman, Gilbert Price, Philip Proctor, John Tracy, Jennifer West

1964–65: Carolyn Coates, Joyce Jillson, Linda Lavin, Luba Lisa, Michael O'Sullivan, Joanna Pettet, Beah Richards, Jaime Sanchez, Victor Spinetti, Nicolas Surovy, Robert Walker, Clarence Williams III
1965–66: Zoe Caldwell, David Carradine, John Cullum, John Davidson, Faye Dunaway, Gloria Foster, Robert Hooks, Jerry Lanning, Richard Mulligan, April Shawhan, Sandra Smith, Lesley Ann Warren
1966–67: Bonnie Bedelia, Richard Benjamin, Dustin Hoffman, Terry Kiser, Reva Rose, Robert Salvio, Sheila Smith, Connie Stevens, Pamela Tiffin, Leslie Uggams, Jon Voight, Christopher Walken
1967–68: David Birney, Pamela Burrell, Jordan Christopher, Jack Crowder (Thalmus Rasulala), Sandy Duncan, Julie Gregg, Stephen Joyce, Bernadette Peters, Alice Playten, Michael Rupert, Brenda Smiley, Russ Thacker
1968–69: Jane Alexander, David Cryer, Blythe Danner, Ed Evanko, Ken Howard, Lauren Jones, Ron Leibman, Marian Mercer, Jill O'Hara, Ron O'Neal, Al Pacino, Marlene Warfield
1969–70: Susan Browning, Donny Burks, Catherine Burns, Len Cariou, Bonnie Franklin, David Holliday, Katharine Houghton, Melba Moore, David Rounds, Lewis J. Stadlen, Kristoffer Tabori, Fredricka Weber
1970–71: Clifton Davis, Michael Douglas, Julie Garfield, Martha Henry, James Naughton, Kipp Osborne, Roger Rathburn, Ayn Ruymen, Jennifer Salt, Joan Van Ark, Walter Willison
1971–72: Jonelle Allen, Maureen Anderman, William Atherton, Richard Backus, Adrienne Barbeau, Cara Duff-MacCormick, Robert Foxworth, Elaine Joyce, Jess Richards, Ben Vereen, Beatrice Winde, James Woods
1972–73: D'Jamin Bartlett, Patricia Elliott, James Farentino, Brian Farrell, Victor Garber, Kelly Garrett, Mari Gorman, Laurence Guittard, Trish Hawkins, Monte Markham, John Rubinstein, Jennifer Warren, Alexander H. Cohen (Special Award)
1973–74: Mark Baker, Maureen Brennan, Ralph Carter, Thom Christopher, John Driver, Conchata Ferrell, Ernestine Jackson, Michael Moriarty, Joe Morton, Ann Reinking, Janie Sell, Mary Woronov, Sammy Cahn (Special Award)
1974–75: Peter Burnell, Zan Charisse, Lola Falana, Peter Firth, Dorian Harewood, Joel Higgins, Marcia McClain, Linda Miller, Marti Rolph, John Sheridan, Scott Stevensen, Donna Theodore, Equity Library Theatre (Special Award)
1975–76: Danny Aiello, Christine Andreas, Dixie Carter, Tovah Feldshuh, Chip Garnett, Richard Kelton, Vivian Reed, Charles Repole, Virginia Seidel, Daniel Seltzer, John V. Shea, Meryl Streep, A Chorus Line (Special Award)
1976–77: Trazana Beverley, Michael Cristofer, Joe Fields, Joanna Gleason, Cecilia Hart, John Heard, Gloria Hodes, Juliette Koka, Andrea McArdle, Ken Page, Jonathan Pryce, Chick Vennera, Eva LeGallienne (Special Award)
1977–78: Vasili Bogazianos, Nell Carter, Carlin Glynn, Christopher Goutman, William Hurt, Judy Kaye, Florence Lacey, Armelia McQueen, Gordana Rashovich, Bo Rucker, Richard Seer, Colin Stinton, Joseph Papp (Special Award)
1978–79: Philip Anglim, Lucie Arnaz, Gregory Hines, Ken Jennings, Michael Jeter, Laurie Kennedy, Susan Kingsley, Christine Lahti, Edward James Olmos, Kathleen Quinlan, Sarah Rice, Max Wright, Marshall W. Mason (Special Award)
1979–80: Maxwell Caulfield, Leslie Denniston, Boyd Gaines, Richard Gere, Harry Groener, Stephen James, Susan Kellermann, Dinah Manoff, Lonny Price, Marianne Tatum, Anne Twomey, Dianne Wiest, Mickey Rooney (Special Award)
1980–81: Brian Backer, Lisa Banes, Meg Bussert, Michael Allan Davis, Giancarlo Esposito, Daniel Gerroll, Phyllis Hyman, Cynthia Nixon, Amanda Plumber, Adam Redfield, Wanda Richert, Rex Smith, Elizabeth Taylor (Special Award)
1981–82: Karen Akers, Laurie Beechman, Danny Glover, David Alan Grier, Jennifer Holliday, Anthony Heald, Lizbeth Mackay, Peter MacNicol, Elizabeth McGovern, Ann Leslie Morrison, Michael O'Keefe, James Widdoes, Manhattan Theatre Club (Special Award)

AARON, JACK. Born May 1, 1933 in NYC. Attended Hunter Col., Actors Workshop. OB in "Swim Low Little Goldfish," "Journey of the 5th Horse," "The Nest," "One Flew Over the Cuckoo's Nest," "The Birds," "The Pornographer's Daughter," "Love Death Plays," "Unlikely Heroes," "Taking Steam."

ABBOTT, CHARLES. Born Aug. 26, 1943 in Chicago, IL. Attended Goodman Theatre School. Debut 1963 OB in "Cindy," followed by "Speed Gets the Poppys," "Where's Charley?," Bdwy in "Blood Red Roses," "The Grand Tour," "Two Gentlemen of Verona."

ABUBA, ERNEST. Born Aug. 25, 1947 in Honolulu, HI. Attended Southwestern Col. Bdwy debut 1976 in "Pacific Overtures," followed by "Loose Ends," OB in "Sunrise," "Monkey Music," "Station J.," "Yellow Fever."

ACKERMAN, LONI. Born Apr. 10, 1949 in NYC. Attended New School. Bdwy debut 1968 in "George M.!," followed by "No, No Nanette," "So Long 174th Street," "Magic Show," "Evita," OB in "Dames at Sea," "Starting Here Starting Now."

ACKROYD, DAVID. Born May 30, 1940 in Orange, NJ. Graduate Bucknell, Yale. Bdwy debut 1971 in "Unlikely Heroes," followed by "Full Circle," "Hamlet," "Hide and Seek," "Children of a Lesser God," OB in "Isadora Duncan Sleeps with the Russian Navy."

ADAMSON, DAVID. Born Nov. 30, 1944 in Winona, MN. Graduate UNI, UNC. Debut 1980 OB in "Kohlhaas," followed by "Sister Aimee," "Happy Birthday, Wanda June."

ADDY, WESLEY. Born Aug. 4, 1913 in Omaha, NE. Attended UCLA. Bdwy debut 1935 in "Panic," followed by "How Beautiful With Shoes," "Hamlet," "Richard II," "Henry IV," "Summer Night," "Romeo and Juliet," "Twelfth Night," "Antigone," "Candida," "Another Part of the Forest," "Galileo," "Leading Lady," "The Traitor," "The Enchanted," "King Lear," "The Strong Are Lonely," "First Gentleman," "South Pacific," "A Stitch in Time," OB in "A Month in the Country," "Candida," "Ghosts," "John Brown's Body," "Curtains," "With Love and Laughter."

AGRESS, TED. Born Apr. 20, 1945 in Brooklyn, NY. Attended Adelphi U. Bdwy debut 1965 in "Hello, Dolly!," followed by "Dear World," "Shenandoah," OB in "Look Me Up," "Around the Corner From the White House."

AHEARN, DAN. Born Aug. 7, 1948 in Washington, DC. Attended Carnegie Mellon. Debut OB 1981 in "Woyzeck," followed by "Brontosaurus Rex," "Billy Liar."

AIDEM, BETSY SUE. Born Oct. 28, 1957 in Eastmeadow, NY. Graduate NYU. Debut 1981 OB in "The Trading Post," followed by "A Different Moon."

AKERS, KAREN. Born Oct. 13, 1945 in NYC. Hunter College grad. Bdwy debut 1982 in "Nine" for which she received a Theatre World Award.

ALDREDGE, TOM. Born Feb. 28, 1928 in Dayton, OH. Attended Dayton U., Goodman Theatre. Bdwy bow 1959 in "The Nervous Set," followed by "UTBU," "Slapstick Tragedy," "Everything in the Garden," "Indians," "Engagement Baby," "How the Other Half Loves," "Sticks and Bones," "Where's Charley?," "Leaf People," "Rex," "Vieux Carre," "St. Joan," "Stages," "On Golden Pond," "The Little Foxes," OB in "The Tempest," "Between Two Thieves," "Henry V," "The Premise," "Love's Labour's Lost," "Troilus and Cressida," "Butter and Egg Man," "Ergo," "Boys in the Band," "Twelfth Night," "Colette," "Hamlet," "The Orphan," "King Lear," "The Iceman Cometh," "Black Angel."

ALDRICH, JANET. Born Oct. 16, 1956 in Hinsdale, IL. Graduate UMiami. Debut OB 1979 in "A Funny Thing Happened on the Way to the Forum," followed by "American Princess."

ALEX, MARILYN. Born Oct. 30, 1930 in Hollywood, CA. Attended RADA. Bdwy debut 1981 in "Deathtrap," OB in "Invitation to a March," "Not Now, Darling."

ALEXANDER, JACE. Born Apr. 7, 1964 in NYC. Attended NYU. Bdwy debut 1983 in "The Caine Mutiny Court Martial."

ALEXANDER, JASON. Born Sept. 23, 1959 in Irvington, NJ. Attended Boston U. Bdwy bow 1981 in "Merrily We Roll Along," OB in "Forbidden Broadway."

ALEXANDER, TERRY. Born Mar. 23, 1947 in Detroit, MI. Graduate Wayne State U. Bdwy debut 1971 in "No Place to Be Somebody," OB in "Rashomon," "The Glass Menagerie," "Breakout," "Naomi Court," "Streamers," "Julius Caesar," "Nongogo," "Sus."

ALICE, MARY. Born Dec. 3, 1941 in Indianola, MS. Debut OB 1967 in "Trials of Brother Jero," followed by "The Strong Breed," "Duplex," "Thoughts," "Miss Julie," "House Party," "Terraces," "Heaven and Hell's Agreement," "In the Deepest Part of Sleep," "Cockfight," "Julius Caesar," "Nongogo," "Second Thoughts," "Spell #7," "Zooman and The Sign," "Glasshouse," "The Ditch," Bdwy 1971 in "No Place to Be Somebody."

ALLEN, FREDERICK. Born Oct. 12, 1958 in London, Eng. Attended New School, HB Studio. Debut 1979 OB in "Widows and Children First," followed by "What's So Beautiful about a Sunset," "Herself as Lust," "Body Parts," "Never Say Die."

ALLEN, KAREN. Born Oct. 5, 1951 in Carrollton, IL. Attended Geo. Wash. U., UMD. Bdwy debut 1982 in "Monday After the Miracle" for which she received a Theatre World Award, OB in "Extremities" (1983).

ALLEN, SETH. Born July 13, 1941 in Brooklyn, NY. Attended Musical Th. Acad. OB in "Viet Rock," "Futz," "Hair," "Candaules Commissioner," "Mary Stuart," "Narrow Road to the Deep North," "More Than You Deserve," "Split Lip," "The Misanthrope," "Hard Sell," "The Wild Duck," "Jungle of Cities," "Egyptology," Bdwy in "Jesus Christ Superstar" (1972).

ALLINSON, MICHAEL. Born in London; attended Lausanne U, RADA. Bdwy bow 1960 in "My Fair Lady," (also 1981 revival), followed by "Hostile Witness," "Come Live With Me," "Coco," "Angel Street," OB in "The Importance of Being Earnest," "Staircase."

ALLISON DEBORAH. Born Apr.3 1955 in Miami, Fl. Graduate Flastateu. Debut 1981 OB in "Tied by the Leg," followed by "Love in the Dark," Bdwy 1981 in "Fools."

ALLMON, CLINTON. Born June 13, 1941 in Monahans, TX. Graduate OkStateU. Bdwy debut 1969 in "Indians," followed by "The Best Little Whorehouse in Texas," "Caine Mutiny Court Martial," OB in "Bluebird," "Khaki Blue," "One Sunday Afternoon."

ALTAY, DERIN. Born Nov. 10, 1954 in Chicago, IL. Attended Goodman School, AmCons. Broadway debut 1981 in "Evita."

AMENDOLIA, DON. Born Feb. 1, 1945 in Woodbury, NJ. Attended Glassboro State Col., AADA. Debut 1966 OB in "Until the Monkey Comes," followed by "Park," "Cloud 9."

AMES, KENNETH. Born Oct. 6, 1961 in Beaumont, TX. Bdwy debut 1982 in "Play Me a Country Song."

AMKRAUT, ALYNNE. Born July 3, 1953 in Amityville, NY. Graduate Syracuse U. Debut 1981 OB in "Godspell," followed by "Women in Tune," "Not Now Darling."

ANDERMAN, MAUREEN. Born Oct. 26, 1946 in Detroit, MI. Graduate UMich. Bdwy debut 1970 in "Othello," followed by "Moonchildren" for which she received a Theatre World Award, "An Evening with Richard Nixon . . . ," "The Last of Mrs. Lincoln," "Seascape," "Who's Afraid of Virginia Woolf?" "A History of the American Film," "The Lady from Dubuque," "The Man Who Came to Dinner," "Einstein and the Polar Bear," "You Can't Take It With You," OB in "Hamlet," "Elusive Angel," "Out of Our Father's House," "Sunday Runners," "Macbeth."

ANDERS, KENNETH. Born Oct. 6, 1955 in Rapid City, SD. Attended UAz. Debut OB 1983 in "The Beggar's Opera."

ANDERSON, ARTHUR. Born Aug. 29, 1922 in Staten Island, NY. Attended AmThWing. Bdwy debut 1937 in "Julius Caesar," followed by "Shoemaker's Holiday," "1776," OB in "Winkelberg," "The Doctor's Dilemma," "Zoo Story," "American Dream," "Gallows Humor," "The Rivals," "The Fantasticks," "American Collage."

ANDERSON, C. B. Born June 18, 1939 in Nashville, TN. Attended UGa. Debut 1980 with BAM Theatre Co. in "The Winter's Tale," followed by "Johnny on a Spot," "The Recruiting Officer," "The Wild Duck," "Jungle of Cities," "Court of Miracles," "The Taming of the Shrew."

ANDERSON, JOEL. Born Nov. 19, 1955 in San Diego, CA. Graduate UUtah. Debut 1980 OB in "A Funny Thing Happened on the Way to the Forum," followed by "Joan of Lorraine."

ANDERSON, MYRA. Born May 12, 1949 in Detroit, MI. Graduate UMich., NYU. Debut 1979 OB in "The Shirt," followed by "Margaret's Bed," "Butterflings Angel," "Trio."

ANDREAS, CHRISTINE. Born Oct. 1, 1951 in Camden, NJ. Bdwy debut 1975 in "Angel Street," followed by "My Fair Lady" for which she received a Theatre World Award, "Oklahoma (1979)," "On Your Toes," OB in "Disgustingly Rich," "Rhapsody in Gershwin," "Alex Wilder: Clues to a Life."

ANDREWS, GEORGE LEE. Born Oct. 13, 1942 in Milwaukee, WI. Debut OB 1970 in "Jacques Brel Is Alive," followed by "Starting Here Starting Now," "Vamps and Rideouts," Bdwy in "A Little Night Music" (1973), "On the 20th Century," "Merlin."

ANDROSKY, CAROL. Born in Pittston, PA. Graduate Cornell U. Bdwy debut 1983 in "You Can't Take It With You."

ANGLIM, PHILIP. Born Feb. 11, 1953 in San Francisco, CA. Yale graduate. Debut OB and Bdwy 1979 in "The Elephant Man" for which he received a Theatre World Award, followed by "Macbeth," OB in "Judgment," "Welded."

ANTHONY, ROBERT. Born May 10, 1941 in Newark, NJ. Attended Boston U., AADA. OB credits: "Jerico-Jim Crow," "Bugs and Veronica," "Dirty Old Man," "Hamlet," "Othello," "Scuba Duba," "Salome," "Love Affairs and Wedding Bells," Bdwy in "Man in the Glass Booth" (1968), "Butterflies Are Free," "Legend."

ARANAS, RAUL. Born Oct. 1, 1947 in Manilla, Phil. Pace U. grad. Debut 1976 OB in "Savages," followed by "Yellow Is My Favorite Color," "49," "Bullet Headed Birds," "Tooth of Crime," "Teahouse." Bdwy 1978 in "Loose Ends."

ARBEIT, HERMAN O. Born Apr. 19, 1925 in Brooklyn, NY. Attended CCNY, HB Studio, Neighborhood Playhouse. Debut 1939 OB in "The Golem," followed by "Awake and Sing," "A Delicate Balance," "Yentl the Yeshiva Boy," "A Yank in Beverly Hills," "Second Avenue Rag," "Taking Steam," Bdwy in "Yentl" (1975).

ARDAO, DAVID. Born July 24, 1951 in Brooklyn, NY. Graduate Rutgers U. Bdwy debut 1981 in "Joseph and the Amazing Technicolor Dreamcoat."

ARMAGNAC, GARY. Born Aug. 17, 1952 in New Jersey. Iona Col. grad. Debut 1981 OB in "A Taste of Honey," followed by "Out of the Night."

ARMEN, REBECCA. Born Apr. 24, 1957 in Norwood, MA. Graduate Wesleyan U, Drama Studio. Debut 1980 OB in "The Winter's Tale," Bdwy in "Alice in Wonderland" (1982).

ARMISTEAD, DIANE. Born May 26, 1936 in Canton, OH. Attended Wooster Col. Debut OB 1979 in "The Old Maid and the Thief," followed by Light Opera of Manhattan, "Principally Pinter/Slightly Satie," Bdwy 1982 in "A Doll's Life."

ARNOLD, DULCIE. Born Nov. 20, 1949 in Neptune, NJ. Graduate Syracuse U. Debut 1980 OB in "Last Summer at Bluefish Cove," followed by "Polycarpe Reincarnate."

ASHER, DAVID. Born June 3, 1953 in Cleveland, OH. Graduate Stanford, Yale. Debut OB 1974 in "The Proposition," Bdwy in "Most Happy Fella" (1979), "Joseph and the Amazing Technicolor Dreamcoat," "Merlin."

ASHER, LAWRENCE. Born July 30, 1948 in Palisades Park, NJ. Graduate Ithaca Col. Debut OB 1974 in "The Proposition," followed by "The Rise of David Levinsky," Bdwy 1979 in "Most Happy Fella."

ASHLEY, ELIZABETH. Born Aug. 30, 1939 in Ocala, FL. Attended Neighborhood Playhouse. Bdwy debut 1959 in "The Highest Tree," followed by "Taker Her, She's Mine" for which she received a Theatre World Award, "Barefoot in the Park," "Ring Round the Bathtub," "Cat on a Hot Tin Roof," "The Skin of Our Teeth," "Legend," "Caesar and Cleopatra," "Hide and Seek," "Agnes of God."

ASHTON, COLLEEN. Born Oct. 25, 1949 in Austin, MN. Attended St. Cloud State Col., PaStateU. Bdwy debut 1982 in "Little Johnny Jones," followed by "Dance a Little Closer," OB in "Broadway Scandals of 1928," "Anything Goes."

ASQUITH, WARD. Born March 21 in Philadelphia, PA. Graduate UPa., Columbia U. OBdwy debut 1979 in "After the Rise," followed by "Kind Lady," "Incident at Vichy," "Happy Birthday, Wanda June."

ATHERTON, WILLIAM. Born July 30, 1947 in Orange, CT. Graduate Carnegie Tech. Debut 1971 OB in "House of Blue Leaves," followed by "The Basic Training of Pavlo Hummel," "Suggs" for which he received a Theatre World Award, "Rich and Famous," "The Passing Game," "Three Acts of Recognition," Bdwy in "The Sign in Sidney Brustein's Window" (1972), "Happy New Year," "The American Clock," "Caine Mutiny Court-Martial."

ATKINSON, PEGGY. Born Oct. 1, 1943 in Brooklyn, NY. Attended Ithaca Col. Bdwy debut 1967 in "Fiddler on the Roof," followed by "Two Gentlemen of Verona," OB in "Boccaccio," "The Faggot," "One Free Smile," "One Cent Plain," "Hostage," "Bags," "Robin Hood," "Bugles at Dawn."

AWAD, JODY. Born Jan. 3, 1959 in Framingham, MA. Graduate Dartmouth Col. Debut 1982 OB in "Going Steady."

AYLWARD, TONY. Born May 30 in NYC. Attended Hunter Col. Debut 1960 OB in "Gay Divorce," followed by "Babes in Arms," "Class Act," "A Hole in the Wall," "Corkscrews."

AYR, MICHAEL. Born Sept. 8, 1953 in Great Falls, MT. Graduate SMU. Debut 1976 OB in "Mrs. Murray's Farm," followed by "The Farm," "Ulysses in Traction," "Lulu" "Cabin 12," "Stargazing," "The Deserter," "Hamlet," "Mary Stuart," "Save Grand Central," "The Beaver Coat," "Richard II," "Great Grandson of Jedediah Kohler," "Domestic Issues," "Time Framed," "The Dining Room," Bdwy 1980 in "Hide and Seek," "Piaf."

BACIGALUPI, DENNIS. Born July 14, 1956 in San Francisco, CA. Attended Juilliard. Debut 1978 OB in "King Lear," followed by "The Music Keeper," Bdwy in "Frankenstein" (1981).

BACKER, BRIAN. Born Dec. 5, 1956 in NYC. Attended Neighborhood Playhouse. Bdwy debut 1981 in "The Floating Light Bulb" for which he received a Theatre World Award.

BACKUS, RICHARD. Born Mar. 28, 1945 in Goffstown, NH. Harvard graduate. Bdwy debut 1971 in "Butterflies are Free," followed by "Promenade, All" for which he received a Theatre World Award, "Ah, Wilderness!," "Camelot" (1981), OB in "Studs Edsel," "Gimme Shelter," "Sorrows of Stephen," "Missing Persons."

BACON, KEVIN. Born July 8, 1958 in Philadelphia, PA. Debut 1978 OB in "Getting Out," followed by "Glad Tidings," "Album," "Flux," "Poor Little Lambs," "Slab Boys."

BADDELEY, HERMIONE. Born Nov. 13, 1906 in Broseley, Eng. Bdwy debut 1961 in "A Taste of Honey," followed by "The Milk Train Doesn't Stop Here Anymore," "I Only Want an answer" (OB), "Canterbury Tales," "Whodunnit."

BADILLO, ROBERTO. Born June 12, 1958 in NYC. Attended Goddard Col. Debut 1983 OB in "The House of Ramon Iglesia."

BADOLATO, DEAN. Born June 6, 1952 in Chicago, IL. Attended UIll. Bdwy debut 1978 in "A Chorus Line," followed by "Pirates of Penzance," "On Your Toes."

BAGDEN, RONALD. Born Dec. 26, 1953 in Philadelphia, PA. Graduate Temple U., RADA. Debut OB 1977 in "Oedipus Rex," followed by "Oh! What A Lovely War!," Bdwy 1980 in "Amadeus."

BAILEY, DENNIS. Born Apr. 12, 1953 in Grosse Point Woods, MI. UDetroit graduate. Debut 1977 OB in "House of Blue Leaves," followed by "Wonderland," "Head over Heels," Bdwy 1978 in "Gemini."

BAINES, HOWARD. Born Nov. 13, 1969 in NYC. Debut 1983 OB in "Sons and Fathers of Sons."

BAKER, BLANCHE. (nee Brocho Freyda Garfein) Dec. 20, 1956 in NYC. Attended Wellesley Col. Bdwy debut 1981 in "Lolita," followed by OB's "Poor Little Lambs," "Hannah."

BAKER, MARK. Born Oct. 2, 1946 in Cumberland, MD. Attended Wittenberg U., Carnegie-Mellon U., Neighborhood Playhouse, AADA. Bdwy debut 1972 in "Via Galactica," followed by "Candide" for which he received a Theatre World Award, "Habeas Corpus," OB in "Love Me, Love My Children," "A Midsummer Night's Dream," "From Rodgers and Hart With Love," "Edgar Allan," "Oh My Broken Hearts and Back."

BAKER, RAYMOND. Born July 9, 1948 in Omaha, NE. Graduate UDenver. Debut 1972 OB in "The Proposition," followed by "Are You Now or Have You Ever Been . . . ," "Character Lines," "Lunch Hour," "Legends of Arthur," "War Babies," "Bathroom Plays," Bdwy in "Crimes of the Heart," "Division Street," "Is There Life After High School?"

BALABAN, ROBERT. Born Aug. 16, 1945 in Chicago, IL. Attended Colgate, NYU. Debut 1967 OB in "You're a Good Man, Charlie Brown," followed by "Up Eden," "White House Murder Case," "Basic Training of Pavlo Hummel," "The Children," "Marie and Bruce," "Three Sisters," Bdwy in "Plaza Suite" (1968), "Some of My Best Friends," "Inspector General."

BALLOU, MARK. Born Oct. 12, 1971 in NYC. Debut 1983 OB in "Happy Birthday, Wanda June."

BALOU, BUDDY. Born in 1953 in Seattle, WA. Joined American Ballet Theatre in 1970, rising to soloist. Joined Dancers in 1977; "A Chorus Line" in 1980.

BANES, LISA. Born July 9, 1955 in Chagrin Falls, OH. Juilliard grad. Debut OB 1980 in "Elizabeth I," followed by "A Call from the East," "Look Back in Anger" for which she received a Theatre World Award, "My Sister in This House," "Antigone," "Three Sisters."

BANSAVAGE, LISA. Born March 22, 1953 in Syracuse, NY. Graduate Carnegie-Mellon, UPittsburgh. Debut 1983 OB in "The Changeling."

BARANSKI, CHRISTINE. Born May 2, 1952 in Buffalo, NY. Graduate Juilliard Sch. Debut OB 1978 in "One Crack Out," followed by "Says I Says He," "The Trouble with Europe," "Coming Attractions," "Operation Midnight Climax," "Sally and Marsha," "A Midsummer Night's Dream," Bdwy 1980 in "Hide and Seek."

BARBER, KEVIN. Born Sept. 16, 1968 in Morristown, NJ. Debut 1982 OB in "Life With Father."

BARBOUR, THOMAS. Born July 25, 1921 in NYC. Graduate Princeton, Harvard. Bdwy debut 1968 in "Portrait of a Queen," followed by "Great White Hope," "Scratch," "The Lincoln Mask," "Kingdoms," OB in "Twelfth Night," "Merchant of Venice," "Admirable Bashful," "The Lady's Not for Burning," "The Enchanted," "Antony and Cleopatra," "The

Saintliness of Margery Kemp," "Dr. Willy Nilly," "Under the Sycamore Tree," "Epitaph for George Dillon," "Thracian Horses," "Old Glory," "Sjt. Musgrave's Dance," "Nestless Bird," "The Seagull," "Wayside Motor Inn," "Arthur," "The Grinding Machine," "Mr. Simian," "The Sorrows of Frederick," "The Terrorists," "Dark Ages," "Royal Bob."

BARCROFT, JUDITH. Born July 6 in Washington, DC. Attended Northwestern U, Stephens Col. Bdwy debut 1965 in "The Mating Dance," followed by "Plaza Suite," "Dinner at 8," "The Elephant Man," OB in "M. Amilcar," "Cloud 9."

BARKER, CHRISTINE. Born Nov. 26 in Jacksonville, FL. Attended UCLA. Bdwy debut 1979 in "A Chorus Line."

BARKER, JEAN. Born Dec. 20, in Philadelphia, PA. Attended UPa., AmThWing. Debut OB 1953 in "The Bald Soprano," followed by "Night Shift," "A Month in the Country," "Portrait of Jenny," "Knucklebones," "About Iris Berman," "Goodnight, Grandpa," Bdwy in "The Innkeepers."

BARKER, MARGARET. Born Oct. 10, 1908 in Baltimore, MD. Attended Bryn Mawr. Bdwy debut 1928 in "Age of Innocence," followed by "Barretts of Wimpole Street," "House of Connelly," "Men in White," "Gold Eagle Guy," "Leading Lady," "Member of the Wedding," "Autumn Garden," "See the Jaguar," "Ladies of the Corridor," "The Master Builder," OB in "Wayside Motor Inn," "The Loves of Cass McGuire," "Three Sisters," "Details without a Map."

BARNES, FRANCES. Born Feb. 24, 1931 in Windber, PA. Graduate PaStateU, Western Reserve U. Debut 1955 in "An Ideal Husband," followed by "Knights Errant," Bdwy in "Waltz of the Toreadors" (1958).

BARON, ROGER. Born Nov. 22, 1946 in Chicago, IL. Graduate Northwestern U. Bdwy debut 1976 in "The Heiress," followed by OB's "The Crucible," "Under Milkwood."

BARONE, JOHN. Born March 14, 1954 in Staten Island, NY. Graduate Wagner Col. Debut 1982 OB in "Robin Hood."

BARRETT, BRENT. Born Feb. 28, 1957 in Quinter, KS. Graduate Carnegie-Mellon. Bdwy debut 1980 in "West Side Story," OB in "Dance a Little Closer," OB in "March of the Falsettos," "Portrait of Jenny," "The Death of Von Richthofen."

BARRETT, LAURINDA. Born in 1931 in NYC. Attended Wellesley Col., RADA. Bdwy debut 1956 in "Too Late the Phalarope," followed by "The Girls in 509," "The Milk Train Doesn't Stop Here Anymore," "UTBU," "I Never Sang For My Father," "Equus," OB in "The Misanthrope," "Palm Tree in a Rose Garden," "All Is Bright," "The Carpenters."

BARRIE, BARBARA. Born May 23, 1931 in Chicago, IL. Graduate UTx. Bdwy debut 1955 in "The Wooden Dish," followed by "Happily Never After," "Company," "Selling of the President," "Prisoner of Second Avenue," "California Suite," "Torch Song Trilogy," OB in "The Crucible," "Beaux Stratagem," "Taming of the Shrew," "Twelfth Night," "All's Well That Ends Well," "Horseman, Pass By," "Killdeer," "Big and Little."

BARROW, BERNARD E. Born Dec. 30, 1927 in NYC. Graduate Syracuse U, Columbia, Yale. Debut OB 1959 in "Billy Budd," followed by "Poor Murderer," "Scuba Duba," "Uncle Vanya," "Hamlet," "Punchy."

BARRY, KATHERINE. Born Sept. 19, 1956 in Washington, DC. Graduate Northwestern U. Debut 1982 OB in "After the Fall."

BARRY, RAYMOND J. Born Mar. 14, 1939 in Hempstead, NY. Graduate Brown U. Debut 1963 OB in "Man Is Man," followed by "Penguin Touquet," "Egyptology," Bdwy 1975 in "The Leaf People," "Hunting Scenes."

BARSKY, BARBARA. Born July 7, 1955 in Winnipeg, Manitoba, Canada. Debut 1982 OB in "Corkscrews."

BARTENIEFF, GEORGE. Born Jan. 24, 1933 in Berlin, Ger. Bdwy bow 1947 in "The Whole World Over," followed by "Venus Is," "All's Well That Ends Well," "Quotations from Chairman Mao Tse-Tung," "The Death of Bessie Smith," "Cop-Out," "Room Service," "Unlikely Heroes," in "Walking to Waldheim," "Memorandum," "The Increased Difficulty of Concentration," "Trelawny of the Wells," "Charley Chestnut Rides the IRT," "Radio (Wisdom): Sophia Part I," "Images of the Dead," "Dead End Kids," "The Blonde Leading the Blonde," "The Dispossessed," "Growing Up Gothic," "Rosetti's Apologetics."

BARTLETT, D'JAMIN. Born May 21 in NYC. Attended AADA. Bdwy debut 1973 in "A Little Night Music" for which she received a Theatre World Award, OB in "The Glorious Age," "Boccaccio," "2 by 5," "Lulu," "Alex Wilder: Clues to Life."

BARTLETT, ROBIN. Born Apr. 22, 1951 in NYC. Graduate Boston U. Bdwy debut 1975 in "Yentl," followed by "The World of Sholem Aleichem," OB in "Agamemnon," "Fathers and Sons," "No End of Blame," "Living Quarters," "After the Fall."

BARTON, DONALD. Born May 2, 1928 in Eastland, TX. Attended UTx. Credits include "Design for a Stained Glass Window," "Paint Your Wagon," "Wonderful Town," "Goldilocks," "Much Ado About Nothing," "The Royal Family," "Deathtrap," "Equus," "The Middle Ages" (OB).

BARTON, FRED. Born Oct. 20, 1958 in Camden, NJ. Graduate Harvard. Debut 1982 OB in "Forbidden Broadway."

BARTZ, JAMES. Born Apr. 23, 1948 in Racine, WI. Graduate UWisc. Bdwy debut 1976 in "Wheelbarrow Closers," OB in "Salome," "Mandragola," "Antigone," "You Are What You Are," "Woman of Iron," "Innocent Thoughts," "Tom Tom," "War and Peace," "Divine Hysteria."

BATES, KATHY. Born June 18, 1948 in Memphis, TN. Graduate S. Methodist U. Debut 1976 OB in "Vanities," followed by "The Art of Dining," Bdwy in "Goodbye Fidel" (1980), "5th of July," "Come Back to the 5 & Dime, Jimmy Dean," " 'night, Mother."

BATTALION, RICHARD. Born June 8, 1955 in Philadelphia, PA. Attended Temple U. Debut 1982 OB in "Meegan's Game," followed by "Beggar's Opera."

BATTISTA, LLOYD. Born May 14, 1937 in Cleveland, OH. Graduate Carnegie Tech. Bdwy debut 1966 in "Those That Play the Clowns," followed by "The Homecoming." OB in "The Flame and the Rose," "Murder in the Cathedral," "The Miser," "Gorky," "Sexual Perversity in Chicago," "King of Schnorrers," "Francis," "The Keymaker," "The Guys in the Truck."

BATTLE, HINTON. Born Nov. 29, 1956 in Neubraecke, Ger. Joined Dance Theatre of Harlem. Bdwy debut 1975 in "The Wiz," followed by "Dancin'," "Sophisticated Ladies," "Dreamgirls."

BAUERS, DEBORAH. Born July 19, 1953 in Nashville, TN. Graduate UColo., Smith Col. Broadway debut 1982 in "Oh! Calcutta!"

BAUGHAN, TERRY. Born Feb. 21, 1951 in Lincoln, NE. Graduate UNeb. Debut 1979 OB in "The Sound of Music," followed by "Anyone Can Whistle," "Colette Collage."

BAUM, SUSAN J. Born July 12, 1950 in Miami, FL. Graduate UFl. Has appeared OB in "The Children's Hour," "Holy Ghosts," "Hay Fever," "Doctor in the House," "Trifles," "Arms and the Man," "Uncle Vanya," "Hedda Gabler," "Close Enough for Jazz," "Colette Collage."

BAXLEY, BARBARA. Born Jan. 1, 1925 in Porterville, CA. Attended Pacific Col., Neighborhood Playhouse. Bdwy debut 1948 in "Private Lives," followed by "Out West of Eighth," "Peter Pan," "I Am a Camera," "Bus Stop," "Camino Real," "Frogs of Spring," "Oh, Men! Oh, Women!," "The Flowering Peach," "Period of Adjustment," "She Loves Me," "Three Sisters," "Plaza Suite," "Me Jack, You Jill," "Best Friend," "Whodunnit," OB in "Brecht on Brecht," "Measure for Measure," "To Be Young, Gifted and Black," "Oh, Pioneers," "Are You Now or Have You Ever . . . ," "Isn't It Romantic."

BEACH, GARY. Born Oct. 10, 1947 in Alexandria, VA. Graduate NCSch. of Arts. Bdwy bow 1971 in "1776," followed by "Something's Afoot," "Moony Shapiro Songbook," "Annie," OB in "Smile, Smile, Smile," "What's a Nice Country Like You . . . ," "Ionescapade," "By Strouse," "A Bundle of Nerves."

BEACHNER, LOUIS. Born June 9, 1923 in Jersey City, NJ. Bdwy bow 1942 in "Junior Miss," followed by "No Time for Sergeants," "Georgy," "The Changing Room," "National Health," "Where's Charley?," "Passion," OB in "Time to Burn," "The Hostage," "Savages," "The Overcoat."

BEALS, FREDERICK. Born July 3, 1916 in Mt. Vernon, NY. Williams Col. graduate. Debut 1978 OB in "Desire under the Elms," followed by "Peace in Our Time," "The Importance of Being Earnest," " 'Dark of the Moon," "The Old Woman Broods," "Caligula," "All the Way Home," "Adam."

BEAN, ORSON. Born July 22, 1928 in Burlington, VT. Bdwy bow 1953 in "Men of Distinction," followed by "John Murray Anderson's Almanac" for which he received a Theatre World Award, "Will Success Spoil Rock Hunter?," "Nature's Way," "Mister Roberts" (CC), "Subways Are for Sleeping," "Say, Darling" (CC), "Never Too Late," "I Was Dancing," "Ilya Darling," OB in "Home Movies," "A Round with Ring," "Make Someone Happy," "I'm Getting My Act Together," "40 Deuce," "A Christmas Carol."

BEAUCHAMP, STEVEN. Born March 26 in Watertown, CT. Graduate Wesleyan U. Debut 1981 OB in "Badgers," followed by "Of Mice and Men."

BECKERMAN, MARA. Born Mar. 22, 1954 in NYC. Graduate Queens Col. Debut 1982 OB in "Charlotte Sweet."

BEDFORD, BRIAN. Born Feb. 16, 1935 in Morley, Eng. Attended RADA. Bdwy debut 1960 in "Five Finger Exercise," followed by "Lord Pengo," "The Private Ear," "The Knack" (OB), "The Astrakhan Coat," "The Unknown Soldier and His Wife," "Seven Descents of Myrtle," "Jumpers," "The Cocktail Party," "Hamlet," "Private Lives," "School for Wives," "The Misanthrope."

BEECHMAN, LAURIE. Born Apr. 4, 1954 in Philadelphia, Pa. Attended NYU. Bdwy debut 1977 in "Annie," followed by "Pirates of Penzance," "Joseph and the Amazing Technicolor Dreamcoat" for which she received a Theatre World Award, "Some Enchanted Evening" (OB), "Pal Joey in Concert."

BEIM, NORMAN. Born Oct. 2 in Newark, NJ. Attended Ohio State U. Debut 1954 OB in "Coriolanus," followed by "Black Visions," "Thieves Carnival," "Ah, Wilderness," "Bojangles," Bdwy 1955 in "Inherit the Wind."

BELL, VANESSA. Born Mar. 20, 1957 in Toledo, OH. Graduate OhU. Bdwy debut 1981 in "Bring Back Birdie," followed by "El Bravo!," "Dreamgirls."

BELUSHI, JAMES Born June 15, 1954 in Chicago, IL. Graduate S.Ill.U. Bdwy debut 1982 in "Pirates of Penzance," OB in "True West" (1983).

BENNETT, HARRY. Born Dec. 25 in Ridgefield, CT. Graduate UCt., Catholic U. Debut 1982 OB in "Not Now, Darling," followed by "Kiss Me, Kate."

BENSON, CINDY. Born Oct. 2, 1951 in Attleboro, MA. Graduate St. Leo Col., UIll. Debut 1981 OB in "Some Like It Cole."

BENTLEY, JOHN. Born Jan. 31, 1940 in Jackson Heights, NY. Graduate AADA. Debut OB 1961 in "King of the Dark Chamber," followed by "As to the Meaning of Words," "West Side Story" (JB), Bdwy in "Mike Downstairs," "Lysistrata," "The Selling of the President," "A Funny Thing Happened on the Way to the Forum" (1972), "West Side Story" (1980).

BERETTA) JOANNE. Born Nov. 14 in San Francisco, CA. Attended SFState Col. Bdwy Debut in "New Faces of 1962," OB in "The Club" "Colette Collage."

BEREZIN, TANYA. Born Mar. 25, 1941 in Philadelphia, PA. Attended Boston U. Debut OB 1967 in "The Sandcastle," followed by "Three Sisters," "Great Nebula in Orion," "him," "Amazing Activity of Charlie Contrare," "Battle of Angels," "Mound Builders," "Serenading Louie," "My Life," "Brontosaurus," "Glorious Morning," "Mary Stuart," "The Beaver Coat," Bdwy in "5th of July" (1981), "Angels Fall."

BERGER, ANNA. Born July 28 in NYC. Attended Geo. Wash. U. Bdwy debut 1950 in "Twilight Walk," followed by "Diamond Lil," "Flowering Peach," "Very Special Baby," "The Rose Tattoo," "Unlikely Heroes," "Gideon," OB in "Tevye and His Daughters," "Silver Tassie," "Juno and the Paycock," "Him," "Dog Beneath the Skin," "Within the Gates."

BERLE, MILTON. Born July 12, 1908 in NYC. Bdwy debut 1920 in "Florodora," followed by "Earl Carroll's Vanities," "Saluta," "Ziegfeld Follies," "See My Lawyer," "The Goodbye People," "Goodnight, Grandpa."

BERMAN, DONALD F. Born Jan. 23, 1954 in NYC. Graduate USyracuse. Debut 1977 OB in "Savages," followed by "Dona Rosita," "The Lady or the Tiger," "The Overcoat," "Steel on Steel."

BERNER, GARY. Born Nov. 29, 1956 in Mt. Kisco, NY. Attended Hampshire Col., Brandeis U. Debut 1979 OB in "Minnesota Moon," followed by "The Runner Stumbles," "Richard II," "The Great Grandson of Jedediah Kohler."

BERNSTEIN, DOUGLAS. Born May 6, 1958 in NYC. Amherst graduate. Debut 1982 OB in "Upstairs at O'Neals."

BERTISH, SUZANNE. Born Aug. 7, 1951 in London, Eng. Attended London Drama School. Bdwy debut 1981 in "Nicholas Nickleby," followed by (OB) "Skirmishes" for which she received a Theatre World Award.

BESSETTE, MIMI. Born Jan. 15, 1956 in Midland, MI. Graduate TCU, RADA. Debut 1978 OB in "The Gift of the Magi," followed by "Bugles at Dawn," Bdwy 1981 in "The Best Little Whorehouse in Texas."

BIGGS, CASEY. Born Apr. 4, 1955 in Toledo, OH. Attended Juilliard. Debut 1981 OB in "Il Campiello," followed by "Twelfth Night," "The Country Wife," "The Cradle Will Rock."

BINNS, EDWARD. Born Sept. 12, 1916 in Philadelphia, PA. Attended Penn State Col., Cleveland Play House. Credits include "Command Decision," "Sundown Beach," "Detective Story," "The Lark," "A View From the Bridge," "Caligula," "Ghosts."

BIRKIN, JOHN. Born July 15, 1953 in NYC. Graduate CUNY, Queens Col. Debut OB 1980 in "Hedda Gabler," followed by "Hamlet."

BIRNEY, DAVID. Born Apr. 23, 1939 in Washington, DC. Graduate Dartmouth, UCLA. OB in "Comedy of Errors," "Titus Andronicus," "King John," "MacBird," "Crime of Passion," "Ceremony of Innocence," Lincoln Center's "Summertree" for which he received a Theatre World Award, "The Miser," "Playboy of the Western World," "Good Woman of Setzuan," "An Enemy of the People" and "Antigone," Bdwy 1983 in "Amadeus."

BIRNEY, REED. Born Sept. 11, 1954 in Alexandria, VA. Attended Boston U. Bdwy debut 1977 in "Gemini," OB in "The Master and Margarita," "Bella Figura," "Winterplay."

BISOGLIO, VAL. Born May 7, 1931 in NYC. Debut OB 1964 in "Kiss Mama," followed by "A View From the Bridge" (1966), "Victims of Duty," Bdwy in "Wait until Dark" (1966).

BIXLER, VALERIE LEIGH. Born Feb. 17, 1956 in Des Moines, IA. Attended Sweet Briar Col., TCU, graduate SMU. Debut 1979 OB in "Telecast," Bdwy 1981 in "The Best Little Whorehouse in Texas."

BLAXILL, PETER. Born Sept. 27, 1931 in Cambridge, MA. Graduate Bard Col. Debut 1967 OB in "Scuba Duba," followed by "The Fantasticks," "The Passion of Antigona Perez," "Oh, Boy!," "From Brooks With Love," Bdwy in "Marat/Sade," "The Littlest Circus," "The Innocents."

BLUM, MARK. Born May 14, 1950 in Newark, NJ. Graduate UPa., UMinn. Debut 1976 OB in "The Cherry Orchard," followed by "Green Julia," "Say Goodnight, Gracie," "Table Settings," "Key Exchange," "Loving Reno."

BODLE, JANE. Born Nov. 12 in Lawrence KS. Attended UUtah. Bdwy debut 1983 in "Cats."

BOFSHEVER, MICHAEL. Born Oct. 12, 1950 in Brooklyn, NY. Graduate Boston U. Debut 1981 OB in "Romance," followed by "Saigon Rose."

BOGOK, GUSTI. Born Sept. 24 in San Francisco, CA. Attended UCLA, Cal Arts, New School. Bdwy debut 1978 in "The King and I," OB in "Don Juan in Hell," "Douglas and Isabel," "Kurt Weill Cabaret," "Mercury Descending," "Lennon."

BONACKI, LOU. Born Apr. 3, 1943 in Brooklyn, NY. Attended Bklyn Col., HB Studio. Debut OB 1970 in "Sonata for Mott St.," followed by "Around the Corner from the White House," "Le Petit Mort."

BONDS, ROBERT. Born Feb. 27, 1933 in Pasadena, CA. Attended LACC. Debut 1975 OB in "Another Language," followed by "Heartbreak House," "The Actors."

BOOCKVOR, STEVEN. Born Nov. 18, 1942 in NYC. Attended Queens Col., Juilliard. Bdwy debut 1966 in "Anya," followed by "A Time for Singing," "Cabaret," "Mardi Gras," "Jimmy," "Billy," "The Rothschilds," "Follies," "Over Here," "The Lieutenant," "Musical Jubilee," "Annie," "Working," "The First," "A Chorus Line."

BORDEN, MARSHALL. Born Aug. 10, 1935 in Howell, MI. Graduate Wayne State U., Detroit U. Debut 1970 on Bdwy in "The Cherry Orchard," followed by "We Interrupt This Program," OB in "In Agony."

BORN, LYNN P. Born Aug. 6, 1956 in Richmond, VA. Attended Northwestern U. Debut 1982 OB in "Catholic School Girls," followed by "Nag and Nell," "Stifled Growls."

BOROWITZ, KATHERINE. Born in Chicago, IL. Graduate Yale, Harvard. Debut 1982 OB in "Cloud 9," followed by "Lennon."

BOSCO, PHILIP. Born Sept. 26, 1930 in Jersey City, NJ. Graduate Catholic U. Credits: "Auntie Mame," "Rape of the Belt," "Ticket of Leave Man," "Donnybrook," "Man for All Seasons," "Mrs. Warren's Profession," with LCRep in "The Alchemist," "East Wind," "Galileo," "St. Joan," "Tiger at the Gate," "Cyrano," "King Lear," "A Great Career," "In the Matter of J. Robert Oppenheimer," "The Miser," "The Time of Your Life," "Camino Real," "Operation Sidewinder," "Amphitryon," "Enemy of the People," "Playboy of the Western World," "Good Woman of Setzuan," "Antigone," "Mary Stuart," "Narrow Road to the Deep North," "The Crucible," "Twelfth Night," "Enemies," "Plough and the Stars," "Merchant of Venice," and "A Streetcar Named Desire," "Henry V," "Threepenny Opera," "Streamers," "Stages," "St. Joan," "The Biko Inquest," "Man and Superman," "Whose Life Is It Anyway," "Major Barbara," "A Month in the Country," "Bacchae," "Hedda Gabler," "Don Juan in Hell," "Inadmissible Evidence," "Eminent Domain," "Misalliance," "Learned Ladies," "Some Men Need Help," "Ah, Wilderness!," "The Caine Mutiny Court Martial."

BOTMA, JACOB. Born Feb. 24, 1957 in Ottawa, Ont., Can. Attended HB Studio. Debut 1981 OB in "The Picture of Dorian Gray," followed by "The Importance of Being Earnest," "Playboy of the Western World," "Dear Brutus," "Jerry Lane Is in Hiding," "The Cenci," "Salome."

BOUTSIKARIS, DENNIS. Born Dec. 21, 1952 in Newark, NJ. Graduate Hampshire Col. Debut 1975 OB in "Another Language," followed by "Funeral March for a One-Man Band," "All's Well That Ends Well," "A Day in the Life of the Czar," Bdwy in "Filumena," "Bent," "Amadeus."

BOVA, JOSEPH. Born May 25 in Cleveland, OH. Graduate Northwestern U. Debut 1959 OB in "On the Town," followed by "Once Upon a Mattress," "House of Blue Leaves," "Comedy," "The Beauty Part," "Taming of the Shrew," "Richard III," "Comedy of Errors," "Invitation to a Beheading," "Merry Wives of Windsor," "Henry V," "Streamers," Bdwy in "Rape of the Belt," "Irma La Douce," "Hot Spot," "The Chinese," "American Millionaire," "St. Joan," "42nd Street."

BOVASSO, JULIE. Born Aug. 1, 1930 in Brooklyn, NY. Attended CCNY. Bdwy in "Monique," "Minor Miracle," "Gloria and Esperanza," OB in "Naked," "The Maids," "The Lesson," "The Typewriter," "Screens," "Henry IV Part I," "What I Did Last Summer."

BOWERS, JEANIE. Born Apr. 18, 1953 in Greenville, OH. Graduate IndU., Miami U. Bdwy debut 1982 in "Nine."

BOWMAN, REGIS. Born Aug. 22, 1935 in Butler, PA. Graduate WVaU. Debut 1980 OB in "Room Service," followed by "T.N.T," "Not Now, Darling."

BOYDEN, PETER. Born July 19, 1945 in Leominster, MA. Graduate St. Anselm Col., Smith Col. Debut OB in "One Flew Over the Cuckoo's Nest," followed by "Nice Girls," "Claw," "Berkeley Square," "Pericles," "Pig!," "Smart Alek," "Booth," Bdwy in "Whoopee!" (1979).

BOYLE, ROBERT. Born Mar. 28, 1950 in Patton, PA. Graduate Carnegie-Mellon U. Debut 1980 OB in "Merton of the Movies" followed by "Pericles," "King of Hearts," "What a Life!," Bdwy in "Alice in Wonderland" (1982).

BOZYK, REIZL (ROSE). Born May 13, 1914 in Poland. Star of many Yiddish productions before 1966 Bdwy debut in "Let's Sing Yiddish," followed by "Sing, Israel, Sing," "Mirele Efros," OB in "Light, Lively and Yiddish," "Rebecca, the Rabbi's Daughter," "Wish Me Mazel-Tov," "Roumanian Wedding," "The Showgirl."

BRASINGTON, ALAN. Born in Monticello, NY. Attended RADA. Bdwy debut 1968 in "Pantagleize," followed by "The Misanthrope," "Cock-a-Doodle Dandy," "Hamlet," "Patriot For Me," "Shakespeare's Cabaret," "Merlin," OB in "Sterling Silver," "Charlotte Sweet."

BRAUN, RALPH. Born Aug. 20, 1946 in Milwaukee, WI. Graduate Carroll Col, UVa. Bdwy debut 1974 in "Irene," followed by "The Music Man," "Copperfield," OB in "Pirates of Penzance," "Nathan the Wise," "The Specialist," "Promises, Promises."

BREED, HELEN LLOYD. Born Jan. 27, 1911 in NYC. Debut 1956 OB in "Out of This World," followed by "Winners," "Exiles," "Something Unspoken," "You Never Can Tell," "Liliom," "The Hollow," "Chalk Garden," "Ring Round the Moon," "Richard II," "Kind Lady," "A Little Night Music," "The Holly and the Ivy."

BREEN, J. PATRICK. Born Oct. 26, 1960 in Brooklyn, NY. Graduate NYU. Debut 1982 OB in "Epiphany," Bdwy in "Brighton Beach Memoirs" (1983).

BRENNAN, MAUREEN. Born Oct. 11, 1952 in Washington, DC. Attended UCin. Bdwy debut 1974 in "Candide" for which she received a Theatre World Award, followed by "Going Up," "Knickerbocker Holiday," "Little Johnny Jones," OB in "Shakespeare's Cabaret."

BRENNAN, TOM. Born Apr. 16, 1926 in Cleveland, OH. Graduate Oberlin, Western Reserve. Debut 1958 OB in "Synge Trilogy," followed by "Between Two Thieves," "Easter," "All in Love," "Under Milkwood," "An Evening with James Purdy," "Golden Six," "Pullman Car Hiawatha," "Are You Now or Have You . . . ," "Diary of Anne Frank," "Milk of Paradise," "Transcendental Love," "The Beaver Coat," "The Overcoat," "Summer," "Asian Shade."

BRENNER, RANDY. Born Oct. 4, 1955 in Philadelphia, PA. Attended Temple U., HB Studio. Debut 1982 OB in "New Faces of 1952."

BRIAN, MICHAEL. Born Nov. 14, 1958 in Utica, NY. Attended Boston Conservatory. Debut 1979 OB in "Kennedy's Children," followed by "Street Scene," "Death of Von Richthofen as Witnessed From Earth."

BRILL, FRAN. Born Sept. 30 in PA. Attended Boston U. Bdwy debut 1969 in "Red, White and Maddox," OB in "What Every Woman Knows," "Scribes," "Naked," "Look Back in Anger," "Knuckle," "Skirmishes."

BROCKLIN, JEFFERY. Born Nov. 10, 1952 in Gate City, VA. Graduate UTn. Debut 1982 OB in "Oh, Johnny!," followed by "Robin Hood."

BROCKSMITH, ROY. Born Sept. 15, 1945 in Quincy, IL. Debut 1971 OB in "Whip Lady," followed by "The Workout," "Beggar's Opera," "Polly," "Threepenny Opera," "The Master and Margarita," "Jungle of Cities," "Don Juan," Bdwy in "The Leaf People" (1975), "Stages," "Tartuffe."

BRODERICK, MATTHEW. Born Mar. 21, 1963 in NYC. Debut OB 1981 in "Torch Song Trilogy," Bdwy 1983 in "Brighton Beach Memoirs" for which he received a Theatre World Award.

BROMKA, ELAINE. Born Jan. 6 in Rochester, NY. Smith Col. graduate. Debut 1975 OB in "The Dybbuk," followed by "Naked," "Museum," "The Son," "Inadmissible Evidence," "The Double Game," "Cloud 9," Bdwy 1982 in "Macbeth."

BROOK, PAMELA. Born Jan. 21, 1947 in London, Ont. Can. Graduate UToronto, UMn. Debut 1976 OB in "The Philanderer," followed by "The Holly and the Ivy," Bdwy in "Goodbye Fidel" (1980).

BROOKES, JACQUELINE. Born July 24, 1930 in Montclair, NJ. Graduate UIowa, RADA. Bdwy debut 1955 in "Tiger at the Gates," followed by "Watercolor," "Abelard and Heloise," OB in "The Cretan Woman" for which she received a Theatre World Award, "The Clandestine Marriage," "Measure for Measure," "Duchess of Malfi," "Ivanov," "Six Characters in Search of an Author," "An Evening's Frost," "Come Slowly, Eden," "The Increased Difficulty of Concentration," "The Persians," "Sunday Dinner," "House of Blue Leaves," "A Meeting by the River," "Owners," "Hallelujah," "Dream of a Blacklisted Actor," "Knuckle," "Mama Sang the Blues," "Buried Child," "On Mt. Chimorazo," "Winter Dancers," "Hamlet," "Old Flames," "The Diviners," "Richard II," "Vieux Carre."

BROOKS, ALAN. Born July 11, 1950 in Bakersfield, CA. Graduate Occidental Col., FlStateU. Debut 1978 OB in "Porno Stars at Home," followed by "Dr. Faustus," "Merchant of Venice," "The Cuchulain Cycle," "The Changeling."

BROOKS, RUTH. Born Nov. 11, 1920 in Omaha, NE. Attended NYCC, New School. Debut OB 1982 in "Orpheus Descending."

BROTHERS, JON. Born Feb. 16, 1957 in Lynn, MA. Graduate Emerson Col. Debut 1980 OB in "The Desert Song," followed by "The Student Prince," "Where's Charley?"

BROWN, GRAHAM. Born Oct. 24 in NYC. Graduate Howard U. OB in "Widower's Houses," "The Emperor's Clothes," "Time of Storm," "Major Barbara," "Land Beyond the River," "The Blacks," "Firebugs," "God Is a (Guess What?)," "An Evening of One Acts," "Man Better Man," "Behold! Cometh the Vanderkellans," "Ride a Black Horse," "The Great MacDaddy," "Eden," "Nevis Mountain Dew," "Season Unravel," "The Devil's Tear," "Sons and Fathers of Sons," "Abercrombie Apocalypse," Bdwy in "Weekend," "Man in the Glass Booth," "River Niger," "Pericles," "Black Picture Show," "Kings."

BROWN, KERMIT. Born Feb. 3, 1937 in Asheville, NC. Graduate Duke U. With APA in "War and Peace," "Man and Superman," "The Show-Off," "Pantagleize," "The Cherry Orchard," OB in "The Millionairess," "Things," "Lulu," "Heartbreak House," "Glad Tidings," "Anyone Can Whistle," "Facade," "The Arcata Promise," "A Midsummer Night's Dream."

BROWN, SHARON. Born Jan. 11, 1962 in NYC. Bdwy debut 1967 in "Maggie Flynn," followed by "Joseph and the Amazing Technicolor Dream Coat."

BROWNE, ROSCOE LEE. Born in 1925 in Woodbury, NJ. Attended Lincoln U, Columbia; Debut OB in "Julius Caesar," followed by "Taming of the Shrew," "Titus Andronicus," "Romeo and Juliet," "Othello," "Aria da Capo," "The Blacks," "Brecht on Brecht," "King Lear," "Winter's Tale," "The Empty Room," "Hell Is Other People," "Benito Cereno," "Troilus and Cressida," "Danton's Death," "Volpone," "Dream on Monkey Mountain," "Behind the Broken Words," Bdwy in "General Seeger" (1962), "Tiger, Tiger Burning Bright," "Ballad of the Sad Cafe," "A Hand Is on the Gate," "My One and Only."

BRUMMEL, DAVID. Born Nov. 1, 1942 in Brooklyn, NY. Bdwy debut 1973 in "The Pajama Game," followed by "Music Is," "Oklahoma!," OB in "Cole Porter," "The Fantasticks."

BRUZZESE, ELIZABETH. Born Aug. 6, 1958 in New Brunswick, NJ. Attended Parsons School. Debut 1981 OB in "Godspell," followed by "Boogie-Woogie Rumble."

BRYAN, KENNETH. Born July 30, 1953 in New Jersey. Graduate IndU. Bdwy debut 1981 in "Joseph and the Amazing Technicolor Dreamcoat."

BRYANT, DAVID. Born May 26, 1936 in Nashville, TN. Attended TnStateU. Bdwy debut 1972 in "Don't Play Us Cheap," followed by "Bubbling Brown Sugar," "Amadeus."

BRYDON, W. B. Born Sept. 20, 1933 in Newcastle, Eng. Debut 1962 OB in "The Long, the Short and the Tall," followed by "Live Like Pigs," "Sjt. Musgrave's Dance," "The Kitchen," "Come Slowly Eden," "The Unknown Soldier and His Wife," "Moon for the Misbegotten," "The Orphan," "Possession," "Total Abandon," Bdwy in "The Lincoln Mask," "Ulysses in Nighttown," "The Father."

BRYGGMAN, LARRY. Born Dec. 21, 1938 in Concord, CA. Attended CCSF, AmThWing. Debut 1962 OB in "A Pair of Pairs" followed by "Live Like Pigs," "Stop, You're Killing Me,", "Mod Donna," "Waiting for Godot," "Ballymurphy," "Marco Polo Sings a Solo," "Brownsville Raid," "Two Small Bodies," "Museum," "Winter Dancers," "The Resurrection of Lady Lester," "Royal Bob," "Modern Ladies of Guanabacoa," Bdwy in "Ulysses in Nighttown," "Checking Out," "Basic Training of Pavlo Hummel," "Richard III."

BUCKLEY, BETTY. Born July 3, 1947 in Big Spring, TX. Graduate TCU. Bdwy debut 1969 in "1776," followed by "Pippin," "Cats," OB in "Ballad of Johnny Pot," "What's a Nice Country Like You . . . ," "Circle of Sound," "I'm Getting My Act Together . . ."

BUFFALOE, KATHARINE. Born Nov. 7, 1953 in Greenville, SC. Graduate NC School of Arts. Bdwy debut 1981 in "Copperfield," followed by "Joseph and the Amazing Technicolor Dreamcoat."

BURCH, SHELLY. Born Mar. 19, 1960 in Tucson, AZ. Attended Carnegie-Mellon U. Bdwy debut 1978 in "Stop the World I Want to Get Off," followed by "Annie," "Nine."

BURKS, STEPHEN. Born July 5, 1956 in Belleville, IL. Graduate Boston U. Debut 1980 on Bdwy in "Division Street," OB in "Steel on Steel."

BURRELL, TERRY. Born Feb. 8, 1952 in Trinidad, WI. Graduate Pace U. Bdwy debut 1977 in "Eubie!," followed by "Dreamgirls."

BURSTYN, ELLEN. Born Dec. 7, 1932 in Detroit, MI. Attended Actors Studio. Bdwy debut 1957 (as Ellen McRae) in "Fair Game," followed by "Same Time Next Year," "84 Charing Cross Road," OB in "The Three Sisters," "Andromeda II."

BURTON, KATE. Born Sept. 10, 1957 in Geneva, Switz. Graduate Brown U., Yale. Bdwy debut 1982 in "Present Laughter," followed by "Alice in Wonderland," OB in "Winners" for which she received a Theatre World Award.

BURTON, RICHARD. Born Nov. 10, 1925 in Pontrhydyfen, S.Wales. Attended Exeter Col., Oxford. Bdwy debut 1950 in "The Lady's Not for Burning" for which he received a Theatre World Award, followed by "Legend of Lovers," "Time Remembered," "Camelot" (1960/1980), "Hamlet," "Equus," "Private Lives."

BURTON, WARREN. Born Oct. 23, 1944 in Chicago, IL. Graduate Wright Col. Bdwy debut 1967 in "Hair," followed by "A Patriot for Me," OB in "P.S. Your Cat Is Dead," followed by "The Truth."

BUSSERT, MEG. Born Oct. 21, 1949 in Chicago, IL. Attended UIll, HB Studio. Bdwy debut 1980 in "The Music Man" for which she received a Theatre World Award, followed by "Brigadoon," "Camelot," "New Moon," "Lola" (OB), "The Firefly."

BYRD, LILLIAN M. Born Dec. 15, 1952 in Memphis, TN. Graduate Memphis State U. Debut 1982 OB in "Murder on the Nile," followed by "110 in the Shade."

Jack Aaron

Loni Ackerman

Ted Agress

Karen Akers

Terry Alexander

Deborah Allison

Maureen
Anderman

Kenneth Anders

Christine Andreas

Philip Anglim

Rebecca Armen

Lawrence Asher

Tony Aylward

Lisa Bansavage

Brian Backer

Judith Barcroft

John Barone

Laurinda
Barrett

Katherine Barry

George Bartenieff

D'Jamin Bartlett

Richard Battalion

Terry Baughan

Louis Beachner

Harry Bennett

Anna Berger

Peter Blaxill

Jane Bodle

Graham Brown

Terry Burrell

CADEN, PAMELA. Born Mar. 14, 1954 in NYC. Graduate NYU, Queens Col. Debut 1982 OB in "A Night of Scenes."

CADIFF, KAY. Born Nov. 11 in Ft. Collins, CO. Attended Kansas State U. Debut 1976 OB in "The Boys from Syracuse," followed by "Oh, Coward!," "Mary," "Romance Is," "Beggar's Opera."

CAHILL, JAMES. Born May 31, 1940 in Brooklyn, NY. Bdwy debut 1967 in "Marat/deSade," followed by "Break a Leg," OB in "The Hostage," "The Alchemist," "Johnny Johnson," "Peer Gynt," "Timon of Athens," "An Evening for Merlin Finch," "The Disintegration of James Cherry," "Crimes of Passion," "Rain," "Screens," "Total Eclipse," "Entertaining Mr. Sloane," "Hamlet," "Othello," "The Trouble with Europe," "Lydie Breeze," "Don Juan," "Bathroom Plays," "Wild Life."

CAHN, CATHY. Born Apr. 26, 1954 in NYC. Graduate Antioch U., AADA. Debut OB 1982 in "Snoopy."

CALLAN, MICHAEL. Born Nov. 22, 1935 in Philadelphia, PA. Bdwy credits include "The Boy Friend," "Catch a Star," "West Side Story," "Pay Joey in Concert."

CALLMAN, NANCY. Born Apr. 12, 1949 in Buffalo, NY. Graduate SUNY/Binghamton, Manhattan Sch. of Music. Bdwy debut 1976 in "1600 Pennsylvania Ave.," followed by "Sweeney Todd," "Nine," OB in "Circa 1900," "Broadway a la Carte," "Hit Tunes from Flop Shows."

CAMERON, HOPE. Born Feb. 21, 1920 in Hartford, Ct. Attended AADA. Bdwy debut 1947 in "All My Sons," followed by "Death of a Salesman," OB in "The Strindberg Brothers," "The Last Days of Lincoln," "Grace," "Skirmishes."

CAMP, JOANNE. Born Apr. 4, 1951 in Atlanta, GA. Graduate FlAtlanticU, Geo WashU. Debut 1981 OB in "The Dry Martini," followed by "Geniuses," for which she received a Theatre World Award.

CANARY, DAVID. Born Aug. 25 in Elwood, IN. Graduate UCin, Cinn. Conservatory. Debut 1960 OB in "Kittywake Island," followed by "The Fantasticks," "The Father," "Hi, Paisano," "Summer," "Blood Moon," Bdwy in "Great Day in the Morning," "Happiest Girl in the World," "Clothes for a Summer Hotel."

CAPUCILLI, BILL. Born Oct. 1, 1951 in Syracuse, NY. Attended Auburn Col. Debut 1983 OB in "The Firebugs."

CAREY, DAVID. Born Nov. 16, 1945 in Brookline, MA. Graduate Boston U, Ohio U. Debut 1969 OB in "Oh, What a Wedding," followed by "Let's Sing Yiddish," "Dad Get Married," "Light, Lively and Yiddish," "Wedding in Shtetl," "Big Winna," "Rebecca, the Rabbi's Daughter," "Wish Me Mazel-Tov," "Roumanian Wedding," "The Showgirl."

CARIOU, LEN. Born Sept. 30, 1939 in Winnipeg. Can. Bdwy debut 1968 in "House of Atreus," followed by "Henry V" and "Applause" for which he received a Theatre World Award, "Night Watch," "A Little Night Music," "Cold Storage," "Sweeney Todd," "Dance a Little Closer," OB in "A Sorrow Beyond Dreams," "Up from Paradise."

CARLIN, CHET. Born Feb. 23, 1940 in Malverne, NY. Graduate Ithaca Col., Catholic U. Bdwy bow 1972 in "An Evening with Richard Nixon . . . ," OB in "Under Gaslight," "Lou Gehrig Did Not Die of Cancer," "Graffiti!," "Crystal and Fox," "Golden Honeymoon," "Arms and the Man," "Arsenic and Old Lace," "The Father."

CARLIN, THOMAS A. Born Dec. 10, 1928 in Chicago, IL. Attended Loyola U. Catholic U. Credits include "Time Limit!," "Holiday for Lovers," "Man in the Dog Suit," "A Cook for Mr. General," "Great Day in the Morning," "A Thousand Clowns," "The Deputy," "Players," OB in "Thieves Carnival," "Brecht on Brecht," "Summer," "Wonderland," "Solitude 40," "Royal Bob."

CARLING, P. L. Born March 31. Graduate Stanford, UCLA. Debut 1955 OB in "The Chairs," followed by "In Good King Charles' Golden Days," "Magistrate," "Picture of Dorian Gray," "The Vise," "Lady From the Sea," "Booth Is Back In Town," "Ring Round the Moon," "Philadelphia, Here I Come," "Sorrows of Frederick," "Biography," "Murder on the Nile," "Three Lost Plays of O'Neill," Bdwy in "The Devils" (1965), "Scratch," "Shenandoah."

CARLISLE, KITTY. Born Sept. 3, 1915 in New Orleans, LA. Attended RADA. Bdwy debut 1932 in "Rio Rita," followed by "Champagne, Sec," "White Horse Inn," "Three Waltzes," "Walk With Music," "The Rape of Lucretia," "Anniversary Waltz," "Kiss Me, Kate" (CC'56), "On Your Toes."

CARLO, JOHANN. Born May 21, 1957 in Buffalo, NY. Attended London's Webber-Douglass Academy. Debut 1978 OB in "Grand Magic," followed by "Artichoke," "Don Juan Comes Back From the War," Bdwy in "Plenty" (1983).

CARLSEN, ALLAN. Born Feb. 7 in Chicago, IL. Attended UPa. Bdwy debut 1974 in "The Freedom of the City," OB in "The Morning After Optimism," "Iphigenia in Aulis," "Peg O' My Heart," "Star Treatment," "Starry Night," "Journey to Gdansk," "Accounts."

CARRADINE, KEITH. Born Aug. 8, 1951 in San Mateo, Ca. Attended ColStateU. Bdwy debut 1969 in "Hair," followed by "Foxfire," OB in "Wake Up, It's Time to Go to Bed."

CARROLL, DANNY. Born May 30, 1940 in Maspeth, NY. Bdwy bow in 1957 in "The Music Man," followed by "Flora the Red Menace," "Funny Girl," "George M!," "Billy," "Ballroom," "42nd Street," OB in "Boys from Syracuse," "Babes in the Woods."

CARROLL, DAVID-JAMES. Born July 30, 1950 in Rockville, Centre, NY. Graduate Dartmouth Col. Debut 1975 OB in "A Matter of Time," followed by "Joseph and the Amazing Technicolor Dreamcoat," "New Tunes," Bdwy in "Rodgers and Hart" (1975), "Where's Charley?," "Oh, Brother!," "7 Brides for 7 Brothers."

CARROLL, DIAHANN. Born July 17, 1935 in NYC. Attended NYU. Bdwy debut 1954 in "House of Flowers," followed by "No Strings," "Agnes of God."

196 CARRUBBA, PHILIP. Born May 3, 1951 in San Francisco, Ca. Graduate SFStateU. Bdwy debut 1981 in "Joseph and the Amazing Technicolor Dreamcoat."

CARRUTHERS, JAMES. Born May 26, 1931 in Morristown, NJ. Attended Lafayette Col., HB Studio. Debut 1959 OB in "Our Town," followed by "Under the Sycamore Tree," "Misalliance," "The Hostage," "Telemachus Clay," "Shadow of a Gunman," "Masks," "Biography: A Game," "Lulu," "Salt Lake City Skyline," "Journey to Gdansk," Bdwy in "Poor Murderer" (1976).

CARTER, DIXIE. Born May 25, 1939 in McLemoresville, TN. Graduate Memphis State U. Debut 1963 OB in "Winter's Tale," followed by "Carousel," "Merry Widow," "The King and I" (LC), "Sextet," "Jesse and the Bandit Queen" for which she received a Theatre World Award, "Fathers and Sons," "A Coupla White Chicks . . . ," "Taken in Marriage," "Buried Inside Extra," Bdwy in "Pal Joey" (1976).

CARTER, MYRA. Born Oct. 27, 1930 in Chicago, IL. Attended Glasgow U. Bdwy debut 1957 in "Major Barbara," followed by "Maybe Tuesday," "Trials of OZ" (OB), "Present Laughter."

CARUSO, BARBARA. Born in East Orange, NJ. Graduate Douglass Col., RADA. Debut 1969 OB in "The Millionairess," followed by "Picture of Dorian Gray," "Wars of the Roses," "Chez Nous," "Ride a Cock Horse," "Inadmissible Evidence," "Ned and Jack," "Candida in Concert," "The 12 Pound Look," "The Browning Version," Bdwy in "Night of the Iguana" (1976).

CASS, PEGGY. Born May 21, 1926 in Boston, MA. Attended Wyndham Sch. Credits include "Touch and Go," "Live Wire," "Bernardine," "Othello," "Henry V," "Auntie Mame" for which she received a Theatre World Award, "A Thurber Carnival," "Children from Their Games," "Don't Drink the Water," "Front Page" (1969), "Plaza Suite," "Once a Catholic," "42nd Street," OB in "Phoenix '55," "Are You Now or Have You Ever Been."

CASSIDY, DAVID. Born Apr. 12, 1950 in NYC. Bdwy debut 1969 in "Fig Leaves Are Falling," followed by "Joseph and the Amazing Technicolor Dreamcoat."

CASSIDY, TIM. Born March 22, 1952 in Alliance, OH. Attended UCincinnati. Bdwy debut 1974 in "Good News," followed by "A Chorus Line."

CASTANG, VERONICA. Born Apr. 22 in London, Eng. Attended Sorbonne. Bdwy debut 1946 in "How's the World Treating You?," followed by "The National Health," "Whose Life Is It Anyway?," OB in "The Trigon," "Sjt. Musgrave's Dance," "Saved," "Water Hens," "Self-Accusation," "Kaspar," "Ionescapade," "Statements After and Arrest under the Immorality Act," "Ride a Cock Horse," "Banana Box," "Bonjour La Bonjour," "A Call From the East," "Close of Play," "Cloud 9," "After the Prize," "David and Paula."

CATES, MADLYN. Born Mar. 8, 1925 in NYC. Attended Queens Col. Debut 1965 OB in "Sunset," followed by "The Kitchen," "Max," Bdwy in "Marat/deSade" (1966), "A Patriot for Me."

CATLETT, MARY JO. Born Sept. 2, 1938 in Denver, CO. Graduate Loretto Hts. Col. Credits include "Along Came a Spider," "Promenade," "Greenwillow," "Fashion," Bdwy in "New Girl in Town," "Fiorello," "Pajama Game," "Hello, Dolly!," "Canterbury Tales," "Different Times," "Lysistrata," "Play Me a Country Song."

CHAIKIN, SHAMI. Born Apr. 21, 1931 in NYC. Debut 1966 OB in "America Hurrah," followed by "Serpent," "Terminal," "Mutation Show," "Viet Rock," "Mystery Play," "Electra," "The Dybbuk," "Endgame," "Bag Lady," "The Haggadah," "Antigone," "Loving Reno," "Early Warnings."

CHALFANT, KATHLEEN. Born Jan. 14, 1945 in San Francisco, CA. Graduate Stanford U. Bdwy debut 1975 in "Dance With Me," followed by OB "Jules Feiffer's Hold Me," "Killings on the Last Line," "The Boor," "Blood Relations."

CHAMBERLAIN, ROBERT. Born May 22 in NYC. Attended CUNY. Debut 1983 OB in "Dwarfs/A Slight Ache."

CHAMBERLIN, MARK. Born June 2, 1955 in Portland, OR. Graduate Whitman Col., AADA. Debut 1980 OB in "Sananda Sez," Bdwy in "84 Charing Cross Road" (1982).

CHAMBERLIN, SALLY. Born Dec. 26 in Cambridge, MA. Graduate Sarah Lawrence Col. Bdwy debut 1949 in "Twelfth Night," OB in "Julius Caesar," "Behind a Mask."

CHAMPAGNE, MICHAEL. Born Apr. 10, 1947 in New Bedford, MA. Graduate SMU, MSU. Debut 1975 OB in "The Lieutenant," followed by "Alinsky," "The Hostage," "Livingstone and Sechele," "A Christmas Carol," "Penelope."

CHANDLER, JEFFREY ALAN. Born Sept. 9 in Durham, NC. Graduate Carnegie-Mellon. Bdwy debut 1972 in "Elizabeth I," followed by "The Dresser," "Whodunnit," OB in "The People vs Ranchman," "Your Own Thing," "Penguin Touquet."

CHAPIN, TOM. Born Mar. 13, 1945 in Charlotte, NC. Graduate SUNY/Plattsburgh. Debut OB 1981 in "Cottonpatch Gospel," Bdwy in "Pump Boys and Dinettes" (1983).

CHAPMAN, ROGER. Born Jan. 1, 1947 in Cheverly, Md. Rollins Col. graduate. Debut 1976 OB in "Who Killed Richard Corey?," followed by "My Life," "Hamlet," "Innocent Thoughts, Harmless Intentions," "Richard II," "The Great Grandson of Jedediah Kohler," "Threads," "Time Framed."

CHARLES, WALTER. Born Apr. 4, 1945 in East Stroudsburg, PA. Graduate Boston U. Bdwy debut 1973 in "Grease," followed by "1600 Pennsylvania Avenue," "Knickerbocker Holiday," "Sweeney Todd," "Cats."

CHARNAY, LYNNE. Born Apr. 1 in NYC. Attended UWisc., Columbia, AADA. Debut 1950 OB in "Came the Dawn," followed by "A Ram's Horn," "In a Cold Hotel," "Amata," "Yerma," "Ballad of Winter Soldiers," "Intimate Relations," "Play Me Zoltan," "Grand Magic," "The Time of Your Life," "Nymph Errant," Bdwy in "Julia, Jake and Uncle Joe" (1961), "A Family Affair," "Broadway," "Inspector General," "Grand Tour."

CHARNEY, EVA. Born June 7 in Brooklyn, NY. Graduate Douglass Coll., Boston U. Debut 1977 OB in "NYC Street Show," followed by "The Wanderers," "Caligula," "I Can't Keep Running . . . ," "Battle of the Giants," "American Heroes," "The Rise of David Levinsky," Bdwy 1977 in "Hair."

CHATER, GORDON. Born Apr. 6, 1922 in London, Eng. Debut 1979 OB in "The Elocution of Benjamin," followed by "The Learned Ladies," "Major Barbara in Concert," Bdwy in "Whodunnit" (1982).

CHEN, TINA. Born Nov. 2 in Chung King, China. Graduate Brown U. Debut 1972 OB in "A Maid's Tragedy," followed by "Family Devotions," Bdwy in "The King and I," "Rashomon," "A Midsummer Night's Dream."

CHILDS, LUCINDA. Born June 26, 1940 in NYC. Graduate Sarah Lawrence. Debut 1977 OB in "I Was Sitting on My Patio . . . ," followed by "The Singular Life of Albert Nobbs."

CHOATE, TIM. Born Oct. 11, 1954 in Dallas, TX. Graduate UTx. Bdwy debut 1979 in "Da," followed by "Crimes of the Heart," OB in "Young Bucks," "Comedians."

CHRIS, MARILYN. Born May 19 in NYC. Appeared in "The Office," "Birthday Party," "7 Descents of Myrtle," "Lenny," OB in "Nobody Hears a Broken Drum," "Fame," "Juda Applause," "Junebug Graduates Tonight," "Man Is Man," "In the Jungle of Cities," "Good Soldier Schweik," "The Tempest," "Ride a Black Horse," "Screens," "Kaddish," "Lady From the Sea," "Bread," "Leaving Home," "Curtains," "Elephants," "The Upper Depths."

CHRISTIAN-JONES, LINDA. Born Mar. 19, 1947 in Tonawanda, NY. Graduate Wake Forest U. Debut 1977 OB in "The Bald Soprano," followed by "Partners."

CHRISTOPHER, JOYCE REEHLING. Born Mar. 5, 1949 in Baltimore, MD. Graduate NCSch of Arts. Debut 1976 OB in "Hot l Baltimore," followed by "Who Killed Richard Cory?," "Lulu," "5th of July," "The Runner Stumbles," "Life and/or Death," "Back in the Race," "Time Framed," "Extremities," Bdwy in "A Matter of Gravity" (1976), "5th of July."

CIESLA, DIANE. Born May 20, 1952 in Chicago, IL. Graduate Clarke Col. Debut 1980 OB in "Uncle Money," followed by "Afternoons in Vegas," "The Taming of the Shrew."

CLARK, BRYAN E. Born Apr. 5, 1929 in Louisville, KY. Graduate Fordham U. Bdwy debut 1978 in "A History of the American Film," followed by "Bent," OB in "Winning Isn't Everything," "Put Them All Together," "Red Rover."

CLARK, CHERYL. Born Dec. 7, 1950 in Boston, MA. Attended Ind. U., NYU. Bdwy debut 1972 in "Pippin," followed by "Chicago," "A Chorus Line."

CLARK, JOSH. Born Aug. 16, 1955 in Bethesda, MD. Attended NCSch. of Arts. Debut 1976 OB in "The Old Glory," followed by "Molly," "Just a Little Bit Less Than Normal," "Rear Column," "The Browning Version," "Accounts," Bdwy in "The Man Who Came to Dinner"(1980), "Alice in Wonderland."

CLARKE, CAITLIN. Born May 3, 1952 in Pittsburgh, PA. Graduate Mt. Holyoke Col., Yale. Debut 1981 OB in "No End of Blame," followed by "Lorenzaccio," "Summer," Bdwy in "Teaneck Tanzi" (1983).

CLARKE, RICHARD. Born Jan. 31, 1933 in England. Graduate UReading. With LCRep in "St. Joan" (1968), "Tiger at the Gates," "Cyrano de Bergerac," Bdwy in "Conduct Unbecoming" (1970), "The Elephant Man," OB in "Old Glory," "Looking-Glass."

CLEMENTE, RENE. Born July 2, 1950 in El Paso, TX. Graduate WestTxStateU. Bdwy debut 1977 in "A Chorus Line," followed by "Dancin'," "Play Me a Country Song," "Cats."

CLOSE, GLENN. Born May 19, 1947 in Greenwich, CT. Graduate William & Mary Col. Bdwy debut 1974 with Phoenix Co. in "Love for Love," "Member of the Wedding," and "Rules of the Game," followed by "Rex," "Crucifer of Blood," "Barnum," OB in "The Crazy Locomotive," "Uncommon Women and Others," "Wine Untouched," "The Winter Dancers," "The Singular Life of Albert Nobbs."

COCO, JAMES. Born Mar. 21, 1930 in NYC. Debut 1956 OB in "Salome," followed by "Moon in the Yellow River," "Squat Betty/The Sponge Room," "That 5 A.M. Jazz," "Lovey," "The Basement," "Fragments," "Witness," "Next," "Monsters (The Transfiguration of Benno Blimpie)," Bdwy in "Hotel Paradiso," "Everybody Loves Opal," "Passage to India," "Arturo Ui," "The Devils," "Man of LaMancha," "The Astrakan Coat," "Here's Where I Belong," "Last of the Red Hot Lovers," "Wally's Cafe," "Little Me," "You Can't Take It With You."

COHEN, JOYCE. Born Nov. 25, 1948 in West Hartford, CT. Graduate UNC. Debut 1975 OB in "Diamond Studs," followed by "It's Called the Sugar Plum." "Of Men and Angels," "Living at Home," "Primal Time," "Happy Birthday, Wanda June," Bdwy in "Once a Catholic" (1979).

COHENOUR, PATTI. Born Oct. 17, 1952 in Albuquerque, NMx. Attended UNMex. Bdwy debut 1982 in "A Doll's Life," followed by "Pirates of Penzance."

COLAHAN, LIBBY. Born Nov. 8, 1942 in California. Graduate UPacific, UCSan Diego. Debut 1983 OB in "Pericles," "Tartuffe," "Play and Other Plays."

COLE, KAY. Born Jan. 13, 1948 in Miami, FL. Bdwy debut 1961 in "Bye Bye Birdie," followed by "Stop the World I Want to Get Off," "Roar of the Greasepaint . . . ," "Hair," "Jesus Christ Superstar," "Words and Music," "Chorus Line," OB in "The Cradle Will Rock," "Two If By Sea," "Rainbow," "White Nights," "Sgt. Pepper's Lonely Hearts Club Band," "On the Swing Shift," "Snoopy."

COLE, NORA. Born Sept. 10, 1953 in Louisville, KY. Attended Beloit Col., Goodman School. Debut 1977 OB in "Movie Buff," followed by "Cartoons for a Lunch Hour," "Boogie-Woogie Rumble," Bdwy in "Your Arms Too Short to Box With God" (1982), "Inacent Black," "Runaways."

COLES, CHARLES HONI. Born Apr. 2, 1911 in Philadelphia, PA. Debut 1933 OB in "Humming Sam," Bdwy in "Gentlemen Prefer Blondes" (1949), "Black Broadway," "My One and Only."

COLLAMORE, JEROME. Born Sept. 25, 1891 in Boston, MA. Debut 1918 with Washington Square Players in "Salome," and subsequently in, among others, "Christopher Bean," "Hamlet," "Romeo and Juliet," "Kind Lady," "Androcles and the Lion," "George Washington Slept Here," "The Would-Be Gentleman," "Cheri," "Abraham Cochran," "That Hat," Bam Co.'s "New York Idea," "Trouping Since 1912," "The Dresser," "Three Sisters," "That's It, Folks."

COLLYER, EVE. Born Nov. 26, 1927 in Pittsburgh, PA. Graduate Carnegie Tech. Bdwy debut 1959 in "The Music Man," followed by "Gideon," "Arturo Ui," "Right Honourable Gentleman," OB in "Way of the World," "Morning's at 7," "The Adding Machine," "Don Juan in Hell," "Diversions," "Love Affairs and Wedding Bells."

COLYER, AUSTIN. Born Oct. 29, 1935 in Brooklyn, NY. Attended SMU. Credits include "Darwin's Theories," "Let It Ride," "Maggie Flynn," "Brigadoon," "The Music Man," "How to Succeed in Business . . . ," "Jimmy," "Desert Song," "Pal Joey," "I Remember Mama," "Show Me Where the Good Times Are," "Where's Charley?"

CONNELL, DAVID. Born Nov. 24, 1935 in Cleveland, OH. Bdwy Bow 1968 in "The Great White Hope," Followed By "Don't Play Us Cheap," OB in "Ballet Behind the Bridge," "Miracle Play," "Time Out of Time," "Champeen!"

CONNELL, GORDON. Born Mar. 19, 1923 in Berkeley, CA. Graduate UCal, NYU. Bdwy debut 1961 in "Subways Are for Sleeping," followed by "Hello, Dolly!," "Lysistrata," OB in "Beggar's Opera," "The Butler Did It," "With Love and Laughter."

CONNELL, JANE. Born Oct. 27, 1925 in Berkeley, CA. Attended UCal. Bdwy debut in "New Faces of 1956," followed by "Drat! The Cat!," "Mame," "Dear World," "Lysistrata," OB in "Shoestring Revue," "Threepenny Opera," "Pieces of Eight," "Demi-Dozen," "She Stoops to Conquer," "Drat!," "The Real Inspector Hound," "The Rivals," "The Rise and Rise of Daniel Rocket."

CONNER, BYRON. Born Dec. 5, 1953 in Gadsden, AL. Graduate Ithaca Col. Debut 1978 OB in "The Taming of the Shrew," followed by "On a Clear Day," "Florodora," "Where's Charley?"

CONNOLLY, MICHAEL. Born Sept. 22, 1947 in Boston, MA. Graduate Fordham U. Bdwy debut 1977 in "Otherwise Engaged," followed by "Break a Leg," "Clothes for a Summer Hotel,," "Copperfield," "Amadeus," OB in "Hijinks."

CONROY, FRANCES. Born in 1953 in Monroe, GA. Attended Dickinson Col., Juilliard, Neighborhood Playhouse. Debut 1978 OB with the Acting Co. in "Mother Courage," "King Lear," "The Other Half," followed by "All's Well That Ends Well," "Othello," "Sorrows of Stephen," "Girls Girls Girls," "Zastrozzi," "Painting Churches," Bdwy 1980 in "The Lady from Dubuque."

CONROY, JARLATH. Born Sept. 30, 1944 in Galway, IR. Attended RADA. Bdwy debut 1976 in "Comedians," followed by "The Elephant Man," "Macbeth," OB in "Translations," "The Wind That Shook the Barley," "Gardenia," "Friends."

CONRY, KATHLEEN. Born Nov. 15, 1947 in Cleveland, OH. Bdwy debut 1968 in "George M!," followed by "No, No Nanette," OB in "The Sign in Sidney Brustein's Window," "Suffragette," "Promises, Promises."

CONVY, BERT. Born July 23, 1935 in St. Louis, MO. Graduate UCLA. Bdwy debut 1959 in "Billy Barnes Revue," followed by "Nowhere To Go But Up," "Morning Sun," "Love and Kisses," "Fiddler On the Roof," "The Impossible Years," "Cabaret," "Shoot Anything with Hair That Moves" (OB), "The Front Page," "Nine."

COOK, JILL. Born FEb. 25, 1954 in Plainfield, NJ. Bdwy debut 1971 in "On the Town," followed by "So Long, 174th Street," "Dancin'," "Best Little Whorehouse in Texas," "Perfectly Frank," OB in "Carnival," "Potholes," "My One and Only."

COOK, LINDA. Born June 8 in Lubbock, TX. Attended Auburn U. Debut 1974 OB in "The Wager," followed by "Hole in the Wall," "Shadow of a Gunman," "Be My Father," "Ghosts of the Loyal Oaks," "Different People, Different Rooms," "Saigon Rose."

COOK, RODERICK. Born 1932 in London. Attended Cambridge U. Bdwy debut 1961 in "Kean," followed by "Roar Like a Dove," "The Girl Who Came to Supper," "Noel Coward's Sweet Potato," "The Man Who Came to Dinner," "Woman of the Year," "Eileen," OB in "A Scent of Flowers," "Oh, Coward!"

COOPER, BOB, JR. Born Sept. 19, 1941 in Grand Rapids, MI. Graduate WesternMiU. Debut 1980 OB in "The Devil's Disciple," followed by "School for Scandal," "The Price of Genius."

COOPER, CHRISTOPHER. Born July 9, 1951 in Kansas City, MO. Attended UMo. Bdwy debut 1980 in "Of the Fields Lately," followed by OB's "A Different Moon."

COPELAND, JOAN. Born June 1, 1922 in NYC. Attended Brooklyn Col., AADA. Debut 1945 OB in "Romeo and Juliet," followed by "Othello," "Conversation Piece," "Delightful Season," "End of Summer," "The American Clock," "The Double Game," Bdwy in "Sundown Beach," "Detective Story," "Not for Children," "Hatful of Fire," "Something More," "The Price," "Two by Two," "Pal Joey," "Checking Out," "The American Clock."

COPELAND, MAURICE. Born June 13, 1911 in Rector, AR. Graduate Pasadena Playhouse. Bdwy debut 1974 in "The Freedom of the City," followed by "The First Monday in October," "Morning's at 7," OB in "Henry V," "Blood Relations."

COPPLE, TY. Born Aug. 3, 1952 in Little Rock, AR. Graduate UArk. Debut 1982 OB in "Andrea's Got Two Boyfriends."

COPPOLA, SAM J. Born July 31, 1935 in NJ. Attended Actors Studio. Debut 1968 OB in "A Present From Your Old Man," followed by "Things That Almost Happen," "Detective Story," "Jungle of Cities," Bdwy 1983 in "The Caine Mutiny Court-Martial."

CORCORAN, DANIEL. Born Oct. 8, 1952 in Capague, NY. Graduate Carnegie-Mellon U., Cal. Inst. of Arts. Debut 1978 OB with the Acting Company in "King Lear," followed by "Broadway," "Leaving Home," "Mother Courage and Her Children," "The Cradle Will Rock."

CORFMAN, CARIS. Born May 18, 1955 in Boston, MA. Graduate FlaStateU, Yale. Debut 1978 OB in "Wings," followed by "Fish Riding Bikes," Bdwy 1980 in "Amadeus."

CORREN, DONALD. Born June 5, 1952 in Stockton, CA. Attended Juilliard. Bdwy debut 1980 in "A Day in Hollywood/A Night in the Ukraine," followed by "Tomfoolery" (OB), "Torch Song Trilogy."

CORTEZ, KATHERINE. Born Sept. 28, 1950 in Detroit, MI. Graduate UNC. Debut 1979 OB in "The Dark at the Top of the Stairs," followed by "Corners," "Confluence," "The Great Grandson of Jedediah Kohler," "A Think Piece," Bdwy in "Foxfire" (1982).

COSTA, JOSEPH. Born June 8, 1946 in Ithaca, NY. Graduate Gettysburg Col., Yale. Debut 1978 OB in "The Show-Off" followed by "The Tempest," "The Changeling."

COSTABILE, RICHARD. Born July 16, 1947 in The Bronx, NY. Graduate Fordham U., Neighborhood Playhouse. Debut 1979 OB in "The Electra Myth," followed by "Twelfth Night," "The Workroom," "Hope With Feathers."

COSTANZA, JOSEPH. Born Aug. 11, 1957 in Brooklyn, NY. Graduate Queens Col. Debut 1983 OB in "Hamlet."

COSTIGAN, KEN. Born Apr. 1, 1934 in NYC. Graduate Fordham U., Yale U. Debut 1960 OB in "Borak," followed by "King of the Dark Chamber," "The Hostage," "Next Time I'll Sing To You," "Curley McDimple," "The Runner Stumbles," "Peg O' My Heart," "The Show-Off," "Midsummer Night's Dream," "Diary of Anne Frank," "Knuckle Sandwich," "Seminary Murder," "Declassee," "Big Apple Messenger," "When We Dead Awaken," "The 12 Pound Look," "The Browning Version," "The Changeling," Bdwy 1962 in "Gideon."

COUNCIL, RICHARD. Born Oct. 1, 1947 in Tampa, FL. Graduate UFla. Debut 1973 OB in "Merchant of Venice," followed by "Ghost Dance," "Look, We've Come Through," "Arms and the Man," "Isadora Duncan Sleeps With the Russian Navy," "Arthur," "The Winter Dancer," "The Prevalence of Mrs. Seal," "Jane Avril," Bdwy in "The Royal Family" (1975), "Philadelphia Story."

COWLES, MATTHEW. Born Sept. 28, 1944 in NYC. Attended Neighborhood Playhouse. Bdwy bow 1966 in "Malcolm," followed by "Sweet Bird of Youth," OB in "King John," "The Indian Wants the Bronx," "Triple Play," "Stop, You're Killing Me!," "The Time of Your Life," "Foursome," "Kid Champion," "End of the War," "Tennessee," "Bathroom Plays," "Touch Black."

COX, CATHERINE. Born Dec. 13, 1950 in Toledo, OH. Wittenberg U. graduate. Bdwy debut 1976 in "Music Is," followed by "Whoopee!" "Oklahoma!," "Shakespeare's Cabaret," "Barnum," OB in "By Strouse," "It's Better With a Band."

CRABTREE, DON. Born Aug. 21, 1928 in Borger, TX. Attended Actors Studio. Bdwy bow 1959 in "Destry Rides Again," followed by "Happiest Girl in the World," "Family Affair," "Unsinkable Molly Brown," "Sophie," "110 In the Shade," "Golden Boy," "Pousse Cafe," "Mahagonny" (OB), "The Best Little Whorehouse in Texas," "42nd Street."

CRAIG, NOEL. Born Jan. 4 in St. Louis, MO. Attended Northwestern U., Goodman Theatre, London Guildhall. Bdwy debut 1967 in "Rosencrantz and Guildenstern Are Dead," followed by "A Patriot For Me," "Conduct Unbecoming," "Vivat! Vivat Regina!," "Going Up," "Dance a Little Closer," OB in "Pygmalion," "Promenade," "Family House," "Inn At Lydda."

CRAIN, STEPHEN. Born Oct. 3, 1952 in Tokyo, Japan. MIT graduate. Bdwy debut 1979 in "Oklahoma!," followed by "The First," "Play Me a Country Song," OB in "The Robber Bridegroom."

CRAWLEY, TOM. Born Aug. 4, 1940 in Central Falls, RI. Graduate UNeb, NYU. Debut 1970 OB in "The Persians," followed by "The Measure Taken," "Ghosts," "The Snob," "Heartbreak House," "Life With Father."

CREST, ROBERT. Born July 21, 1938 in Pecos, TX. Attended Trinity U., Pasadena Playhouse. Debut 1969 OB in "The Fantasticks," followed by "Servant of Two Masters," "Andorra," "Under Milk Wood."

CRISWELL, KIM. Born July 19, 1957 in Hampton, VA. Graduate UCin. Bdwy debut 1981 in "The First," followed by "Nine."

CRITT, C. J. Born Carol Jane Crittenden on Apr. 6, 1954 in Portland, OR. Graduate AMDA. Debut 1979 OB in "Thighs," followed by "Plain and Fancy," "Crisp," "Promises, Promises," Bdwy 1982 in "Waltz of the Stork."

CRIVELLO, ANTHONY. Born Aug. 2, 1955 in Milwaukee, WI. Bdwy debut 1982 in "Evita," OB in "The Juniper Tree."

CROFOOT, LEONARD JOHN. Born Sept. 20, 1948 in Utica, NY. Bdwy debut 1968 in "The Happy Time," followed by "Come Summer," "Gigi," "Barnum," OB in "Circus," "Joseph and the Amazing Technicolor Dreamcoat."

CROMWELL, JAMES. Born Jan. 27, 1940 in Los Angeles, CA. Attended Middlebury Col., Carnegie Tech. Debut 1960 OB in "Port Royal," followed by "AC/DC," "Three Acts of Recognition," "Hamlet," Bdwy in "Othello" ('71).

CRONYN, HUME. Born July 18, 1911 in London, Can. Bdwy debut 1934 in "Hipper's Holiday," followed by "Boy Meets Girl," "High Tor," "Room Service," "There's Always a Breeze," "Escape This Night," "Off to Buffalo," "Three Sisters," "Weak Link," "Retreat to Pleasure," "Mr. Big," "Survivors," "Fourposter," "Madam, Will You Walk" (OB), "The Honeys," "A Day by the Sea," "Man in the Dog Suit," "Triple Play," "Big Fish, Little Fish," "Hamlet," "The Physicists," "A Delicate Balance," "Hadrian VII," "Promenade All," "Noel Coward in Two Keys," "Krapp's Last Tape," "Happy Days," "Act Without Words," "The Gin Game," "Foxfire."

CRONYN, TANDY. Born Nov. 27, 1945 in Los Angeles, CA. Attended London's Central School. Bdwy debut 1969 in "Cabaret," followed by LC's "Playboy of the Western World," "Good Woman of Setzuan," "An Enemy of the People," and "Antigone," OB in "An Evening With the Poet-Senator," "Winners."

CROTHERS, JOEL. Born Jan. 28, 1941 in Cincinnati, OH. Harvard graduate. Bdwy debut 1953 in "The Remarkable Mr. Pennypacker," followed by "A Case of Libel," "Barefoot in the Park," "The Jockey Club Stakes," OB in "Easter," "The Office Murders," "Torch Song Trilogy."

CROTTY, EDWARD. Born Sept. 12, 1941 in New Orleans, LA. Graduate Loyola U. Debut 1978 OB in "Once More With Feeling," followed by "Bugles at Dawn."

CRYER, DAVID. Born Mar. 8, 1936 in Evanston, IL. Attended DePauw U. OB in "The Fantasticks," "Streets of New York," "Now Is the Time for All Good Men," "Whispers On the Wind," "The Making of Americans," "Portfolio Revue," Bdwy in "110 In the Shade," "Come Summer" for which he received a Theatre World Award, "1776" "Ari," "Leonard Bernstein's Mass," "Desert Song," "Evita."

CULLISON, BARRY. Born Sept. 11, 1949 in Vincennes, IN. Attended Goodman Theatre School. Bdwy debut in "Bedroom Farce" (1979), followed by OB in "Cloud 9" (1982).

CULLIVER, KAREN. Born Dec. 30, 1959 in Florida. Attended Stetson U. Bdwy debut 1983 in "Show Boat."

CULLUM, JOHN. Born Mar. 2, 1930 in Knoxville, TN. Graduate U. Tenn. Bdwy bow 1960 in "Camelot," followed by "Infidel Caesar," "The Rehearsal," "Hamlet," "On a Clear Day You Can See Forever" for which he received a Theatre World Award," "Man of LaMancha," "1776," "Vivat! Vivat Regina!," "Shenandoah," "Kings," "The Trip Back Down," "On the 20th Century," "Deathtrap," OB in "Three Hand Reel," "The Elizabethans," "Carousel," "In the Voodoo Parlor of Marie Leveau," "The King and I" (JB), "Whistler."

CUMMINGS, GRETEL. Born July 3 in Bolzano, Italy. Attended Antioch Col. Debut 1964 OB in "Home Movies," followed by "Two Camps by Koutoukas," "Penguin Touquet," "Etiquette," "Egyptology," Bdwy in "Inner City," "Lolita, My Love," "Stages," "Agamemnon."

CUNLIFFE, JERRY. Born May 16, 1935 in Chicago, IL. Attended UChicago. Debut 1957 OB in "Anatole," followed by "Antigone," "Difficult Woman," "Tom Paine," "Futz," "Cherry Orchard," "Etiquette," Bdwy in "Elizabeth I" (1972).

CUNNINGHAM, JOHN. Born June 22, 1932 in Auburn, NY. Graduate of Yale and Dartmouth. OB in "Love Me Little," "Pimpernel," "The Fantasticks," "Love and Let Love," "The Bone Room," "Dancing in the Dark," "Father's Day," "Snapshot," "Head Over Heels," "Quartermaine's Terms," Bdwy in "Hot Spot," "Zorba," "Company," "1776," "Rose."

CURTIS, KEENE. Born Feb. 15, 1925 in Salt Lake City, UT. Graduate UUtah. Bdwy bow 1949 in "Shop at Sly Corner," with APA in "School for Scandal," "The Tavern," "Anatole," "Scapin," "Right You Are," "Importance of Being Earnest," "Twelfth Night," "King Lear," "Seagull," "Lower Depths," "Man and Superman," "Judith," "War and Peace," "You Can't Take It With You," "Pantagleize," "Cherry Orchard," "Misanthrope," "Cocktail Party," "Cock-a-Doodle Dandy," and "Hamlet," "A Patriot for Me," "The Rothschilds," "Night Watch," "Via Galactica," "Annie," "Division Street," OB in "Colette," "Ride Across Lake Constance."

CWIKOWSKI, BILL. Born Aug. 4, 1945 in Newark, NJ. Graduate Smith and Monmouth Col. Debut 1972 OB in "Charlie the Chicken," followed by "Summer Brave," "Desperate Hours," "Mandrogola," "Two by Noonan," "Soft Touch," "Innocent Pleasures," "3 From the Marathon," "Two Part Harmony," "Bathroom Plays," "Little Victories," "Dolphin Position."

DABDOUB, JACK. Born Feb. 5 in New Orleans, LA. Graduate Tulane U. OB in "What's Up," "Time for the Gentle People," "The Peddler," "The Dodo Bird," "Annie Get Your Gun," "Lola," Bdwy in "Paint Your Wagon" (1952), "My Darlin' Aida," "Happy Hunting," "Hot Spot," "Camelot," "Baker St.," "Anya," "Her First Roman," "Coco," "Man of LaMancha," "Brigadoon" ('80), "Moose Murders."

DAHMS, GAIL. Born June 26, 1957 in Kitchener, Ont. Can. Attended HB Studio. Debut 1982 OB in "The Guys in the Truck."

DALTON, LEZLIE. Born Aug. 12, 1952 in Boston, MA. Attended Pasadena Playhouse, UCLA. Debut 1980 OB in "Annie and Arthur," followed by "After Maigret."

D'ALTORIO, VICTOR. Born Jan. 10, 1957 in Garfield Heights, OH. Graduate Northwestern U. Debut 1982 OB in "The Coarse Acting Show."

DALY, JOSEPH. Born Apr. 7, 1930 in Oakland, CA. Debut 1959 OB in "Dance of Death," followed by "Roots," "Sjt. Musgrave's Dance," "Viet Rock," "Dark of the Moon," "Shadow of a Gunman," "Hamlet," "The Ride Across Lake Constance," "A Doll's House," "Native Bird," "Yeats Trio," "Mecca," "Marching to Georgia," "Comedians."

DAMON, CATHRYN. Born Sept. 11 in Seattle, WA. Bdwy debut 1954 in "By the Beautiful Sea," followed by "The Vamp," "Shinbone Alley," "A Family Affair," "Foxy," "Flora the Red Menace," "UTBU," "Come Summer," "Criss-Crossing," "A Place for Polly," "Last of the Red Hot Lovers," "Passion," OB in "Boys From Syracuse," "Secret Life of Walter Mitty," "Show Me Where the Good Times Are," "Effect of Gamma Rays on Man-in-the-Moon Marigolds," "Siamese Connections," "Prodigal," "Down by the River . . . ," "Sweet Bird of Youth," "The Cherry Orchard."

DANIAS, STARR. Born March 18, 1949 in NYC. Performed with Joffrey Ballet before OB debut 1981 in "El Bravo," followed by "On Your Toes" (Bdwy 1983).

DANIELLE, MARLENE. Born Aug. 16 in NYC. Bdwy debut 1979 in "Sarava," followed by "West Side Story," "Marlowe," "Damn Yankees" (JB), "Cats," OB in "Little Shop of Horrors."

DANSON, RANDY. Born Apr. 30, 1950 in Plainfield, NJ. Graduate Carnegie-Mellon. Debut 1978 OB in "Gimme Shelter," followed by "Big and Little," "The Winter Dancers," "Time Steps," "Casualties," "Red and Blue," "The Resurrection of Lady Lester," "Jazz Poets at the Grotto," "Plenty."

DANTUONO, MICHAEL. Born July 30, 1942 in Providence, RI. Debut 1974 OB in "How to Get Rid of It," followed by "Maggie Flynn," "Charlotte Sweet," "Berlin to Broadway," Bdwy 1977 in "Caesar and Cleopatra," "Can-Can" ('81).

DANZER, KATHY. Born July 23, 1951 in Townsend, MT. Graduate UMont. Debut 1978 OB in "Curse of the Starving Class," Bdwy in "Crimes of the Heart" (1982).

D'ARCY, MARY. Born in 1956 in Yardville, NJ. Graduate Glassboro State Col. Bdwy debut 1980 in "The Music Man," OB in "Florodora," "Upstairs at O'Neal's."

DARKE, REBECCA. Born Dec. 6, 1935 in Brooklyn, NY. Debut 1958 OB in "The Midnight Caller," followed by "Who'll Save the Plowboy," "Undercover Man," "Party for Divorce," "A Piece of Blue Sky," "Hey Rube," "Glory! Hallelujah!," "Orpheus Descending," Bdwy in "The Basic Training of Pavlo Hummel" ('77).

DARLING, CANDY. Born March 6, 1954 in Toronto, Can. Bdwy debut 1976 in "Very Good Eddie," followed by "Censored Scenes from King Kong," "Whoopee," "Dreamgirls."

DARLOW, CYNTHIA. Born June 13, 1949 in Detroit, MI. Attended NCSchool of Arts, PennStateU. Debut 1974 OB in "This Property Is Condemned," followed by "Portrait of a Madonna," "Clytemnestra," "Unexpurgated Memoirs of Bernard Morgandigler," "Actors Nightmare," "Sister Mary Ignatius Explains It All," Bdwy in "Grease" (1976).

DAVID, DANIEL. Born May 7, 1960 in Torrance, CA. Attended Carnegie-Mellon U. Bdwy debut 1982 in "Cleavage."

DAVID, REGINA. Born in Denver, CO. Graduate UWy. Debut 1963 OB in "Six Characters in Search of an Author," followed by "Beelch," "Istanboul," "Moondreamers," "Subject to Fits," "Wedding Band," "Confetti and Italian Ice."

DAVIDSON, JACK. Born July 17, 1936 in Worcester, MA. Graduate Boston U. Debut 1968 OB in "Moon for the Misbegotten," followed by "Big and Little," "The Battle of Angels," "Midsummer Night's Dream," "Hot l Baltimore," "A Tribute to Lili Lamont," "Ulysses in Traction," "Lulu," "Hey, Rube," "In the Recovery Lounge," "The Runner Stumbles," "Winter Signs," "Hamlet," "Mary Stuart," "Ruby Ruby Sam Sam," "The Diviners," "Marching to Georgia," "Hunting Scenes from Lower Bavaria," "Richard II," "The Great Grandson of Jedediah Kohler," "Buck," "Time Framed," Bdwy in "Capt. Brassbound's Conversion" (1972), "Anna Christie."

DAVIDSON, RICHARD M. Born May 10, 1940 in Hamilton, Ont., Can. Graduate UToronto, LAMDA. Debut 1978 OB in "The Beasts," followed by "The Bacchae," "The Broken Pitcher," "Knights Errant," "The Entertainer," Bdwy in "The Survivor" ('81)

DAVIES, DAVID. Born Feb. 5, 1941 in Washington, DC. Graduate UMd., Wayne State U. Debut 1971 OB in "Hamlet," followed by "Warbeck," "Back Bog Beast Bait," "The Redeemer," "A Soldier's Play," "Manhattan Made Me," "About Heaven and Earth."

DAVIS, ANDREW. Born Aug. 9, 1950 in San Antonio, TX. Graduate UNew Orleans, Yale. Bdwy debut 1978 in "Crucifer of Blood," OB in "Word of Mouth," "Says I Says He," "Dreck/Vile," "Justice," "Mercenaries."

DAVIS, CLAYTON. Born May 18, 1948 in Pensacola, FL. Graduate FlStateU, Princeton. Debut 1978 OB in "Oklahoma!," followed by "Oh, Johnny," "Where's Charley?"

DAVIS, DONNA. Born June 28, 1949 in Elkin, NC. Graduate UNC. Bdwy debut 1978 in "Angel," followed by "Filumena," OB in "Getting Out," "Radical Solutions," "The Mousetrap," "A Difficult Borning."

DAVIS, MICHAEL ALLEN. Born Aug. 23, 1953 in San Francisco, CA. Attended Clown Col. Bdwy debut 1981 in "Broadway Follies" for which he received a Theatre World Award, followed by "Sugar Babies."

DAVIS, SHEILA KAY. Born May 30, 1956 in Daytona, FL. Graduate Spelman Col. Debut 1982 OB in "Little Shop of Horrors."

DAVIS, SYLVIA. Born Apr. 10, 1910 in Philadelphia, PA. Attended Temple U., AmThWing. Debut 1949 OB in "Blood Wedding," followed by "Tobacco Road," "Orpheus Descending," "Autumn Garden," "Madwoman of Chaillot," "House of Bernarda Alba," "My Old Friends," "Max," Bdwy in "Nathan Weinstein, Mystic, CT." (1966), "Xmas in Las Vegas."

DAWSON, CURT. Born Dec. 5, 1941 in Kansas. Graduate RADA. Debut 1968 OB in "Futz," followed by "Boys in the Band," "Not Now, Darling," "White Nights," "Enter a Free Man," "You Never Can Tell," "Donna Rosita," "The Penultimate Problem of Sherlock Holmes," "Ah, Men," Bdwy in "Absurd Person Singular" (1975), "Alice in Wonderland."

DAWSON, DAVID. Born Feb. 22, 1922 in Brooklyn, NY. Graduate CCNY. Debut 1965 OB in "Hogan's Goat," followed by "Some Rain," Bdwy in "The Freaking Out of Stephanie Blake" (1967).

DAWSON, SUZANNE. Born Jan. 19, 1951 in Montreal, Can. Attended Boston Consv. Debut 1980 OB in "Chase a Rainbow," followed by "New Faces of 1952."

DAYTON, R. MICHAEL. Born Oct. 19, 1944 in Troy, NY. Attended HB Studio. Debut 1981 OB in "Eternal Love," followed by "La Summer."

DEAN, FELICITY. Born Jan. 24, 1959 in London, Eng. Attended Oxford U. Bdwy debut 1982 in "Good."

DEARBORN, DALTON. Born Oct. 1, 1930 in Nantucket, MA. Debut 1957 OB in "Mary Stuart," followed by "The Makropoulos Secret," "Undercover Man," "MacBird," "The 12 Pound Look," "The Browning Version," Bdwy in "Venus Is" (1966).

de BANZIE, LOIS. Born May 4 in Glasgow, Scot. Bdwy debut 1966 in "Elizabeth the Queen," followed by "Da," "Morning's at 7," OB in "Little Murders," "Mary Stuart," "People Are Living There," "Ride Across Lake Constance," "The Divorce of Judy and Jane," "What the Butler Saw," "Man and Superman," "The Judas Applause," "The Dining Room."

DEERING, SALLY. Born Nov. 7, 1952 in Jersey City, NJ. Attended AADA. Debut 1983 OB in "Balzaminov's Wedding."

DeFELICE, AURELIA. Born Apr. 2 in NYC. Attended Northwestern U. Debut 1968 OB in "Scarlet Lullaby," followed by "Evenings With Chekhov," "The Anniversary," "On the High Road," "The Wedding," "June Moon," "The Hostage," "The Transgressor Rides Again," "Cold Feet," "Broadway," "Neighbors," "In Agony," "The Killing of Sister George."

DeFONTE, ANTHONY. Born Oct. 23, 1947 in Chicago, IL. Attended LACC, UWisc. Bdwy debut 1982 in "The Queen and the Rebels."

DeKOVEN, ROGER. Born Oct. 22, 1907 in Chicago, IL. Attended UChicago, Northwestern, Columbia. Bdwy bow 1926 in "Juarez and Maximilian," followed by "Mystery Man," "Once In a Lifetime," "Counselor-at-Law," "Murder in the Cathedral," "Eternal Road," "Brooklyn U.S.A.," "The Assassin," "Joan of Lorraine," "Abie's Irish Rose," "The Lark," "Hidden River," "Compulsion," "The Miracle Worker," "Fighting Cock," "Herzl," "Strider," OB in "Deadly Game," "Steal the Old Man's Bundle," "St. Joan," "Tiger At the Gates," "Walking To Waldheim," "Cyrano de Bergerac," "An Enemy of the People," "Ice Age," "Prince of Homburg," "Biography: A Game," "Strider," "Ivanov," "13."

DELANEY, KIM. Born Nov. 29, 1961 in Philadelphia, PA. Debut 1983 OB in "Loving Reno."

DELANY, DANA. Born Mar. 13, 1956 in NYC. Graduate Wesleyan U. Bdwy debut 1980 in "A Life," followed by "Blood Moon."

DE LA PENA, GEORGE. Born in NYC in 1956. Performed with American Ballet Theatre before Bdwy debut 1981 in "Woman of the Year," followed by "On Your Toes."

DeLUCA, JOHN. Born Sept. 6 in Orange, NJ. Graduate Boston U. Bdwy debut 1980 in "Dancin'," followed by OB in "The Boogie-Woogie Rumble of a Dream Deferred."

DeMIRJIAN, DENISE. Born July 8, 1952 in Los Angeles, CA. Graduate CalInst of Arts. Debut 1978 OB in "Cartoons," followed by "No Strings," "Oh, Baby!"

DEMPSEY, JEROME. Born Mar. 1, 1929 in St. Paul, MN. Toledo U graduate. Bdwy bow 1959 in "West Side Story," followed by "The Deputy," "Spofford," "Room Service," "Love Suicide at Schofield Barracks," "Dracula," "Whodunnit," OB in "Cry of Players," "Year Boston Won the Pennant," "The Crucible," "Justice Box," "Trelawny of the Wells," "The Old Glory," "Six Characters in Search of an Author," "Threepenny Opera," "Johnny On the Spot," "The Barbarians," "He and She," "Midsummer Night's Dream," "The Recruiting Officer," "Oedipus the King," "The Wild Duck," "The Fuehrer Bunker," "Entertaining Mr. Sloane," "Clownmaker."

DeMUNN, JEFFREY. Born Apr. 25, 1947 in Buffalo, NY. Graduate Union Col. Debut 1975 OB in "Augusta," followed by "A Prayer for My Daughter," "Modigliani," "Chekhov Sketchbook," "A Midsummer Night's Dream," "Total Abandon," Bdwy in "Comedians" (1976), "Bent," "K2."

DENNIS, RONALD. Born Oct. 2, 1944 in Dayton, OH. Debut 1966 OB in "Show Boat," followed by "Of Thee I Sing," "Moon Walk," "Please Don't Cry," Bdwy in "A Chorus Line" (1975), "My One and Only."

DENNIS, SANDY. Born Apr. 27, 1937 in Hastings, NE. Bdwy debut 1957 in "The Dark At the Top of the Stairs," followed by "Face of a Hero," "The Complaisant Lover," "A Thousand Clowns" for which she received a Theatre World Award, "Any Wednesday," "Daphne in Cottage D," "How the Other Half Loves," "Let Me Hear You Smile," "Absurd Person Singular," "Same Time Next Year," "Supporting Cast," "Come Back To the 5 & Dime, Jimmy Dean," OB in "Burning Bright," "Buried Inside Extra."

DEROSKI, BONNIE. Born June 8, 1961 in Neptune, NJ. Debut 1977 OB in "Landscape of the Body," followed by "New England Legend," "Did You See the Elephant?," "Partners."

DESAI, SHELLY. Born Dec. 3, 1935 in Bombay, India. Graduate OkStateU. Debut 1968 OB in "The Indian Wants the Bronx," followed by "Babu," "Wonderful Year," "Jungle of Cities," "Gandhi," "Savages," "Cuchulain," "Hamlet," "Merchant of Venice," "Fanshen," "Grunts," Bdwy 1981 in "A Talent for Murder."

DeSHIELDS, ANDRE. Born Jan. 12, 1946 in Baltimore, MD. Graduate UWi. Bdwy debut 1973 in "Warp," followed by "Rachel Lily Rosenbloom," "The Wiz," "Ain't Misbehavin'," OB in "2008½," "Jazzbo Brown," "The Soldier's Tale," "The Little Prince."

DEVINE, LORETTA. Born Aug. 21 in Houston, TX. Graduate UHouston, Brandeis U. Bdwy debut 1977 in "Hair," followed by "A Broadway Musical," "Dreamgirls," OB in "Godsong," "Lion and the Jewel," "Karma," "The Blacks," "Mahalia."

DEVLIN, JAY. Born May 8, 1929 in Ft. Dodge, IA. OB in "The Mad Show," "Little Murders," "Unfair to Goliath," "Ballymurphy," "Front Page," "Fasnacht Day," "Bugles at Dawn," Bdwy 1978 in "King of Hearts."

DEWHURST, COLLEEN. Born June 3, 1926 in Montreal, Can. Attended Downer Col., AADA. Bdwy debut 1952 in "Desire Under the Elms," followed by "Tamburlaine the Great," "The Country Wife," "Caligula," "All the Way Home," "Great Day in the Morning," "Ballad of the Sad Cafe," "More Stately Mansions," "All Over," "Mourning Becomes Electra," "Moon for the Misbegotten," "Who's Afraid of Virginia Woolf?," "An Almost Perfect Person," "The Queen and the Rebels," "You Can't Take It With You," OB in "The Taming of the Shrew," "The Eagle Has Two Heads," "Camille," "Macbeth," "Children of Darkness." for which she received a Theatre World Award, "Antony and Cleopatra," "Hello and Goodbye," "Good Woman of Setzuan," "Hamlet," "Are You Now or Have You Ever . . . ?," "Taken in Marriage."

DILLON, DENNY. Born May 18, 1951 in Cleveland, OH. Graduate Syracuse U. Bdwy debut 1974 in "Gypsy," followed by "The Skin of Our Teeth," "Harold and Maude," "My One and Only."

DILLON, MIA. Born July 9, 1955 in Colorado Springs, CO. Graduate Penn State U. Bdwy debut 1977 in "Equus," followed by "Da," "Once a Catholic," "Crimes of the Heart," OB in "The Crucible," "Summer," "Waiting for the Parade," "Crimes of the Heart," "Fables for Friends," "Scenes from La Vie de Boheme," "Three Sisters."

DINELLI, MICHAEL. Born Jan. 22, 1953 in Los Angeles, CA. Debut 1976 OB in "In the Boom Boom Room," followed by "Extremities," Bdwy in "The Basic Training of Pavlo Hummel" (1977).

DIXON, ED. Born Sept. 2, 1948 in Oklahoma. Attended OkU. Bdwy in "The Student Prince," followed by "No, No, Nanette," "Rosalie in Concert," OB in "By Bernstein," "King of the Schnorrers."

DIXON, MacINTYRE. Born Dec. 22, 1931 in Everett, MA. Graduate Emerson Col. Bdwy debut 1965 in "Xmas in Las Vegas," followed by "Cop-Out," "Story Theatre," "Metamorphosis," "Twigs," "Over Here!," "Once In a Lifetime," "Alice in Wonderland," OB in "Quare Fellow," "Plays for Bleecker St.," "Stewed Prunes," "Cat's Pajamas," "Three Sisters," "3 X 3," "Second City," "Mad Show," "Meow!," "Lotta," "Rubbers," "Conjuring an Event," "His Majesty the Devil," "Tomfoolery."

DIXON, OLIVER. Born Dec. 9 in Colquitt, GA. Graduate FlStateU. Bdwy debut 1983 in "The Caine Mutiny Court-Martial."

DOBRES, MARCIA-ANNE. Born Sept. 21, 1953 in Philadelphia, PA. Attended American U. Debut 1980 OB in "A Funny Thing Happened on the Way to the Forum," followed by "Life With Father."

DODSON, JACK. Born May 16, 1931 in Pittsburgh, PA. Graduate Carnegie-Mellon U. Debut 1957 OB in "The Country Wife," followed by "Our Town," "The Balcony," "Under Milkwood," "Infancy," "Six Characters in Search of an Author," Bdwy in "Hughie" (1964), "You Can't Take It With You" (1983).

DODSON, COLLEEN. Born June 29, 1954 in Chicago, IL. Graduate UIl. Debut 1981 OB in "The Matinee Kids," Bdwy 1982 in "Nine."

DOLINER, ROY. Born June 27, 1954 in Boston, MA. Attended Tufts U. Debut 1977 OB in "Don't Cry Child, Your Father's an American," followed by "Zwi Kanar Show," "Big Bad Burlesque," "Lysistrata," "Rats."

DONENBERG, BENJAMIN. Born Mar. 8, 1957 in Chicago, IL. Graduate Juilliard. Debut 1980 OB in "How It All Began," followed by "Henry IV Part I," Bdwy in "Amadeus" (1982).

DONNELLY, DONAL. Born July 6, 1931 in Bradford, Eng. Bdwy debut 1966 in "Philadelphia, Here I Come," followed by "A Day in the Death of Joe Egg," "Sleuth," "The Faith Healer," "The Elephant Man," OB in "My Astonishing Self," "The Chalk Garden."

DORFMAN, ROBERT. Born Oct. 8, 1950 in Brooklyn, NY. Attended CUNY, HB Studio. Debut 1979 OB in "Say Goodnight, Gracie," followed by "America Kicks," "Winterplay."

DORWARD, MARY ANNE. Born June 29, 1958 in Berkeley, CA. Graduate UBerkeley. Debut 1982 OB in "T.N.T.," followed by "Transformations," "Snoopy."

DOUGLASS, PI. Born in Sharon, CT. Attended Boston Consv. Bdwy debut 1969 in "Fig Leaves Are Falling," followed by "Hello, Dolly!," "Georgy," "Purlie," "Ari," "Jesus Christ Superstar," "Selling of the President," "The Wiz," OB in "Of Thee I Sing," "Under Fire," "The Ritz."

DOWNING, VIRGINIA. Born Mar. 7 in Washington, DC. Attended Bryn Mawr. OB in "Juno and the Paycock," "Man With the Golden Arm," "Palm Tree in a Rose Garden," "Play With a Tiger," "The Wives," "The Idiot," "Medea," "Mrs. Warren's Profession," "Mercy Street," "Thunder Rock," "Pygmalion," "First Week in Bogota," "Rimers of Eldritch," "Les Blancs," "Shadow of a Gunman," "All the Way Home," "A Winter's Tale," "Billy Liar," Bdwy in "Father Malachy's Miracle" (1937), "Forward the Heart," "The Cradle Will Rock," "A Gift of Time," "We Have Always Lived in a Castle."

DOYLE, JACK. Born June 7, 1955 in Brooklyn, NY. Graduate Adelphi U. Debut 1982 OB in "New Faces of '52."

DREYFUSS, RICHARD. Born Oct. 29, 1947 in Brooklyn, NY. Bdwy debut 1969 in "But Seriously," followed by "Total Abandon," OB in "Line," "Julius Caesar," "Othello."

DRISCHELL, RALPH. Born Nov. 26, 1927 in Baldwin, NY. Attended Carnegie-Tech. Bdwy in "Rhinoceros," "All in Good Time," "Rosencrantz and Guildenstern Are Dead," "The Visit," "Chemin de Fer," "Ah, Wilderness," "Stages," "The American Clock," "The Survivor," OB in "Playboy of the Western World," "The Crucible," "The Balcony," "Time of Vengeance," "Barroom Monks," "Portrait of the Artist," "Abe Lincoln in Illinois," "The Caretaker," "A Slight Ache," "The Room," "The Year Boston Won the Pennant," "The Time of Your Life," "Camino Real," "Operation Sidewinder," "Beggar on Horseback," "Threepenny Opera," "Henry IV Part II," "A Midsummer Night's Dream," "Rock Island."

DRIVAS, ROBERT. Born Nov. 20, 1943 in Chicago, IL. Bdwy debut 1958 in "The Firstborn," followed by "One More River," "The Wall," "Lorenzo," "Irregular Verb to Love," "And Things That Go Bump In the Night," "The Ritz," "The Man Who Had Three Arms," OB in "Mrs. Dally Has a Lover" for which he received a Theatre World Award, "Sweet Eros," "Where Has Tommy Flowers Gone," "A Breeze From the Gulf," "Monsters(Sideshow)."

DRUMMOND, ALICE. Born May 21, 1929 in Pawtucket, RI. Attended Pembroke Col. Bdwy debut 1963 in "Ballad of the Sad Cafe," followed by "Malcolm," "The Chinese," "Thieves," "Summer Brave," "Some of My Best Friends," "You Can't Take It With You," OB in "Royal Gambit," "Go Show Me a Dragon," "Sweet of You to Say So," "Gallows Humor," "American Dream," "Giants' Dance," "Carpenters," "Charles Abbot & Son," "God Says There Is No Peter Ott," "Enter a Free Man," "Memory of Two Mondays," "Secret Service," "Boy Meets Girl," "Savages," "Killings On the Last Line," "Knuckle," "Wonderland."

DUDLEY, CRAIG. Born Jan. 22, 1945 in Sheepshead Bay, NY. Graduate AADA, AmThWing. Debut 1970 OB in "Macbeth," followed by "Zou," "Othello," "War and Peace."

DUFF-MacCORMICK, CARA. Born Dec. 12 in Woodstock, Can. Attended AADA. Debut 1969 OB in "Love Your Crooked Neighbor," followed by "The Wager," "Macbeth," "A Musical Merchant of Venice," "Ladyhouse Blues," "The Philanderer," "Bonjour, La, Bonjour," "Journey to Gdansk," "The Dining Room," Bdwy in "Moonchildren" (1972) for which she received a Theatre World Award, "Out Cry," "Animals."

DUKES, DAVID. Born June 6, 1945 in San Francisco, CA. Attended Mann Col. Bdwy debut 1971 in "School for Wives," followed by "Don Juan," "The Play's the Thing," "The Visit," "Chemin de Fer," "Holiday," "Rules of the Game," "Love for Love," "Travesties," "Dracula," "Bent," "Amadeus," OB in "Rebel Women."

DULLEA, KEIR. Born May 30, 1936 in Cleveland, NJ. Attended Neighborhood Playhouse. Debut 1959 OB in "Season of Choice," followed by "Sweet Prince," Bdwy in "Dr. Cook's Garden," "Butterflies Are Free," "P.S.: Your Cat Is Dead."

DUNNE, GRIFFIN. Born June 8, 1955 in NYC. Attended Neighborhood Playhouse. Debut 1980 OB in "Marie and Bruce," followed by "Coming Attractions," "Hooters."

EASLEY, DOUGLAS. Born Jan. 26, 1929 in Chattanooga, TN. Attended MiStateU., Goodman Theatre. Debut 1960 OB in "Shadow of Heroes," followed by "Boogie-Woogie Rumble," Bdwy in "Elizabeth the Queen" (1966), "Of Love Remembered."

EASTON, EDWARD. Born Oct. 21, 1942 in Moline, IL. Graduate Lincoln Col., UIl., Neighborhood Playhouse. Debut 1967 OB in "Party on Greenwich Avenue," followed by "Middle of the Night," "Summer Brave," "Sunday Afternoon."

eda-YOUNG, BARBARA. Born Jan. 30, 1945 in Detroit, MI. Bdwy debut 1968 in "Lovers and Other Strangers," OB in "The Hawk," LCRep's "The Time of Your Life," "Camino Real," "Operation Sidewinder," "Kool Aid" and "A Streetcar Named Desire," "The Gathering," "The Terrorists," "Drinks Before Dinner," "Shout Across the River," "After Stardrive," "Birdbath," "Crossing the Crab Nebula," "Maiden Stakes," "Come Dog Come Night," "Two Character Play."

EDE, GEORGE. Born Dec. 22, 1931 in San Francisco, CA. Bdwy debut 1969 in "A Flea in Her Ear," followed by "Three Sisters," "The Changing Room," "The Visit," "Chemin de Fer," "Holiday," "Love for Love," "Rules of the Game," "Member of the Wedding," "Lady from the Sea," "A Touch of the Poet," "Philadelphia Story," OB in "The Philanderer," "The American Clock," "The Broken Pitcher, "No End of Blame."

EDEIKEN, LOUISE. Born June 23, 1956 in Philadelphia, PA. Graduate GeoWashU. Bdwy debut 1982 in "Nine."

EDENFIELD, DENNIS. Born July 23, 1946 in New Orleans, LA. Debut 1970 OB in "The Evil That Men Do," followed by "I Have Always Believed in Ghosts," "Nevertheless They Laugh," Bdwy in "Irene" ('73), "A Chorus Line."

EDMEAD, WENDY. Born July 6, 1956 in NYC. Graduate NYCU. Bdwy debut 1974 in "The Wiz," followed by "Stop the World . . . ," "America," "Dancin'," "Encore," "Cats."

EDMONDS, LOUIS. Born Sept. 24, 1923 in Baton Rouge, LA. Attended Carnegie Tech. OB in "Life in Louisiana," "Way of the World," "The Cherry Orchard," "Uncle Vanya," "The Duchess of Malfi," "Ernest in Love," "The Rapists," "Amoureuse," "The Interview," "The Wisteria Trees," Bdwy in "Candide," "Maybe Tuesday," "The Killer," "Passage to India," "Fire!," "Otherwise Engaged."

EDWARDS, BRANDT. Born Mar. 22, 1947 in Holly Springs, MS. Graduate UMiss. NY debut off and on Bdwy 1975 in "A Chorus Line."

EDWARDS, PAIGE. Born Dec. 12, 1916 in Springfield, MA. Bdwy debut 1944 in "Embezzled Heaven," followed by "Can-Can," "The Ritz" (1983).

EDWARDS, RANDALL. Born June 15 in Atlanta, GA. Attended CalInst of the Arts. Debut 1983 OB in "Upstairs at O'Neal's."

EDWARDS, SUSAN. Born Aug. 14, 1950 in Levittown, NY. Graduate Hofstra U. Bdwy debut 1976 in "Bubbling Brown Sugar," followed by "The Suicide," "Torch Song Trilogy," OB in "Jazz Babies," "Boys from Syracuse," "Scrambled Feet."

EDWIN, MICHAEL. Born June 15, 1953 in Reading, PA. Graduate West Chester State Col. Debut 1983 OB in "The Robber Bridegroom."

EHLERS, MICHAEL. Born Mar. 24, 1962 in Chicago, IL. Debut 1982 OB in "New Faces of 1952."

EISENBERG, NED. Born Jan. 13, 1957 in NYC. Attended CalInst of Arts, HB Studio. Debut 1980 OB in "The Time of the Cuckoo," followed by "Our Lord of Lynchville."

ELDREDGE, LYNN. Born July 25, 1955 in Holden, MA. Graduate San Francisco State U. Debut 1982 OB in "Charlotte Sweet."

ELEY, STEPHANIE. Born Nov. 3, 1951 in Hominy, OK. Graduate NCSch of Arts. Bdwy debut 1981 in "Dreamgirls," followed by "My One and Only."

ELLIN, DAVID. Born Jan. 10, 1925 in Montreal, Can. Attended AADA. Bdwy in "Swan Song," "West Side Story," "Education of Hyman Kaplan," "Light, Lively and Yiddish," OB in "Trees Die Standing," "Mirele Efros," "End of All Things Natural," "Yoshe Kalb," "Fiddler on the Roof" (JB), "Rebecca, the Rabbi's Daughter," "Wish Me Mazel-Tov," "Roumanian Wedding," "The Showgirl."

ELLIOTT, ALICE. Born Aug. 22, 1950 in Durham, NC. Graduate Carnegie-Mellon, Goodman Theatre. Debut 1972 OB in "In the Time of Harry Harass," followed by "American Gothic," "Bus Stop," "As You Like It," "My Early Years."

ELLIOTT, PATRICIA. Born July 21, 1942 in Gunnison, CO. Graduate U. Colo., London Academy. Debut with LCRep 1968 in "King Lear," and "A Cry of Players," followed OB in "Henry V," "The Persians," "A Doll's House," "Hedda Gabler," "In Case of Accident," "Water Hen," "Polly," "But Not for Me," "By Bernstein," "Prince of Homburg," "Artichokes," "Wine Untouched," "Misalliance," Bdwy bow 1973 in "A Little Night Music" for which she received a Theatre World Award, followed by "The Shadow Box," "Tartuffe," "13 Rue de L'Amour," "The Elephant Man."

ELLIS, FRASER. Born May 1, 1957 in Boulder, CO. Graduate UCo. Bdwy debut 1982 in "A Chorus Line."

ELLIS, SCOTT. Born Apr. 19, 1957 in Washington, DC. Attended Goodman Theatre. Bdwy debut in "Grease," followed by "Musical Chairs," OB in "Mrs. Dally Has a Lover," "Hijinks," "110 In the Shade," "A Midsummer Night's Dream."

ELMORE, STEVE. Born July 12, 1936 in Niangua, MO. Debut 1961 in "Madame Aphrodite," followed by "Golden Apple," "Enclave," Bdwy in "Camelot," "Jenny," "Fade In Fade Out," "Kelly," "Company," "Nash at 9," "Chicago," "42nd St."

ELSTON, ROBERT. Born May 29, 1934 in NYC. Graduate Hunter Col., CCNY. Bdwy debut 1958 in "Maybe Tuesday," followed by "Tall Story," "Golden Fleecing," "Spoon River Anthology," "You Know I Can't Hear You When . . . ," "Vivat! Vivat Regina!," OB in "Undercover Man," "Conditioned Reflex," "archy and mehitabel," "Notes from the Underground," "After Many a Summer," "Portrait of a Man."

ENSLEY, EVERETT. Born June 21, 1931 in NYC. Debut 1964 OB in "Automation," followed by "Mummers Play," "My Sister, My Sister," "One Last Look," "A Yank in Beverly Hills," "Blues for Mr. Charlie."

EPSTEIN, PIERRE. Born July 27, 1930 in Toulouse, FR. Graduate UParis. Bdwy debut 1962 in "A Shot In the Dark," followed by "Enter Laughing," "Bajour," "Black Comedy," "Thieves," "Fun City," "Filumena," "Plenty," OB in "Incident at Vichy," "Threepenny Opera," "Too Much Johnson," "Second City," "People vs Ranchman," "Promenade," "Cakes With Wine," "Little Black Sheep," "Comedy of Errors," "A Memory of Two Mondays," "They Knew What They Wanted," "Museum," "The Bright and Golden Land," "Manny," "God Bless You, Mr. Rosewater."

ESPOSITO, GIANCARLO. Born Apr. 26, 1958 in Copenhagen, Den. Bdwy debut 1968 in "Maggie Flynn," followed by "The Me Nobody Knows," "Lost In the Stars," "Seesaw," "Merrily We Roll Along," OB in "Zooman and the Sign" for which he received a Theatre World Award, "Keyboard," "Who Loves the Dancer," "House of Ramon Iglesias."

ESTERMAN, LAURA. Born Apr. 12 in NYC. Attended Radcliffe, LAMDA. Debut 1969 OB in "The Time of Your Life," followed by "Pig Pen," "Carpenters," "Ghosts," "Waltz of the Toreadors," "Macbeth," "The Seagull," "Rubbers," "Yanks 3 Detroit 0," "Golden Boy," "Out of Our Father's House," "The Master and Margarita," "Chinchilla," "Dusa, Fish, Stas and Vi," "Midsummer Night's Dream," "Recruiting Officer," "Oedipus the King," "Two Fish in the Sky," "Mary Barnes," Bdwy in "God's Favorite" (1974), "Teibele and Her Demon," "The Suicide."

ESTEY, SUELLEN. Born Nov. 21 in Mason City, IA. Graduate Stephens Col., Northwestern U. Debut 1970 OB in "Some Other Time," followed by "June Moon," "Buy Bonds Buster," "Smile, Smile, Smile," "Carousel," "The Lullaby of Broadway," "I Can't Keep Running," "The Guys in the Truck," Bdwy 1972 in "The Selling of the President," followed by "Barnum."

ETJEN, JEFF. Born June 12, 1953 in Chicago, IL. Graduate Rollins Col. Debut 1983 OB in "Forbidden Broadway."

EVANS, PETER. Born May 27, 1950 in Englewood, NJ. Graduate Yale, London Central School of Speech. Debut OB 1975 in "Life Class," followed by "Streamers," "A Life in the Theatre," "Don Juan Comes Back From the War," "The American Clock," "Geniuses," "Transfiguration of Benno Blimpie," Bdwy in "Night and Day" (1979), "Children of a Lesser God."

EVANS, SCOTT. Born Oct. 18, 1955 in Irvington-on-Hudson, NY. Graduate Boston U. Bdwy debut 1983 in "Moose Murders."

FAHEY, LEE ANNE. Born Apr. 7 in Chicago, IL. Graduate Chicago Inst., Goodman School. Bdwy debut 1969 in "Play It Again, Sam," OB in "Talking With."

FAIRCHILD, MORGAN. Born Patsy McClenny in 1950 in Dallas, TX. Debut 1982 OB in "Geniuses."

FARIN, PAUL. Born July 1, 1947 in NYC. Graduate St. Michael's Catholic U. Debut 1980 OB in "Elizabeth and Essex" followed by "The Evangelist," "Gospel According to Al."

FARRAR, MARTHA. Born Apr. 22, 1928 in Buffalo, NY. Graduate Smith Col. Bdwy debut 1953 in "A Pin to See the Peepshow." OB in "The Cretan Woman," "Easter," "Half-Life," "Touched," "Between Us."

FARWELL, JONATHAN. Born Jan. 9, 1932 in Lansing, MI. Graduate Ithaca Col., Yale. Debut 1961 OB in "A Midsummer Night's Dream," followed by "Home Remedies," Bdwy in "Morning's at Seven" (1980), "Amadeus."

FAWCETT, ALLEN. Born in 1947 in Schenectady, NY. Bdwy debut 1982 in "Joseph and the Amazing Technicolor Dreamcoat."

FAWCETT, FARRAH. Born Feb. 2, 1947 in Texas. Debut 1983 OB in "Extremities."

FAYE, JOEY. Born July 12, 1910 in NYC. Bdwy bow 1938 in "Sing Out the News," followed by "Room Service," "Meet the People," "The Man Who Came to Dinner," "The Milky Way," "Boy Meets Girl," "Streets of Paris," "Allah Be Praised," "Duchess Misbehaves," "Tidbits of 1948," "High Button Shoes," "Top Banana," "Tender Trap," "Man of LaMancha," "70 Girls 70," OB in "Lyle," "Naomi Court," "Awake and Sing," "Coolest Cat in Town," "The Ritz."

FEAGAN, LESLIE. Born Jan. 9, 1951 in Hinckley, OH. Graduate Ohio U. Debut 1978 OB in "Can-Can," followed by "Merton of the Movies," "Promises, Promises."

FEINSTEIN, ALAN. Formerly Alan Yorke, Laurence Feinstein. Born Sept. 10, 1948 in NYC. Attended LACC. Bdwy debut 1966 in "Malcolm," followed by "Zelda," "Streetcar Named Desire" (1973), "A View From the Bridge" (1983), OB in "Iphigenia in Aulis," "Come Back, Little Sheba," "Light Up the Sky," "Seahorse," "Papers," "Shoot Anything with Hair That Moves," "The Sandcastle."

FELDER, CLARENCE. Born Sept. 2, 1938 in St. Matthew, SC. Debut 1964 OB in "The Room," followed by "Are You Now or Have You Ever Been," "Claw," "Henry V," "Winter Dancers," "Goose and Tomtom," "Don Juan," Bdwy in "Red, White and Maddox," "Love for Love," "Rules of the Game," "Golden Boy," "A Memory of Two Mondays," "They Knew What They Wanted," "The Queen and the Rebels," "Teaneck Tanzi."

FENNING, STEPHEN. Born Jan. 6 in Washington, DC. Attended AMDA. Bdwy debut 1972 in "Hair," followed by "You're a Good Man, Charlie Brown," OB in "Morality," "Narrow Road to the Deep North," "Godspell," "Snoopy."

FERRELL, CONCHATA. Born Mar. 28, 1943 in Charleston, WVa. Graduate Marshall U. Debut 1973 OB in "The Hot l Baltimore," followed by "The Sea Horse" for which she received a Theatre World Award, "Battle of Angels," "Elephant in the House," "Wine Untouched," "Time Framed."

FICKINGER, STEVEN. Born Apr. 29, 1960 in Chicago, IL. Graduate UCLA. Debut 1982 OB in "Louisiana Summer," followed by "The Robber Bridegroom."

FIELDING, ANNE. Born Jan. 30, 1943 in NYC. Has appeared OB in "Ivanov," "Monserrat," "Romeo and Juliet," "A Midsummer Night's Dream," "Hedda Gabler," "School for Wives," "School for Scandal," "The Flattering Word."

FIERSTEIN, HARVEY. Born June 6, 1954 in Brooklyn, NY. Graduate Pratt Inst. Debut 1971 OB in "Pork," followed by "International Stud," "Fugue In a Nursery," Bdwy 1982 in "Torch Song Trilogy." for which he received a Theatre World Award.

FIGUEROA, LAURA. Born Feb. 2, 1948 in San Turce, PR. Attended Pace Col. Bdwy debut 1969 in "Does a Tiger Wear a Necktie?," OB in "The Ox Cart," "Theatre in the Street."

FILIPOV, ALEXANDER. Born Mar. 19, 1947 in Moscow, R. Attended Leningrad Kirov School. With ABT, San Francisco Ballet before Bdwy debut 1983 in "On Your Toes."

FINKEL, FYVUSH. Born Oct. 9, 1922 in Brooklyn, NY. Bdwy debut 1970 in "Fiddler On the Roof" (also 1981 revival), OB in "Gorky," "Little Shop of Horrors."

FIRESTONE, ROCHELLE. Born June 14, 1949 in Kansas City, MO. Graduate NYU, HB Studio. Debut 1974 OB in "A Funny Thing Happened on the Way to the Forum," followed by "One Flew Over the Cuckoo's Nest," "The Apple Tree," "The Little Match Girl Makes It Big."

FIRMENT, MARILYN. Born Feb. 18 in Elyria, OH. Graduate Boston Consv. Debut 1976 OB in "Panama Hattie," followed by "The Gilded Cage."

FISHER, CARRIE. Born Oct. 21, 1956 in Los Angeles. Bdwy debut 1973 in "Irene," followed by "Agnes of God."

FITE, MARK. Born Jan. 24, 1954 in Raceland, LA. Graduate USouthernMs. Bdwy debut 1982 in "Cleavage."

FITZGERALD, FERN. Born Jan. 7, 1947 in Valley Stream, NY. Bdwy debut 1976 in "Chicago," followed by "A Chorus Line."

FITZPATRICK, JIM. Born Nov. 26, 1950 in Omaha, NE. Attended UNeb. Debut 1977 OB in "Arsenic and Old Lace" (ELT), followed by "Merton of the Movies" (ELT), "Oh, Boy!," "Time and the Conways," "Street Scene," "Duchess of Malfi."

FLANAGAN, KIT. Born July 6 in Pittsburgh, PA. Graduate Northwestern U. Debut 1979 OB in "The Diary of Anne Frank," followed by "An Evening with Dorothy Parker," "Still Life," "Cloud 9."

FLANAGAN, PAULINE. Born June 29, 1925 in Sligo, Ire. Debut 1958 OB in "Ulysses in Nighttown," followed by "Pictures in the Hallway," "Later," "Antigone," "The Crucible," "The Plough and the Stars," "Summer," "Close of Play," Bdwy in God and Kate Murphy," "The Living Room," "The Innocents," "The Father," "Medea," "Steaming."

FLANINGAM, LOUISA. Born May 5, 1945 in Chester, SC. Graduate UMd. Debut 1971 OB in "The Shrinking Bride," Bdwy in "Magic Show," "Most Happy Fella" (1979), "Play Me a Country Song."

FLEISCHMAN, MARK. Born Nov. 25, 1935 in Detroit, MI. Attended UMi. Bdwy Debut 1955 in "Tonight in Samarkand," followed by "A Distant Bell," "The Royal Family," "The World of Sholom Aleichem," OB in "What Every Woman Knows," "Lute Song," "The Beautiful People," "Big Fish, Little Fish," "Incident at Vichy."

FLOREK, DAVE. Born May 19, 1953 in Dearborn, MI. Graduate Eastern MiU. Debut 1976 OB in "The Collection," followed by "Richard III," "Much Ado About Nothing," "Young Bucks," "Big Apple Messenger," "Death of a Miner," "Marvelous Gray," "Journey to Gdansk," Bdwy 1980 in "Nuts."

FLORZAK, DENNIS. Born July 18, 1947 in Buffalo, NY. Graduate Ithaca Col. Debut 1978 OB in "Masterpieces," followed by Bdwy in "Moose Murders" (1983).

FOGARTY, MARY. Born in Manchester, NH. Debut 1959 OB in "The Well of Saints," followed by "Shadow and Substance," "Nathan, the Wise," "Bonjour La Bonjour," "Family Comedy," Bdwy in "The National Health," "Watch on the Rhine" (1980), "Of the Fields Lately."

FORBES, BRENDA. Born Jan. 14, 1909 in London, Eng. Bdwy debut 1931 in "Barretts of Wimpole St.," followed by "Candida," "Lucrece," "Flowers of the Forest," "Pride and Prejudice," "Storm Over Patsy," "Heartbreak House," "One for the Money," "Two for the Show," "Three to Make Ready," "Yesterday's Magic," "Morning Star," "Suds In Your Eyes," "Quadrille," "The Reluctant Debutante," "Loves of Cass McGuire," "Darling of the Day," "The Constant Wife," "My Fair Lady," OB in "Busybody."

FORBES, KATHLEEN. Born Nov. 17, 1951 in Bermuda. Graduate SUNY/Buffalo. Debut 1983 OB in "About Heaven and Earth," followed by "Manhattan Made Me."

FORD, BARRY. Born Mar. 27, 1933 in Oakland, CA. Graduate CaStateU. Debut 1972 OB in "Ruddigore," followed by "The Devil's Disciple," "Nymph Errant," "After You've Gone."

FORSYTHE, HENDERSON. Born Sept. 11, 1917 in Macon, MO. Attended UIowa. Debut 1956 OB in "The Iceman Cometh," followed by "The Collection," "The Room," "A Slight Ache," "Happiness Cage," "Waiting for Godot," "In Case of Accident," "Not I," "An Evening With the Poet-Senator," "Museum," "How Far Is It to Babylon," "Wild Life," Bdwy in "The Cellar and the Well" (1950), "Miss Lonelyhearts," "Who's Afraid of Virginia Woolf?," "Malcolm," "Right Honourable Gentleman," "Delicate Balance," "Birthday Party," "Harvey," "Engagement Baby," "Freedom of the City," "Texas Trilogy," "Best Little Whorehouse in Texas."

FOSTER, FRANCES. Born June 11 in Yonkers, NY. Bdwy debut 1955 in "The Wisteria Trees," followed by "Nobody Loves an Albatross," "Raisin in the Sun," "The River Niger," "First Breeze of Summer," OB in "Take a Giant Step," "Edge of the City," "Tammy and the Doctor," "The Crucible," "Happy Ending," "Day of Absence," "An Evening of One Acts," "Man Better Man," "Brotherhood," "Akokawe," "Rosalee Pritchett," "Sty of the Blind Pig," "Ballet Behind the Bridge," "Good Woman of Setzuan" (LC), "Behold! Cometh the Vanderkellans," "Origin," "Boesman and Lena," "Do Lord Remember Me," "Nevis Mountain Dew," "Daughters of the Mock," "Big City Blues," "Zooman and the Sign," "Sleep Beauty," "Do Lord Remember Me."

FOUQUET, PAUL. Born Oct. 13, 1954 in Rochester, NY. Graduate UDayton. Debut 1982 OB in "Divine Fire," followed by "Salome."

FOWKES, CONARD. Born Jan. 4, 1933 in Washington, DC. Yale graduate. Bdwy bow 1958 in "Howie," followed by "The Wall," "Minor Miracle," "All the Girls Came Out to Play," OB in "Look Back in Anger," "That Thing at the Cherry Lane," "America Hurrah," "The Reckoning," "Istanboul," "Sleep," "Domino Courts," "Wild Life."

FOWLER, CLEMENT. Born Dec. 27, 1924 in Detroit, MI. Graduate Wayne State U. Bdwy debut 1951 in "Legend of Lovers," followed by "The Cold Wind and the Warm," "Fragile Fox," "The Sunshine Boys," "Hamlet (1964), OB in "The Eagle Has Two Heads," "House Music," "Transfiguration of Benno Blimpie."

FOX, NANCY. Born Sept. 23, 1952 in Houston, TX. Attended NYU. Bdwy debut 1970 in "Minnie's Boys," followed by "7 Brides for 7 Brothers," OB in "You're a Good Man, Charlie Brown."

FRANKLIN, NANCY. Born in NYC. Debut 1959 OB in "Buffalo Skinner," followed by "Power of Darkness," "Oh, Dad, Poor Dad . . . ," "Theatre of Peretz," "Seven Days of Mourning," "Here Be Dragons," "Beach Children," "Safe Place," "Innocent Pleasures," "Loves of Cass McGuire," "After the Fall," Bdwy in "Never Live Over a Pretzel Factory" (1964), "Happily Never After," "The White House," "Charlie and Algernon."

FRANKS, MICHELE. Born Feb. 3 in Tulsa, OK. Graduate UAk. Debut 1981 OB in "Anything Goes," followed by "The Ventriloquist."

FRANZ, ELIZABETH. Born June 18, 1941 in Akron, OH. Attended AADA. Debut 1965 OB in "In White America," followed by "One Night Stands of a Noisy Passenger," "The Real Inspector Hound," "Augusta," "Yesterday Is Over," "Actor's Nightmare," "Sister Mary Ignatius Explains It All," Bdwy in "Rosencrantz and Guildenstern Are Dead," "The Cherry Orchard," "Brighton Beach Memoirs."

FRANZ, JOY. Born in 1944 in Modesto, CA. Graduate UMo. Debut 1969 OB in "Of Thee I Sing," followed by "Jacques Brel Is Alive . . . ," "Out of This World," "Curtains," "I Can't Keep Running in Place," "Tomfoolery," "Penelope," Bdwy in "Sweet Charity," "Lysistrata," "A Little Night Music," "Pippin," "Musical Chairs."

FRATANTONI, DIANE. Born Mar. 29, 1956 in Wilmington, DE. Bdwy debut 1979 in "A Chorus Line."

FREEMAN, MORGAN. Born June 1, 1937 in Memphis, TN. Attended LACC. Bdwy bow 1967 in "Hello, Dolly!" followed by "The Mighty Gents," OB in "Ostrich Feathers," "Niggerlovers," "Exhibition," "Black Visions," "Cockfight," "White Pelicans," "Julius Caesar," "Coriolanus," "Mother Courage," "The Connection," "The World of Ben Caldwell," "Buck."

FREEMAN, YVETTE. Born Oct. 1, 1950 in Chester, PA. Graduate UDe. Debut 1976 OB in "Let My People Come," followed by "Rats," Bdwy in "Ain't Misbehavin' " (1979).

FRENCH, ARTHUR. Born in NYC. Attended Brooklyn Col. Debut 1962 OB in "Raisin' Hell in the Sun," followed by "Ballad of Bimshire," "Day of Absence," "Happy Ending," "Jonah," "Black Girl," "Ceremonies in Dark Old Men," "An Evening of One Acts," "Man Better Man," "Brotherhood," "Perry's Mission," "Rosalee Pritchett," "Moonlight Arms," "Dark Tower," "Brownsville Raid," "Nevis Mt. Dew," "Julius Caesar," "Friends," "Court of Miracles," Bdwy in "Ain't Supposed to Die a Natural Death," "The Iceman Cometh," "All God's Chillun Got Wings," "The Resurrection of Lady Lester," "You Can't Take It With You."

GABLE, JUNE. Born June 5, 1945 in NYC. Carnegie Tech graduate. OB in "Macbird," "Jacques Brel Is Alive and Well . . . ," "A Day in the Life of Just About Everyone," "Mod Donna," "Wanted," "Lady Audley's Secret," "Comedy of Errors," "Chinchilla," "Star Treatment," "Coming Attractions," Bdwy in "Candide" (1974), "The Ritz," "Moose Murders."

GAINES, BOYD. Born May 11, 1953 in Atlanta, GA. Juilliard graduate. Debut 1978 OB in "Spring Awakening," followed by "A Month in the Country" for which he received a Theatre World Award, BAM Theatre Co.'s "Winter's Tale," "The Barbarians," and "Johnny On a Spot," "Vikings."

GALARNO, BILL. Born Mar. 1, 1938 in Saginaw, MI. Attended Pittsburgh Playhouse. Debut 1962 OB in "Nathan the Wise," followed by "Pantagleize," "The Sound of Music," "Candide," "Pictures at an Exhibition."

GALLAGHER, HELEN. Born in 1926 in Brooklyn, NY. Bdwy debut 1947 in "Seven Lively Arts," followed by "Mr. Strauss Goes to Boston," "Billion Dollar Baby," "Brigadoon," "High Button Shoes," "Touch and Go," "Make a Wish," "Pal Joey," "Guys and Dolls," "Finian's Rainbow," "Oklahoma!," "Pajama Game," "Bus Stop," "Portofino," "Sweet Charity," "Mame," "Cry for Us All," "No, No, Nanette," "A Broadway Musical," "Sugar Babies," OB in "Hothouse," "Tickles by Tucholsky," "The Misanthrope," "I Can't Keep Running in Place," "Red Rover," "Tallulah."

GALLAGHER, PETER. Born Aug. 19, 1955 in NYC. Graduate Tufts U. Bdwy debut 1977 in "Hair," followed by "A Doll's Life" for which he received a Theatre World Award.

GANTRY, DONALD. Born June 11, 1936 in Philadelphia, PA. Attended Temple U. Bdwy debut 1961 in "One More River," followed by "Ah, Wilderness," "The Queen and the Rebels," OB in "The Iceman Cometh," "Children of Darkness," "Here Come the Clowns," "Seven at Dawn," "Long Day's Journey Into Night," "Enclave," "Bags."

GARBER, VICTOR. Born Mar. 16, 1949 in London, Can. Debut 1973 OB in "Ghosts" for which he received a Theatre World Award, followed by "Joe's Opera," "Cracks," Bdwy in "Tartuffe," "Deathtrap," "Sweeney Todd," "They're Playing Our Song," "Little Me."

GARDENIA, VINCENT. Born Jan. 7, 1923 in Naples, It. Debut 1955 OB in "In April Once," followed by "Man with the Golden Arm," "Volpone," "Brothers Karamazov," "Power of Darkness," "Machinal," "Gallows Humor," "Theatre of the Absurd," "Lunatic View," "Little Murders," "Passing Through from Exotic Places," "Carpenters," "Buried Inside Extra," Bdwy in "The Visit" (1958), "Rashomon," "The Cold Wind and the Warm," "Only in America," "The Wall," "Daughter of Silence," "Seidman & Son," "Dr. Fish," "Prisoner of Second Avenue," "God's Favorite," "California Suite," "Ballroom."

GARDNER, JEFFREY HOLT. Born Nov. 18, 1962 in NYC. Attended SUNY/Purchase. Bdwy debut 1982 in "The Queen and the Rebels," OB in "Berlin to Bdwy" (1982), followed by "Bentley's War."

GARDNER, LAURA, Born Mar. 17, 1951 in Flushing, NY. Graduate Boston U., Rutgers U. Debut 1979 OB in "The Office Murders," followed by "Welded," "Living Quarters," "Beggar's Opera."

GARFIELD, JULIE. Born Jan. 10, 1946 in Los Angeles, CA. Attended UWi, Neighborhood Playhouse. Debut 1969 OB in "Honest-to-God Schnozzola," followed by "East Lynne," "The Sea," "Uncle Vanya" for which she received a Theatre World Award, "Me and Molly," "Chekhov Sketchbook," "Rosario and the Gypsies," "Occupations," "Modern Ladies of Guanabacoa," Bdwy in "The Good Doctor," "Death of a Salesman," "The Merchant."

GARLAND, GEOFF. Born June 10, 1932 in Warrington, Eng. OB in "The Hostage," "Trelawny of the Wells," "Timon of Athens," "Waiting for Godot," "Billy Liar," Bdwy in "Hamlet," "Imaginary Invalid," "Touch of the Poet," "Tonight at 8:30," "Front Page," "Capt. Brassbound's Conversion," "Cyrano," "My Fat Friend," "Sly Fox," "The Dresser," "Alice In Wonderland."

GARLAND, JAMIL K. Born Oct. 19, 1951 in Shreveport, LA. Attended Laney Col., Bdwy debut 1980 in "Your Arms Too Short to Box With God" (also 1982), OB in "Macbeth," "Helen," "Miss Truth," "Raisin," "Boogie-Woogie Rumble."

GARRISON, DAVID. Born June 30, 1952 in Long Branch, NJ. Graduate Boston U. Debut OB in "Joseph and the Amazing Technicolor Dreamcoat," followed by "Living At Home," "Geniuses," Bdwy in "A History of the American Film," "A Day in Hollywood/A Night in the Ukraine," "Pirates of Penzance," "Snoopy," "Torch Song Trilogy."

GARSIDE, BRAD. Born June 2, 1958 in Boston, MA. Graduate NTexState U. Debut 1983 OB in "Forbidden Broadway."

GARTEN, LIBBY. Born Nov. 19, 1957 in Raleigh, NC. Graduate Wake Forest U. Debut 1983 OB in "The Robber Bridegroom."

GARZA, TROY. Born Aug. 20, 1954 in Hollywood, CA. Attended RADA. Bdwy debut 1977 in "A Chorus Line," followed by "Got Tu Go Disco," OB in "Fourtune," "Paris Lights."

GAVON, IGORS. Born Nov. 14, 1937 in Latvia. Bdwy bow 1961 in "Carnival," followed by "Hello Dolly!" "Marat/deSade," "Billy," "Sugar," "Mack and Mabel," "Musical Jubilee," "Strider," OB in "Your Own Thing," "Promenade," "Exchange," "Nevertheless They Laugh," "Polly," "The Boss," "Biography: A Game," "Murder in the Cathedral."

GEFFNER, DEBORAH. Born Aug. 26, 1952 in Pittsburgh, PA. Attended Juilliard, HB Studio. Debut 1978 OB in "Tenderloin," Bdwy in "Pal Joey," "A Chorus Line."

GELFER, STEVEN. Born Feb. 21, 1949 in Brooklyn, NY. Graduate NYU, IndU. Debut 1968 OB and Bdwy in "The Best Little Whorehouse in Texas," followed by "Cats."

GENELLE, JOANNE. Born Nov. 21, 1956 in Brooklyn, NY. Attended Queens Col. Debut 1982 OB in "Get Happy," followed by "The Larry Loeber Show," Bdwy in "Dance a Little Closer" (1983).

GENTLES, AVRIL. Born Apr. 2, 1929 in Upper Montclair, NJ. Graduate UNC. Bdwy debut 1955 in "The Great Sebastians," followed by "Nude With Violin," "Present Laughter," "My Mother, My Father and Me," "Jimmy Shine," "Grin and Bare It," "Lysistrata," "Texas Trilogy," "Show Boat" (1983), OB in "Dinny and the Witches," "The Wives," "Now Is the Time," "Man With a Load of Mischief," "Shay," "Winter's Tale," "Johnny On a Spot," "The Barbarians," "The Wedding," "Nymph Errant."

GERROLL, DANIEL. Born Oct. 16, 1951 in London, Eng. Attended Central Sch. of Speech. Debut 1980 OB in "The Slab Boys," followed by "Knuckle" and "Translations" for which he received a Theatre World Award, "The Caretaker," "Scenes from La Vie de Boheme," Bdwy in "Plenty" (1982).

GETTY ESTELLE. Born July 25, 1923 in NYC. Attended New School. Debut 1971 OB in "The Divorce of Judy and Jane," followed by "Widows and Children First," "Table Settings," "Demolition of Hannah Fay," "Never Too Old," "A Box of Tears," "Hidden Corners," "I Don't Know Why I'm Screaming," "Under the Bridge There's a Lonely Place," "Light Up the Sky," "Pocketful of Posies," "Fits and Starts," Bdwy 1982 in "Torch Song Trilogy."

GILBERT, RONNIE. Born Sept. 7 in NYC. Bdwy debut 1968 in "The Man in the Glass Booth," OB in "America Hurrah," "Hector the Heroic," "Hot Buttered Roll," "Viet Rock," "Tourists and Refugees," "Antigone," "Trespassing," "Lies and Secrets," "Aladin."

GILDIN, KENNETH. Born Feb. 2, 1955 in NYC. Graduate Tufts U. Debut 1978 OB in "Oklahoma!," followed by "On a Clear Day You Can See Forever," "Primal Time."

GILFORD, JACK. Born July 25, 1907 in NYC. Bdwy debut 1940 in "Meet the People," followed by "They Should Have Stood in Bed," "Count Me In," "The Live Wire," "Alive and Kicking," "Once Over Lightly," "Diary of Anne Frank," "Romanoff and Juliet," "The Tenth Man," "A Funny Thing Happened on the Way to the Forum," "Cabaret," "3 Men on a Horse," "No, No Nanette," "The Sunshine Boys," "Sly Fox," "Supporting Cast," "The World of Sholom Aleichem," OB in "Three Sisters."

GILL, TERI. Born July 16, 1954 in Long Island City, NY. Graduate USIU. Bdwy debut 1976 in "Going Up," followed by "Evita," "A Doll's Life," OB in "Allegro."

GILPIN, JACK. Born May 31, 1951 in Boyce, VA. Harvard graduate. Debut 1976 OB in "Goodbye and Keep Cold," followed by "Shay," "The Soft Touch," "Beyond Therapy," "The Lady or the Tiger," "The Middle Ages," "The Rise of Daniel Rocket," Bdwy in "Lunch Hour" ('80).

GIONSON, MEL. Born Feb. 23, 1954 in Honolulu, HI. Graduate UHi. Debut 1979 OB in "Richard II," followed by "Sunrise," "Monkey Music," "Behind Enemy Lines," "Station J." "Teahouse," "A Midsummer Night's Dream."

GIRARDEAU, FRANK. Born Oct. 19, 1942 in Beaumont. TX. Attended Rider Col, HB Studio. Debut 1972 OB in "22 Years," followed by "The Solider," "Hughie" "An American Story," "El Hermano," "Dumping Ground," "Daddies," "Accounts."

GLEASON, JAMES. Born Sept. 30, 1952 in NYC. Graduate Santa Fe Col. Debut 1982 OB in "Guys in the Truck," followed by "Corkscrews!," Bdwy in "Guys in The Truck" (1983).

GLOVER, JOHN. Born Aug. 7, 1944 in Kingston, NY. Attended Towson State Col. Debut 1969 OB in "A Scent of Flowers," followed by "Government Inspector," "Rebel Women," "Treats," "Booth," Bdwy in "The Selling of the President," "Great God Brown," "Don Juan," "The Visit," "Chemin de Fer," "Holiday," "The Importance of Being Earnest," "Frankenstein," "Whodunnit."

GLYNN, CARLIN. Born Feb. 19, 1940 in Cleveland, OH. Attended Sophie Newcomb Col., Actors Studio. Debut 1959 OB in "Waltz of the Toreadors," followed by "Cassatt," "Winterplay," Bdwy 1978 in "The Best Little Whorehouse in Texas" for which she received a Theatre World Award.

GODFREY, LYNNIE. Born Sept. 11, 1952 in NYC. Graduate Hunter Col. Debut 1976 OB in "I Paid My Dues," followed by "Two Fish in the Sky," Bdwy 1978 in "Eubie!"

GOETZ, PETER MICHAEL. Born Dec. 10, 1941 in Buffalo, NY. Graduate SUNY/Fredonia, Southern ILU. Debut 1980 OB in "Jail Diary of Albie Sachs," followed by Bdwy in "Ned and Jack" (1981), "Beyond Therapy," "The Queen and the Rebels," "Brighton Beach Memoirs."

GOLD, DAVID. Born Feb. 2, 1929 in NYC. Attended Antioch Col. Bdwy bow 1955 in "Red Roses for Me," followed by "Copper and Brass," "New Girl in Town," "Redhead," "Greenwillow," "Do Re Mi," "We Take the Town," "Little Me," "Pleasures and Palaces," "Drat! The Cat!," "Sweet Charity," "Education of Hyman Kaplan," "Lorelei," "On Your Toes," OB in "The Trial," "Metamorphosis," "If Five Years Pass," "Carefree Tree," "Dandelion Wine."

GOLDSMITH, MERWIN. Born Aug. 7, 1937 in Detroit, MI. Graduate UCLA, Old Vic. Bdwy debut 1970 in "Minnie's Boys," followed by "The Visit," "Chemin de Fer," "Rex," "Dirty Linen," "The 1940's Radio Show," "Slab Boys," OB in "Hamlet as a Happening," "Chickencoop Chinaman," "Wanted," "Comedy," "Rubbers," "Yankees 3 Detroit 0," "Trelawny of the Wells," "Chincilla," "Real Life Funnies," "Big Apple Messenger."

GOODMAN, JOHN. Born June 20, 1952 in St. Louis, MO. Graduate Southwest MoStateU. Debut 1978 OB in "A Midsummer Night's Dream," followed by "The Chisholm Trail," "Henry IV Part II," "Ghosts of the Loyal Oaks," "Half a Lifetime."

GOODMAN, LISA. Born in Detroit, MI. Attended UMi. Debut 1982 OB In "Talking With," followed by "The First Warning," "The Show-Off."

GOODMAN, MARGARET. Born Oct. 10, 1936 in Knoxville, TN. Graduate Bryn Mawr, New Eng. Consv. Debut 1976 OB in "Follies," followed by "Louisiana Summer."

GOODMAN, ROBYN. Born Aug. 24, 1947 in NYC. Graduate Brandeis U. Debut 1973 OB in "When You Comin' Back, Red Ryder?" followed by "Richard III," "Museum," "Bits and Pieces," "Fishing," "Flux," "Something Different."

GOOTENBERG, AMY. Born Feb. 29, 1952 in Boston, MA. Graduate Middlebury Col., Catholic U. Debut 1980 OB in "The Time of the Cuckoo," followed by "Firebugs."

GORDON, KEITH. Born Feb. 3, 1961 in NYC. Debut 1976 OB in "Secrets of the Rich," followed by "A Traveling Companion," "Suckers," "Gimmer Shelter," "Sunday Runners," "Album," "The Buddy System," "Back to Back."

GORSHIN, FRANK. Born Apr. 5, 1933 in Pittsburg, PA. Bdwy debut 1969 in "Jimmy," followed by "Whodunnit."

GOSSETT, ROBERT. Born Mar. 3, 1954 in The Bronx, NY. Attended AADA. Debut 1973 OB in "One Flew over the Cuckoo's Nest," followed by "The Amen Corner," "Weep Not for Me," "Colored People's Time," "A Soldier's Play," "Sons and Fathers of Sons," "Manhattan Made Me."

GOULD, ELLIOTT. Born Aug. 29, 1938 in Brooklyn, NY. Attended Columbia U. Bdwy debut 1957 in "Rumple," followed by "Say, Darling," "Irma La Douce," "I Can Get It for You Wholesale," "Drat! The Cat!," "Little Murders," "Guys in the Truck" (previews only).

GOULD, GORDON. Born May 4, 1930 in Chicago, IL. Graduate Yale, Cambridge (Eng.). Bdwy debut 1965 in "You Can't Take It With You," followed by "War and Peace," "Right You Are," "The Wild Duck," "Pantagleize," "Exit the King," "The Show-Off," "School for Wives," "Freedom of the City," "Strider," "Amadeus," OB in "Man and Superman," "Scapin," "Impromptu at Versailles," "The Lower Depths," "The Tavern," "Judith," "Naked," "Tatyana Repina," "The Middle Ages."

GRAAE, JASON. Born May 15, 1958 in Chicago, IL. Graduate Cincinnati Consv. Debut 1981 OB in "Godspell," followed by "Snoopy," Bdwy 1982 in "Do Black Patent Leather Shoes Really Reflect Up?"

GRAHAM, DEBORAH. Born Jan. 20, 1959 in Speedway, IN. Graduate UCinn. Debut 1982 OB in "Snoopy."

GRAMMIS, ADAM. Born Dec. 8, 1947 in Allentown, PA. Graduate Kutztown State Col. Bdwy debut 1971 in "Wild and Wonderful," followed by "Shirley MacLaine Show," "A Chorus Line," OB in "Dance Continuum," "Joseph and the Amazing Technicolor Dreamcoat."

GRAVES, RUTHANNA. Born Sept. 14, 1957 in Philadelphia, PA. Attended NYU. Debut 1980 OB in "Mother Courage," followed by "Boggie-Woogie Rumble."

GRAY, SAM. Born July 18, 1923 in Chicago, IL. Graduate Columbia U. Bdwy debut 1955 in "Deadfall," followed by "Six Fingers in a Five Finger Glove," "Saturday, Sunday, Monday," "Golda," "A View from the Bridge," OB in "Ascent of F-6," "Family Portrait," "One Tiger on a Hill," "Shadow of Heroes," "The Recruiting Officer," "The Wild Duck," "Jungle of Cities," "3 Acts of Recognition," "Returnings."

Pamela Caden

Bill Capucilli

Myra Carter

Bob Chamberlain

Sally Chamberlin

Jeffrey Alan Chandler

Gordon Chater

Gail Dahms

Daniel David

Sheila Kay Davis

R. Michael Dayton

Aurelia DeFelice

Denise DeMirjian

Ronald Dennis

Loretta Devine

Michael Dinelli

Virginia Downing

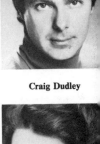
Craig Dudley

Edward Easton

Louise Edeiken

David Ellin

Suellen Estey

Jeff Etjen

Lee Anne Fahey

Rochelle Firestone

Dennis Florzak

Nancy Franklin

Arthur French

Libby Garten

Sam Gray

203

GRAYSON, LEE. Born July 9, 1947 in Brooklyn, NY. Attended Hofstra U. Debut 1979 OB in "I'm Getting My Act Together . . .," followed by "Lennon."

GREEN, PETER. Born Dec. 16, 1955 in NYC. Graduate SUNY/Purchase. Debut 1979 OB in "The City Suite," followed by "Badgers," "Primal Time."

GREENAN, DAVID. Born Sept. 21 in Burlington, VT. Graduate Boston U, UCLA. Debut 1980 OB in "Plain and Fancy," followed by "Twelfth Night," "Murder in the Cathedral," "Under Milk Wood," "Wives."

GREENBERG, MITCHELL. Born Sept. 19, 1950 in Brooklyn, NY. Graduate Harpur Col., Neighborhood Playhouse. Debut 1979 OB in "Two Grown Men," followed by "Scrambled Feet," "A Christmas Carol," Bdwy in "A Day in Hollywood/A Night in the Ukraine" (1980), "Can-Can" (1981).

GREENE, ELLEN. Born Feb. 22 in NYC. Attended Ryder Col. Debut 1973 in "Rachel Lily Rosenbloom," followed OB by "In the Boom Boom Room," "Threepenny Opera," "The Nature and Purpose of the Universe," "Teeth 'n' Smiles," "The Sorrows of Stephen," "Disrobing the Bride," "The Little Shop of Horrors," Bdwy 1981 in "The Little Prince and the Aviator."

GREENE, GAYLE. Born Jan. 22, 1948 in NYC. Graduate Carnegie Tech. Debut 1975 OB in "The Love Death Plays of William Inge," followed by "Secret Thighs of New England Women," "The Incognita," "Returnings."

GREENE, JAMES. Born Dec. 1, 1926 in Lawrence, MA. Graduate Emerson Col. OB in "The Iceman Cometh," "American Gothic," "The King and the Duke," "The Hostage," "Plays for Bleecker Street," "Moon in the Yellow River," "Misalliance," "Government Inspector" "Baba Goya," LCRep 2 years, "You Can't Take It With You," "School for Scandal," "Wild Duck," "Right You Are," "The Show-Off," "Pantagleize," "Festival of Short Plays," "Nourish the Beast," "One Crack Out," "Artichoke," "Othello," "Salt Lake City Skyline," "Summer," "The Rope Dancers," "Frugal Repast," "Bella Figura," "The Freak," Bdwy in "Romeo and Juliet," "Girl on the Via Flaminia," "Compulsion," "Inherit the Wind," "Shadow of a Gunman," "Andersonville Trial," "Night Life," "School for Wives," "Ring Round the Bathtub," "Great God Brown," "Don Juan," "Foxfire."

GREENE, REUBEN. Born Nov. 24, 1938 in Philadelphia, PA. With APA in "War and Peace," "You Can't Take It with You," and "Pantagleize," OB in "Jerico-Jim Crow," "Happy Ending," "Boys in the Band," "Twilight Dinner," "Adam."

GREENHILL, SUSAN. Born March 19 in NYC. Graduate UPa, Catholic U. Bdwy debut 1982 in "Crimes of the Heart," followed by OB in "Hooters," "Our Lord of Lynchville."

GREENHOUSE, MARTHA. Born June 14 in Omaha, NE. Attended Hunter Col., Theatre Wing. Bdwy debut 1942 in "Sons and Soldiers," followed by "Dear Me, the Sky Is Falling," "Family Way," "Woman Is My Idea," "Summer Brave," OB in "Clerambard," "Our Town," "3 by Ferlinghetti," "No Strings," "Cackle," "Philistines," "Ivanov," "Returnings."

GREER, MICHAEL. Born Apr. 20, 1943 in Galesburg, IL. Attended AmThWing. Debut 1969 OB in "Fortune and Men's Eyes," followed by "The Ritz."

GREGORIO, ROSE. Born in Chicago, IL. Graduate Northwestern, Yale. Debut 1962 OB in "The Days and Nights of Beebee Fenstermaker," followed by "Kiss Mama," "The Balcony," "Bivouac at Lucca," "Journey to the Day," "Diary of Anne Frank," "Weekends Like Other People," Bdwy in "The Owl and the Pussycat," "Daphne in Cottage D," "Jimmy Shine," "The Cuban Thing," "The Shadow Box," "A View from the Bridge."

GRIER, DAVID ALAN. Born June 30, 1955 in Detroit, MI. Graduate UMich, Yale. Bdwy debut 1981 in "The First" for which he received a Theatre World Award, OB in "A Soldier's Play."

GRIESEMER, JOHN. Born Dec. 5, 1947 in Elizabeth, NJ. Graduate Dickinson Col, URI. Debut 1981 OB in "Turnbuckle," followed by "Death of a Miner," "Little Victories."

GRIFFIN, SEAN G. Born Oct. 14, 1942 in Limerick, Ire. Graduate Notre Dame, UKan. Bdwy debut 1974 in "The National Health," followed by "Poor Murder" "Ah, Wilderness!," "Ned and Jack," "The Queen and the Rebels."

GRIMES, FRANK. Born in 1947 in Dublin, IRE. Attended Abbey Theatre School. Bdwy debut 1970 in "Borstal Boy," followed by OB's "The Holly and the Ivy."

GRIMES, TAMMY. Born Jan, 30, 1934 in Lynn, MA. Attended Stephens Col., Neighborhood Playhouse. Debut 1956 in OB "The Littlest Revue," followed by "Clerambard," "Molly," "Trick," "Are You Now or Have You Ever Been," "Father's Day," "A Month in the Country," Bdwy in "Look After Lulu" (1959) for which she received a Theatre World Award, "The Unsinkable Molly Brown," "Rattle of a Simple Man," "High Spirit," "The Only Game in Town," "Private Lives," "Musical Jubilee," "California Suite," "Tartuffe," "42nd Street," "Pal Joey in Concert,".

GROENER, HARRY. Born Sept. 10, 1951 in Augsburg. Ger. Graduate UWash. Bdwy debut 1979 in "Oklahoma!" for which he recieved a Theatre World Award, followed by "Oh, Brother!," "Is There Life after High School," "Cats," OB in "Beside the Seaside."

GROLLMAN, ELAINE. Born Oct. 22, 1928 in The Bronx, NY. Debut 1974 OB in "Yentl the Yeshiva Boy," followed by "Kaddish," "The Water Hen," "Millions of Miles," "Come Back, Little Sheba," "Biography: A Game," "House Music," "The Workroom," Bdwy in "Yentl."

GROSS, MICHAEL. Born in 1947 in Chicago, IL. UIll and Yale graduate. Debut 1978 OB in "Sganarelle," followed by "Othello," "Endgame," "The Wild Duck" "Oedipus the King." "Put Them All Together," "No End of Blame," "Geniuses," "Territorial Rites." Bdwy in "Bent." ('79), "The Philadelphia Story."

GUARDINO, LAWRENCE. Born Sept. 4 in NYC. Graduate Wagner Col. Debut 1974 OB in "The Sirens," followed by "Golden Boy," "Bullpen," Bdwy in "The Guys in the Truck" (1983).

GUASP, JULIO. Born July 25, 1942 in Puerto Rico. Attended AADA. Debut 1969 OB in "Your Own Thing," followed by "The Cowboy and the Legend," "Whatever Happens Don't Leave."

GUIDO, MICHAEL. Born Jan. 13, 1950 in Woodside, NY. Graduate U South FL., Brandeis U. Debut 1982 OB in "The Workroom."

GUNTON, BOB. Born Nov. 15, 1945 in Santa Monica, CA. Attended UCal. Debut 1971 OB in "Who Am I?," followed by "The Kid," "Desperate Hours," "Tip-Toes," "How I Got That Story," "Hamlet," "Death of Von Richthofen," Bdwy in "Happy End" (1977), "Working," "King of Hearts," "Evita," "Passion."

GUTIERREZ, ANNA MARIE. Born in Santa Barbara, CA. Graduate San Diego State U. Debut 1982 OB in "New Faces of 1952."

GUTIERREZ, GERALD. Born Feb. 3, 1950 in Brooklyn, NY. Graduate SUNY/Stonybrook, Juilliard. Debut 1972 OB in "School for Scandal," followed by "Lower Depths," "U.S.A.," "The Hostage," "The Time of Your Life," "The Cradle Will Rock," Bdwy in "Measure for Measure," (1977), "Beggar's Opera," "Scapin," "Three Sisters."

GWYNNE, FRED. Born July 10, 1926 in NYC. Graduate Harvard. Bdwy debut 1952 in "Mrs. McThing," followed by "Love's Labour's Lost," "Frogs of Spring," "Irma La Duce," "Here's Love," "The Lincoln Mask," "Cat on a Hot Tin Roof," "Texas Trilogy," "Angel," "Players," "Whodunnit," OB in "More Than You Deserve," "Fair Game," "Grand Magic," "Salt Lake City Skyline."

HABER, MARTIN. Born Apr. 11, 1928 in NYC. Graduate NYU. Debut 1983 OB in "Goodnight, Grandpa."

HACK, STEVEN. Born Apr. 20, 1958 in St. Louis MO. Attended CalArts, AADA. Debut 1978 OB in "The Coolest Cat in Town," followed by Bdwy in "Cats" (1982).

HADARY, JONATHAN. Born Oct. 11, 1948 in Chicago, IL. Attended Tufts U. Debut 1974 OB in "White Nights," followed by "El Grande de Coca-Cola," "Songs from Pins and Needles," "God Bless You, Mr. Rosewater," "Pushing 30," "Scrambled Feet," "Coming Attractions," "Tomfoolery," Bdwy 1977 in "Gemini" (also OB), "Torch Song Trilogy."

HAGAN, PETER. Born Oct. 3, 1954 in Alexandria, VA. Graduate UVa. Debut 1980 OB in "Class Enemy," followed by "Scenes from American Life."

HAGUE, MELANIE. Born Jan. 30, 1952 in Bangor, ME. Graduate Ohio U. Debut 1982 OB in "Looking-Glass."

HALL, DAVIS. Born Apr. 10, 1946 in Atlanta, GA. Graduate Northwestern U. Bdwy debut 1973 in "Butley," followed by "Dogg's Hamlet and Cahoot's MacBeth," OB in "The Promise," "Dreamboats."

HALL, GEORGE. Born Nov. 19, 1916 in Toronto. Can. Attended Neighborhood Playhouse. Bdwy bow 1946 in "Call Me Mister," followed by "Lend an Ear," "Touch and Go," "Live Wire," "The Boy Friend," "There's a Girl in My Soup," "An Evening with Richard Nixon . . . ," "We Interrupt This Program," "Man and Superman," "Bent," OB in "The Balcony," "Ernest in Love," "A Round with Rings," "Family Pieces," "Carousel," "The Case Against Roberta Guardino," "Marry Me!" Marry Me!" "Arms and the Man," "The Old Glory," "Dancing for the Kaiser," "Casualties," "The Seagull," "A Stitch in Time," "Mary Stuart," "No End of Blame," "Hamlet," "Colette Collage."

HALL, STEVE. Born June 4, 1958 in Washington, DC. Attended NCShool for Arts. Bdwy debut 1981 in "Marlowe," OB in "T.N.T.", followed by "Colette Collage."

HALLER, TOBIAS. Born Sept. 30, 1951 in Baltimore, MD. Graduate Towson State Col. Debut 1971 OB in "Now There's Just the Three of Us," followed by "The Screens," "Gorey Stories," "The Madman and the Nun," "Frozen Assets," Bdwy in "The Last of Mrs. Lincoln," "Gorey Stories."

HAMILL, MARK. Born Sept. 25, 1952 in Oakland, CA. Attended LACC. Bdwy debut 1981 in "The Elephant Man," followed by "Amadeus" (1983).

HAMILL, MARY. Born Dec. 29, 1943 in Flushing, NY. Graduate UDallas. Debut 1969 OB in "Spiro Who?," followed by "What the Butler Saw," "Siamese Connections," "Trelawny of the Wells," "A Difficult Borning," Bdwy in "4 on a Garden," "P.S.: Your Cat Is Dead," "Talley's Folly."

HAMMIL, JOHN. Born May 9, 1948 in NYC. Attended UCLA. Bdwy debut 1972 in "Purlie," followed by "Oh! Calcutta!," "Platinum," "They're Playing Our Song," "Woman of the Year," OB in "El Grande de Coca-Cola," "Songs from the City Streets."

HANAN, STEPHEN. Born Jan. 7, 1947 in Washington, DC. Graduate Harvard, LAMDA. Debut 1978 OB in "All's Well That Ends Well," followed by "Taming of the Shrew," Bdwy in "Pirates of Penzance" (1978), "Cats."

HANDLER, EVAN. Born Jan. 10, 1961 in NYC. Attended Juilliard. Debut 1979 OB in "Biography: A Game," followed by "Strider," "Final Orders," Bdwy in "Solomon's Child."

HANNAFIN, DANIEL P. Born Feb. 8, 1933 in NYC. Attended Juilliard. On Bdwy in "Camelot," "Flora the Red Menace," "Baker Street," CC revivals of "South Pacific," "Wonderful Town," "Brigadoon," "Oklahoma!" and "The Tenth Man," "West Side Story" (JB).

HANNING, GERALDINE. Born in Cleveland, OH. Graduate CtCol. Western Reserve U. Debut 1954 OB in "Praise of Folly," followed by "In Good King Charles' Golden Days," "Philanderer," "Lysistrata," "Alcestis Comes Back," "Under the Gaslight," "One for the Money," "The Constant Wife," "From Brooks with Love."

HANSEN, LARRY. Born Mar. 11, 1952 in Anacortes, WA. Graduate Western Wash. U. Debut 1978 OB in "Can-Can," Bdwy in "Show Boat" (1983).

HANSEN, RANDY. Born Jan. 30, 1953 in Audubon, IA. Graduate UNIa., Ind U. Debut 1980 OB in "Elizabeth and Essex," Bdwy in "Show Boat" (1983).

HAO, WILLIAM. Born Aug. 10, 1953 In Hololulu, HI. Attended Chaminade Col., Leeward Col. Debut 1981 OB in "The Shining House," followed by "Gaugin in Tahiti," "Teahouse," "A Midsummer Night's Dream."

HARDY, WILLIAM. Born Jan. 19, 1933 in Houston, TX. Attended UHouston, Debut 1983 OB in "Joan of Lorraine."

HARGROVE, BRIAN. Born Apr. 2, 1956 in Edgecombe County, NC. Graduate UNC, Juilliard. Debut 1981 OB in "How It All Began," followed by "Henry IV Part I," "Boiling Point," "Never Say Die," "The Three Sisters," "Vieux Carre."

HARLEY, LUCILLE FUTRELL. Born Jan. 28, 1945 in Suffolk, VA. Attended Manhattan Community Col. Bdwy debut 1964 in "Black Nativity," followed by "Bubbling Brown Sugar," OB in "God's Trombone," "Miss Waters, To You."

HARMON, JENNIFER. Born Dec. 3, 1943 in Pasadena, CA. Attended UMiss. With APA in "Right You Are," "You Can't Take It With You," "War and Peace," "Wild Duck," "School for Scandal," OB in "The Effect of Gamma Rays. . . ," "The Hot 1 Baltimore," "Learned Ladies," "The Holly and the Ivy."

HARNEY, BEN. Born Aug. 29, 1952 in Brooklyn, NY. Bdwy debut 1971 in "Purlie," followed by "Pajama Game," "Tree-Monisha," "Pippin," "Dreamgirls," OB in "Don't Bother Me I Can't Cope," "The Derby," "The More You Get."

HARPER, CHARLES THOMAS. Born Mar. 29, 1949 in Carthage, NY. Graduate Webster Col. Debut 1975 OB in "Down by the River . . . ," followed by "Holy Ghosts," "Hamlet," "Mary Stuart," "Twelfth Night," "The Beaver Coat," "Richard II," "Great Grandson of Jedediah Kohler," "Applause," Bdwy in "Passion" (1973).

HARPER, JAMES. Born Oct. 8, 1948 in Bell, CA. Attended Marin Col., Juilliard. Bdwy debut 1973 in "King Lear," followed by "The Robber Bridegroom," "The Time of Your Life," "Mother Courage," "Edward II," OB in "A Midsummer Night's Dream," "Recruiting Officer," "The Wild Duck," "The Jungle of Cities," "The Cradle Will Rock."

HARPER, RON. Born Jan. 12, 1936 in Turtle Creek, PA. Princeton graduate. Debut OB 1955 in "3 by Dylan Thomas," followed by "A Palm Tree in a Rose Garden," "Meegan's Game," "Red Rover," Bdwy in "Sweet Bird of Youth," "Night Circus," "6 Rms Riv Vu."

HARRIS, BAXTER. Born Nov. 18, 1940 in Columbus, KS. Attended UKan. Debut 1967 OB in "America Hurrah," followed by "The Reckoning," "Wicked Women Revue," "More than You Deserve," "Pericles," "him," "Battle of Angels," "Down by the River," "Selma," "Ferocious Kisses," "Three Sisters," "Gradual Clearing," "Dolphin Position."

HARRIS, CYNTHIA. Born in NYC. Graduate Smith Col. Bdwy debut 1963 in "Natural Affection," followed by "Any Wednesday," "Best Laid Plans," "Company," OB in "The Premise," "3 by Wilder," "America Hurrah," "White House Murder Case," "Mystery Play," "Bad Habits," "Merry Wives of Windsor," "Beauty Part," "Jules Feiffer's Hold Me," "Second Avenue Rag," "Cloud 9."

HARRIS, NIKI. Born July 20, 1948 in Pittsburgh, PA. Graduate Duquesne U. Bdwy debut 1980 in "A Day in Hollywood/A Night in the Ukraine," followed by "My One and Only."

HARRIS, SKIP. Born Oct. 27, 1952 in Hempstead, NY. Graduate UCinn. Bdwy debut 1979 in "Sweeney Todd," followed by "Alice in Wonderland."

HART, KITTY CARLISLE. See Carlisle.

HART, PAUL E . Born July 20, 1939 in Lawrence, MA. Graduate Merrimack Col. Debut 1977 OB in "Turandot," followed by "Darkness at Noon," "Light Shines in the Darkness," "Pictures at an Exhibition," Bdwy 1981 in "Fiddler on the Roof."

HART, ROXANNE. Born in 1952 in Trenton, NJ. Attended Skidmore, Princeton U. Bdwy debut 1977 in "Equus," followed by "Loose Ends," "Passion," OB in "A Winter's Tale," "Johnny On a Spot," "The Purging," "Hedda Gabler," "Waiting for the Parade."

HARUM, EIVIND. Born May 24, 1944 in Stavanger, Norway. Attended Utah State U. Credits include "Sophie," "Foxy," "Baker Street," "West Side Story" ('68), "A Chorus Line," "Woman of the Year."

HAUSMAN, ELAINE. Born June 8, 1949 in Sacramento, CA. Graduate UCal, Juilliard. Bdwy debut 1975 in "The Robber Bridegroom," followed by "Edward II," "The Time of Your Life," "Three Sisters," "Brigadoon," OB in "Top Girls."

HAVOC, JUNE. Born Nov. 8, 1916 in Seattle, WA. Bdwy debut 1936 in "Forbidden Melody," followed by "The Women," "Pal Joey," "Mexican Hayride," "Sadie Thompson," "The Ryan Girl," "Dunnigan's Daughter," "Dream Girl," "Affairs of State," "Infernal Machine," "Beaux Stratagem," "The Warm Peninsula," "Dinner at 8," "Habeas Corpus," "Annie."

HAWKINS, TRISH. Born Oct. 30, 1945 in Hartford, CT. Attended Radcliffe, Neighborhood Playhouse. Debut OB 1970 in "Oh! Calcutta!" followed by "Iphigenia," "The Hot l Baltimore" for which she received a Theatre World Award, "him," "Come Back, Little Sheba," "Battle of Angels," "Mound Builders," "The Farm," "Ulysses in Traction," "Lulu," "Hogan's Folly," "Twelfth Night," "A Tale Told," "Great Grandson of Jedediah Kohler," "Time Framed," Bdwy 1977 in "Some of My Best Friends," "Talley's Folly" (1979).

HAYNES, TIGER. Born Dec. 13, 1907 in St. Croix, VI. Bdwy bow 1956 in "New Faces," followed by "Finian's Rainbow," "Fade Out—Fade In," "The Pajama Game," "The Wiz," "A Broadway Musical," "Comin' Uptown," OB in "Turns," "Bags," "Louis."

HEALD, ANTHONY. Born Aug. 25, 1944 in New Rochelle, NY. Graduate MiStateU. Debut 1980 OB in "The Glass Menagerie," followed by "Misalliance" for which he received a Theatre World Award, "The Caretaker," "The Fox," "Quartermaine's Terms," Bdwy in "The Wake of Jamey Foster" (1982).

HEARD, CORDIS. Born July 27, 1944 in Washington, DC. Graduate Chatham Col. Bdwy debut 1973 in "Warp," followed by "The Elephant Man," "Macbeth," OB in "Vanities," "City Junket," "Details without a Map."

HEARD, JOHN. Born Mar. 7, 1946 in Washington, DC. Graduate Clark U. Debut 1974 OB in "The Wager," followed by "Macbeth," "Hamlet," "Fishing," "G. R. Point" for which he received a Theatre World Award, "The Creditors," "The Promise," "Othello," "Split," "Chekhov Sketchbook," Bdwy in "Warp" (1973), "Total Abandon."

HEARN, GEORGE. Born June 18, 1934 in St. Louis, MO. Graduate Southwestern Col. OB in "Macbeth," "Antony and Cleopatra," "As You Like It," "Richard III," "Merry Wives of Windsor," "Midsummer Night's Dream," "Hamlet," "Horseman, Pass By," Bdwy in "A Time for Singing," "The Changing Room," "An Almost Perfect Person," "I Remember Mama," "Watch on the Rhine," "Sweeney Todd," "A Doll's Life," "Whodunnit."

HEBERT, RICH. Born Dec. 14, 1956 in Quincy, MA. Graduate Boston U. Debut 1978 OB in "The Rimers of Eldritch," followed by "110 in the Shade," Bdwy in "Rock 'n' Roll! The First 5000 Years" (1982).

HEFFERNAN, JOHN. Born May 30, 1934 in NYC. Attended CCNY, Columbia, Boston U. Bdwy debut 1963 in "Luther," followed by "Tiny Alice," "Postmark Zero," "Woman Is My Idea," "Morning, Noon and Night," "Purlie," "Bad Habits," "Lady from the Sea," "Knock Knock," "Sly Fox," "The Suicide," "Alice in Wonderland," OB in "The Judge," "Julius Caesar," "Great God Brown," "Lysistrata," "Peer Gynt," "Henry IV," "Taming of the Shrew," "She Stoops to Conquer," "The Plough and the Stars," "Octoroon," "Hamlet," "Androcles and the Lion," "A Man's a Man," "Winter's Tale," "Arms and the Man," "St. Joan," "Memorandum," "Invitation to a Beheading," "The Sea," "Shadow of a Gunman," "Johnny on a Spot," "Barbarians."

HEINEMAN, LAURIE. Born Aug. 4 in Chicago, IL. Graduate Radcliffe Col. Debut 1959 in "The Miracle Worker," OB in "The Orphan" (1973), followed by "Close Relations," "The American Clock," "Letters Home," "Goodnight, Grandpa."

HEIST, KARL. Born June 14, 1950 in West Reading, PA. Graduate McMurry Col. Debut 1976 OB in "Fiorello!," followed by "Silk Stockings," "Winterville," "The Death of Von Richthofen."

HENDERSON, JO. Born in Buffalo, NY. Attended WMiU. OB in "Camille," "Little Foxes," "An Evening with Merlin Finch," "20th Century Tar," "A Scent of Flowers," "Revival," "Dandelion Wine," "My Life," "Ladyhouse Blues," "Fallen Angels," "Waiting for the Parade," "Threads," "Bella Figura," "Details without a Map," "The Middle Ages," "Time Framed," Bdwy in "Rose" (1981), "84 Charing Cross Road."

HENDRICKSON, STEVE. Born Sept. 29, 1954 in Schenectady, NY. Graduate Yale U. Debut 1982 OB in "Herself as Lust," followed by "Lorenzaccio," Bdwy in "The Misanthrope" (1983).

HENNING, DEBBY. Born Jan. 13, 1955 in White Plains, NY. Attended Cooper Union. Bdwy debut 1983 in "Merlin."

HENNING, DOUG. Born May 3, 1947 in Winnipeg, Can. Graduate McMaster U. Bdwy debut 1974 in "The Magic Show," followed by "Merlin."

HENRITZE, BETTE. Born May 3 in Betsy Layne, KY. Graduate UTenn. OB in "Lion in Love," "Abe Lincoln in Illinois," "Othello," "Baal," "Long Christmas Dinner," "Queens of France," "Rimers of Eldritch," "Displaced Person," "Acquisition," "Crime of Passion," "Happiness Cage," "Henry VI," "Richard III," "Older People," "Lotta," "Catsplay," "A Month in the Country," Bdwy in "Jenny Kissed Me" (1948), "Pictures in the Hallway," "Giants, Sons of Giants," "Ballad of the Sad Cafe," "The White House," "Dr. Cook's Garden," "Here's Where I Belong," "Much Ado about Nothing," "Over Here," "Angel Street," "Man and Superman," "Macbeth" (1981), "Present Laughter."

HERRMANN, EDWARD. Born July 21, 1943 in Washington, DC. Graduate Bucknell U., LAMDA. Debut 1970 OB in "The Basic Training of Pavlo Hummel," followed by "Midsummer Night's Dream," "Gardenia," Bdwy in "Moonchildren" ('72), "Mrs. Warren's Profession," "Philadelphia Story," "Plenty."

HESS, ELIZABETH. Born July 17, 1953 in Ontario, Can. Graduate York U. Debut 1982 OB in "The Frances Farmer Story."

HIBBERT, EDWARD. Born Sept. 9, 1955 in NYC. Attended Hurstpierpoint Col., RADA. Bdwy debut 1982 in "Alice in Wonderland," followed by OB in "Candida in Concert."

HILBOLDT, LISE. Born Jan. 7, 1954 in Racine, WI. Attended UWisc., London's Webber-Douglas Acad. Bdwy debut 1981 in "To Grandmother's House We Go," followed by "Top Girls" (OB).

HILLIARD, RYAN. Born Jan. 20, 1945 in Ashtabula, OH. Graduate Kent State U. Debut 1971 OB in "Godspell," followed by "The Boar," "Under Milk Wood," "The Madwoman of Chaillot," "Behind a Mask."

HILLNER, JOHN. Born Nov. 5, 1952 in Evanston, IL. Graduate Dension U. Debut 1977 OB in "Essential Shepard," followed by Bdwy in "They're Playing Our Song," "Little Me," "Woman of the Year."

HILTON, RICHARD. Born June 25, 1950 in Kalamazoo, MI. Graduate WMichU. Debut 1981 OB in "Feiffer's People," followed by Bdwy (1982) in "Joseph and the Amazing Technicolor Dreamcoat."

HINES, GREGORY. Born Feb. 14, 1946 in NYC. Bdwy debut 1954 in "The Girl in Pink Tights," followed by "Eubie!" for which he received a Theatre World Award, "Comin' Uptown," "Black Broadway," "Sophisticated Ladies."

HINES, PATRICK. Born Mar. 17, 1930 in Burkesville, TX. Graduate TexU. Debut OB in "Duchess of Malfi," followed by "Lysistrata," "Peer Gynt," "Henry IV," "Richard III," "Hot Grog," BAM's "A Winter's Tale," "Johnny on a Spot," "Barbarians," "The Wedding" Bdwy in "The Great God Brown," "Passage to India," "The Devils," "Cyrano," "The Iceman Cometh," "A Texas Trilogy," "Caesear and Cleopatra," "Amadeus."

HIRSCHORN, LARRY. Born Aug. 31, 1958 in Oceanside, NY. Graduate Ithaca Col. Debut 1983 OB in "Promises, Promises."

HOBEL, MARA. Born June 18, 1971 in NYC. Bdwy debut 1983 in "Moose Murders."

HODES, RYN. Born Dec. 28, 1956 in NYC. Graduate NYU. Debut 1979 OB in "Miradolina," followed by "Boy Meets Swan," "A Collier's Friday Night," "Suicide in B Flat," "Kaspar," "Fanshen."

HOFFMAN, PHILIP. Born May 12, 1954 in Chicago, IL. Graduate UIll. Bdwy debut 1981 in "The Moony Shapiro Songbook," followed by "Is There Life after High School?" OB in "The Fabulous '50's."

HOFMAIER, MARK. Born July 4, 1950 in Philadelphia, PA. Graduate UAZ. Debut 1978 OB in "A Midsummer Night's Dream," followed by "Marvelous Gray."

HOGAN, JONATHAN. Born June 13, 1951 in Chicago, IL. Graduate Goodman Theatre. Debut OB 1972 in "The Hot l Baltimore," followed by "Mound Builders," "Harry Outside," "Cabin 12," "5th of July," "Glorious Morning," "Innocent Thoughts, Harmless Intentions," "Sunday Runners," "Threads," "Time Framed," Bdwy in "Comedians" (1976), "Otherwise Engaged," "5th of July," "The Caine Mutiny Court-Martial."

HOLBROOK, HAL. Born Feb. 17, 1925 in Cleveland, OH. Graduate Denison U. Bdwy debut 1961 in "Do You Know the Milky Way?," followed by "The Glass Menagerie," "Mark Twain Tonight," "The Apple Tree," "I Never Sang for My Father," "Man of La Mancha," "Does A Tiger Wear a Necktie?," OB in "Henry IV," "Richard II," "Abe Lincoln in Illinois," "Marco Millions," "Incident at Vichy," "Tartuffe," "After the Fall," "Lake of the Woods," "Buried Inside Extra."

HOLLIDAY, JENNIFER. Born Oct. 19, 1960 in Houston, TX. Bdwy debut 1980 in "Your Arms Too Short to Box with God," followed by "Dreamgirls" for which she received a Theatre World Award.

HOLM, CELESTE. Born Apr. 29, 1919 in NYC. Attended UCLA, UChicago. Bdwy debut 1938 in "Glorianna," followed by "The Time of Your Life," "Another Sun," "Return of the Vagabond," "8 O'Clock Tuesday," "My Fair Ladies," "Papa Is All," "All the Comforts of Home," "Damask Cheek," "Oklahoma!," "Bloomer Girl," "She Stoops to Conquer," "Affairs of State," "Anna Christie," "The King and I," "His and Hers," "Interlock," "Third Best Sport," "Invitation to a March," "Mame," "Candida," "Habeas Corpus," "The Utter Glory of Morrissey Hall," OB in "A Month in the Country," "Paris Was Yesterday," "With Love and Laughter."

HOLMES, GEORGE. Born June 3, 1935 in London, Eng. Graduate ULondon. Debut 1978 OB in "The Changeling," followed by "Love from a Stranger," "The Hollow," "The Story of the Gadsbys," "Learned Ladies."

HOLMES, SCOTT. Born May 30, 1952 in West Grove, PA. Graduate Catawba Col. Bdwy debut 1979 in "Grease," followed by "Evita."

HOPE, STEPHEN. Born Jan 23, 1957 in Savannah, GA. Attended ULouisville, CinConsv. Bdwy debut 1982 in "Joseph and the Amazing Technicolor Dreamcoat."

HORMANN, NICHOLAS. Born Dec. 22, 1944 in Honolulu, HI. Graduate Oberlin Col., Yale. Bdwy debut 1973 in "The Visit," followed by "Chemin de Fer," "Holiday," "Love for Love," "Rules of the Game," "Member of the Wedding," "St. Joan," "Moose Murders," OB in "Ice Age," "Marco Polo," "Artichoke," "Looking-Glass," "The Dining Room"

HORNE, GEOFFREY. Born Aug. 22, 1933 in Argentina. Graduate UCal/Berkeley. Debut 1954 OB in "High Named Today," followed by Bdwy in "Too Late the Phalarope" (1956), "Strange Interlude," "Merrily We Roll Along," "The Caine Mutiny Court-Martial."

HOSBIEN, JAMES. Born Sept. 24, 1946 in Benton Harbor, MI. Graduate UMich. Debut 1972 OB in "Dear Oscar," followed by "Darrell and Carol and Kenny and Jenny," "Corkscrews!," Bdwy 1977 in "Annie."

HOUGHTON, KATHARINE. Born Mar. 10, 1945 in Hartford, CT. Graduate Sarah Lawrence Col. Bdwy debut 1965 in "A Very Rich Woman," followed by "The Front Page" (1969), OB in "A Scent of Flowers" for which she received a Theatre World Award, "To Heaven in a Swing."

HOUSEMAN, JOHN. Born Sept. 22, 1902 in Bucharest, Romania. Attended Clifton Col. Made acting debut 1983 OB in "The Cradle Will Rock."

HOWARD, ALAN. Born Mar. 21, 1951 in Rockville Centre, NY. Bdwy debut 1960 in "The Wall," followed by "Garden of Sweets," "A Gift of Time," "Playroom," "Good," OB in "King of the Whole Damn World," "Square in the Eye," "Titus Andronicus," "A Certain Young Man," "Whitsuntide."

HOXIE, RICHMOND. Born July 21, 1946 in NYC. Graduate Dartmouth Col., LAMDA. Debut 1975 OB in "Shaw for an Evening," followed by "The Family," "Justice," "Landscape with Waitress," "3 from the Marathon," "The Slab Boys," "Vivien," "Operation Midnight Climax," "The Dining Room," "Daddies."

HOXIT, LINDA C. Born Mar. 13, 1953 in Bremerton, WA. Attended Olympic Col., USF, UCLA, USC. Bdwy debut 1982 in "Seven Brides for Seven Brothers."

HUBBARD, ELIZABETH. Born Dec. 22 in NYC. Graduate Radcliffe Col. Bdwy debut 1940 in "Tis of Thee," followed by "Crazy with the Heat," "Something for the Boys," "One Touch of Venus," "Calico Wedding," "Mermaids Singing," "Temporary Island," "Story for Strangers," "Two Blind Mice," "Rose Tattoo," "The Crucible," "Witness for the Prosecution," "Third Best Sport," "Rhinoceros," "Mother Courage and Her Children," "Fair Game for Lovers," "A Murderer among Us," "Murder among Friends," "Present Laughter," "Dance a Little Closer," OB in "American Dream," "Sandbox," "Picnic on the Battlefield," "Theatre of the Absurd," "Child Buyer," "A Corner of the Bed," "Someone's Comin' Hungry," "Increased Difficulty of Concentration," "American Hamburger League," "Slow Memories," "Last Analysis," "Dear Oscar," "Hocus-Pocus," "Lessons," "The Art of Dining," "Second Avenue Rag."

HUGHES, BARNARD. Born July 16, 1915 in Bedford Hills, NY. Attended Manhattan Col. Credits: OB in "Rosmersholm," "A Doll's House," "Hogan's Goat," "Lime," "Older People," "Hamlet," "Merry Wives of Windsor," "Pericles," "Three Sisters," "Translations," Bdwy in "The Ivy Green," "Dinosaur Wharf," "Teahouse of the August Moon," "A Majority of One," "Advise and Consent," "The Advocate," "Hamlet," "I Was Dancing," "Generation," "How Now, Dow Jones?," "Wrong Way Light Bulb," "Sheep on the Runway," "Abelard and Heloise," "Much Ado about Nothing," "Uncle Vanya," "The Good Doctor," "All over Town," "Da," "Angels Fall."

HUGHES, LAURA. Born Jan 28, 1959 in NYC. Graduate Neighborhood Playhouse. Debut 1980 OB in "The Diviners," followed by "A Tale Told," "Time Framed."

HUGHES, MICHAELA. Born Mar. 31, 1957 in Morristown, NJ. Attended HB Studio. With Eliot Feld Ballet before Bdwy debut 1983 in "On Your Toes."

HUGHES, TRESA. Born Sept. 17, 1929 in Washington, DC. Attended Wayne U. Appeared OB in "Electra," "The Crucible," "Hogan's Goat," "Party on Greenwich Avenue," "Fragments," "Passing Through from Exotic Places," "Beggar on Horseback," "Early Morning," "The Old Ones," "Holy Places," "Awake and Sing," "Standing on My Knees," "Modern Ladies of Guanabacoa," Bdwy in "Miracle Worker," "Devil's Advocate," "Dear Me, The Sky Is Falling," "Last Analysis," "Spofford," "Man in the Glass Booth," "Prisoner of Second Avenue," "Tribute," "A View from the Bridge."

HULCE, THOMAS. Born Dec. 6, 1953 in Plymouth, MI. Graduate NCSch. of Arts. Bdwy debut 1975 in "Equus," followed by OB "A Memory of Two Mondays," "Julius Casear," "Twelve Dreams," "The Rise and Rise of Daniel Rocket."

HULSWIT, MART. Born May 24, 1940 in Maracaibo, Ven. Attended Hobart Col., AADA. Debut 1961 OB in "Romeo and Juliet," followed by "Richard II," "Merchant of Venice," "The Tempest," "King Lear," "Macbeth," "In Celebration," "Summer People," Bdwy in "Present Laughter" (1982).

HUNT, ANNETTE. Born Jan. 31, 1938 in Hampton, VA. Graduate VaIntermontCol. Debut 1957 OB in "Nine by Six," followed by "Taming of the Shrew," "Medea," "Anatomist," "Misanthrope," "The Cherry Orchard," "Electra," "Last Resort," "The Seducers," "A Sound of Silence," "Charades," "Dona Rosita," "Rhinestone," "Where's Charley?," Bdwy in "All the Girls Came Out to play" (1972).

HUNT, LINDA. Born Apr. 2, 1945 in Morristown, NJ. Attended Goodman Th. Debut 1975 OB in "Down by the River . . .," followed by "The Tennis Game," "Metamorphosis in Miniature," "Little Victories," "Top Girls," Bdwy in "Ah, Wilderness!" (1975).

HUNTER, HOLLY. Born Mar. 20, 1958 in Atlanta, GA. Graduate Carnegie-Mellon U. Debut 1981 OB in "Battery," Bdwy in "Crimes of the Heart" (1982), "The Wake of Jamey Foster."

HUNTER, KIM. Born Nov. 12, 1922 in Detroit, MI. Attended Actors Studio. Debut 1947 in "A Streetcar Named Desire," followed by "Darkness at Noon," "The Chase," "The Children's Hour," "The Tender Trap," "Write Me a Murder," "Weekend," "Penny Wars," "The Women," "To Grandmother's House We Go," OB in "Come Slowly, Eden," "All Is Bright," "The Cherry Orchard," "When We Dead Awaken," "Territorial Rites."

HURLEY, JOHN PATRICK. Born May 7, 1949 in Salt Lake City, UT. Graduate UUtah. Debut 1982 OB in "Inserts," followed by "Sharing."

HURT, MARY BETH. Born in 1948 in Marshalltown, IA. Attended UIa, NYU. Debut 1972 OB in "More Than You Deserve," followed by "As You Like it," "Trelawny of the Wells," "The Cherry Orchard," "Love for Love," "Member of the Wedding," "Boy Meets Girl," "Secret Service," "Father's Day," Bdwy in "Crimes of the Heart." (1981), "The Misanthrope."

HURT, WILLIAM. Born Mar. 20, 1950 in Washington, D.C. Graduate Tufts U., Juilliard. Debut 1976 OB in "Henry V," followed by "My Life," "Ulysses in Traction," "Lulu," "5th of July," "The Runner Stumbles." He received a 1978 Theatre World Award for his performances with Circle Repertory Theatre, followed by "Hamlet," "Mary Stuart," "Childe Byron," "The Diviners," "Richard II," "The Great Grandson of Jedediah Kohler," "A Midsummer Night's Dream."

HUTTON, BILL Born Aug. 5, 1950 in Evansville, In. Graduate UEvansville. Debut 1979 OB in "Festival," Bdwy 1982 in "Joseph and the Amazing Technicolor Dreamboat,"

HYMAN, ROBERT. Born Nov. 10, 1956 in Boston, MA. Graduate Stanford U. Bdwy debut 1982 in "Joseph and the Amazing Technicolor Dreamcoat."

INGE, MATTHEW. Born May 29, 1950 in Fitchburg, MA. Attended Boston U., Harvard. Bdwy debut 1976 in "Fiddler on the Roof," followed by "A Chorus Line."

INGRAM, TAD. Born Sept. 11, 1948 in Pittsburgh, PA. Graduate Temple U., LAMDA. Debut 1979 OB in "Biography: A Game," followed by "The Possessed," "Gospel according to Al," "Death of Von Richthofen."

INNES, LAURA. Born Aug. 16, 1957 in Pontiac, MI. Graduate Northwestern U. Debut 1982 OB in "Edmond."

IRIZARRY, VINCENT. Born Nov. 12, 1959 in Queens, NY. Attended Berkeley Col., Strasberg Inst. Debut 1982 OB in "The Death of Von Richthofen . . .," followed by "Lennon."

IRVING, GEORGE S. Born Nov. 1, 1922 in Springfield, MA. Attended Leland Powers Sch. Bdwy bow 1943 in "Oklahoma!," followed by "Call Me Mister," "Along 5th Ave.," "Two's Company," "Me and Juliet," "Can-Can," "Shinbone Alley," "Bells Are Ringing," "The Good Soup," "Tovarich," "A Murderer Among Us," "Alfie," "Anya," "Galileo," "4 on a Garden" "An Evening with Richard Nixon," "Irene," "Who's Who in Hell," "All Over Town," "So Long 174th St," "Once in a Lifetime," "I Remember Mama," "Copperfield," "Pirates of Penzance," "On Your Toes," "Rosalie in Concert," "Pal Joey in Concert."

IVANEK, ZELJKO. Born Aug. 15, 1957 in Lujubljana, Yugo, Graduate Yale U, LAMDA. Bdwy debut 1981 in "The Survivor," followed by "Brighton Beach Memoirs," OB in "Cloud 9."

IVEY, DANA. Born Aug. 12, 1941 in Atlanta, GA. Graduate Rollins Col, LAMDA. Bdwy debut 1981 in "Macbeth" (LC), followed by "Present Laughter," OB in "A Call from the East," "Vivien," "Dumping Ground," "Pastorale," "Two Small Bodies." "Candida in Concert," "Major Barbara in Concert," "Quartermaine's Terms.

IVEY, JUDITH. Born Sept. 4, 1951 in El Paso, TX. Bdwy debut 1979 in "Bedroom Farce," followed by "Steaming," OB in "Dusa, Fish, Stas and Vi," "Sunday Runners."

JABLONS, KAREN. Born July 19, 1951 in Trenton, NJ. Juilliard graduate. Debut 1969 OB in "The Student Prince," followed by "Sound of Music," "Funny Girl," "Boys from Syracuse," "Sterling Silver," "People in Show Business Make Long Goodbyes," "In Trousers," Bdwy in "Ari," "Two Gentlemen of Verona," "Lorelei," "Where's Charley?," "A Chorus Line."

JACKEL, PAUL. Born June 30, 1952 in Winchester, MA. Graduate Harvard U. Debut 1983 OB In "The Robber Bridegroom."

JACKSON, ANNE. Born Sept. 3, 1926 in Allegheny, PA. Attended Neighborhood Playhouse. Bdwy debut 1945 in "Signature," followed by "Yellow Jack," "John Gabriel Borkman," "The Last Dance," "Summer and Smoke," "Magnolia Alley," "Love Me Long," "Lady from the Sea," "Never Say Never," "Oh, Men! Oh, Women!," "Rhinoceros" "Luv," "The Exercise," "Inquest," "Promenade All," "Waltz of the Toreadors," "Twice around the Park" OB In "The Tiger," "The Typist," "Marco Polo Sings a Solo," "Diary of Anne Frank."

JACKSON, DAVID. Born Dec. 4, 1948 in Philadelphia, PA. Bdwy debut 1980 in "Eubie!," followed by "My One and Only."

JACKSON, ERNESTINE. Born Sept. 18, in Corpus Christi, TX. Graduate Del Mar Col., Juilliard. Debut 1966 in "Show Boat" (LC), followed by "Finian's Rainbow," "Hello, Dolly!," "Applause," "Jesus Christ Superstar," "Tricks," "Raisin" for which she received a Theatre World Award, "Guys and Dolls," "Bacchae," OB in "Louis," "Some Enchanted Evening."

JACKSON, RUFUS E. Born June 9, 1956 in Latta, SC. Attended John Jay Col. Bdwy debut 1982 in "Your Arms Too Short to Box with God," followed by OB in "The Boogie-Woogie Rumble of a Dream Deferred."

JACOBS, MAX. Born Apr. 28, 1937 in Buffalo, NY. Graduate UAz. Bdwy debut 1965 in "The Zulu and the Zayda," OB in "Full Circle," "The Working Man," "Hallowed Halls," "The Man in the Glass Booth," "Different People Different Rooms."

JACOBS, RUSTY. Born July 10, 1967 in NYC. Debut OB in 1979 in "Tripletale," followed by "Glory! Hallelujah!" "What a Life!" Bdwy 1979 in "Peter Pan."

JACOBSON, JOANNE. Born Dec. 19, 1937 in Cambridge, MA. Graduate Barnard Col. Debut 1958 OB in "Don't Destroy Me," followed by "Naomi Court," "Summertree," "Fish Riding Bikes."

JACOBY, MARK. Born May 21 in Johnson City, TN. Graduate GaStateU,FlaStateU, St. JohnsU. Debut 1982 OB in "Eileen in Concert."

JAMES, CLIFTON. Born May 29, 1921 in Spokane, WA. Attended OreU., Actors Studio. Has appeared in "The Time of Your Life" (CC), "The Cave Dwellers," "Great Day in the Morning," "Andorra," "And Things That Go Bump in the Night," "The Trial of Lee Harvey Oswald," "Shadow Box," "Total Abandon," OB in "The Coop," "American Buffalo."

JAMES, ELMORE. Born May 3, 1954 in NYC. Graduate SUNY/Purchase. Debut 1970 OB in "Moon on a Rainbow Shawl," followed by "The Ups and Downs of Theopholus Maitland," "Carnival," "Until the Real Thing Comes Along," "A Midsummer Night's Dream," Bdwy in "But Never Jam Today" (1979), "Your Arms Too Short to Box with God."

JAMES, FRANCESCA. Born Jan. 23 in Montebello, CA. Attended Carnegie-Mellon U. Bdwy debut 1971 in "The Rothschilds," OB in "The Father," "Life of Galileo," "The Truth."

JAMES, JESSICA. Born Oct. 31, 1933 in Los Angeles, CA. Attended USC. Bdwy debut 1970 in "Company," followed by "Gemini," "Little Me," "42nd Street," OB in "Nourish the Beast," "Hothouse," "Loss of Innocence," "Rebirth Celebration of the Human Race," "Silver Bee," "Gemini."

JAMES, LINDA. Born Feb. 24, 1955 in Jamaica, NY. Graduate Queens Col. Debut 1978 OB in "Never Jam Today" and Bdwy 1979, followed by "Comin' Uptown," "Your Arms Too Short to Box with God."

JAMESON, MICHAEL. Born Nov. 7, 1945 in Wilmington, DE. Graduate UDel., IndU. Debut 1975 OB in "Liberty Call," followed by "You Bet Your Sweet Ass I'm a Lady," "Liberty Call" (1983).

JAMROG, JOSEPH. Born Dec. 21, 1932 in Flushing, NY. Graduate CCNY. Debut 1970 OB in "Nobody Hears a Broken Drum," followed by "Tango," "And Whose Little Boy Are You?," "When You Comin' Back, Red Ryder?," "Drums at Yale," "The Boy Friend," "Love, Death Plays," "Too Much Johnson," "A Stitch in Time," "Pantagleize," "Final Hours," "Returnings."

JARCHOW, BRUCE A. Born May 19, 1948 in Evanston, IL. Graduate Amherst Col. Debut 1982 OB in "Edmond."

JASPER, ZINA. Born Jan. 29, 1939 in The Bronx, NY. Attended CCNY. Bdwy debut 1967 in "Something Different," followed by "Paris Is Out," OB in "Saturday's Children," "Moon-dreamers," "A Dream Out of Time," "Quail Southwest," "On Green Pond," "Artichoke," "My Mother, My Father and Me," "A Different Moon."

JAY, MARY. Born Dec. 23, 1939 in Brooklyn, NY. Graduate UMe, AmThWing. Debut 1962 OB in "Little Mary Sunshine," followed by "Toys in the Attic," "Telecast," "Sananda Sez," "Soul of the White Ant," "The Quilling of Prue," Bdwy in "The Student Gypsy," "Candida" (1981).

JAY-ALEXANDER, RICHARD. Born May 24, 1953 in Syracuse, NY. Graduated S.IllU. Debut 1975 OB in "Boy Meets Boy," Bdwy 1979 in "Zoot Suit," followed by "Amadeus."

JECKO, TIMOTHY. Born Jan. 24, 1938 in Washington, DC. Yale Graduate. Bdwy debut 1980 in "Annie," followed by "Woman of the Year."

JENKINS, TIMOTHY. Born Dec. 5, 1949 in Detroit, MI. Graduate Mercy Col., Catholic U. Debut 1980 OB in "Room Service," followed by "The Quilling of Prue."

JENNER, JAMES. Born Mar. 5, 1953 in Houston, TX. Attended UTx, LAMDA. Debut 1980 OB in "Kind Lady," followed by "Station J.," "Yellow Fever."

JENNINGS, KEN. Born Oct. 10, 1947 in Jersey City, NJ. Graduate St. Peter's Col. Bdwy debut 1975 in "All God's Chillun Got Wings," followed by "Sweeney Todd" for which he received a Theatre World Award, "Present Laughter."

JEROME, TIMOTHY. Born Dec. 29, 1943 in Los Angeles, CA. Graduate Ithaca Col. Bdwy debut 1969 in "Man of La Mancha," followed by "The Rothschilds," "Creation of the World . . . ," "Moony Shapiro Songbook," OB in "Beggar's Opera," "Pretzels," "Civilization and Its Discontents," "The Little Prince," "Colette Collage."

JETER, MICHAEL. Born Aug. 26, 1952 in Lawrenceburg, TN. Graduate Memphis State U. Bdwy debut 1978 in "Once in a Lifetime," OB in "The Master and Margarita," "G. R. Point" for which he received a Theatre World Award, "Alice in Concert," "El Bravo," "Cloud 9," "Greater Tuna."

JILER, JOHN. Born Apr. 4, 1946 in NYC. Graduate U. Hartford. Debut 1982 OB in "The Frances Farmer Story," followed by "Trouble/Idle Hands."

JOHANNES, MARK. Born Aug. 9, 1956 in Norfolk, NE. Graduate Wayne State U. Debut 1983 OB in "Behind a Mask."

JOHNSON, ARCH. Born Mar. 14, 1931 in Minneapolis, MN. Attended UPa., Neighborhood Playhouse. Debut 1952 OB in "Down in the Valley," followed by "St. Joan," "Purple Dust," "Knucklebones," Bdwy in "Mrs. McThing," "Bus Stop," "The Happiest Millionaire," "West Side Story" (1957 & 1980).

JOHNSON, DAVID CALE. Born Dec. 28, 1947 in El Paso, TX. Attended AmConsvTheatre. Bdwy debut 1975 in "Shenandoah," followed by "My Fair Lady" (1981), "A Doll's Life."

JOHNSON, KNOWL. Born Sept. 16, 1970 in Greenwich, CT. Debut 1982 OB in "A Christmas Carol," Bdwy in "Merlin" (1983).

JOHNSON, KURT. Born Oct. 5, 1952 in Pasadena, CA. Attended LACC, Occidental Col. Debut 1976 OB in "Follies," followed by "Walking Papers," "A Touch of Marble," "A Midsummer Night's Dream," Bdwy in "Rockabye Hamlet" (1976), "A Chorus Line," "A Stitch in Time."

JOHNSON, LYNN. Born Aug. 13, 1957 in Camden, NJ. Graduate UCLA, Juilliard. Debut 1981 OB in "How It All Began," followed by "Henry IV Part I," "The Singular Life of Albert Nobbs," Bdwy in "The Queen and the Rebels" (1982).

JOHNSON, PAGE. Born Aug. 25, 1930 in Welch, WV. Graduate Ithaca Col. Bdwy bow in 1951 in "Romeo and Juliet," followed by "Electra," "Oedipus," "Camino Real," "In April Once" for which he received a Theatre World Award, "Red Roses for Me," "The Lovers," "Equus," "You Can't Take It With You," OB in "The Enchanted," "Guitar," "4 in 1," "Journey of the Fifth Horse," APA's "School for Scandal," "The Tavern," and "The Seagull," "Odd Couple," "Boys In The Band," "Medea," "Deathtrap," "Best Little Whorehouse in Texas."

JONES, EDDIE. Born in Washington, PA. Debut 1960 OB in "Dead End," followed by "Curse of the Starving Class," "The Ruffian on the Stair," "An Act of Kindness," "Big Apple Messenger," "The Skirmishers," "Maiden Stakes," "The Freak," "Knights Errant," "Slacks and Tops," Bdwy in "That Championship Season" ('74), "Devour the Snow."

JONES, JAMES EARL. Born Jan. 17, 1931 in Arkabutla, MS. Graduate MiU. OB in "The Pretender," "The Blacks," "Clandestine on the Morning Line," "The Apple," "Midsummer Night's Dream," "Moon on a Rainbow Shawl" for which he received a Theatre World Award, "P.S. 193," "Last Minstrel," "Love Nest," "Bloodknot," "Othello," "Baal," "Danton's Death," "Boesman and Lena," "Hamlet," "Cherry Orchard," Bdwy in "The Egghead," "Sunrise at Campobello," "The Cool World," "A Hand Is on the Gate," "The Great White Hope," "Les Blancs," "King Lear," "The Iceman Cometh," "Of Mice and Men," "Paul Robeson," "Lesson from Aloes," "Othello," "Master Harold and the Boys."

JONES, JEFFREY. Born Sept. 28, 1947 in Buffalo, NY. Graduate Lawrence U., LAMDA. Debut 1973 OB in "Lotta," followed by "The Tempest," "Trelawny of the Wells," "Secret Service," "Boy Meets Girl," "Scribes," "Cloud 9," "The Death of Von Richthofen."

JONES, JEN. Born Mar. 23, 1927 in Salt Lake City, UT. Attended UUt. Debut 1960 OB in "Drums Under the Window," followed by "Long Voyage Home," "Diff'rent," "Creditors," "Look at Any Man," "I Knock at the Door," "Pictures in the Hallway," "Grab Bag," "Bo Bo," "Oh, Dad, Poor Dad . . . ," Bdwy in "Dr. Cook's Garden," "But Seriously," "Eccentricities of a Nightingale," "Music Man" ('80).

JONES, LEILANI. Born May 14, 1957 in Honolulu, HI, Graduate UHi. Debut 1981 OB in "El Bravo," followed by "The Little Shop of Horrors."

JONES, NEAL. Born Jan. 2, 1960 in Wichita, KS. Attended Webster Col. Debut 1981 OB in "The Dear Love of Comrades," followed by "The Tavern," "Spring's Awakening," "Billy Liar," "Groves of Academe," Bdwy in "Macbeth" (1982).

JONES, REED. Born June 30, 1953 in Portland, OR. Graduate USIU. Bdwy debut 1979 in "Peter Pan," followed by "West Side Story," "America," "Play Me a Country Song," "Cats."

JOSEPH, STEPHEN. Born Aug. 27, 1952 in Shaker Heights, OH. Graduate Carnegie-Mellon, FlaStateU. Debut 1978 OB in "Oklahoma!," followed by "Is Paris Flaming?"

JOSLYN, BETSY. Born Apr. 19, 1954 in Staten Island, NY. Graduate Wagner Col. Debut 1976 OB in "The Fantasticks," Bdwy in "Sweeney Todd" (1979), "A Doll's Life."

JOY, ROBERT. Born Aug. 17, 1951 in Montreal, Can. Graduate Nfd. Memorial U. Oxford U. Debut 1978 OB in "The Diary of Anne Frank," followed by "Fables for Friends," "Lydie Breeze," "Sister Mary Ignatius Explains It All," "Actor's Nightmare," "What I Did Last Summer," "The Death of Von Richthofen."

JOYCE, STEPHEN. Born Mar. 7, 1933 in NYC. Attended Fordham U. Bdwy debut 1966 in "Those That Play the Clowns," followed by "The Exercise," "The Runner Stumbles," "Devour the Snow," "The Caine Mutiny Court-Martial," OB in "Three Hand Reel," "Galileo," "St. Joan," "Stephen D" for which he received a Theatre World Award, "Fireworks," "School for Wives," "Savages," "Scribes," Daisy."

JULIA, RAUL. Born Mar. 9, 1940 in San Juan, PR. Graduate UPR. OB in "Macbeth," "Titus Andronicus," "Theatre in the Streets," "Life Is a Dream," "Blood Wedding," "Ox Cart," "No Exit," "Memorandum," "Frank Gagliano's City Scene," "Your Own Thing," "Persians," "Castro Complex," "Pinkville," "Hamlet," "King Lear," "As You Like It," "Emperor of Late Night Radio," "Threepenny Opera," "The Cherry Orchard," "Taming of the Shrew," "Othello," "The Tempest," Bdwy in "The Cuban Thing," "Indians," "Two Gentlemen of Verona," "Via Galactica," "Where's Charley?," "Dracula," "Betrayal," "Nine."

KAGAN, DIANE. Born in Maplewood, NJ. Graduate FlaStateU. Debut 1963 OB in "Asylum," followed by "Days and Nights of Beebeee Fenstermaker," "Death of a Well-Loved Boy," "Mme. de Sade," "Blue Boys," "Alive and Well in Argentina," "Little Black Sheep," "The Family," "Ladyhouse Blues," "Scenes from the Everyday Life," "Marvelous Gray," Bdwy in "Chinese Prime Minister," "Never Too Late," "Any Wednesday," "Venus Is," "Tiger at the Gates," "Vieux Carre."

KAHLER, CHRIS. Born Nov. 18 in Cheyenne, WY. Attended ColStateU, UKan. Debut 1983 OB in "Where's Charley?"

KALEMBER, PATRICIA. Born Dec. 30, 1956 in Schenectady, NY. Graduate InU. Debut 1981 OB in "The Butler Did It," followed by "Sheepskin," "Playboy of the Western World."

KAN, LILAH. Born Sept. 4, 1931 in Chicago, IL. Attended UCBerkeley, NYU. Debut 1974 OB in "Year of the Dragon," followed by "Pursuit of Happiness," "G.R. Point," "Primary English Class," "The Blind Young Man," "Paper Angels," "Liberty Call."

KANAR, ZWI. Born July 17, 1931 in Skalbmierz, Poland. Debut 1978 OB in solo mime show, followed by "Run, Jacob, Run!"

KANE, BRADLEY. Born Sept. 29, 1973 in New Rochelle, NY. Debut 1982 OB in "Scraps," followed by "Sunday in the Park with George," Bdwy in "Evita" (1983).

KANSAS, JERI. Born Mar. 10, 1955 in Jersey City, NJ. Debut 1978 OB in "Gay Divorce," Bdwy 1979 in "Sugar Babies," followed by "42nd Street."

KAPEN, BEN. Born July 2, 1928 in NYC. Graduate NYU. Bdwy debut 1968 in "The Happy Time," followed by "The Man in the Glass Booth," "Penny Wars," "Animals," OB in "No Trifling with Love," "Good News," "A Memory of Two Mondays," "They Knew What They Wanted," "Deli's Fable," "Inserts."

KAREN, LYNDA. Born Feb. 14, 1953 in Fort Myers, FL. Graduate USouthFla. Debut 1978 OB in "Company," followed by "Christmas Spectacular," "Season's Reasons," Bdwy in "Show Boat" (1983).

KARFO, ROBIN. Born Oct. 14 in NYC. Attended Lehman Col., NYU. Debut 1981 OB in "And I Ain't Finished Yet," followed by "Scenes from La Vie de Boheme," "Friends Too Numerous to Mention."

KARRAS, DEMETRA. Born Sept. 24, 1954 in Miami, FL. Attended Barry Col., Catholic U., RADA. Debut 1982 OB in "The Guys in the truck," followed by "The Quilling of Prue."

KATSULAS, ANDREAS. Born May 18, 1946 in St. Louis, MO. Graduate St. Louis U, IndU. Debut 1982 OB in "Zastrozzi," followed by "Don Juan," "A Midsummer Night's Dream."

KAUFMAN, MICHAEL. Born July 28, 1950 in Washington, DC. Graduate UWi. Debut 1978 OB in "Hooters," followed by "First Thirty," "Warriors from a Long Childhood," "Scenes from La Vie de Boheme," "Man Overboard," Bdwy 1980 in "Gemini."

KAVA, CAROLINE. Born in Chicago, IL. Attended Neighborhood Playhouse. Debut 1975 OB in "Gorky," followed by "Threepenny Opera," "The Nature and Purpose of the Universe," "Disrobing the Bride," "Marching Song," "Domestic Issues," "Little Victories," "Cloud 9," Bdwy in "Stages" (1978).

KAVANAUGH, RICHARD. Born in 1943 in NYC. Bdwy debut 1977 in "Dracula," followed by "Hothouse," OB in "Learned Ladies."

KAYE, JUDY. Born Oct. 11, 1948 in Phoenix, AZ. Attended UCLA, Ariz. State U. Bdwy debut 1977 in "Grease," followed by "On the 20th Century" for which she received a Theatre World Award, "Moony Shapiro Songbook," "Oh, Brother!," OB in "Eileen in Concert," "Can't Help Singing," "Four to Make Two."

KEAL, ANITA. Born in Philadelphia, PA. Graduate Syracuse U. Debut 1956 OB in "Private Life of the Master Race," followed by "Brothers Karamazov," "Hedda Gabler," "Witches Sabbath," "Six Characters in Search of an Author," "Yes, My Darling Daughter," "Speed Gets the Poppys," "You Didn't Have to Tell Me," "Val Christie and Others," "Do You Still Believe The Rumor," "Farmyard," "Merry Wives of Scarsdale," "Exiles," "Fish Riding Bikes."

KEITH, LAWRENCE (LARRY). Born Mar. 4, 1931 in Brooklyn, NY. Graduate Bklyn. Col., IndU. Bdwy debut 1960 in "My Fair Lady," followed by "High Spirits," "I Had a Ball," "Best Laid Plans," "Mother Lover," OB in "The Homecoming," "Conflict of Interest," "Brownsville Raid," "M. Amilcar," "The Rise of David Levinsky."

KEITH, PAUL. Born June 1, 1944 in Chicago, IL. Graduate UCLA. Debut 1971 OB in "Unfair to Goliath," followed by "Beggar's Opera," "Secret Affairs of Mildred Wild," "Look Me Up," Bdwy in "Show Boat" (1983).

KELLER, JEFF. Born Sept. 8, 1947 in Brooklyn, NY. Graduate Monmouth Col. Bdwy debut 1974 in "Candide," followed by "Fiddler on the Roof," "On the 20th Century," "The 1940's Radio Show," "Dance a Little Closer," OB in "Bird of Paradise," "Charlotte Sweet."

KENNEDY, LAURIE. Born Feb. 14, 1948 in Hollywood CA. Graduate Sarah Lawrence Col. Debut 1974 OB in "End of Summer," followed by "A Day in the Death of Joe Egg," "Ladyhouse Blues," "He and She," "The Recruiting Officer," "Isn't It Romantic," Bdwy in "Man and Superman" (1978), for which she received a Theatre World Award, "Major Barbara."

KENNEDY, TARA. Born Aug. 8, 1971 in Yonkers, NY. Bdwy debut 1979 in "I Remember Mama," followed by "Annie," OB in "Looking-Glass."

KENNY, JACK. Born Mar. 9, 1958 in Chicago, IL. Attended Juilliard. Debut 1983 OB in "Pericles," followed by "Tartuffe," "Play and Other Plays."

KENYON, LAURA. Born Nov. 23, 1948 in Chicago, IL. Attended USCal. Debut 1970 OB in "Peace," followed by "Carnival," "Dementos," "The Trojan Women," Bdwy in "Man of La Mancha" (1971), "On the Town," "Nine."

KEPROS, NICHOLAS. Born Nov. 8, 1932 in Salt Lake City, UT. Graduate UUt. RADA. Debut 1958 OB in "The Golden Six," followed by "Wars of Roses," "Julius Caesar," "Hamlet," "Henry IV," "She Stoops to Conquer," "Peer Gynt," "Octaroon," "Endicott and the Red Cross," "The Judas Applause," "Irish Hebrew Lesson," "Judgment at Havana," "The Millionairess," "Androcles and the Lion," "The Redemptor," "Othello," Bdwy "St. Joan" (1968), "Amadeus."

KERNER, NORBERTO. Born July 19, 1929 in Valparaiso, Chile. Attended Piscator Workshop, Goodman Theatre. Debut 1971 OB in "Yerma," followed by "I Took Panama," "The F. M. Sale," "My Old Friends," "Sharon Shashanovah," "The Blood Wedding," "Crisp," "The Great Confession."

KERNS, LINDA. Born June 2, 1953 in Columbus, OH. Attended Temple U, AADA. Debut 1981 OB in "Crisp," Bdwy 1982 in "Nine."

KERSHAW, WHITNEY. Born Apr. 10, 1962 in Orlando, FL. Attended Harkness, Joffrey Ballet Schools. Debut 1981 OB in "Francis," Bdwy in "Cats" (1982).

KILLMER, NANCY. Born Dec. 16, 1936 in Homewood, IL. Graduate Northwestern U. Bdwy debut 1969 in "Coco," followed by "Goodtime Charley," "So Long, 174th Street," "A Little Night Music," "Sweeney Todd," "Alice in Wonderland," OB in "Exiles," "Mrs. Murray's Farm," "Pillars of Society," "Threads," "A Tale Told."

KIMBALL, WENDY. Born July 4 in NYC. Attended Hofstra U, Neighborhood Playhouse. Bdwy debut 1980 in "The Music Man," followed by "Annie," OB in "Louisiana Summer."

KIMBROUGH, CHARLES. Born May 23, 1936 in St. Paul, MN. Graduate IndU, Yale. Bdwy bow 1969 in "Cop-Out," followed by "Company," "Love for Love," "Rules of the Game," "Candide," "Mr. Happiness," "Same Time, Next Year," OB in "All in Love," "Struts and Frets," "Troilus and Cressida," "Secret Service," "Boy Meets Girl," "Drinks Before Dinner," "The Dining Room."

KING, GINNY. Born May 12, 1957 in Atlanta, GA. Attended NCSch. of Arts. Bdwy debut 1980 in "42nd Street."

KINGSLEY, PETER. Born Aug. 14, 1945 in Mexico City, MX. Graduate Hamilton Col., LAMDA. Debut 1974 OB in "The Beauty Part," followed by "Purification," "Moliere in Spite of Himself," "Old Man Joseph and His Family," Bdwy 1980 in "Amadeus."

KINGLSEY, SUSAN. Born Mar. 1, 1946 in Middlesboro, KY. Graduate UKy, FlaStateU, LAMDA. Debut 1978 OB in "Getting Out" for which she received a Theatre World Award, Bdwy in "The Wake of Jamey Foster" (1982).

KIPP, EMILY. Born July 19 in NYC. Bdwy debut 1956 in "Auntie Mame," followed by "The Gazebo," "Sweet Bird of Youth," "Face of a Hero," "Midgie Purvis," "Freedom of the City," OB in "Kind Lady," "Merry Wives of Scarsdale."

KIRK, ALYSON. Born Jan. 14, 1970 in Waldwick, NJ. Bdwy debut 1982 in "Annie."

KIRSCH, CAROLYN. Born May 24, 1942 in Shreveport, LA. Bdwy debut 1963 in "How to Succeed . . .," followed by "Folies Bergere," "La Grosse Valise," "Skyscraper," "Breakfast at Tiffany's," "Sweet Charity," "Hallelujah, Baby!," "Dear World," "Promises, Promises," "Coco," "Ulysses in Nighttown," "A Chorus Line," OB in "Silk Stockings," "Telecast."

KIRWIN, TERRY. Born Oct. 30 in Fort Wayne, IN. Graduate Purdue U. Debut 1982 OB in "Snoopy."

KITT, EARTHA. Born Jan. 26, 1928 in North, SC. Appeared with Katherine Dunham before Bdwy debut in "New Faces of 1952," followed by "Mrs. Patterson," "Shinbone Alley," "Timbuktu!," OB in "New Faces of 1952."

KLAR, GARY. Born Mar. 24, 1947 in Bridgeport, CT. Graduate UAz. Debut 1982 OB in "The Last of the Knucklemen," followed by "Vatzlav," "The Guys in the Trucks" (also Bdwy 1983).

KLEIN, SALLY. Born Jan. 21 in Toledo, OH. Graduate UAz. Bdwy Debut 1981 in "Merrily We Roll Along," followed by "Agnes of God."

KLETTER, LAWRENCE. Born Apr. 7, 1935 in NYC. Graduate Hunter Col. Debut 1982 OB in "Rhinestone."

KLIBAN, KEN. Born July 26, 1943 in Norwalk, CT. Graduate UMiami, NYU. Bdwy debut 1967 in "War and Peace," followed OB in "Puppy Dog Tails," "Istanbul," "Persians," "Home," "Elizabeth the Queen," "Judith," "Man and Superman," "Boom Boom Room," "Ulysses in Traction," "Lulu," "The Beaver Coat," "Troilus and Cressida," "Richard II," "Great Grandson of Jedediah Kohler," "It's Only a Play," "Time Framed."

KLUNIS, TOM. Born in San Francisco, CA. Bdwy debut 1961 in "Gideon," followed by "The Devils," "Henry V," "Romeo and Juliet," "St. Joan," "Hide and Seek," "Bacchae," "Plenty," OB in "The Immoralist," "Hamlet," "Arms and the Man," "Potting Shed," "Measure for Measure," "Romeo and Juliet," "The Balcony," "Our Town," "Man Who Never Died," "God Is My Ram," "Rise Marlow," "Iphigenia in Aulis," "Still Life," "The Master and Margarita," "As You Like It," "The Winter Dancers," "When We Dead Awaken," "Vieux Carre."

KMECK, GEORGE. Born Aug. 4, 1949 in Jersey City, NJ. Attended Glassboro State Col. Bdwy debut 1981 in "Pirates of Penzance," followed by "On Your Toes."

KNIGHT, LILY. Born Nov. 30, 1956 in Baltimore, MD. Graduate NYU. Debut 1980 OB in "After the Revolution," followed by "The Wonder Years," Bdwy in "Agnes of God" (1983).

KNOBELOCH, JIM. Born Mar. 18, 1950 in Belleville, IL. Graduate S.Ill.U. Debut 1983 OB in "Joan of Lorraine."

KOLBA, MICHAEL. Born Oct. 1, 1947 in Moorhead, MN. Graduate Moorhead U, UHawaii. Debut 1976 OB in "The Cherry Orchard," followed by "Measure for Measure," "The Balcony," "The Further Inquiry."

KOLINSKI, JOSEPH. Born June 26, 1953 in Detroit MI. Attended UDetroit, HB Studio. Bdwy debut 1980 in "Brigadoon," followed by "Dance a Little Closer," OB in "Hijinks!"

KOONS, JON. Born July 15, 1962 in NYC. Attended Fordham U, Wagner Col. Debut 1983 OB in "The Ritz."

KORDER, HOWARD. Born Nov. 24, 1957 in NYC. Graduate SUNY/Binghamton. Debut 1982 OB in "Booth," followed by "Love in the Dark," "Action."

KOREY, ALEXANDRA. Born May 14 in Brooklyn, NY. Graduate Columbia U. Debut 1976 OB in "Fiorello!," followed by "Annie Get Your Gun," "Jerry's Girls," "Rosalie in Concert," "America Kicks Up Its Heels," "Gallery," Bdwy in "Hello, Dolly!" (1978), "Show Boat" (1983).

KOSNIK, BRIAN. Born Nov. 20, 1955 in Cleveland, OH. Graduate Goodman School. Debut 1980 OB in "Ricochet," followed by "Taking in the Grave Outdoors."

KOTLISKY, MARGE. Born Feb. 19 in Chicago, IL. Attended NorthwesternU, UMiami. Debut 1982 OB in "Edmond."

KOVITZ, RANDY. Born Sept. 28, 1955 in Arlington, VA. Graduate Carnegie-Mellon. Debut 1981 in "Macbeth" (LC), followed by "Othello" (1982), OB in "A Prelude to Hamlet."

KRESS, RONNA. Born Dec. 29, 1959 in Pittsburgh, PA. Graduate Boston U. Debut 1982 OB in "Twelfth Night," followed by "The Country Wife," "Pericles," "Tartuffe."

KURNITZ, JULIE. Born Sept. 8, 1942 in Mt. Vernon, NY. Attended UWisc, NYU. Debut 1968 OB in "In Circles," followed by "Peace," "Joan," "The Faggot," "Not Back with the Elephants," "Coronation of Poppae," Bdwy in "Minnie's Boys" (1970), "Gorey Stories."

KURTH, WALLY. Born July 31, 1958 in Billings, MT. Attended Loretto Hts. Col., UCLA. Bdwy debut in "Pirates of Penzance" (1982).

KURTZ, MARCIA JEAN. Born in The Bronx, NY. Juilliard graduate. Debut 1966 OB in "Jonah," followed by "America Hurrah," "Red Cross," "Muzeeka," "The Effects of Gamma Rays . . .," "The Year Boston Won the Pennant," "The Mirror," "The Orphan," "Action," "The Dybbuk," "Ivanov," Bdwy in "The Chinese and Dr. Fish," "Thieves."

LaCHANCE, MANETTE. Born Apr. 1, 1958 in Los Angeles, CA. Attended El Camino Col. Bdwy debut 1981 in "Can-Can," followed by "Dancin'," "Seven Brides for Seven Brothers," OB in "Time Pieces."

LACHOW, STAN. Born Dec. 20, 1931 in Brooklyn, NY. Graduate Roger Williams U. Debut 1977 OB in "Come Back, Little Sheba," followed by "Diary of Anne Frank," "Time of the Cuckoo," "Angelus," Bdwy in "On Golden Pond."

LAGERFELT, CAROLYN. Born Sept. 23 in Paris. Graduate AADA. Bdwy debut 1971 in "The Philanthropist," followed by "4 on a Garden," "Jockey Club Stakes," "The Constant Wife," "Otherwise Engaged," "Betrayal," OB in "Look Back in Anger," "Close of Play," "Sea Anchor," "Quartermaine's Terms."

LAHTI, CHRISTINE. Born Apr. 4, 1950 in Detroit, MI. Graduate UMich, HB Studio. Debut 1979 OB in "The Woods" for which she received a Theatre World Award. Bdwy 1980 in "Loose Ends," followed by "Division Street," "Scenes and Revelations," "Present Laughter."

LAMANNA, MARK. Born Dec. 20, 1959 in Syracuse, NY. Attended SUNY/Buffalo. Debut 1981 OB in "Eternal Love," Bdwy in "Dance a Little Closer" (1983).

LANCE, RORY. Born Apr. 10, 1954 in Brooklyn, NY. Graduate Brooklyn Col. Debut 1978 OB in "She Stoops to Conquer," followed by "Twelfth Night," "The Seagull," "The Miser," "Uncle Vanya," "Don Juan," "Empire Builders."

LANDFIELD, TIMOTHY. Born Aug. 22, 1950 in Palo Alto, CA. Graduate Hampshire Col. Bdwy debut 1977 in "Tartuffe," followed by "Crucifer of Blood," OB in "Actor's Nightmare," "Sister Mary Ignatius Explains It All," "Charlotte Sweet."

LANE, NATHAN. Born Feb. 3, 1956 in Jersey City, NJ. Debut 1978 OB in "A Midsummer Night's Dream," Bdwy in "Present Laughter" (1982) followed by "Merlin."

LANG, STEPHEN. Born July 11, 1952 in NYC. Graduate Swarthmore Col. Debut 1975 OB in "Hamlet," followed by "Henry V," "Shadow of a Gunman," "A Winter's Tale," "Johnny On a Spot," "Barbarians," "Ah, Men," "Clownmaker," "Hannah," Bdwy 1977 in "St. Joan."

LANGELLA, FRANK. Born Jan. 1, 1940 in Bayonne, NJ. Graduate Syracuse U. Debut 1963 OB in "The Immoralist," followed by "The Old Glory," "Good Day," "White Devil," "Yerma," "Iphigenia in Aulis," "A Cry of Players," "Prince of Homburg," Bdwy in "Seascape," "Dracula," "Amadeus," "Passion."

LANSBURY, ANGELA. Born Oct. 16, 1925 in London, Eng. Bdwy debut 1957 in "Hotel Paradiso," followed by "A Taste of Honey," "Anyone Can Whistle," "Mame," "Dear World," "Gypsy," "The King and I" (1978), "Sweeney Todd," "A Little Family Business."

LARSON, JILL. Born Oct. 7, 1947 in Minneapolis, MN. Graduate Hunter Col. Debut 1980 OB in "These Men," followed by "Peep," "Serious Bizness," "It's Only a Play," "Red Rover," Bdwy in "Romantic Comedy" ('80).

LARSON, LISBY. Born Oct. 23, 1951 in Washington, DC. Graduate UKs. Debut 1976 OB in "The Boys from Syracuse," followed by "Some Enchanted Evening," Bdwy in "The Five O'Clock Girl" (1981), "Eileen in Concert," "The Firefly in Concert."

LASKY, ZANE. Born Apr. 23, 1953 in NYC. Attended Manhattan Col., HB Studio. Debut 1973 OB in "The Hot l Baltimore," followed by "The Prodigal," "Innocent Thoughts, Harmless Intentions," "Time Framed," Bdwy in "All Over Town" (1974).

LAUGHLIN, SHARON. Graduate UWVa. Bdwy debut 1964 in "One by One," followed by "The Heiress," OB in "Henry IV," "Huui, Huui," "Mod Donna," "Subject to Fits," "The Minister's Black Veil," "Esther," "Rag Doll," "Four Friends," "Heartbreak House," "Marching Song," "Declassee," "Frozen Assets."

LAURENCE, PAULA. Born Jan. 25 in Brooklyn, NY. Bdwy debut 1936 in "Horse Eats Hat," followed by "Dr. Faustus," "Junior Miss," "Something for the Boys," "One Touch of Venus," "Cyrano de Bergerac," "The Liar," "Season in the Sun," "Tovarich," "The Time of Your Life," "Beggar's Opera," "Hotel Paradiso," "Night of the Iguana," "Have I Got a Girl for You," "Ivanov," "Rosalie in Concert," OB in "7 Days of Mourning."

LAURIA, DAN. Born Apr. 12, 1947 in Brooklyn, NY. Graduate SConnState, UConn. Debut 1978 OB in "Game Plan," followed by "All My Sons," "Marlon Brando Sat Here," "Home of the Brave," "Collective Portraits," "Dustoff," "Niagara Falls," "Punchy."

LAYMAN, TERRY. Born Jan. 12, 1948 in Charlotte, NC. Graduate Wake Forest U. Debut 1980 OB in "Room Service," followed by "In the Matter of J. Robert Oppenheimer," "Ferocious Kisses," "The Butter and Egg Man."

LAYNE, MARY. Born June 20, 1950 in Colorado, TX. Attended Houston Baptist Col., UHouston. Bdwy debut 1975 in "The Royal Family," followed by "The Misanthrope," OB in "The Fox."

LEARY, DAVID. Born Aug. 8, 1939 in Brooklyn, NY. Attended CCNY. Debut 1969 OB in "Shoot Anything That Moves," followed by "Macbeth," "The Plough and the Stars," "Emigres," "Sus," Bdwy in "The National Health," "Da," "The Lady from Dubuque," "Piaf."

LEARY, ROBIN. Born Apr. 15 in Laredo, TX. Attended Bristol Old Vic School. Debut 1982 OB in "The Workroom."

LECESNE, JAMES. Born Nov. 24, 1954 in NJ. Debut 1982 OB in "One Man Band," followed by "Cloud 9."

LEDERER, SUZANNE. Born Sept. 29, 1948 in Great Neck, NY. Graduate Hofstra U. Bdwy debut 1974 in "The National Health," followed by "Ah, Wilderness!" "Days in the Trees," "Amadeus," OB in "Treats."

LEE, EUGENE. Born July 16, 1953 in New Brunswick, NJ. Attended Southwest TexStateU. Debut 1981 OB in "Home," followed by "A Soldier's Play," "Back to Back," "Sons and Fathers of Sons," "About Heaven and Earth," "Manhattan Made Me."

LEEDS, LYDIA. Born May 22, 1955 in NYC. Graduate Hofstra U. Debut 1980 OB in "Romeo and Juliet," followed by "The Tenth Man."

LEESEBERG, BETTYANN. Born July 12 in Wyandotte, MI. Graduate Capital U., OhioU. Debut 1981 OB in "The Rimers of Eldritch," followed by "Four to Make Two," "Ah, Wilderness."

LeFEVRE, ADAM. Born Aug. 11, 1950 in Albany, NY. Graduate Williams Col., UIa. Debut OB 1981 in "Turnbuckle," followed by "Badgers," "Goose and Tomtom," "In the Country."

LeGALLIENNE, EVA. Born Jan. 11, 1899 in London, Eng. Bdwy debut 1915 in "Mrs. Boltay's Daughters," followed by "Bunny," "Melody of Youth," "Mr. Lazarus," "Saturday to Monday," "Lord and Lady Algy," "Off Chance," "Lusmore," "Elsie Janis and Her Gang," "Not So Long Ago," "Liliom," "Sandro Botticelli," "The Rivals," "The Swan," "Assumption of Hannele," "LaVierge Folle," "Call of Life," "Master Builder," "John Gabriel Borkman," "Saturday Night," "Cradle Song," "Inheritors," "Good Hope," "First Stone," "Improvisations in June," "Hedda Gabler," "Would-Be Gentleman," "Cherry Orchard," "Peter Pan," "Sunny Morning," "Seagull," "Living Corpse," "Romeo and Juliet," "Siegfried," "Alison's House," "Camille," "Dear Jane," "Alice in Wonderland" (1932/1947/1982), "L'Aiglon," "Rosmersholm," "Women Have Their Way," "Prelude to Exile," "Mme. Capet," "Frank Fay's Music Hall," "Uncle Harry," "Therese," "Henry VIII," "What Every Woman Knows," "Ghosts," "The Corn Is Green," "Starcross Story," "Southwest Corner," "Mary Stuart," "Exit the King," "The Royal Family," "To Grandmother's House We Go."

LEIBMAN, RON. Born Oct. 11, 1937 in NYC. Attended Ohio Wesleyan, Actors Studio. Bdwy debut 1963 in "Dear Me, the Sky Is Falling," followed by "Bicycle Ride to Nevada," "The Deputy," "We Bombed in New Haven" for which he received a Theatre World Award, "Cop-Out," "I Ought to Be in Pictures," OB in "The Academy," "John Brown's Body," "Scapin," "The Premise," "Legend of Lovers," "Dead End," "Poker Session," "Transfers," "Room Service," "Love Two," "Rich and Famous," "Children of Darkness," "Non Pasquale."

LEIGHTON, RICHARD. Born Jan. 27, 1945 in Lakeland, FL. Graduate Hunter Col. Bdwy debut in "Talent 1965," followed by "To Broadway With Love," OB in "Shadow of a Gunman," "Long Christmas Dinner," "Rats," "Gypsies," "Color of the Wind," "Tuba Players," "Miss Jairus," "Dark at the Top of the Stairs," "Julius Caesar," "The Tempest," "A Month in the Country," "Devil's Disciple," "Modigliani," "It's Only a Play," "Buck."

LeMASSENA, WILLIAM. Born May 23, 1916 in Glen Ridge, NJ. Attended NYU. Bdwy bow 1940 in "Taming of the Shrew," followed by "There Shall Be No Night," "The Pirate," "Hamlet," "Call Me Mister," "Inside U.S.A.," "I Know My Love," "Dream Girl," "Nina," "Ondine," "Fallen Angels," "Redhead," "Conquering Hero," "Beauty Part," "Come Summer," "Grin and Bare It," "All Over Town," "A Texas Trilogy," "Deathtrap," OB in "The Coop," "Brigadoon," "Life With Father," "F. Jasmine Addams," "The Dodge Boys," "Ivanov."

LENCH, KATHERINE. Born Dec. 3, 1956 in Los Angeles, CA. Debut 1982 OB in "Oh, Johnny!" followed by "Summers Past."

LeNOIRE, ROSETTA. Born Aug. 8, 1911 in NYC. Attended AmThWing. Bdwy debut 1936 in "Macbeth," followed by "Bassa Moona," "Hot Mikado," "Marching With Johnny," "Janie," "Decision," "Three's A Family," "Destry Rides Again," "Finian's Rainbow," "South Pacific," "Sophie," "Tambourines to Glory," "Blues for Mr. Charlie," "Great Indoors," "Lost In the Stars," "The Royal Family," "You Can't Take It With You," OB in "Bible Salesman," "Double Entry," "Clandestine on the Morning Line," "Cabin In the Sky," "Lady Day," "Show Boat," "Cry of Players," "Streetcar Named Desire!"

LEON, JOSEPH. Born June 8, 1923 in NYC. Attended NYU, UCLA. Bdwy debut 1950 in "Bell, Book and Candle," followed by "Seven Year Itch," "Pipe Dream," "Fair Game," "Gazebo," "Julia, Jake and Uncle Joe," "Beauty Part," "Merry Widow," "Henry, Sweet Henry," "Jimmy Shine," "All Over Town," "California Suite," "The Merchant," "Break a Leg," "Once a Catholic," "Fools," OB in "Come Share My House," "Dark Corners," "Interrogation of Havana," "Are You Now or Have You Ever Been," "Second Avenue Rag," "Buck," "Ah, Wilderness"

LERITZ, LAWRENCE R. Born Sept. 26, 1955 in Alton, IL. Attended Juilliard, AmBallet School. Bdwy debut 1981 in "Fiddler on the Roof."

LeROUX, MADELEINE. Born May 28, 1946 in Laramie, WY. Graduate UCapetown. Debut 1969 OB in "Moondreamers," followed by "Dirtiest Show in Town," "Rain," "Troilus and Cressida," "2008½," "Glamour, Glory, Gold," "Lisping Judas," "Why Hanna's Skirt Won't Stay Down," "Women Behind Bars," "Buck," Bdwy in "Lysistrata" (1972), "Clothes for a Summer Hotel."

LESTER, BARBARA. Born Dec. 27, 1928 in London, Eng. Graduate Columbia U. Bdwy debut 1956 in "Protective Custody," followed by "Legend of Lizzie," "Luther," "Inadmissible Evidence," "Johnny-No-Trump," "Grin and Bare It," "Abelard and Heloise," "One in Every Marriage," "Butley," "Man and Superman," "Faith Healer," "Present Laughter," OB in "Electra," "Queen After Death," "Summer of the 17th Doll," "Richard II," "Much Ado About Nothing," "One Way Pendulum," "Biography," "Heartbreak House," "Hedda Gabler."

LESTER, BETTY. Born Dec. 1 in Grand Island, NE. Graduate UNeb., Columbia. Debut 1952 OB in "Merry-Go-Round," followed by "Three in One," "Streetcar Named Desire," "Medea," "Divine Hysteria."

LeSTRANGE, PHILIP. Born May 9, 1942 in The Bronx, NY. Graduate Catholic U, Fordham U. Debut 1970 OB in "Getting Married," followed by "Erogenous Zones," "The Quilling of Prue."

LEVINE, ANNA KLUGER. Born Sept. 18, 1955 in NYC. Attended Actors Studio. Debut 1975 OB in "Kid Champion," followed by "Uncommon Women and Others," "City Sugar," "A Winter's Tale," "Johnny-On-a-Spot," "The Wedding," "American Days," "The Singular Life of Albert Nobbs."

LEVINE, RICHARD S. Born July 16, 1954 in Boston, MA. Graduate Juilliard. Debut 1978 OB in "Family Business," followed by "Magic Time," "It's Better With a Band," Bdwy in "Dracula," "Rock 'n Roll: The First 5000 Years."

LEWIS, TODD. Born May 26, 1952 in Chicago, IL. Graduate Lewis U. Debut 1979 OB in "Flying Blind," followed by "Willy and Sahara," "Sawney Bean."

LEWIS, VICKI. Born Mar. 17, 1960 in Cincinnati, OH. Graduate CinConsv. Bdwy debut 1982 in "Do Black Patent Leather Shoes Really Reflect Up?," followed by OB in "Snoopy," "A Bundle of Nerves."

LIEBERMAN, RICK. Born May 10, 1950 in NYC. Graduate CornellU. Debut 1979 OB in "Justice," followed by "Split," "Scenes from La Vie de Boheme," "A Midsummer Night's Dream," "Hamlet."

LIGON, TOM. Born Sept. 10, 1945 in New Orleans, LA. Bdwy debut 1969 in "Angela," followed by "Love Is a Time of Day," OB in "Your Own Thing," "A Place without Mornings," "God Says There Is No Peter Ott," "Geniuses."

LINDLEY, AUDRA. Born Sept. 24, 1923 in Los Angeles, CA. Has appeared in "Comes the Revolution," "Heads or Tails," "Hear That Trumpet," "The Young and the Fair," "Venus Is," "Spofford," "Fire!," OB in "Elba."

LINDO, DELROY. Born Nov. 18, 1952 in London, Eng. Debut 1979 OB in "Spell #7," followed by "Les Blancs," Bdwy in "Master Harold . . . and the boys" (1983).

LINDSEY, GENE. Born Oct. 26, 1936 in Beaumont, TX. Graduate Baylor U. OB in "By Jupiter," "Gogo Loves You," "Bernstein's Theatre Songs," "Deer Park," "Troubles in Tahiti," "Columbus," "Ramblings," "Unsung Cole," "Trixie True," "Sharing," Bdwy in "My Daughter, Your Son," "Cactus Flower."

LIPTON, MICHAEL. Born Apr. 27, 1925 in NYC. Attended Queens Col. Credits include "Caesar and Cleopatra," "The Moon Is Blue," "Sing Me No Lullaby," "Wake Up, Darling," "Tenth Man," "Separate Tables," "Inquest," "Loose Ends," OB in "Lover," "Trigon," "Long Christmas Dinner," "Hamp," "Boys in the Band," "Justice Box," "Cold Storage," "Heartbreak House," "Buck."

LITTLE, ALAN DAVID. Born June 8, 1954 in Atlanta, GA. Debut 1979 OB in "God Bless You, Mr. Rosewater," followed by "The Wisteria Trees."

LITTLE, CLEAVON. Born June 1, 1939 in Chickasha, OK. Attended San Diego State U. AADA. Debut 1967 in "MacBird," followed by "Hamlet," "Someone's Coming Hungry," "Ofay Watcher," "Scuba Duba," "Narrow Road to the Deep North," "Great MacDaddy," "Joseph and the Amazing Technicolor Dreamcoat," "Resurrection of Lady Lester," "Keyboard," "Two Fish in the Sky," Bdwy in "Jimmy Shine," "Purlie," "All Over Town," "The Poison Tree."

LIZZUL, ANTHONY JOHN. Born Jan. 11 in The Bronx, NY. Graduate NYU. Debut 1977 OB in "The Cherry Orchard," followed by "The Prophets," "Lady Windermere's Fan," "Revenger's Tragedy," "Twelfth Night," "Night Talk," "The Butterfingers Angel."

LO, RANDON. Born June 12, 1949 in Oakland, CA. Graduate UCalBerkeley. Bdwy debut 1978 in "Stop the World, I Want to Get Off," followed by "Joseph and the Amazing Techncolor Dreamcoat."

LoBIANCO, TONY. Born Oct. 19, 1936 in NYC. Bdwy debut 1966 in "The Office," followed by "Royal Hunt of the Sun," "The Rose Tattoo," "90 Day Mistress," "Goodbye People," "A View From the Bridge," OB in "Threepenny Opera," "Answered the Flute," "Camino Real," "Oh, Dad, Poor Dad . . . ," "Journey to the Day," "Zoo Story," "Nature of the Crime," "Incident at Vichy," "Tartuffe," "Yankees 3 Detroit 0."

LOCKWOOD, GORDON. (formerly Gordon Halliday) Born Apr. 2, 1952 in Providence, RI. Graduate AADA. Bdwy debut in "Shenandoah" (1975), OB in "Promises, Promises," "The Gilded Cage," "Blue Island."

LODGE, LILY. Born in 1934 in NYC. Graduate Wellesley Col., RADA. Debut 1954 OB in "Easter," followed by "The Music Crept by Me," "Ladies at the Alamo," "Crab Quadrille," "Choices," "After You've Gone," Bdwy in "Cyrano de Bergerac" (1955), "What Every Woman Knows," "The Wisteria Trees," "The Good Soup."

LONG, AVON. Born June 18, 1910 in Baltimore, MD. Attended New Eng. Consv. Bdwy debut 1942 in "Porgy and Bess," followed by "Memphis Bound," "Carib Song," "Beggar's Holiday," "Don't Play Us Cheap," "Bubbling Brown Sugar," OB in "Ballad of Jazz Street," "The Wisteria Trees."

LONG, JODI. Born in NYC, graduate SUNY/Purchase. Bdwy debut 1963 in "Nowhere to Go but Up," followed by "Loose Ends," "Bacchae," OB in "Fathers and Sons," "Family Devotions," "Rohwer," "A Midsummer Night's Dream," "Tooth of Crime."

LONGWELL, KAREN. Born Feb. 7, 1955 in Ithaca, NY. Graduate Fredonia State Col., Ithaca Col. Debut 1983 OB in "The Robber Bridegroom."

LOPEZ, PRISCILLA. Born Feb. 26, 1948 in The Bronx, NY. Bdwy debut 1966 in "Breakfast at Tiffany's," followed by "Henry, Sweet Henry," "Lysistrata," "Company," "Her First Roman," "The Boy Friend," "Pippin," "A Chorus Line," "A Day in Hollywood/A Night in the Ukraine," "Nine," OB in "What's a Nice Country Like You . . .," "Key Exchange," "Buck," "Extremities."

LORRING, JOAN. Born Apr. 17, 1931 in Hong Kong. Bdwy debut 1950 in "Come Back, Little Sheba," followed by "Autumn Garden," "Dead Pigeon," "A Clearing in the Woods," OB in "Awake and Sing," "Without Willie."

LOTI, ELISA. Born Aug. 26 in Guayaquil, Ecuador. Graduate Vassar. Bdwy debut 1961 in "Rhinoceros," OB in "Come Share My House" for which she received a Theatre World Award, followed by "The Laundry," "Lucky Rita," "A Murder Is Announced," "Enter Laughing."

LOUDON, DOROTHY. Born Sept. 17, 1933 in Boston, MA. Attended Emerson Col., Syracuse U. Debut 1961 OB in "World of Jules Feiffer," Bdwy 1963 in "Nowhere to Go but Up" for which she received a Theatre World Award, followed by "Noel Coward's Sweet Potato," "Fig Leaves Are Falling," "Three Men on a Horse," "The Women," "Annie," "Ballroom," "West Side Waltz."

LOUISE, MARY. Born July 10 in Baltimore, MD. Attended AmThWing. Debut 1962 OB in "Fly Blackbird," followed by "Unsung Cole," "Suddenly the Music Starts," "Miss Waters to You," Bdwy in "Funny Girl," "Sweet Charity," "Jimmy," "God's Favorite," "Side by Side by Sondheim," "Hello, Dolly!"

LOVELACE, CINDIE. Born Aug. 31, 1958 in Baltimore, MD. Graduate Boston U., Neighborhood Playhouse, LAMDA. Debut 1980 OB in "Forget the Alamo," followed by "Long Day's Journey into Night," "Irish Coffee," "Teach Me How to Cry," "Billy Liar," "American Collage."

LOW, MAGGIE. Born Apr. 23, 1957 in Nyack, NY. Debut 1982 OB in "Catholic School Girls," followed by "Action."

LOWE, LARRY. Born Feb. 10, 1946 in Cleveland, OH. Attended Philander Smith Col., AADA. Debut 1973 OB in "Holy Moses," followed by "Pop," "The Prodigal Sister," "Opening Night."

LOWERY, MARCELLA. Born Apr. 27, 1945 in Jamaica, NY. Graduate Hunter Col. Debut 1967 OB in "Day of Absence," followed by "American Pastoral," "Ballet Behind the Bridge," "Jamimma," "A Recent Killing," "Miracle Play," "Welcome to Black River," "Anna Lucasta," "Baseball Wives," "Louis," Bdwy in "A Member of the Wedding" ('75), "Lolita."

LUCAS, HOWARD. Born Apr. 10, 1937 in Harrisburg, PA. Debut 1972 OB in "Rosencrantz and Guildenstern Are Dead," followed by "The Tempest," "Measure for Measure," "The Devils," "Macbeth," "Twelfth Night," "Revenger's Tragedy," "Cuchulain," "Merchant of Venice," "Dr. Faustus," "Wild Oats," "Faust," "The Ghost Sonata," "Balloon," "Danton's Death."

LUDWIG, KAREN. Born Oct. 9, 1942 in San Francisco, CA. Bdwy debut 1964 in "The Deputy," followed by "The Devils," "Bacchae," OB in "Trojan Women," "Red Cross," "Muzeeka," "Huui, Huui," "Our Last Night," "Seagull," "Museum," "Nasty Rumors," "Daisy," "Gethsemene Springs," "After the Revolution," "Before She Is Even Born," "Exiles."

LUDWIG, SALEM. Born July 31, 1915 in Brooklyn, NY. Attended Bklyn. Col. Bdwy bow 1946 in "Miracle in the Mountains," followed by "Camino Real," "Enemy of the People," "All You Need Is One Good Break," "Inherit the Wind," "Disenchanted," "Rhinoceros," "Three Sisters," "The Zulu and the Zayda," "Moonchildren," "American Clock," OB in "Brothers Karamazov," "Victim," "Troublemaker," "Man of Destiny," "Night of the Dunce," "Corner of the Bed," "Awake and Sing," "Prodigal," "Babylon," "Burnt Flowerbed," "American Clock," "Friends Too Numerous to Mention."

LUGENBEAL, CAROL. Born July 14, 1952 in Detroit, MI. Graduate U.S. International U. Bdwy debut 1974 in "Where's Charley?" followed by "On the 20th Century," "Evita."

LUM, ALVIN. Born May 28, 1931 in Honolulu, HI. Attended U Hi. Debut 1969 OB in "In the Bar of a Tokyo Hotel," followed by "Pursuit of Happiness," "Monkey Music," "Flowers and Household Gods," "Station J," "Double Dutch," "Teahouse," Bdwy in "Lovely Ladies, Kind Gentlemen," "Two Gentlemen of Verona."

LuPONE, PATTI. Born Apr. 21, 1949 in Northport, NY. Juilliard graduate. Debut 1972 OB in "School for Scandal," followed by "Women Beware Women," "Next Time I'll Sing to You," "Beggar's Opera," "Scapin," "Robber Bridegroom," "Edward II," "The Woods," "Edmond," "America Kicks Up Its Heels," "The Cradle Will Rock," Bdwy in "The Water Engine" (1978), "Working," "Evita."

LuPONE, ROBERT. Born July 29, 1956 in Brooklyn, NY. Juilliard graduate. Bdwy debut 1970 in "Minnie's Boys," followed by "Jesus Christ Superstar," "The Rothschilds," "Magic Show," "A Chorus Line," "St. Joan," OB in "Charlie Was Here," "Twelfth Night," "In Connecticut," "Snow Orchid," "Lennon," "Black Angel," "The Quilling of Prue," "Time Framed."

LUSTIK, MARLENA. Born Aug. 22, 1944 in Milwaukee, WI. Attended Marquette U. Bdwy debut 1966 in "Pousse Cafe," followed by "Days in the Trees," OB in "The Effect of Gamma Rays . . .," "Billy Liar," "One Flew over the Cuckoo's Nest."

LUTE, DENISE. Born Aug. 2, 1954 in NYC. Attended HB Studio. Debut 1975 OB in "Harry Outside," followed by "Green Fields," "Peep," "My Prince My King," "Living Quarters."

LUZ, FRANC. (aka Frank C.) Born Dec. 22 in Cambridge, MA. Attended NMxStateU. Debut 1974 OB in "The Rivals," followed by "Fiorello!," "The Little Shop of Horrors," Bdwy 1979 in "Whoopee!"

LYDIARD, ROBERT. Born Apr. 28, 1944 in Glen Ridge, NJ. Graduate FlaAtlanticU. Debut 1968 OB in "You're a Good Man, Charlie Brown," followed by "Johnny Johnson," "Dear Oscar," "Oh, Lady! Lady!," "Winterville," "Not Now Darling," Bdwy in "Hello, Dolly!" (1978).

LYND, BETTY. Born in Los Angeles, CA. Debut 1968 OB in "Rondelay," followed by "Love Me, Love My Children," Bdwy in "The Skin of Our Teeth" (1975), "A Chorus Line."

LYNDECK, EDMUND. Born Oct 4, 1925 in Baton Rouge, LA. Graduate Montclair State Col., Fordham U. Bdwy debut 1969 in "1776," followed by "Sweeney Todd," "A Doll's Life," "Merlin," OB in "The King and I" (JB), "Mandragola," "A Safe Place," "Amoureuse," "Piaf: A Remembrance," "Children of Darkness."

MACHRAY, ROBERT. Born May 4, 1945 in San Diego, CA. Attended Yale, NYU. Debut 1972 OB in "Servant of Two Masters," followed by "Looking-Glass."

MACKAY, LIZBETH. Born March 7 in Buffalo, NY. Graduate Adelphi U., Yale. Bdwy debut 1981 in "Crimes of the Heart" for which she received a Theatre World Award.

MacKENZIE, WENNDY LEIGH. Born Oct. 19, 1955 in Los Angeles, CA. Attended LACC, UCLA. Debut 1965 in "Oliver," Bdwy in "Platinum"(1978), "Rock 'n' Roll: The First 5000 Years."

MacMILLAN, ANN. Born Apr. 7, 1942 in Scotland. Attended RADA. Debut 1979 OB in "Merry Wives of Windsor," followed by "The Winslow Boy," "Learned Ladies."

MacNICOL, PETER. Born April 10 in Dallas, TX. Attended UMn. Bdwy debut 1981 in "Crimes of the Heart" for which he received a Theatre World Award.

MACY, W. H. Born Mar. 13, 1950 in Miami, FL. Graduate Goddard Col. Debut 1980 OB in "The Man in 605," followed by "Twelfth Night," "The Beaver Coat," "A Call from the East," "Sittin'," "Shoeshine," "The Dining Room," "Speakeasy," "Wild Life."

MAGGART, BRANDON. Born Dec. 12, 1933 in Carthage, TN. Graduate UTn. OB in "Sing Muse!," "Like Other People," "Put It in Writing" for which he received a Theatre World Award, "Wedding Band," "But Not For Me," "Romance," "Potholes," "Nurse Jane Goes to Hawaii," Bdwy in "Kelly"(1965), "New Faces of 1968," "Applause," "Lorelei," "We Interrupt This Program," "Musical Chairs."

MAGNUSON, MERILEE. Born June 11, 1951 in Tacoma, WA. Attended UCal/Irvine. Bdwy debut 1973 in "Gigi," followed by "Irene," "The Best Little Whorehouse in Texas," "My One and Only," OB in "Dancing in the Dark."

MAGUIRE, GEORGE. Born Dec. 4, 1946 in Wilmington, DE. Graduate UPa. Debut 1975 OB in "Polly," followed by "Follies," "Antigone," "Primary English Class," "Sound of Music," "Richard III," Bdwy in "Canterbury Tales"(1980).

MAHAFFEY, VALERIE. Born June 16, 1953 in Sumatra, Indonesia. Graduate UTx. Debut 1975 OB in "Father Uxbridge Wants to Marry," followed by "Bus Stop," "Black Tuesday," "Scenes and Revelations," (also Bdwy), "Twelve Dreams," "Translations," "Butter and Egg Man," "Top Girls," Bdwy in "Rex," "Dracula," "Fearless Frank."

MAHER, JOSEPH. Born Dec. 29, 1933 in Westport, Ire. Bdwy bow 1964 in "The Chinese Prime Minister," followed by "The Prime of Miss Jean Brodie," "Henry V," "There's One in Every Marriage," "Who's Who in Hell," "Days in the Trees," "Spokesong," "Night and Day," "84 Charing Cross Road," OB in "The Hostage," "Live Like Pigs," "Importance of Being Earnest," "Eh?," "Local Stigmatic," "Mary Stuart," "The Contractor," "Savages," "Entertaining Mr. Sloane."

MAIS, MICHELE. Born July 30, 1954 in NYC. Graduate CCNY. Debut 1975 OB in "Godspell," followed by "Othello," "Superspy," "Yesterday Continued," "We'll Be Right Back," "Que Ubo?," "El Bravo!," "Opening Night," Bdwy 1979 in "Zoot Suit."

MAKAROVA, NATALIA. Born Nov. 21, 1940 in Leningrad. Joined American Ballet Theatre in 1970. Bdwy debut in "On Your Toes" (1983) for which she received a Theatre World Award.

MALKOVICH, JOHN. Born Dec. 9, 1953 in Christopher, IL. Attended EastIllU, IllStateU. Debut 1982 OB in "True West" for which he received a Theatre World Award.

MANGANO, NICK. Born Oct. 22, 1958 in Brooklyn, NY. Attended Hofstra U. Debut 1981 in "Oh! Calcutta!"

MANN, RONALD. Born Apr. 4, 1956 in Fresno, CA. Graduate UPacific. OB in "Sally," "Welcome to the Moon," "Miss Waters to You."

MANNINO, ANTHONY. Born June 16, 1944 in Altoona, PA. Graduate CalState, UCLA. Debut 1975 OB in "Kid Champion," followed by "Max."

MANSELL, LILENE. Born Aug. 4, 1944 in Beaver Falls, PA. Graduate Carnegie Tech. Debut 1983 OB in "Ivanov."

MARADEN, FRANK. Born Aug. 9, 1944 in Norfolk, VA. Graduate UMn., MichStateU. Debut 1980 OB with BAM Theatre Co. in "A Winter's Tale," "Johnny on a Spot," "Barbarians" "The Wedding," "Midsummer Night's Dream," "The Recruiting Officer," "The Wild Duck," "Jungle of Cities," "Three Acts of Recognition," "Don Juan," "The Workroom," "Egyptology."

MARADEN, MARTI. Born June 22, 1945 in El Centro, CA. Attended UMn., MiStateU. Debut 1980 OB in "A Winter's Tale," followed by "Barbarians," "He and She," "Waiting for the Parade," "Blood Relations."

MARCH, ELLEN. Born Aug. 18, 1948 in Brooklyn, NY. Graduate AMDA. Debut 1967 OB in "Pins and Needles," followed by "I Can't Keep Running in Place," "Something Different," Bdwy in "Grease," "Once in a Lifetime," "The Floating Light Bulb."

MARCHAND, NANCY. Born June 19, 1928 in Buffalo, NY. Graduate Carnegie Tech. Debut 1951 in CC's "Taming of the Shrew," followed by "Merchant of Venice," "Much Ado about Nothing," "Three Bags Full," "After the Rain," "The Alchemist," "Yerma," "Cyrano de Bergerac," "Mary Stuart," "Enemies," "The Plough and the Stars," "40 Carats," "And Miss Reardon Drinks a Little," "Veronica's Room," OB in "The Balcony," "Children," "Taken in Marriage," "Morning's at 7," "Sister Mary Ignatius Explains It All."

MARCHETTI, WILL. Born Nov. 11, 1933 in San Francisco, CA. Attended HB Studio. Debut 1983 OB in "Fool for Love."

MARCUS, JEFFREY. Born Feb. 21, 1960 in Harrisburg, PA. Attended Carnegie-Mellon U. Bdwy debut 1982 in "Almost an Eagle."

| Mitchell Greenberg | Gayle Greene | David Alan Grier | Anna Marie Gutierrez | Steven Hack | Mary Hamill |

| Geraldine Hanning | William Hao | Lucille Futrell Harley | Tiger Haynes | Laurie Heineman | George Holmes |

| John Patrick Hurley | Laura Innes | Vincent Irizarry | Ernestine Jackson | Mark Jacoby | Francesca James |

| Linda James | Page Johnson | Patricia Kalember | Zwi Kanar | Anita Keal | Wally Kurth |

| Rory Lance | Lisby Larson | James Lecesne | Elisa Loti | Peter MacNicol | Lilene Mansell |

211

MARGULIES, DAVID. Born Feb. 19, 1937 in NYC. Graduate CCNY. Debut 1958 OB in "Golden Six," followed by "Six Characters in Search of an Author," "Tragical Historie of Dr. Faustus," "Tango," "Little Murders," "Seven Days of Mourning," "Last Analysis," "An Evening with the Poet Senator," "Kid Champion," "The Man with the Flower in His Mouth," "Old Tune," "David and Paula," Bdwy in "The Iceman Cometh" (1973), "Zalmen or the Madness of God," "Comedians," "Break a Leg," "West Side Waltz."

MARINOS, PETER. Born Oct. 2, 1951 in Pontiac, MI. Graduate MiStateU. Bdwy debut 1976 in "Chicago," followed by "Evita."

MARKS, JACK R. Born Feb. 28, 1935 in Brooklyn, NY. Debut 1975 OB in "Hamlet," followed by "A Midsummer Night's Dream," "Getting Out," "Basic Training of Pavlo Hummel," "We Bombed in New Haven," "Angel Street," "Birthday Party," "Tarzan and Boy," "Goose and Tomtom," "The Carpenters," Bdwy 1982 in "The Queen and the Rebels."

MARR, RICHARD. Born May 12, 1928 in Baltimore, MD. Graduate UPa. Bdwy in "Baker Street," "How to Succeed . . .," "Here's Where I Belong," "Coco," "The Constant Wife," "So Long, 174th St.," OB in "Sappho," "Pilgrim's Progress," "Pimpernel," "Witness," "Antiquities," "Two by Tennessee," "King of Hearts," "What a Life!," "Primal Time."

MARRELLA, LANI. Born Sept. 8, 1960 in Orleans, France. Attended Catholic U. Debut 1982 OB in "Louisiana Summer."

MARSHALL, LARRY. Born Apr. 3, 1944 in Spartanburg, SC. Attended Fordham U., New Eng. Cons. Bdwy debut in "Hair," followed by "Two Gentlemen of Verona," "A Midsummer Night's Dream," "Rockabye Hamlet," "Porgy and Bess," "A Broadway Musical," "Comin' Uptown," "Oh, Brother!," OB in "Spell #7," "Jus' Like Livin'," "The Haggadah," "Lullabye and Goodnight," "Aladin."

MARSHALL, ROB. Born Oct. 17, 1960 in Madison, WI. Graduate Carnegie-Mellon U. Debut 1982 OB in "Boogie-Woogie Rumble of a Dream Deferred."

MARTENS, LORA JEANNE. Born in Glen Ellyn, IL. Graduate IllWesleyanU. Bdwy debut 1980 in "Onward Victoria," followed by "The Five O'Clock Girl," OB in "Skyline."

MARTIN, GEORGE. Born Aug. 15, 1929 in NYC. Bdwy debut 1970 in "Wilson in the Promise Land," followed by "The Hothouse," "Plenty," "Total Abandon."

MARTIN, LEILA. Born Aug. 22, 1932 in NYC. Bdwy debut 1944 in "Peepshow," followed by "Two on the Aisle," "Wish You Were Here," "Guys and Dolls," "Best House in Naples," "Henry, Sweet Henry," "The Wall," "Visit to a Small Planet," "The Rothschilds," "42nd Street," OB in "Ernest in Love," "Beggar's Opera," "King of the U.S.," "Philemon," "Jerry's Girls."

MARTIN, LUCY. Born Feb. 8, 1942 in NYC. Graduate Sweet Briar Col. Debut 1962 OB in "Electra," followed by "Happy as Larry," "The Trojan Women," "Iphigenia in Aulis," "Wives," Bdwy in "Shelter" (1973), "Children of a Lesser God."

MARTIN, MILLICENT. Born June 8, 1934 in Romford, Eng. Attended Italia Conti Sch. Bdwy debut 1954 in "The Boy Friend," followed by "Side by Side by Sondheim," "King of Hearts," "42nd Street."

MARTIN, NICHOLAS. Born June 10, 1938 in Brooklyn, NY. Graduate Carnegie Tech. Bdwy in "The Wild Duck," "You Can't Take It with You," "Right You Are," "School for Scandal," "Pantagleize," "The Man Who Came to Dinner," "Alice in Wonderland," OB in "The Millionairess."

MARTYN, GREG. Born Jan. 21, 1957 in London, Eng. Attended RADA. Debut 1982 OB in "Barbarians," followed by "Lennon."

MASSA, STEVE. Born July 20, 1955 in Mansfield, OH. Graduate OhU. Debut 1982 on Bdwy in "Alice in Wonderland."

MASTERS, BEN. Born May 6, 1947 in Corvallis, OR. Graduate UOr. Debut 1970 OB in "Boys in the Band," followed by "What the Butler Saw," "The Cherry Orchard," "Key Exchange," Bdwy in "Capt. Brassbound's Conversion," "Plenty."

MATHERS, JAMES. Born Oct. 31, 1936 in Seattle, WA. Graduate UWa., Beverly Col. Debut 1983 OB in "Happy Birthday, Wanda June."

MATSUSAKA, TOM. Born Aug. 8 in Wahiawa, HI. Graduate MiStateU. Bdwy bow 1968 in "Mame," followed by "Ride the Winds," "Pacific Overtures," OB in "Agamemnon," "Chu Chem," "Jungle of Cities," "Santa Anita '42," "Extenuating Circumstances," "Rohwer," "Teahouse."

MATZ, JERRY. Born Nov. 15, 1935 in NYC. Graduate Syracuse U. Debut 1965 OB in "The Old Glory," followed by "Hefetz," "A Day Out of Time," "A Mad World, My Masters," "Rise of David Levinsky."

MAURER, LISA. Born Jan. 20 in NYC. Debut 1978 OB in "The Hallway," followed by "The House of Ramon Iglesia," "The Dolphin Position."

MAY, BEVERLY. Born Aug. 11, 1927 in East Wellington, BC, Can. Graduate Yale U. Debut 1976 OB in "Female Transport," followed by "Bonjour La Bonjour," "My Sister in This House," Bdwy 1977 in "Equus," followed by "Once in a Lifetime," "Whose Life Is It Anyway?," "Rose," "Curse of an Aching Heart," "Slab Boys."

MAZUMDAR, MAXIM. Born Jan. 27, 1953 in Bombay, India. Graduate Loyola Col., McGill U. Debut 1981 OB in "Oscar Remembered," followed by "a/k/a Tennessee."

MAZZIE, MARIN. Born Oct. 9, 1960 in Rockford, IL. Graduate Western MiU. Debut 1983 OB in "Where's Charley?"

McCALL, NANCY. Born Jan. 12, 1948 in Atlanta, GA. Graduate Northwestern U. Debut 1975 OB in "Godspell," followed by "Heebie Jeebies," Bdwy 1982 in "Nine."

McCANN, CHRISTOPHER. Born Sept. 29, 1952 in NYC. Graduate NYU. Debut 1975 OB in "The Measures Taken," followed by "Ghosts," "Woyzzeck," "St. Joan of the Stockyards," "Buried Child," "Dwelling in Milk," "Tongues," "3 Acts of Recognition," "Don Juan," "Michi's Blood."

McCARTY, MICHAEL. Born Sept. 7, 1946 in Evansville, IN. Graduate InU., MiStateU. Debut 1976 OB in "Fiorello!," "The Robber Bridegroom," Bdwy in "Dirty Linens," "King of Hearts," "Amadeus."

McCHESNEY, MART. Born Jan. 27, 1954 in Abilene, TX. Graduate Webster Col. Consv. Debut 1979 OB in "Making Peace," followed by "Sometime Soon," "Grunts."

McCLAIN, MARCIA. Born Sept. 30, 1949 in San Antonio, TX. Graduate Trinity U. Debut 1972 OB in "Rainbow," followed by "A Bistro Car on the CNR" "The Derby," "Etiquette," Bdwy in "Where's Charley?"(1974) for which she received a Theatre World Award.

McCORMICK, MICHAEL. Born July 24, 1951 in Gary, IN. Graduate NorthwesternU. Bdwy debut 1964 in "Oliver!," followed by OB in "Coming Attractions," "Tomfoolery," "The Regard of Flight," "Charlotte Sweet."

McCRACKEN, JEFF. Born Sept. 12, 1952 in Chicago, IL. Debut 1981 OB in "In Connecticut," followed by "Am I Blue," "Thymus Vulgaris," "Confluence," "Breakfast with Les and Bess."

McCRANE, PAUL. Born Jan. 19, 1961 in Philadelphia, PA. Debut 1977 OB in "Landscape of the Body," followed by "Dispatches," "Split," "Hunting Scenes," "Crossing Niagara," "Hooters," Bdwy in "Runaways," "Curse of an Aching Heart."

McDONNELL, MARY. Born in 1952 in Ithaca, NY. Graduate SUNY/Fredonia. Debut OB 1978 in "Buried Child," followed by "Letters Home," "Still Life," "Death of a Miner," "Black Angel."

McDONOUGH, ANN. Born in Portland, ME. Graduate Towson State. Debut 1975 OB in "Trelawny of the Wells," followed by "Secret Service," "Boy Meets Girl," "Scribes," "Uncommon Women," "City Sugar," "Fables for Friends," "The Dining Room," "What I Did Last Summer," "The Rise of Daniel Rocket," "The Middle Ages."

McDONOUGH, STEPHEN. Born Oct. 27, 1958 in Brooklyn, NY. Graduate SUNY/Potsdam. Debut 1981 OB in "The Fantasticks," followed by "Teach Me How to Cry."

McGOVERN, ELIZABETH. Born July 18, 1961 in Evanston, IL. Attended Juilliard. Debut 1981 OB in "To Be Young, Gifted and Black," followed by "Hotel Play," "My Sister in This House" for which she received a Theatre World Award.

McGOVERN, MAUREEN. Born July 27, 1949 in Youngstown, OH. Bdwy debut 1981 in "Pirates of Penzance," followed by "Nine."

McGRATH, J. ANDREW. Born Nov. 17, 1955 in New Castle, PA. Graduate WVaU., Juilliard. Debut 1983 OB in "Pericles," followed by "Tartuffe."

McGUIRE, MITCHELL. Born Dec. 26, 1936 in Chicago, IL. Attended Goodman Th., Santa Monica City Col. OB in "The Rapists," "Go, Go, God Is Dead," "Waiting for Lefty," "The Bond," "Guns of Carrar," "Oh! Calcutta!," "New York! New York!," "What a Life!," "Butter and Egg Man."

McGUIRK, SEAN. Born Mar. 12, 1952 in Boston, MA. Graduate UMa, AADA, Debut 1982 OB in "Applause," followed by "Lola," "The Robber Bridegroom."

McHATTIE, STEPHEN. Born Feb. 3 in Antigonish, NS. Graduate Acadia U., AADA. Bdwy debut 1968 in "The American Dream," followed by "The Misanthrope," OB in "Henry IV," "Richard III," "The Persians," "Pictures in the Hallway," "Now There's Just the Three of Us," "Anna K," "Twelfth Night," "Mourning Becomes Electra," "Alive and Well in Argentina," "The Iceman Cometh," "Winter Dancers," "Casualties," "Three Sisters."

McINERNEY, BERNIE, Born Dec. 4, 1936 in Wilmington, DE. Graduate UDel., Catholic U. Bdwy debut 1972 in "That Championship Season," followed by "Curse of an Aching Heart," OB in "Life of Galileo," "Losing Time," "3 Friends," "The American Clock," "Father Dreams," "Winners."

McKEEHAN, MAYLA. Born Dec. 8 in Barboursville, KY. Graduate FlaStateU. Debut 1979 OB in "Big Bad Burlesque," followed by "God Bless You, Mr. Rosewater," "Anyone Can Whistle," "Facade," "Colette Collage."

McKEON, DOUG. Born June 10, 1966 in Pompton Plains, NJ. Debut 1974 OB in "Dandelion Wine," Bdwy in "Truckload"(1975), "Brighton Beach Memoirs."

McKIERNAN, KATHLEEN. Born in NYC. Graduate Mt. St. Vincent, Catholic U. Debut 1973 OB in "Last Chance Saloon," followed by "The Crucible," "Native Son," "Sunday Afternoon."

McKINLEY, PHILIP WILLIAM. Born June 22, 1952 in Avon, IL. Debut 1982 OB in "Applause," followed by "Babes in Toyland," "Letters to Ben," "Homeseekers," "New Faces of '52."

McKINNEY, TOM. Born May 5, 1943 in Lufkin, TX. Graduate SMU. Debut 1981 OB in "Florodora," followed by "The Gilded Cage."

McLAUGHLIN, JACK. Born Sept. 3, 1938 in Arlington, MA. Graduate Boston Col., Harvard, NYU, HB Studio. Debut 1972 OB in "A God and a Machine," followed by "The Prophets," "Dancers on My Ceiling," "Tale without Title."

McLEAN, ANN. Born July 30, 1954 in Palo Alto, CA. Attended San Francisco State U. Bdwy debut 1980 in "Blackstone Magic Show," OB in "Ah, Wilderness."

McMARTIN, JOHN. Born in Warsaw, IN. Attended Columbia U. Debut 1959 OB in "Little Mary Sunshine" for which he received a Theatre World Award, followed by "Too Much Johnson," "The Misanthrope," Bdwy in "Conquering Hero," "Blood, Sweat and Stanley Poole," "Children from Their Games," "Rainy Day in Newark," "Sweet Charity," "Follies," "Great God Brown," "Don Juan," "The Visit," "Chemin de Fer," "Love for Love," "Rules of the Game," "Happy New Year," "Solomon's Child," "A Little Family Business."

McMILLAN, LISA. Born May 28, 1955 in Oregon. Graduate Juilliard. Debut 1980 OB in "City Junket," followed by "Moose Murders" (Bdwy 1983).

McMURRAY, SAM. Born Apr. 15, 1952 in NYC. Graduate WaU. Debut 1975 OB in "The Taking of Miss Janie," followed by "Merry Wives of Windsor," "Clarence," "Ballymurphy," "The Connection," "Translations," "Man Overboard," "Comedians."

McNALLY, JEAN. Born May 29, 1959 in Hinsdale, IL. Graduate Boston U., RADA. Bdwy debut 1982 in "Amadeus."

McNAUGHTON, STEPHEN. (Formerly Steve Scott) Born Oct. 11, 1949 in Denver, CO. Graduate UDenver. Debut 1971 OB in "The Drunkard," followed by "Summer Brave," "Monsters," "Chase a Rainbow," "Two on the Isles," "Hamlet," Bdwy in "The Ritz"(1976), "Shenandoah," "Cheaters," "Da," "Best Little Whorehouse in Texas," "Joseph and the Amazing Technicolor Dreamcoat."

McNEELY, ANNA. Born June 23, 1950 in Tower Hill, IL. Graduate McKendree Col. Bdwy debut 1982 in "Little Johnny Jones," followed by "Cats."

McQUEEN, ARMELIA. Born Jan. 6, 1952 in North Carolina. Attended HB Studio, Bklyn. Consv. Bdwy debut 1978 in "Ain't Misbehavin'" for which she received a Theatre World Award, OB in "Can't Help Singing."

McRAE, CALVIN. Born Feb. 14, 1955 in Toronto, Can. Attended London Guildhall. Bdwy debut 1971 in "Anne of Green Gables," followed by "Music Man," "A Broadway Musical," "Going Up," "A Chorus Line," "Sophisticated Ladies."

McTIGUE, MARY. Born Sept. 5 in Webster City, IA. Graduate Clarke Col. Debut 1979 OB in "Vanities," followed by "Who's Happy Now," "Disintegration of James Cherry," "Marriage of Bette and Boo," "Scenes from American Life," "Richard III," "Long Voyage Home."

MEEK, JOE. Born Nov. 10, 1944 in Bremerton, WA. Attended UWa. Debut 1981 OB in "Two Gentlemen of Verona," followed by "Edward II," "The Pink Comb," "Taming of the Shrew."

MEISTER, FREDERIKKE. Born Aug. 18, 1951 in San Francisco, CA. Graduate NYU. Debut 1978 OB in "Museum," followed by "Dolphin Position."

MELLOR, STEPHEN. Born Oct. 17, 1954 in New Haven, CT. Graduate Boston U. Debut 1980 OB in "Paris Lights," followed by "Coming Attractions," "Plenty," "Tooth of Crime."

MENDILLO, STEPHEN. Born Oct. 9, 1942 in New Haven, CT. Graduate Colo. Col., Yale. Debut 1973 OB in "Nourish the Beast," followed by "Gorky," "Time Steps," "The Marriage," "Loot," "Subject to Fits," "Wedding Band," "As You Like It," "Fool for Love," Bdwy in "National Health"(1974), "Ah, Wilderness," "A View from the Bridge."

MERCADO, HECTOR JAIME. Born in 1949 in NYC. Attended Harkness Ballet School, HB Studio. Bdwy debut 1960 in "West Side Story," followed by "Mass," "Dr. Jazz," "1600 Pennsylvania Avenue," "Your Arms Too Short to Box with God," "West Side Story"(1980), "Cats," OB in "Sancocho," "People in Show Business Make Long Goodbyes."

MEREDITH, JAN. Born Sept. 21, 1949 in Birmingham, AL. Graduate UAla. Debut 1982 OB in "The Raspberry Picker," followed by "The Ritz."

MERRILL, DINA. Born Dec. 29, 1925 in NYC. Attended AADA, AMDA, Geo. Wash. U. Bdwy debut 1975 in "Angel Street," followed by "On Your Toes," OB in "Are You Now or Have You Ever Been," "Suddenly Last Summer."

MERSON, SUSAN. Born Apr. 25, 1950 in Detroit, MI. Graduate Boston U. Bdwy debut 1974 in "Saturday Sunday Monday," followed by "Children of a Lesser God," OB in "Vanities," "Loves of Shirley Abramovitz," "Reflections of a China Doll," "Delmore," "The Misunderstanding," "Dolphin Position," "Modern Ladies of Guanabacoa."

MERYL, CYNTHIA. Born Sept. 25, 1950 in NYC. Graduate InU. Bdwy debut 1976 in "My Fair Lady," followed by "Nine," OB in "Before Sundown," "The Canticle," "The Pirate," "Dames at Sea," "Gay Divorce," "Sterling Silver," "Anthing Goes."

MESEROLL, KENNETH. Born Apr. 15, 1952 in NJ. Attended UWisc. Debut 1979 OB in "Funeral Games," followed by "Saved," Bdwy in "Plenty"(1982).

MICKENS, JAN. Born Feb. 16, 1939 in NYC. Attended Juilliard. Debut 1973 OB in "Thoughts," followed by "My One and Only"(Bdwy 1983).

MILGRIM, LYNN. Born Mar. 17, 1944 in Philadelphia, PA. Graduate Swarthmore Col, Harvard U. Debut 1969 OB in "Frank Gagliano's City Scene," followed by "Crimes of Passion," "Macbeth," "Charley's Aunt," "The Real Inspector Hound," "Rib Cage," "Museum," "Bits and Pieces," "What Would Jeanne Moreau Do?," "Talking With," "Win/Lose/-Draw," Bdwy in "Otherwise Engaged," "Bedroom Farce."

MILLER, AMY. Born Nov. 4, 1953 in Grand Rapids, MI. Graduate MiStateU. Debut 1975 OB in "Tuscaloosa's Calling Me . . .," followed by "Tan Shoes and Pink Shoelaces," Bdwy in "Do Black Patent Leather Shoes Really Reflect Up?"

MILLER, ANN. Born Apr. 12, 1923 in Chireno, TX. Bdwy debut 1940 in "George White's Scandals," followed by "Mame," "Sugar Babies."

MILLER, BETTY. Born Mar. 27, 1925 in Boston, MA. Attended UCLA. OB in "Summer and Smoke," "Cradle Song," "La Ronde," "Plays for Bleecker St.," "Desire under the Elms," "The Balcony," "The Power and the Glory," "Beaux Stratagem," "Gandhi," "Girl on the Via Flaminia," "Hamlet," "Summer," Bdwy in "You Can't Take It With You," "Right You Are," "The Wild Duck," "The Cherry Orchard," "A Touch of the Poet," "Eminent Domain," "The Queen and the Rebels."

MILLER, COURT. Born Jan. 29, 1952 in Norwalk, CT. Debut 1980 OB in "Elizabeth and Essex," followed by "Welded," Bdwy in "The First," "Torch Song Trilogy."

MILLER, JONATHAN. Born Nov. 22, 1954 in Allison Park, PA. Graduate Duke U, Ohio U. Bdwy debut 1983 in "Amadeus."

MILLER, MARTHA. Born Aug. 30, 1929 in New Bedford, MA. Graduate Carnegie-Mellon U. Debut 1956 OB in "House of Connelly," followed by "A Place without Morning," "Julius Caesar," "Major Barbara," "In the Summer House," "Merry Wives of Windsor," "Rimers of Eldritch," "Heartbreak House," "Importance of Being Earnest," "Who'll Save the Plowboy?," Bdwy in "Happy End"(1977), "Morning's at 7."

MILLER, NANCY. Born Apr. 15, 1955 in Washington, DC. Debut 1983 OB in "Where's Charley?"

MILLER, RUTH. Born June 25 in Chicago, IL. Graduate UChicago, Western Reserve. Debut 1980 OB in "Not Like Him," followed by "The Truth," Bdwy 1982 in "Come Back to the 5 & Dime, Jimmy Dean."

MILLIGAN, JOHN. Born in Vancouver, Can. Attended Bristol Old Vic. Credits include: "Matchmaker," "First Gentleman," "Lock Up Your Daughters," "Love and Libel," "Man and Boy," "The Devils," "Portrait of a Queen," OB in "One Way Pendulum," "John Brown's Body," "When You Comin' Back, Red Ryder?," "Esther," "Veronica's Room," "Without Willie."

MILVANEY, BILL. Born Mar. 10, 1953 in Armonk, NY. Graduate Princeton U. Debut 1983 OB in "Oh, Baby."

MINDELL, JON. Born Mar. 4, 1941 in Buffalo, NY. Graduate Syracuse U. Debut 1982 OB in "Who'll Save the Plowboy?" followed by "His Royal Legacy," "Things of the Heart."

MINER, JAN. Born Oct. 15, 1917 in Boston, MA. Debut 1958 OB in "Obligato," followed by "Decameron," "Dumbbell People," "Autograph Hound," "A Lovely Sunday for Creve Coeur," "The Music Keeper," Bdwy in "Viva Madison Avenue"(1960), "Lady of the Camelias," "The Freaking Out of Stephanie Blake," "Othello," "The Milk Train Doesn't Stop Here Anymore," "Butterflies Are Free," "The Women," "Pajama Game," "Saturday Sunday Monday," "The Heiress," "Romeo and Juliet," "Watch on the Rhine."

MINOT, ANNA. Born in Boston, MA. Attended Vassar Col. Bdwy debut 1942 in "The Strings, My Lord, Are False," followed by "The Russian People," "The Visitor," "The Iceman Cometh," "Enemy of the People," "Love of Four Colonels," "Trip to Bountiful," "Tunnel of Love," "Ivanov," OB in "Sands of the Niger," "Getting Out," "Vieux Carre."

MISTRETTA, SAL. Born Jan. 9, 1945 in Brooklyn, NY. Ithaca Col. graduate. Bdwy debut 1976 in "Something's Afoot," followed by "On the 20th Century," "Evita."

MITCHELL, GREGORY. Born Dec. 9, 1951 in Brooklyn, NY. Graduate Juilliard. Principal with Feld Ballet before Bdwy debut (1983) in "Merlin."

MITZMAN, MARCIA. Born Feb. 28, 1959 in NYC. Attended SUNY/Purchase, Neighborhood Playhouse. Debut 1978 OB in "Promises, Promises," followed by "Taming of the Shrew," "Around the Corner from the White House," Bdwy in "Grease"(1979).

MIYAMOTO, ANNE. Born in Honolulu, HI. Graduate UHi., NYU. Debut 1962 OB in "Yanks Are Coming," followed by "And the Soul Shall Dance," "Roshwer," "Cries and Whispers," Bdwy in "The Basic Training of Pavlo Hummel" (1977).

MOFFAT, DONALD. Born Dec. 26, 1930 in Plymouth, Eng. Attended RADA. Bdwy bow 1957 in "Under Milk Wood," followed by "Much Ado about Nothing," "The Tumbler," "Duel of Angels," "Passage to India," "The Affair," "Father's Day," OB in "The Bald Soprano," "Jack," "The Caretaker," "Misalliance," with APA in "You Can't Take It with You," "War and Peace," "Right You Are," "The Wild Duck," "The Cherry Orchard," "Cock-a-doodle Dandy," and "Hamlet," "Painting Churches."

MOFFET, SALLY. Born Apr. 21, 1931 in NYC. Attended Friend's Acad. Bdwy debut 1948 in "The Young and Fair," OB in "Under Milk Wood."

MOKAE, ZAKES. Born Aug. 5, 1935 in Johannesburg, SA. Attended St. Peter's Col., RADA. Debut 1970 OB in "Boesman and Lena," followed by "Fingernails Blue as Flowers," "The Cherry Orchard," Bdwy in "A Lesson from Aloes"(1980), "Master Harold . . . and the boys."

MONAGHAN, KELLY. Born Oct. 22, 1944 in NYC. Graduate Yale U. Debut 1971 OB in "One Flew over the Cuckoo's Nest," followed by "After the Fall," "Wives," Bdwy in "Butley"(1973).

MONSON, LEX. Born Mar. 11, 1926 in Grindstone, PA. Attended DePaul U, UDetroit. Debut 1961 OB in "The Blacks," followed by "Pericles," "Macbeth," "See How They Run," "Telemachus Clay," "Keyboard," "Oh My Mother Passed Away," "The Confession Stone," "Linty Lucy," "Burnscape," Bdwy in "Moby Dick," "Trumpets of the Lord," "Watch on the Rhine."

MOODY, NAOMI. Born Sept. 23, 1953 in Memphis, TN. Graduate Hampton Inst. Bdwy debut 1976 in "Porgy and Bess," followed by "Sophisticated Ladies," "Porgy and Bess"(1983).

MOONEY, DEBRA. Born in Aberdeen, SD. Graduate Auburn, UMinn. Debut 1975 OB in "Battle of Angels," followed by "The Farm," "Summer and Smoke," "Stargazing," "Childe Byron," "Wonderland," "A Think Piece," "What I Did Last Summer," "The Dining Room," Bdwy 1978 in "Chapter 2," followed by "Talley's Folly."

MOONEY, WILLIAM. Born in Bernie, MO. Attended UCol. Bdwy debut 1961 in "A Man for All Seasons," followed by "A Place for Polly," OB in "Half Horse, Half Alligator," "Strike Heaven on the Face," "Conflict of Interest," "Overnight," "Brownsville Raid," "The Truth," "The Upper Depths."

MOOR, BILL. Born July 13, 1931 in Toledo, OH. Attended Northwestern, Dennison U. Bdwy debut 1964 in "Blues for Mr. Charlie," followed by "Great God Brown," "Don Juan," "The Visit," "Chemin de Fer," "Holiday," "P.S. Your Cat Is Dead," "Night of the Tribades," "Water Engine," "Plenty," OB in "Dandy Dick," "Love Nest," "Days and Nights of Beebee Fenstermaker," "The Collection," "The Owl Answers," "Long Christmas Dinner," "Fortune and Men's Eyes," "King Lear," "Cry of Players," "Boys in the Band," "Alive and Well in Argentina," "Rosmersholm," "The Biko Inquest," "A Winter's Tale," "Johnny on a Spot," "Barbarians," "The Purging," "Potsdam Quartet."

MOORE, JONATHAN. Born Mar. 24, 1923 in New Orleans, LA. Attended Piscator School. Debut 1961 OB in "After the Angels," followed by "Berkeley Square," "Checking Out," "The Biko Inquest," Bdwy in "Dylan," "1776," "Amadeus."

MOORE, MAUREEN. Born Aug. 12, 1951 in Wallingford, CT. Bdwy debut 1974 in "Gypsy," followed by "Do Black Patent Leather Shoes Really Reflect Up?," "Amadeus," OB in "Unsung Cole," "By Strouse."

MORAN, DON. Born in Wilkes-Barre, PA. Graduate Emerson Col. OB credits include "The Drunkard," "The Firebugs," "Brides of Dracula," "Love and Let Love," "Where's Charley?"

MORANZ, BRAD. Born Aug. 29, 1952 in Houston, TX. Bdwy debut in "A Day in Hollywood/A Night in the Ukraine"(1981), OB in "Little Shop of Horrors."

MORANZ, JANNET. (formerly Horsley) Born Oct. 13, 1954 in Los Angeles, CA. Attended CaStateU. Bdwy debut 1980 in "A Chorus Line."

MORATH, KATHY. (aka Kathryn) Born Mar. 23, 1955 in Colorado Springs, CO. Graduate Brown U. Debut 1980 OB in "The Fantasticks," followed by "Dulcy," "Snapshot," "Alice in Concert," "A Little Night Music," "The Little Prince," Bdwy in "Pirates of Penzance" (1982).

MORDEN, ROGER. Born Mar. 21, 1939 in Iowa City, IA. Graduate Coe Col., Neighborhood Playhouse. Debut 1964 OB in "Old Glory," followed by "3 by Ferlinghetti," "Big Broadcast," "The Incognita," "Bravo!," "Dead Giveaway," "Marvelous Gray," Bdwy in "Man of La Mancha."

MORELAND, RAWLEIGH E. Born July 23, 1952 in Hamilton, OH. Graduate Valdosta-StateCol., UCinn. Debut 1982 OB in "A Night of Scenes."

MORGAN, ALISON. Born Aug. 8, 1958 in NYC. Debut 1980 OB in "Plain and Fancy," followed by "Eternal Love," "American Princess."

MORIARTY, MICHAEL. Born Apr. 5, 1941 in Detroit, MI. Graduate Dartmouth, LAMDA. Debut 1963 OB in "Antony and Cleopatra," followed by "Peanut Butter and Jelly," "Long Day's Journey into Night," "Henry V," "Alfred the Great," "Our Father's Failing," "G. R. Point," " Love's Labour's Lost," "Dexter Creed," Bdwy in "Trial of the Catonsville 9," "Find Your Way Home" for which he received a Theatre World Award, "Richard III," "The Caine Mutiny Court-Martial."

MORRIS, MARTI. Born June 8, 1949 in Clarksburg, WV. Graduate UWVa. Debut 1972 OB in "The Fantasticks," followed by "Riverwind," Bdwy in "Candide"(1974), "Alice in Wonderland"(1982).

MORRISEY, BOB. Born Aug 15, 1946 in Somerville, MA. Attended UWi. Debut 1974 OB in "Ionescapade," followed by "Company," "Anthing Goes," "Philistines," Bdwy in "The First"(1981), "Cats."

MORRISON, ANN LESLIE. Born Apr. 9, 1956 in Sioux City, IA. Attended Boston Cons., Columbia U. Debut 1980 OB in "Dream Time," followed by "All of the Above," "Forbidden Broadway," Bdwy 1981 in "Merrily We Roll Along" for which she received a Theatre World Award.

MORRISON, JANET. Born May 9 in Rochester, NY. Graduate Temple U. Debut 1980 OB in "Last Summer at Blue Fish Cove," followed by "Pictures at an Exhibition," "Lady Windermere's Fan," "Chamber Music."

MORSE, ROBERT. Born May 18, 1931 in Newton, MA. Bdwy debut 1955 in "The Matchmaker" followed by "Say, Darling" for which he received a Theatre World Award, "Take Me Along," "How to Succeed in Business . . .," "Sugar," "So Long, 174th St.," OB in "More of Loesser," "Eileen in Concert."

MORSE, ROBIN. Born July 8, 1963 in NYC. Bdwy debut 1981 in "Bring Back Birdie," followed by "Brighton Beach Memoirs."

MORTON, JOE. Born Oct. 18, 1947 in NYC. Attended Hofstra U. Debut 1968 OB in "A Month of Sundays," followed by "Salvation," "Charlie Was Here and Now He's Gone," "G. R. Point," "Crazy Horse," "A Winter's Tale" "Johnny on a Spot," "Midsummer Night's Dream," "The Recruiting Officer," "Oedipus the King," "The Wild Duck," "Rhinestone," Bdwy in "Hair," "Two Gentlemen of Verona," "Tricks," "Raisin" for which he received a Theatre World Award, "Oh, Brother!"

MUENZ, RICHARD. Born in Hartford, CT, in 1948. Attended Eastern Baptist College. Bdwy debut 1976 in "1600 Pennsylvania Avenue," followed by "The Most Happy Fella," "Camelot," "Rosalie in Concert."

MUNDY, MEG. Born in London, Eng. Attended Inst. of Musical Art. Bdwy debut 1936 in "Ten Million Ghosts," followed by "Hoorah for What," "The Fabulous Invalid," "Three to Make Ready," "How I Wonder," "The Respectful Prostitute" for which she received a Theatre World Award, "Detective Story," "Love's Labour's Lost," "Love Me a Little," "Philadelphia Story," "You Can't Take It with You," OB in "Lysistrata," "Rivers Return."

MURNEY, CHRISTOPHER. Born July 20, 1943 in Narragansett, RI. Graduate URI, PaStateU. Bdwy debut 1973 in "Tricks" followed by "Mack and Mable," OB in "As You Like It," "Holeville," "The Lady or the Tiger," "Bathroom Plays," "Two Fish in the Sky," "Wild Life."

MURPHY, PETER. Born Sept. 13, 1925 in Glenarm, Ire. Attended ULondon, RADA. Debut 1956 OB in "The Comedian," followed by "Macbeth," "Ghosts," "The Fantasticks," "When We Dead Awaken," "Dancing for the Kaiser," "Heartbreak House," "Primal Time."

MURPHY, ROSEMARY. Born Jan. 13, 1927 in Munich, Ger. Attended Neighborhood Playhouse, Actors Studio. Bdwy debut 1950 in "Tower Beyond Tragedy," followed by "Look Homeward, Angel," "Period of Adjustment," "Any Wednesday," "Delicate Balance," "Weekend," "Death of Bessie Smith," "Butterflies Are Free," "Ladies at the Alamo," "Cheaters," "John Gabriel Borkman," OB in "Are You Now or Have You Ever Been," "Learned Ladies."

MURPHY, SEAMUS. Born in Philadelphia, PA. Attended Juilliard. Bdwy debut 1967 in "Hair," OB in "Butterfingers Angel . . .," "Shulamith."

MURPHY, SEAN. Born Sept. 10, 1956 in Topeka, KS. Graduate UKs. Bdwy debut 1982 in "Little Me."

MURPHY, STEPHANIE. Born Feb. 2 in NYC. Graduate Smith Col. Debut 1981 OB in "Badgers," followed by "Buddies," "Boogie-Woogie Rumble."

MURRAY, BRIAN. Born Oct. 9, 1939 in Johannesburg, SA. Debut 1964 OB in "The Knack," followed by "King Lear," "Ashes," "The Jail Diary of Albie Sachs," "A Winter's Tale," "Barbarians," "The Purging," "Midsummer Night's Dream," "The Recruiting Officer," "The Arcata Promise," "Candida in Concert," Bdwy in "All in Good Time," "Rosencrantz and Guildenstern Are Dead," "Sleuth," "Da."

MURRAY, JANE. Born May 10, 1954 in Santa Monica, CA. Graduate Occidental Col. Bdwy debut 1982 in "Ghosts."

MURRAY, MARC. Born Jan. 25, 1955 in NYC. Attended Ithaca Col., HB Studio. Debut 1978 OB in "Godsong," followed by "Fall of Masada," "The Importance of Being Earnest," "A Marriage Proposal," "Danton's Death," "The Ditch."

MURRAY, MARY GORDON. Born Nov. 13, 1953 in Ridgewood, NJ. Attended Ramapo Col., Juilliard. Bdwy debut 1976 in "The Robber Bridegroom," followed by "Grease," "I Love My Wife," "Little Me," "Play Me a Country Song."

MYERS, JENNIFER S. Born Dec. 21, 1959 in Detroit, MI. Graduate Northwestern U. Debut 1983 OB in "Where's Charley?"

NADEL, BARBARA. Born Dec. 18, 1947 in New Haven, CT. Graduate Simmons Col. Bdwy debut 1980 in "Barnum," followed by OB in "Divine Hysteria."

NAHRWOLD, THOMAS. Born June 25, 1954 in Ft. Wayne, IN. Attended USIntnlU, AmConsTheatre. Bdwy debut 1982 in "84 Charing Cross Road," followed OB by "A Midsummer Night's Dream."

NAKAHARA, RON. Born July 20, 1947 in Honolulu, HI. Attended UHI, Tenri U. Debut 1981 OB in "Danton's Death," followed by "Flowers and Household Gods," "A Few Good Men," "Rohwer," "A Midsummer Night's Dream," "Teahouse."

NASTASI, FRANK. Born Jan. 7, 1923 in Detroit, MI. Graduate Wayne U, NYU. Bdwy debut 1963 in "Lorenzo," followed by "Avanti," OB in "Bonds of Interest," "One Day More," "Nathan the Wise," "The Chief Things," "Cindy," "Escurial," "The Shrinking Bride," "Macbird," "Cakes with the Wine," "Metropolitan Madness," "Rockaway Boulevard," "Scenes from La Vie de Boheme," "Agamemnon," "Happy Sunset Inc," "3 Last Plays of O'Neill," "Taking Steam."

NAUGHTON, AMANDA. Born Nov. 23, 1965 in NYC. Attended HB Studio. Debut 1982 OB in "Life with Father."

NAVIN, JOHN P., JR. Born July 24, 1968 in Philadelphia, PA. Bdwy debut 1980 in "Peter Pan," followed by "Almost an Eagle."

NAVIN, SARAH. Born June 2, 1970 in Philadelphia, PA. Debut 1981 OB in "The Captivity of Pixie Shedman."

NAYLOR, PETER. Born Feb. 20, 1950 in NYC. Attended LAMDA. Debut 1970 OB in "Wars of the Roses," followed by "Pavilion," "Compulsion," "The Cold Wind and the Warm," "Reflected Glory," "Rhinestone."

NAYYAR, HARSH. Born Feb. 6 in New Delhi, India. Graduate NCStateU., NYU. Debut 1974 OB in "Jungle of Cities," followed by "Twelfth Night," "Comedians," "The Verandah," Bdwy in "A Meeting by the River"(1979).

NEIL, DIANNE. Born Apr. 7, 1955 in Boston, MA. Attended NtlThInst. Debut 1974 OB in "Four Little Girls," followed by "The Ride Across Lake Constance," "Rocket to the Moon," "Asian Shade."

NELSON, CHRISTOPHER. Born Apr. 29, 1944 in Duluth, MN. Bdwy debut 1968 in "Cabaret," followed by "Promises, Promises," "Follies," OB in "The Changeling."

NELSON, MARK. Born Sept. 26, 1955 in Hackensack, NJ. Graduate Princeton U. Debut 1977 OB in "The Dybbuk," followed by "Green Fields," "The Keymaker," Bdwy 1981 in "Amadeus."

NEVILLE, JOHN. Born May 2, 1925 in London, Eng. Attended RADA. Bdwy debut 1956 in "Romeo and Juliet," followed by "Richard II," "Hamlet," "Twelfth Night," "Sherlock Holmes," "Ghosts."

NEWMAN, ELLEN. Born Sept. 5, 1950 in NYC. Attended San Diego State U., London Central School. Debut 1972 OB in "Right You Are," followed by "Benya the King," LCRep's "Merchant of Venice," "Streetcar Named Desire," "The Importance of Being Earnest," "A Midsummer Night's Dream," "The Guys in the Truck," Bdwy in "Othello" (1982), "84 Charing Cross Road."

NEWMAN, PHYLLIS. Born Mar. 19, 1935 in Jersey City, NJ. Attended Western Reserve U. Bdwy debut 1953 in "Wish You Were Here," followed by "Bells Are Ringing," "First Impressions," "Subways Are for Sleeping," "The Apple Tree," "On the Town," "Prisoner of Second Avenue," "Madwoman of Central Park West," OB in "I Feel Wonderful," "Make Someone Happy," "I'm Getting My Act Together," "Red Rover."

NEWMAN, STEPHEN D. Born Jan. 20, 1943 in Seattle, WA. Graduate Stanford U. Debut 1971 OB in "Hamlet," followed by "School for Wives," "Beggar's Opera," "Pygmalion," "In the Voodoo Parlor," "Richard III," "Santa Anita '42," "Polly," Bdwy in "An Evening with Richard Nixon." (1972), "Emperor Henry IV," "Habeas Corpus," "Rex," "Dirty Linen," "Dogg's Hamlet, Cahoot's Macbeth," "The Misanthrope."

NEWTON, JOHN. Born Nov. 2, 1925 in Grand Junction, CO. UWash. graduate. Debut 1951 OB in "Othello," followed by "As You Like It," "Candida," "Candaules Commissioner," "Sextet," LCRep's "The Crucible" and "A Streetcar Named Desire," "The Rivals," "The Subject Was Roses," "The Brass Ring," "Hadrian VII," "The Best Little Whorehouse in Texas," "A Midsummer Night's Dream," Bdwy in "Weekend," "First Monday in October," "Present Laughter."

NICASTRO, MICHELLE. Born Mar. 31, 1960 in Washington, DC. Graduate Northwestern U. Bdwy debut in "Merlin" (1983).

NILES, MARY ANN. Born May 2, in NYC. Attended Miss Finchley's Ballet Acad. Bdwy debut in "Girl from Nantucket," followed by "Dance Me A Song," "Call Me Mister," "Make Mine Manhattan," "La Plume de Ma Tante," "Carnival," "Flora the Red Menace," "Sweet Charity," "George M!," "No, No, Nanette," "Irene," "Ballroom," OB in "The Boys from Syracuse," CC's "Wonderful Town" and "Carnival."

NIXON, CYNTHIA. Born Apr. 9, 1966 in NYC. Debut 1980 in "The Philadelphia Story" (LC) for which she received a Theatre World Award, OB in "Lydie Breeze."

NOLAN, KATHLEEN. Born Sept.27, 1933 in St. Louis, MO. Attended Neighborhood Playhouse. Bdwy debut 1954 in "Peter Pan," followed by "Love in E-Flat," OB in "Accounts."

NORCIA, PATRIZIA. Born Apr. 6, 1954 in Rome, Italy. Graduate Hofstra U., Yale. Debut 1978 OB in "Sganarelle," followed by "The Master and Margarita," "The Loves of Cass McGuire," "Fanshen," "The Price of Genius."

NORTH, ALAN. Born Dec. 23, 1927 in NYC. Attended Columbia U. Bdwy bow 1955 in "Plain and Fancy," followed by "South Pacific," "Summer of the 17th Doll," "Requiem for a Nun," "Never Live over a Pretzel Factory," "Dylan," "Spofford," "The American Clock," OB in "Finian's Rainbow," "The Music Man," "Annie Get Your Gun," "The American Clock," "Comedians."

NOVY, NITA. Born June 13 in Wilkes-Barre, PA. Graduate DukeU. Bdwy debut 1960 in "Gypsy," followed by "Sound of Music," "Grease," "Harold and Maude," OB in "How to Succeed," "Maggie Flynn," "Too Much Johnson," "Wives."

NUTE, DON. Born Mar. 13, in Connellsville, PA. Attended Denver U. Debut OB 1965 in "The Trojan Women" followed by "Boys in the Band," "Mad Theatre for Madmen," "The Eleventh Dynasty," "About Time," "The Urban Crisis," "Christmas Rappings," "The Life of a Man," "A Look at the Fifties."

NYE, CARRIE. Attended Stephens Col., Yale U. Bdwy debut 1960 in "Second String," followed by "Mary, Mary," "Half a Sixpence," "A Very Rich Woman," "Cop-Out," "The Man Who Came to Dinner," OB in "Ondine," "Ghosts," "Importance of Being Earnest," "Trojan Women," "Real Inspector Hound," "a/k/a Tennessee," "The Wisteria Trees."

O'BRIEN, SYLVIA. Born May 4 in Dublin, Ire. Debut 1961 OB in "O Marry Me," followed by "Red Roses for Me," "Every Other Evil," "3 by O'Casey," "Essence of Woman," "Dear Oscar," "Dona Rosita," "Returnings," Bdwy in "The Passion of Joseph D," "The Right Honourable Gentleman," "Loves of Cass McGuire," "Hadrian VII," "Conduct Unbecoming," "My Fair Lady," "Da."

O'CONNELL, PATRICIA. Born May 17 in NYC. Attended AmThWing. Debut 1958 OB in "The Saintliness of Margery Kemp," followed by "Time Limit," "An Evening's Frost," "Mrs. Snow," "Electric Ice," "Survival of St. Joan," "Rain," "Rapists," "Who Killed Richard Cory?," "Misalliance," "The Singular Life of Albert Nobbs," Bdwy in "Criss-Crossing," "Summer Brave," "Break a Leg," "The Man Who Came to Dinner."

O'CONNELL, PATRICK. Born July 7, 1957 in Norwalk, Ct. Juilliard graduate. Debut 1982 OB in "Twelfth Night," followed by "The Country Wife," "Never Say Die," "How It All Began."

O'CONNOR, DONALD. Born Aug. 28, 1925 in Chicago, IL. Bdwy debut 1981 in "Bring Back Birdie," followed by "Show Boat."

O'CONNOR, GLYNNIS. Born Nov. 19, 1955 in NYC. Attended SUNY/Purchase. Debut 1983 OB in "Domestic Issues."

O'CONNOR, KEVIN. Born May 7 in Hololulu, HI. Attended UHi., Neighborhood Playhouse. Debut 1964 OB in "Up to Thursday," followed by "Six from La Mama," "Rimers of Eldritch," "Tom Paine," "Boy on the Straightback Chair," "Dear Janet Rosenberg," "Eyes of Chalk," "Alive and Well in Argentina," "Duet," "Trio," "The Contractor," "Kool Aid," "The Frequency," "Chucky's Hunch," "Birdbath," "The Breakers," "Crossing the Crab Nebula," "Jane Avril," "Inserts," Bdwy in "Gloria and Esperanza," "The Morning after Optimism," "Figures in the Sand," "Devour the Snow," "The Lady from Dubuque."

O'DONNELL, PATRICIA. Born Nov. 25, 1952 in Miami, FL. Graduate Temple U. Debut 1981 OB in "Peer Gynt," followed by "The Cherry Orchard," "King Lear," "Ghost Sonata," "The Changeling."

OEHLER, GRETCHEN. Born in Chicago, IL. Attended Goodman Theatre. Debut 1971 OB in "The Homecoming," followed by "I'm Okay," Bdwy in "Dracula" (1977).

O'HALLORAN, BRIAN. Born May 20, 1952 in San Jose, Ca. Graduate Principia. Col., RADA. Bdwy debut 1977 in "Caesar and Cleopatra," OB in "Shay," "Strawberry Fields," "Lysistrata," "Kiss Me, Kate."

O'HARA, JENNY. Born Feb. 24 in Sonora, CA. Attended Carnegie Tech. Bdwy debut 1964 in "Dylan," OB in "Hang Down Your Head and Die," "Play with a Tiger," "Arms and the Man," "Sambo," "My House Is Your House," "The Kid," "The Fox."

O'HARA, PAIGE. Born May 10, 1956 in Ft. Lauderdale, FL. Debut 1975 OB in "The Gift of the Magi," followed by "Company," Bdwy in "Show Boat" (1983).

O'KEEFE, MICHAEL. Born Apr. 24, 1955 in Westchester, NY. Attended NYU. Debut 1974 OB in "The Killdeer," Bdwy 1981 in "5th of July," followed by "Mass Appeal" for which he received a Theatre World Award.

OLIN, KEN. Born July 30, 1954 in Chicago, IL. Graduate UPa. Debut 1978 OB in "Taxi Tales," followed by "Lorenzaccio."

OLIVER, LYNN. Born Sept. 18 in San Antonio, TX. Graduate UTx, UHouston. Debut 1970 OB in "Oh! Calcutta!," followed by "In the Boom Boom Room," "Redhead," "Blood," "Two Noble Kinsmen," "Curtains," "The Blonde Leading the Blonde," Bdwy in "Dance with Me" (1975).

OLSON, JAMES. Born Oct. 8, 1930 in Evanston, IL. Attended Northwestern, Actors Studio. Bdwy bow 1955 in "The Young and the Beautiful," followed by "The Sin of Pat Muldoon," "J. B.," "The Chinese Prime Minister," "Three Sisters," "Slapstick Tragedy," "Of Love Remembered," OB in "Twelve Dreams," "Winterplay."

O'MALLEY, ETAIN. Born Aug. 8 in Dublin, Ire. Attended Vassar Col. Debut 1964 OB in "The Trojan Women," followed by "Glad Tidings," "God of Vengeance," "A Difficult Borning," Bdwy in "The Cherry Orchard" (1968), "The Cocktail Party," "The Misanthrope," "The Elephant Man," "Kingdoms," "The Queen and the Rebels," "84 Charing Cross Road."

O'NEILL, GENE. Born Apr. 7, 1951 in Philadelphia, PA. Graduate Loyola U. Bdwy debut 1976 in "Poison Tree," followed by "Best Little Whorehouse in Texas," OB in "Afternoons in Vegas," "The Slab Boys," "No End of Blame," "Three Sisters."

ORBACH, JERRY. Born Oct. 20, 1935 in NYC. Attended Northwestern U. Bdwy debut 1961 in "Carnival," followed by "Guys and Dolls," "Carousel," "Annie Get Your Gun," "The Natural Look," "Promises Promises," "6 Rms Riv Vu," "Chicago," "42nd Street," OB in "Threepenny Opera," "The Fantasticks," "The Cradle Will Rock," "Scuba Duba."

O'REILLY, CIARAN. Born Mar. 13, 1959 in Ireland. Attended Carmelite Col., Juilliard. Debut 1978 OB in "Playboy of the Western World," followed by "Summer," "Freedom of the City," "Famine," "Interrogation of Ambrose Fogarty."

OSCAR, GAIL. Born in Cleveland OH. Graduate Ithaca Col. Debut 1972 OB in "How to Succeed in Business," followed by "Do I Hear a Waltz?," "Corkscrews."

O'SULLIVAN, MAUREEN. Born May 17, 1911 in Roscommon, Ire. Bdwy debut 1962 in "Never Too Late," followed by "The Subject Was Roses," "Keep It in the Family," "Front Page," "Charley's Aunt," "No Sex, Please, We're British," "Morning's at 7," "Eileen in Concert."

O'SULLIVAN-MOORE, EMMETT. Born Oct. 3, 1919 in New Orleans, LA. Graduate LaStateU. Debut 1982 OB in "Bottom of the Ninth," followed by "Who'll Save the Plowboy?"

OTTO, LIZ. Born in Coral Gables, FL. Graduate UFla. Debut 1963 OB in "The Plot Against the Chase Manhattan Bank," followed by "I Dreamt I Dwelt in Bloomingdale's," "One for the Money," "Two," "Nurse Jane Goes to Hawaii."

OUSLEY, ROBERT. Born July 21, 1946 in Waco, TX. Debut 1975 OB in "Give Me Liberty," followed by "Coronation of Poppae," Bdwy in "Sweeney Todd" (1979), "Othello" (1982).

OVERMIRE, LAURENCE. Born Aug. 17, 1957 in Rochester, NY. Graduate Muskingum Col, UMn. Debut 1982 OB in "Don Jaun," followed by Bdwy in "Amadeus" (1982).

OWENS, ELIZABETH. Born Feb. 26, 1938 in NYC. Attended New School, Neighborhood Playhouse. Debut 1955 OB in "Dr. Faustus Lights the Lights," followed by "Chit Chat on a Rat," "The Miser," "The Father," "Importance of Being Earnest," "Candida," "Trumpets and Drums," "Oedipus," "Macbeth," "Uncle Vanya," "Misalliance," "Master Builder," "American Gothics," "The Play's the Thing," "The Rivals," "Death Story," "The Rehearsal," "Dance on a Country Grave," "Othello," "Little Eyolf," "The Winslow Boy," "Playing with Fire," "The Chalk Garden," "The Entertainer," Bdwy in "The Lovers," "Not Now Darling," "The Play's the Thing."

PACE, MICHAEL. Born Aug. 26, 1949 in Kansas City, MO. Graduate Carnegie Tech. Debut 1971 OB in "Shekina," followed by "Marry Me a Little," "Tied by the Leg," Bdwy in "Rock 'n Roll: The First 5000 Years."

PAGAN, PETER. Born July 24, 1921 in Sydney, Aust. Attended Scots Col. Credits include "Escapade," "Portrait of a Lady," "The Dark Is Light Enough," "Child of Fortune," "Hostile Witness," OB in "Busybody."

PAGANO, GIULIA. Born July 8, 1948 in NYC. Attended AADA. Debut 1977 OB in "The Passion of Dracula," followed by "Heartbreak House," "The Winslow Boy," "Miss Julie," "Playing with Fire," "Out of the Night," Bdwy in "Medea" (1982).

PAGE, GERALDINE. Born Nov. 22, 1924 in Kirkskville, MO. Attended Goodman Theatre. Debut 1945 OB in "Seven Mirrors," followed by "Yerma," "Summer and Smoke," "Macbeth," "Look Away," "The Stronger," "The Human Office," Bdwy in "Midsummer" (1953) for which she received a Theatre World Award, "The Immoralist," "The Rainmaker," "Innkeepers," "Separate Tables," "Sweet Bird of Youth," "Strange Interlude," "Three Sisters," "P.S. I Love You," "The Great Indoors," "White Lies," "Black Comedy," "The Little Foxes," "Angela," "Absurd Person Singular," "Clothes for a Summer Hotel," "Agnes of God."

PAGE, KEN. Born Jan. 20, 1954 in St. Louis, MO. Attended Fontbonne Col. Bdwy debut 1976 in "Guys and Dolls" for which he received a Theatre World Award followed by "Ain't Misbehavin'," "Cats," OB in "Louis," "Can't Help Singing."

PALIFERRO, TOM. Born Apr. 16, 1940 in Chicago, IL. Graduate DePaul U, Goodman Theatre. Debut 1982 OB in "Between Friends," followed by "Children of Darkness," "Ah, Wilderness," "Broken Heart," Bdwy in "The Caine Mutiny Court-Martial" (1983).

PARKER, ELLEN. Born Sept. 30, 1949 in Paris, France. Graduate Bard Col. Debut 1971 OB in "James Joyce Liquid Memorial Theatre," followed by "Uncommon Women and Others," "Dusa, Fish, Stas and Vi," "A Day in the Life of the Czar," Bdwy in "Equus," "Strangers," "Plenty."

PARKER, NORMAN. Born in Brooklyn, NY. Graduate CCNY. Debut 1971 OB in "Basic Training of Pavlo Hummel," followed by "Something Different," "My Three Angels," "The Castro Complex," Bdwy in "Chapter Two" (1977).

PARKER, PATRICIA. Born Jan. 29, 1953 in Elizabeth City, NC. Graduate Converse Col., Eastman School of Music. Bdwy debut 1982 in "A Doll's Life."

PARKER, PAULA. Born Aug. 14, 1950 in Chicago, IL. Graduate S. Ill.U. Debut 1971 OB in "The Debate," followed by "Maggie Flynn," "Metropolitan Madness," "Suffragette," "Four to Make Two."

PARKER, ROXANN. Born Apr. 24, 1948 in Los Angeles, CA. Graduate USCal. Debut 1979 OB in "Festival," followed by "New Faces of '52."

PARKER, VIVECA. Born Mar. 7, 1956 in Montgomery, AL. Graduate Catholic U. Debut 1979 OB in "Don Juan Comes Back from the War," followed by "Hitting Town," "Principally Pinter," "A Midsummer Night's Dream," Bdwy in "John Gabriel Borkman" (1980).

PARKS, KATHERINE. Born May 11, 1946 in Louisville, KY. Graduate Stephens Col., UMo. Debut 1978 OB in "Old Man Joseph and His Family," followed by "Moliere in spite of Himself," "Feelers."

PARSONS, ESTELLE. Born Nov. 20, 1927 in Lynn, MA. Attended Boston U, Actors Studio. Bdwy debut 1956 in "Happy Hunting," followed by "Whoop-Up!," "Beg, Borrow or Steal," "Mother Courage," "Ready When You Are, C.B.," "Malcolm," "The 7 Descents of Myrtle," "And Miss Reardon Drinks a Little," "The Norman Conquests," "Ladies at the Alamo," "Miss Margarida's Way," "Pirates of Penzance," OB in "Demi-Dozen," "Pieces of 8," "Threepenny Opera," "Automobile Graveyard," "Mrs. Dally Has a Lover" for which she received a Theatre World Award, "Next Time I'll Sing to You," "Come to the Palace of Sin," "In the Summer House," "Monopoly," "The East Wind," "Galileo," "Peer Gynt," "Mahagonny," "People Are Living There," "Barbary Shore," "Oh Glorious Tintinnabulation," "Mert and Paul," "Elizabeth and Essex," "Dialogue for Lovers," "New Moon in Concert," "Orgasmo Adulto Escapes from the Zoo."

PASEKOFF, MARILYN. Born Nov. 7, 1949 in Pittsburgh, PA. Graduate Boston U. Debut 1975 OB in "Godspell," followed by "Words," "Forbidden Broadway."

PASSELTINER, BERNIE. Born Nov. 21, 1931 in NYC. Graduate Catholic U. OB in "Square in the Eye," "Sourball," "As Virtuously Given," "Now Is the Time for All Good Men," "Rain," "Kaddish," "Against the Sun," "End of Summer," "Yentl, the Yeshiva Boy," "Heartbreak House," "Every Place Is Newark," "Isn't It Romantic," "Buck," Bdwy in "The Office," "The Jar," "Yentl."

PATTERSON, JAY. Born Aug. 22 in Cincinnati, OH. Attended OhU. Bdwy debut 1983 in "K2."

PATTERSON, RAYMOND. Born Oct. 1, 1955 in Richmond, VA. Graduate UMd. Bdwy Debut in "Hair" (1977), followed by "Comin' Uptown," "Rock 'n' Roll: the First 5000 Years," OB in "The Tempest," "The Architect and the Emperor of Assyria," "A Book of Etiquette," "Arturo Ui," "Battle of the Giants," "American Heroes," "Child of the Sun."

PATTON, LUCILLE. Born in NYC, attended Neighborhood Playhouse. Bdwy debut 1946 in "A Winter's Tale," followed by "Topaze," "Arms and the Man," "Joy to the World," "All You Need Is One Good Break," "Fifth Season," "Heavenly Twins," "Rhinoceros," "Marathon '33," "The Last Analysis," "Dinner at 8," "La Strada," "Unlikely Heroes," "Love Suicide at Schofield Barracks," OB in "Ulysses in Nighttown," "Failures," "Three Sisters," "Yes, Yes, No, No," "Tango," "Mme. deSade," "Apple Pie," "Follies," "Yesterday Is Over," "My Prince My King," "I Am Who I Am," "Double Game."

PAUL, LINDA. Born June 1, 1962 in Wayne, NJ. Debut 1983 OB in "Where's Charley?"

PAYTON-WRIGHT, PAMELA. Born Nov. 1, 1941 in Pittsburgh, PA. Graduate Birmingham Southern Col., RADA. Bdwy debut 1967 in "The Show-Off," followed by "Exit the King," "The Cherry Orchard," "Jimmy Shine," "Mourning Becomes Electra," "The Glass Menagerie," "Romeo and Juliet," OB in "The Effect of Marigolds on . . .," "The Crucible," "The Seagull," "Don Juan."

PEARSON, PAULETTA. Born Sept. 28 in NC. Attended NCSch. of Arts, NTxStateU. Bdwy debut 1977 in "Jesus Christ Superstar," followed by "Shakespeare's Cabaret," OB in "Jule Styne Revue," "Sweet Main Street," "Ethel Waters Story," "Helen of Troy," "Frimbo," "Jerry's Girls," "Children of the Sun," "Vamps and Rideouts," "Rhinestone."

PEARSON, SCOTT. Born Dec. 13, 1941 in Milwaukee, WI. Attended Valparaiso U, UWisc. Bdwy debut 1966 in "A Joyful Noise," followed by "Promises, Promises," "A Chorus Line."

PEARTHREE, PIPPA. Born Sept. 23, 1956 in Baltimore, MD. Attended NYU, Bdwy debut 1977 in "Grease," followed by "Whose Life Is It Anyway?," OB in "American Days," "Hunting Scenes from Lower Bavaria," "And I Ain't Finished Yet," "The Dining Room," "The Singular Life of Albert Nobbs," "Hamlet."

PELLEGRINO, SUSAN. Born June 3, 1950 in Baltimore, MD. Attended CCSan Francisco, CalStateU. Debut 1982 OB in "The Wisteria Trees," followed by "Steel on Steel."

PEN, POLLY. Born Mar. 11, 1954 in Chicago, IL. Graduate Ithaca Col. Debut 1978 OB in "The Taming of the Shrew," followed by "The Gilded Cage," "Charlotte Sweet," Bdwy in "The Utter Glory of Morrissey Hall."

PENDLETON, AUSTIN. Born Mar. 27, 1940 in Warren, OH. Attended Yale. Debut 1962 OB in "Oh, Dad, Poor Dad . . .," followed by "The Last Sweet Day's of Isaac," "Three Sisters," "Say Goodnight, Gracie," "The Office Murders," "Up from Paradise," "The Overcoat," "Two Character Play," Bdwy in "Fiddler on the Roof," "Hail Scrawdyke," "The Little Foxes," "American Millionaire," "The Runner Stumbles."

PENN, SEAN. Born Aug. 17, 1960 in California. Bdwy debut 1981 in "Heartland," followed by "Slab Boys."

PENNER, RALPH. Born Dec. 9, 1947 in NYC. Graduate Yale U. Debut 1973 OB in "Spoon River Anthology," followed by "Applesauce."

PENTECOST, GEORGE. Born July 15, 1939 in Detroit, MI. Graduate Wayne State, UMi. With APA in "Scapin," "Lower Depths," "The Tavern," "School for Scandal," "Right You Are," "War and Peace," "The Wild Duck," "The Show-Off," "Pantagleize," and "The Cherry Orchard," OB in "The Boys in the Band," "School for Wives," "Twelfth Night," "Enemies," Bdwy in "The Merry Wives of Windsor," "The Rivals," "The Visit," "Chemin de Fer," "Holiday," "The Misanthrope."

PERALTA, CRAIG. Born Nov. 27, 1954 in Hollywood, CA. Bdwy debut 1982 in "Seven Brides for Seven Brothers."

PEREZ, LAZARO. Born Dec. 17, 1945 in Havana, Cuba. Bdwy debut 1969 in "Does a Tiger Wear a Necktie?," followed by "Animals," OB in "Romeo and Juliet," "12 Angry Men," "Wonderful Years," "Alive," "G. R. Point," "Primary English Class," "The Man and the Fly," "The Last Latin Lover."

PERKINS, DON. Born Oct. 23, 1928 in Boston, MA. Graduate Emerson Col. OB in "Drums under the Window," "Henry VI," "Richard III," "The Dubliners," "The Rehearsal," "Fallen Angels," "Our Lord of Lynchville," Bdwy in "Borstal Boy" (1970).

PERRI, PAUL. Born Nov. 6, 1953 in New Haven, CT. Attended Elmira Col., UMe, Juilliard. Debut 1979 OB in "Say Goodnight, Gracie," followed by "Henry VI," "Agamemnon," "Julius Caesar," "Waiting for Godot," Bdwy in "Bacchae," "Macbeth," "A View from the Bridge."

PERRIN, SCOTT. Born June 7, 1967 in NYC. Debut 1982 OB in "Life with Father."

PERRY, ELIZABETH. Born Oct. 15, 1937 in Pawtuxet, RI. Attended RISU, AmThWing. Bdwy debut 1956 in "Inherit the Wind," followed by "The Women," with APA in "The Misanthrope," "Hamlet," "Exit the King," "Beckett" and "Macbeth," OB in "Royal Gambit," "Here Be Dragons," "Lady from the Sea," "Heartbreak House," "Him," "All the Way Home," "The Frequency," "Fefu and Her Friends," "Out of the Broomcloset," "Ruby Ruby Sam Sam," "Did You See the Elephant?," "Last Stop Blue Jay Lane," "A Difficult Borning."

PERRY, KEITH. Born Oct. 28, 1931 in Des Moines, IA. Graduate Rice U. Bdwy debut 1965 in "Pickwick," followed by "I'm Solomon," "Copperfield," OB in "Epicene, the Silent Woman," "Hope with Feathers."

PESATURO, GEORGE. Born July 29, 1949 in Winthrop, MA. Graduate Manhattan Col. Bdwy debut 1976 in "A Chorus Line," OB in "The Music Man" (JB).

PESOLA, STEVE. Born Nov. 6, 1956 in Torrance, CA. Attended USCB, AADA. Debut 1983 OB in "Hannah."

PETERS, BERNADETTE. Born Feb. 28, 1948 in Jamaica, NY. Bdwy debut 1967 in "Girl in the Freudian Slip," followed by "Johnny No-Trump," "George M!" for which she received a Theatre World Award, "La Strada," "On the Town," "Mack and Mabel," OB in "Curley McDimple," "Penny Friend," "Most Happy Fella," "Dames at Sea," "Nevertheless They Laugh," "Sally and Marsha."

PETERS, GEORGE J. Born Mar. 23, 1923. On Bdwy in "Medea," "Caesar and Cleopatra," OB in "Climate of Eden," "Independence Day," "Streamers," "Sunday Afternoon."

PETERSEN, ERIKA. Born Mar. 24, 1949 in NYC. Attended NYU. Debut 1963 OB in "One Is a Lonely Number," followed by "I Dreamt I Dwelt in Bloomingdale's," "F. Jasmine Addams," "The Dubliners," "P.S.: Your Cat Is Dead," "The Possessed," "Murder in the Cathedral," "The Further Inquiry."

PETERSON, CHRIS. Born Nov. 19, 1962 in Malden, MA. Bdwy debut 1983 in "On Your Toes."

PETERSON, LENKA. Born Oct. 16, 1925 in Omaha, NE. Attended UIowa. Bdwy debut 1946 in "Bathsheba," followed by "Harvest of Years," "Sundown Beach," "Young and Fair," "The Grass Harp," "The Girls of Summer," "The Time of Your Life," "Look Homeward, Angel," "All the Way Home," "Nuts," OB in "Mrs. Minter," "American Night Cry," "Leaving Home," "The Brass Ring," "Father Dreams," "El Bravo!"

PETERSON, RICHARD. Born Apr. 25, 1945 in Palo Alto, CA. Graduate Boston U. Debut 1972 OB in "Antony and Cleopatra," followed by "Titanic," "Twelfth Night," "Looking Glass,"

PHELPS, DWAYNE. Born Dec. 18, 1958 in Houston, TX. Bdwy debut 1975 in "Treemonisha," followed by "It's So Nice to Be Civilized," "Your Arms Too Short to Box with God," OB in "Boogie-Woogie Rumble."

PHILLIPS, BARY. Born Nov. 29, 1954 in Indianapolis, IN. Graduate IndU. Debut 1981 OB in "Raisin," followed by "While We're Young," "Cries and Whispers."

PHILLIPS, GARRISON. Born Oct. 8, 1929 in Tallahassee, FL. Graduate UWVa. Debut 1956 OB in "Eastward in Eden," followed by "Romeo and Juliet," "Time of the Cuckoo," "Triptych," "After the Fall," Bdwy 1980 in "Clothes for a Summer Hotel."

PIDDOCK, JIM. Born Apr. 8, 1956 in Rochester, Eng. Graduate London U. Bdwy debut in "Present Laughter" (1982), OB in "The Boy's Own Story."

PIERCE, HARVEY. Born June 24, 1917 in NYC. Graduate NYU. OB credits include "The Gentle People," "Native Son," "The Country Girl," "Men in White," "To Bury a Cousin," "Time of the Cuckoo," "Doctor's Office Disco," "Taking Steam."

PIETROPINTO, ANGELA. Born Feb. 5, in NYC. Graduate NYU. OB credits include "Henry IV," "Alice in Wonderland," "Endgame," "Our Late Night," "The Sea Gull," "Jinxs Bridge," "The Mandrake," "Marie and Bruce," "Green Card Blues," "3 by Pirandello," "The Broken Pitcher," "A Midsummer Night's Dream," Bdwy 1980 in "The Suicide."

PINA, LIONEL, JR. Born Mar. 10, 1956 in NYC. Graduate CCNY. Bdwy debut 1980 in "West Side Story," followed by OB in "The House of Ramon Iglesias," "American Collage."

PINCHOT, BRONSON. Born May 20, 1959 in NYC. Graduate Yale. Debut 1982 OB in "Poor Little Lambs," followed by "Mr. Joyce Is Leaving Paris."

PINHASIK, HOWARD. Born June 5, 1953 in Chicago, IL. Graduate OhU. Debut 1978 OB in "Allegro," followed by "Marya," "The Meehans," "Street Scene." "Collette Collage."

PINKINS, TONYA. Born May 30, 1962 in Chicago, IL. Attended Carnegie-Mellon U. Bdwy debut 1981 in "Merrily We Roll Along," OB in "Five Points," "A Winter's Tale."

PINZA, CARLA. Born Feb. 2, 1942 in Puerto Rico. Attended Hunter Col. Bdwy debut 1968 in "The Cuban Thing," followed by "Two Gentlemen of Verona," OB in "The Oxcart," "House of Flowers," "The Orchestra," "Servant of Two Masters," "Marriage Proposal," "House of Ramon Iglesias."

PITONIAK, ANNE. Born Mar. 30, 1922 in Westfield, MA. Attended UNC Women's Col. Debut 1982 OB in "Talking With," followed by Bdwy in "'night, Mother" (1983) for which she received a Theatre World Award.

PLACE, DALE. Born Feb. 27, 1950 in Hastings, MI. Graduate Oakland U. Debut 1983 OB in "Starstruck," followed by "Happy Birthday, Wanda June."

PLANK, SCOTT. Born Nov. 11, 1958 in Washington, DC. Attended NCSch of Arts. Bdwy debut 1981 in "Dreamgirls," followed by "A Chorus Line."

PLAYTEN, ALICE. Born Aug. 38, 1947 in NYC. Attended NYU. Bdwy debut 1960 in "Gypsy" followed by "Oliver," "Hello, Dolly!," "Henry Sweet Henry," for which she received a Theatre World Award, "George M!," OB in "Promenade," "The Last Sweet Days of Isaac," "National Lampoon's Lemmings," "Valentine's Day," "Pirates of Penzance," "Up from Paradise," "A Visit," "Sister Mary Ignatius Explains It All," "An Actor's Nightmare," "That's It, Folks."

PLUMMER, AMANDA. Born Mar. 23, 1957 in NYC. Attended Middlebury Col., Neighborhood Playhouse. Debut 1979 OB in "Artichoke," followed by "A Month in the Country," "A Taste of Honey" for which she received a Theatre World Award, "Alice in Concert," "A Stitch in Time," Bdwy in "A Taste of Honey," "Agnes of God."

POGGI, JACK. Born June 14, 1928 in Oakland, CA. Graduate Harvard, Columbia U. Debut 1962 OB in "This Side of Paradise," followed by "The Tavern," "Dear Janet Rosenberg," "House Music," "The Closed Door," "Ghosts," "Uncle Vanya," "Tiger at the Gates," "Wars of Roses."

POOLE, ROY. Born Mar. 31, 1924 in San Bernardino, Ca. Graduate Stanford U. Bdwy debut 1950 in "Now I Lay Me Down to Sleep," followed by "St. Joan," "The Bad Seed," "I Knock at the Door," "Long Day's Journey into Night," "Face of a Hero," "Moby Dick," "Poor Bitos," "1776," "Scratch," "Once a Catholic," OB in "27 Wagons Full of Cotton," "A Memory of Two Mondays," "Secret Service," "Boy Meets Girl," "Villager," "Quartermaine's Terms."

PORTER, BRETT. Born Dec. 31, 1956 in Guelph, Ont. Can. Graduate UTn. Debut 1982 OB in "Hamlet."

PORTER, CAROLYN. Born Oct. 13, 1950 in Pittsburgh, PA. Graduate Denison U, PennStateU, WayneStateU. Debut 1982 OB in "The Course Acting Show."

POSER, LINDA. Born March 10 in Los Angeles, CA. Graduate SanFranciscoStateU. Debut 1973 OB in "Call Me Madam," followed by "The Boy Friend," Bdwy in "On the 20th Century" (1978), "The Grand Tour," "Onward Victoria," "Copperfield," "Dance a Little Closer."

POTTER, DON. Born Aug. 15, 1932 in Philadelphia, PA. Debut 1961 OB in "What a Killing," followed by "Sunset," "You're a Good Man, Charlie Brown," "One Cent Plain," "The Ritz," Bdwy in "Gypsy" (1974), "Snow White," "Moose Murders."

POTTER, DUKE. Born Feb. 21, 1954 in Brooklyn, NY. Graduate Temple U. Debut 1981 OB in "Death Takes a Holiday," followed by "Pictures at an Exhibition."

PRESCOTT, KEN. Born Dec. 28, 1945 in Omaha, NE. Attended Omaha U, UUtah. Bdwy debut 1971 in "No, No Nanette," followed by "That's Entertainment," "Follies," "Lorelei," "42nd Street."

PRESTON, WILLIAM. Born Aug. 26 1921 in Columbia, PA Graduate PennStateU. Debut 1972 OB in "We Bombed in New Haven," followed by "Hedda Gabler," "Whisper into My Good Ear," "A Nestless Bird," "Friends of Mine," "Iphigenia in Aulis," "Midsummer," "The Fantasticks," "Frozen Assets."

PRICE, LONNY. Born Mar. 9, 1959 in NYC. Attended Juilliard. Debut 1979 OB in "Class Enemy" for which he received a Theatre World Award, Bdwy 1980 in "The Survivor," followed by "Merrily We Roll Along," "Master Harold and the boys."

PRINCE, WILLIAM. Born Jan. 26, 1913 in Nicholas, NY. Attended Cornell U. Bdwy debut 1937 in "The Eternal Road," followed by "Richard II," "Hamlet," "Ah, Wilderness," "Guest in the House," "Across the Board on Tomorrow Morning," "Eve of St. Mark," "John Loves Mary," "Forward the Heart," "As You Like It," "I Am a Camera," "Affair of Honor," "Third Best Sport," "Highest Tree," "Venus at Large," "Strange Interlude," "Ballad of the Sad Cafe," "Little Foxes," "Man with Three Arms," OB in "Stephen D," "Mercy Street," "The Caretaker," "Tausk."

PROTASOFF, MARGARITA. Born Dec. 22, 1956 in Hong Kong. Attended Mexico City U. Debut 1982 OB in "Stifled Growls," followed by "Dear Mrs. Attison."

PUDENZ, STEVE. Born Sept. 25, 1947 in Carroll, IA. Graduate UIa. Debut 1980 OB in "Dona Rosita," followed by "Dick Deterred."

PUMA, MARIE. Born in Brooklyn, NY. Graduate CUNY. Debut 1969 OB in "Romeo and Jeannette," followed by "Purification," "Naked," "La Morsa," "Hamlet."

QUINN, CHERYL. Born Mar. 14, 1951 in Baltimore, MD. Graduate UMBC, UMd. Debut 1982 OB in "Nomad," followed by "A Night of Scenes."

QUINN, PATRICK. Born Feb. 12, 1950 in Philadelphia, PA Graduate Temple. U. Bdwy debut 1976 in "Fiddler on the Roof," followed by OB in "It's Better with a Band."

RABB, ELLIS Born June 20, 1930 in Memphis, TN. Attended Carnegie Tech., Yale. Debut 1956 in "A Midsummer Night's Dream," followed by "The Misanthrope," "Mary Stuart," "The Tavern," "Twelfth Night," "The Importance of Being Earnest," "King Lear," "Man and Superman," "The Tavern," "Twelfth Night," "The Importance of Being Earnest," "King Lear," "Man and Superman," "Life in the Theatre," Bdwy in "Look after Lulu," "Jolly's Progress," "Right You Are," "Scapin," "Impromptu at Versailles," "Lower Depths," "School for Scandal," "Pantagleize," "Cock-a-Doodle Dandy," "Hamlet," "The Royal Family," "The Man Who Came to Dinner," "You Can't Take It With You."

RAE, AUDREE. Born Feb. 12, 1942 in North Shields, Eng. Debut 1962 OB in "One Way Pendulum," followed by "Something Different," Bdwy in "Clothes for a Summer Hotel" (1980).

RAIKEN, LAWRENCE. Born Feb. 5, 1949 in Long Island, NY. Graduate Wm. & Mary Col., UNC. Debut 1979 OB in "Wake Up, It's Time to Go to Bed," "Rise of David Levinsky," Bdwy 1981 in "Woman of the Year."

RAINER, JOHN. Born May 10, 1946 in Stoke-on-Trent, Staffordshire, Eng. Attended RADA. Debut 1981 OB in "The Lady's Not for Burning," followed by "The Enchanted," "The Crunch."

RAMAKER, JULIANNE (a.k.a. Julie) Born Aug. 16, 1952 in LaCross, WI. Graduate Drake U. OB in "The Real Inspector Hound," "Doctor in the House," "Hay Fever," "Shakespeare Pastiche," "Arms and the Man," "Uncle Vanya," "Twelfth Night," "A Midsummer Night's Dream."

RAMOS, RAMON. Born Nov. 17, 1948 in Bayamon, PR. Graduate Brooklyn Col., LAMDA. Bdwy debut 1983 in "A View from the Bridge."

RAMSAY, REMAK. Born Feb. 2, 1937 in Baltimore, MD. Graduate Princeton U. Debut 1964 OB in "Hang Down Your Head and Die," followed by "The Real Inspector Hound," "Landscape of the Body," "All's Well That Ends Well" (CP), "Rear Column," "The Winslow Boy," "The Dining Room," Bdwy in "Half a Sixpence," "Sheep on the Runway," "Lovely Ladies, Kind Gentlemen," "On the Town," "Jumpers," "Private Lives," "Dirty Linen," "Every Good Boy Deserves Favor," "Save Grand Central," "Quartermaine's Terms."

RAMSEY, MARION. Born May 10 in Philadelphia, PA. Bdwy debut 1969 in "Hello, Dolly!," followed by "The Me Nobody Knows," "Rachel Lily Rosenbloom," "Eubie!," "Rock 'n' Roll," OB in "Soon," "Do It Again," "Wedding of Iphigenia," "2008½."

RANDEL, MELISSA. Born June 16, 1955 in Portland, ME. Graduate UCal/Irvine. Bdwy debut 1980 in "A Chorus Line."

RANDELL, RON. Born Oct. 8, 1920 in Sydney, Aust. Attended St. Mary's Col. Bdwy debut 1949 in "The Browning Version," followed by "Harlequinade," "Candida," "World of Suzie Wong," "Sherlock Holmes," "Mrs. Warren's Profession," "Measure for Measure," "Bent," OB in "Holy Places," "After You've Gone."

RAPHAEL, JAY E. Born Sept. 4, 1943 in NYC. Graduate Brooklyn Col., Northwestern, MiStateU. OB in "Wings," followed by "A Christmas Carol," "Taming of the Shrew," "The Scarecrow."

RASCHE, DAVID. Born Aug. 7, 1944 in St. Louis, MO. Graduate Elmhurst Col., U. Chicago. Debut 1976 OB in "John," followed by "Snow White," "Isadora Duncan Sleeps with the Russian Navy," "End of the War," "A Sermon," "Routed," "Geniuses," "Dolphin Position," Bdwy in "Shadow Box" (1977), "Loose Ends," "Lunch Hour."

RASHOVICH, GORDANA. Born Sept. 18 in Chicago, IL. Graduate Roosevelt U, RADA. Debut 1977 OB in "Fefu and Her Friends" for which she received a Theatre World Award, followed by "Selma."

RAWLS, HARDY. Born Nov. 18, 1952 in Jacksonville, FL Graduate FlaAtlanticU, UCLA. Debut 1982 OB in "Who'll Save the Plowboy?"

REAGAN, DEBORAH. Born Mar. 14, 1955 in Wayne, PA. Attended UDel. Debut 1979 OB in "The Proposition," followed by "The Sidle Show," "Corral," "Bathroom Plays," Bdwy in "Barnum" (1982), "Gemini."

REAMS, LEE ROY. Born Aug. 23, 1942 in Covington, KY. Graduate U. Cinn. Cons. Bdwy debut 1966 in "Sweet Charity," followed by "Oklahoma!" (LC), "Applause," "Lorelei," "Show Boat" (JB), "Hello Dolly!" (1978), "42nd Street," OB in "Sterling Silver," "Potholes," "The Firefly in Concert."

REAUX, ANGELINA. Born Jan. 23, 1954 in Houston, TX. Graduate Northwestern U. Debut 1979 OB in "King of Schnorrers," followed by "My Heart Is in the East."

REBHORN, JAMES. Born Sept. 1, 1948 in Philadelphia, PA. Graduate Wittenberg U, Columbia U. Debut 1972 OB in "Blue Boys," "Are You Now Or Have You Ever Been," "Trouble with Europe," "Othello," "Hunchback of Notre Dame," "Period of Adjustment," "The Freak," "Half a Lifetime," "Touch Black."

REDFIELD, ADAM. Born Nov. 4, 1959 in NYC. Attended NYU. Debut 1977 OB in "Hamlet," followed by "Androcles and the Lion," "Twelfth Night," "Reflected Glory," "Movin' Up," "The Unicorn," Bdwy 1980 in "A Life" for which he received a Theatre World Award.

REED, GAVIN. Born June 3, 1935 in Liverpool, Eng. Attended RADA. Debut 1974 OB in "The Taming of the Shrew," followed by "French without Tears," "Potsdam Quarter," "Two Fish in the Sky," Bdwy in "Scapino" (1974), "Some of My Best Friends."

REED, MARGARET. Born Nov. 15, 1956 in Calinas, CA. Graduate UCal/Santa Barbara, Cornell U. Debut 1983 OB in "Pericles," followed by "Tartuffe," "Play and Other Plays."

REED, PAMELA. Born Apr. 2, 1949 in Tacoma, WA. Graduate UWa. Bdwy debut 1978 in "November People," OB in "The Curse of the Starving Class," "All's Well That Ends Well," "Seduced," "Getting Out," "The Sorrows of Stephen," "Standing on My Knees."

REEHLING, JOYCE. See Christopher, Joyce Reehling.

REEVES, MARI. Born Mar. 1, 1952 in Denver, CO. Graduate UMiami. Debut 1972 OB in "Dear Janet Rosenberg," followed by "Southern Ladies and Gentlemen," "Lunchtime," "Stampin'," "The Double R," "Pictures at an Exhibition."

REGAN, MOLLY. Born Oct. 8 in Mankato, MN. Graduate Northwestern U. Debut 1979 OB in "Say Goodnight, Gracie," followed by "Etiquette."

REID, CRISTINE. Born Sept. 4, 1950 in Chicago, IL. Graduate SUNY/Fredonia, FlaStateU. Debut 1982 OB in "Send Her to the Beast."

REILEY, ORRIN. Born Aug. 12, 1946 in Santa Monica, CA. Graduate UCLA. Bdwy debut 1969 in "Dear World," followed by "Man of La Mancha," "Applause," "On the Town," "Seesaw," "Knickerbocker Holiday," "You Can't Take It with You."

REILLY, JACQUELINE. Born Oct. 31 in Philadelphia, PA. Graduate Kent State U, AADA. Debut 1976 OB in "I Paid My Dues," followed by "American Heroes," "Celebration," "Jacques Brel Is Alive . . ."

REISNER, CHRIS. Born Aug. 31, 1951 in NYC. Attended HB Studio. Debut 1978 OB in "Can-Can," followed by "The More You Get," "Promises, Promises."

REISSA, ELEANOR. Born May 11 in Brooklyn, NY. Graduate Brooklyn Col. Debut 1979 OB in "Rebecca, the Rabbi's Daughter," followed by "That's Not Funny, That's Sick," "The Rise of David Levinsky."

REMME, JOHN. Born Nov. 21, 1935 in Fargo, ND. Attended UMn. Debut 1972 OB in "One for the Money," followed by "Anything Goes," "The Rise of David Levinsky," Bdwy in "The Ritz" (1975), "The Royal Family," "Can-Can," "Alice in Wonderland."

RENDERER, SCOTT. Born in Palo Alto, CA. Graduate Whitman Col. Bdwy debut in "Teaneck Tanzi" (1983).

RESSEGUIE, LEW. Born May 3, 1932 in Brooklyn, NY. Attended Duke U. Debut 1982 OB in "I Take These Women," followed by "Four to Make Two," "Promises, Promises."

REY, ANTONIA. Born Oct. 12, 1927 in Havana, Cuba. Graduate Havana U. Bdwy debut 1964 in "Bajour," followed by "Mike Downstairs," "Engagement Baby," "The Ritz," OB in "Yerma," "Fiesta in Madrid," "Camino Real" (LC), "Back Dog Beast Bait," "Rain," "42 Seconds from Broadway," "Streetcar Named Desire" (LC), "Poets from the Inside," "Blood Wedding," "Missing Persons," "Crisp," "The Last Latin Lover."

REYNOLDS, DEBBIE. Born Apr. 1, 1932 in El Paso, TX. Bdwy debut 1973 in "Irene," followed by "The Debbie Reynolds Show," "Woman of the Year."

REYNOLDS, JEFFREY. Born Dec.7, 1955 in Long Island, NY. Graduate IndU. Bdwy debut 1980 in "West Side Story," followed by "Seven Brides for Seven Brothers."

RICE, SARAH. Born Mar. 5, 1955 in Okinawa. Attended AzStateU. Debut 1974 OB in "The Fantasticks," followed by "The Enchantress," Bdwy 1979 in "Sweeney Todd" for which she received a Theatre World Award.

RICH, JAMES. Bron Apr. 29, 1955 in Boston, MA. Attended Boston U. Debut 1975 OB in "Let My People Come," followed by "Livin' Dolls," Bdwy in "Hair" (1977), "The Best Little Whorehouse in Texas," "Joseph and the Amazing Technicolor Dreamcoat."

RICH, SYLVESTER. Born May 24, 1950 in Geneva, NY. Attended UHouston. Debut 1983 OB in "Dick Deterred."

RICHARDS, CAROL. Born Dec. 26 in Aurora, IL. Graduate Northwestern U, Columbia U. Bdwy debut 1965 in "Half a Sixpence," followed by "Mame," "Last of the Red Hot Lovers," "Company," "Cats."

RICHARDS, JESS. Born Jan. 23, 1943 in Seattle, WA. Attended UWash. Bdwy debut 1966 in "Walking Happy," followed by "South Pacific" (LC) "Two by Two," "On the Town" for which he received a Theatre World Award, "Mack and Mabel," "Musical Chairs," "A Reel American Hero," "Barnum," OB in "One for the Money," "Lovesong," "A Musical Evening with Josh Logan," "The Lullaby of Broadway," "All Night Strut!," "Station Joy."

RICHARDS, PAUL-DAVID. Born Aug. 31, 1935 in Bedford, IN. Graduate IndU. Bdwy debut 1959 in "Once Upon a Mattress," followed by "Camelot," "It's Superman!," "A Joyful Noise," "1776," "Devour the Snow," "My One and Only," OB in "Black Picture Show," "Devour the Snow."

RICHARDSON, PATRICIA. Born Feb. 23 in Bethesda, MD. Graduate SMU. Bdwy debut 1974 in "Gypsy," followed by "Loose Ends," "The Wake of Jamey Foster," OB in "Coroner's Plot," "Vanities," "Hooters," "The Frequency," "Fables for Friends,"

RICHERT, WANDA. Born Apr. 18, 1958 in Chicago, IL. Bdwy debut 1980 in "42nd Street" for which she received a Theatre World Award.

RICHWOOD, PATRICK. Born Nov. 6, 1962 in Burbank, CA. Debut 1983 OB in "The Robber Bridegroom."

RIEGELMAN, RUSTY. Born Sept. 9, 1948 in Kansas City, MO. Attended UCincinnati. Bdwy debut in "This Was Burlesque" (1981), followed by OB in "Not Now Darling."

RILEY, LARRY. Born June 21, 1952 in Memphis, TN. Graduate Memphis State U. Bdwy debut 1978 in "A Broadway Musical," followed by "I Love My Wife," "Night and Day," "Shakespeare's Cabaret," OB in "Street Songs," "Amerika," "Plane Down," "Sidewalkin'," "Frimbo," "A Soldier's Play," "Maybe I'm Doing It Wrong."

RINEHART, ELAINE. Born Aug. 16, in San Antonio, TX. Graduate NC Sch of Arts. Debut 1975 OB in "Tenderloin," followed by "Native Son," "Joan of Lorraine," "Dumping Ground," "Fairweather Friends," Bdwy in "The Best Little Whorehouse in Texas."

RINGHAM, NANCY. Born Nov. 16, 1954 in Minneapolis, MN. Graduate St. Olaf Col., Oxford U. Bdwy debut 1954 in "My Fair Lady" (also 1981), OB in "That Jones Boy," "Bugles at Dawn," "Not-so-New Faces of '82," "Trouble in Tahiti."

RISEMAN, NAOMI. Born Oct. 6, 1930 in Boston, MA. Graduate NYU, Columbia U. Debut 1959 OB in "Boo Hoo East Lynn," followed by "Merry Wives of Windsor," "The Lady's Not for Burning," "Romeo and Juliet," "Ernest in Love," "Will the Mail Train Run Tonight?," "Once in a Lifetime," "Promenade," "Heartbreak House," "About Heaven and Earth," "The Closed Door," Bdwy in "Status Quo Vadis" (1973), "How to Be a Jewish Mother," "Fiddler on the Roof."

RISKIN, SUSAN. Born Sept. 24, 1936 in Los Angeles, CA. Graduate UCLA. Debut 1974 in "The Sea Horse," Bdwy in "Agnes of God" (1982).

RIVERA, CHITA. Born Jan. 23, 1933 in Washington, DC. Bdwy debut 1950 in "Guys and Dolls," followed by "Call Me Madam," "Can-Can," "Seventh Heaven," "Mr. Wonderful," "West Side Story," "Bye Bye Birdie," "Bajour," "Chicago," "Bring Back Birdie," "Merlin," OB in "Shoestring Revue,"

ROBARDS, JASON. Born July 26, 1922 in Chicago, IL. Attended AADA. Bdwy debut 1947 with D'Oyly Carte, followed by "Stalag 17," "The Chase," "Long Day's Journey into Night," for which he received a Theatre World Award, "The Disenchanted," "Toys in the Attic," "Big Fish, Little Fish," "A Thousand Clowns," "Hughie," "The Devils," "We Bombed in New Haven," "The Country Girl," "Moon for the Misbegotten," "A Touch of the Poet," "You Can't Take It with You," OB in "American Gothic," "The Iceman Cometh," "After the Fall," "But for Whom Charlie," "Long Day's Journey into Night."

ROBARE, MARY C. Born May 23, 1959 in Havelock, NC. Bdwy debut 1982 in "Little Me," followed by "on Your Toes"

ROBBINS, JANA. Born Apr. 18, 1947 in Johnstown, PA. Graduate Stephens Col. Bdwy debut 1974 in "Good News," followed by "I Love My Wife," "Crimes of the Heart," OB in "Tickles by Tucholsky," "Tip-Toes," "All Night Strut!," "Colette Collage."

ROBBINS, JANE MARLA. Born Nov. 2, 1944 in NYC. Graduate Bryn Mawr. Bdwy debut 1969 in "Morning, Noon and Night," OB in "The Bear," "Beyond Desire," "Deep Six the Briefcase," "Dear Nobody," "Richard III," "Jane Avril."

ROBBINS, REX. Born in Pierre, SD. Bdwy debut 1964 in "One Flew over the Cuckoo's Nest," followed by "Scratch," "The Changing Room," "Gypsy," "Comedians," "An Almost Perfect Person," "Richard III," "You Can't Take It with You," OB in "Servant of Two Masters," "The Alchemist," "Arms and the Man," "Boys in the Band," "A Memory of Two Mondays," "They Knew What They Wanted," "Secret Service," "Boy Meets Girl," "Three Sisters," "The Play's the Thing," "Julius Caesar," "Henry IV Parts 1 and 2," "The Dining Room."

ROBERTS, BILL. Born May 25, 1948 in Sealy, TX. Graduate Sam Houston State U. Debut 1976 OB in "Maggie Flynn," followed by "Twelfth Night," "Murder in the Cathedral," Bdwy in "Amadeus" (1982).

ROBERTS, GRACE. Born Nov. 9, 1935 in NYC. Debut 1956 OB in "Out of This World," followed by "Affairs of Anatol," "Beethoven/Karl," "Friends Too Numerous to Mention," "Applesauce."

ROBERTS, RALPH. Born Aug. 17 in Salisbury, NC. Attended UNC. Bdwy debut 1948 in "Angel Street," followed by "4 Chekhov Comedies," "SS. Glencairn," "Madwoman of Chaillot," "Witness for the Prosecution," "The Lark," "Bells Are Ringing," "The Milk Train Doesn't Stop Here Anymore," "Love Suicide at Shofield Barracks," "A Texas Trilogy," OB in "Siamese Connections," "Fishing," "Joan of Lorraine."

ROBERTS, TONY. Born Oct. 22, 1939 in NYC. Graduate Northwestern U. Bdwy bow 1962 in "Something About a Soldier," followed by "Take Her, She's Mine," "Last Analysis," "Never Too Late," "Barefoot in the Park," "Don't Drink the Water," "How Now, Dow Jones," "Play It Again, Sam," "Promises, Promises," "Sugar," "Absurd Person Singular," "Murder at the Howard Johnson's," "They're Playing Our Song," OB in "The Cradle Will Rock," "Losing Time," "The Good Parts," "Time Framed."

ROBERTSON, CLIFF. Born Sept. 9, 1925 in La Jolla, CA. Attended Antioch Col. Bdwy debut 1953 in "Late Love," followed by "The Wisteria Trees," "Orpheus Descending" for which he received a Theatre World Award, "Rosalie in Concert."

ROBERTSON, LILLIE. Born Sept. 5, 1953 in Houston, TX. Graduate Carnegie-Mellon U. Debut 1979 OB in "The Guardsman," followed by "Casualties," "The Chinese Viewing Pavilion," Bdwy in "Moose Murders" (1983).

ROBINSON, MARTIN P. Born Mar. 9, 1954 in Dearborn, MI. Graduate WiStateU, AADA. Debut 1980 OB in "The Haggadah," followed by "Yellow Wallpaper," "The Lady's Not for Burning," "Little Shop of Horrors."

ROCCO, MARY. Born Sept. 12, 1933 in Brooklyn, NY. Graduate Queens Col., CCNY. Debut 1976 OB in "Fiorello!," followed by "The Constant Wife," "Archy and Mehitabel," "Sweethearts," Bdwy in "Show Boat" (1983).

ROCKAFELLOW, MARILYN. Born Jan. 22, 1939 in Middletown, NJ. Graduate Rutgers U. Debut 1976 OB in "La Ronde," followed by "The Art of Dining," "One Act Play Festival," "Open Admissions," "Bathroom Plays," Bdwy 1980 in "Clothes for a Summer Hotel."

RODRIGUEZ, ROLAND. Born Apr. 14, 1959 in Cuero, TX. Debut 1983 OB in "The Ritz," followed by "Measure for Measure."

ROGERS, BRENT. Born Feb. 15, 1955 in Dayton, OH. Attended MiamiU, Wright State U. Debut 1982 OB in "Bugles at Dawn."

ROGERS, HARRIET. Born Dec. 25, 1910 in St. Regis Falls, NY. Graduate Emerson Col. Debut 1965 OB in "Live Like Pigs," followed by "Richard II," "It's Only a Play," Bdwy in "Richard III" (1979), "Morning's at 7."

ROGERS, KEN LEIGH. Born Aug. 2, 1951 in NYC. Attended Southern Ill.U., RADA. Bdwy debut in "Hello, Dolly!" (1975), followed by "A Chorus Line," "My One and Only."

ROONEY, MICKEY. Born Sept. 23, 1920 in Brooklyn, NY. As a child, appeared in vaudeville with his parents Joe Yule and Nell Brown. Bdwy debut 1979 in "Sugar Babies," for which he received a Special Theatre World Award.

ROOS, CASPER. Born Mar. 21, 1925 in The Bronx, NY. Attended Manhattan School of Music. Bdwy debut 1959 in "First Impressions," followed by "How to Succeed in Business . . . ," "Mame," "Brigadoon," "Shenandoah," "My One and Only," OB in "Street Scene."

ROOSA, ROBIN. Born May 6, 1954 in Urbana, OH. Debut 1978 OB in "Dylan," followed by "Laughs, Etc.," "Loving Reno."

ROSE, CRISTINE. Born Jan. 31, 1951 in Lynwood, CA. Graduate Stanford U. Debut 1979 OB in "The Miracle Worker," followed by "Don Juan Comes Back from the War," "Hunting Scenes from Bavaria," "Three Acts of Recognition," "Winterplay."

ROSE, GEORGE. Born Feb. 19, 1920 in Bicester, Eng. Bdwy debut with Old Vic 1946 in "Henry IV," followed by "Much Ado about Nothing," "A Man for All Seasons," "Hamlet," "Royal Hunt of the Sun," "Walking Happy," "Loot," "My Fair Lady," (CC'68), "Canterbury Tales," "Coco," "Wise Child," "Sleuth," "My Fat Friend," "My Fair Lady," "She Loves Me," "Peter Pan," BAM's "The Play's the Thing," "The Devil's Disciple," and "Julius Caesar," "The Kingfisher," "Pirates of Penzance," "Dance a Little Closer."

ROSENBLATT, MARCELL. Born July 1, in Baltimore, MD. Graduate UNC, Yale. Debut 1979 OB in "Vienna Notes," followed by "Sorrows of Stephen," "The Dybbuk," "Twelfth Night," "Second Avenue Rag," "La Boheme," "Word of Mouth," "Twelve Dreams," "Don Juan," "A Midsummer Night's Dream."

ROSENBLATT, SELMA. Born Jan. 21, 1926 in NYC. Graduate Hunter Col. Debut 1982 OB in "Primal Time," followed by "The Coarse Acting Show," "Gertie's Gone."

ROSENFELD, CAROL. Born Apr. 27, 1938 in Philadelphia, PA. Graduate UPa. Debut 1979 in "Street Scene," followed by "The Ladies Should Be in Bed," "The Matchmaker," "Question Marks and Periods."

ROSS, ALAN J. Born Dec. 3, 1953 in New Haven, CT. Graduate UCt. Debut 1981 OB in "The Italian Straw Hat," followed by "Bloody Mary."

ROSS, HOWARD. Born Aug. 21, 1934 in NYC. Attended Juilliard, NYU. Bdwy debut in "Oliver" (1965), followed by "1600 Pennsylvania Avenue," "Carmelina," OB in "Jacques Brel Is Alive . . . ," "Beggar's Opera," "Philemon," "Isadora Duncan Sleeps with the Russian Navy," "The Further Inquiry."

ROTHMAN, JOHN. Born June 3, 1949 in Baltimore, MD. Graduate Wesleyan U, Yale. Debut 1978 OB in "Rats Nest," followed by "The Impossible H. L. Mencken," "The Buddy System," "Rosario and the Gypsies," "Italian Straw Hat," "Modern Ladies of Guanabacoa."

ROUNDS, DAVID. Born Oct. 9, 1930 in Bronxville, NY. Attended Denison U. Bdwy debut 1965 in "Foxy," followed by "Child's Play" for which he received a Theatre World Award, "The Rothschilds," "The Last of Mrs. Lincoln," "Chicago," "Romeo and Juliet," "Morning's at 7," OB in "You Never Can Tell," "Money," "The Real Inspector Hound," "Epic of Buster Friend," "Enter a Free Man," "Metamorphosis in Miniature," "Herringbone."

ROWE, DEE ETTA. Born Jan. 29, 1953 in Lewiston, ME. Graduate UHartford. Bdwy debut 1979 in "Most Happy Fella," followed by "Nine."

ROWEN, MARK. Born Oct. 28, 1956 in Chicago, IL. Graduate UTn., RADA. Debut 1982 OB in "Hooters."

ROWLES, POLLY. Born Jan. 10, 1914 in Philadelphia, PA. Attended Carnegie Tech. Bdwy debut 1938 in "Julius Caesar," followed by "Richard III," "Golden State," "Small Hours," "Gertie," "Time Out for Ginger," "Wooden Dish," "Goodbye Again," "Auntie Mame," "Look After Lulu," "A Mighty Man Is He," "No Strings," "Best Laid Plans," "Killing of Sister George," "40 Carats," "The Women," "Steaming," OB in "Older People," "Mrs. Warren's Profession," "The Show-Off."

RUBINSTEIN, JOHN. Born Dec. 8, 1946 in Los Angeles, CA. Attended UCLA. Bdwy debut 1972 in "Pippin" for which he received a Theatre World Award, followed by "Children of a Lesser God," "Fools," "The Soldier's Tale," "The Caine Mutiny Court-Martial."

RUCKER, BO. Born Aug. 17, 1948 in Tampa, FL. Debut 1978 OB in "Native Son" for which he received a Theatre World Award, followed by "Blues for Mr. Charlie," "Streamers," "Forty Deuce," "Dustoff."

RUDRUD, KRISTIN. Born May 23, 1955 in Fargo, ND. Graduate Moorhead State U, LAMDA. Debut 1981 OB in "A Midsummer Night's Dream," Bdwy 1981 in "Amadeus."

RUISINGER, THOMAS. Born May 13, 1930 in Omaha, NE. Graduate SMU, Neighborhood Playhouse. Bdwy debut 1959 in "Warm Peninsula," followed by "The Captain and the Kings," "A Shot in the Dark," "Frank Merriwell," "The Importance of Being Earnest," "Snow White," "Manhattan Showboat," "A Stitch in Time," OB in "The Balcony," "Thracian Horses," "Under Milk Wood," "Characters in Search of an Author," "Papers," "As to the Meaning of Words," "Damn Yankees" (JB), "The Holly and the Ivy."

RUSKIN, JEANNE. Born Nov. 6 in Saginaw, MI. Graduate NYU. Bdwy debut 1975 in "Equus," OB in "Says I, Says He," "Cassatt," "Inadmissible Evidence," "Hedda Gabler," "Misalliance," "Winners."

RUSSO, JAMES. Born Apr. 23, 1953 in NYC. Debut 1975 OB in "Welcome to Andromeda," followed by "Deathwatch," "Marat/Sade," "Extremities" for which he received a Theatre World Award.

RUSSO, KAREN. Born Jan. 14, 1961 in Washington, DC. Graduate UMd. Debut 1982 OB in "The Mothers," followed by "A Night of Scenes."

RUSSOM, LEON. Born Dec. 6, 1941 in Little Rock, AR. Attended Southwestern U. Debut 1968 OB in "Futz," followed by "Cyrano de Bergerac," "Boys in the Band," "Oh! Calcutta!," "Trial of the Catonsville 9," "Henry VI," "Richard III," "Shadow of a Gunman," "The New York Idea," "Three Sisters," "Old Flames," "Loving Reno," "Ruffian on the Stair," "Royal Bob," "Our Lord of Lynchville."

RYDER, RICHARD. Born Aug. 20, 1942 in Rochester, NY. Attended Colgate,U., Pratt Inst. Bdwy debut 1972 in "Oh! Calcutta!," followed by "Via Galactica," OB in "Rain," "Oh, Pshaw!," "The Dog Beneath the Skin," "Polly," "Lovers," "Green Pond," "Piano Bar," "She Loves Me," "Upstairs at O'Neal's."

SABELLICO, RICHARD. Born June 29, 1951 in NYC. Attended C.W. Post Col. Bdwy debut 1974 in "Gypsy," followed by "Annie," OB in "Gay Divorce," "La Ronde," "Manhattan Breakdown," "From Brooks with Love."

SABIN, DAVID. Born Apr. 24, 1937 in Washington, DC. Graduate Catholic U. Debut 1965 OB in "The Fantasticks," followed by "Now Is the Time for All Good Men," "Threepenny Opera," "You Never Can Tell," "Master and Margarita," Bdwy in "The Yearling," "Slapstick Tragedy," "Jimmy Shine," "Gantry," "Ambassador," "Celebration," "Music Is," "The Water Engine," "The Suicide," "Othello," "Dance a Little Closer."

SACHS, ANN. Born Jan. 23, 1948 in Boston, MA. Graduate Carnegie Tech. Bdwy debut 1970 in "Wilson in the Promise Land," followed by "Dracula," "Man and Superman," OB in "Tug of War," "Sweetshoppe Miriam," "Festival of American Plays," "Clownmaker," "A Think Piece."

SACKS, DAVIA. Born July 10 in Flushing, NY. Attended Dade Jr. Col. Debut 1973 OB in "Swiss Family Robinson," followed by "Zorba," Bdwy in "Fiddler on the Roof" (1976), "Evita."

SADLER, WILLIAM (BILL). Born Apr. 13, 1950 in Buffalo, NY. Graduate S.U.C.-/Genesco, Cornell U. Debut 1975 OB in "Ivanov," followed by "Limbo Tales," "Chinese Viewing Pavilion," "Lennon," "Necessary Ends," "Hannah."

SADOFF, FRED. Born Oct. 21, 1926 in Brooklyn, NY. Attended Bklyn Col., Neighborhood Playhouse, Actors Studio. Bdwy debut 1949 in "South Pacific," followed by "Wish You Were Here," "Camino Real," OB in "The Collyer Brothers at Home," "Period Piece," "Hannah."

SAFIER, ALAN. Born June 3, 1949 in Cleveland, OH. Graduate Ohio U. Debut 1980 OB in "Goodnight, Gracie," followed by "New Faces of '52."

SAINT, EVA MARIE. Born July 4, 1924 in Newark, NJ. Attended Bowling Green State U., Actors Studio. Bdwy debut 1953 in "The Trip to Bountiful," for which she received a Theatre World Award, followed by "The Lincoln Mask," OB in "Duet for One" (1983).

SANDERS, JAY O. Born Apr. 16, 1953 in Austin, TX. Graduate SUNY/Purchase. Debut 1976 OB in "Henry V," followed by "Measure for Measure," "Scooping," "Buried Child," "Fables for Friends," "In Trousers," "Girls Girls Girls," "Twelfth Night," "Geniuses," Bdwy in "Loose Ends" (1979), "The Caine Mutiny Court-Martial."

SANTIAGO, SAUNDRA. Born Apr. 13, 1957 in NYC. Graduate UMiami, SMU. Debut on Bdwy in "A View From the Bridge" (1983).

SAPUTO, PETER J. Born Feb 2, 1939 in Detroit, MI. Graduate EMiU, Purdue U. Debut 1977 OB in "King Oedipus," followed by "Twelfth Night," "Bon Voyage," "Happy Haven," "Sleepwalkers," "Humulus the Mute," "The Freak," "Promises, Promises," Bdwy in "Once in a Lifetime."

SARANDON, SUSAN. Born Oct. 4, 1946 in NYC. Graduate Catholic U. Bdwy debut 1972 in "An Evening with Richard Nixon," OB in "A Coupla White Chicks . . . ," "Extremities."

Richard Marr

Lora Jeanne Martens

Steve McDonough

Elizabeth McGovern

Jan Mickens

Ann Leslie
Morrison

Jennifer S. Myers

Harsh Nayyar

Mary Ann Niles

Don Nute

Cynthia Nixon

Patrick O'Connell

Brian O'Halloran

Paige O'Hara

Robert Ousley

Roxann Parker

Scott Pearson

Susan Pellegrino

Carla Pinza

Ken Prescott

Cheryl Quinn

Patrick Quinn

Julie Ramaker

Adam Redfield

Orrin Reiley

Sarah Rice

Ken Leigh Rogers

Robin Roosa

Bo Rucker

Saundra Santiago

219

SARDI, GEORGE. Born July 9, 1924 in Baltimore, MD. Debut 1983 OB in "The Ritz."

SAUCIER, CLAUDE-ALBERT. Born Oct. 9, 1953 in Berlin, NH. Graduate Dartmouth Col. Debut 1977 OB in "A Midsummer Night's Dream," followed by "Veronica's Room," "Madwoman of Chaillot," "Sjt. Musgrave's Dance," Bdwy in "Alice in Wonderland" (1982).

SAUNDERS, NICHOLAS. Born June 2, 1914 in Kiev, Russia. Bdwy debut 1942 in "Lady in the Dark" followed by "A New Life," "Highland Fling," "Happily Ever After," "The Magnificent Yankee," "Anastasia," "Take Her, She's Mine," "A Call on Kuprin," "Passion of Josef D.," OB in "An Enemy of the People," "End of All Things Natural," "The Unicorn in Captivity," "After the Rise," "All My Sons," "My Great Dead Sister," "The Investigation," "Past Tense," "Scenes and Revelations," "Zeks," "Blood Moon," "Family Comedy."

SAVELLA, MARCIA. Born Nov. 6, 1947 in Cranston, RI. Graduate UCt. Bdwy debut 1973 in "The Iceman Cometh," OB in "Circus," "Cowpokes," "Eleanor and Franklin," "A Night Out," "Happy Birthday, Wanda June."

SBARGE, RAPHAEL. Born Feb. 12, 1964 in NYC. Attended HB Studio. Debut 1981 OB in "Henry IV Part I," followed by "The Red Snake," "Hamlet," Bdwy in "The Curse of an Aching Heart."

SCHACT, SAM. Born Apr. 19, 1936 in The Bronx, NY. Graduate CCNY. OB in "Fortune and Men's Eyes," "Cannibals," "I Met a Man," "The Increased Difficulty of Concentration," "One Night Stands of a Noisy Passenger," "Owners," "Jack Gelber's New Play," "The Master and Margarita," "Was It Good for You?," "True West," Bdwy in "The Magic Show," "Golda."

SCHAFER, DENISE. Born May 17 in DeKalb, IL. Graduate Northwestern U. Debut 1982 OB in "New Faces of '52."

SCHAFFNER, LESTER J. Born Nov. 6 in NYC. Graduate Hofstra U. Debut 1982 OB in "Ah, Wilderness," followed by "Before Caesar," "The Actors,"

SCHAUT, ANN LOUISE. Born Nov. 21, 1956 in Minneapolis, MN. Attended UMn. Bdwy debut 1981 in "A Chorus Line."

SCHEINE, RAYNOR. Born Nov. 10 in Emporia, VA. Graduate VaCommonwealthU. Debut 1978 OB in "Curse of the Starving Class," followed by "Blues for Mr. Charlie," "Salt Lake City Skyline," "Mother Courage," "The Lady or the Tiger," "Bathroom Plays," "Wild Life."

SCHENK, ERNIE. Born Nov. 4, 1940 in Newark, NJ. Graduate Bloomfield Col., NYU. Debut 1969 OB in "Makbeth," followed by "Goose and Tom Tom," "Under Milk Wood," Bdwy in "Shenandoah" (1978).

SCHERER, SUSAN. Born Sept. 18, 1948 in New Orleans, LA. Graduate LaStateU. Debut OB 1973 in "Call Me Madam," followed by "Busybody."

SCHILKE, MICHAEL. Born Dec. 10, 1953 in Sulphur, OK. Graduate Dennison U., UCin. Debut 1978 OB in "Tribute to Women," followed by "On a Clear Day You Can See Forever," "Plain and Fancy," "Beggar's Opera," "Eileen in Concert," "The Happy Time."

SCHLAMME, MARTHA. Born Sept. 25 in Vienna, Aust. Debut 1963 OB in "The World of Kurt Weill," followed by "A Month of Sundays," "Mata Hari," "Beethoven and Karl," "Aspirations," "God of Vengeance," "Twilight Cantata," Bdwy in "Fiddler on the Roof," "Threepenny Opera," "Solitaire/Double Solitaire," "A Kurt Weill Cabaret."

SCHMIDT, STEPHEN. Born Dec. 24, 1955 in Cincinnati, OH. Graduate NYU. Debut 1980 OB in "Fair Play for Eve," followed by "The Robber Bridegroom."

SCHRAMM, DAVID. Born Aug. 14, 1946 in Louisville, KY. Attended Western KyU., Juilliard. Debut 1972 OB in "School for Scandal," followed by "Lower Depths," "Women Beware Women," "Mother Courage," "King Lear," "Duck Variations," "The Cradle Will Rock," Bdwy in "Three Sisters," "Next Time I'll Sing to You," "Edward II," "Measure for Measure," "The Robber Bridegroom," "Bedroom Farce," "Goodbye, Fidel," "The Misanthrope."

SCHULL, REBECCA. Born Feb. 22 in NYC. Graduate NYU. Bdwy debut 1976 in "Herzl," followed by "Golda," OB in "Mother's Day," "Fefu and Her Friends," "On Mt Chimborazo," "Mary Stuart," "Balzamov's Wedding," "Before She Is Ever Born," "Exiles."

SCHULTZ, CAROL. Born Feb. 12 in Chicago, IL. Graduate Case Western Reserve U., UIll. Debut 1982 OB in "Peer Gynt," followed by "The Cherry Orchard," "King Lear," "Ghost Sonata."

SCHULTZ, CATHERINE. Born Jan. 11, 1954 in Pittsburgh, PA. Graduate Chatham Col. Debut 1978 OB in "Arturo Ui," followed by "Refrigerators," "Mopealong," "Love's Labour's Lost," "Soap."

SCHWARTZ, MICHAEL. Born Apr. 21, 1944 in San Diego, CA. Attended AzStateU. Debut 1982 OB in "Svelte Anna," followed by "Bottoms Up, Donald Duck," "Never Say Die," "After the Fall."

SCHWEID, CAROLE. Born Oct. 5, 1946 in Newark, NJ. Graduate Boston U, Juilliard. Bdwy debut 1970 in "Minnie's Boys," followed by "A Chorus Line," "Street Scene," OB in "Love Me, Love My Children," "How to Succeed in Business . . . ," "Silk Stockings," "Children of Adam," "Upstairs at O'Neal's," "Not-So-New Faces of '82."

SCOTT, GEORGE C. Born Oct. 18, 1927 in Wise, VA. Debut 1957 OB in "Richard III" for which he received a Theatre World Award, followed by "As You Like It," "Children of Darkness," "Desire under the Elms," Bdwy in "Comes a Day," "Andersonville Trial," "The Wall," "General Seegar," "The Little Foxes," "Plaza Suite," "Uncle Vanya," Death of a Salesman," "Sly Fox," "Tricks of the Trade," "Present Laughter."

SEAMAN, JANE. Born Nov. 18 in Bellevue, OH. Graduate Stanford U, Wittenberg U. Debut 1982 OB in "Street Scene."

SEAMON, EDWARD. Born Apr. 15, 1937 in San Diego, CA. Attended San Diego State Col. Debut 1971 OB in "The Life and Times of J. Walter Smintheous," followed by "The Contractor," "The Family," "Fishing," "Feedlot," "Cabin 12," "Rear Column," "Devour the Snow," "Buried Child," "Friends," "Extenuating Circumstances," "Confluence," "Richard II," "Great Grandson of Jedediah Kohler," "Marvelous Gray," "Time Framed," Bdwy in "The Trip Back Down," "Devour the Snow," "The American Clock."

SEFF, RICHARD. Born Sept. 23, 1927 in NYC. Attended NYU. Bdwy debut 1951 in "Darkness at Noon," followed by "Herzl," OB in "Big Fish, Little Fish," "Modigliani," "Childe Byron," "Richard II," "Time Framed."

SEGAL, KATHRIN KING. Born Dec. 8, 1947 in Washington, DC. Attended HB Studio. Debut 1969 OB in "Oh! Calcutta!," followed by "The Drunkard," "Alice in Wonderland," "Pirates of Penzance," "Portfolio Revue," "Philomen," "Butter and Egg Man."

SEIDEL, VIRGINIA. Born July 26 in Harvey, IL. Attended Roosevelt U. Bdwy debut 1975 in "Very Good Eddie" for which she received a Theatre World Award, OB in "Hoofers," "Charlotte Sweet," "Where's Charley?"

SEIDMAN, JOHN. Born Oct. 11, 1949 in Miami, FL. Graduate NYU. Debut 1982 on Bdwy in "Alice in Wonderland."

SELDES, MARIAN. Born Aug. 23, 1928 in NYC. Attended Neighborhood Playhouse. Bdwy debut 1947 in "Medea," followed by "Crime and Punishment," "That Lady," "Tower Beyond Tragedy," "Ondine," "On High Ground," "Come of Age," "Chalk Garden," "The Milk Train Doesn't Stop Here Anymore," "The Wall," "A Gift of Time," "A Delicate Balance," "Before You Go," "Father's Day," "Equus," "The Merchant," "Deathtrap," OB in "Different," "Ginger Man," "Mercy Street," "Isadora Duncan Sleeps With the Russian Navy," "Painting Churches."

SEPPE, CHRISTOPHER. Born Sept. 19, 1955 in Brooklyn, NY. Debut 1979 OB in "The Fantasticks," followed by "Charlotte Sweet."

SERRANO, CHARLIE. Born Dec. 4, 1952 in Rio Piedras, PR. Attended Brooklyn Col. Debut 1978 OB in "Allegro" followed by "Mama, I Want to Sing," "El Bravo," Bdwy in "Got Tu Go Disco," "Joseph and the Amazing Technicolor Dreamcoat."

SERRECCHIA, MICHAEL. Born Mar. 26, 1951 in Brooklyn, NY. Attended Brockport State U. Teachers Col. Bdwy debut 1972 in "The Selling of the President," followed by "Heathen!" "Seesaw," "A Chorus Line," OB in "Lady Audley's Secret."

SETRAKIAN, ED. Born Oct. 1, 1928 in Jenkintown, WV. Graduate Concord Col., NYU. Debut 1966 OB in "Drums in the Night," followed by "Othello," "Coriolanus," "Macbeth," "Hamlet," "Baal," "Old Glory," "Futz," "Hey Rube," "Seduced," "Shout Across the River," "American Days," "Sheepskin," "Inserts," Bdwy in "Days in the Trees," "St. Joan," "The Best Little Whorehouse in Texas."

SEVERS, WILLIAM. Born Jan. 8, 1932 in Britton, OK. Attended Pasadena Playhouse, Columbia Col. Bdwy debut 1960 in "Cut of the Axe," OB in "The Moon Is Blue," "Lulu," "Big Maggie," "Mixed Doubles," "The Rivals," "The Beaver Coat," "Twister," "Midnight Mass," "Gas Station," "Firebugs."

SEVIER, JACK. Born Apr. 1, 1925 in Chattanooga, TN. Graduate UChattanooga, UNC. Bdwy debut 1959 in "Destry Rides Again," followed by "My Fair Lady" (1981), OB in "American Princess."

SEVRA, ROBERT. Born Apr. 15, 1945 in Kansas City, MO. Graduate Stanford U., UMi. Debut 1972 OB in "Servant of Two Masters," followed by "Lovers," Bdwy in "Charlie and Algernon" (1980), "Torch Song Trilogy."

SHAFFER, LOUISE. Born July 5 in New Haven, CT. Attended Yale, HB Studio. Bdwy debut 1966 in "First One Asleep Whistle," followed by "We Have Always Lived in a Castle," "The Women," OB in "The Butter and Egg Man."

SHAKAR, MARTIN. Born Jan. 1, 1940 in Detroit, MI. Attended Wayne State U. Bdwy bow 1969 in "Our Town," OB in "Lorenzaccio," "Macbeth," "The Infantry," "Americana Pastoral," "No Place to be Somebody," "World of Mrs. Solomon," "And Whose Little Boy Are You," "Investigation of Havana," "Night Watch," "Owners," "Actors," "Richard III," "Transfiguration of Benno Blimpie," "Jack Gelber's New Play," "Biko Inquest," "Second-Story Sunlight," "Secret Thighs of New England Women," "After the Fall."

SHALDENE, VALERIE. Born July 25, 1960 in Neptune, NJ. Attended USCal. Debut 1982 OB in "A Place on the Magdalena Flats."

SHALLO, KAREN. Born Sept. 28, 1946 in Philadelphia, PA. Graduate PaStateU. Debut 1973 OB in "Children of Darkness," followed by "Moliere in spite of Himself," "We Won't Pay!," "The Overcoat," "Angelus," Bdwy 1980 in "Passione."

SHANGOLD, JOAN. Born Mar. 28 in Albany, NY. Debut 1977 OB in "The Crucible," followed by "Love's Labor's Lost," "13."

SHAPIRO, DEBBIE. Born Sept. 29, 1954 in Los Angeles, CA. Graduate LACC. Bdwy debut 1979 in "They're Playing Our Song," followed by "Perfectly Frank," "Blues in the Night," OB in "They Say It's Wonderful," "New Moon in Concert."

SHASHY, SUSAN. Born May 3, 1955 in Jacksonville, FL. Graduate UDenver. Debut 1981 OB in "Dog and Suds," followed by "Transformations."

SHAW, MARCIE. Born June 19, 1954 in Franklin Square, NY. Attended UIl. Bdwy debut 1980 in "Pirates of Penzance," OB in "A Midsummer Night's Dream."

SHAWHAN, APRIL. Born Apr. 10, 1940 in Chicago, IL. Debut 1964 OB in "Jo," followed by "Hamlet," "Oklahoma," "Mod Donna," "Journey to Gdansk," Bdwy in "Race of Hairy Men," "3 Bags Full" (1966) for which she received a Theatre World Award, "Dinner at 8," "Cop-Out," "Much Ado about Nothing," "Over Here," "Rex," "A History of the American Film."

SHEA, JOHN V. Born Apr. 14 in North Conway, NH. Graduate Bates Col., Yale. Debut OB 1974 in "Yentl, the Yeshiva Boy," followed by "Gorky," "Battering Ram," "Safe House," "The Master and Margarita," "Sorrows of Stephen," "American Days," "The Dining Room," Bdwy in "Yentl" (1975) for which he received a Theatre World Award, "Romeo and Juliet," "A Soldier's Tale."

SHELLEY, CAROLE. Born Aug. 16, 1939 in London, Eng. Bdwy debut 1965 in "The Odd Couple," followed by "Astrakhan Coat," "Loot," "Noel Coward's Sweet Potato," "Hay Fever," "Absurd Person Singular," "The Norman Conquests," "The Elephant Man," "The Misanthrope," OB in "Little Murders," "The Devil's Disciple," "The Play's the Thing," "Double Feature," "Twelve Dreams."

SHELTON, SLOANE. Born Mar. 17, 1934 in Asheville, NC. Attended Berea Col., RADA. Bdwy debut 1967 in "The Imaginary Invalid," followed by "A Touch of the Poet," "Tonight at 8:30," "I Never Sang for My Father," "Sticks and Bones," "The Runner Stumbles," "Shadow Box," "Passione," OB in "Androcles and the Lion," "The Maids," "Basic Training of Pavlo Hummel," "Play and Other Plays," "Julius Caesar," "Chieftains," "Passione," "The Chinese Viewing Pavilion," "Blood Relations."

SHEPARD, JOAN. Born Jan. 7 in NYC. Graduate RADA. Bdwy debut 1940 in "Romeo and Juliet," followed by "Sunny River," "The Strings, My Lord, Are False," "This Rock," "Foolish Notion," "A Young Man's Fancy," "My Romance," "Member of the Wedding," OB in "Othello," "Plot Against the Chase Manhattan Bank," "Philosophy in the Boudoir," "Knitters in the Sun," "School for Wives," "Importance of Being Earnest."

SHEPARD, JOHN. Born Dec. 9, 1932 in Huntington Park, CA. Graduate UCal/Irvine. Debut 1982 OB in "Scenes from La Vie de Boheme," Bdwy in "A View From the Bridge" (1983).

SHEPHERD, GWENDOLYN J. Born Oct. 20 in East Meadowbrook, NY. Graduate NYU, FordhamU. Bdwy debut 1983 in "Porgy and Bess."

SHIELDS, DALE. Born Nov. 4, 1952 in Cleveland, OH. Graduate Ohio U. Debut 1976 OB in "Sing America," followed by "Fashion," "Contributions," "Anyone Can Whistle," "Liberty Call."

SHORT, SYLVIA. Born Oct. 22, 1927 in Concord, MA. Attended Smith Col., Old Vic. Debut 1954 OB in "The Clandestine Marriage," followed by "Golden Apple," "Passion of Gross," "Desire Caught by the Tail," "City Love Story," "Family Reunion," "Beaux Stratagem," "Just a Little Bit Less Than Normal," "Nasty Rumors," "Says I, Says He," "Milk of Paradise," "The Broken Pitcher," "After You've Gone," Bdwy in "King Lear" (1956), "Hide and Seek."

SHROPSHIRE, NOBLE. Born Mar. 2, 1946 in Cartersville, GA. Graduate LaGrange Col., RADA. Debut 1976 OB in "Hound of the Baskervilles," followed by "The Misanthrope," "The Guardsman," "Oedipus Cycle," "Gilles de Rais," "Leonce and Lena," "King Lear," "Danton's Death."

SHULTZ, PHILIP. Born July 24, 1953 in NYC. Graduate NYU. Debut 1974 OB in "Patience," followed by "Rehearsal," "The Coolest Cat in Town," "Basement Skylight," "Guys and Dolls," "Bugles at Dawn," "The Coarse Acting Show."

SHUMAN, JOHN. Born Aug. 10 in Boston, MA. Debut 1975 OB in "The Hot l Baltimore," followed by "Moonchildren," "The Taming of the Shrew," Bdwy in "13 Rue de l'Amour" (1978).

SIDNEY, P. JAY. Bdwy debut 1934 in "Dance with Your Gods," followed by "20th Century," "Carmen Jones," "Green Pastures," "Run, Little Chillun," "Jeb," "Cool World," "The Winner," "The Playroom," "First Monday in October," OB in "The Octoroon," "Goodnight, Grandpa."

SIEGLER, BEN. Born Apr. 9, 1958 in Queens, NY. Attended HB Studio. Debut 1980 OB in "Innocent Thoughts, Harmless Intentions," followed by "Threads," "Many Happy Returns," "Snow Orchid," "The Diviners," "What I Did Last Summer," "Time Framed," Bdwy 1981 in "5th of July."

SINKYS, ALBERT. Born July 10, 1940 in Boston, MA. Attended Boston U, UCLA. Debut 1981 OB in "In the Matter of J. Robert Oppenheimer," followed by "The Caine Mutiny Court-Martial," "Man in the Glass Booth."

SISTI, MICHELAN. Born May 27, 1949 in San Juan, PR. Graduate UBuffalo. Debut 1979 OB in "A Midsummer Night's Dream," followed by "All of the Above," Bdwy in "Fiddler on the Roof" (1981).

SKINNER, MARGO. Born Jan. 3, 1950 in Middletown, OH. Graduate Boston U. Debut 1980 OB in "Missing Persons," followed by "The Dining Room," "Mary Barnes."

SLATER, CHRISTIAN. Born Aug. 18, 1969 in NYC. Bdwy debut 1980 in "The Music Man," followed by "Copperfield," "Macbeth," "Merlin," OB in "Between Daylight and Boonville."

SLOAN, GARY. Born July 6, 1952 in New Castle, IN. Graduate Wheaton Col., SMU. Debut 1982 OB in "Faust," followed by "Wild Oats," "Balloon," "Danton's Death."

SLUTSKER, PETER. Born Apr. 17, 1958 in NYC. Graduate UMi. Bdwy debut 1983 in "On Your Toes."

SMALL, LARRY. Born Oct. 6, 1947 in Kansas City, MO. Attended Manhattan School of Music. Bdwy debut 1971 in "1776," followed by "La Strada," "Wild and Wonderful," "A Doll's Life," OB in "Plain and Fancy."

SMALL, NEVA. Born Nov. 17, 1952 in NYC. Bdwy debut 1964 in "Something More," followed by "The Impossible Years," "Henry, Sweet Henry," "Frank Merriwell," "Something's Afoot," OB in "Ballad for a Firing Squad," "Tell Me Where the Good Times Are," "How Much, How Much," "F. Jasmine Addams," "Macbeth," "Yentl the Yeshiva Boy," "Life Is Not a Doris Day Movie."

SMITH, ANNA D. Born Sept. 18, 1950 in Baltimore, MD. Graduate Beaver Col, AmConTh. Debut 1980 OB in "Mother Courage," followed by "Mercenaries."

SMITH, COTTER. Born May 29, 1949 in Washington, DC. Graduate Trinity Col. Debut 1980 OB in "The Blood Knot," followed by "Death of a Miner," "A Soldier's Play."

SMITH, GEDDETH. Born Feb. 28, 1934 in Columbia, SC. Graduate USC. OB in "The Golden Six," "Fashion," "Joan at the Stake," "Imaginary Invalid," "A Touch of the Poet," "Tonight at 8:30," Bdwy in "Alice in Wonderland" (1983).

SMITH, LIONEL MARK. Born Feb. 5, 1946 in Chicago, IL. Attended Goodman ThSchool. Debut 1982 OB in "Edmond."

SMITH, LOIS. Born Nov. 3, 1930 in Topeka, KS. Attended UWa. Bdwy debut 1952 in "Time Out for Ginger," followed by "The Young and the Beautiful," "Wisteria Trees," "Glass Menagerie," "Orpheus Descending," "Stages," OB in "Sunday Dinner," "Present Tense," "The Iceman Cometh," "Harry Outside," "Hillbilly Women," "Touching Bottom," "Tennessee," "The Articulated Man," "Hannah."

SMITH, MICHAEL PETER. Born Aug. 14, 1951 in Worcester, MA. Graduate Northeastern U. Bdwy debut 1976 in "Equus," OB in "Mr. Scrooge," "Ah, Wilderness," "Chamber Music," "Dark of the Moon."

SMITH, NICK. Born Jan. 13, 1932 in Philadelphia, PA. Attended Boston U. Debut 1963 OB in "The Blacks," followed by "Man Is Man," "The Connection," "Blood Knot," "No Place to Be Somebody," "Androcles and the Lion," "So Nice They Named It Twice," "In the Recovery Lounge," "Liberty Call."

SMITH, SHEILA.) Born Apr. 3, 1933 in Conneaut, OH. Attended Kent State U., Clevelnd Play House. Bdwy debut 1963 in "Hot Spot," followed by "Mame" for which she received a Theatre World Award, "Follies," "Company," "Sugar," "Five O'Clock Girl," "42nd Street," OB in "Taboo Revue" "Anything Goes," "Best Foot Forward," "Sweet Miami," "Fiorello," "Taking My Turn."

SMITH-CAMERON, J. Born Sept. 7 in Louisville, KY. Attended FlaStateU. Bdwy debut 1982 in "Crimes of the Heart," OB in "Asian Shade."

SMITROVICH, BILL. Born May 16, 1947 in Bridgeport, CT. Graduate UBridgeport, Smith Col. Bdwy debut 1980 in "The American Clock," OB in "Zeks," "Never Say Die."

SMITS, JIMMY. Born July 9, 1955 in NYC. Graduate Brooklyn Col, Cornell U. Debut 1982 OB in "Hamlet," followed by "Little Victories," "Buck."

SNOVELL, WILLIAM. Born June 2, 1956 in Baltimore, MD. Graduate Catholic U. Debut 1982 OB in "Black Angel," Bdwy in "Passion" (1983).

SNYDER, NANCY E. Born Dec. 2, 1949 in Kankakee, IL. Graduate Webster Col., Neighborhood Playhouse. Bdwy debut 1976 in "Knock, Knock," followed by "Angels Fall," OB in "The Farm," "My Life," "Lulu," "Cabin 12," "5th of July," "My Cup Runneth Over," "Glorious Morning," "Stargazing," "Time Framed."

SOD, TED. Born May 12, 1951 in Wilkes-Barre, PA. Graduate King's Col. Debut 1976 OB in "Henry V," followed by "Savages," "City Junket," "A Midsummer Night's Dream," "Recruiting Officer," "Jungle of Cities," "The Wild Duck," "Buck."

SOHMERS, BARBARA. Born July 7 in NYC. Attended Antioch Col. Debut 1955 OB in "The Trial," followed by "Spring's Awakening," "Threepenny Opera," "Elba," Bdwy in "Ned and Jack" (1981).

SOMERS, BRETT. Born July 11, 1927 in New Brunswick, Can. Attended AmThWing, Actors Studio. Bdwy debut 1958 in "Maybe Tuesday," OB in "My Prince My King" (1982), "Night Fishing in Beverly Hills."

SOMMER, JOSEF. Born June 26, 1934 in Griefswald, Ger. Graduate Carnegie Tech. Bdwy bow 1970 in "Othello," followed by "Children, Children," "Trial of the Catonsville 9," "Full Circle," "Who's Who in Hell," "Shadow Box," "Spokesong," "The 1940s Radio Show," "Whose Life Is It Anyway?," OB in "Enemies," "Merchant of Venice," "The Dog Ran Away," "Drinks Before Dinner," "Lydie Breeze," "Black Angel."

SOREL, ANITA. Born Oct. 25, in Hollywood, CA. Graduate UUtah, CalState/Long Beach. Debut 1980 OB in "The Time of the Cuckoo" (ELT) followed by "Bourgeois Gentlemen," "Hedda Gabler," "Merry Wives of Scarsdale."

SOREL, THEODORE. Born Nov. 14, 1936 in San Francisco, CA. Graduate College of Pacific. Bdwy debut 1977 in "Sly Fox," followed by "Horowitz and Mrs. Washington," "A Little Family Business," OB in "Arms and the Man," "Moon Mysteries," "A Call from the East," "Hedda Gabler."

SPACKMAN, TOM. Born Oct. 4, 1950 in Binghamton, NY. Graduate WayneStateU. Debut 1981 OB in "Peer Gynt," followed by "King Lear," "Ghost Sonata," "Faust," "Wild Oats."

SPANO, NEALLA. Born Sept. 26, 1958 in NYC. Graduate Northwestern U. Debut 1981 OB in "Lady Windermere's Fan," followed by "The Night Is Young," "The Coarse Acting Show."

SPARER, KATHRYN C. Born Jan 5, 1956 in NYC. Graduate UChicago. Debut 1982 OB in "Beside the Seaside," followed by "About Iris Berman," "The Rise of Daniel Rocket."

SPECHT, PATTI. Born Aug. 13, 1954 in San Diego, CA. Graduate OhioStateU. Debut 1979 OB in "Svengali," followed by "A Pearl of Great Price."

SPIEGEL, BARBARA. Born Mar. 12 in NYC. Debut 1969 in LCRep's "Camino Real," "Operation Sidewinder" and "Beggar on Horseback," OB in "Feast for Flies," "Museum," "Powder," "The Bleachers," "Nightshift," "Cassatt," "Rope Dancers," "Friends Too Numerous to Mention."

SPINDELL, AHVI. Born June 26, 1954 in Boston, MA. Attended Ithaca Col. UNH, Juilliard. Bdwy debut 1977 in "Something Old, Something New," OB in "Antony and Cleopatra," "Forty Deuce," "Alexandriad."

SPOLAN, JEFFREY. Born July 14, 1947 in NYC. Graduate Adelphi U. Debut 1982 OB in "Yellow Fever."

SQUIBB, JUNE. Born Nov. 6 in Vandalia, IL. Attended Cleveland Play House, HB Studio. Debut 1956 OB in "Sable Brush," followed by "The Boy Friend," "Lend an Ear," "Another Language," "Castaways," "Funeral March for a One-Man Band," "Gorey Stories," "Blues for Mr. Charlie," "The Workroom," Bdwy in "Gypsy" (1960), "The Happy Time," "Gorey Stories."

STAHLHUTH, GAYLE. Born Aug. 11, 1950 in Indianapolis, IN. Graduate IndCentralU. Debut 1981 OB in "Lou," followed by "Sholom Aleichem," "Jimmy the Veteran," "Cries and Whispers."

STANLEY, GORDON. Born Dec. 20, 1951 in Boston, MA. Graduate Brown U., Temple U. Debut 1977 OB in "Lyrical and Satirical," followed by "Allegro," "Elizabeth and Essex," "Two on the Isles," Bdwy in "Onward Victoria" (1980), "Joseph and the Amazing Technicolor Dreamcoat."

STANNARD, NICK. Born Dec. 2, 1948 in Cohasset, MA. Attended Carnegie-Mellon U. Debut 1975 OB in "Wings," followed by "Beyond Therapy," "I Am Who I Am," Bdwy in "Dracula" (1979).

STANSBURY, HOPE. Born Nov. 23, 1949 in London, Eng. OB in "Henry and Henrietta," "Just Before the War with the Eskimos," "Run to the Sea," "Chocolates," "Couchmates," "Paderefski," "Howies," "Women Behind Bars," "Inserts."

STAPLETON, MAUREEN. Born June 21, 1925 in Troy, NY. Attended HB Studio. Bdwy debut 1946 in "Playboy of the Western World," followed by "Antony and Cleopatra," "Detective Story," "Bird Cage," "The Rose Tattoo" for which she received a Theatre World Award, "The Emperor's Clothes," "The Crucible," "Richard III," "The Seagull," "27 Wagons Full of Cotton," "Orpheus Descending," "The Cold Wind and the Warm," "Toys in the Attic," "Glass Menagerie" (1965 & 1975), "Plaza Suite," "Norman, Is That You?," "Gingerbread Lady," "Country Girl," "Secret Affairs of Mildred Wild," "The Gin Game," "The Little Foxes" (1981).

STARK, SALLY. Born May 28, 1938 in Riverhead, NY. Attended St. Elizabeth Col. Debut 1967 OB in "Babes in Arms," followed by "Your Own Thing," "Dames at Sea," Bdwy in "A Little Family Business" (1982).

STATTEL, ROBERT. Born Nov. 20, 1937 in Floral Park, NY. Graduate Manhattan Col. Debut 1958 OB in "Heloise," followed by "When I Was a Child," "Man and Superman," "The Storm," "Don Carlos," "Taming of the Shrew," "Titus Andronicus," "Henry IV," "Peer Gynt," "Hamlet," LCRep's "Danton's Death," "Country Wife," "Caucasian Chalk Circle," and "King Lear," "Iphigenia in Aulis," "Ergo," "The Persians," "Blue Boys," "The Minister's Black Veil," "Four Friends," "Two Character Play," "The Merchant of Venice," "Cuchulain," "Oedipus Cycle," "Gilles de Rais," "Woyzeck," "King Lear," "The Fuehrer Bunker," "Learned Ladies," "Domestic Issues."

STEFAN, MARK. Born Sept. 17, 1972 in NYC. Debut 1981 OB in "Sister Mary Ignatius Explains It All for You," "Actor's Nightmare," followed by "The Workroom."

STEFFY, DON. Born Sept. 30, 1950 in Canton, OH. Graduate KentStateU. Bdwy debut 1982 in "Seven Brides for Seven Brothers," followed by "On Your Toes."

STEINBERG, ROY. Born Mar. 24, 1951 in NYC. Graduate Tufts U., Yale. Debut 1974 OB in "A Midsummer Night's Dream," followed by "Firebugs," "The Doctor in Spite of Himself," "Romeo and Juliet," "After the Rise," "Our Father," "Zeks," "In Agony," Bdwy in "Wings."

STEINER, SHERRY. Born Sept. 29, 1948 in NYC. Graduate Chatham Col. Debut 1978 OB in "Catsplay," followed by "Safe House," "Frankie and Annie," "Sorrows of Stephen," "A Winter's Tale," "Barbarians," "The Purging," "Cloud 9," Bdwy in "Piaf" (1981).

STENARD, DEBORAH. Born Sept. 18, 1956 in Springfield, MA. Graduate York U. Debut 1982 OB in "The Coarse Acting Show."

STENBORG, HELEN. Born Jan. 24, 1925 in Minneapolis, MN. Attended Unter Col. OB in "A Doll's House," "A Month in the Country," "Say Nothing," "Rosmersholm," "Rimers of Eldritch," "Trial of the Catonsville 9," "The Hot l Baltimore," "Pericles," "Elephant in the House," "A Tribute to Lili Lamont," "Museum," "5th of July," "In the Recovery Lounge," "The Chisholm Trail," "Time Framed," Bdwy in "Sheep on the Runway" (1970), "Da," "A Life."

STENDER, DOUGLAS. Born Sept. 14, 1942 in Nanticoke, PA. Graduate Princeton U, RADA. Bdwy debut 1973 in "The Changing Room," OB in "New England Eclectic."

STERNE, RICHARD. Born Feb. 26, 1942 in Philadelphia, PA. Graduate Northwestern U. Bdwy bow 1964 in "Hamlet," followed by "Crown Matrimonial," "Alice in Wonderland," OB in "Beyond Desire," "Naked."

STERNER, STEVE. Born May 5, 1951 in NYC. Attended CCNY. Bdwy debut 1980 in "Clothes for a Summer Hotel" followed by "Oh, Brother!," OB in "Lovesong," "Vagabond Stars," "Fabulous '50's," "My Heart Is in the East."

STERNHAGEN, FRANCES. Born Jan. 13, 1932 in Washington, DC. Vassar graduate, OB in "Admirable Bashful," "Thieves' Carnival," "Country Wife," "Ulysses in Nighttown." "Saintliness of Margery Kemp," "The Room," "A Slight Ache," "Displaced Person," "Playboy of the Western World," "The Prevalence of Mrs. Seal," "Summer," Bdwy in "Great Day in the Morning," "Right Honorable Gentleman," with APA in "Cocktail Party," and "Cock-a-Doodle Dandy," "The Sign in Sidney Brustein's Window," "Enemies," (LC) "The Good Doctor," "Equus," "Angel," "On Golden Pond," "The Father," "Grownups."

STEVENS, ALLAN. Born Nov. 30, 1949 in Los Angeles, CA. Attended LAMDA. Bdwy debut 1975 in "Shenandoah," followed by "Kings," OB in "It's Wilde!," "Frozen Assets."

STEVENS, FISHER. Born Nov. 27, 1963 in Chicago, IL. Attended NYU. Bdwy debut 1982 in "Torch Song Trilogy," followed by "Brighton Beach Memoirs."

STEVENS, JESS R. Born Dec. 7, 1951 in Elyria, OH. Attended Antioch Col., KentStateU. Debut 1978 OB in "King of the Castle," followed by "Engaged."

STEVENS, LEON B. Born Jan. 13, 1926 in Manchester, NH. Graduate UNH. Debut 1957 in "Inherit the Wind," followed by "The Wall," "A Gift of Time," "Diamond Orchid," "The Investigation," "The Caine Mutiny Court-Martial."

STILLMAN, RICHARD. Born Nov. 24, 1954 in Midland, MI. Graduate Dartmouth Col. Debut 1979 OB in "Hamlet," followed by "Sea-Dream," "The Gilded Cage," Bdwy in "The Curse of an Aching Heart."

STOCK, BARBARA. Born May 26, 1956 in Illinois. Graduate IndU. Bdwy debut 1983 in "Nine."

STOECKLE, ROBERT. Born Sept. 21, 1947 in Port Chester, NY. Graduate Hartt Col. Bdwy debut 1980 in "Canterbury Tales," OB in "110 in the Shade," "A Midsummer Night's Dream."

STOLLER, AMY. Born March 7 in NYC. Attended Mills Col. Debut 1982 OB in "The Sea Anchor," followed by "La Belle au Bois."

STONEBURNER, SAM. Born Feb. 24, 1934 in Fairfax, VA. Graduate Georgetown U., AADA. Debut 1960 OB in "Ernest in Love," followed by "Foreplay," "Anyone Can Whistle," "Twilight Cantata," Bdwy in "Different Times" (1972), "Bent," "Macbeth" (1981), "The First."

STORCH, LARRY. Born Jan. 8, 1923 in NYC. Bdwy debut 1958 in "Who Was That Lady I Saw You With?," followed by "Porgy and Bess" (1983), OB in "The Littlest Revue" (1956).

STOUT, MARY. Born Apr. 8, 1952 in Huntington, WV. Graduate Marshall U. Debut 1980 OB in "Plain and Fancy" followed by "Crisp," "A Christmas Carol," Bdwy 1981 in "Copperfield."

STOUT, STEPHEN. Born May 18, 1952 in Berwyn, IL. Graduate SMU. Bdwy debut 1981 in "Kingdoms," followed by OB in "Cloud 9."

STRASSER, ROBIN. Born May 7, 1945 in NYC. Bdwy debut 1963 in "Irregular Verb to Love," followed by "The Country Girl," "Chapter Two," OB in "A Meeting by the River," "Loving Reno."

STROMAN, GUY. Born Sept. 11, 1951 in Terrell, TX. Graduate TxChristianU. Bdwy debut 1979 in "Peter Pan," followed by OB in "Glory! Hallelujah!," "Berlin to Broadway."

STRYKER, CHRISTOPHER. Born Jan. 3, 1963 in NYC. Attended Actors Inst. Bdwy debut in "Torch Song Trilogy" (1982).

SULLIVAN, BRAD. Born Nov. 18, 1931 in Chicago, IL. Graduate UMe., AmThWing. Debut 1961 OB in "Red Roses for Me," followed by "South Pacific," "Hot-House," "Leavin' Cheyenne," Bdwy in "Basic Training of Pavlo Hummel" (1977), "Working," "The Wake of Jamey Foster," "The Caine Mutiny Court-Martial."

SUNG, ELIZABETH. Born Oct. 14, 1954 in Hong Kong. Graduate Juilliard. Debut 1982 OB in "Station J," followed by "A Midsummer Night's Dream."

SUROVY, NICOLAS. Born June 30, 1944 in Los Angeles, CA. Attended Northwestern U., Neighborhood Playhouse. Debut 1964 in "Helen" for which he received a Theatre World Award, followed by "Sisters of Mercy," "Cloud 9," Bdwy in "Merchant," "Crucifer of Blood," "Major Barbara," "You Can't Take It with You."

SWAIN, ELIZABETH. Born Aug. 6, 1941 in England. Bdwy debut 1968 in "The Crucible," followed by "Charley's Aunt," "Crown Matrimonial," OB in "Tango," "The Quilling of Prue."

SWANN, ELAINE. Born May 9 in Baltimore, MD. Attended UNC. Bdwy debut 1957 in "The Music Man," followed by "Greenwillow," "A Thurber Carnival," "My Mother, My Father and Me," "Jennie," "Agatha Sue, I Love You," OB in "Miss Stanwyck Is Still in Hiding," "Oh, Boy!," "Vieux Carre."

SWARBRICK, CAROL. Born Mar. 20, 1948 in Inglewood, CA. Graduate UCLA, NYU. Debut 1971 OB in "Drat!," followed by "The Glorious Age," Bdwy in "Side by Side by Sondheim," "Whoopee!," "42nd Street."

SWEDEEN, STACI. Born Jan. 28, 1956 in Mt. Vernon, WA. Attended UWa. Debut 1981 OB in "What the Butler Saw," followed by "New Faces of '52."

SWIFT, ALLEN. Born Jan. 16, 1924 in NYC. Debut 1961 OB in "Portrait of the Artist," followed by "Month of Sundays," "Where Memories Are Magic," "My Old Friends," "Divine Fire," "Royal Bob," Bdwy in "The Student Gypsy" (1963), "Checking Out."

SWOPE, TRACY BROOKS. Born Feb. 20, 1952 in NYC. Attended Neighborhood Playhouse, AADA. Bdwy debut 1968 in "Woman Is My Idea," followed by "A Little Family Business."

SYKES, ROSEMARY. Born Jan. 12 in Manchester, CT. Graduate State U/Albany, Neighborhood Playhouse. Debut 1981 OB in "The Diviners," followed by "Three Lost Plays of O'Neill."

SZLOSBERG, DIANA. Born Aug. 18, 1957 in NYC. Graduate FlStateU. Debut 1981 OB in "Seesaw," followed by "Loose Joints."

TALBOT, SHARON. Born Mar. 12, 1949 in Denver, CO. Graduate DenverU. Bdwy debut 1975 in "Musical Jubilee," OB in "Housewives Cantata," "The Angel and the Dragon."

TALMAN, ANN. Born Sept. 13, 1957 in Welch, WVa. Graduate PaStateU. Debut 1980 OB in "What's So Beautiful about a Sunset over Prairie Avenue?," followed by "Louisiana Summer," "Winterplay," Bdwy in "The Little Foxes" (1981).

TANDY, JESSICA. Born June 7, 1909 in London, Eng. Attended Greet Acad. Bdwy debut 1930 in "The Matriarch," followed by "Last Enemy," "Time and the Conways," "White Steed," "Geneva," "Jupiter Laughs," "Anne of England," "Yesterday's Magic," "A Streetcar Named Desire," "Hilda Crane," "The Fourposter," "The Honeys," "A Day by the Sea," "Man in the Dog Suit," "Triple Play," "Five Finger Exercise," "The Physicists," "A Delicate Balance," "Home," "All Over," "Camino Real," "Not I," "Happy Days," "Noel Coward in Two Keys," "The Gin Game," "Rose," "Foxfire."

TARANTINA, BRIAN. Born Mar. 27, 1959 in NYC. Debut 1980 OB in "Innocent Thoughts and Harmless Intentions," followed by "Time Framed," Bdwy 1983 in "Angels Fall" for which he received a Theatre World Award.

TARLETON, DIANE. Born Oct. 25, in Baltimore, MD. Graduate UMd. Bdwy debut 1965 in "Anya," followed by "A Joyful Noise," "Elmer Gantry," "Yentl," "Torch Song Trilogy," OB in "A Time for the Gentle People," "Spoon River Anthology," "International Stud," "Too Much Johnson," "To Bury a Cousin," "A Dream Play."

TATUM, MARIANNE. Born Feb. 18, 1951. in Houston, TX. Attended Manhattan School of Music. Debut 1971 OB in "Ruddigore," followed by "The Sound of Music," "The Gilded Cage," Bdwy 1980 in "Barnum" for which she received a Theatre World Award.

TAYLOR, ELIZABETH. Born Feb. 27, 1932 in London, Eng. Bdwy debut 1981 in "The Little Foxes," for which she received a Special Theatre World Award, followed by "Private Lives" (1983).

TAYLOR, HOLLAND. Born Jan. 14, 1943 in Philadelphia, PA. Graduate Bennington Col. Bdwy debut 1965 in "The Devils," followed by "Butley," "We Interrupt This Program," "Something Old, Something New," "Moose Murders," OB in "Poker Session," "The David Show," "Tonight in Living Color," "Colette," "Fashion," "Nightlight," "Children," "Breakfast with Les and Bess."

TAYLOR, JENNIFER. Born June 15, 1956 in Paris, Fr. Graduate Viterbo Col. Debut 1982 OB in "Teach Me How to Cry," followed by "Merry Wives of Scarsdale."

TAYLOR-MORRIS, MAXINE. Born June 26 in NYC. Graduate NYU. Debut 1977 OB in "Counsellor-at-Law," followed by "Manny," "The Devil's Disciple," "Fallen Angels," "Billy Liar," "Uncle Vanya," "What the Butler Saw," "The Subject Was Roses," "Goodnight, Grandpa."

TEETER, LARA. Born in 1955 in Tulsa, OK. Graduate OkCityU. Bdwy debut in "The Best Little Whorehouse in Texas," followed by "Pirates of Penzance," "7 Brides for 7 Brothers," "On Your Toes."

TEITEL, CAROL. Born Aug. 1, 1929 in NYC. Attended AmTh Wing. Bdwy debut 1957 in "The Country Wife," followed by "The Entertainer," "Hamlet," "Marat/deSade," "A Flea in Her Ear," "Crown Matrimonial," "All Over Town," OB in "Way of the World," "Juana La Loca," "An Evening with Ring Lardner," "Misanthrope," "Shaw Festival," "Country Scandal," "The Bench," "Colombe," "Under Milk Wood," "7 Days of Mourning," "Long Day's Journey into Night," "The Old Ones," "Figures in the Sand," "World of Sholom Aleichem," "Big and Little," "Duet," "Trio," "Every Good Boy Deserves Favor" (LC) "Fallen Angels," "A Stitch in Time," "Faces of Love," "Keymaker," "Learned Ladies," "Major Barbara in Concert," "Baseball Wives."

TESTA, MARY. Born June 4, 1955 in Philadelphia, PA. Attended URI. Debut 1979 OB in "In Trousers," followed by "Company," "Life Is Not a Doris Day Movie," "Not-so-New Faces of '82," "American Princess," Bdwy 1980 in "Barnum."

THACKER, RUSS. Born June 23, 1946 in Washington, DC. Attended Montgomery Col. Bdwy debut 1967 in "Life with Father," followed by "Music! Music!," "Grass Harp," "Heathen," "Home Sweet Homer," "Me Jack You Jill," OB in "Your Own Thing" for which he received a Theatre World Award. "Do Black Patent Leather Shoes Really Reflect Up?," "Dear Oscar," "Once I Saw a Boy Laughing," "Tip-Toes," "Oh Coward!," "New Moon in Concert," "The Firefly in Concert," "Rosalie in Concert," "Some Enchanted Evening."

THOMAS, JAY. Born July 12, 1948 in Kermit, TX. Graduate Jacksonville U. Debut 1983 OB in "The Transfiguration of Benno Blimpie."

THOMAS, RAYMOND ANTHONY. Born Dec. 19, 1956 in Kentwood, LA. Graduate UTx/El Paso. Debut 1981 OB in "Escape to Freedom," followed by "The Sun Gets Blue," "Blues for Mr. Charlie."

THOMAS, WILLIAM, JR. Born in Columbus, OH. Graduate OhStateU. Debut 1972 OB in "Touch," followed by "Natural," "Godspell," "Poor Little Lambs," "Loose Joints," "Not-So-New Faces of '81." Bdwy in "Your Arms Too Short to Box with God" (1976).

THOME, DAVID. Born July 24, 1951 in Salt Lake City, UT. Bdwy debut 1971 in "No, No, Nanette," followed by "Different Times," "Good News," "Rodgers and Hart," "A Chorus Line," "Dancin'," "Dreamgirls."

THOMPSON, EVAN. Born Sept. 3, 1931 in NYC. Graduate UCal. Bdwy bow 1969 in "Jimmy," OB in "Mahagonny," "Treasure Island," "Knitters in the Sun," "Half-Life," "Fasnacht Day," "Importance of Being Earnest."

THOMPSON, LAUREN. Born in 1950. Attended PaStateU., Pittsburgh Playhouse. Bdwy debut 1979 in "Dracula," followed by "A Life," "Whodunnit."

THOMPSON, OWEN. Born Sept. 16, 1962 in Los Angeles, CA. Debut 1974 OB in "The Trojan Women," followed by "The Importance of Being Earnest," "She Loves Me," "The Browning Version," "King John," "Richard III."

THOMPSON, WEYMAN. Born Dec. 11, 1950 in Detroit, MI. Graduate Wayne State U, UDetroit. Bdwy debut 1980 in "Clothes for a Summer Hotel," followed by "Dreamgirls."

THORNTON, ANGELA. Born in Leeds, Eng. Attended Webber-Douglas School. Bdwy debut 1956 in "Little Glass Clock," followed by "Nude with Violin," "Present Laughter," "Hostile Witness," OB in "The Mousetrap," "Big Broadcast," "Mary Barnes."

THORSON, LINDA. Born June 18, 1947 in Toronto, Can. Graduate RADA. Bdwy debut 1982 in "Steaming" for which she received a Theatre World Award.

TOBIAS, BARBARA. Born Nov, 8, 1954 in Boston, MA. Graduate UCal/Irvine. Debut 1982 OB in "Nymph Errant," followed by "West Side Story."

TOBIE, ELLEN. Born Mar. 26 in Chambersburg, PA. Graduate OH WesleyanU. Wayne State U. Debut 1981 OB in "The Chisholm Trail Went Through Here," followed by "Welded." "Talking With," "The Entertainer."

TOMEI, CONCETTA. Born Dec. 30, 1945 in Kenosha, WI. Graduate UWisc, Goodman School. Debut 1979 OB in "Little Eyolf," followed by "Cloud 9," "Lumiere," Bdwy 1979 in "The Elephant Man."

TONER, THOMAS. Born May 25, 1928 in Homestead, PA. Graduate UCLA. Bdwy debut 1973 in "Tricks," followed by "The Good Doctor," "All Over Town," "A Texas Trilogy," "The Inspector General," OB in "Pericles," "Merry Wives of Windsor," "A Midsummer Night's Dream," "Richard III," "My Early Years."

TOREN, SUZANNE. Born Mar. 15, 1947 in NYC. Graduate CCNY, UWis. Bdwy debut 1980 in "Goodbye Fidel," OB in "Who'll Save the Plowboy?," "The Further Inquiry."

TORN, RIP. Born Feb. 6, 1931 in Temple, TX. Graduate UTx. Bdwy bow 1956 in "Cat on a Hot Tin Roof," followed by "Sweet Bird of Youth" for which he received a Theatre World Award, "Daughter of Silence," "Strange Interlude," "Blues for Mr. Charlie," "Country Girl," "Glass Menagerie," OB in "Chaparral," "The Cuban Thing," "The Kitchen," "Deer Park," "Dream of a Blacklisted Actor," "Dance of Death," "Macbeth," "Barbary Shore," "Creditors," "Seduced," "The Man and the Fly," "Terrible Jim Fitch," "Village Wooing."

TORREN, FRANK. Born Jan. 5, 1939 in Tampa, FL. Attended UTampa, AADA. Debut 1964 OB in "Jo," followed by "No Corner in Heaven," "Treasure Island," "Open Season for Butterflies," "Brownstone Urge," "The Meehans," "Where's Charley?"

TORRES, ANDY. Born Aug. 10, 1945 in Ponce, PR. Attended AMDA. Bdwy debut 1969 in "Indians," followed by "Purlie," "Don't Bother Me, I Can't Cope," "The Whiz," "Guys and Dolls," "Your Arms Too Short to Box with God," "Reggae," OB in "Billy Noname," "Suddenly the Music Starts," "Louis."

TORRES, MARK. Born May 7, 1955 in Brownsville, TX. Graduate InU, Temple U. Bdwy debut 1980 in "Amadeus."

TREAT, MARTIN. Born May 9, 1945 in Yreka, CA. Graduate UOr. Debut 1977 OB in "Heartbreak House," followed by "The Balcony," "Cuchulian Cycle," "Dr. Faustus," "A Dream Play," "The Danube," "Further Inquiry."

TREBOR, ROBERT. Born June 7, 1953 in Philadelphia, PA. Graduate Northwestern U. Debut 1980 OB in "City Junket," followed by "The Changeling," "The New Living Newspaper."

TRIGGER, IAN. Born Sept. 30, 1942 in England. Graduate RADA. Debut 1973 OB in "The Taming of the Shrew," followed by "Scapino," "True History of Squire Jonathan," "Slab Boys," "Cloud 9," Bdwy in "Scapino," "Habeas Corpus," "13 Rue de l'Amour."

TROOBNICK, GENE. Born Aug. 23, 1926 in Boston, MA. Attended Ithaca Col, Columbia U. Bdwy debut 1960 in "Second City," followed by "The Odd Couple," "Before You Go," "The Time of Your Life," OB in "Dynamite Tonight," "A Gun Play," "Tales of the Hasidim," "Wings," "Sganarelle," "Damien," "The Workroom."

TROY, LOUISE. Born Nov. 9 in NYC. Attended AADA. Debut 1955 OB in "The Infernal Machine," followed by "Merchant of Venice," "Conversation Piece," "Salad Days," "O, Oysters!," "A Doll's House," "Last Analysis," "Judy and Jane," "Heartbreak House," Bdwy in "Pipe Dream" (1955), "A Shot in the Dark," "Tovarich," "High Spirits," "Walking Happy," "Equus," "Woman of the Year."

TRUMBULL, ROBERT. Born Feb. 8, 1938 in San Rafael, CA. Graduate UCal/Berkeley. Debut 1983 in "Guys in the Truck" (Off and on Bdwy).

TUNE, TOMMY. Born Feb. 28, 1939 in Wichita Falls, TX. Graduate UTx. Bdwy debut 1965 in "Baker Street," followed by "A Joyful Noise," "How Now Dow Jones," "Seesaw," "My One and Only," OB in "Ichabod."

TURQUE, MIMI. Born Sept. 30, 1939 in Brooklyn, NY. Graduate Brooklyn Col. Bdwy debut 1945 in "Carousel," followed by "Seeds in the Wind," "The Enchanted," "Cry of the Peacock," "Anniversary Waltz," "Carnival," "Man of LaMancha," OB in "Johnny Summit," "The Dybbuk," "Romeo and Juliet," "The Happy Journey," "God Bless You, Mr. Rosewater," "13."

TWAIN, MICHAEL. Born Nov. 1, 1936 in Lawrence, NY. Graduate OhioStateU. Debut 1956 in "Mr. Roberts," followed OB in "Kill the One-Eyed Man," "Duchess of Malfi," "Recess," "The Empire Builders," "Pictures at an Exhibition."

TWIGGY. Born Lesley Hornby Sept. 19, 1949 in London, Eng. Bdwy debut 1983 in "My One and Only."

TWOMEY, ANNE. Born June 7, 1951 in Boston, MA. Graduate Temple U. Debut 1975 OB in "Overruled," followed by "The Passion of Dracula," "When We Dead Awaken," "Vieux Carre," Bdwy 1980 in "Nuts" for which she received a Theatre World Award, "To Grandmother's House We Go."

ULLMANN. LIV. Born Dec. 16, 1938 in Touro, Japan. Debut 1975 in "A Doll's House," followed by "Anna Christie," "I Remember Mama," "Ghosts."

ULLRICK, SHARON. Born Mar. 19, 1947 in Dallas, TX. Graduate SMU. Debut 1980 OB in "Vanities," Bdwy 1981 in "Crimes of the Heart."

UNGER, DEBORAH. Born July 2, 1953 in Philadelphia, PA. Graduate UPittsburg, FlStateU. Debut 1981 OB in "Seesaw," Followed by "The Rise of David Levinsky."

VALE, MICHAEL. Born June 28, 1922 in Brooklyn, NY. Attended New School. Bdwy debut 1961 in "The Egg" followed by "Cafe Crown," "Last Analysis," "The Impossible Years," "Saturday Sunday Monday," "Unexpected Guests," "California Suite," OB in "Autograph Hound," "Moths," "Now There's the Three of Us," "Tall and Rex," "Kaddish," "42 Seconds from Broadway," "Sunset," "Little Shop of Horrors."

VALENTINE, JAMES. Born Feb. 18, 1933 in Rockford, IL. Attended ULondon, Central Sch. of Drama. Bdwy debut 1958 in "Cloud 7," followed by "Epitaph for George Dillon," "Duel of Angels," "Ross," "Caesar and Cleopatra," "The Importance of Being Earnest," "Camelot" (1980/1981), "Alice in Wonderland."

VANCE, DANA. Born June 23, 1952 in Steubenville, OH. Graduate WVaU. Debut 1981 OB in "An Evening with Sheffman and Vance," Bdwy in "Teaneck Tanzi" (1983).

VAN DER LINDE, LAUREL. Born Mar. 7, 1952 in Cleveland, OH. Graduate UCLA. Bdwy debut in "My Fair Lady" (1976), followed by "Seven Brides for Seven Brothers."

VAN NOSTRAND, AMY. Born Apr. 11, 1953 in Providence, RI. Graduate Brown U. Bdwy debut in "The Hothouse" (1982).

VAN PATTEN, JOYCE. Born Mar. 9 in Kew Gardens, NY. Bdwy bow 1941 in "Popsy," followed by "This Rock," "Tomorrow the World," "The Perfect Marriage," "The Wind Is 90," "Desk Set," "A Hole in the Head," "Murder at the Howard Johnson's," "I Ought to Be in Pictures," "Supporting Cast," "Brighton Beach Memoirs." OB in "Between Two Thieves," "Spoon River Anthology," "The Seagull."

VENORA, DIANE. Born in 1952 in Hartford, CT. Graduate Juilliard. Debut 1981 OB in "Penguin Touquet," followed by "A Midsummer Night's Dream," "Hamlet."

VICKERY, JOHN. Born in 1951 in Alameda, CA. Graduate UCaBerkeley, UCaDavis. Debut 1981 in "Macbeth" (LC), followed by "Ned and Jack," "Eminent Domain," OB in "American Days," "A Call from the East," "Henry IV Part I," "Looking-Glass," "The Death of Von Richthofen."

VIDNOVIC, MARTIN. Born Jan. 4, 1948 in Falls Church, VA. Attended Cincinnati Consv. Debut 1972 OB in "The Fantasticks," followed by "Some Enchanted Evening," Bdwy in "Home Sweet Homer," "The King and I" (1977), "Oklahoma!" (1979), "Brigadoon" (1980).

VINOVICH, STEVE. Born Jan. 22, 1945 in Peoria, IL. Graduate UIl, UCLA, Juilliard. Debut 1974 OB in "The Robber Bridegroom," followed by "King John," "Father Uxbridge Wants to Marry," "Hard Sell," "Ross," "Double Feature," Bdwy in "Robber Bridegroom" (1976) "The Magic Show," "The Grand Tour," "Loose Ends," "A Midsummer Night's Dream."

VIPOND, NEIL. Born Dec. 24, 1929 in Toronto, Can. Bdwy debut 1956 in "Tamburlaine the Great," followed by "Macbeth," OB in "Three Friends," "Sunday Runners," "Hamlet" (ELT), "Routed," "Mr. Joyce Is Leaving Paris."

VIRTA, RAY. Born June 18, 1958 in L'Anse, MI. Debut 1982 OB in "Twelfth Night," followed by "The Country Wife," "Dubliners," "Pericles," "Tartuffe."

VITA, MICHAEL. Born in NYC Studied at HB Studio. Bdwy debut 1967 in "Sweet Charity," followed by "Golden Rainbow," "Promises, Promises," "Cyrano," "Chicago," "Ballroom," "Charlie and Algernon," "A Doll's Life," "On Your Toes." OB in "Sensations," "That's Entertainment," "Rocket to the Moon," "Nymph Errant."

VITELLA, SEL. Born July 7, 1934 in Boston, MA. Graduate San Francisco Inst. of Music. Debut 1975 OB in "The Merchant of Venice," followed by "Gorey Stories," "Jane Eyre," Bdwy in "Something's Afoot" (1976), "Gorey Stories."

VOET, DOUG. Born Mar. 1, 1951 in Los Angeles, CA. Graduate BYU. Bdwy debut in "Joseph and the Amazing Technicolor Dreamcoat" (1982).

VOIGTS, RICHARD. Born Nov. 25, 1934 in Streator, IL. Graduate InU, Columbia U. Debut 1979 OB in "The Constant Wife," followed by "Company," "The Investigation," "Dune Road," "The Collection," "Miracle Man," "As Time Goes By," "Silence," "Station J." "Frozen Assets," "Happy Birthday, Wanda June."

VON DOHLEN, LENNY. Born Dec. 22, 1958 in Augusta, GA. Graduate Loretto Heights Col. Debut 1982 OB in "Cloud 9," followed by "Twister," "Asian Shade."

VON SCHERLER, SASHA. Born Dec. 12 in NYC. Bdwy debut 1959 in "Look after Lulu," followed by "Rape of the Belt," "The Good Soup," "Great God Brown," "First Love," "Alfie," "Harold," "Bad Habits," OB in "Admirable Bashful," "The Comedian," "Conversation Piece," "Good King Charles' Golden Days," "Under Milk Wood," "Plays for Bleecker St.," "Ludlow Fair," "Twelfth Night," "Sondra," "Cyrano de Bergerac," "Crimes of Passion," "Henry VI," "Trelawny of the Wells," "Screens," "Soon Jack November," "Pericles," "Kid Champion," "Henry V," "Comanche Cafe," "Museum," "Grand Magic," "The Penultimate Problem of Sherlock Holmes," "Keymaker," "Hunting Scenes from Lower Bavaria," "Slacks and Tops."

VOSBURGH, DAVID. Born Mar. 14, 1938 in Coventry, RI. Attended Boson U. Bdwy debut 1968 in "Maggie Flynn," followed by "1776," "A Little Night Music," "Evita," "A Doll's Life," OB in "Smith."

WAARA, SCOTT. Born June 5, 1957 in Chicago, IL. Graduate SMU. Debut 1982 OB in "The Rise of Daniel Rocket," followed by "The Dining Room."

WAGER, MICHAEL. Born Apr. 29, 1925 in NYC. Graduate Harvard U. Bdwy debut 1949 in "A Streetcar Named Desire," followed by "Small Hours," "Bernardine," "Merchant of Venice," "Misalliance," "The Remarkable Mr. Pennypacker," "Othello," "Henry IV," "St. Joan," "Firstborn," "The Cradle Will Rock," "Three Sisters," "The Cuban Thing," OB in "Noontide," "Brecht on Brecht," "Sunset," "Penny Friend," "Trelawny of the Wells," "Taming of the Shrew," "Inn at Lydda," "Richard III," "Rhinestone."

WAITE, JOHN THOMAS. Born Apr. 19, 1948 in Syracuse, NY. Attended Syracuse U. Debut 1976 OB in "The Fantasticks," Bdwy in "Amadeus" (1982).

WALDECK, NONA. Born Feb. 2, 1956 in Cincinnati, OH. Graduate Edgecliff Col., OhioU. Debut 1982 OB in "The Coarse Acting Show."

WALDHORN, GARY. Born July 3, 1943 in London, Eng. Attended Yale U. Bdwy debut 1982 in "Good."

WALDRON, MICHAEL. Born Nov. 19, 1949 in West Orange, NJ. Graduate Columbia U. Debut 1979 in "Mary," followed by "Dulcy," "Romance Is," "New Faces of '52."

WALDROP, MARK. Born July 30, 1954 in Washington, DC. Graduate Cincinnati Consv. Debut 1977 OB in "Movie Buff," Bdwy in "The Grand Tour," "Evita."

WALKER, GERALD. Born Dec. 8, 1948 in Bridgeport, CT. Debut 1982 OB in "The Holly and the Ivy."

WALL, BRUCE. Born July 14, 1956 in Bath, Eng. Graduate UToronto, RADA. Debut 1979 OB in "Class Enemy," followed by "The Browning Version," "Candida in Concert," "Major Barbara in Concert."

WALLACE, LEE. Born July 15, 1930 in NYC. Attended NYU. Debut 1966 OB in "Journey of the Fifth Horse," followed by "Saturday Night," "An Evening with Garcia Lorca," "Macbeth," "Booth Is Back in Town," "Awake and Sing," "Shepherd of Avenue B," "Basic Training of Pavlo Hummel," "Curtains," "Elephants," "Goodnight, Grandpa," Bdwy in "Secret Affairs of Mildred Wild," "Molly," "Zalmen, or the Madness of God," "Some of My Best Friends."

WALLACH, ELI. Born Dec.7, 1915 in Brooklyn, NY. Graduate UTx, CCNY. Bdwy debut 1945 in "Skydrift," followed by "Henry VIII," "Androcles and the Lion," "Alice in Wonderland," "Yellow Jack," "What Every Woman Knows," "Antony and Cleopatra," "Mr. Roberts," "Lady from the Sea," "The Rose Tattoo" for which he received a Theatre World Award, "Mlle. Colombe," "Teahouse of the August Moon," "Major Barbara," "The Cold Wind and the Warm," "Rhinoceros," "Luv," "Staircase," "Promenade All," "Waltz of the Toreadors," "Saturday, Sunday, Monday," "Every Good Boy Deserves Favor," "Twice Around the Park," OB in "The Diary of Anne Frank."

WALSH, TENNEY. Born Oct. 18, 1963 in New Haven, CT. Attended Yale U. Debut 1981 OB in "The Wild Duck," followed by "A Think Piece."

WALTERS, FREDERICK. Born July 19, 1930 in Schenectady, NY. Graduate Centenary Col., Rutgers U. Debut 1979 OB in "Biography: A Game," followed by "A Midsummer Night's Dream," "Not Now, Darling."

WANDEL, PETER. Born Oct. 15, 1955 in Buffalo, NY. Attended SUNY/Purchase. Bdwy debut 1980 in "The Music Man," followed by "Dance a Little Closer."

WANN, JIM. Born Aug. 30, 1948 in Chattanooga, TN. Graduate UNC. Debut 1975 OB in "Diamond Studs," Bdwy 1982 in "Pump Boys & Dinettes."

WARD, DOUGLAS TURNER. Born May 5, 1930 in Burnside, LA. Attended UMi. Bdwy bow 1959 in "A Raisin in the Sun," followed by "One Flew over the Cuckoo's Nest," "Last Breeze of Summer," OB in "The Iceman Cometh," "The Blacks," "Pullman Car Hiawatha," "Bloodknot," "Happy Ending," "Day of Absence," "Kongi's Harvest," "Ceremonies in Dark Old Men," "The Harangues," "The Reckoning," "Frederick Douglass through His Own Words, "River Niger," "Brownsville Raid," "The Offering," "Old Phantoms," "The Michigan," "About Heaven and Earth."

WARNER, AMY. Born June 29, 1951 in Minneapolis, MN. Graduate Principia Col. Debut 1982 OB in "Faust," followed by "Ghost Sonata," "Wild Oats."

WARREN, JENNIFER LEIGH. Born Aug. 29 in Dallas, TX. Graduate Dartmouth Col. Debut 1982 OB in "Little Shop of Horrors."

WASHINGTON, DENZEL. Born Dec. 28, 1954 in Mt. Vernon, NY. Graduate Fordham U. Debut 1975 OB in "The Emperor Jones," followed by "Othello," "Coriolanus," "Mighty Gents," "Becket," "Spell #7," "Ceremonies in Dark Old Men," "One Tiger To a Hill," "A Soldier's Play."

WASHINGTON, MELVIN. Born Dec. 19 in Brooklyn, NY. Attended CCNY, HB Studio. Debut 1980 OB in "Streamers," followed by "Something to Live For," Bdwy in "My One and Only" (1983).

WASSERMAN, ALLAN. Born May 16, 1952 in The Bronx, NY. Graduate Boston U. Bdwy debut 1977 in "The Basic Training of Pavlo Hummel," OB in "Coming Attractions," "Saigon Rose," "Cappella," "Saturday Night at the War."

WATERSTON, SAM. Born Nov. 15, 1940 in Cambridge, MA. Yale graduate. Bdwy bow 1963 in "Oh Dad, Poor Dad," followed by "First One Asleep Whistle," "Halfway Up the Tree," "Indians," "Hay Fever," "Much Ado about Nothing," "Lunch Hour," OB in "As You Like It," "Thistle in My Bed," "The Knack," "Fitz," "Biscuit," "La Turista," "Posterity for Sale," "Ergo," "Muzeeka," "Red Cross," "Henry IV," "Spitting Image," "I Met a Man," "Brass Butterfly," "Trial of the Catonsville 9," "Cymbeline," "Hamlet," "A Meeting by the River," "The Tempest," "A Doll's House," "Measure for Measure," "Chez Nous," "Waiting for Godot," "Gardenia," "Three Sisters."

WATKINS, DANIEL. Born Oct. 12, 1950 in Lynchburg, VA. Attended NCSchool of Arts. Debut 1979 OB in "The Wait," followed by "Come Back to the 5 & Dime, Jimmy Dean," "Lorenzaccio."

WATSON, DOUGLASS. Born Feb. 24, 1921 in Jackson, GA. Graduate UNC. Bdwy bow 1947 in "The Iceman Cometh," followed by "Antony and Cleopatra," for which he received a Theatre World Award, "Leading Lady," "Richard III," "The Happiest Years," "That Lady," "Wisteria Trees," "Romeo and Juliet," "Desire under the Elms," "Sunday Breakfast," "Cyrano de Bergerac," "Confidential Clerk," "Portrait of a Lady," "The Miser," "The Young and Beautiful," "Little Glass Clock," "Country Wife," "Man for All Seasons," "Chinese Prime Minister," "Marat/deSade," "Prime of Miss Jean Brodie," "Pirates of Penzance," "Over Here," "Philadelphia Story," OB in "Much Ado about Nothing," "King Lear," "As You Like It," "Hunger," "Dancing for the Kaiser," "Money," "My Life," "Sightlines," "Glorious Morning," "Hamlet," "Upside Down on the Handlebars."

WEATHERS, PATRICK. Born Jan. 22, 1954 in Hattiesburg, MS. Graduate SMsU. Debut 1981 OB in "Daisy the Shopping Bag Lady," Bdwy in "Rock 'n' Roll: the First 5000 Years."

WEAVER, FRITZ. Born Jan. 19, 1926 in Pittsburgh, PA. Graduate UChicago. Bdwy debut 1955 in "Chalk Garden," for which he received a Theatre World Award, followed by "Protective Custody," "Miss Lonelyhearts," "All American," "Lorenzo," "The White House," "Baker Street," "Child's Play," "Absurd Person Singular," "Angels Fall," OB in "The Way of the World," "White Devil," "Doctor's Dilemma," "Family Reunion," "The Power and the Glory," "The Great God Brown," "Peer Gynt," "Henry IV," "My Fair Lady" (CC), "Lincoln," "The Biko Inquest," "The Price," "Dialogue for Lovers," "A Tale Told," "Time Framed."

WEAVER, LYNN. Born May 17 in Paris, TN. Graduate UTn, Neighborhood Playhouse. Debut 1981 OB in "The Italian Straw Hat," followed by "Tiger at the Gates."

WEBER, FREDRICKA. Born Dec. 22, 1940 in Beardstown, IL. Attended Northwestern U. Bdwy debut 1965 in "Those That Play the Clowns," OB in "Upstairs at the Downstairs," "The Last Sweet Days of Isaac" for which she received a Theatre World Award, "Two."

WEDDELL, MIMI. Born Feb. 15, 1915 in Williston, ND. OB credits include "Woman of No Importance," "Trelawny of the Wells," "Little Eyolf," "A Doll's House," "Hedda Gabler," "Balzamov's Wedding."

WEDGEWORTH, ANN. Born Jan. 21, 1935 in Abilene, TX. Bdwy debut 1958 in "Make a Million," followed by "Blues for Mr. Charlie," "Last Analysis," "Thieves," "Chapter Two," OB in "Chapparal," "The Crucible," "Days and Nights of Beebee Fenstermaker," "Ludlow Fair," "Line," "Elba."

WEEKS, JAMES RAY. Born Mar. 21, 1942 in Seattle, WA. Graduate UOre., AADA. Debut 1972 in LCR's "Enemies," "Merchant of Venice," and "A Streetcar Named Desire," followed by OB's "49 West 87th," "Feedlot," "The Runner Stumbles," "Glorious Morning," "Just the Immediate Family," "The Deserter," "Life and/or Death," "Devour the Snow," "Innocent Thoughts, Harmless Intentions," "The Diviners," "A Tale Told," "Confluence," "Richard II," "Great Grandson of Jedediah Kohler," "Black Angel," Bdwy in "My Fat Friend," "We Interrupt This Program," "Devour the Snow."

WEST, CARYN. Born June 23, 1954 in Washington, DC. Graduate Stanford U, Temple U. Bdwy debut in "Crimes of the Heart" (1982), OB in "As You Like It."

WEST, MATT. Born Oct. 2, 1958 in Downey, CA. Attended Pfiffer-Smith School. Bdwy debut in "A Chorus Line" (1980).

WESTENBERG, ROBERT. Born Oct. 26, 1953 in Miami Beach, FL. Graduate Fresno State U. Debut 1981 OB in "Henry IV Part I," followed by "The Death of Von Richthofen," "Hamlet."

WESTFALL, RALPH DAVID. Born July 2, 1934 in North Lewisburg, OH. Graduate OhWesleyanU, SUNY/New Paltz. Debut 1977 OB in "Richard III," followed by "Importance of Being Earnest," "Anyone Can Whistle," "A Midsummer Night's Dream."

WESTON, MARK. Born Feb. 13, 1931 in The Bronx, NY. Attended UWi. Debut 1955 in "Billy Budd," followed by "The Trial of Mary Surratt," "Come Back, Little Sheba," "Time Limit," OB in "36," "Getting Mama Married."

WETTIG, PATRICIA. Born Dec. 4, in Cincinnati, OH. Graduate Temple U. Debut 1980 OB in "Innocent Thoughts, Harmless Intentions," followed by "The Woolgatherer," "Childe Byron," "A Tale Told," "Threads," "The Dining Room."

WHITE, ALICE. Born Jan. 6, 1945 in Washington, DC. Graduate Oberlin Col. Debut 1977 OB in "The Passion of Dracula," followed by "La Belle au Bois."

WHITE, JOAN. Born Dec. 3 in Alexandria, Egypt. Attended RADA. Bdwy debut 1962 in "A Passage to India," followed by "Alice in Wonderland," OB in "Stephen D."

WHITMORE, JAMES. Born Oct. 1, 1922 in White Plains, NY. Attended Yale U. Bdwy debut 1947 in "Command Decision," followed by "A case of Libel," "Inquest," "Will Rogers U.S.A.," "Bully," "Almost an Eagle," OB in "Elba."

WHITTON, MARGARET. (formerly Peggy). Born Nov. 30 in Philadelphia, PA. Debut 1973 OB in "Baba Goya," followed by "Arthur," "The Wager," "Nourish the Beast," "Another Language," "Chinchilla," "Othello," "The Art of Dining," "One Tiger to a Hill," "Henry IV Parts 1 & 2," "Don Juan," Bdwy in "Steaming" (1982).

WIDDOES, JAMES. Born Nov. 15, 1953 in Pittsburgh, PA. Attended NYU. Debut 1977 OB in "Wonderful Town," Bdwy 1982 in "Is There Life after High School?" for which he received a Theatre World Award, followed by "Caine Mutiny Court-Martial."

WIDDOES, KATHLEEN. Born Mar. 21, 1939in Wilmington, DE. Attended Paris Theatre des Nations. Bdwy debut 1958 in "The Firstborn," followed by "World of Suzie Wong," "Much Ado about Nothing," "The Importance of Being Earnest," OB in "Three Sisters," "The Maids," "You Can't Take It with You," "To Clothe the Naked," "World War 2½," "Beggar's Opera," "As You Like It," "A Midsummer Night's Dream," "One Act Play Festival," "Hamlet."

WIEST, DIANE. Born Mar. 28, 1948 in Kansas City, MO. Attended UMd. Debut 1976 OB in "Ashes," followed by "Leave It to Beaver Is Dead," "The Art of Dining" for which she received a Theatre World Award, "Bonjour La Bonjour," "Three Sisters," Bdwy in "Frankenstein" (1980), "Othello," "Beyond Therapy."

WIGGINS, TUDI. Born Oct. 10 in Victoria, BC, Can. Bdwy debut 1968 in "The Prime of Miss Jean Brodie," OB in "Looking-Glass," "Knights Errant."

WILKINSON, KATE. Born Oct. 25 in San Francisco, CA. Attended San Jose State Col. Bdwy debut 1967 in "Little Murders," followed by "Johnny No-Trump," "Watercolor," "Postcards," "Ring Round the Bathtub," "The Last of Mrs. Lincoln," "Man and Superman," "Frankenstein," "The Man Who Came to Dinner," OB in "La Madre," "Ernest in Love," "Story of Mary Surratt," "Bring Me a Warm Body," "Child Buyer," "Rimers of Eldritch," "A Doll's House," "Hedda Gabler," "Real Inspector Hound," "The Contractor," "When the Old Man Died," "The Overcoat," "Villager," "Good Help Is Hard to Find," "Lumiere."

| Raphael Sbarge | Carol Schultz | Ed Setrakian | Gwendolyn J. Shepherd | P. Jay Sidney | Sheila Smith |

| Kathryn C. Sparer | Nick Stannard | Elaine Swann | William Thomas, Jr. | Concetta Tomei | Andy Torres |

| Mark Torres | Mimi Turque | Michael Twain | Anne Twomey | James Valentine | Deborah Unger |

| Laurel van der Linde | Neil Vipond | Sasha von Scherler | Melvin Washington | Tudi Wiggins | Nicholas Woodeson |

| Nicholas Wyman | Ginny Yang | Peter Yoshida | Nancy Youngblut | Alan Zampese | Janet Zarish |

225

WILKOF, LEE. Born June 25, 1957 in Canton, OH. Graduate UCincinnati. Debut 1977 OB in "Present Tense," followed by "Little Shop of Horrors."

WILLIAMS, CURT. Born Nov. 17, 1935 in Mt. Holly, NJ. Graduate Oberlin Col., UMiami. Debut 1964 OB in "The Fantasticks," followed by "Pinafore," "Mikado," "Night Must Fall," "The Hostage," "Macbeth," "Ice Age," "Colored People's Time," "About Heaven and Earth," Bdwy 1970 in "Purlie."

WILLIAMS, ELLIS. Born June 28, 1951 in Brunswick, GA. Graduate Boston U. Debut 1977 OB in "Intimation," followed by "Spell #7," "Mother Courage," Bdwy in "The Basic Training of Pavlo Hummel," "Pirates of Penzance," "Solomon's Child," "Trio."

WILLIAMS, L B Born May 7, 1949 in Richmond, VA. Graduate Albion Col. Debut 1976 in "Equus," OB in "Spa," "Voices," "5 on the Backhand Side," "Chameleon," "Mercenaries."

WILLIAMS, TREAT. Born in 1952 in Rowayton, CT. Bdwy debut 1976 in "Grease," followed by "Over Here," "Once in a Lifetime," "Pirates of Penzance," OB in "Randy Newman's Maybe I'm Doing It Wrong," "Some Men Need Help."

WILLIAMSON, NICOL. Born Sept. 14, 1938 in Hamilton, Scot. Bdwy Debut 1965 in "Inadmissible Evidence" followed by "Plaza Suite," "Hamlet," "Uncle Vanya," "Macbeth," OB in "Nicol Williamson's Late Show," "Inadmissible Evidence," "The Entertainer."

WILSON, ALEXANDER. Born Sept. 12, 1948 in Port Swepstone, SAfr. Graduate SUNY. Debut 1983 in "The Other Side of the Swamp."

WILSON, CARRIE. Born Sept. 15, 1944 in Philadelphia, PA. Graduate Barnard Col., Neighborhood Playhouse. Debut 1969 OB in "Promenade," followed by "School for Wives," "School for Scandal."

WILSON, DOLORES. Born Aug. 9 in Philadelphia, PA. Bdwy debut 1965 in "The Yearling," followed by "Fiddler on the Roof," "Cry for Us All," "I Remember Mama," "Annie," "The Ritz."

WILSON, ELIZABETH. Born Apr. 4, 1925 in Grand Rapids, MI. Attended Neighborhood Playhouse. Bdwy debut 1953 in "Picnic," followed by "Desk Set," "Tunnel of Love," "Big Fish, Little Fish," "Sheep on the Runway," "Sticks and Bones," "Secret Affairs of Mildred Wild," "Importance of Being Earnest," "Morning's at 7," "You Can't Take It with You," OB in "Plaza 9," "Eh?," "Little Murders," "Good Woman of Setzuan," "Uncle Vanya," "Threepenny Opera," "All's Well That Ends Well," "Taken in Marriage."

WILSON, K.C. Born Aug. 10, 1945 in Miami, FL. Graduate AADA. Debut 1973 OB in "Little Mahagonny," followed by "The Tempest," "Richard III," "Macbeth," "Threepenny Opera," "The Passion of Dracula," "Francis," "Robin Hood."

WILSON, MARY LOUISE. Born Nov. 12, 1936 in New Haven, CT. Graduate Northwestern U. Bdwy debut 1963 in "Hot Spot," followed by "Flora the Red Menace," "Criss-Crossing," "Promises, Promises," "The Women," "Gypsy," "The Royal Family," "Importance of Being Earnest," "Philadelphia Story," "Fools," "Alice in Wonderland," OB in "Our Town," "Upstairs at the Downstairs," "Threepenny Opera," "A Great Career," "Whispers on the Wind," "Beggar's Opera," "Buried Child," "Sister Mary Ignatius Explains It All," "Actor's Nightmare."

WILSON, ROY ALAN. Born Jan. 5, 1945 in Portland, OR. Graduate UPugetSound, UWa. Debut 1957 in "The Music Man," followed by "1776," "Fiddler on the Roof," OB in "Robin Hood."

WILSON, TREY. Born Jan, 21, 1948 in Houston, TX. Bdwy debut 1979 in "Peter Pan," followed by "Tintypes," "The First," "Foxfire."

WINDE, BEATRICE. Born Jan. 6 in Chicago, IL. Debut 1966 OB in "In White America," followed by "June Bug Graduates Tonight," "Strike Heaven on the Face," "Divine Comedy," "Crazy Horse," "My Mother, My Father and Me," "Steal Away," Bdwy 1971 in "Aint Supposed to Die a Natural Death" for which she received a Theatre World Award.

WINGATE, MARTHA. Born July 28, 1953 in Boston, MA. Attended WesternWaStateU, UWa. Bdwy debut 1977 in "Hair," followed by OB in "The Death of Von Richthofen."

WINSTON, LEE. Born Mar. 14, 1941 in Great Bend, KS. Graduate UKs. Debut 1966 OB in "The Drunkard," followed by "Little Mahagonny," "Good Soldier Schweik," "The Adopted Moon," "Miss Waters to You," Bdwy in "Show Boat" (1966), "1600 Pennsylvania Avenue."

WINTERS, TIME. Born Feb. 3, 1956 in Lebanon, OR. Graduate Lane Com. Col., Stephens Col. Debut 1981 OB in "Nathan the Wise," followed by "Round and Round the Garden," "Fanshen," Bdwy in "Amadeus" (1983).

WINTERS, WARRINGTON. Born July 28, 1909 in Bigstone Country, MN. Graduate UMn. Debut 1975 OB in "Another Language," followed by "A Night at the Black Pig," "Uncle Vanya," "Richard III," "Livin' at the Raccoon Lodge."

WINTERS, WENDEE. Born Aug. 15 in Chicago, IL. Graduate UCLA. Debut 1982 OB in "Forbidden Broadway."

WIRTH, DANIEL. Born Oct. 3, 1955 in Bay City, MI. Graduate Central MiU, UCal. Debut 1982 OB in "Twelfth Night," followed by "The Country Wife," "Dubliners," "Hamlet."

WISNISKI, RON. Born Aug. 11, 1957 in Pittsburgh, PA. Graduate UPittsburgh. Debut 1983 OB in "Promises, Promises."

WOHL, DAVID. Born Sept. 22, 1953 in Brooklyn, NY. Debut 1981 OB in "The Buddy System," followed by "Awake and Sing," "Portrait of Jenny."

WOLF, CATHERINE. Born May 25 in Abington, PA. Attended Carnegie-Tech, Neighborhood Playhouse. Bdwy debut 1976 in "The Innocents," followed by "Otherwise Engaged," OB in "A Difficult Borning," "I Can't Keep Running in Place," "Cloud 9."

WOODESON, NICHOLAS. Born in England and graduate of USussex, RADA. Debut 1978 OB in "Strawberry Fields," followed by "The Taming of the Shrew," Bdwy in "Man and Superman" (1978), "Piaf," "Good."

WOODS, LAUREN K. Born Nov. 19, 1939 in Providence, RI. Graduate Rutgers U, Amherst Col. Debut 1980 OB in "The Ballad of Boris K," followed by "The Guys in the Truck," "Movie of the Month," "Four to Make Two."

WOODS, RICHARD. Born May 9, 1923 in Buffalo, NY. Graduate Ithaca Col. Bdwy in "Beg, Borrow or Steal," "Capt. Brassbound's Conversion," "Sail Away," "Coco," "Last of Mrs. Lincoln," "Gigi," "Sherlock Holmes," "Murder among Friends," "The Royal Family," "Deathtrap," "Man and Superman," "The Man Who Came to Dinner," "The Father," "Present Laughter," "Alice in Wonderland," "You Can't Take It with You," OB in "The

Crucible," "Summer and Smoke," "American Gothic," "Four-in-one," "My Heart's in the Highlands," "Eastward in Eden," "The Long Gallery," "The Year Boston Won the Pennant," "In the Matter of J. Robert Oppenheimer" (LC), with APA in "You Can't Take It With You," "War and Peace," "School for Scandal," "Right You Are," "The Wild Duck," "Pantagleize," "Exit the King," "The Cherry Orchard," "Cock-a-doodle Dandy," and "Hamlet," "Crimes and Dreams."

WOOTERS, JOAN Born Dec. 15, 1951 in Boston, MA. Graduate Rollins Col. Debut 1982 OB in "The Dining Room."

WRIGHT, AMY. Born Apr. 15, 1950 in Chicago, IL. Graduate Beloit Col. Debut 1977 OB in "The Stronger," followed by "Nightshift," "Hamlet," "Miss Julie," "Slacks and Tops," "Terrible Jim Fitch," "Village Wooing," "The Stronger," "Time Framed," Bdwy in "5th of July" (1980).

WRIGHT, MARY CATHERINE. Born Mar. 19, 1948 in San Francisco, CA. Attended CCSF, SFState Col. Bdwy debut 1970 in "Othello," followed by "A History of the American Film," "Tintypes," OB in "East Lynne," "Mimi Lights the Candle," "Marvin's Gardens," "The Tempest," "The Doctor in Spite of Himself," "Love's Labour's Lost," "Pushcart Peddlers," "Sister Mary Ignatius Explains It All," "Actor's Nightmare."

WRIGHT, REBECCA. Born Dec. 5 in Springfield, OH. With Joffrey Ballet, ABT before Bdwy debut 1983 in "Merlin."

WYMAN, NICHOLAS. Born May 18, 1950 in Portland, ME. Graduate Harvard U. Bdwy debut 1975 in "Very Good Eddie," followed by "Grease," "The Magic Show," "On the 20th Century," "Whoopee!" "My Fair Lady" (1981), OB in "Paris Lights," "When We Dead Awaken," "Charlotte Sweet."

YANCEY, KIM. Born Sept. 25, 1959 in NYC. Graduate CCNY. Debut 1978 OB in "Why Lillie Won't Spin," followed by "Escape to Freedom," "Dacha," "Blues for Mr. Charlie."

YANG, GINNY. Born Apr. 22, 1952 in Korea. Graduate Catawba Col. Debut 1980 OB in "F.O.B.," followed by "Peking Man," "Extenuating Circumstances," Bdwy in "Plenty" (1982).

YEOMAN, JOANN. Born Mar. 19, 1948 in Phoenix, AZ. Graduate AzStateU, Purdue U. Debut 1974 OB in "The Boy Friend," followed by "Texas Starlight," "Ba Ta Clan," "A Christmas Carol."

YONOWSKY, MAURICE. Born July 5, 1930 in The Bronx, NY. Attended UMd, AADA. Debut 1956 OB in "Jephthah the Gileadite," followed by "Family Portrait," "One Thursday Last May," "Blue Bird," "Sans Everything," "NY Transit Authority," "Drawn by Night," "Treasure," "Eternal Song of Walt Whitman," "Hamburger without Relish," "The Actors."

YOSHIDA, PETER. Born May 28, 1945 in Chicago, IL. Graduate UIll., Princeton U., AADA. Debut 1965 OB in "Coriolanus," followed by "Troilus and Cressida," "Santa Anita '42," "Pursuit of Happiness," "Servant of Two Masters," "The Peking Man," "Monkey Music," "Station J," "Double Dutch."

YOST, JOHN. Born Jan. 30 in NYC. Graduate CCNY. Bdwy debut 1979 in "Evita."

YOUNGBLUT, NANCY. Born Feb. 14, 1953 in Waterloo, IA. Graduate St. Catherine Col., UGa. Debut 1983 OB in "D.C. Al Fine."

YULIN, HARRIS. Born Nov. 5, 1937 in Calif. Attended USCal. Debut 1963 OB in "Next Time I'll Sing to You," followed by "A Midsummer Night's Dream," "Troubled Waters," "Richard III," "King John," "The Cannibals," "Lesson from Aloes," "Hedda Gabler," "Barnum's Last Life," Bdwy in "Watch on the Rhine" (1980)

ZACHARY, ALAINA. Born Oct 6, 1946 in Cleveland, OH. Graduate Boston U. Debut 1971 OB in "The Proposition," followed by "Secrets," "El Bravo!" Bdwy in "Grease" (1972), "Nine."

ZAGNIT, STUART. Born Mar. 28, 1952 in New Brunswick, NJ. Graduate Montclair State Col. Debut 1978 OB in "The Wager," followed by "Manhattan Transference," "Women in Tune," "Enter Laughing."

ZALOOM, PAUL. Born Dec. 14, 1951 in Brooklyn, NY. Graduate Goddard Col. Debut 1979 OB in "Fruit of Zaloom," followed by "Zalooming Along," "Zaloominations!", "Crazy as Zaloom."

ZAMPESE, ALAN. Born Feb. 1 in Trenton, NJ. Attended Piscator Workshop. Bdwy debut 1976 in "Bubbling Brown Sugar," OB in "The Herne's Egg" (1961), "Merry Wives of Windsor," "Teach Me How to Cry," "Arms and the Man," "See How They Run."

ZANG, EDWARD. Born Aug. 19, 1934 in NYC. Graduate Boston U. OB in "Good Soldier Schweik," "St. Joan," "Boys in the Band," "The Reliquary of Mr. and Mrs. Potterfield," "Last Analysis," "As You Like It," "More than You Deserve," "Polly," "Threepenny Opera," BAM Co.'s "New York Idea," "The Misanthrope," "Banana Box," "The Penultimate Problem of Sherlock Holmes," Bdwy in "Crucifier of Blood," "Amadeus," "Alice in Wonderland."

ZARISH, JANET. Born Apr. 21, 1954 in Chicago, IL. Graduate Juilliard. Debut 1981 OB in "Villager," followed by "Playing With Fire," "Royal Bob."

ZETTLER, STEPHEN. Born Dec. 21, 1947 in New Jersey. Debut 1981 OB in "The Amazin' Casey Stengel," followed by "A Soldier's Play."

ZIEMBA, KAREN. Born Nov. 12, 1957 in St. Joseph, MO. Graduate UAkron. Debut 1981 OB in "Seesaw," Bdwy 1982 in "A Chorus Line."

ZORICH, LOUIS. Born Feb. 12, 1924 in Chicago, IL. Attended Roosevelt U. OB in "Six Characters in Search of an Author," "Crimes and Crimes," "Henry V," "Thracian Horses," "All Women Are One," "Good Soldier Schweik," "Shadow of Heroes," "To Clothe the Naked," "Sunset," "A Memory of Two Mondays," "They Knew What They Wanted," "The Gathering," "True West," "The Tempest," "Come Dog, Come Night," Bdwy in "Becket," "Moby Dick," "The Odd Couple," "Hadrian VII," "Moonchildren," "Fun City," "Goodtime Charley," "Herzl."

ZURICH, TOM. Born Oct.28, 1959 in Freeport, NY. Graduate Dartmouth Col. Debut 1982 OB in "Going Steady."

ZUTZ, CARL. Born Mar. 18, 1953 in Manitowoc, WI. Graduate Dartmouth Col. Debut 1982 OB in "The Regard of Flight," followed by "Transformations," "Melissa While She Sleeps," "Mame," "Craig's Wife."

MABEL ALBERTSON, 81, stage, film and tv actress, died Sept. 28, 1982 of Alzheimer's disease in Santa Monica, CA. On Broadway she appeared in "The Return of Ulysses," "The Egg" and "Xmas in Las Vegas," among others. She had appeared regularly on such tv series as "The Tom Ewell Show," "Those Whiting Girls" and "Bewitched." No reported survivors.

BRANDY ALEXANDER, 38 Maine-born nightclub and stage performer, died July 30, 1982 of cancer in NYC. He had appeared in "Jewel Box Revue," "Triple Play," "Save It for Your Death Bed," and "Let My People Come." No reported survivors.

JOHN ALEXANDER, 85, Kentucky-born stage and screen actor, died July 13, 1982 in NYC during a board meeting of the Actors Fund. After making his debut at 11 in "Elmer Brown," he subsequently appeared in "The Mirage," "Cyrano de Bergerac," "Jamboree," "Marathon," "The Tragedy of Ages," "The Petrified Forest," "Nowhere Bound," "Mid West," "Swing Your Lady," "Red Harvest," "The Greatest Show on Earth," "All the Living," "Kiss the Boys Goodbye," "Morning's at Seven," "Out from Under," "Arsenic and Old Lace," "Hilda Crane," "Ondine," "Teahouse of the August Moon," "The Gondoliers," "Visit to a Small Planet," "Never Too Late." He retired in 1962. No reported survivors.

GEORGE BALANCHINE, 79, ne Georgi Balanchivadez in Russia, died April 30, 1983 of pneumonia resulting from a progressive neurological disorder. One of ballet's greatest choreographic geniuses, co-founder and artistic director of the NY City Ballet, also directed and choreographed for the musical comedy theatre. His Broadway credits include "On Your Toes," "Ziegfeld Follies," "Babes in Arms," "I Married an Angel," "The Boys from Syracuse," "Keep Off the Grass," "Lousiana Purchase," "Cabin in the Sky," "The Lady Comes Across," "Rosalinda," "The Merry Widow," "What's Up," "Dream with Music," "Song of Norway," "The Chocolate Soldier," "Where's Charley?," "Romeo and Juliet," "Courtin' Time," "A Midsummer Night's Dream," "The Winter's Tale" and "The Merry Wives of Windsor." He was married and divorced four times, to ballerinas Tamara Geva, Vera Zorina, Maria Tallchief, Tanaquil LeClercq. Surviving is his brother, Russian composer Andrei Balanchivadze. Burial was in Sag Harbor, Long Island, NY.

BEVERLY BAYNE, 87, Minneapolis-born stage and screen actress, died Aug. 18, 1982 of natural causes in Scottsdale, AZ. Her stage credits include "Once in a Lifetime," "As Husbands Go," "The Shining Hour," "Claudia," "From 8 to 12," "Escapade," "Gala Night," "Pied Piper," "Only the Young," "Symphony," "I Like It Here," "Loco," "The Cup of Trembling." She was married and divorced from actor Francis X. Bushman and businessman Charles T. Hvass. No reported survivors.

INGRID BERGMAN, Swedish-born stage, film and tv actress, died of cancer in London on her 67th birthday, Aug. 29, 1982. Although her fame came from luminous characterizations on screen, she also performed on stage, making her Bdwy debut in 1940 in "Liliom," followed by "Joan of Lorraine," "More Stately Mansions," "Capt. Brassbound's Conversion," and "The Constant Wife" in 1975. She was divorced from Dr. Peter Lindstrom, Roberto Rossellini, and Lars Schmidt. Surviving are four children: Pia Lindstrom, Ingrid, Isabella and Roberto Rossellini. After cremation, her ashes were scattered at her summer home in Sweden on the islet of Dannholmen.

KARL N. BERNSTEIN, 89, Brooklyn-born theatrical press agent, died Jan. 1, 1983 of a heart ailment in NYC. After serving as a vaudeville critic, he switched to publicizing Broadway productions for more than 50 years. He had been in retirement for several years. He is survived by his son, producer-manager Ira B. Bernstein and four grandchildren.

VALERIE BETTIS, 62, Texas-born modern dancer, choreographer, teacher and actress, died Sept. 26, 1982 in NYC after a brief illness. She was the first modern dancer to choreograph for a classical ballet company in 1947 with "Virginia Sampler" for Ballet Russe de Monte Carlo, subsequently she choreographed "Where I Lay Dying," "Yerma," "The Golden Round," "Winesburg, Ohio," "Beggar's Holiday," "Two on the Aisle," "Peer Gynt," "Ulysses in Nighttown," "Green Mansions." She had appeared in "Inside U.S.A." for which she received a Theatre World Award, "Great to Be Alive," "Bless You All," "Threepenny Opera," and "Back to Methuselah" in 1958. She was divorced from her first husband, pianist Bernardo Segall, and her second, Arthur Schmidt, died in 1969. Surviving are her mother and a brother, both of Dallas, TX.

JAMES HUBERT "EUBIE"BLAKE, 100, legendary ragtime composer, died of natural causes Feb. 12, 1983 in his Brooklyn home. Born in Baltimore, he began his career at 15 playing piano in a bordello, and composing songs, subsequently writing hundreds of familiar tunes. In 1978 a Broadway musical "Eubie!" was produced using his songs. He had helped bring the first black musical "Shuffle Along" to Bdwy in 1921 and it ran for 14 months, followed by "Chocolate Dandies," "Elsie," "Blackbirds of 1930." He was in retirement from 62 to 86 when a retrospective album brought him back into the spotlight. His two wives predeceased him, and he left no immediate survivors.

JAMES BRODERICK, 55, New Hampshire-born stage, screen and tv actor, died of cancer Nov. 1, 1982 in New Haven, CT. After his 1953 Broadway debut in "Maggie," he appeared in "Johnny No Trump," "Let Me Hear You Smile," "A View from the Bridge," "Johnny Johnson," "A Touch of the Poet," "Two by Saroyan," "Firebugs," "The Time of Your Life," "Scenes from American Life," and "Wedding Band." For 5 years he was the father in tv's "Family" series. He had also appeared in "Frenner," "The Bold Ones," "Run for Your LIfe," "The F.B.I. Story" and "Gunsmoke." Surviving are his widow, two daughters, and actor-son Matthew.

KAY BUCKLEY 60, Philadelphia-born stage and film actress, died of cancer, Nov. 2, 1982 in Los Angeles, CA. After appearing on Broadway in "Naked Genius," "Let's Face It," "Burlesque" and "Sally," she went to Hollywood and performed in several films before retiring after her marriage in 1952 to Milton A. Pickman who survives. She also leaves a son and daughter.

WAYNE CARSON, 55, actor, director, stage manager, died July 4, 1982 in his NYC home. Among the 35 productions with which he was involved are "School for Wives," "Desk Set," "The Pleasure of His Company," "A Far Country," "Mary, Mary," "Poor Richard," "The Odd Couple," "Dumas and Son," "The Promise," "Staircase," "The Exercise," "Mother's Kisses," "Hadrian VII," "How the Other Half Loves," "Old Times," "Night Watch," "Finishing Touches," "Absurd Person Singular," "Who's Afraid of Virginia Woolf?," "Golda," "Dracula," "Bedroom Farce," "Romantic Comedy," "Lunch Hour," "Supporting Cast," "Grown-Ups," "Medea" (1982). Surviving are his widow, actress Martha Randall, two sons and a daughter.

ROBERT CHRISTIAN, 42, Los Angeles-born stage, screen and tv actor, died of cancer Jan. 27, 1983 in NYC. Included among his many NYC appearances are "The Happening," "Fortune and Men's Eyes," "Boys in the Band," "Mary Stuart," "Narrow Road to the Deep North," "Twelfth Night," "Terraces," "Blook Knot" for which he received an Obie Award, "Boesman and Lena," "Julius Caesar," "Coriolanus," "Mother Courage," "We Bombed in New Haven," "Does a Tiger Wear a Necktie?," "An Evening with Richard Nixon . . .," "All God's Chillun" and "Piaf" (1981). He had roles on tv's "Amos 'n' Andy," "Andy Griffith Show," and "Another World." His mother survives.

KENDALL CLARK, 70, stage, screen and tv actor, died Jan. 28, 1983 after a long illness in his home in Vero Beach, FL. After his 1935 Bdwy debut with Eva LeGallienne in "L'Aiglon" and "Camille," he appeared in "End of Summer," "Ghost of Yankee Doodle," "Fifth Column," "George Washington Slept Here," "Home of the Brave," "The Eagle Has Two heads," "St. Joan," "The Shrike," "Richard III," "The Desperate Hours," "The Taming of the shrew," "Auntie Mame," "The First Mrs. Fraser," and "Who's Afraid of Virginia Woolf?" A sister survives.

PHILIP O. COOK, 58, former actor-dancer, and director of Actors Equity Association's interviews and auditions department, died Nov. 23, 1982 in NYC after a long illness. His theatre credits include "Oklahoma" (1951), "Kiss Me, Kate," "Mr. Roberts," "Walk Tall," "Seventh Heaven," "Kismet," "South Pacific," "Wish You Were Here," "Brigadoon," "The King and I," "Plain and Fancy," "Pajama Game," "Can-Can," "Guys and Dolls." He had also appeared in night clubs and on tv. Surviving are his mother and two brothers.

ROBERT COOTE, 73, London-born actor on stage, screen and tv, died of a heart attack in his sleep Nov. 25, 1982 at the NY Athletic Club where he lived. After his 1953 Broadway debut in "The Love of Four Colonels," he appeared in "Dear Charles," "My Fair Lady" (as Col. Pickering in 1956 and 1976), "Camelot," "Jockey Club Stakes," and "Bedroom Farce." He is survived by a sister.

TONI DARNAY, 61, actress on stage, screen, radio and tv, died of cancer Jan. 5, 1983 in her NYC home. Born Mercy Mustell, in Chicago, her NY debut was 1942 Off-Broadway in "Name Your Poison," subsequently appearing in "When the Bough Breaks," "Nocturne in Daylight," "The Gold Watch," "Possibilities," "Dead Giveaway," "The Sound of Music," "Sadie Thompson," "Affair of Honor," "Life with Father," "The Women," "Molly," "The Heiress," "Vieux Carre." She is survived by her husband, Hobe Morrison, legitimate editor and critic for *Variety*, two sons, and a daughter.

REGINALD DENHAM, 89, London-born actor, playwright, director, died Feb. 4, 1983 after a stroke in Englewood, NJ. He came to Broadway in 1929 to direct "Rope's End," followed by "Ladies in Retirement" which he co-authored, "Yesterday's Magic," "The Two Mrs. Carrolls," "Obsession," "Temper the Wind," "Gramercy Ghost," "Dial M for Murder," "The Bad Seed," "Hostile Witness," "Janus." With his third wife, Mary Orr, he wrote "The Platinum Set," "Sweet Peril," "Minor Murder," "Wallflower," "Dead Giveaway," and more than 100 tv scripts. He also wrote "Give Me Yesterday," "Suspect," "Dark Hammock," "Round Trip" and "Be Your Age." He leaves his widow, and two daughters.

RUTH DONNELLY, 86, New Jersey-born stage and film character comedienne, died Nov. 17, 1982 in NYC. She began her career at 17 as a chorus girl, subsequently appearing in "A Scrap of Paper," "Going Up," "A Prince There Was," "As You were," "Meanest Man in the World," "Madeleine and the Movies," "The Crooked Square," "Cheaper to Marry," "If I Was Rich," "So Was Napoleon," "She Means Business," "The Riot Act," "No, No, Nanette." She was the widow of Basil de Guichard. A sister survives.

TOM DRAKE, 64, Brooklyn-born stage, screen and tv actor, died of cancer, Aug. 11, 1982 in Torrance, CA. Using his real name of Alfred Alderdice, he made his Broadway debut in 1938 in "June Night," followed by "Central Casting," "Dance Night," "Run, Sheep, Run," "Clean Beds" and "Janie." Divorced from singer-actress Christopher Curtis, a sister survives.

HILTON EDWARDS, 79, London-born actor, director, and co-founder of Dublin Gate Theater, died Nov. 18, 1982 in a Dublin hospital. He began his career on the London stage and appeared with the Old Vic company. In New York he played in and/or directed "John Bull's Other Island," "The Old Lady Says No," "Where Stars Walk," "Philadelphia, Here I Come!" and "The Loves of Cass McGuire." No reported survivors.

227

FAYE EMERSON, 65, Louisiana-born stage, screen and tv actress, died March 9, 1983 of cancer in Deya, Majorca where she had lived for many years. After her 1948 Broadway debut in "The Play's the Thing," she appeared in "Parisienne," "The Heavenly Twins," "Protective Custody," "Back to Methuselah," "Mary Stuart" and "Elizabeth the Queen." She was hostess of her own tv show for several years. She was married and divorced three times. A son survives.

LEHMAN ENGEL, 71, Mississippi-born composer, director and teacher, died of cancer Aug. 29, 1982 in his Manhattan home. He had conducted more than 100 Broadway musicals, including some of the biggest hits, such as "Show Boat," "Brigadoon," "Annie Get Your Gun," "Fanny," "Guys and Dolls" and "Carousel." He was the recipient of two "Tony" awards for conducting: "The Consul" in 1950 and "Wonderful Town" in 1953. He also composed incidental music for more than 40 productions, including "Murder in the Cathedral" and "A Streetcar Named Desire." Four cousins survive in Jackson, Miss., where he was cremated.

PAUL FEIGAY, 64, Broadway and tv producer, died Feb. 26, 1983 in his home in Brewster, NY. His first production was "On the Town" in 1944, followed by "Billion Dollar Baby," "Land's End," "Me and Molly," and "Do You Know the Milky Way?" For tv he produced "Omnibus" series. A sister and a brother survive.

NEIL FITZGERALD, 90, Ireland-born stage, screen and tv actor, died June 15, 1982 in Princeton, NJ. After his Broadway debut in 1940 in "Leave Her to Heaven," he appeared in "Ten Little Indians," "The Wookey," "Without Love," "Plan M," "You Touched Me," "The Play's the Thing," "Design for a Stained Glass Window," "High Ground," "To Dorothy a Son," "Mr. Pickwick," "Witness for the Prosecution," "Little Moon of Alban," "Hadrian VII," "Mundy Scheme," "All Over," "Portrait of the Artist," "Murderous Angels," "The Contractor." Reported survivors in Ireland.

HENRY FONDA, 77, Nebraska-born actor on stage, screen and tv, died of a chronic heart disease in Los Angeles on Aug. 12, 1982. He made his Broadway debut in 1929's "Game of Love and Death," followed by "I Loved You Wednesday," "Forsaking All Others," "New FAces of 1934," "The Farmer Takes a Wife," "Mr. Roberts," "Point of No Return," "Caine Mutiny Court Martial," "Two for the Seesaw," "Silent Night, Lonely Night," "Critics Choice," "A Gift of Time," "Generation," "Our Town, "Clarence Darrow" and "First Monday in October." Surviving are his fifth wife, two daughters, Amy and Jane, and a son Peter. He was cremated.

EDUARD FRANZ, 80, Milwaukee-born character actor on stage, screen and tv, died Feb. 10, 1983 after a long illness in Los Angeles. A member of the original Provincetown Players, and subsequently on Broadway in "Miss Swan Expects," "Farm of Three Echoes," "The Russian People," "Cafe Crown," "Outrageous Fortune," "The Cherry Orchard," "Embezzled Heaven," "The Stranger," "Home of the Brave," "The Big Two," "The Egghead," "Those That Play the Clowns," "In the Matter of J. Robert Oppenheimer." His widow survives.

ROSALINDE FULLER, 90, England-born stage actress, died in her sleep Sept. 15, 1982 in London. After touring the U.S. in 1913 with her sisters, she returned in 1919 and appeared on Broadway in "Greenwich Village Follies," "Pinwheel Revue," "What's in a Name?," "A Christmas Carol," "The Champion," Ophelia to John Barrymore's Hamlet in 1922, "The Farmer's Wife," "Patience," "Love for Love," "Call of Life," "The Fountain," "Lost," "The Squall," "Unknown Warrior," "Murder on Account." A sister survives.

ERNEST GRAVES, 64, Chicago-born stage, screen and tv actor, died of cancer June 1, 1983 in NYC. He made his Broadway debut in Maurice Evans' 1941 "Macbeth," subsequently appearing in "The Russian People," "Othello," "Cyrano de Bergerac," "As You Like It," "Eastward in Eden," "Venus Is," "Ceremony of Innocence," "Poor Murderer," "Golda," "Dylan," "Tiger at the Gates" and "Third Best Sport." Surviving are his widow and a daughter.

PENELOPE HUBBARD, 81, retired actress, died Feb. 17, 1983 in Toledo, Ohio, where she worked as an interior designer. She appeared in such plays as "The Royal Family," "After Tomorrow," "House Party," "Hoosiers Abroad," "Aloma of the South Seas," and "London Calling." No immediate survivors.

ARTHUR HUGHES, 89, Illinois-born character actor on stage, screen, radio and tv, died of pneumonia Dec. 28, 1982 in NYC. After his 1923 Broadway debut in "King Lear," he appeared in "Man and the Masses," "Out of Step," "Rosmersholm," "A Man's Man," "Easter," "An American Tragedy," "Wall Street," "The Queen's Husband," "Harlem," "Subway Express," "Elizabeth the Queen," "Mourning Becomes Electra," "Tight Britches," "New Faces of 1936," "Behind the Red Lights," "Censored," "Quiet Please!," "My Fair Ladies," "Cuckoos on the Hearth," "Winesburg, Ohio," "Man in the Dog Suit" and "How Now, Dow Jones." For 23 years he starred on radio as Bill in "Just Plain Bill." His widow survives.

GRACE KELLY, Princess Grace of Monaco, 52, died Sept. 14, 1982 in Monte Carlo of a cerebral hemorrage and other injuries sustained in an accident when her car plunged off a mountain road. After training at American Academy of Dramatic Art, she made her Broadway debut in 1949 in "The Father" for which she received a Theatre World Award, followed by "To Be Continued." Hollywood beckoned and she appeared in films until her marriage to Prince Rainier of Monaco in 1956. She leaves her husband, a son and two daughters. Interment was in the Monaco cathedral.

JOSEPH KIPNESS, 71, Russia-born producer and restaurateur, died of cancer Nov. 18, 1982 in NYC. His Broadway productions include "Bright Lights of 1944," "Star Spangled Family," "High Button Shoes," "All You Need Is One Good Break," "Women of Twilight," "Be Your Age," "La Plume de Ma Tante," "Have I Got a Girl for You," "I Had a Ball," "La Grosse Valise," "But Seriously," "Applause," "Seesaw," and "I Love My Wife." Surviving are his widow, two daughters, and a son.

ADELAIDE KLEIN, 82, actress on stage, screen, radio and tv, died of a brain tumor March 18, 1983 in NYC. Her credits include "Double Dummy," "Brooklyn U.S.A.," "Uncle Harry," "Collector's Item," "The Immoralist," "Once Upon a Tailor," "Anna Christie," "Jane Eyre," "The Secret Concubine," "Poppa Is All." She is survived by her husband, Norman Annenberg.

HANK LADD, 73, Chicago-born performer on stage, radio, tv and night clubs, writer and production supervisor, died of a stroke June 9, 1982 in his Hollywood home. On Broadway he had appeared in "Priorities of 1942," "New Priorities of 1943," "Angel in the Wings," "Along Fifth Avenue," "Skits-Oh-Frantics" and two Earl Carroll Vanities. He had his own tv show series, "The Arrow Show.' He was married to vaudevillian Francetta Malloy who predeceased him.

MAX LEAVITT, 77, actor, director, producer, and founder of the Lemonade Opera, died Nov. 7, 1982 in NYC. His Broadway appearances include "The Moon Is a Gong," "The Centuries," "Family Portrait," "Twelfth Night," "Catherine Was Great," "Winter Soldiers," "The Milky Way," "Broken Hearts of Broadway," "Lute Song." Surviving are a sister and a brother.

JEAN LeBOUVIER, 62, stage and television actress, died April 6, 1983 in Van Nuys, CA. She had appeared in "A Streetcar Named Desire," "The Plough and the Stars," "Caucasian Chalk Circle," "Mrs. Warren's Profession," "The Burning," and "Protective Custody." She is survived by her husband, Richard Welsh.

WILL LEE, 74, Brooklyn-born character actor on stage, screen, and tv, and a teacher, died of a heart attack Dec. 7, 1982 in NYC. After his 1935 Broadway debut in "The Young Go First," he appeared in "Boy Meets Girl," "Family Portrait," "The Strings, My Lord, Are False," "The Shrike," "The Time of Your Life," "Johnny Johnson," "Night Music," "Heavenly Express," "Lily of the Valley," "Golden Boy," "Mexican Hayride," "Dream Girl," "Once Upon a Mattress," "Carnival," "As We Forgive Our Debtors," "Strange Bedfellows," "Jenny Kissed Me," "World of Sholom Aleichem," "The Last Analysis," "Incident at Vichy," "Deer Park," and "Enemies." He was Mr. Hooper on Tv's "Sesame Street" for 13 years. He is survived by a sister.

SUSAN LITTLER, 33, British-born stage, screen and tv actress, died of cancer July 11, 1982 in London. In 1979 she was nominated for a "Tony" Award for her Broadway performance in "Bedroom Farce." She is survived by her parents and a sister.

EUGENE LORING, 72, Milwaukee-born LeRoy Kerpestein, dancer, choreographer, director, died Aug. 30, 1982 after a long illness in Kingston, NY. He danced with American Ballet, Ballet Caravan and Ballet Theatre before founding Dance Players. On Broadway he appeared in "The Beautiful People" and choreographed "Carmen Jones," "Buttrio Square," and "Ice Capades of 1958 and 1966." He is probably best remembered for his classic ballet "Billy the Kid," first performed in 1938 by Ballet Caravan. A brother and sister survive.

DONALD MADDEN, 49, a Manhattan-born classical actor, died of cancer Jan. 22, 1983 in Central Islip, NY. For his debut in the 1959 production of "Julius Caesar" he received a Theatre World Award, and subsequently appeared in "Look Back in Anger," "First Impressions," "Lysistrata," "Pictures in the Hallway," "Henry IV," "She Stoops to Conquer," "The Plough and the Stars," "Hamlet," "Octoroon," "Ceremony of Innocence," "Henry VI," Richard III,"'A Doll's House,''Hedda Gabler," "Step on a Crack," "The Milk Train Doesn't Stop Here Anymore," "In the Bar of a Tokyo Hotel," "Richard III," The Philanderer," "Scribes," "Trick," "Jungle of Cities." He is survived by a cousin.

PATRICK MAGEE, 58, Ireland-born actor on stage and film, died of natural causes, Aug. 14, 1982, in his London home. In 1965 he received a "Tony" Award for his portrayal of the Marquis de Sade in the Royal Shakespeare Company's production of "Marat/Sade." His widow and two children survive.

VIVIEN MERCHANT, 53, British actress nee Ada Thompson, died of alcoholism Oct. 3, 1982 in her London home. She appeared in New York to critical praise in the Royal Shakespeare Company's "The Homecoming." She was divorced from playwright Harold Pinter, and leaves a son, Daniel.

ROBERT MERRIMAN, 66, Illinois-born actor, director, producer, designer, teacher, died of a heart attack Feb. 2, 1983 in Bennington, VT. He began his career as a child actor and appeared in over 200 productions, winning a Vernon Rice Award for his performance in "Idiot's Delight." He received a "Tony" Award for his Off-Broadway production of "Thieves Carnival" at the Cherry Lane Theatre. No reported survivors.

MICHAEL MILLER, 71, Los Angeles-born stage, film and tv actor, died of a heart ailment while on location in Harpers Ferry, WVa., May 4, 1983. After his 1961 New York debut in "Under Milk Wood," he appeared in "The Lesson," "A Memory of Two Mondays," "Little Murders," "Tom Paine," "Morning, Noon and Night," "Enemy of the People," "Whitsuntide," "Say When," "Case against Roberta Guardino," "Dandelion Wine," "Museum," "Ivanov," "Black Comedy," "The Trial of Lee Harvey Oswald" and "Past Tense." He is survived by his widow and three sons.

WORTHINGTON MINER, 82, stage and tv actor, director, producer, died Dec. 11, 1982 in NYC. His acting career began in 1925 in "Cyrano de Bergerac," his directing in 1929 with "Up Pops the Devil," followed by "Reunion in Vienna," "I Loved You Wednesday," "Both Your Houses," "Revenge with Music," "Blind Alley," "Let Freedom Ring," "Bury the Dead," "Jane Eyre," "On Your Toes," "Father Malachy's Miracle," "Jeremiah" which he wrote, "Susannah and the Elders," "Home Is the Hero" and "For Love or Money." He also served as president of the American Academy of Dramatic Arts. Surviving are a son and two daughters.

John Alexander	George Balanchine	Beverly Bayne	Ingrid Bergman	Eubie Blake	James Broderick

Wayne Carson	Robert Christian	Kendall Clark	Robert Coote	Toni Darnay	Ruth Donnelly

Faye Emerson	Neil Fitzgerald	Henry Fonda	Eduard Franz	Grace Kelly	Will Lee

Eugene Loring	Donald Madden	Vivien Merchant	Michael Miller	Cathleen Nesbitt	Selena Royle

Martha Sleeper	Walter Slezak	Shepperd Strudwick	Fred Stuthman	Gloria Swanson	Mark Syers

CATHLEEN NESBITT, 93, English-born actress on stage, screen and tv, died of natural causes Aug. 2, 1982 at her home in London. She had appeared in approximately 300 plays. After her 1911 Broadway debut in "Well of the Saints," she appeared in "Justice," "Hush," "Such Is Life," "Magic," "Garden of Paradise," "General Post," "Saving Grace," "Diversion," "The Cocktail Party," "Gigi," "Sabrina Fair," "Portrait of a Lady," "Anastasia," "My Fair Lady" (1956 & 1981), "The Sleeping Prince," "Second String," "Romulus" and "Uncle Vanya." She is survived by a son and a daughter.

PHILIP OBER, 80, Alabama-born stage, screen and tv actor, died of lung cancer Sept. 13, 1982 in Santa Monica, CA. After his Broadway debut in "The Animal Kingdom" (1932), he appeared in "She Loves Me Not," "Personal Appearance," "Spring Dance," "Without Warning," "The Hill Between," "Kiss the Boys Goodbye," "Out from Under," "Mr. and Mrs. North," "Junior Miss," "The Two Mrs. Carrolls," "Doctor's Degree," "Craig's Wife," "Dear Ruth" and "Light Up the Sky." He is survived by his second wife.

LEE PATRICK, 71, New York-born stage, screen and tv actress, died of a heart seizure Nov. 21, 1982 in her Laguna Beach, CA., home. Her Broadway career began at the age of 13 and her credits include "The Green Beetle," "Undercurrent," "Bachelor's Brides," "It All Depends," "Baby Mine," "Matrimonial Bed," "Nightstick," "June Moon," "Rock Me, Julie," "Friendship," "Little Women," "Blessed Event," "Shooting Star," "Knock on Wood," "Abide with Me." and "Stage Door." She is survived by her husband of 45 years, Tom Wood.

JACK PEARL, 88, stage and radio comedian, died Dec. 25, 1982 in his native Manhattan, NYC. His career began at the age of 12 in "School Days," followed by "Dancing Girl," "A Night in Paris," "Artists and Models," "Pleasure Bound," "International Revue," "Ziegfeld Follies of 1931," "Pardon My English," "One Flight Down" and "All for All." His greatest impact was on radio where he was Baron Munchhausen and popularized the expression "Vas you dere, Sharlie?" He also appeared in two films. His widow survives.

HELEN STERN RICHARDS, 66, Texas-born publicity agent and manager, died April 9, 1983 of complications following lung surgery. She had been press agent for many Broadway productions, including "Don Juan in Hell," "West Side Story," "Pajama Game," "Purlie," "Shenandoah." She is survived by a son, press agent Jeffrey Richards.

SELENA ROYLE, 78, NYC-born stage and screen actress who began her career at 17 on Broadway, died April 23, 1983 in Guadalajara, Mexico, where she had been in retirement since 1955. Her Broadway credits include "Lancelot and Elaine," "Golden Days," "Her Temporary Husband," "Peer Gynt," "She Stoops to Conquer," "Paradise," "Thunder in the Air," "Merchant of Venice," "Heat Wave," "When Ladies Meet," "Days Without End," "Goodbye Please," "Mad Morning," "Meet the Prince," "On Stage," "Among Those Sailing," "Curtain Call," "Reno," and "Young Mr. Disraeli." Her husband, actor Georges Renavent, died in 1968. A sister survives.

NANCY RYAN, 79, London-born actress, died May 23, 1983 after a long illness in Glen Cove, NY. She had appeared in "The Last of Mrs. Cheyney," "The Happy Husband," "The High Road," "Forsaking All Others," "No More Ladies," "Something Gay" and "Once Is Enough." Her husband, Carl F. Holmes, survives.

HOWARD SACKLER, 52, Brooklyn-born playwright and director, died Oct. 12, 1982 in his studio in Ibiza, Spain. He received the 1969 Pulitzer Prize and "Tony" Award for "The Great White Hope" that starred James Earl Jones on Broadway and film. He also wrote "Goodbye Fidel" and "Semmelweiss." Surviving are his widow, a son and a daughter.

SIDNEY SKOLSKY, 78, Manhattan-born Broadway and Hollywood reporter, died May 3, 1983 after a long illness in Los Angeles, CA. His column "Tintypes" appeared in national papers for over 50 years. He had been in retirement for seven years. Surviving are his widow and two daughters.

MARTHA SLEEPER, 72, Illinois-born stage and film actress, died of a heart attack Mar. 25, 1983 at her home in Beaufort, SC. After her Broadway debut (1929) in "Stepping Out," she appeared in "Dinner at Eight," "Good Men and True," "Russet Mantel," "Double Dummy," "Save Me the Waltz," "I Must Love Someone," "The Cream in the Well," "The Land Is Bright," "The Perfect Marriage," "The Rugged Path," and "Christopher Blake." She is survived by her third husband, Col. Howard Stelling.

WALTER SLEZAK, 80, Vienna-born actor on stage, screen and tv, shot himself in the head with a revolver April 21, 1983 in his home in Flower Hill, LI, NY., after becoming increasingly depressed over a series of illnesses. He was a matinee idol in Germany before making his Broadway debut (1930) in "Meet My Sister." Other productions include "Music in the Air," "Ode to Liberty," "May Wine," "A Doll's House," "I Married an Angel," "The Trojan Women," "Somewhere in France," "Little Dark Horse," "My Three Angels," "Fanny" for which he received a "Tony" Award, "The First Gentleman" and "The Gazebo." Surviving are his widow, a son, and two daughters, including actress Erika Slezak.

SHEPPERD STRUDWICK, 75, NC-born stage, screen and tv actor, died of cancer Jan. 15, 1983 in his Manhattan home. He had more than 35 leading roles on Broadway, 28 in road companies and 75 in stock. During the 1940's he sometimes used the name John Shepperd. His NY credits include "Falstaff," "Life Line," "Both Your Houses," "Yellow Jacket," "Biography," "Jig Saw," "Trelawny of the 'Wells'," "Let Freedom Ring," "End of Summer," "As You Like It," "The Three Sisters," "Christopher Blake," "Affairs of State," "The Bat," "Ladies of the Corridor," "The Doctor's Dilemma," "The Sea Gull," "Night Circus," "Only in America," "Who's Afraid of Virginia Woolf?," "The Devils," "Measure for Measure," "Galileo," "The Price," "Eccentricities of a Nightingale," "To Grandmother's House We Go" and "Morning's at Seven." Surviving are his widow, and a son by a previous marriage.

FRED STUTHMAN, 63, California-born stage, screen and tv actor, died of natural causes July 7, 1982 in his home in Santa Monica, CA. After a successful career as a radio announcer, he became an actor. His New York credits include "Hamlet," "Uncle Vanya," "Charles Abbot & Son," "She Stoops to Conquer," "Master Builder," "Taming of the Shrew," "Misalliance," "Merchant of Venice," "Conditions of Agreement," "The Play's the Thing," "Ghosts," "The Father," "Hot 1 Baltimore," "Cherry Orchard," "The Devil's Disciple," "Bonjour, La, Bonjour," "Sherlock Holmes" and "Fools." No reported survivors.

GLORIA SWANSON, 84, Chicago-born Gloria May Josephine Svensson, actress on stage and film, died of a heart ailment Apr. 4, 1983 in New York City. After her Broadway debut (1945) in "A Goose for the Gander," she appeared in "Twentieth Century," "Anta Album," "Nina," and "Butterflies Are Free." She was cremated. Surviving are her sixth husband, and two daughters by previous marriages.

MARK SYERS, 30, actor-singer, was killed in an auto collision near his home in New Jersey on May 15, 1983. After his 1976 Broadway Debut in "Pacific Overtures," he appeared in "Jesus Christ Superstar" (1977), "Evita," "Under Fire." He is survived by his parents, a sister and two brothers.

MAURICE TURET, 73, New York press agent, died March 23, 1983 in NYC. He began his career doing publicity for Yiddish theatre, making the transition to Broadway in 1944 with "Stars on Ice." Surviving are his widow and two daughters.

BETTY WALKER, 54, actress, singer, comedienne on stage, screen and tv, died July 26, 1982 after a lengthy illness in her Manhattan home. She had appeared on Broadway in "Springtime Folly," "Middle of the Night," "The Passion of Josef D," and "Ready When You Are, C.B." She was well known for her tv monologues beginning "Hello Ceil?" A sister and a brother survive.

CHARLES WALTERS, 70, film director, and former Broadway singer-dancer, died Aug. 13, 1982 after a long illness at his home in Malibu, CA. Before going to Hollywood, he appeared on Broadway in "New Faces of 1933," "The Tale of the Wolf," "Strange Interlude," "No More Frontier," "Parade," "Jubilee," "So Proudly We Hail," "The Show Is On," "Between the Devil," "I Married an Angel" and "DuBarry Was a Lady." He choreographed "Let's Face It," "Banjo Eyes," "St. Louis Woman." An adopted son survives.

ALAN WEBB, 75, actor on stage and film, died June 22, 1982 in Sussex, Eng. Born in York, Eng., he made his Broadway debut in 1936 in "Tonight at 8:30," followed by "George and Margaret," "The Winslow Boy," "Nina," "The Deep Blue Sea," "The Genius and the Goddess," "The Night of the Iguana," "Heartbreak House," "The Chinese Prime Minister," "UTBU," "We Have Always Lived in the Castle," and "I Never Sang for My Father." No reported survivors.

JOHN WILLIAMS, 80, British actor on stage, film and tv, died of an aneurism May 5, 1983 in his La Jolla, CA. home. After his Broadway debut (1924) in "The Fake," he appeared in "Ghost Train," "Mixed Doubles," "The High Road," "Ten Minute Alibi," "Dodsworth," "Call It a Day," "No Time for Comedy," "Claudia," "Anne of the Thousand Days," "The Velvet Glove," "Venus Observed," "Dial 'M' for Murder" for which he received a "Tony," Donaldson, and NY Drama Critics awards, 'Elmer the Great," "The Tavern," "Once in a Lifetime," "Barchester Towers," "Miss Swan Expects," "Let's Face It," "A Family Affair," "Barefoot Boy with Cheek," "The Men We Marry," "On Your Toes" (1954), "The Dark Is Light Enough," "Ross," "The New York Idea," "The Chinese Prime Minister," and "Hay Fever" (1970). His widow survives.

TENNESSEE WILLIAMS, 71, America's greatest playwright since Eugene O'Neill, died March 25, 1983 from choking on a plastic bottle cap in his NYC hotel suite. He was born Thomas Lanier Williams in Columbus, MS. but grew up in St. Louis. He was the author of two Pulitzer Prize winning plays, "A Streetcar Named Desire" and "Cat on a Hot Tin Roof," and wrote more than twenty others, including "The Glass Menagerie," "The Rose Tattoo," "Orpheus Descending," "Summer and Smoke," "The Night of the Iguana," "Camino Real," "Sweet Bird of Youth," "The Milk Train Doesn't Stop Here Anymore," "Battle of Angels," "You Touched Me," "Period of Adjustment," "Slapstick Tragedy," "Two Character Play," "Vieux Carre," "The Seven Descents of Myrtle," "In the Bar of a Tokyo Hotel" and "Clothes for a Summer Hotel." His last play, "A House Not Meant to Stand," was premiered in 1982 at the Goodman Theatre in Chicago. He is survived by a sister and a brother. Interment was in St. Louis, Mo.

KEITH WINTER, 76, playwright born in North Wales, died Feb. 17, 1983 in Englewood, NJ. His first Broadway production was "The Rats of Norway," in 1933, and subsequently he wrote "The Shining Hour," "The Ringmaster," "Worse Things Happen at Sea," "Old Music" and "We at the Cross Roads." No reported survivors.

Alan Webb   John Williams   Tennessee Williams

INDEX

243

244